An Introduction to Design Patterns in C++ with Qt™, 2nd Edition

An Introduction to Design Patterns in C++ with Qt™, 2nd Edition

Alan Ezust and Paul Ezust

PRENTICE
HALL

Upper Saddle River, NJ · Boston · Indianapolis · San Francisco
New York · Toronto · Montreal · London · Munich · Paris · Madrid
Cape Town · Sydney · Tokyo · Singapore · Mexico City

The publisher offers excellent discounts on this book when ordered in quantity for bulk purchases or special sales, which may include electronic versions and/or custom covers and content particular to your business, training goals, marketing focus, and branding interests. For more information, please contact:

U.S. Corporate and Government Sales
(800) 382-3419
corpsales@pearsontechgroup.com

For sales outside the United States please contact:

International Sales
international@pearson.com

Visit us on the Web: informit.com/ph

Library of Congress Cataloging-in-Publication Data:

Ezust, Alan.
 An introduction to design patterns in C++ with QT / Alan Ezust, Paul Ezust. -- 2nd ed.
    p. cm.
 Includes bibliographical references and index.
 ISBN 978-0-13-282645-7 (hardback : alk. paper)
 1. C++ (Computer program language) 2. Software patterns. 3. Computer software--Reusability. I. Ezust, Paul. II. Title.
 QA76.73.C153E94 2011
 005.13'3--dc23

                    2011018378

Tux is created by Larry Ewing, lewing@isc.tamu.edu, using GIMP.

Qt and the Qt logo are trademarks of Nokia Corporation and/or its subsidiaries in Finland and other countries.

ISBN-13: 978-0-132-82645-7
ISBN-10: 0-132-82645-3
Text printed in the United States on recycled paper at Courier in Westford, Massachusetts.
Third printing, May 2015

Editor-in-Chief: Mark Taub
Acquisitions Editor: Debra Williams Cauley
Managing Editor: Kristy Hart
Project Editor: Jovana San Nicolas-Shirley
Copy Editor: Apostrophe Editing Services
Indexer: Cheryl Lenser
Proofreader: Gill Editorial Services
Publishing Coordinator: Kim Boedigheimer
Cover Designer: Alan Clements
Compositor: Nonie Ratcliff

This book is dedicated to Miriam Ezust, without whom none of our work would have been possible.

Contents

Foreword

I still remember how I first got to know C++ and Qt. It was around 15 years ago while working on my diploma thesis. Most of the development we did at that time was done in Fortran and C. I was working on a Linux system with FVWM as a window manager. One day I read an article about KDE—a cool, new open source project to create a desktop environment for Linux. Being not really happy with the user interface that Linux had to offer, I went to download, compile, and install the package.

KDE used Qt as the underlying framework. After some time as a user, I started contributing to the KDE project. Although I had studied object-oriented programming at university, it was only when I started developing for KDE with Qt that I really learned and understood many of the concepts.

C++ as a programming language is in some ways incomplete. Most other languages such as Java, Python, or C# come with a rather complete set of frameworks. The scope of the C++ standard library is, however, limited to low-level functionality, containers, and algorithms.

Combining a powerful and complex language such as C++ with a standard library that is limited in scope but makes extensive use of all the advanced features of C++ creates an extremely steep learning curve for developers who want to start developing in C++.

This is where Qt can help. Qt is a comprehensive, high-quality framework for professional application development. It covers most of the functionality that is missing from the standard library, such as threading, Unicode support, XML handling, and most important, ways to create graphical user interfaces (GUIs).

When I did my first bits of coding in C++, I was using Qt. Qt made it easy for me to start on my first projects and made it easy to learn new concepts of the C++ language while developing real applications. It was actually a lot of fun to work with Qt, so I soon migrated all my work from other languages to using Qt and C++.

Qt has always focused on trying to provide an intuitive and easy-to-use API set. The focus of the framework has always been on helping application developers to get their work done. This focus has, however, often led to rather clean implementations of certain design patterns. The signal/slot mechanism, for example, makes object-oriented programming extremely easy and intuitive.

This book tries to teach C++ and Qt together. With Qt, creating visible results is easy, usually only requiring a few lines of code. This helps overcome the complexity of C++ as a language, makes learning it more enjoyable, and motivates students to continue learning.

To become a good novelist, one must first read many good novels. To become a good composer, one must first listen to good music. The same thing applies to software developers. Working with an expertly designed library is important to becoming a good software developer. Having the source code for this library available helps developers understand many details, and it can be a place to find inspiration and maybe even solutions to some problems. Qt being LGPL[1] licensed makes this source code available to everybody.

Every C++ student should learn the language in conjunction with Qt. This book is committed to bringing this synergy to students. Qt users tend to be passionate about the framework, and Paul and Alan Ezust are no exception. This second edition of their book covers even more Qt technologies with more screenshots of the developed applications.

Learning application development has never been easier than it is today. Qt comes in an all-encompassing and integrated free package that provides an integrated development environment (IDE), a compiler, a debugger, the Qt library, tools, and documentation with tons of examples and demos.

Previously, many emerging software developers got stuck along the way because there was no proper guidance or the result of the hard coding work was not rewarding enough. With Qt you can create more with less coding. Bringing your software onto another platform like a mobile phone, embedded hardware, Mac, Windows, Linux desktop, and others is only a recompile away. The people who build Qt do everything possible to make developers' lives as easy as possible. Alan and Paul's book can give you, the developer, the guidance you need.

We hope that you enjoy the journey to becoming a C++ developer [who can] one day contribute to KDE or one of the many other open source projects using Qt. Maybe you can write Qt software for a living, as many thousands of developers do

---

[1] GNU Lesser General Public License

today. The opportunity is there—the number of jobs for skilled Qt engineers is increasing every year.

This text is not only for those new to C++ and Qt. Experienced software developers can also obtain much value from the many surprising new ideas contained in Paul and Alan's work. The book also serves as a good lookup resource due to the large index.

Today Qt development takes place in the open with both Qt's own engineers and the large community of contributors working on the same code repository. We hope one day you will contribute code to Qt or add to the Qt ecosystem in another way as Paul and Alan have done with this excellent new book.

—Lars Knoll
Director of Qt Research and Development

Preface

C++ had been in use for many years before it was standardized in 1989, which makes it a relatively mature language compared to others in popular use today. It is an important language for building fast, efficient, mission-critical systems. C++ is also one of the most flexible languages around, giving developers many choices of programming styles for uses ranging from high-level GUI code to low-level device drivers.

For a few years in the early 90s, C++ was the most popular object-oriented (OO) language in use, and many computer science (CS) students were introduced to object-oriented programming (OOP) via C++. This was because C++ provided a relatively easy transition to OOP for C programmers, and many CS professors had been teaching C previously.

Starting around 1996, Java gained favor over C++ as the first OO language for students to learn. There are a number of reasons that Java gained so much popularity.

- The language itself is simpler than C++.
- The language has built-in garbage collection, so programmers do not need to concern themselves with memory deallocation.
- A standard set of GUI classes is included in the development kit.
- The built-in String class supports Unicode.
- Multithreading is built into the language.
- It is easier to build and "plug in" Java Archives (JARs) than it is to recompile and relink libraries.
- Many Web servers provide Java application programming interfaces (APIs) for easy integration.
- Java programs are platform independent (Wintel, Solaris, MacOS, Linux, *nix, etc.).

Many of these benefits can be achieved with C++ used with Qt.

- Qt provides a comprehensive set of GUI classes that run faster, look better, and are more flexible than Java's Swing classes.
- Signals and slots are easier to use than (Action|Event|Key)Listener interfaces in Java.
- Qt has a plugin architecture that makes it possible to load code into an application without recompiling or relinking.
- Qt provides foreach, which makes iteration through collections simpler to read and write.

Although Qt does not provide garbage collection, it provides a variety of alternatives you can use to avoid the need to delete heap objects directly:

- Containers (see Section 6.8) that support reference counting and copy on write
- Parents and children (see Section 8.2)
- QPointer, and QSharedPointer, and QWeakReference (see Section 19.11).
- Subobjects (see Section 2.14)
- Stack objects (see Section 20.3)

Using C++ with Qt comes close to (and sometimes exceeds) Java in ease of use, comprehensiveness, and convenience. It significantly exceeds Java in the areas of speed and efficiency, making everything from processing-intensive server applications to high-speed graphics-intensive games possible.

Another benefit of learning C++ with Qt comes from Qt's widespread use in open source projects. There is already a great wealth of free open source code that you can learn from, reuse, and perhaps help to improve.

How to Use This Book

Part I contains the meat of the course: introduction to C++, UML, Qt core, QObjects, Widgets, Model-View, SQL, XML, and design patterns. This Part is designed to avoid forward referencing as much as possible, and it presents the topics in an order and a level of detail that should not overwhelm someone who is new to C/C++.

For completeness and for reference, Part II covers in more depth some of the "dry" but important C++ features that were introduced in Part I. By the time you have reached this point, these ideas should be a lot easier to understand.

At the end of each chapter, you will find exercises and review questions. Most of the programming exercises have solutions available to instructors on our Web site. For the questions, if the answers are not in the preceding chapter, then often there are pointers on where to find them. If this book is used for a course, these questions could be asked by the student or by the teacher, in the classroom or on an exam.

A Note About Formats

What you are reading now is only one of a number of possible versions available. Because the document was originally written in XML, using a "literal programming" style, we can generate a variety of different versions (bulleted slides, paragraphed textbook, with or without solutions, etc.) in a variety of different formats (HTML, pdf, ps, htmlhelp).

Each programming example is extracted from working source code. The Web version provides a hyperlink from each code excerpt to its full source file. This makes it easy to try the examples yourself. The text and listings in the Web version also contain hyperlinks from each library ClassName to its class documentation page.

Preface to the Second Edition

It is hard to know when a book is "finished," especially when writing about a subject (Qt) that is also under constant development. So, like Qt, our book has been under constant development since its conception.

Since the publication of the first edition, Trolltech released Qt 4.2, Nokia purchased Trolltech, Nokia released Qt 4.7.3, and Alan became a Nokia Certified Qt Specialist.

In the second edition, there are improvements in every chapter. Many eyeballs have scrutinized it, and we have rewritten a number of examples and explanations. We have added new exercises and review questions, some with handouts and solutions.

The first part of the book has been rearranged to introduce Qt earlier than before. We decided to take advantage of some of Qt's static convenience functions to write simple dialog-based applications prior to fully covering classes, functions, etc. File Streams have also been introduced earlier so that we could present more interesting examples and assignments.

Widgets, Main Windows, Models and Views, Reflection, Threads, and Databases have all been rewritten to use new classes that have been added to Qt since our first edition went to press. The Models and Views chapter has been revised and now explains the use of Delegates, `QXmlStreamReader`, `QStandardItemModel`, `QFileSystemModel`, `QColumnView`, sorting and filtering, cut and paste, and drag and drop.

The section on threads has been completely rewritten to highlight the advantages of using `QtConcurrent` algorithms rather than managing the QThreads directly from your code.

The Dynamic Forms chapter is gone. Instead, we show how to design forms manually and with the assistance of QtCreator/Designer, pointing out various techniques of integrating designer forms with user code.

The media player examples and exercises have been rewritten to use Phonon.[1]

The FileVisitor example, which was originally developed back in the Qt3 days, has outlived its usefulness now that we have QDirIterator. The section on Iteration is new, and there is no longer a section devoted to the rarely used Visitor pattern. Instead, we emphasize the Iterator pattern.

Some classes we placed in our libraries have been simplified or adapted to use the capabilities of the newest Qt components. We show new smart and shared pointers and how to use them.

More design patterns have been introduced and described. For each pattern, we have either provided an implementation (perhaps as an exercise) or, where appropriate, we have pointed out the Qt classes that implement or use the pattern.

Tips and best practices have been taken from various sources, including Nokia's official Qt training material, and are made available to you here. All of the examples in this edition have been tested with Qt 4.7.

---

[1] Make sure that the libphonon-dev package has been installed if you plan to work with those materials.

Acknowledgments

Thanks to the many authors and contributors involved in the following open source projects, for making the free tools, for answering questions, and for writing good docs. We reused each of these programs to make this book:

- jEdit[1]
- Umbrello[2]
- Firefox[3]
- Doxygen[4]
- dia[5]
- imagemagick[6]
- graphviz[7]
- KDE,[8] amarok,[9] taglib[10]
- docbook,[11] docbook-xsl[12]
- xsltproc, xmllint, gnu xml libs[13]

---

[1] http://jedit.sourceforge.net

[2] http://uml.sourceforge.net/index.php

[3] http://www.mozilla.org/products/firefox/

[4] http://www.stack.nl/~dimitri/doxygen/

[5] http://www.gnome.org/projects/dia/

[6] http://www.imagemagick.org/script/index.php

[7] http://www.research.att.com/sw/tools/graphviz/

[8] http://www.kde.org/

[9] http://amarok.kde.org/

[10] http://developer.kde.org/~wheeler/taglib.html

[11] http://www.docbook.org/

[12] http://docbook.sourceforge.net/projects/xsl/

[13] http://xmlsoft.org/XSLT/xsltproc2.html

- subversion[14] git[15]
- MoinMoin[16]
- Bugzilla[17]
- Apache httpd,[18] ant,[19] fop[20]
- pidgin[21]
- Python[22]
- ReportLab PyRXP[23]
- QtCreator[24]
- mysql[25]
- GNU Emacs[26]
- Linux,[27] gcc,[28] gdb[29]
- valgrind[30]

Thanks to Norman Walsh [docbook] and Bob Stayton [docbookxsl] for developing and documenting a superb system of publishing tools. Thanks to the rest of the docbook community for help and guidance.

---

[14] http://subversion.tigris.org/

[15] http://git-scm.com/

[16] http://moinmoin.wikiwikiweb.de/

[17] http://www.bugzilla.org/

[18] http://httpd.apache.org/

[19] http://ant.apache.org/

[20] http://xmlgraphics.apache.org/fop/

[21] http://www.pidgin.im/

[22] http://www.python.org

[23] http://www.reportlab.org/pyrxp.html

[24] http://qt.nokia.com/products/developer-tools/

[25] http://www.mysql.com/

[26] http://www.gnu.org/software/emacs/emacs.html

[27] http://www.kernel.org/

[28] http://gcc.gnu.org/

[29] http://www.gnu.org/software/gdb/gdb.html

[30] http://valgrind.org/

Thanks to the volunteers @debian.org for keeping testing up to date and still stable enough to be a productive development platform. Thanks to irc.freenode. net for bringing together a lot of good brains.

Thanks to Emily Ezust for wordsmithing skills and for getting us started with Qt in the first place. Thanks to the reviewers who provided input and valuable feedback on the text: Johan Thelin, Stephen Dewhurst, Hal Fulton, David Boddie, Andy Shaw, and Jasmin Blanchette. Thanks to Matthias Ettrich for the vision and motivation. Thanks to the Trolls@Nokia for writing good docs, producing QtCreator, answering questions on the mailing lists, and porting Qt over to mobile devices.

Thanks to the editorial and production staff at Prentice Hall for their meticulous reading of our book and for helping us to find the errors that were distributed throughout the text.

Thanks to Chris Craig, Chris Gaal, and the other gurus at ics.com for feedback and technical assistance. Thanks to ics.com for bringing together a team of Qt experts who are a pleasure to work with.

Finally, thanks to Suffolk University, a source of great support throughout this project. Thanks also to the students who took CMPSC 331/608 using the evolving versions of this book since fall 2003 and to our colleagues at many universities who used various forms of our book for their classes and who provided us with a stream of valuable bug reports and feedback.

Rationale for the Book

At Suffolk University, we buck the popular trend and continue teaching object-oriented programming using C++. For many years we taught a standard one-semester OOP/C++ course that had the CS1-CS2 sequence as prerequisite and a data structures and algorithms course as corequisite. Our CS1-CS2 sequence was based on the C programming language for many years and is now taught in Java. In the OOP course, students developed substantial mastery of the core C++ language, the Standard Template Library (STL), and an understanding of key OO concepts such as encapsulation, refactoring, and tool development. However, we found that STL is a library that often overwhelms students and causes them to spend too much time on low-level programming constructs and template issues. In addition, the naming conventions used do not encourage the kind of programming style we prefer.

Furthermore, STL does not provide a basis for writing applications with GUIs, so another framework would have to be used anyway.

During the summer of 2003, while Qt 3.2 was the current version, we decided to develop a book that would approach OOP/C++ at a higher level. We wanted to provide a substantial introduction to GUI programming using the multiplatform Qt framework and to introduce and use some important design patterns. When Qt 4.0 was released, we did some extensive rewriting to accommodate the code-breaking improvements that it introduced.

We designed this book first as a textbook to be used in a university class, but we did so in an extensible way and included lots of information that can make it useful for readers with a wide range of backgrounds: from those who already program in C or another procedural language and want to learn OO and GUI programming, to those who have no C background but are familiar with Basic, Java, Python, or another programming language and want to learn C++. The first part of the book is aimed at familiarizing all audiences with basic C++ elements, OO concepts, UML, and the core Qt classes.

We believe that readers understand ideas best when they apply them, and we found this to be especially true with design patterns. Many of the Qt classes or code examples are concrete implementations of some of the more popular design patterns described in [Gamma95]. For each design pattern that we discuss, we make available the source code for our example and include exercises that challenge readers to reuse, refine, and extend that code.

Reuse of libraries requires an understanding not only of libraries but of modular software, the linker, and library design. We have included substantial advice distilled from experience (ours and our students') and from online discussion communities. We found that this helped our students cope with most of the problems they encountered in courses based on early versions of this book.

We used evolving versions of this book in Suffolk University's OOP/C++ course each semester during the academic years 2003–2004 through 2010–2011, with increasingly promising results and with much valuable feedback from our students. In the earlier version of this course (prior to 2003), students typically would write thousands of lines of code for their programming projects. By contrast, with the emphasis now on code reuse and the exploitation of robust tool libraries, student programming projects have fewer lines of student code but are much more interesting and, we feel, provide a much more valuable learning experiences.

There are many C++ books in print that either teach C++ or teach Qt, but we found that the C++ books use a variety of different programming styles, and they emphasize some topics that we do not often use with Qt. All the Qt books we have seen assume prior C++ knowledge. This book, by contrast, assumes no C or C++ programming experience, and it covers the language features of C++ that you need to know to use Qt classes as early as possible in the examples and assignments. It can be used as a textbook for teaching C++ and design patterns, with an emphasis on code design and reuse.

As far as we know, there are no other university-level C++ textbooks that contain Qt examples and provide review questions, exercises, solutions, and lecture slides for instructors. Code examples, lab handouts, and other useful materials can be downloaded from our [dist] directory (the URL for which can be found in the "Bibliography" at the end of this book).

About the Authors

Alan Ezust received his M.Sc in computer science from McGill University in Montreal. He currently works as a Nokia Certified Qt Specialist for ICS (www.ics.com), a company that specializes in delivering training and professional services on Qt software. He honed his teaching and courseware development skills at Learnix, and later at Objectivity, where he taught and/or wrote courses in Python, UNIX, C, C++, Java, Perl, Design Patterns, Froglogic Squish, and Object Oriented Databases. He lives in Victoria, BC, Canada.

Paul Ezust (Cambridge, Massachusetts) chaired Suffolk University's Department of Mathematics and Computer Science for more than 30 years, leading development of computer science curricula based on Association for Computing Machinery guidelines. He has done extensive outside consulting, contract programming, and research in computational mathematics.

Our book, which was originally going to be an extrapolation of a course that Paul had developed and refined for about eight years, has evolved into one that represents a complete paradigm shift for him and a totally different approach to teaching OOP, thanks to gentle but persistent pressure from Alan. Since 2003, the evolving, published, Chinese, and open source versions have been used successfully in classrooms at Suffolk and at other universities in Australia, China, Russia, South Africa, Taiwan, the United States, and the European Union. This edition adds new topics and refinements that have been enabled by the many new frameworks and classes that have been added to Qt since the first edition went to print.

PART I

Design Patterns and Qt

Chapter 1

C++ Introduction

In this chapter, the C++ language is introduced. Basic concepts such as keywords, literals, identifiers, declarations, native types, and type conversions are defined. Some history and evolution are discussed, along with the relationship between C++ and the C language. Some Standard Library and Qt classes are introduced.

1.1 Overview of C++

C++ was originally written as an extension of C by means of a series of preprocessor macros and known as *C with Classes*.[1] After many years of evolution and refinement, it now extends C by adding several higher-level features such as strong typing, data abstraction, references, operator and function overloading, and considerable support for object-oriented programming.

C++ retains the key features that have made C such a popular and successful language: speed, efficiency, and a wide range of expressiveness that enables programming at many levels, from the lowest level (such as direct operating system calls or bitwise

---

[1] http://www.research.att.com/~bs/bs_faq.html#invention

operations) to the highest level (such as manipulating containers of large complex objects).

A fundamental design decision was made at the beginning for C++: New language features should not cause a runtime penalty for C code that does not use them.[2] There are many advanced features in C++ that enable the programmer to write readable, reusable, object-oriented programs; and using those features invariably causes the compiler to do lots of extra work. But longer compile times is a small price to pay for the power and maintainability of the resulting code. Some features have a runtime cost if they are used, but a C program compiled by a C++ compiler should run just as fast as it would if compiled by a C compiler.

1.2   A Brief History of C++

C++ was designed by Bjarne Stroustrup while he was working for AT&T Bell Labs, which eventually packaged and marketed it. Initial versions of the language were made available internally at AT&T beginning in 1981. C++ evolved steadily in response to user feedback.

The first edition of Stroustrup's book, *The C++ Programming Language*, was published in early 1986. After the release of Version 2.0 in 1989, C++ was rapidly acknowledged as a serious, useful language. Work began that year to establish an internationally recognized language standard for it. In 1997, a committee of the American National Standards Institute (ANSI) completed and published internally the *Draft Standard - The C++ Language, X3J16/97-14882, Information Technology Council (NSITC), Washington, DC.*

In June 1998, the draft standard was unanimously accepted by the representatives of the 20 principal nations that participated in the nine-year ANSI/ISO (International Standards Organization) effort. The third edition of Stroustrup's book [Stroustrup97] was published in 1997. It is widely regarded as the definitive C++ reference.

Ongoing work to refine the standard is being done by the ISO with the International Electrotechnical Commission (IEC), an international standards and conformity assessment body for all fields of electrotechnology. In 2005, a *Technical Report 1*, also known as "tr1," was published, containing many extensions to the C++ language and standard library. In 2010, the international standardization working group on C++ was

---

[2] Unfortunately, exception-handling broke this rule and does cause a bit of overhead if enabled. This is why many libraries do not use exceptions.

named ISO/IEC JTC1/SC22/WG21. A 2010 version of the C++ Draft Standard[3] is freely available online. **C++0x** is the unofficial name of the "next version of C++," due to be finalized sometime in 2011.

1.3 C++ First Example

Throughout this book, code examples explain and illustrate important programming and object oriented program (OOP) issues. The aim in each case is to use a minimal example to illustrate the ideas and techniques briefly and efficiently. Example 1.1 provides a quick overview of some elementary C++ syntax.

EXAMPLE 1.1   src/early-examples/example0/fac.cpp

```
/* Computes and prints n! for a given n.
   Uses several basic elements of C++. */

#include <iostream>                                                    1
int main() {                                                          2
    using namespace std;                                             3
    // Declarations of variables
    int factArg = 0 ;                                                4
    int fact(1) ;                                                    5
    do {                                                             6
        cout << "Factorial of: ";                                   7
        cin >> factArg;                                              8
        if ( factArg < 0 ) {
            cout << "No negative values, please!" << endl;
        }                                                            9
    } while (factArg < 0) ;                                         10
    int i = 2;
    while ( i <= factArg ) {                                       11
        fact = fact * i;
        i = i + 1;
    }                                                              12
    cout << "The Factorial of " << factArg << " is: " << fact << endl;
    return 0;                                                      13
}                                                                  14
```

1 Standard C++ library—In older versions of C++, you might find <iostream.h> instead, but that version is regarded as "deprecated"; i.e., its use is discouraged.

---

[3] http://www.open-std.org/jtc1/sc22/wg21/docs/papers/2010/n3225.pdf

2 Start of function `main`, which returns an `int`

3 Permits you to use the symbols cin, cout, and endl without prefixing each name with std::

4 C-style initialization syntax

5 C++ style initialization syntax

6 Start of `do..while` loop

7 Write to standard output

8 Read from standard input and convert to `int`

9 End of `if` block

10 If `false`, break out of `do` loop

11 Start of `while` loop

12 End of `while` block

13 When main returns `0`, that normally means "no errors"

14 End of `main` block

On most platforms, you can compile and run this program using the ubiquitous GNU C compiler, gcc. The command to compile a C++ program is g++, which is a program that calls gcc, treats `.c` and `.h` files as C++ source files and automatically links to the C++ library.

To maximize the amount of diagnostic information available from the compilation process, use the command-line option, -Wall.

```
src/early-examples/example0> g++ -Wall fac.cpp
src/early-examples/example0> g++ -Wall -o execFile fac.cpp
```

-Wall enables all possible warnings about constructions that might be considered questionable even if they conform to the standard.

In the second version, the optional switch argument -o *execFile* is used to specify the name of the generated executable. If you omit that option, as in the first version, the compiler produces an executable file named a.out.[4] In either case, if there already exists a file in the same directory with the name of your target executable (e.g., if you are recompiling), the compiler quietly and automatically overwrites it.

---

[4] On Windows, with mingw, it creates a file called an.exe.

These are just two of the most commonly used compiler options. On a *nix system, you can view the **manual page**, a summary of command options and how they are used, by typing the command

```
    man g++
```
or
```
    info g++
```

On most systems this command enables you to browse the online documentation for g++ one screen at a time. For more complete gcc documentation, visit the GNU online document center.[5]

After it has been compiled successfully, the program can be run by typing the name of the executable file. Here is an example on a *nix platform:

```
src/early-examples/example0> ./a.out
Factorial of: -3
No negative values, please!
Factorial of: 5
The Factorial of 5 is: 120
src/early-examples/example0>
```

This short program uses several of the language elements that show up in most C++ programs.

1.3.1   Comments

C++ has single-line comments as in Java. Any text between // and the end of the line is a comment. C-style comment-delimiters for multiline comments can also be used. The text between /* and */ is a comment.

#include

To reuse functions, types, or identifiers from libraries, use the preprocessor directive #include.[6] As in C, all preprocessor directives begin with the pound sign character # and are evaluated just before the compiler compiles your code. In this example,

---

[5] http://www.gnu.org/software/gcc/onlinedocs/

[6] Discussed in Section C.2.

the included header <iostream> contains the Standard Library definitions for input/output.

using namespace

Symbols from the Standard Library (Appendix B, "Standard Headers") are enclosed in the namespace std.

   A **namespace** (Section 20.4) is a collection of classes, functions, and objects that can be addressed with a named prefix. The **using** declaration tells the compiler to add all symbols from the specified namespace (std) into the global namespace.

1.3.2   Declaring and Initializing Variables

Variable declarations come in three styles in C++ :

```
type-expr   variableName;
type-expr   variableName = init-expr;
type-expr   variableName (init-expr);
```

   In the first form, the variable might not be initialized. The third form is an alternative syntax for the second.

1.3.3   Selection

C++ provides the usual assortment of syntax variations for selection and control structures, which Section 19.2.2 discusses.

1.3.4   Iteration

Example 1.1 uses two of the three iteration structures provided by C++. Section 19.2.3 discusses all three.

1.4   Standard Input and Output

In Example 1.1, the directive

```
#include <iostream>
```

enabled you to use predefined global input (istream) and output (ostream) objects.

1. `cin`, **console input**, the keyboard by default.

2. `cout`, **console output**, the console screen by default.

3. `cerr`, **console error**, another output stream to the console screen that flushes more often and is normally used for error messages.

In Example 1.1, we used the global `ostream` object, `cout`. We also called one of its member functions, `operator<<()`. This function overloads the `<<` operator and is used to insert data into the output stream, so we call it the **insertion** operator.[7] The syntax for that output statement is also quite interesting. Instead of using the rather bulky function notation

```
cout.operator<<("Factorial of: ");
```

we invoked the same function using the more elegant and readable *infix* syntax:

```
cout << "Factorial of: ";
```

This operator can be **chained** (used on multiple values) and is predefined for use with many built-in types, as you see in the next output statement.

```
cout << "The cost is $" << 23.45 << " for " << 6 << " items." << '\n';
```

In Example 1.2, you can see the `operator>>()` used for input with the `istream` object `cin` in an analogous way to the way we used `<<` for output with the `ostream` object `cout`. Because the effect of this operator is to extract data from the input stream, we call it the *extraction* operator.[8]

EXAMPLE 1.2   src/iostream/io.cpp

```
#include <string>
#include <iostream>

int main() {
    using namespace std;
    const int THISYEAR = 2011;
```

---

[7] We discuss overloaded functions and operators further in Section 5.1. This particular operator already has a name and definition from C. It is the *left shift* operator. For example, n `<<` 2 shifts the bits of the int n two positions to the left and fills the vacated bits with zeros—effectively multiplying n by 4.

[8] This time we have overloaded the *right shift* operator. n `>>` 2 shifts the bits of the int n two positions to the right, effectively dividing by 4, and fills the vacated bits appropriately depending on whether n is signed or unsigned.

```
string yourName;
int birthYear;

cout << "What is your name? "  << flush;
cin >> yourName;

cout << "What year were you born? " ;
cin >> birthYear;

cout << "Your name is " << yourName
        << " and you are approximately "
        << (THISYEAR - birthYear)
        << " years old. " << endl;
}
```

The symbols `flush` and `endl` are **manipulators**[9] from the `std` namespace.

In Example 1.2, we use the `string` class,[10] also from the C++ Standard Library. We discuss this type and demonstrate some of its functions later in Section 1.8.

NOTE

For Windows/MSVC Users

By default, MSVC generates applications with no console support. This means that you cannot use the standard i/o/error streams unless you tell MSVC to build a console application. See the note "CONFIG += console (for MSVC Users)" in Section 1.6.

1.4.1   Exercises: Standard Input and Output

1. In the [dist] directory, we have provided a tarball named `src.tar.gz` that contains all the code examples in this book. An extremely valuable practice that you should adopt is to take each code example, build and run it to see how it is supposed to behave, and then break it by making various changes to see what happens. Sometimes you can learn how the compiler responds to a particular

---

[9] Manipulators are function references that can be inserted into an input or output stream to modify its state. We discuss these further in Section 1.9.

[10] We discuss classes in detail in Chapter 2, "Top of the `class`." For now, you can think of a class as a data type with built-in functions.

syntax error that your change produced. The compiler can be your best friend if you can learn to understand its language. Other times you can see how the runtime behavior of the program is affected by a particular logic error that you produced. In each case, the experience can strengthen your understanding of C++ programming.

2. Using Example 1.2, do the following experiments:

- First, compile and run it, to see its normal behavior.
- What happens if you enter a non-numeric value for the birth year?
- What happens if you enter a name like `Curious George` as your name?
- What happens if you remove the following line?

  ```
  using namespace std;
  ```

- Replace the statement

  ```
  cin >> yourName;
  ```

  with the statement

  ```
  getline(cin, yourName);
  ```

  and try `Curious George` again.

- Can you explain the differences in behavior between `cin >>` and `getline()`? We discuss this in Section 1.8.
- Add some more questions to the program that require a variety of numerical and string answers and test the results.

1.5 Introduction to Functions

Every modern programming language has a way for programmers to define functions. Functions enable you to divide a program into manageable components instead of presenting it as a large, complex monolith. This enables you to develop and test small components individually or in small groups and makes it easier to build and maintain software. Functions also provide a way to write reusable code for specific tasks. For example, Example 1.1 computes the factorial of a given number *inside* the `main()`

function. Example 1.3 shows how to extract the code for computing factorials and transform it into a reusable function.

EXAMPLE 1.3   src/early-examples/fac2.cpp

```
#include <iostream>

long factorial(long n) {
    long ans = 1;
    for (long i = 2; i <= n; ++i) {
        ans = ans * i;
        if (ans < 0) {
            return -1;
        }
    }
    return ans;
}


int main() {
    using namespace std;
    cout << "Please enter n: " << flush;
    long n;                                                     1
    cin >> n;                                                   2

    if (n >= 0) {
        long nfact = factorial(n);
        if (nfact < 0) {
            cerr << "overflow error: "
                << n << " is too big." << endl;
        }
        else {
            cout << "factorial(" << n << ") = "
                << nfact << endl;
        }
    }
    else {
        cerr << "Undefined:   "
            << "factorial of a negative number: " << n << endl;
    }
    return 0;
}
```

1 long `int`

2 read from `stdin`, try to convert to `long`

With the exception of constructors and destructors,[11] discussed in Chapter 2, and conversion operators, discussed in Section 19.9.1, every function must have

- A return type (which may be `void`)
- A name
- An ordered, comma-separated list (which may be empty) of the types of the function's parameters
- A body (a block of zero or more statements enclosed in {braces})

The first three are the function's interface, and the last is its implementation.

In Example 1.3, the function definition appears above the statement that invokes it; however, it may not always be possible or desirable to place a function definition before every instance in which it is called. C and C++ allow a function to be called before it has been defined, as long as the function has been **declared** prior to the call.

The mechanism for declaring a function (i.e., describing to the compiler how it is to be invoked) is the **function prototype**. A function prototype includes the following information:

- Function's return type
- Function's name
- Function's parameter list

In other words, it includes everything except the function's body. Here are a few prototypes.

```
int toCelsius(int fahrenheitValue);
QString toString();
double grossPay(double hourlyWage, double hoursWorked);
```

Remember, a function must be declared or defined before it is used for the first time so that the compiler can set up calls to it properly. We discuss declarations and definitions in more detail in Section 20.1. It is an error to omit the return type (even

---

[11] A constructor must not have a return type and may have an empty body. A destructor must not have a return type, must have an empty parameter list, and may have an empty body.

if it is `void`) except for the `main()` function, in which case the return type implicitly defaults to `int`.

Although parameter names are optional in function prototypes, it is good programming practice to use them. They constitute an effective and efficient part of the documentation for a program.

A simple example can help to show why parameter names should be used in function prototypes. Suppose you needed a function to set a `Date` with values for the year, month, and day. If you presented the prototype as `setDate(int, int, int)`, the programmer working with `Dates` would not know immediately from the prototype alone in what order to list the three values when calling that function. Because at least three of the possible orderings are in common use somewhere on the planet, there is no "obvious" answer that would eliminate the need for more information. As you can see in Section 2.2, the definition of a member function is usually kept in a separate file from the declaration (and might not be accessible), so a programmer might have some difficulty figuring out how to call the function. By giving the parameters good names, that problem is eliminated and the function has, at least partially, documented itself.[12]

Function Overloading

C++ permits **overloading** of function names. This enables programmers to attach the same function name to different implementations with different parameters.

The **signature** of a function consists of its name and its parameter list. In C++, the return type is *not* part of the signature.

A function name is overloaded if two or more functions within a given scope have the same name but different signatures. It is an error to have two functions in the same scope with the same signature but different return types. Overloading requires the compiler to determine, by analyzing the argument list, which version of an overloaded function gets executed in response to a function call. Because the decision is entirely based upon the argument list, it is easy to see why the compiler cannot permit functions with the same signature but different return types to coexist in the same scope. We discuss that decision process in Section 5.1. In the meantime, Example 1.4 provides some function calls to ponder.

---

[12] In Section 15.2 we discuss an example in which it can be advantageous to omit some parameter names.

EXAMPLE 1.4   src/functions/overload-not.cpp

```cpp
#include <iostream>
using namespace std;

void foo(int n) {
  cout << n << " is a nice number." << endl;
}


int main() {
   cout << "before call: " << 5 << endl;
   foo(5);
   cout << "before call: " << 6.7 << endl;
   foo(6.7);
   cout << "before call: " << true << endl;
   foo(true);
}
```

Here there is only one function, but we call it with three different numerical types. In this case, automatic type conversions permit the function to be called three times.

```
src/functions> g++ overload-not.cpp
src/functions> ./a.out
before call: 5
5 is a nice number.
before call: 6.7
6 is a nice number.
before call: 1
1 is a nice number.
src/functions>
```

This output shows some of the harsh realities of numerical types. First, when a floating point number gets converted to an int, its fractional part (the decimal point and all digits to the right of it) is discarded. Even though 6.7 is closer to 7 than to 6, no rounding takes place. Second, the bool value true is displayed as 1 (and false is displayed as 0). If you want to see the word true (or false), you need to add code to output the appropriate strings as shown in Example 1.5.

Now, you'll use overloaded functions.

EXAMPLE 1.5   src/functions/overload.cpp

```cpp
#include <iostream>
using namespace std;

void foo(int n) {
  cout << n << " is a nice int." << endl;
}

void foo(double x) {
  cout << x << " is a nice double." << endl;
}

void foo(bool b) {
    cout << "Always be " << (b?"true":"false") << " to your bool." << endl;
}

int main() {
  foo(5);
  foo(6.7);
  foo(true);
}
```

With three overloaded versions of the function, no type conversions are necessary when using the same `main()` function.

Notice the use of the conditional operator in the third version of foo().[13]

```
src/functions> g++ overload.cpp
src/functions> ./a.out
5 is a nice int.
6.7 is a nice double.
Always be true to your bool.
src/functions>
```

Chapter 5, "Functions," discusses in more detail the many interesting and useful features of C++ functions.

---

[13] The ternary conditional operator, `testExpr ? valueIfTrue : valueIfFalse`, provides a terse way to insert a simple choice into an expression. If `testExpr` has a nonzero value (e.g., `true`), the value immediately to the right of the question mark (?) is returned. If `testExpr` has value 0 (e.g., `false`), the value to the right of the colon (:) is returned.

1.5.1   Exercises: Introduction to Functions

1. Locate the code for Example 1.3 in the `src` tree and then
   - Build and test that program with a variety of input values, including some non-numeric values.
   - Determine the largest input value that can produce a valid output.
   - Change the program so that it can produce valid results for larger input values.
   - Modify the program so that it cannot produce invalid results.
   - Explore the effects of using the statement

     ```
     if (cin >> n)  {  ...  }
     ```

   to enclose the processing of n in this program. In particular, try entering non-numeric data after the prompt. This is an example of the use of a conversion operator, which is discussed in more detail in Section 19.9.1.

   - Modify the program so that it can accept values from the user until the value 9999 is entered.

2. Write definitions for the functions

   ```
   double toCelsius(double fahrenheitTemp);
   double toFahrenheit(double celsiusTemp);
   ```

   and then write a program that enables the user to obtain temperature conversions (in either direction) between Celsius and Fahrenheit.

1.6   qmake, **Project Files, and** Makefile

C++ applications are generally composed of many source files, header files, and external libraries. During the normal course of project development, source files and libraries get added, changed, or removed. To build an executable that reflects the current state of the project, such changes require all affected files to be compiled and the resulting object files to be properly linked. This changing-rebuilding process typically happens many times.

Keeping track of all the parts of such a project requires a mechanism that precisely specifies the input files involved, the tools needed to build, the intermediate targets and their dependencies, and the final executable target.

The most widely used utility for handling the job of building a project is **make**.[14] make reads the details of the project specifications and the instructions for the compiler from a **Makefile**, which resembles a shell script but contains (at a minimum)

- **Rules** for building certain kinds of files (e.g., to get a .o file from a .cpp file, you must run gcc -c on the .cpp file)
- **Sources** and **Headers** lists that contain the names of all source and header files needed by the project
- **Targets** that specify which executables (or libraries) must be built
- **Dependencies** that list which targets need to be rebuilt when certain files get changed

The make command, by default, loads the file named Makefile from your current working directory and performs the specified build steps (**compiling** and **linking**).

The immediate benefit of using make is that it recompiles only the files that have changed or are affected by any changes, rather than blindly recompiling every source file every time. Figure 1.1 shows the steps involved in building a Qt application.

With Qt, it is not necessary for the programmer to write Makefiles. Qt provides a tool called qmake to generate Makefiles for you. It is still necessary to somehow run make and understand its output. Most IDEs run make (or something similar) at the click of a button and either display or filter its output.

To create a Makefile, qmake requires a **project file**. A project file describes the project by listing all of the other files, and all the options and file locations, that are needed to build the project. It is much simpler than a Makefile and can easily be created by the user. Although a programmer can easily create one, qmake can also generate a simple project file with the command qmake -project When this command is issued, qmake lists all source files (*.cpp) in the current working directory as SOURCES and all header files (*.h) in that directory as HEADERS. The resulting project file will be given the name that follows the optional -o switch. If that switch and its argument are not present,

---

[14] Depending on your development environment, you may find variants of make, such as mingw32-make, gmake, or cmake. In MS Dev Studio, you'll find nmake.

qmake uses the name of the current working directory to name the project file and also, eventually, the executable file.

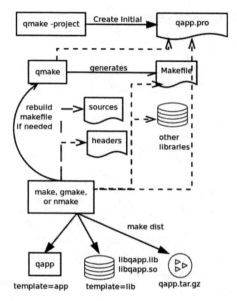

FIGURE 1.1 (q)make build steps

After the project file has been created, the command qmake creates a Makefile based on the project file. The command make can then attempt to build an executable by following the instructions in the Makefile.[15] The name of the executable is specified by the TARGET variable. It defaults to the name of the project.

The following transcript shows how to use qmake to build the same little program that we discussed, compiled, and ran in Example 1.1. The files that are created after each step of the build process are italicized.

---

[15] To produce a Makefile in MacOSX, you need to add the line CONFIG -= app_bundle to the project file, and you need to type qmake -spec macx-g++ instead of just qmake.

```
src/early-examples/example0> ls
fac.cpp
src/early-examples/example0> qmake -project
src/early-examples/example0> ls
example0.pro fac.cpp
src/early-examples/example0> cat example0.pro

TEMPLATE = app
TARGET =
DEPENDPATH += .
INCLUDEPATH += .

# Input
SOURCES += fac.cpp
src/early-examples/example0> qmake
src/early-examples/example0> ls
example0.pro fac.cpp Makefile
src/early-examples/example0> make
g++ -c -pipe -O2 -Wall -W -D_REENTRANT -DQT_NO_DEBUG -DQT_GUI_LIB
   -DQT_CORE_LIB -DQT_SHARED -I/usr/share/qt4/mkspecs/linux-g++ -I.
   -I/usr/include/qt4/QtCore -I/usr/include/qt4/QtCore
   -I/usr/include/qt4/QtGui -I/usr/include/qt4/QtGui -I/usr/include/qt4
   -I. -I. -I. -o fac.o fac.cpp
g++ -o example0 fac.o  -L/usr/lib -lQtGui -lQtCore -lpthread
src/early-examples/example0> ls
example0 example0.pro fac.cpp fac.o Makefile
src/early-examples/example0>
```

Notice that you can see the arguments passed to the compiler when you run make. If any errors are encountered, you will also see them. Now you can run this application.

```
src/early-examples/example0> ./example0
Factorial of: 10
The Factorial of 10 is: 3628800
src/early-examples/example0> ./example0
Factorial of: -3
No negative values, please!
Factorial of: 0
The Factorial of 0 is: 1
src/early-examples/example0>
```

Instead of running the compiler directly from the command line, you should henceforth use qmake and make, which greatly simplify the build process—especially when a project involves multiple source and header files and libraries.

Section C.1 discusses the `make` command and `Makefiles` in a bit more detail.

The project file can be thought of as a map of the project, containing references to all files and locations required for building your application or library. Like other source code files, this is both human-readable and machine-readable. *The .pro file is the first place to look when you encounter* not found *or* undefined *messages during the build process (especially at link time).* For further details we recommend that you read Qt's guide to qmake.[16]

As you add more source-code, header, or library modules to your project, you must edit the `.pro` file and add the new items to the appropriate SOURCES, HEADERS, and LIBS lists. The same documentation standards that apply to C++ source code should be applied to project files (where comments begin with #).

In Example 1.6, you can see common qmake variable settings that can be helpful to add to all of your projects. By placing a copy of this file in a convenient location and adding the line

```
include (/path/to/wherever you put/common.pri)
```

to your project file, you can save yourself some typing.

EXAMPLE 1.6   src/common.pri

```
# required if you want to see qDebug () messages
CONFIG += debug

# place auto-generated files in "invisible" subdirectories
win32 {
    MOC_DIR = _moc
    UI_DIR = _ui
    OBJECTS_DIR = _obj
} else {
    UI_DIR = .ui
    MOC_DIR = .moc
    OBJECTS_DIR = .obj
}

# rules below apply to TEMPLATE=app projects only:
app {
    # place executable in same folder:
    DESTDIR=$$OUT_PWD
```

---

[16] http:// doc.qt.nokia.com/latest/qmake-manual.html

```
# don't place executables in an app bundle on mac os
# this also permits console apps to work on the mac
mac {
    CONFIG -= app_bundle
}

# Open a console for stdin, stdout, and stderr Windows:
win32 {
    CONFIG += console
}
}
```

NOTE

`CONFIG += console` (for MSVC Users)

The line `CONFIG += console`, only necessary on Windows platforms, tells the compiler to build a "console" application, which can interact with the user via standard input/output streams. If you use MS Dev studio, this is equivalent to selecting Project Properties - Configuration Properties - Linker - System - Subsystem - Console. Without this option, you will not see messages to `qDebug()`, `stdout`, or `stderr`.

NOTE

`CONFIG -= app_bundle` (for Mac OSX)

```
For console apps on the Mac, you can prevent the creation of an "app bundle" that
places your executable in a subdirectory by adding the line CONFIG -= app_bundle
```

in your project file. That will also permit interactions with standard I/O. You can then use the command line

```
qmake -spec macx-g++
```

to produce a `Makefile`. The command `make>` can then produce a single executable for your app.

1.6.1   `#include`: Finding Header Files

The three ways to `#include` a library header file are

```
#include <headerFile>
#include "headerFile"
#include "path/to/headerFile"
```

The angle brackets (<>) indicate that the preprocessor must look (sequentially) in the directories listed in the **include path** for the file.

A quoted filename indicates that the preprocessor should look for *headerFile* in the including file's directory first. A quoted path indicates that the preprocessor should check the path directory first. The path information can be absolute or relative (to the including file's directory). If no file is found at the specified location, the directories listed in the include path are searched for *headerFile*.

If versions of the file exist in more than one directory in the include path, the search stops as soon as the first occurrence of the file has been found. If the file is not found in any of the directories of the search path, then the compiler reports an error.

When the compiler was installed, it was told where to find the header files in the C++ Standard Library. For other libraries, you can expand the search path by adding the switch `-I/path/to/headerfile` to the invocation of the compiler.

If you use an IDE, there will be a `Project->Settings->Preprocessor`, or `Project->Options->Libraries` configuration menu that lets you specify additional include directories, which get passed as `-I` switches to the compiler at build time.

With qmake, as you will soon see, you can add `INCLUDEPATH += ` *dirName* lines to the project file. These directories end up in the generated `Makefile` as `INCPATH` macros, which *then* get passed on to the compiler/preprocessor at build time.

---

qmake -r

Some project files are `SUBDIRS`, which means they run both qmake and make recursively down the tree. If you have an old `Makefile` from a previous version of Qt and want to force all `Makefiles` to be regenerated immediately, invoke qmake `-r`, to recursively generate all `Makefiles` down the file tree.

⚔ **TIP**

In general, it is a good idea to #include non-Qt header files *after* Qt header files. Because Qt defines many symbols (for the compiler and for the preprocessor), this can make it easier to avoid (or locate) name clashes.

For more information about the preprocessor and how it is used, see Section C.2.

1.7   Getting Help Online

In addition to the Qt Online Documentation,[17] which includes links to API docs and also to articles and documentation for related Qt products, there are many online resources available to you. Here are a few.

1. The Qt Interest Mailing List[18] provides a developer community and searchable archives. Searching on a class you are trying to use, or an error message you do not understand, can often give you useful results.

2. Qt Developer Network[19] has technical articles and tutorials about Qt.

3. QtCentre[20] is a Web-based online community site devoted to C++ programming using Qt. It puts you in touch with people all over the planet who use Qt and help one another out. There are numerous forums, projects, and FAQ. This site is constantly monitored by key Qt developers who often participate in forum discussions, make announcements, and give useful advice.

4. ics.com[21] is a training and consulting partner of Nokia, providing on-site consulting and consulting services for people who need Qt expertise. This is a shameless plug, because one of the authors is employed there.

5. If you encounter a seemingly intractable error with an error message that is not too long, try pasting it into Google.

1.8   Strings

When working with string data in C++, you have three choices:

1. `const char*`, or C-style strings, which are used mainly when you are interfacing with C libraries, and rarely otherwise. They are a frequent source of runtime errors and should be avoided.

2. `string`, from the C++ standard library, which is available everywhere.

3. `QString`, which is preferred over STL strings, because it has a richer API and is easier to use. Its implementation supports lazy copy-on-write (or implicit

---

[17] Qt Online Documentation: http://doc.qt.nokia.com/

[18] Qt Mailing Lists: http://lists.qt.nokia.com/

[19] Qt Developer Network: http://developer.qt.nokia.com/wiki

[20] Qt Centre http://www.qt.centre.org/

[21] http://www.ics.com

sharing, explained later in Section 11.5) so functions can receive QString arguments and return QStrings by value without paying the penalty of allocating and copying the string's memory each time. Further, QString's built-in support for the Unicode standard[22] facilitates internationalization.

Example 1.7 demonstrates basic usage of STL strings.

EXAMPLE 1.7   src/generic/stlstringdemo.cpp

```
#include <string>
#include <iostream>

int main() {
    using namespace std;
    string s1("This "), s2("is a "), s3("string.");
    s1 += s2;                                                      1
    string s4 = s1 + s3;
    cout << s4 << endl;
    string s5("The length of that string is: ");
    cout << s5 << s4.length() << " characters." << endl;
    cout << "Enter a sentence: " << endl;
    getline(cin, s2);                                              2
    cout << "Here is your sentence: \n" << s2 << endl;
    cout << "The length of your sentence is: " << s2.length() << endl;
    return 0;
}
```

1 Concatenation
2 s2 will get the entire line.

Here is the compile and run:

```
src/generic> g++ -Wall stlstringdemo.cpp
src/generic> ./a.out
This is a string.
The length of that string is 17
Enter a sentence:
20 years hard labor
Here is your sentence:
20 years hard labor
The length of your sentence is: 20
src/generic>
```

---

[22] Unicode Standard http://www.unicode.org/standard/standard.html

Observe that we used

```
getline(cin, s2)
```

to extract a `string` from the standard input stream. The same example, rewritten to use Qt instead of STL, is shown in Example 1.8. It produces the same output.

EXAMPLE 1.8   src/qstring/qstringdemo.cpp

```
#include <QString>
#include <QTextStream>

QTextStream cout(stdout);                                          1
QTextStream cin(stdin);

int main() {
    QString s1("This "), s2("is a "), s3("string.");
    s1 += s2;  // concatenation
    QString s4 = s1 + s3;
    cout << s4 << endl;
    cout << "The length of that string is " << s4.length() << endl;
    cout << "Enter a sentence with whitespaces: " << endl;
    s2 = cin.readLine();                                           2
    cout << "Here is your sentence: \n" << s2 << endl;
    cout << "The length of your sentence is: " << s2.length() << endl;
    return 0;
}
```

1 Define `QTextStream`s that look like C++ standard iostreams.

2 not iostream, `QTextStream::readLine()`!

Observe that, this time, we used

```
s2 = cin.readLine()
```

to extract a `QString` from the standard input stream.

1.9   Streams

Streams are objects used for reading and writing. The Standard Library defines `<iostream>`. Qt defines `<QTextStream>` for the equivalent functionality.

You already saw before that `iostream` defines the three global streams:

- `cin`—console input (keyboard)
- `cout`—console output (screen)
- `cerr`—console error (screen)

Also defined in `<iostream>` are *manipulators*, such as `flush` and `endl`. Manipulators are implicit calls to functions that can change the state of a stream object in various ways. A manipulator can be added to

- An output stream to change the way the output data is formatted.
- An input stream to change the way the input data is interpreted.

Example 1.9 demonstrates the use of manipulators applied to the console output stream.

EXAMPLE 1.9   src/stdstreams/streamdemo.cpp

```cpp
#include <iostream>

int main() {
    using namespace std;
    int num1(1234), num2(2345) ;
    cout << oct << num2 << '\t'
            << hex << num2 << '\t'
             << dec << num2
             << endl;
    cout << (num1 < num2) << endl;
    cout << boolalpha
             << (num1 < num2)
             << endl;
    double dub(1357);
    cout << dub << '\t'
             << showpos << dub << '\t'
             << showpoint << dub
             << endl;
    dub = 1234.5678;
    cout << dub << '\t'
             << fixed << dub << '\t'
             << scientific << dub << '\n'
             << noshowpos << dub
             << endl;
}
```

Output:

```
4451       929       2345
1
true
1357       +1357      +1357.00
+1234.57              +1234.567800      +1.234568e+03
1.234568e+03
```

It is easy to define QTextStreams with the same names as their equivalent iostream counterparts. Because console input and output streams are often used primarily for debugging purposes, Qt provides a global function, qDebug(), that facilitates sending messages to the console (whatever that may be) with a flexible interface demonstrated in Example 1.10.

EXAMPLE 1.10   src/qtstreams/qtstreamdemo.cpp

```cpp
#include <QTextStream>
#include <QDebug>

QTextStream cin(stdin);
QTextStream cout(stdout);
QTextStream cerr(stderr);

int main() {
    int num1(1234), num2(2345) ;
    cout << oct << num2 << '\t'
            << hex << num2 << '\t'
             << dec << num2
             << endl;
    double dub(1357);
    cout << dub << '\t'
            << forcesign << dub << '\t'
            << forcepoint << dub
            << endl;
    dub = 1234.5678;
    cout << dub << '\t'
            << fixed << dub << '\t'
            << scientific << dub << '\n'
            << noforcesign << dub
            << endl;
```

```
    qDebug() << "Here is a debug message with " << dub << "in it." ;
    qDebug("Here is one with the number %d in it.", num1 );
}
```

Output:

```
4451      929      2345
1357     +1357    +1357.00
+1234.57          +1234.567800      +1.234568e+03
1.234568e+03
Here is a debug message with  1234.57 in it.

Here is one with the number 1234 in it.
```

The symbols stdin, stdout, and stderr come from the C standard library. Note that QTextStream also provides manipulators, some of which are spelled the same as the ones used in Example 1.9 with iostream.

1.10   File Streams

Streams are used for reading from or writing to files, network connections, and strings. One useful feature of streams is that they make it easy to produce strings from mixed types of data. Example 1.11 creates some strings from characters and numerics and writes them to a file.

EXAMPLE 1.11   src/stl/streams/streams.cpp

```
[ . . . . ]

#include <iostream>
#include <sstream>
#include <fstream>

int main() {
    using namespace std;
    ostringstream strbuf;

    int lucky = 7;
    float pi=3.14;
    double e=2.71;
```

```
cout << "An in-memory stream" << endl;
strbuf << "luckynumber: " << lucky << endl
       << "pi: " << pi << endl
       << "e: " << e << endl;

string strval = strbuf.str();                                    1
cout << strval;

ofstream outf;                                                   2
outf.open("mydata");                                            3
outf << strval ;
outf.close();
```

1 Convert the stringstream to a string.

2 An output file stream.

3 Creates (or overwrites) a disk file for output.

After the strings have been written, you have a couple of choices of how to read them. You can use simple input operators to read from the file and, because there is whitespace between records, the insertion operator might look like Example 1.12.

EXAMPLE 1.12   src/stl/streams/streams.cpp

```
[ . . . . ]

    cout << "Read data from the file - watch for errors." << endl;
    string newstr;
    ifstream inf;                                               1
    inf.open("mydata");
    if(inf) {   /*Make sure the file exists before attempting to read.*/
      int lucky2;
      inf >> newstr >> lucky2;
      if (lucky != lucky2)
        cerr << "ERROR! wrong " << newstr << lucky2  << endl;
      else
        cout << newstr << " OK" << endl;

      float pi2;
      inf >> newstr >> pi2;
      if (pi2 != pi)
        cerr << "ERROR! Wrong " << newstr << pi2 << endl;
      else
        cout << newstr << " OK" << endl;
```

```
    double e2;
    inf >> newstr >> e2;
    if (e2 != e)
      cerr << "ERROR: Wrong " << newstr << e2 <<  endl;
    else
      cout << newstr << " OK" << endl;
    inf.close();
  }
```

1 An input file stream

You can read files line-by-line and deal with each line as a single string, as shown in
Example 1.13.

EXAMPLE 1.13   src/stl/streams/streams.cpp

```
[ . . . . ]

    cout << "Read from file line-by-line" << endl;
    inf.open("mydata");
    if(inf) {
      while (not inf.eof()) {
        getline(inf, newstr);
        cout << newstr << endl;
      }
      inf.close();
    }
    return 0;
}
```

Example 1.14 does the same things using Qt files, strings, and streams. This example also uses two other Qt types: QString, which provides a powerful and flexible string
representation, and QFile, which provides an interface for handling files.

EXAMPLE 1.14   src/qtstreams/files/qdemo.cpp

```
#include <QTextStream>
#include <QString>
#include <QFile>

QTextStream cout(stdout);
QTextStream cerr(stderr);
```

```
int main() {
  QString str, newstr;
  QTextStream strbuf(&str);                                        1

  int lucky = 7;
  float pi = 3.14;
  double e = 2.71;

  cout << "An in-memory stream" << endl;
  strbuf << "luckynumber: " << lucky << endl
         << "pi: " << pi << endl
         << "e: " << e << endl;


  cout << str;

  QFile data("mydata");
  data.open(QIODevice::WriteOnly);                                 2
  QTextStream out(&data);                                          3
  out << str ;
  data.close();

  cout << "Read data from the file - watch for errors." << endl;
  if(data.open(QIODevice::ReadOnly)) {                             4
    QTextStream in(&data);                                         5
    int lucky2;
    in >> newstr >> lucky2;
    if (lucky != lucky2)
      cerr << "ERROR! wrong " << newstr << lucky2  << endl;
    else
      cout << newstr << " OK" << endl;


    float pi2;
    in >> newstr >> pi2;
    if (pi2 != pi)
      cerr << "ERROR! Wrong " << newstr << pi2 << endl;
    else
      cout << newstr << " OK" << endl;


    double e2;
    in >> newstr >> e2;
    if (e2 != e)
      cerr << "ERROR: Wrong " << newstr << e2 <<  endl;
    else
      cout << newstr << " OK" << endl;
```

```
        data.close();
    }

    cout << "Read from file line-by-line" << endl;
    if(data.open(QIODevice::ReadOnly)) {
        QTextStream in(&data);                                    6
        while (not in.atEnd()) {
            newstr = in.readLine();
            cout << newstr << endl;
        }
        data.close();
    }
    return 0;
}
```

1 `strbuf` is initialized with the address of `str`.

2 Creates (or overwrites) a disk file for output.

3 An output file stream.

4 Make sure the file exists before attempting to read.

5 An input file stream.

6 An input file stream.

Section 1.15.1 discusses the *address-of operator*, used to initialize `strbuf`.

1.10.1   Exercises: File Streams

1. Run the program excerpted in Example 1.11 as written and then
   - Modify it so that it gets the filename from the user as an STL string `fileName` before writing or reading. You need to use the function `fileName.c_str()` to convert the string to a form acceptable to the `open()` function.
   - Modify it so that it makes sure that the file specified by the user does not already exist (or that it is okay to overwrite if it does exist) before opening it for output.
   - Explain what happens if you read the individual numbers with variables of the wrong type (e.g., `int` instead of `float` or `double`) in the "watch for errors" section.
   - Explain what happens if you read only with numerical variables and do not use the `newstr` variable in the "watch for errors" block.

2. Do the same thing for the program in Example 1.14.

1.11   Qt Dialogs for User Input/Output

Example 1.15 shows a rewrite of the first C++ example, using standard Qt dialogs instead of standard input/output and QString instead of Standard Library strings. We include this example here, even though the code contains a few things that have not been discussed yet so that you can see another way to ask for input and present output, using Qt graphical user interface (GUI) convenience functions.

EXAMPLE 1.15   src/early-examples/example1/fac1.cpp

```
#include <QtGui>

int main (int argc, char* argv[]) {                              1
    QApplication app(argc, argv);                                2
    QTextStream cout(stdout);                                    3

    // Declarations of variables
    int answer = 0;                                              4

    do {
        // local variables to the loop:
        int factArg = 0;
        int fact(1);
        factArg = QInputDialog::getInt(0, "Factorial Calculator",
            "Factorial of:", 1);                                 5
        cout << "User entered: " << factArg << endl;
        int i=2;
        while (i <= factArg) {
            fact = fact * i;
            ++i;
        }
        QString response = QString("The factorial of %1 is %2.\n%3")
            .arg(factArg).arg(fact)                              6
            .arg("Do you want to compute another factorial?");   7
        answer = QMessageBox::question(0, "Play again?", response,
            QMessageBox::Yes | QMessageBox::No);                 8
    } while (answer == QMessageBox::Yes);
    return EXIT_SUCCESS;
}
```

1 Start of function `main` which returns `int`.

2 Start of every Qt GUI application.

3 Create a `QTextStream` to standard output.

4 Must be defined outside the `do` loop because it is used in the condition outside the `do` block.

5 Pop up dialog, wait for user to enter an integer, return it.

6 Each `%n` is replaced with an `arg()` value.

7 Long statements can continue on multiple lines, as long as they are broken on token boundaries.

8 Bitwise or of two values.

This program uses the Qt types (classes) listed next.

- `QApplication`—A single object that needs to exist in Qt GUI applications.
- `QInputDialog`—For asking questions of the user.
- `QMessageBox`—For sending responses back to the user.
- `QString`—A unicode string class. This example uses the powerful `QString` function `arg()`, which enables you to format parameterized values (`%1`, `%2`, etc.) into the string.
- `QTextStream`—For streaming to/from text files. In this example, we defined a variable called `cout` that goes to the same place (`stdout`) as the `iostream cout` from the C++ standard library. If you intend to get user input from dialogs and other widgets, there is no need for `cin` anymore.

The code in Example 1.15 contains items discussed in the following sections:

- Command-line arguments (`argc` and `argv`)—Section 1.13.1
- Classes and scope resolution operators (`::`)—Section 2.2
- Static member functions—Section 2.9
- Pointers—Section 1.15
- Optional arguments—Section 5.2

When you run this application, you first see an input dialog like Figure 1.2.

FIGURE 1.2   `QInputDialog` - Getting an int

The input "widget" inside the dialog box is called a **spin box** and is implemented as `QSpinBox`. It displays the current value and, if the user clicks on the up or down button located at the right end of the display space, it displays other acceptable choices. The user could also press the up or down arrow key. The implementation is flexible and can easily be customized (e.g., by specifying the minimum and maximum acceptable values). After the user enters a number and clicks OK, the dialog box is replaced with a `QMessageBox` that pops up with the calculated result, as you see in Figure 1.3.

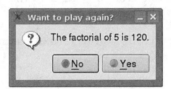

FIGURE 1.3   `QMessageBox` Question

More About Project Files

Any application that uses Qt classes needs a *project file*. Recall that a project file describes the project by listing all the files and all the options and file locations that are needed to build the project. Because this is a simple application, the project file is also quite simple, as shown in Example 1.16.

EXAMPLE 1.16   src/early-examples/example1/example1.pro

```
TEMPLATE = app
include (../../common.pri)
SOURCES += fac1.cpp
```

The first line, TEMPLATE = app, indicates that qmake should start with a templated Makefile suited for building applications. If this project file were for a library, you would see TEMPLATE = lib to indicate that a Makefile library template should be used instead. A third possibility is that you might have your source code distributed among several subdirectories, each having its own project file. In such a case you might see TEMPLATE = subdirs in the project file located in the parent directory, which would cause a Makefile to be produced in the parent directory and in each subdirectory.

The second line includes the optional common project settings from Example 1.6. Finally, the source file is listed in SOURCES.

1.11.1   Exercises: Qt Dialogs for User Input/Output

The exercises in this section are based on Example 1.15. You can find most answers in the Qt Reference API Documentation.

1. How can you fix the program so that it performs no calculation and exits the loop if the user clicks Cancel?

2. At the moment, the program does not check to see if the user enters a negative number. How can you fix it to ensure that negative numbers are never accepted?

1.12   Identifiers, Types, and Literals

Identifiers are names that are used in C++ programs for functions, parameters, variables, constants, classes, and types.

An **identifier** consists of a sequence of letters, digits, and underscores that does not begin with a digit. An identifier cannot be a reserved keyword. See Appendix A, "C++ Reserved Keywords," for a list of them. The standard does not specify a limit to the length of an identifier, but certain implementations of C++ examine only the first 31 characters to distinguish between identifiers.

A **literal** is a constant value that appears somewhere in a program. Because every value has a *type*, every literal has a type also. It is possible to have literals of each of the native data types and also character string literals. Table 1.1 shows some examples of literals and their types.

TABLE 1.1   Examples of Literals

Literal	Meaning
5	`int` literal
5u	u or U specifies unsigned int
5L	l or L specifies `long int` after an integer
05	Octal `int` literal
0x5	Hexadecimal `int` literal
true	`bool` literal
5.0F	f or F specifies single precision floating point literal
5.0	`double` precision floating point literal
5.0L	l or L specifies `long double` if it comes after a floating point
'5'	`char` literal (ASCII 53)
"50"	`const char*` containing the chars `'5'` `'0'` and `'\0'`
"any" "body"	"anybody"
'\a'	Alert
'\\'	Backslash
'\b'	Backspace
'\r'	Return (or Enter)
'\''	Single quote
'\"'	Double quote
'\f'	Formfeed (newpage)
'\t'	Tab
'\n'	Newline `char` literal
"\n"	Newline followed by null terminator (`const char*`)
'\0'	Null character
'\v'	Vertical tab
"a string with newline\n"	Another `const char*`

String literals are special in C++, due to its historical roots in the C language. Example 1.17 shows how certain characters need to be escaped inside double-quoted string delimiters.

EXAMPLE 1.17   src/early-examples/literals/qliterals.cpp

```
#include <QTextStream>
#include <QString>
```

```
int main() {
    const char* charstr = "this is one very long string "
                " so I will continue it on the next line";
    QTextStream cout(stdout);
    QString str = charstr;                                        1
    cout << str << endl;
    cout << "\nA\tb\\c\'d\"" << endl;
    return 0;
}
```

1 C-style strings can be converted to QString.

Building and running this program produce the following output.

```
src/early-examples/literals> qmake -project
src/early-examples/literals> qmake
src/early-examples/literals> make
g++ -c -pipe -O2 -Wall -W -D_REENTRANT -DQT_NO_DEBUG -DQT_GUI_LIB
  -DQT_CORE_LIB -DQT_SHARED -I/usr/share/qt4/mkspecs/linux-g++ -I.
  -I/usr/include/qt4/QtCore -I/usr/include/qt4/QtCore
  -I/usr/include/qt4/QtGui -I/usr/include/qt4/QtGui
  -I/usr/include/qt4 -I. -I. -I. -o qliterals.o qliterals.cpp
g++ -o literals qliterals.o  -L/usr/lib -lQtGui -lQtCore -lpthread
src/early-examples/literals> ./literals
```

The output should look something like this:

```
this is one very long string so I will continue it on the next line

A       b\c'd"
```

Notice that this program shows a way to control the lengths of lines when dealing with string literals. They can be broken at any whitespace character and are concatenated automatically using this syntax.

1.12.1   Exercises: Identifiers, Types, and Literals

Modify Example 1.17 so that, with a single output statement, the output becomes:
1. GNU stands for "GNU's Not UNIX".
2.
   ```
           Title 1        "Cat Clothing"
           Title 2        "Dog Dancing"
   ```

1.13   C++ Simple Types

The simple types supported in C/C++ are listed in Table 1.2.

C/C++ also provides a special symbol that signifies the absence of type information: `void`.

C++ simple types can (variously) be modified by the following keywords to produce other simple types.

- `short`
- `long`
- `signed`
- `unsigned`[23]

TABLE 1.2   Simple Types Hierarchy

byte/char Types	Integral Types	Floating Point Types
bool	short int	float
char	unsigned short	double
signed char	int	long double
unsigned char	unsigned int	
wchar_t	anyType*	
	long int	
	unsigned long	

C++ compilers allow you to omit `int` from the type names `short int`, `long int`, and `unsigned int`. You can also omit `signed` from most types because that is the default.

C++ Object Size

Object size in C++ is expressed in terms of the size of `char`. In this metric, the size of `char` is 1. Because the range of values for a particular type depends on the underlying architecture of the compiler's platform, the ANSI/ISO standard for C++ does not specify the size of any of the types displayed in Table 1.2. It guarantees only that a given type (e.g., `int`) must not be smaller than one that appears above it (e.g., `short`) in the table.

---

[23] For further discussion of the differences between signed and unsigned integral types, see Section 19.5.

There is a special operator, `sizeof()`, that returns the number of char-sized memory cells that a given expression requires for storage. On most systems, a single char is stored as an 8-bit *byte*. Unlike most functions, the `sizeof()` operator can take arguments that are value expressions *or* type expressions. Example 1.18 shows how `sizeof()` can be used and some of the values it returns on a 32-bit x86 system.

EXAMPLE 1.18   src/early-examples/size/qsize.cpp

```cpp
#include <QString>
#include <QTextStream>
#include <QChar>
#include <QDate>

int main() {
    QTextStream cout(stdout);
    char array1[34] = "This is a dreaded C array of char";
    char array2[] = "if not for main, we could avoid it entirely.";
    char* charp = array1;                                              1
    QString qstring = "This is a unicode QString. Much preferred." ;
    Q_ASSERT (sizeof(i) == sizeof(int));
    cout << "  c type sizes: \n";
    cout << "sizeof(char) = " << sizeof(char) << '\n';
    cout << "sizeof(wchar_t) = " << sizeof(wchar_t) << '\n';
    cout << "sizeof(int) = " << sizeof(int) << '\n';
    cout << "sizeof(long) = " << sizeof(long) << '\n';
    cout << "sizeof(float) = " << sizeof(float) << '\n';
    cout << "sizeof(double) = " << sizeof(double) << '\n';
    cout << "sizeof(double*) = " << sizeof(double*) << '\n';
    cout << "sizeof(array1) = " << sizeof(array1) << '\n';
    cout << "sizeof(array2) = " << sizeof(array2) << '\n';
    cout << "sizeof(char*) = " << sizeof(charp) << endl;
    cout << "  qt type sizes: \n";
    cout << "sizeof(QString) = " << sizeof(QString) << endl;
    cout << "sizeof(qint32) = " << sizeof (qint32) << "\n";           2
    cout << "sizeof(qint64) = " << sizeof(qint64) << '\n';           3
    cout << "sizeof(QChar) = " << sizeof (QChar) << endl;            4
    cout << "sizeof(QDate) = " << sizeof(QDate) << endl;
    cout << "qstring.length() = " << qstring.length() << endl;       5
    return 0;

}
```

Output:

```
(example run on 32-bit system)
sizeof(char) = 1
sizeof(wchar_t) = 4
sizeof(int) = 4
sizeof(long) = 4
sizeof(float) = 4
sizeof(double) = 8
sizeof(double*) = 4
sizeof(array1) = 34
sizeof(array2) = 45
sizeof(char*) = 4
  qt type sizes:
sizeof(QString) = 4
sizeof(qint32) = 4
sizeof(qint64) = 8
sizeof(QChar) = 2
sizeof(QDate) = 4
qstring.length() = 42
```

1 Pointer to first element of array.

2 Guaranteed to be 32 bits on all platforms.

3 Guaranteed to be 64 bits on all platforms.

4 Twice as big as a char

5 For # of bytes, be sure to take into account the size of QChar.

Notice that all pointers are the same size, regardless of their type.

In the output, you can see that sizeof(qstring) is only 4 bytes, but it is a complex class that uses dynamic memory, so you must call length() to get the number of QChar in the string. Because a QChar is twice the size of char, you need to double the length to compute the actual size of QString in memory. Under the covers, QString can share memory with other strings that have the same value, so after a copy, the dynamic memory does not "belong" exclusively to one QString object.

The ranges of values for the integral types (bool, char, int) are defined in the standard header file limits.h. On a typical *nix installation, that file can be found in a subdirectory of /usr/include.

NOTE

Initialization of Basic-Typed Variables

When a variable is of a basic type, it must be initialized. Uninitialized variables of basic types have undefined values on program startup. They may have initial value 0 when running in a debugger and have garbage values when run in other envrionments.

1.13.1   `main` and Command-Line Arguments

`main()` is a function that is called at program startup. If you want the program to accept command-line arguments, you must define `main` with its full parameter list.

C and C++ permit some flexibility in the way that arguments are defined in `main()`, so you may see it defined in a variety of ways:

```
int main(int argc, char* argv[])
int main(int argCount, char ** argValues)
int main(int argc, char * const argv[])
```

All these forms are valid, and they each define two parameters: an `int` to contain the number of command-line arguments and an array of C-style strings to contain the actual arguments. These parameters contain enough information to reconstruct the command-line arguments passed into the program from the parent process.[24] Example 1.19 is a simple `main` program that prints its command-line arguments.

EXAMPLE 1.19   src/clargs/clargs-iostream/clargs.cpp

```
#include <iostream>
#include <cstdlib>                                              1

int main (int argc, char* argv[]) {
    using namespace std;
    cout << "argc = " << argc << endl;
    for (int i = 0; i < argc; ++i) {
        cout << "argv# " << i << " is " << argv[i] << endl;
    }
    int num = atoi(argv[argc - 1]);
    cout << num * 2 << endl;
    return 0;
}
```

---

[24] The process that called `main()` (e.g., a command-line shell, a window manager, etc.).

1 for `atoi()`

`argv`, the **argument vector**, is an array (Section 21.4) that contains all the command-line strings. In other words, because each command-line string is itself an array of `char`, `argv` is an array of `char` arrays. `argc`, the **argument count**, is the number of `char` arrays in `argv`.

`main()` needs to return an `int` to the parent process. In *nix systems, the return value of a process is called its **exit status**. Presumably, the parent process can use the exit status to decide what to do next.[25] The return value should be 0 if all went well, or a nonzero error code if something went wrong. This can be accomplished in a few different ways.

- With an explicit

  ```
  return 0;
  ```

  statement, as we do in most of our examples.
- If there is no return statement in the `main()` block, 0 will be returned by default when the closing brace } is reached. Example 1.20 demonstrates this.
- For maximum portability, programs strictly adhering to the C++ standard should

  ```
  #include <cstdlib>
  ```

  and then explicitly terminate `main()` with

  ```
  return EXIT_SUCCESS;
  ```

  as in Section 1.11.

NOTE

Try not to confuse this interpretation of 0 with the `bool` value `false`, which is also equal to 0.

If you run this program with command-line arguments, you will see something like this in the output:

---

[25] We discuss programs that control various separate processes in in Section 17.1.

```
clargs> ./clargs spam eggs "space wars" 123
argc = 5
argv# 0 is ./clargs
argv# 1 is spam
argv# 2 is eggs
argv# 3 is space wars
argv# 4 is 123
246
```

The first argument is the name of the executable. The other arguments are taken from the command line as strings separated by spaces or tabs. To pass a string that contains spaces as a single argument, you must enclose the string in quotes.

The last argument looks like the number 123. In fact, it is the string representation of that number. If you need to calculate with that number, it would be necessary to use a suitable function to convert the string "123" to the number 123.

Processing Command-Line Arguments with Qt

In Example 1.20, we have rewritten Example 1.19 to set up and access the command-line arguments using Qt types and avoiding the use of arrays. The two applications produce the same output.

EXAMPLE 1.20   src/clargs/qt/clargs.cpp

```cpp
#include <QTextStream>
#include <QCoreApplication>
#include <QStringList>

int main (int argc, char* argv[]) {
    QCoreApplication app(argc, argv);
    QTextStream cout(stdout);
    QStringList arglst = app.arguments();
    cout << "argc = " << argc << endl;
    for (int i=0; i<arglst.size(); ++i) {
        cout << QString("argv#%1 is %2").arg(i).arg(arglst[i]) << endl;
    }
    int num = arglst[argc - 1].toInt();
    cout << num * 2 << endl;
}
```

Most applications that employ Qt types should define an object of type
`QCoreApplication` or `QApplication` as early as possible in `main()`.[26] Section 8.3 discusses the reasons for this and the distinctions between those two types in more detail.

The `QCoreApplication app` is initialized with the argument `count` and the argument `vector`. app silently converts the `char` arrays in `argv` to `QStrings` and stores those
strings in a `QStringList` (Section 4.2.1). You can then access and process the command-
line arguments by using `app` to call the `arguments()` function. Using higher-level data
structures like these eliminates the need to work with `char` arrays, which reduces the
risk of memory corruption.[27]

Notice the use of the `QString` function `toInt()`.

1.13.2 Arithmetic

Every programming language provides support for basic arithmetic operations and
expressions. For each of its native numerical types, C++ provides these four basic arithmetic operators:

- Addition (+)
- Subtraction (-)
- Multiplication (*)
- Division (/)

These operator symbols are used to form expressions in the standard infix syntax
that you learned in math class.

C++ provides shortcut operators that combine each of the basic operators with the
assignment operator (=) so that, for example, it is possible to write

```
x += y;
```

instead of

```
x = x + y;
```

C++ also provides unary increment (++) and decrement (--) operators that can
be used with integral types. If one of these operators is applied to a variable on its
left side (prefix), then the operation is performed before the rest of the expression is

---

[26] Applications that use only types such as `QString`, `QStringList`, and `QTextStream` do not need a `QCoreApplication`.

[27] First read Section 1.15 and then Chapter 21, "Memory Access." Bjarne Stroustrup also has some helpful advice on this subject.

evaluated. If it is applied to a variable on its right side (postfix), then the operation is performed after the rest of the expression is evaluated. Modern compilers usually produce a shorter block of machine code when compiling the prefix operator than when compiling the postfix operator, so prefix operators are recommended over postfix operators when it doesn't matter whether the operation takes place before or after the expression is evaluated. Example 1.21 through Example 1.25 demonstrate the use of the C++ arithmetic operators.

EXAMPLE 1.21   src/arithmetic/arithmetic.cpp

```
[ . . . . ]


#include <QTextStream>

int main() {
    QTextStream cout(stdout);
    double x(1.23), y(4.56), z(7.89) ;
    int i(2), j(5), k(7);
    x += y ;
    z *= x ;
    cout << "x = " << x << "\tz = " << z
            << "\nx - z = " << x - z << endl ;
```

Integer division is handled as a special case. The result of dividing one `int` by another produces an `int` quotient and an `int` remainder. The operator `/` is used to obtain the quotient. The operator `%` (called the **modulus operator**) is used to obtain the remainder. Example 1.22 demonstrates the use of these integer arithmetic operators.

EXAMPLE 1.22   src/arithmetic/arithmetic.cpp

```
[ . . . . ]


    cout << "k / i = " << k / i
            << "\tk % j = " << k % j << endl ;
    cout << "i = " << i << "\tj = " << j << "\tk = " << k << endl;
    cout << "++k / i = " << ++k / i << endl;
    cout << "i = " << i << "\tj = " << j << "\tk = " << k << endl;
    cout << "i * j-- = " << i * j-- << endl;
    cout << "i = " << i << "\tj = " << j << "\tk = " << k << endl;
```

Mixed expressions, if valid, generally produce results of the widest of the argument types.[28] In Example 1.23, you can see that the result of a `double` divided by an `int` is a `double`.

EXAMPLE 1.23   src/arithmetic/arithmetic.cpp

```
[ . . . . ]

    cout << "z / j = " << z / j << endl ;
```

Conversions are discussed further in Chapter 19, "Types and Expressions."

C++ also provides a full set of boolean operators to compare numeric expressions. Each of these operators returns a `bool` value of either `false` or `true`.

- Less than (`<`)
- Less than or equal to (`<=`)
- Equal to (`==`)
- Not equal to (`!=`)
- Greater than (`>`)
- Greater than or equal to (`>=`)

A `bool` expression can be negated with the unary `not` (`!`) operator. Expressions can be formed with two or more `bool` expressions using the **conjunction** and **disjunction** operators

- and (`&&`)
- or (`||`)

EXAMPLE 1.24   src/arithmetic/arithmetic.cpp

```
[ . . . . ]

    /*   if () ... else   approach */
    if (x * j <= z)
        cout << x * j << " <= " << z << endl ;
    else
        cout << x * j << " > " << z << endl;
```

---

[28] See Table 1.2 for relative type widths.

In addition to the binary boolean operators, Example 1.25 uses the **conditional-expression**.

```
(boolExpr) ? expr1 : expr2
```

returns *expr1* if *boolExpr* is true, and otherwise returns *expr2*.

EXAMPLE 1.25   src/arithmetic/arithmetic.cpp

```
[ . . . . . ]

    /* conditional operator approach */
    cout << x * k
            <<( (x * k < y * j) ? " < " : " >= ")
            << y * j << endl;
    return 0;
}
```

Example 1.26 shows the output of this program.

EXAMPLE 1.26   src/arithmetic/arithmetic.cpp

```
[ . . . . . ]
```

Output:

```
x = 5.79        z = 45.6831
x - z = -39.8931
k / i = 3       k % j = 2
i = 2    j = 5   k = 7
++k / i = 4
i = 2    j = 5   k = 8
i * j-- = 10
i = 2    j = 4   k = 8
z / j = 11.4208
23.16 <= 45.6831
46.32 >= 18.24
```

1.13.3   Exercises: C++ Simple Types

1. Write a short program that asks the user to enter a Celsius value and then computes the equivalent Fahrenheit temperature. It should use a QInputDialog to get the value from the user and a `QMessageBox` to display the result. After that, it should print out a table of Celsius to Fahrenheit values from 0 to 100 by increments of 5, to the console output.

2. If you `#include <cstdlib>`, you can use the `rand()` function, which generates a sequence of uniformly distributed pseudo-random `long int` values in the range 0 to `RAND_MAX`. It works by computing the next number in its sequence from the last number that it generated. The function call

```
srand(unsigned int seed)
```

sets the first value of the sequence that `rand()` generates to `seed`. Write a short program that tests this function. Ask the user to supply the `seed` from the keyboard and then generate a list of pseudo-random numbers.

3. If you want your program's behavior to change each time you run it, you can use `srand(time(0))` to seed the `rand()` function. Because the function call `time(0)` returns the number of seconds since some initial starting point, the `seed` will be different each time you run the program. This enables you to write programs that have usefully unpredictable behavior patterns.

There is no particular advantage to calling `srand()` more than once when you execute your program. In fact, because a computer can do many things in a single second, repeated calls to `srand()` might even reduce the apparent randomness of your program.

Write a program that simulates a dice game that the user can play with the computer. Here are the rules to apply to your game:

- The game is about repeated "throws" of a pair of dice.
- Each die has six faces, numbered 1 through 6.
- A throw results in a number that is the total of the two top faces.
- The first throw establishes the player's number.
- If that number is 7 or 11, the player automatically wins.
- If that number is 2, the player automatically loses.
- Otherwise, the player continues throwing until she wins (by matching her number) or loses (by throwing a 7 or an 11).

4. Write a program that accepts two values from the user (customer): the total purchase amount and the amount submitted for payment.

Each of these values can be stored in a variable of type double. Compute and display the change that will be given to the user. Express the change in terms of the number of $10 bills, $5 bills, $1 bills, quarters, dimes, nickels, and pennies. (Presumably, this output could be sent to a machine that dispenses those items automatically.)

For example, if the total purchase amount is $73.82 and the customer pays with a $100 bill, the change should be two $10 bills, a $5 bill, a $1 bill, no quarters, a dime, a nickel, and three pennies.

 TIP

Convert the amount owed to the customer into pennies, which can be stored as an int. Use integer division operators.

---

5. Write a program to play the following game, which the user plays against the computer.

   This game is played on an imaginary game board that has numbered spaces arranged in a circle.[29] For example, here is what a game board with 12 spaces might look like.

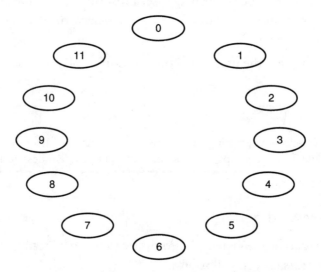

---

[29] No graphics are required for this exercise. The game board is described only to help you picture the setup in your mind.

- When the program starts, the user is asked to specify how many spaces there are on the game board. There must be at least five spaces.

- The computer then randomly selects two spaces (excluding space numbers 0 and 1): One of the selected spaces is **The Goal**. The other is **The Pit**.

- The computer announces the two special spaces.

- Play then starts from space #0: Each player, in turn, "rolls" a pair of dice and "moves" to another space by advancing N spaces (where N is the number that came up on the dice). For example, using the sample game board with 12 spaces, if the user rolled a 10 (6 plus 4) on her first turn and a 7 (3 + 4) on her second turn, then she would land on space #5. That's where she would start on her next turn.

- The user and the computer take turns rolling the dice and moving around the board. Each move is displayed on the screen (as text, not graphics; e.g., "You are now on space #3").

- The game continues until one player lands on **The Goal** (and wins the game) or on **The Pit** (and loses the game).

- The computer announces the outcome of each game and keeps track of each player's wins and losses.

- The user can choose single play (user must press Enter for each roll of the dice) or continuous play (dice are automatically rolled and play continues until someone wins).

- After each game the user can choose to quit or play another game.

 TIP

Do Problem 2 before attempting this problem. You may also need the suggestion at the beginning of Problem 3 and, perhaps, some ideas from that problem description.

1.14 The Keyword `const`

Declaring an entity to be `const` tells the compiler to make it "read-only." `const` can be used in many contexts, as you will soon see.

Because it cannot be assigned to, a `const` object must be properly initialized when it is first declared. For example:

```
const int x = 33;
const int v[] = {3, 6, x, 2 * x};    // a const array
```

Working with the preceding declarations:

```
++x ;              // error
v[2] = 44;         // error
```

No storage needs to be allocated for a const initialized with an int or some other simple type unless its address is taken. More generally, if the initializer for a const is a constant expression that can be evaluated at compile time, and the compiler knows every use of it, it might not be necessary to allocate space for it.

It is good programming style to use const entities instead of embedding numeric literals (sometimes called "magic numbers") in your code. This can gain you flexibility later when you need to change the values. In general, isolating constants improves the maintainability of your programs. For example, instead of writing something like this:

```
for(i = 0; i < 327; ++i) {
    ...
}
```

use something like this:

```
// const declaration section of your code
const int SIZE = 327;
...
for(i = 0; i < SIZE; ++i) {
    ...
}
```

 NOTE

In some C/C++ programs, you might see constants defined as preprocessor macros like this:

```
#define STRSIZE 80
[...]
char str[STRSIZE];
```

Preprocessor macros get replaced before the compiler sees them. Using macros instead of constants means that the compiler cannot perform the same level of type checking as it can with proper const expressions. Generally, const expressions are preferred to macros for defining constant values in C++ programs. Other uses of the preprocessor can be found in Section C.2.

1.15   Pointers and Memory Access

C and C++ distinguish themselves from many other languages by permitting direct access to memory through the use of pointers. This section explains the basic pointer operations and modifiers and introduces dynamic memory usage. Pointers can seem complicated at first. We discuss pointer use and misuse in more detail in Chapter 21.

1.15.1   The Unary Operators & and *

An **object** (in the most general sense) is a chunk of memory that can hold data. A **variable** is an object with a name recognized by the compiler. A variable's name can be used as if it is the object itself. For example, if you say

```
int  x  =  5;
```

you can use x to stand for the integer object whose value is 5, and you can manipulate the integer object directly through the name x. For example:

```
++x ;  // symbol x now refers to an integer with value 6
```

Each object has a memory address (where its data begins). The **unary & operator**, also known as the **address-of operator**, when applied to any object, returns the memory address of that object. For example: &x returns the memory address of x.

An object that holds the memory address of another object is called a **pointer**. We say that the pointer **points** to the object at the stored memory address.

```
int*  y  =  &x ;
```

In this example, y points to the integer x. The asterisk * following the type name int indicates that y is a pointer to **int.**

Here the int pointer y is initialized to the address of the int variable x. One of the powerful features of pointers is that, subject to rules that we will explore shortly, it is possible for a pointer of one type to hold the address of an object of a different (but related) type.

Zero (0), often represented by the macro NULL in C programs, is a special value that can be legally assigned to a pointer, usually when it is initialized or after it has been deleted. 0 is not the address of an object. A pointer that stores the value 0 is called a

null pointer. Stroustrup recommends the use of 0 rather than the macro NULL in C++ programs.

A pointer to a simple type uses exactly the amount of memory as a pointer to a large, complicated object. That size is usually the same as sizeof(int) on that machine.

The **unary * operator**, also known as the **dereference operator**, when applied to a non-null pointer, returns the object at the address stored by the pointer.

CAUTION

The symbol * is used in two different ways in connection with pointers:

· It can serve as a *type modifier*, in a pointer variable definition.

· It can be used as the dereference operator.

EXAMPLE 1.27   src/pointers/pointerdemo/pointerdemo.cpp

```cpp
#include <QTextStream>

int main() {
    QTextStream cout(stdout);
    int x = 4;
    int* px = 0 ;                                        1
    px = &x;
    cout << "x = " << x
        << " *px = " << *px                              2
        << " px = " << px
        << " &px = " << &px << endl;
    x = x + 1;
    cout << "x = " << x
        << " *px = " << *px
        << " px = " << px << endl;
    *px = *px + 1;
    cout << "x = " << x
        << " *px = " << *px
        << " px = " << px << endl;
    return 0;

}
```

Output:

```
OOP> ./pointerdemo
x = 4 *px = 4 px = 0xbffff514 &px = 0xbffff510
x = 5 *px = 5 px = 0xbffff514
x = 6 *px = 6 px = 0xbffff514
OOP>
```

1 Type modifier

2 Unary dereference operator

When Example 1.27 is run at different times or on different machines, the memory addresses are likely to be different.

The variable x accesses its data *directly*, but the variable px accesses the same data *indirectly*. This is why the word *indirection* is often used to characterize the process of accessing data through a pointer. The relationship between the two variables, x and px, is illustrated in Figure 1.4.

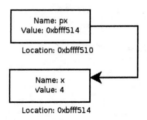

FIGURE 1.4   Pointer Demo

Because whitespace is ignored by the compiler, the location of whitespace can help or confuse the reader. To improve readability and maintainability of C++ code that contains pointer declarations, we recommend that

- Each pointer has its own declaration.
- The asterisk is placed immediately to the right of the type name.

    ```
    T* ptr;
    ```

This declaration is unambiguous: ptr is a pointer to type T.

1.15.2   Operators `new` and `delete`

C++ has a mechanism that permits storage to be allocated dynamically at runtime. This means that the programmer does not need to anticipate the memory needs of a program in advance and make allowances for the maximum amount of memory that might be needed by the program. Dynamic allocation of storage at runtime is a powerful tool that helps to build programs that are efficient and flexible.

The `new` operator allocates storage from the **heap** (also known as dynamic storage) and returns a pointer to the newly allocated object. If for some reason it is not possible for the memory to be allocated, an exception is thrown.[30]

The `delete` operator releases dynamically allocated memory and returns it to the heap. `delete` should be applied only to pointers returned by `new`, or to null pointers. Heap memory that is no longer needed should be released for reuse. Failure to do so can result in crippling memory leaks.

In general, the code that calls `new` should document, or be physically located near, the code that frees the memory. The goal is to keep memory management code as simple and reliable as possible.

Dereferencing a null, deleted, or uninitialized pointer causes a runtime error, usually a segmentation fault or, in Windows, a general protection fault (GPF). It is the responsibility of the programmer to make sure that this cannot happen. We will discuss techniques to ensure that such errors are avoided.

 The ability to manage memory gives the programmer great power. But with great power comes great responsibility.

The syntax of the `new` and `delete` operators is demonstrated in the code fragment shown in Example 1.28.

---

[30] We discuss this situation in an article on our Web site.

EXAMPLE 1.28   src/pointers/newdelete/ndsyntax.cpp

```
#include <iostream>
using namespace std;

int main() {
  int* ip = 0;                                              1
  delete ip;                                                2
  if(ip) cout << "non-null" << endl;
  else cout << "null" << endl;
  ip = new int;                                             3
  int* jp = new int(13);                                    4
  //[...]
  delete ip;                                                5
  delete jp;
}
```

1 Null pointer.

2 Has no effect at all—`ip` is still null.

3 Allocate space for an `int`.

4 Allocate and initialize.

5 Without this, we have a memory leak.

Null pointers are actually quite useful in programs. Even though it is a fatal runtime error to attempt to dereference a null pointer, it is perfectly legal to check to see if a pointer is null. For example, it is common practice for a function to search for an item in a container of pointers and, if the search is successful, return a pointer to that item. If the search is not successful, it still must return a pointer. In that case, returning a null pointer is a good choice. Of course, you must be careful to check the return value of such a function before dereferencing it to make sure it is not null. After a pointer has been deleted, assignment is the only legal operation that can be performed with it. We recommend immediately assigning the value 0 to a deleted pointer if no other choice is feasible.

NOTE

Qt, the Standard Library, and Boost.org each provide a variety of classes and functions to help manage and clean up heap memory. In addition to container classes, each library has one or more **smart pointer** class(es). A smart pointer is an object that stores and manages a pointer to a heap object. It behaves much like an ordinary pointer except that it automatically deletes the heap object at the appropriate time. Qt has `QPointer`, the standard library has `std::auto_ptr`, and Boost has a `shared_ptr`. Using one of these classes makes C++ memory management much easier and safer than it used to be.

1.15.3   Exercises: Pointers and Memory Access

1. Predict the output of Example 1.29.

EXAMPLE 1.29   src/pointers/newdelete1/newdelete1.cpp

```
#include <QTextStream>

int main() {
    QTextStream cout(stdout);
    const char tab = '\t';
    int n = 13;
    int* ip = new int(n + 3);
    double d = 3.14;
    double* dp = new double(d + 2.3);
    char c = 'K';
    char* cp = new char(c + 5);
    cout << *ip << tab << *dp << tab << *cp << endl;
    int* ip2 = ip;
    cout << ip << tab << ip2 << endl;
    *ip2 += 6;
    cout << *ip << endl;
    delete ip;
    cout << *ip2 << endl;
    cout << ip << tab << ip2 << endl;
    return 0;
}
```

Compile and run the code. Explain the output, especially the last two lines.

2. Modify Example 1.28 to do some arithmetic with the value pointed to by `jp`. Assign the result to the location in memory pointed to by `ip`, and print the result. Print out the values from different places in the program. Investigate how your compiler and runtime system react to placement of the output statements.

3. Read Chapter 21 and do experiments with the code examples.

1.16   Reference Variables

You observed earlier that an object (in the most general sense) is a contiguous region of storage. An **lvalue** is an expression that refers to an object. Examples of lvalues are variables, array cells, and dereferenced pointers. In essence, an lvalue is anything with a memory address that can be given a name. By contrast, temporary or constant expressions such as i+1 or 3 are not lvalues.

In C++, a **reference** provides a mechanism for assigning an alternative name to an lvalue. References are especially useful for avoiding making copies when copying is costly or unnecessary, for example, when passing a large object as a parameter to a function. A reference must be initialized when it is declared, and the initializer must be an lvalue.

To create a reference to an object of type SomeType, a variable must be declared to be of type SomeType&. For example:

```
int n;
int& rn = n;
```

The ampersand & following the int indicates that rn is an **int reference**. The reference variable rn is an alias for the actual variable n. Note that the & is being used here as a **type modifier** in a declaration, rather than as an operator on an lvalue.

For its entire life, a reference variable will be an alias for the actual lvalue that initialized it. This association cannot be revoked or transferred. For example:

```
int a = 10, b = 20;
int& ra = a;            // ra is an alias for a
ra = b;                 // this causes a to be assigned the value 20

const int c = 45;       // c is a constant: its value is read-only.
const int& rc = c;      // legal but probably not very useful.
rc = 10;                // compiler error - const data may not be changed.
```

You have surely noticed that the use of the ampersand in this section might be confused with its use in the earlier section on pointers. To avoid confusion, just remember these two facts:

1. The address-of operator applies to an object and returns its address. Hence, it appears only on the right side of an assignment or in an initializing expression for a pointer variable.

2. In connection with references, the ampersand is used only in the declaration of a reference. Hence, it appears only between the type name and the reference name as it is declared.

NOTE

For reference declarations, we recommend placing the ampersand immediately to the right of the type name:

```
Type& ref(initLval);
```

1.17   `const*` and `*const`

Suppose that you have a pointer `ptr` storing the address of a variable `vbl`:

```
Type* ptr = &vbl;
```

When using a pointer, two objects are involved: the pointer itself and the object pointed to. That means there are three possible layers of protection that can be imposed with `const`:

1. If you want to make sure that `ptr` cannot point to any other memory location (i.e., cannot store a different address), you can write it one of two ways:

```
Type* const ptr = &vbl;
Type* const ptr(&vbl);
```

The pointer is a `const`, but the addressed object can be changed.

2. If you want to make sure that the value of `vbl` cannot be changed by dereferencing `ptr`, you can write it in two ways:

```
const Type* ptr = &vbl;
const Type* ptr(&vbl);
```

In this case, the addressed object is a constant, but the pointer is not.

3. If you want to impose *both* kinds of protection, you can write

```
const Type* const ptr = &vbl;
const Type* const ptr(&vbl);
```

Here is a good way to remember which is which: Read each of the following definitions from right to left (starting with the defined variable).

```
const char* x = &p;        /* x is a pointer to const char */
char* const y = &q;        /* y is a const pointer to char */
const char* const z = &r;  /* z is a const pointer to a const char */
```

Volatile

volatile is another keyword that can modify variables and pointer definitions. It can be used in the same places that const can be used. volatile can be thought of as almost the opposite of const: It marks something that can be modified at any time, perhaps by another program or another thread. It is a hint to the compiler that there should be no optimization during access to it.

It can be used for variables, but more commonly, it is used for pointers. Like const, it can be applied to the pointer or the addressed memory. To declare a regular pointer to volatile memory, use this form:

```
volatile char* vcharptr;
```

To declare a volatile pointer to regular memory, use this form:

```
char* volatile vptrchar;
```

Example 1.30 demonstrates the two kinds of protection.

EXAMPLE 1.30   src/constptr/constptr.cpp

```
#include <QTextStream>

int main() {
    QTextStream cout(stdout);
    int m1(11), m2(13);
    const int* n1(&m1);
    int* const n2(&m2);
    // First snapshot
    cout << "n1 = " << n1 << '\t' << *n1 << '\n'
         << "n2 = " << n2 << '\t' << *n2 << endl;
    n1 = &m2;
    //*n1 = 15;                                           1
    m1 = 17;                                              2
    //n2 = &m1;                                           3
    *n2 = 16;                                             4
    // Second snapshot
    cout << "n1 = " << n1 << '\t' << *n1 << '\n'
```

```
        << "n2 = " << n2 << '\t' << *n2 << endl;
    return 0;

}
```

Output:

```
src/constptr> ./constptr
n1 = 0xbffff504 11
n2 = 0xbffff500 13
n1 = 0xbffff500 16
n2 = 0xbffff500 16
src/constptr>
```

1 Error: assignment of read-only location

2 m2 is an ordinary int variable; okay to assign

3 Error: assignment of read-only variable n2

4 Okay to change target

Figure 1.5 shows two snapshots of memory at the noted spots in Example 1.29 to help clarify what is happening when the program runs. Notice that the program produces a memory leak.

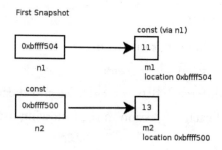

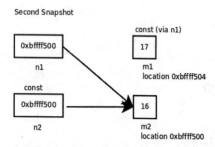

FIGURE 1.5   Memory Snapshots

An object that is read-only when accessed through one pointer may be changeable when accessed through another pointer. This fact is commonly exploited in the design of functions.

```
char* strcpy(char* dst, const char* src); // strcpy cannot change *src
```

It is okay to assign the address of a variable to a pointer to const. It is an error to assign the address of a const object to an unrestricted (i.e., non-const) pointer variable because that would allow the const object's value to be changed.

```
int a = 1;
const int c = 2;
const int* p1 = &c;    // okay
const int* p2 = &a;    // okay
int* p3 = &c;          // error
*p3 = 5;               // error
```

It is good programming practice to use const to protect pointer and reference parameters that do not need to be altered by the action of a function. Read-only reference parameters provide the power and efficiency of pass-by-reference with the safety of pass-by-value (Section 5.5).

1.18   Review Questions

1. What is a stream? What kinds of streams are there?

2. Give one reason to use an ostrstream.

3. What is the main difference between getline and the >> operator?

4. What is the type of each expression in the following list?

    1. 3.14
    2. 'D'
    3. "d"
    4. 6
    5. 6.2f
    6. "something stringy"
    7. false

5. In Example 1.31, identify the type and value of each numbered item.

EXAMPLE 1.31   src/types/types.cpp

```
#include <QTextStream>

int main() {
        QTextStream cout(stdout);
        int i = 5;
        int j=6;
        int* p = &i;                                            1
        int& r=i;
        int& rpr=(*p);                                          2
        i = 10;
        p = &j;                                                 3
        rpr = 7;                                                4

        r = 8;
        cout << "i=" << i << " j=" << j << endl;                5
        return 0;
}
```

1 *p: _____

2 *p: _____

3 *p: _____

4 rpr: _____

5 i: _____ j: _____

6. What is the difference between a pointer and a reference?

7. What is the keyword `const` used for? Why and how would you use it in a program?

8. What is the `address-of` operator? Why and how would you use it in a program?

9. What is the `dereference` operator? Why and how would you use it in a program?

10. What is a null pointer? Why would you define one in a program?

11. What is a memory leak? What would cause one in a program?

12. What might cause a segmentation fault (or, in Windows, a general protection fault)?

13. What are the possible uses of `const` when dealing with pointers?

14. What is a function's signature?

15. What is meant by the term "function overloading"?

16. Why is it an error to have two functions with the same signature but different return types in one scope?

17. Why does `main(int argc, char* argv[])` sometimes have parameters? What are they used for?

1.18.1   Points of Departure

1. See Section 21.1 to learn more about how pointers can be used or misused.

2. See Chapter 19 to learn more about how pointers and types can be converted.

Chapter 2

Top of the class

This chapter provides an introduction to classes and objects and how member functions operate on objects. Classes and objects can be arranged in different structures, and this chapter presents some ways to describe the relationships between them. UML is introduced. static and const members are explained. Constructors, destructors, copy operations, and friends are discussed.

2.1 First, There Was struct

In the C language, the struct keyword enables the programmer to define a structured chunk of memory that can store a heterogeneous set of data. Example 2.1 shows the definition of a structured piece of memory composed of smaller chunks of memory.

EXAMPLE 2.1   src/structdemo/demostruct.h

```
[ . . . . ]
struct Fraction {
    int numer, denom;
    string description;
};
[ . . . . ]
```

Each smaller chunk (`numer`, `denom`, `description`) of the `struct` is accessible by name. The smaller chunks are called **data members** or, sometimes, **fields**. Code that is external to the `struct` definition is called **client code**. Example 2.2 shows how client code can use a `struct` as a single entity.

EXAMPLE 2.2   src/structdemo/demostruct.cpp

```
[ . . . . ]
void printFraction(Fraction f) {                                     1
    cout << f.numer << "/" << f.denom << endl;
    cout << " =? " << f.description << endl;
}
int main() {
    Fraction f1;
    f1.numer = 4;
    f1.denom = 5;
    f1.description = "four fifths";
    Fraction f2 = {2, 3, "two thirds"};                              2

    f1.numer = f1.numer + 2;                                         3
    printFraction(f1);
    printFraction(f2);
    return 0;
}
```

Output:

```
6/5
=? four fifths
2/3
=? two thirds
```

1 Passing a struct by value could be expensive if it has large components.

2 Member initialization.

3 Client code can change individual data members.

The `printFraction()` function in this application displays the individual data members on the screen in its own peculiar way. Notice also that the client code was able to produce a `Fraction` that has an incorrect description.

2.2   Class Definitions

C++ has another datatype called `class` that is similar to `struct`. A `class` definition looks like this:

```
class ClassName {
    public:
         publicMembers
    private:
         privateMembers
};
```

The first line of the class definition is called the **classHead**.

The features of a class include **data members**, **member functions**, and **access specifiers** (`public, private, protected`). Member functions are used to initialize, manipulate, or otherwise manage the data members. Chapter 5, "Functions," discusses functions in more detail, especially those features found in C++ but not in some other languages. For now, we will use functions in ways that should be clear from the context and familiar to you from your earlier experience with other languages.

After you have defined a class, you can use the class name as a **type** for variables, parameters, and returns from functions. Variables of a class type are called **objects**, or **instances**, of the class.

Member functions for class *ClassName* specify the *behavior* of all objects of type *ClassName*. Each member function can access all other members of the class. Non-member functions can only manipulate objects indirectly by calling member functions.

The set of values of the data members of an object is called the *state* of the object.

2.2.1   Header Files

To define a class (or any other type), you should place its definition in a **header file**, preferably with the same name as the class, and with the `.h` extension. Example 2.3 shows a header file that contains a class definition.

EXAMPLE 2.3   src/classes/fraction/fraction.h

```
#ifndef _FRACTION_H_
#define _FRACTION_H_

#include <QString>
```

```
class Fraction {
public:
    void set(int numerator, int denominator);
    double toDouble() const;
    QString toString() const;
private:
    int m_Numerator;
    int m_Denominator;
};


#endif
```

Header files are included in other files by the preprocessor. To prevent a header file from accidentally being included more than once in any compiled file, *wrap* it with `#ifndef`-`#define` ... `#endif` preprocessor macros (Section C.2).

Generally, you should place the definitions of member functions outside the class definition in a separate **implementation file** with the **.cpp** extension.

Example 2.4 is an implementation file that contains definitions of the functions declared in Example 2.3.

EXAMPLE 2.4   src/classes/fraction/fraction.cpp

```
#include <QString>
#include "fraction.h"


void Fraction::set(int nn, int nd) {
    m_Numerator = nn;
    m_Denominator = nd;
}

double Fraction::toDouble() const {
    return 1.0 * m_Numerator / m_Denominator;
}

QString Fraction::toString() const {
  return QString("%1 / %2").arg(m_Numerator).arg(m_Denominator);
}
```

Every identifier has a **scope** (Section 20.2), a region of code in which a name is "known" (or *visible*) and accessible. In earlier examples, you saw identifiers with block scope, which extended from the line in which the identifier was declared down to the end of the code block that contained that declaration. The identifier was not visible above the declaration or below the end of that block.

Class member names have **class scope**. To begin with, class scope includes the entire class definition, regardless of where in that class definition the member name was declared. It also extends into the implementation (.cpp) file. The definition of any class member outside the class definition requires a **scope resolution operator** of the form `ClassName::` before its name. The scope resolution operator tells the compiler that the scope of the class extends beyond the class definition and includes the code between the symbol `::` and the closing brace of the function definition.

For example, the members `Fraction::m_Numerator` and `Fraction::m_Denominator` are visible inside the definitions of `Fraction::toString()` and `Fraction::toDouble()` even though they are declared in a separate file.

It is often necessary to display an object, save it to a file, or send it over a network to another program. There are many ways to perform all these operations. The `toString()` member function typically returns a string containing a "snapshot" of the current state of an object. You can use that string for debugging, display, storage, transmission, or conversion purposes. To increase flexibility, you can give the `toString()` function one or more parameters that permit the string to have a variety of formats. Many Qt classes have done this; for example, `QDate::toString()` returns a variety of date formats depending on which `Qt::DateFormat` is passed in as an argument.

You should make a practice of supplying most of your classes that have data members with a `toString()` member function. Generally, your class definitions should *not* have member functions that display or transmit the values of data members (e.g., `display()`, `print()`, `saveToFile()`, `readFromFile()`, etc.).[1]

2.3   Member Access Specifiers

Thus far you have worked with **class definition code** kept in header files that contain class definitions and other declarations, and with **class implementation code** kept in the header's corresponding .cpp files that contain definitions missing from the header file. There is a third category of code as it relates to a given class. **Client code** is code that is outside the scope of the class but which uses objects or members of that class. Generally, client code includes the header file that contains the class definition. In

---

[1] General purpose, stream-oriented serialization of data for both input and output is discussed further in Section 7.4.1.

Example 2.5, you can see that `fraction.h` contains class definition code of `Fraction` and is itself a client of `QString`.

EXAMPLE 2.5   src/classes/fraction/fraction.h

```
#ifndef _FRACTION_H_
#define _FRACTION_H_

#include <QString>


class Fraction {
public:
    void set(int numerator, int denominator);
    double toDouble() const;
    QString toString() const;
private:
    int m_Numerator;
    int m_Denominator;
};


#endif
```

The access specifiers, `public`, `protected`, and `private`, are used in a class definition to specify where in a program the affected members can be accessed. The following list provides an informal first approximation of the definitions of these three terms. Refinements are contained in footnotes.

- A `public` member can be accessed (using an object of the class)[2] anywhere in a program that `#includes` the `class` definition file.

- A `protected` member can be accessed inside the definition of a member function of its own class, or a member function of a *derived* class.[3]

- A `private` member is only accessible by member functions of its own class.[4]

Class members are `private` by default. If there is no access specifier preceding a member declaration in a class definition, the member is private.

---

[2] `public static` members can be accessed without an object. We discuss this in Section 2.9.
[3] Chapter 6, "Inheritance and Polymorphism," discusses derived classes.
[4] Private members are also accessible by `friends` of the class, which we discuss in Section 2.6.

> ### Accessibility and Visibility
>
> There is a subtle difference between **accessibility** and **visibility**. A named item is visible throughout its scope. Accessibility applies to class members. For a named class member to be accessible, it must first be visible. Not all visible items are accessible. Accessibility depends on the member access specifiers `public`/`private`/`protected`.

Example 2.6 uses some `Fraction` client code to demonstrate accessibiliby and visibility errors in a variety of ways. This example also focuses on *block scope*. A variable (not a class member) declared inside a block is visible and accessible only between its declaration and the closing brace. In the case of a function, the block that contains the function definition also includes the function's parameter list.

EXAMPLE 2.6   src/classes/fraction/fraction-client.cpp

```
#include <QTextStream>
#include "fraction.h"

int main() {
    const int DASHES = 30;
    QTextStream cout(stdout);

    {                                                                     1
        int i;
        for (i = 0; i < DASHES; ++i)
            cout << "=";
        cout << endl;
    }

    cout << "i = " << i << endl;                                          2
    Fraction f1, f2;
    f1.set(3, 4);
    f2.set(11,12);                                                        3
    f2.m_Numerator = 12;                                                  4
    cout << "The first fraction is: " << f1.toString() << endl;
    cout << "\nThe second fraction, expressed as a double is: "
        << f2.toDouble() << endl;
    return 0;
}
```

1 Nested scope, inner block.

2 Error: `i` no longer exists, so it is not visible in this scope.

3 Set through a member function.

4 Error, `m_Numerator` is visible but not accessible.

The relationship between `struct` and `class` in C++ can now be clearly described. Stroustrup defines a `struct` to be a `class` whose members are by default `public`, so that

```
struct T { ...
```

is equivalent to:

```
class T {public: ...
```

In particular, a `struct` in C++ can have member functions and data. C++ programmers tend to prefer using `class` instead of `struct` for most purposes, perhaps because of its bias in favor of `private` access. `struct` seems to be used mostly for applications in which data items need to be grouped together but member functions are not needed.

2.4 Encapsulation

Encapsulation is the first conceptual step in object-oriented programming. It involves

- Packaging data with the functions that can operate on that data in well-named classes
- Providing clearly named and well-documented `public` functions that enable users of the class to do whatever needs to be done with objects of this class
- Hiding implementation details

The set of `public` function prototypes in a class is called its **public interface**. The set of non-`public` class members, together with the member function definitions, is called its **implementation**.

One immediate advantage of encapsulation is that it permits the programmer to use a consistent naming scheme for the members of classes. For example, there are many different classes for which it might make sense to have a data member that contains the unit cost of the particular instance or, as previously mentioned, a member function named `toString()`. Because class member names are not visible outside the class scope, you can safely adopt the convention of using the names `m_unitCost` and `toString()` in every class that needs such members.[5]

2.5 Introduction to UML

A modern, object-oriented application rests upon a foundation of well-designed classes. In most projects, general purpose libraries (such as Qt) and task-specific libraries supply some of the classes. The programmer supplies the others. The Unified Modeling Language (UML) is the most commonly used language for object-oriented design. It permits a designer to describe the project using a rich variety of diagrams. We use UML diagrams because "a picture is said to be worth about 1k words." For example, UML class diagrams can show the important or relevant elements of classes, and the relationships between them, in a concise and intuitive way. Other kinds of UML diagrams can illustrate how classes collaborate with one another and how users interact with class objects. In this book you will use only a small subset of UML.

Most of our diagrams were created with a design tool called Umbrello.[6] For a good overview of UML, we recommend "The Umbrello UML Modeller Handbook," available from the help menu of Umbrello. A more complete reference that provides maximal content and minimal bulk is [Fowler04].

Figure 2.1 shows a class diagram with only one class: `Person`. Notice that the declarations appear as *name : type*, Pascal-style, rather than the more familiar C++/Java style, where the names come after the types. This is to help with readability. Because we tend to read from left to right, this syntax can help you see the member names faster. Notice also that `public` members are preceded by a plus sign (+) and `private` members are preceded by a minus sign (-).

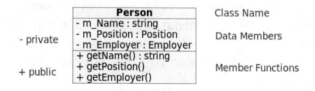

FIGURE 2.1   Person Class

---

[5] The compiler will not be confused because it embeds the name of the class inside the complete name that it gives to each data member.
[6] http://uml.sourceforge.net

2.5.1   UML Relationships

UML is especially good at describing relationships between classes. Jumping ahead a bit to Example 2.22, we will describe an important relationship in UML. In that example we introduce a `Point` class to represent a geometric point on the screen, and a `Square` class to represent a geometric shape on the screen. `Point` has two `int` data members, and `Square` has two `Point` data members. The two `Point` data members, because they are class objects, are regarded as **subobjects** of `Square`. The Square object is regarded as the **parent** of its `Point` subobjects; when a `Square` object is destroyed, so are its subobjects. That makes the subobjects **components** of the parent object, and the relationship is called **composition**. In Figure 2.2, the filled-in diamonds indicate that the instances of that class are *composed* (at least partially) of instance(s) of the class on the other end of the relationship connector.

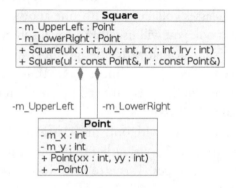

FIGURE 2.2   Composition

2.6   Friends of a Class

Now that you know about accessibility rules, you need to know how to occasionally break them. The **friend** mechanism makes it possible for a class to allow nonmember functions to access its private data. The keyword `friend` is followed by a class or a function declaration. `friend` declarations are located inside a class definition. Here are some syntax examples.

```
class Timer {
    friend class Clock;
    friend void Time::toString();
    friend ostream& operator <<(ostream& os, const Timer& obj);
    [...]
```

```
private:
   long m_Elapsed;
};
```

A `friend` can be a class, a member function of another class, or a nonmember function. In the preceding example, the class `Clock` is a `friend`, so all `Clock` member functions can access `Timer::m_Elapsed`. `Time::toString()` is a `friend` of `Timer` and is assumed (by the compiler) to be a valid member of class `Time`. The third `friend` is a nonmember function, an overloaded **insertion operator**, which inserts its second argument into the output stream and returns a reference to the stream so that the operation can be chained.

Breaking encapsulation can compromise the maintainability of your programs, so you should use the `friend` mechanism sparingly and carefully. Typically, `friend` functions are used for two purposes.

1. For Factory methods when you want to enforce creational rules (Section 16.1) on a class.

2. For global operator functions such as `operator<<()` and `operator>>()` when you do not want to make the operator a member function or do not have write-access to the class definition.

2.7   Constructors

A **constructor**, sometimes abbreviated *ctor*, is a special member function that controls the process of object initialization. Each constructor must have the same name as its class. Constructors do not return anything and do not have return types.

There is a special syntax for constructor definitions:

```
ClassName::ClassName( parameterList )
        :initList                                         1
        {
            constructor body
        }
```

   1 Optional but important. Do not omit this even though the compiler does not care.

Between the closing parenthesis of the parameter list and the opening brace of a function body, an optional member initialization list can be given. A **member initialization list** begins with a colon (:) and is followed by a comma-separated list of member initializers, each of the form

```
memberName(initializingExpression)
```

If (and only if) no constructor is specified in a class definition, the compiler will supply one that looks like this:

```
ClassName::ClassName()
    { }
```

A constructor that can be called with no arguments is referred to as a **default constructor**. A default constructor gives **default initialization** to an object of its class. Any data member that is not explicitly initialized in the member initialization list of a constructor is given default initialization by the compiler.

Classes can have several constructors, each of which initializes in a different (and presumably useful) way. Example 2.7 has three constructors.

EXAMPLE 2.7   src/ctor/complex.h

```
#include <string>
using namespace std;

class Complex {
 public:
    Complex(double realPart, double imPart);
    Complex(double realPart);
    Complex();
    string toString() const;
 private:
    double m_R, m_I;
};
```

Example 2.8 contains the implementation with some client code.

EXAMPLE 2.8   src/ctor/complex.cpp

```
#include "complex.h"
#include <iostream>
#include <sstream>
using namespace std;

Complex::Complex(double realPart, double imPart)
    :   m_R(realPart), m_I(imPart)                          1
{
    cout << "complex(" << m_R << "," << m_I << ")" << endl;
}
```

```
Complex::Complex(double realPart) :
    m_R(realPart), m_I(0) {
}


Complex::Complex() : m_R(0.0), m_I(0.0) {


}

string Complex::toString() const {
    ostringstream strbuf;
    strbuf << '(' << m_R << ", " << m_I << ')';
    return strbuf.str();
}

int main() {
    Complex C1;
    Complex C2(3.14);
    Complex C3(6.2, 10.23);
    cout << C1.toString() << '\t' << C2.toString()
        << C3.toString() << endl;
}
```

1 Member initialization list.

The default constructor for this class gives default initialization to the two data members of the object C1. That initialization is the same kind that would be given to a pair of variables of type `double` in the following code fragment:

```
double x, y;
cout << x << '\t' << y << endl;
```

QUESTION

What would you expect to be the output of that code?

What happens if you leave out the member initialization list? For example, consider the following constructor definition:

```
Complex(double realPart, double imPart) {
   m_R = realPart;
   m_I = imPart;
}
```

Each of the data members is first given default initialization and then given an assigned value. No error was made but the initialization was, essentially, wasted processing.

Look at one more example, which refers to Figure 2.2 and, for the sake of demonstration, assume that, as you see in the `Point` class diagram, there is only one `Point` constructor in the class definition. Further suppose that you define a `Square` constructor without a member initialization list.

```
Square::Square(const Point& ul, const Point& lr) {
   m_UpperLeft = ul;
   m_LowerRight = lr;
}
```

Because you did *not* explicitly define a default constructor for the `Point` class, and you *did* define a two parameter constructor, the `Point` class has no default constructor. Consequently, the compiler reports an error in this `Square` constructor.

2.8 Destructors

A **destructor**, sometimes abbreviated **dtor**, is a special member function that automates cleanup actions *just before* an object is destroyed.

When Is an Object Destroyed?

· When a local (automatic) object goes out of scope (e.g., when a function call returns).

· When an object created by the `new` operator is specifically destroyed by the use of the operator `delete`.

· Just before the program terminates, all objects with `static` storage are destroyed.

The destructor's name is the classname preceded by the tilde (~) character. It has no return type and takes no parameters. Therefore, a class can only have one destructor. If the class definition contains no destructor definition, the compiler supplies one that looks like this:

```
ClassName::~ClassName()
    { }
```

Section 2.9 shows a less trivial example of a destructor.

When Do You Need to Write a Destructor?

In general, a class that directly manages or shares an external resource (opens a file, opens a network connection, creates a process, etc.) needs to free the resource at some appropriate time. Such classes are usually wrappers that are responsible for object cleanup.

Qt's container classes make it easy for you to avoid writing code that directly manages dynamic memory.

You do *not* need a destructor if your class

- Has simple type members that are not pointers
- Has class members with properly defined destructors
- Is a certain kind of Qt class satisfying certain conditions[7]

The default compiler-generated destructor calls the destructors on each of its class members, in the order that they are listed in the class definition, just before the object is destroyed. The default destructor does not delete allocated memory when destroying pointer members.

2.9 The Keyword static

The keyword **static** can be applied to local variables, class members, and global variables/functions. In each case, static means something different.

---

[7] Such classes are discussed at length starting in Chapter 8, "QObject, QApplication, Signals, and Slots."

static Local Variables

The keyword static can be applied to a local variable declaration to give the variable **static storage class** (Section 20.3).

A local static variable is created only once and initialized the first time its declaration statement is processed by the running program. It is destroyed when the program terminates. A nonlocal static is created once, when the object module is loaded into memory, and is destroyed when the program terminates.

static Class Members

A static data member is a piece of data associated with the class itself rather than one that belongs to a particular object. It does not affect the sizeof() an object of the class. Each object of a class maintains its own set of non-static data members, but there is only one instance of a static data member, and it is shared by all objects of the class.

static members are preferable to (and can generally replace the use of) global variables because they do not add unnecessary names to the global namespace.

Global Namespace Pollution

Adding names to the global scope (e.g., by declaring global variables or global functions) is called **global namespace pollution** and is regarded as bad programming style. There are many good reasons to avoid declaring global variables in your programs. One is that it increases the likelihood of name collisions and confusion. Some experts use the number of global names in a program as an inverse measure of the program's quality (the lower the number, the higher the quality).

---

static class members must be declared static in (and only in) the class definition.

EXAMPLE 2.9   src/statics/static.h

```
[ . . . . ]
class Thing {
public:
    Thing(int a, int b);
    ~Thing();
    void display() const ;
    static void showCount();
```

```
private:
    int m_First, m_Second;
    static int s_Count;
};
[ . . . . ]
```

Figure 2.3 shows a UML class diagram for class Thing from Example 2.9.

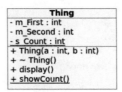

FIGURE 2.3   UML Class Definition with static

Notice that the static members are underlined in the diagram.

A class member function that does not in any way access the non-static data members of the class can (and should) be declared static. In Example 2.9, the static data member is a private counter that keeps track of the number of Thing objects that exist at any given moment. The public static member function displays the current value of the static counter.

Each static data member must be initialized (defined) once *outside* the class definition, preferably in the corresponding class implementation file.[8] Example 2.10 shows how to initialize and use static members.

EXAMPLE 2.10   src/statics/static.cpp

```
#include "static.h"
#include <iostream>

int Thing::s_Count = 0;                                    1

Thing::Thing(int a, int b)
        : m_First(a), m_Second(b) {
    ++s_Count;
}
```

---

[8] The exception to this rule is a static const int, which can be initialized in the class definition.

```
Thing::~Thing() {
    --s_Count;
}

void Thing::display() const {
    using namespace std;
    cout << m_First << "$$" << m_Second;
}

void Thing::showCount() {                                    2
    using namespace std;
    cout << "Count = " << s_Count << endl;
}
```

1 Must initialize static member!

2 Static function.

> ### NOTE
>
> Notice that the term `static` does not appear in the definitions of `s_Count` or `showCount()`. For the definition of `s_Count`, the keyword `static` would mean something quite different: It would change the scope of the variable from global to file-scope (see Section 20.2). For the function definition, it is simply redundant.

Block-Scope Static

`statics` defined inside a function or a block of code are initialized when they are executed for the first time.

```
long nextNumber() {
    int localvar(24);
    static long statNum = 1000;
    cout << statNum + localvar;
    return ++statNum;
}
```

The first call to `nextNumber()` initializes `localvar` to 24 and `statNum` to 1000, displays 1024 on the screen, and returns 1001. When the function returns, `localvar` is destroyed but `statNum` is not. Each time this function is called, `localvar` gets created and initialized to 24 again. The static variable statNum persists between calls and holds onto the value that it obtained in the last call. So, for example, the next time the function is called, 1025 is displayed and 1002 is returned.

static Initialization

A static object that is not defined in a block or function is initialized when its corresponding object module[9] is loaded for the first time. Most of the time, this is at program startup, before main() starts. The order in which modules get loaded and variables get initialized is implementation-dependent, so you should never make an initialization depend on the initial value of a static from a different file, even if you list that file first when compiling.

A static object is constructed once and persists until the program terminates. A static data member is a static object that has class scope.

In Example 2.11, we use an internal block so that we can introduce some local objects that will be destroyed before the program ends.

EXAMPLE 2.11   src/statics/static-test.cpp

```
#include "static.h"

int main() {
    Thing::showCount();                              1
    Thing t1(3,4), t2(5,6);
    t1.showCount();                                  2
    {                                                3
        Thing t3(7,8), t4(9,10);
        Thing::showCount();                          4
    }                                                5

    Thing::showCount();
    return 0;
}
```

1 At this point, no objects exist, but all class statics have been initialized.

2 Access through object.

3 An inner block of code is entered.

---

[9] Chapter 7, "Libraries and Design Patterns"

4 Access through class scope resolution operator.

5 End inner block.

Here is the compile and run:

```
src/statics> g++ -Wall static.cpp static-test.cpp
src/statics> ./a.out
Count = 0
Count = 2
Count = 4
Count = 2
src/statics>
```

Static Globals

`static`, when applied to global functions and variables, does not operate in the way you might expect. Instead of changing the storage class, `static` tells the linker not to export the symbol to the rest of the program. This gives the symbol **file scope**, which is discussed in Section 20.2.

2.10   Class Declarations and Definitions

Bidirectional relationships not very different from Figure 2.4 appear quite often in classes. To implement them, the compiler needs to have some knowledge of each class before defining the other. At first, you might think that each header file should include the other, as shown in Example 2.12.

FIGURE 2.4   Bidirectional Relationship

EXAMPLE 2.12 src/circular/badegg/egg.h

```
[ . . . . ]
#include "chicken.h"
class Egg {
 public:
    Chicken* getParent();
};
[ . . . . ]
```

The problem becomes clear when you look at Example 2.13, which analogously includes egg.h.

EXAMPLE 2.13 src/circular/badegg/chicken.h

```
[ . . . . ]
#include "egg.h"

class Chicken {
 public:
    Egg* layEgg();
};
[ . . . . ]
```

The preprocessor does not permit circular dependencies such as these. In this example, neither header file needed to include the other. In each case, doing so created an unnecessarily strong dependency between header files.

Under the right conditions, C++ permits you to use a **forward class declaration** instead of including a particular header.

EXAMPLE 2.14 src/circular/goodegg/egg.h

```
[ . . . . ]
class Chicken;                                          1
class Egg {
 public:
    Chicken* getParent();                               2
};
[ . . . . ]
```

1 Forward class declaration.

2 Okay in declarations if they are pointers.

A forward class declaration enables you to refer to a symbol without having its full definition available. It is an implicit promise to the compiler that the definition of the class will be `included` when it is needed. Classes that are declared but not defined can only be used as types for pointers or references, as long as they are not dereferenced in the file.

We define `getParent()` in the source code module, `egg.cpp`, shown in Example 2.15. Notice that the `.cpp` file can `#include` both header files without causing a circular dependency between them. The `.cpp` file has a strong dependency on both headers, while the header files have no dependency on one another.

EXAMPLE 2.15   src/circular/goodegg/egg.cpp

```
#include "chicken.h"
#include "egg.h"

Chicken* Egg::getParent() {
    return new Chicken();                                    1
}
```

1 Requires definition of Chicken.

Thus, forward class declarations make it possible to define bidirectional relationships, such as the one in Example 2.15, without creating circular `#includes`. We located the dependencies in the source code modules that actually needed them instead of in the header files.

In Java, you can create circular strong bidirectional dependencies between two (or more) classes. In other words, each class can import and use (dereference references to) the other. This kind of circular dependency makes both classes much more difficult to maintain because changes in either one can break the other. This is one situation where C++ protects the programmer better than Java does: You cannot create such a relationship accidentally.

Java also offers a forward class declaration, but it is rarely used because Java programs do not use separate header and implementation files.

For further details, see Section C.2.

2.11   Copy Constructors and Assignment Operators

C++ gives almost god-like powers to the designer of a class. Object "life cycle" management means taking complete control over the behavior of objects during birth, reproduction, and death. You have already seen how constructors manage the birth of an object and how destructors are used to manage the death of an object. This section investigates the reproduction process: the use of copy constructors and assignment operators.

A **copy constructor** is a constructor that has a prototype like this:

```
ClassName(const ClassName & x);
```

The purpose of a copy constructor is to create an object that is an exact copy of an existing object of the same class.

An **assignment operator** for a class overloads the symbol = and gives it a meaning that is specific to the class. There is one particular version of the assignment operator that has the following prototype:

```
ClassName& operator=(const ClassName& x);
```

Because it is possible to have several overloaded versions of the `operator=()` in a class, we call this particular version the **copy assignment operator**.

The version of `Fraction` in Example 2.16 has three `static` counters, defined in Example 2.17, so that you can count the total number of times each member function is called. This should help you better understand when objects are copied.

EXAMPLE 2.16   src/lifecycle/copyassign/fraction.h

```
[ . . . . ]
class Fraction {
 public:
    Fraction(int n, int d) ;                          1
    Fraction(const Fraction& other) ;                 2
    Fraction& operator=(const Fraction& other) ;      3
    Fraction multiply(Fraction f2) ;
    static QString report() ;
 private:
    int m_Numer, m_Denom;
    static int s_assigns;
    static int s_copies;
    static int s_ctors;
};
[ . . . . ]
```

1 Regular constructor

2 Copy constructor

3 Copy assignment operator

EXAMPLE 2.17   src/lifecycle/copyassign/fraction.cpp

```
[ . . . . ]
int Fraction::s_assigns = 0;                                    1
int Fraction::s_copies = 0;
int Fraction::s_ctors = 0;

Fraction::Fraction(const Fraction& other)
    :  m_Numer(other.m_Numer), m_Denom(other.m_Denom) {
    ++s_copies;
}

Fraction& Fraction::operator=(const Fraction& other) {
    if (this != &other) {                                      2
        m_Numer = other.m_Numer;
        m_Denom = other.m_Denom;
        ++s_assigns;
    }
    return *this;                                              3
}
[ . . . . ]
```

1 Static member definitions.

2 `operator=()` should always do nothing in the case of self-assignment.

3 `operator=()` should always return `*this` to allow for chaining, i.e., a=b=c.

Example 2.18 uses this class to create, copy, and assign some objects.

EXAMPLE 2.18   src/lifecycle/copyassign/copyassign.cpp

```
#include <QTextStream>
#include "fraction.h"

int main() {
    QTextStream cout(stdout);
    Fraction twothirds(2,3);                                   1
    Fraction threequarters(3,4);
    Fraction acopy(twothirds);                                 2
    Fraction f4 = threequarters;                               3
```

```
    cout << "after declarations - " << Fraction::report();
    f4 = twothirds;                                              4
    cout << "\nbefore multiply - " << Fraction::report();
    f4 = twothirds.multiply(threequarters);                      5
    cout << "\nafter multiply - " << Fraction::report() << endl;
    return 0;
}
```

1 Using 2-arg constructor.

2 Using copy constructor.

3 Also using copy constructor.

4 Assignment.

5 Several objects are created here.

Here is the output of this program:

```
copyassign> ./copyassign
after declarations -  [assigns: 0 copies: 2 ctors: 2]
before multiply -  [assigns: 1 copies: 2 ctors: 2]
after multiply -  [assigns: 2 copies: 3 ctors: 3]
copyassign>
```

Question

As you can see, the call to multiply creates three Fraction objects. Can you explain why?

Compiler-Supplied Versions

It is important to know that the compiler will supply default versions of the copy constructor or the copy assignment operator if one or both are missing from the class definition. The compiler-supplied default versions are public and have the following prototypes for a class *T*:

```
T::T(const T& other);
T& T::operator=(const T& other);
```

Both of these default versions make an exact copy of the value of each data member. For a class whose data members are all simple or value types, such as int, double, QString, etc., the compiler-supplied versions are probably okay. But *if a class has pointer or object*[10] *members, it is necessary to write both copy constructors and copy assignment operators that are specifically designed for that class.* You will see later[11] that it is sometimes necessary to *prevent* copies from being made of objects of certain classes. In such a case, both the copy constructor and the copy assignment operator must be declared `private` and given appropriate noncopying definitions to prevent the compiler from supplying `public` versions.

2.12   Conversions

A constructor that can be called with a single argument (of a different type) is a **conversion constructor** because it defines a **conversion** from the argument type to the constructor's class type.

EXAMPLE 2.19   src/ctor/conversion/fraction.cpp

```
class Fraction {
public:
    Fraction(int n)                                                    1
        : m_Numer(n), m_Denom(1) {}
    Fraction(int n, int d )
        : m_Numer(n), m_Denom(d) {}
    Fraction times(const Fraction& other) {
        return Fraction(m_Numer * other.m_Numer, m_Denom * other.m_Denom);
    }
private:
    int m_Numer, m_Denom;
};
int main() {
    int i;
    Fraction frac(8);                                                  2
    Fraction frac2 = 5;                                                3
    frac = 9;                                                          4
    frac = (Fraction) 7;                                               5
    frac = Fraction(6);                                                6
    frac = static_cast<Fraction>(6);                                   7
    frac = frac2.times(19);                                            8
    return 0;
}
```

1 Single argument `ctor` defines a conversion from `int`.

2 Conversion constructor call.

---

[10] Section 8.1

[11] Chapter 8

3 Copy int (calls conversion `ctor`, too).

4 Conversion followed by assignment.

5 C-style typecast (deprecated).

6 Explicit temporary; also a C++ typecast.

7 Preferred ANSI-style typecast.

8 Implicit call to the conversion constructor.

In the `main()` function of Example 2.19, the `Fraction` variable `frac` is initialized with a single `int`. The matching constructor is the one-parameter version. Effectively, it converts the integer `8` to the fraction `8/1`.

The prototype for a conversion constructor typically looks like this:

```
ClassA::ClassA(const ClassB& bobj);
```

The conversion constructor for *ClassA* is automatically called when an object of that class is required, and when such an object can be created by that constructor from the value of *ClassB* that was supplied as an initializer or assigned value.

For example, if `frac` is a properly initialized `Fraction` as defined in Example 2.19, you can write the statement

```
frac = frac.times(19);
```

Because `19` is not a `Fraction` object (as required by the `times()` function definition), the compiler checks to see whether it can be converted to a `Fraction`. Because you have a conversion constructor, this is indeed possible.

`Fraction::operator=()` is not defined, so the compiler uses a default assignment operator that it supplied:

```
Fraction& operator=(const Fraction& fobj);
```

This assignment operator performs a memberwise assignment from each data member of `fobj` to the corresponding member of the host object.

So, that statement calls three `Fraction` member functions:

1. `Fraction::operator=()` to perform the assignment.

2. `Fraction::times()` to perform the multiplication.

3. `Fraction::Fraction(19)` to convert `19` from `int` to `Fraction`.

The temporary `Fraction` object returned by the `times()` function exists just long enough to complete the assignment and is then automatically destroyed.

You can simplify the class definition for `Fraction` by eliminating the one-parameter constructor and providing a default value for the second parameter of the two-parameter constructor. Because it can be called with only one argument, it satisfies the definition of conversion constructor.

EXAMPLE 2.20   src/ctor/conversion/fraction.h

```
class Fraction {
public:
    Fraction(int n, int d = 1)
              : m_Numer(n), m_Denom(d) {}
    Fraction times(const Fraction& other) {
        return Fraction(m_Numer* other.m_Numer, m_Denom* other.m_Denom);
    }

private:
    int m_Numer, m_Denom;
};
```

Ordinarily, any constructor that can be called with a single argument of a different type is a conversion constructor that has the implicit mechanisms discussed previously. If the implicit mechanisms are not appropriate for some reason, it is possible to suppress them. The keyword `explicit` prevents the compiler from automatically using that constructor for implicit conversions.[12]

---

explicit

The keyword `explicit` can be placed before a single argument constructor in the class definition to prevent automatic conversion from being used by the compiler. This is useful if the argument is not anything like the class it is constructing, or if there is something akin to a parent-child relationship between them. Classes generated by QtCreator place this keyword before the generated custom widget constructors, and it is advisable that you do the same with your `QWidget`-derived classes.

---

[12] Section 19.8.4 informally discusses an example.

2.13   const **Member Functions**

When a class member function `ClassX::f()` is invoked through an object `objx`

```
objx.f();
```

we refer to `objx` as the **host object**.

The `const` keyword has a special meaning when it is applied to a (non-`static`) class member function. Placed after the parameter list, `const` becomes part of the function signature and guarantees that the function will not change the state of the host object.

A good way to look at the way `const` modifies member functions is to realize that each non-`static` member function has an implicit parameter, named `this`, which is a pointer to the host object. When you declare a member function to be `const`, you are telling the compiler that, as far as the function is concerned, `this` is a pointer to `const`.

To explain how `const` changes the way a function is invoked, we look at how the original C++ to C preprocessor dealt with member functions. Because C did not support overloaded functions or member functions, the preprocessor translated the function into a C function with a "mangled" name that distinguished itself from other functions by encoding the full signature in the name. The mangling process also added an extra implicit parameter to the parameter list: `this`, a pointer to the host object. Example 2.21 shows how member functions might be seen by a linker after a translation into C.

EXAMPLE 2.21   src/const/constmembers/constmembers.cpp

```
#include <QTextStream>
#include <QString>

class Point {
  public:
    Point(int px, int py)
      : m_X(px), m_Y(py) {}

    void set(int nx, int ny) {                              1
        m_X = nx;
        m_Y = ny;
    }
    QString toString() const {                              2
        // m_X = 5;                                         3
        m_Count++;                                          4
        return QString("[%1,%2]").arg(m_X).arg(m_Y);
```

```
    }
  private:
    int m_X, m_Y;
    mutable int m_Count;                                  5
};


int main() {
    QTextStream cout(stdout);
    Point p(1,1);
    const Point q(2,2);
    p.set(4,4);                                           6
    cout << p.toString() << endl;
    //q.set(4,4);                                         7
    return 0;
}
```

1 C version: `_Point_set_int_int(Point* this, int nx, int ny)`.

2 C version: `_Point_toString_string_const(const Point* this)`.

3 Error: `this->m_X = 5,` `*this` is const.

4 Okay, member is mutable.

5 `mutable` can be changed in a `const` method.

6 Okay to reassign p.

7 Error! `const` object cannot call non-`const` methods.

In a real compiler, the mangled names for `set` and `print` would be compressed significantly to save space and hence be less understandable to a human reader. Notice that **mutable** members can be modified inside `const` member functions, but regular data members cannot.

You can think of the `const` in the signature of `print()` as a modifier of the invisible `this` parameter that points to the host object. This means that the memory pointed to by `this` cannot be changed by the action of the `print()` function. The reason that the assignment `x = 5;` produces an error is that it is equivalent to `this->x = 5;`. The assignment violates the rules of `const`.

Suppose that you need to work with a project that contains classes that do not use `const` correctly. When you start to add `const` to member functions, parameters, and pointers that need it, you may find that those changes generate a cascade of compiler errors that prevent you from building the project until `const` has been correctly added throughout the project. When const has finally been added to all the correct places, you can say that your classes are **const correct**.

2.14   Subobjects

An object can contain another object, in which case the contained object is considered to be a **subobject**. In Example 2.22, each `Square` has two `Point` subobjects.

EXAMPLE 2.22   src/subobject/subobject.h

```
[ . . . . ]
class Point {
 public:
    Point(int xx, int yy) : m_x(xx), m_y(yy){}
    ~Point() {
       cout << "point destroyed: ("
             << m_x << "," << m_y << ")" << endl;
    }
 private:
    int m_x, m_y;
};

class Square {
 public:
    Square(int ulx, int uly, int lrx, int lry)
    : m_UpperLeft(ulx, uly), m_LowerRight (lrx, lry)     1
    {}

    Square(const Point& ul, const Point& lr) :
    m_UpperLeft(ul), m_LowerRight(lr) {}                 2
 private:
    Point m_UpperLeft, m_LowerRight;                     3
};

[ . . . . ]
```

1 Member initialization is required here because there is no default ctor.

2 Initialize members using the implicitly generated `Point` copy ctor.

3 Embedded subobjects.

Whenever an instance of `square` is created, each of its subobjects is created with it so that all three objects occupy a contiguous chunk of memory. When a `square` instance is destroyed, all its subobjects are also destroyed.

The `square` is *composed* of two `Point` objects. Because `Point` has no default constructor[13] you must properly initialize each `Point` subobject in the member initialization list of `square`.[14]

Example 2.23 is the client code that creates instances of the classes discussed.

EXAMPLE 2.23   src/subobject/subobject.cpp

```cpp
#include "subobject.h"

int main() {
    Square sq1(3,4,5,6);
    Point p1(2,3), p2(8, 9);
    Square sq2(p1, p2);
}
```

Even though no destructor was defined for `square`, each of its `Point` subobjects was properly destroyed whenever the containing object was. As you observed in Section 2.5.1, this is an example of **composition**, which is discussed in more detail in Section 6.9.

```
point destroyed: (8,9)
point destroyed: (2,3)
point destroyed: (8,9)
point destroyed: (2,3)
point destroyed: (5,6)
point destroyed: (3,4)
```

2.15   Exercise: Classes

1. Examples 2.24 through 2.26 are part of a single program. Use them together for the following problems.

---

[13] Why not?

[14] Why can't you simply initialize m_x and m_y here?

EXAMPLE 2.24   src/early-examples/thing/thing.h

```
#ifndef THING_H_
#define THING_H_

class Thing {
 public:
    void set(int num, char c);
    void increment();
    void show();
 private:
    int m_Number;
    char m_Character;
};
#endif
```

EXAMPLE 2.25   src/early-examples/thing/thing.cpp

```
#include <QTextStream>
#include "thing.h"


void Thing::set(int num, char c) {
  m_Number = num;
  m_Character = c;
}

void Thing::increment() {
  ++m_Number;
  ++m_Character;
}

void Thing::show() {
  QTextStream cout(stdout);
  cout << m_Number << '\t' << m_Character << endl;
}
```

EXAMPLE 2.26   src/early-examples/thing/thing-demo.cpp

```cpp
#include <QTextStream>
#include "thing.h"


void display(Thing t, int n) {
    int i;
    for (i = 0; i < n; ++i)
        t.show();
}


int main() {
  QTextStream cout(stdout);
  Thing t1, t2;
  t1.set(23, 'H');
  t2.set(1234, 'w');
  t1.increment();
  //cout << t1.m_Number;
  display(t1, 3);
  //cout << i << endl;
  t2.show();
  return 0;
}
```

a. Uncomment the two commented lines of code in Example 2.26, and try to build the program using the commands

```
qmake -project
qmake
make
```

Explain the difference between the errors reported by the compiler.

b. Add public member functions to the definition of the class Thing so that the data members can be kept private, and the client code can still output their values.

2. Given the UML diagram in Figure 2.5, define the class, and each member function specified, for an enhanced Fraction class. You can use Example 2.4 as a starting point.

Fraction
- m_Numerator : int
- m_Denominator : int
+ set(numerator : int, denominator : int)
+ toString() : QString
+ toDouble() : double
+ add(other : const Fraction&) : Fraction
+ subtract(other : const Fraction&) : Fraction
+ multiply(other : const Fraction&) : Fraction
+ divide(other : const Fraction&) : Fraction

FIGURE 2.5   Fraction Class Diagram

Write some client code to test all the new operations and verify that proper calculations are done.

3. Suppose that you want to write an application for a company that matches employers and job seekers. A first step would be to design appropriate classes. Look at Figure 2.6 as a starting point. In this diagram, the Person has two subobjects: Employer and Position.

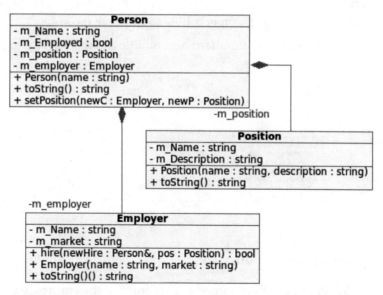

FIGURE 2.6   The Company Chart

To do this exercise, you need to use forward class declarations (Section 2.10).

a. Write classes for `Person`, `Position`, and `Employer`, as described in Figure 2.6.

b. For `Person::getPosition()` and `getEmployer()`, create and return something funny if the person has not yet been hired by a company.

c. For the `hire(...)` function, set the `Person`'s state so that future calls to `getPosition()` and `getEmployer()` give the correct result.

d. In the `main()` program, create at least two Employers: the "StarFleet Federation" and the "Borg."

e. Create at least two employees: Jean-Luc Picard and Wesley Crusher.

f. For each class, write a `toString()` function that gives you a `string` representation of the object.

g. Write a main program that creates some objects and then prints out each company's list of employees.

4. Critique the design shown in Figure 2.6. What problems do you see with it? In particular, how would you write `Employer::getEmployees()` or `Position::getEmployer()`? Suggest how to improve its design.

5. Define a class to represent a modern automobile as suggested by Figure 2.7.

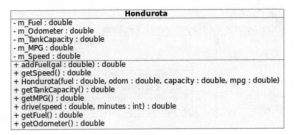

Hondurota
- m_Fuel : double
- m_Odometer : double
- m_TankCapacity : double
- m_MPG : double
- m_Speed : double
+ addFuel(gal : double) : double
+ getSpeed() : double
+ Hondurota(fuel : double, odom : double, capacity : double, mpg : double)
+ getTankCapacity() : double
+ getMPG() : double
+ drive(speed : double, minutes : int) : double
+ getFuel() : double
+ getOdometer() : double

FIGURE 2.7   Hondurota

Here are some features of this class.

- In addition to the four named data members, the constructor should initialize the speed. Zero seems reasonable; it would be awkward to construct a moving automobile.

- The `drive()` function should be reasonably smart:

  - It should not permit the car to drive if there is no fuel.

  - It should adjust the odometer and the fuel amount correctly.

  - It should return the amount of fuel left in the tank.

  - The `addFuel()` function should adjust the fuel amount correctly and return the resulting amount of fuel in the tank. `addFuel(0)` should fill the tank to its capacity.

Write client code to test this class.

6. The previous problem really did not use the speed member. The `drive()` function assumed an average speed and used an average fuel consumption rate. Now use the speed member to make things a bit more realistic.

Add a member function to the `Hondurota` class that has the prototype

```
double highwayDrive(double distance, double speedLimit);
```

The return value is the elapsed time for the trip.

When driving on a highway, it is usually possible to travel at or near the speed limit. Unfortunately, various things happen that can cause traffic to move more slowly—sometimes much more slowly.

Another interesting factor is the effect that changing speed has on the fuel consumption rate. Most modern automobiles have a speed that is optimal for fuel efficiency (e.g., 45 mph). Calculating how long it will take to travel a particular distance on the highway and how much fuel the trip will consume is the job of this new function.

- Write the function so that it updates the speed, the odometer, and the fuel amount every minute until the given distance has been traveled.

- Use 45 mph as the speed at which fuel is consumed precisely at the stored `m_FuelConsumptionRate`.

- Use an adjusted consumption rate for other speeds, increasing the rate of consumption by 1% for each mile per hour that the speed differs from 45 mph.

- Your car should stop if it runs out of fuel.

- Assume that you are traveling at the speed limit, except for random differences that you compute each minute by generating a random speed adjustment between -5 mph and +5 mph. Don't allow your car to drive faster than 40 mph above the speed limit. Of course, your car should not drive slower than 0 mph. If a random speed adjustment produces an unacceptable speed, generate another one.

Write client code to test this function.

7. Be the computer and predict the output of Example 2.28 (which is client code for Example 2.27).

EXAMPLE 2.27   src/statics/static3.h

```cpp
#ifndef _STATIC_3_H_
#define _STATIC_3_H_

#include <string>
using namespace std;

class Client {
 public:
    Client(string name) : m_Name(name), m_ID(s_SavedID++)
        { }
    static int getSavedID() {
        if(s_SavedID > m_ID) return s_SavedID;
        else return 0;
    }
    string getName() {return m_Name;}
    int getID() {return m_ID; }
 private:
    string m_Name;
    int m_ID;
    static int s_SavedID ;
};

#endif
```

EXAMPLE 2.28 src/statics/static3.cpp

```cpp
#include "static3.h"
#include <iostream>

int Client::s_SavedID(1000);

int main() {
    Client cust1("George");
    cout << cust1.getID() << endl;
    cout << Client::getName() << endl;
}
```

8. Design and implement a `Date` class based on Figure 2.8, subject to the following restrictions and suggestions.

Date
- m_DaysSinceBaseDate : int
+ Date()
+ Date(y : int, m : int, d : int)
+ set(y : int, m : int, d : int)
+ toString(brief : bool)
+ setToToday()
+ getWeekDay() : string
+ lessThan(d : const Date&) : bool
+ equals(d : const Date&) : bool
+ daysBetween(d : const Date&) : int
+ addDays(days : int) : Date
+ leapYear(year : int) : bool
+ monthName(month : int) : string
+ yearDays(year : int) : int
+ monthDays(month : int, year : int) : int
- ymd2dsbd(y : int, m : int, d : int) : int
- getYMD(y : int&, m : int&, d : int&)

FIGURE 2.8 Date UML Class Diagram

- Each `Date` must be stored as a single integer equal to the number of days since the fixed base date, January 1, 1000 (or some other date if you prefer). Call that data member `m_DaysSinceBaseDate`.

- The base year should be stored as a `static int` data member (e.g., 1000 or 1900).

- The class has a constructor and a set function that have year, month, day parameters. These three values must be used to compute the number of days from the base date to the given date. We have specified a private member function named `ymd2dsbd()` to do that calculation for both.

- The `toString()` function returns a representation of the stored date in some standard string format that is suitable for display (e.g., yyyy/mm/dd).

This involves reversing the computation used in the ymd2dsbd() function described earlier. We have specified a private member function named getYMD() to do that calculation. We have also suggested a parameter for the toString() function (bool brief) to provide a choice of date formats.

- We have specified some static utility functions (e.g., leapyear()) that are static because they do not affect the state of any Date objects.

- Make sure you use the correct rule for determining whether a given year is a leap year!

  - Create a file named date.h to store your class definition.

  - Create a file named date.cpp that contains the definitions of all the functions declared in date.h.

  - Write client code to test your Date class thoroughly.

  - Your class should handle "invalid" dates in a reasonable way (e.g., year earlier than the base year, month or day out of range, etc.).

  - Here is the code for setToToday() that uses the system clock to determine today's date. You need to #include <time.h> (from the C Standard Library) to use this code.

    ```
    void Date::setToToday() {
      struct tm *tp = 0;
      time_t now;
      now = time(0);
      tp = localtime(&now);
      set(1 + tp->tm_mon, tp->tm_mday, 1900 + tp->tm_year);
    }
    ```

  - The getWeekDay() function returns the name of the week day corresponding to the stored date. Use this in the fancy version of toString(). Hint: Jan 1, 1900, was a Monday.

9. Consider the class shown in Example 2.29.

EXAMPLE 2.29   src/destructor/demo/thing.h

```
#ifndef THING_H_
#define THING_H_
```

```
#include <iostream>
#include <string>
using namespace std;

class Thing {
 public:
    Thing(int n) : m_Num(n) {

    }
    ~Thing() {
        cout << "destructor called: "
            << m_Num << endl;
    }

 private:
    string m_String;
    int m_Num;
};
#endif
```

The client code in Example 2.30 constructs several objects in various ways and destroys most of them.

EXAMPLE 2.30   src/destructor/demo/destructor-demo.cpp

```
#include "thing.h"

void function(Thing t) {
    Thing lt(106);
    Thing* tp1 = new Thing(107);
    Thing* tp2 = new Thing(108);
    delete tp1;
}

int main() {
    Thing t1(101), t2(102);
    Thing* tp1 = new Thing(103);
    function(t1);
    {                                        1
        Thing t3(104);
        Thing* tp = new Thing(105);
    }
    delete tp1;
    return 0;
}
```

1 Nested block/scope.

Here is the output of this program.
```
destructor called: 107
destructor called: 106
destructor called: 101
destructor called: 104
destructor called: 103
destructor called: 102
destructor called: 101
```

a How many objects were created but not destroyed?

b Why does 101 appear twice in the list?

2.16   Review Questions

1. Describe at least one difference between a `class` and a `struct`.

2. How does class scope differ from block scope?

3. Describe two situations where it is okay to use `friend` functions.

4. How does a `static` data member differ from a non-`static` data member?

5. What is the difference between a `static` member function and a non-`static` member function?

6. What does it mean to declare a member function to be `const`?

7. Explain what would happen (and why) if a class `T` could have a copy constructor with the following prototype?

   ```
   T::T(T other);
   ```

8. Some of the lines marked in Example 2.31 have errors. There are multiple choices for the answers shown in Example 2.32.

EXAMPLE 2.31   src/quizzes/constquiz.cpp

```
#include <iostream>

class Point {
  public:
  Point(int px, int py)
```

```
          : m_X(px), m_Y(py) {}                               1

     void set(int nx, int ny) {
         m_X = nx;
         m_Y = ny;
     }
     void print() const {
         using namespace std;
         cout << "[" << m_X << "," << m_Y << "]";
         m_printCount ++;                                      2
     }
   private:
     int m_X, m_Y;
     int m_printCount;                                         3
};

int main() {
    Point p(1,1);
    const Point q(2,2);
    p.set(4,4);                                                4
    p.print();
    q.set(4,4);                                                5
    q.print();                                                 6
    return 0;
}
```

1 _____

2 _____

3 _____

4 _____

5 _____

6 _____

EXAMPLE 2.32   src/quizzes/constquiz-questions.txt

1. What are the errors?
    a. Not allowed here.
    b. m_pointCount is missing here, causing a compiler error.
    c. Missing semicolon in the {}.
    d. m_pointCount is missing here, causing a runtime error.
    e. Nothing is wrong.

2. What are the errors?
   a. Nothing is wrong.
   b. m_printCount needs to be const.
   c. m_printCount needs to be explicit.
   d. Compiler error - can't change m_printCount.
   e. m_printCount needs to be volatile.

3. What is the error?
   a. Nothing is wrong.
   b. m_printCount needs to be volatile.
   c. m_printCount needs to be const.
   d. m_printCount needs to be mutable.
   e. m_printCount needs to be explicit.

4. What are the errors?
   a. Can't call const member.
   b. Can't call non-const member.
   c. Nothing is wrong.
   d. Set needs to be const.
   e. Set needs to be volatile.

5. What are the errors?
   a. Can't call const member.
   b. Can't call non-const member.
   c. Set needs to be volatile.
   d. q needs to be non-const.
   e. Set needs to be volatile.

6. What is the error?
   a. Nothing is wrong.
   b. Can't call non-const member.
   c. print needs to be const.
   d. q needs to be explicit.
   e. Can't call const member.

9. Find the errors in Example 2.33 and answer the questions in Example 2.34.

EXAMPLE 2.33   src/quizzes/statics-quiz.cpp

```
// wadget.h:

class Wadget {
```

```
public:
    Wadget(double a, double b);
    void print();
    static double calculation();
    static int wadgetCount();

private:
    double m_d1, m_d2;
    static int m_wadgetCount;
};

// wadget.cpp:

Wadget::Wadget(double a, double b)
:  m_d1(a), m_d2(b) {
    m_wadgetCount ++;
}

static int wadgetCount() {
    return m_wadgetCount;
}

double Wadget::calculation() {
    return d1*d2 + m_wadgetCount;
}
[ . . . . ]
```

EXAMPLE 2.34   src/quizzes/statics-quiz.txt

```
1. There are a number of problems with the code in Example 2.33.
The first is that it will not link because of a missing
definition of m_wadgetCount. How do we fix that problem?

    a. wadget.h inside class definition:
        static int m_wadgetCount = 0;
    b. wadget.h: outside class definition:
        static int Wadget::m_wadgetCount = 0;
    c. wadget.cpp: top of file
        int Wadget::m_wadgetCount = 0;
    d. wadget.cpp: top of file
        static int Wadget::m_wadgetCount = 0;
```

e. wadget.cpp member initialization list:
```
   Widget::Widget()
    :  m_d1(a), m_d2(b), m_wadgetCount(0)
        { m_wadgetCount ++; }
```

}

2. For the declaration of
        static int Widget::wadgetCount()
   What does the static here mean?

   a. Function must be defined in a .cpp file
   b. Function can only be called on static objects
   c. Function must be called with Widget:: scope resolution
   d. Function name has file scope
   e. Function can only access static members

3. For the definition of
        static int Widget::wadgetCount()
   What does the static here mean?
   a. Function can only access static members
   b. Function can only be called on static objects
   c. Function must be called with Widget:: scope resolution
   d. Function name is exported to the linker
   e. Function name is not exported to the linker

4. What can we say about the definition of Widget::calculation()?

   a. d1 and d2 are not accessible from the static method
   b. Missing a 'static' before the function definition
   c. There is nothing wrong with this.
   d. Both a and b
   e. Function name is not exported to the linker (error)

Chapter 3

Introduction to Qt

This chapter introduces some style guidelines and naming conventions that will be used in the rest of this book. The Qt Core module is introduced with examples and exercises that use Qt stream and date classes.

Qt is a modular system of classes and tools that makes it easier for you to write smaller modules of code. It provides an almost complete replacement for STL classes/ types, builds/runs on more compilers than code written using C++0x, and supports some of the same features without requiring a modern compiler. This chapter explains how to start reusing Qt.

Inside the Qt source archive, there is a collection of Examples and Demos. Some- times we will refer to them, and they have paths which fall under the `examples/` or `demos/` path prefix. If you are using the Qt SDK or a Qt installed with Linux, you may need to run the package manager to install them. Figure 3.1 shows the *Getting Started* page from the Qt Creator Welcome screen.

FIGURE 3.1   Qt Creator Welcome Screen

NOTE

Appendix, "C++/Qt Setup," has some tips for getting quickly set up on various platforms.

3.1   Style Guidelines, Naming Conventions

C++ is a powerful language that supports many different programming styles. The coding style used in most Qt programs is not "pure" C++. Instead, it is common to see a combination of macros and preprocessor trickery to achieve a higher-level dynamic language that has a lot in common with Java and Python. In fact, to take full advantage of Qt's power and simplicity, we have abandoned the Standard Library entirely.

In any serious collaborative programming project, there are likely to be style guidelines to improve the readability, reusability, maintainability, and reliability of the code produced. The semi-official Qt programming style guidelines are described in [qtapistyle] and [kdestyle]. Here is a summary of the style guidelines that we have adopted.

- Names are sequences of letters and numerical digits, the first of which must not be a digit.
- The underscore character (_) can be used also, but we discourage the use of that character except for class data members.
- Class names begin with a capital letter: `class Customer`
- Function names begin with a lowercase letter.
- Use **CamelCase** to form multi-word names by joining the words together and capitalizing the interior word beginnings; e.g., `class MetaDataLoader`, `void getStudentInfo()`
- Constants are capitalized and created, preferably, as `enum` values in a class scope. Global constants and macros are usually all `CAPS`.
- Each class name should be a noun or a noun phrase: `class LargeFurryMammal` for example.
- Each function name should be a verb or a verb phrase: `processBookOrder()` for example.
- Each `bool` variable name should produce a reasonable approximation of a sentence when used in an `if()` statement: `bool isQualified` for example.

We have adopted a modified Hungarian notation for our data members, in which we use a common prefix so that data members are always clearly visible in the code:

- data members: `m_Color`, `m_Width`—prepend lowercase `m_`
- `static` data members: `s_Singleton`, `s_ObjCount`—prepend lowercase `s_`

For each attribute, we have naming conventions for their corresponding getters/setters.

- Non-boolean getters: `color()` or `getColor()`[1]
- Boolean getters: `isChecked()` or `isValid()`
- setter: `setColor(const Color& newColor)`

A consistent naming convention greatly improves the readability and maintainability of a program.

3.1.1   Other Coding Standards

Following are some other coding standards that have been in widespread use. Keep in mind, the style most relevant to Qt programming is still `[qtapistyle]`.

---

[1] The latter is Java style; the former is Qt style. Both conventions are widely used. Try to follow one convention consistently in your code. (We are not consistent in this book because we want to expose you to different conventions.)

- C and C++ style archives[2]
- Coding Standards Generator[3]

3.2   The Qt Core Module

Qt is a large library consisting of several smaller libraries, or *modules*. The most popular ones are

- `core`, including `QObject`, `QThread`, `QFile`, `QVariant`, and so forth
- `gui`, all classes derived from `QWidget` plus some related classes
- `xml`, for parsing and serializing XML
- `sql`, for communicating with SQL databases
- `phonon`, for playing multimedia files
- `webkit`, for using an embedded Web browser, QtWebkit

Except for `core` and `gui`, these modules need to be "enabled" in `qmake` project files. For example:

```
QT += xml  # to use the xml module
QT -= gui  # to not use QWidgets
QT += sql  # to use SQL module
```

Section 3.2.1 will introduce some of the core library classes.

3.2.1   Streams and Dates

In several of our earlier examples, you saw instances of `QTextStream`, which behaves in a similar way to the C++ Standard Library's global `iostream` objects. When we use them to facilitate interactions with standard input (the keyboard) and output (the screen), we like to give them the familiar names `cin`, `cout`, and `cerr`. We have placed these definitions, along with some other useful functions, into a namespace so that they can be easily `#included` in any program.

EXAMPLE 3.1   src/qstd/qstd.h
```
[ . . . . . ]
namespace qstd {

    // declared but not defined:
```

---

[2] http://www.chris-lott.org/resources/cstyle/
[3] http://www.rosvall.ie/CSG/

```
    extern QTextStream cout;
    extern QTextStream cin;
    extern QTextStream cerr;

    // function declarations:
    bool yes(QString yesNoQuestion);
    bool more(QString prompt);
    int promptInt(int base = 10);
    double promptDouble();
    void promptOutputFile(QFile& outfile);
    void promptInputFile(QFile& infile);
};
[ . . . . ]
```

Example 3.1 declares the `iostream`-like `QTextStream` objects, and Example 3.2 contains the required definitions of these `static` objects.

EXAMPLE 3.2   src/qstd/qstd.cpp

```
[ . . . . ]

QTextStream qstd::cout(stdout, QIODevice::WriteOnly);
QTextStream qstd::cin(stdin, QIODevice::ReadOnly);
QTextStream qstd::cerr(stderr, QIODevice::WriteOnly);

/* Namespace members are like static class members */
bool qstd::yes(QString question) {
    QString ans;
    cout << QString(" %1 [y/n]? ").arg(question);
    cout.flush();
    ans = cin.readLine();
    return (ans.startsWith("Y", Qt::CaseInsensitive));
}
```

`QTextStream` works with Unicode `QString` and other Qt types, so we use it instead of `iostream` in most of our examples henceforth. Example 3.3 uses `QTextStream` objects and functions from the `qstd namespace`. It also uses some of the `QDate` member functions and displays dates in several different formats.

EXAMPLE 3.3   src/qtio/qtio-demo.cpp

```
[ . . . . ]
#include <qstd.h>

int main() {
```

```
using namespace qstd;
QDate d1(2002, 4,1), d2(QDate::currentDate());
int days;
cout << "The first date is: " << d1.toString()
        << "\nToday's date is: "
        << d2.toString("ddd MMMM d, yyyy")<< endl;

if (d1 <  d2)
    cout << d1.toString("MM/dd/yy") << " is earlier than "
            << d2.toString("yyyyMMdd") << endl;

cout << "There are " << d1.daysTo(d2)
        << " days between "
        << d1.toString("MMM dd, yyyy") << " and "
        << d2.toString(Qt::ISODate)  << endl;

cout << "Enter number of days to add to the first date: "
        <<  flush;
days = promptInt();
cout << "The first date was " << d1.toString()
        << "\nThe computed date is "
        <<  d1.addDays(days).toString() << endl;
cout << "First date displayed in longer format: "
        << d1.toString("dddd, MMMM dd, yyyy")  << endl;
[ . . . . ]
```

You can build and run this program from its directory in the src tree. The project file listed in Example 3.4 finds the qstd header and implementation files by using relative paths.

EXAMPLE 3.4   src/qtio/qtio.pro

```
CONFIG += debug console
DEFINES += QT_NOTHREAD_DEBUG

CONFIG -= moc
INCLUDEPATH += . ../qstd
DEPENDPATH += ../qstd

# Input
SOURCES += qtio-demo.cpp qstd.cpp
HEADERS += qstd.h
```

Here is the output of this program.

```
The first date is: Mon Apr 1 2002
Today's date is: Wed January 4, 2006
04/01/02 is earlier than 20060104
There are 1374 days between Apr 01, 2002 and 2006-01-04
Enter number of days to add to the first date: : 1234
The first date was Mon Apr 1 2002
The computed date is Wed Aug 17 2005
First date displayed in longer format: Monday, April 01, 2002
```

3.3   QtCreator—An IDE for Qt Programming

QtCreator is a cross-platform, Integrated Development Environment (IDE) that has been designed to facilitate development of C++ applications that use Qt. As you would expect, it includes a good C++ code editor that provides smart code completion, context-sensitive help using the Qt Assistant facilities, error/warning messages as you type, and rapid code navigation tools. In addition, the Qt Designer, which enables drag and drop form layout and design, is fully integrated into QtCreator. QtCreator has a visual debugger and project build/management tools, plus some very handy code generation and navigation features. There are QtCreator tutorial videos available on YouTube.[4]

If you still want to use your favorite IDE, and that happens to be xcode, MS dev studio, or Eclipse, then you are in luck! You can download Qt integration packages that will give your favorite IDE similar features to those offered in QtCreator. QtCreator can be installed on Windows, Mac, and Linux platforms by downloading either a binary package or a source package from qt.nokia.com downloads.[5] QtCreator is included in the Qt Software Development Kit (SDK), which includes Qt and everything else you need to start developing in Qt very quickly.

The project file used by QtCreator is the qmake .pro file. You can avoid the use of command-line tools entirely by creating and/or editing existing project files in QtCreator.

   NOTE

By default, Qt Creator imports projects and builds in a **shadow build directory**. This means that intermediate files and the executable are placed not with the source, but somewhere else. Furthermore, the program runs from that directory by default.

[4] http://www.youtube.com/view_play_list?p=22E601663DAF3A14
[5] http://qt.nokia.com/downloads

To see/change the build or run directory of a project, select Projects mode (Figure 3.2) and click the Build tab to change Qt versions, build directory, or other build settings. Click the Run tab to change the Run directory or other run settings.

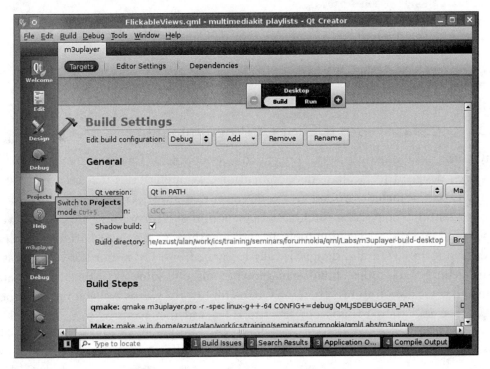

FIGURE 3.2   Qt Creator Projects Mode

3.4   Exercises: Introduction to Qt

1. Write a fuel consumption calculator that can convert in either direction between miles-per-gallon and liters-per-100km.

   For example, a car that can drive 34 miles on one (U.S.) gallon of fuel will consume 6.92 liters of fuel if it is driven 100km.

   Feel free to use QInputDialog and QMessageBox as demonstrated in Section 1.11.

2. Ask the user for a birthdate, and calculate her current age. Hints: use QInputDialog::getText(), convert result from QString to QDate, and compare to QDate::currentDate(). Alternately, you can create a dialog that presents a QDateEdit to get a proper date from the user.

3.5 Review Questions

1. What is `QTextStream`, and how can you reuse it?
2. What is the purpose of the `QT` variable in the `qmake` project file? What are possible values?
3. Why should you use `QTextStream` instead of `iostream` in your programs?

3.5.1 Points of Departure

1. Visit the Unicode Web site, and explain what it is and why it is important that `QString` supports the Unicode standard.
2. Explore the `QTextStream` documentation, and write short programs that test the ways that you can read data from text files.
3. Find out how `QTextStream` can be used to support different character sets.

Chapter 4

Lists

Whenever possible, you should use lists instead of arrays. This chapter introduces containers and discusses various ways of grouping things in lists and how to iterate through them.

4.1 Introduction to Containers

There are many occasions when it is necessary to deal with collections of things. The classic approach in languages like C is to use arrays (Section 21.4) to store such collections. In C++, arrays are regarded as evil.

Following are a few good reasons to avoid using arrays in C++:

- Neither the compiler nor the runtime system checks array subscripts to make sure that they are within the correct range.

- A programmer using an array has the responsibility to write extra code to do the range checking.

- Arrays are either fixed in size or must use dynamic memory from the heap. With heap arrays, the programmer is responsible for making sure that, under all possible circumstances, the memory gets properly deallocated when the array is destroyed.

- To do this properly requires deep knowledge of C++, exceptions, and what happens under exceptional circumstances.
- Inserting, prepending, or appending elements to an array can be expensive operations (in terms of both runtime and developer time).

The Standard Library and Qt both provide the programmer with lists that safely resize themselves as needed and perform range checking. `std::list` and `QList` are the most basic generic containers in their respective libraries. They are similar to each other in *interface* (the way they are used from client code). They differ in **implementation** (the way they behave at runtime). Both libraries also provide several other generic containers that are optimized for particular types of applications.

We used the term **generic containers** because

1. **Generics** are classes or functions that accept template (Section 11.1) parameters so that they can be used with different types of data.

2. **Containers** (Section 6.8) are objects that can *contain* other objects.

To use a generic container, client code must contain a declaration that answers the question: "Container of what?" For example:

```
QList<double>  doubleList;
QList<Thing>  thingList;
```

`QList` supports many operations. As with any class you reuse, we recommend that you read the API docs to get an overview of its full capabilities. With a single function call, items can be added, removed, swapped, queried, cleared, moved, located, and counted in a variety of ways.

4.2 Iterators

Any time you have a container of `Things`, sooner or later, you need to loop through the container and do something with (or to) each individual `Thing`. An **iterator** is an object that provides indirect access to each element in a container. It is specifically designed to be used in a loop.

Qt supports the following styles of iteration:

- Qt style `foreach` loops, similar to Perl and Python
- Java 1.2 style `Iterator`, which always points between elements

- Standard Library style *ContainerType*::iterator
- Hand-made while or for loops that use the getters of the container
- QDirIterator, for iterating through entries in a directory structure

STL-style iterators behave more like pointers than do Java-style iterators. One important difference between iterators and pointers is that there is no iterator value that corresponds to the null value for pointers. For example, a function that uses pointers to search for something in a collection of items can return a null pointer if the search fails. There is no corresponding, generally recognizable iterator value to return that would indicate an unsuccessful iterator-based search.

The Iterator Pattern

A class, function, or programming element that provides a generic way to access elements of a collection sequentially without being type-restricted is an implementation of the Iterator design pattern.[1] C++ iterators, Java-style iterators, and foreach loops are all examples of the Iterator pattern.

There are many classes in Qt that provide specialized iteration for various types of data, such as QDirIterator, QSortFilterProxyModel, QTreeWidgetItemIterator, and QDomNodeList. When an iterator is introduced, its definition must contain enough information to enable it to move from one item to the next in the container.

Section 4.2.1 demonstrates the various styles of iteration available in C++ with Qt.

4.2.1   QStringList **and Iteration**

For text processing, it is useful to work with lists of strings. A QStringList is actually a QList<QString> so you can use the QList public interface.[2] In addition, QStringList has some string-specific convenience functions, such as indexOf(), join(), and replaceInStrings().

Converting between lists and individual strings is quite easy with Perl-like split() and join() functions. Example 4.1 demonstrates lists, iterations, split(), and join().

---

[1] We discuss design patterns in more detail in Section 7.4.

[2] In fact, QStringList is *derived* from QList<QString> so it *inherits* QList's entire public interface. We discuss derivation and inheritance in (Chapter 6, "Inheritance and Polymorphism").

EXAMPLE 4.1   src/containers/lists/lists-examples.cpp

```cpp
#include <QStringList>
#include <QDebug>

/* Some simple examples using QStringList, split, and join */

int main() {

    QString winter = "December, January, February";
    QString spring = "March, April, May";
    QString summer = "June, July, August";
    QString fall = "September, October, November";

    QStringList list;
    list << winter;                                              1
    list += spring;                                              2
    list.append(summer);                                        3
    list << fall;

    qDebug() << "The Spring months are: " << list[1] ;


    QString allmonths = list.join(", ");                         4
    qDebug() << allmonths;

    QStringList list2 = allmonths.split(", ");
    /* Split is the opposite of join. Each month will have its own element. */

    Q_ASSERT(list2.size() == 12);                                5

    foreach (const QString &str, list) {                         6
        qDebug() << QString(" [%1] ").arg(str);
    }

    for (QStringList::iterator it = list.begin();
         it != list.end(); ++it) {                               7
        QString current = *it;                                   8
        qDebug() << "[[" << current << "]]";
    }

    QListIterator<QString> itr (list2);                          9
    while (itr.hasNext()) {                                      10
        QString current = itr.next();
```

```
        qDebug() << "{" <<  current << "}";
    }


    return 0;
}
```

1 Append operator 1.

2 Append operator 2.

3 Append member function.

4 From list to string—join with a , delimiter.

5 Q_ASSERTions abort the program if the condition is not satisfied.

6 Qt foreach loop—similar to Perl/Python and Java 1.5 style for loops.

7 C++ STL-style iteration.

8 Pointer-style dereference.

9 Java 1.2 style iterator.

10 Java iterators point between elements.

Following is the output of Example 4.1:

```
src/containers/lists> ./lists
The Spring months are:  "March, April, May"
"December, January, February, March, April, May, June, July, August, September,
October, November"
" [December, January, February] "
" [March, April, May] "
" [June, July, August] "
" [September, October, November] "
[[ "December, January, February" ]]
[[ "March, April, May" ]]
[[ "June, July, August" ]]
[[ "September, October, November" ]]
{ "December" }
{ "January" }
{ "February" }
{ "March" }
{ "April" }
{ "May" }
{ "June" }
{ "July" }
{ "August" }
```

```
{ "September" }
{ "October" }
{ "November" }
/src/containers/lists>
```

Qt tries to accommodate programmers who have various habits and styles. For example, `QList::Iterator` is just a `typedef` (alias) for `QList::iterator`, providing two different ways to refer to the STL-style `iterator` class. The `QListIterator` and QMutableListIterator classes provide Java-style iterators that point *between* list elements and access particular elements with `previous()` and `next()`.

4.2.2 `QDir, QFileInfo, QDirIterator`

A **directory**, sometimes called a **folder**, is a container for files. Because a directory can also contain other directories, it has a natural **tree** structure. A directory can also contain **symbolic links** (called **symlinks**) that point to other files or directories. A symlink is a reference that can be used instead of the name or path for most operations that handle files or directories.

Qt provides several platform-independent ways to traverse a directory tree. The classes `QDir` and `QFileInfo` enable you to obtain a list of the contents of a directory and then get information about each entry. Example 4.2 shows a recursive function that uses these classes to visit selected items in a directory. It can determine whether an item is a file, a directory, or a symlink and, depending on the parameter choices, process the item appropriately. The first parameter identifies the directory that is to be traversed. The second parameter determines whether the function should recursively descend into any subdirectories that it finds in the directory. The third parameter determines whether the function should process the symlinks that it finds in the directory. The main goal of this particular function is to locate mp3 files and add their paths to a list.

EXAMPLE 4.2   src/iteration/whyiterator/recurseadddir.cpp

```
[ . . . . . ]
void recurseAddDir(QDir d, bool recursive=true, bool symlinks=false ) {
    d.setSorting( QDir::Name );
    QDir::Filters df = QDir::Files | QDir::NoDotAndDotDot;
    if (recursive) df |= QDir::Dirs;
    if (not symlinks) df |= QDir::NoSymLinks;
    QStringList qsl = d.entryList(df, QDir::Name | QDir::DirsFirst);
```

```
    foreach (const QString &entry, qsl) {
        QFileInfo finfo(d, entry);
        if ( finfo.isDir() ) {
            QDir sd(finfo.absoluteFilePath());
            recurseAddDir(sd);
        } else {
            if (finfo.completeSuffix()=="mp3")
                addMp3File(finfo.absoluteFilePath());                1
        }
    }
}
[ . . . . ]
```

1 Nonreusable part

The application listed in Example 4.3 reuses `QDirIterator` to accomplish the same thing with fewer lines of code.

EXAMPLE 4.3   src/iteration/diriterator/diriterator.cpp

```
[ . . . . ]
int main (int argc, char* argv[]) {
    QCoreApplication app(argc, argv);
    QDir dir = QDir::current();
    if (app.arguments().size() > 1) {
        dir = app.arguments()[1];
    }
    if (!dir.exists()) {
        cerr << dir.path() << " does not exist!" << endl;
        usage();
        return -1;
    }
    QDirIterator qdi(dir.absolutePath(),
            QStringList() << "*.mp3",
            QDir::NoSymLinks | QDir::Files,
            QDirIterator::Subdirectories );
    while (qdi.hasNext()) {
        addMp3File(qdi.next());
    }
}
[ . . . . ]
```

There is an important difference between the two applications. In Example 4.2, the call to the project-specific function, `addMp3File()`, occurs inside the definition of the function, `recurseAddDir()`, that manages the iteration, severely limiting the reusability of that function. In Example 4.3, `QDirIterator` manages the iteration. The call to `addMp3File()` occurs in the client code for `QDirIterator` (`main()`) and, thus, can have no effect on the reusability of that class. Using the iterator pattern in appropriate places can make your code much simpler and easier to reuse.

4.3 Relationships

When there is a **one-to-one** or a **one-to-many** correspondence between objects of certain types, we use a variety of connecting lines to describe a **relationship** between them in a UML class diagram.

In Figure 4.1, the line connecting the classes expresses a particular relationship between them.

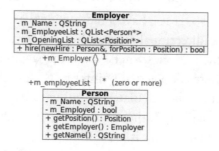

FIGURE 4.1   One-to-Many Relationship

In the context described by this diagram, there can be many `Person` instances working for exactly one `Employer`. This can be denoted by the multiplicity specifier at each end of the relationship: `1` at the `Employer` end, and `*` at the `Person` end. The `*` takes on its regular expression definition, of "0 or more" (Section 14.3).

Revisiting Figure 2.6, another set of relationships is revealed when you look at the company from the `Employer`'s viewpoint. Figure 4.2 shows three kinds of relationships.

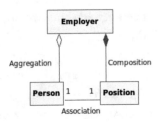

FIGURE 4.2   The Employer's View of the Company

1. There is a **composition** relationship (the filled diamond) between `Employer` and `Position`. It indicates that the `Employer` owns or *manages* the `Position`, and the `Position` should not exist without the `Employer`.

2. There is an **aggregation** relationship (the empty diamond) from the `Employer` to its employees. The `Employer` groups a collection of `Persons` and gets them to do things during working hours. In an aggregation relationship, the lifetimes of the objects on either end are not related to one other.

3. The `Person` and the `Position` have a bidirectional **assocation** between them. An association is a bidirectional relationship and does not specify anything about implementation, ownership, or management between objects. It is possible that there is no actual pointer in `Person` that points to its `Employer` because it can be calculated by going to its `Position` and calling `Position::getEmployer()`. Although the diagram indicates a 1:1 relationship between `Person` and `Position`, it is possible that a `Person` can hold multiple `Positions`, or an `Employer` may hire many `Persons` for the same `Position`. If you want to describe a system that can handle such cases, then the cardinality of this association should be many-to-many.

4.3.1   Relationships Summary

You have seen three kinds of relationships:

- Association (purely for navigation)
- Aggregation (containment without management)
- Composition (containment with management)

A composite relationship is a strong one, which also describes parent-child and (managed) container-contained relationships. In addition, each relationship can have the following properties:

- **Cardinality**—Can be one-to-one, one-to-many, or many-to-many. Often, a number (1, 1..5, *) next to the end of the line segment specifies this.
- **Navigability**—Can be unidirectional or bidirectional. Unidirectional relationships may have arrows instead of diamonds on the line segments between classes.

Figure 4.3 shows an example using containment and unidirectional relationships.

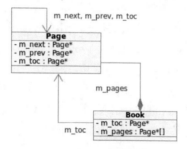

FIGURE 4.3   Books and Pages

In this diagram, a `Book` is a (managed) container of `Page` pointers but, additionally, the pages have their own navigation relationships. Perhaps a reader (or browser) would benefit from direct navigation links to neighboring pages and to the table of contents. Each of these is a unidirectional relationship, so you could show three self-pointing arrows and the diagram would not be incorrect.

For the `m_pages` relationship, there is no reverse relationship shown, so this could describe a unidirectional or a bidirectional containment relationship. If there is need for the `Page` to navigate to its containing `Book` object, you should make the directionality more clear in the diagram. You could do this by labeling the other end of the relationship, and/or by adding an `m_Book` attribute to the `Page` class.

4.4   Exercise: Relationships

1. In these exercises, you implement some relationships loosely based on Figure
   4.2. The diagram is only a starting point. To complete the assignment, you
   need to add some members to the classes.

   a. Implement an `Employer::findJobs()` function to return a list of all open
      `Position`s.

   b. Implement a `Person::apply(Position*)` function to call
      `Employer::hire()`, and return the same result as `hire()`, if successful.

   c. To make things interesting, have the `Employer::hire()` function randomly
      return `false` half of the time.

   d. For the `Person` methods that return information about employment, be
      sure to handle the case where the `Person` is not employed yet, and return
      something meaningful.

   e. Create some more test `Employer` objects (Galactic Empire and Rebel
      Forces), `Person` objects (Darth Vader, C3PO, Data), and `Position` objects
      (Tie Fighter Pilot, Protocol Android, Captain) in your client code.

   f. Define a `static QList<Person*> s_unemploymentLine` in class `Person`,
      and ensure that all persons without a job are on it.

   g. Make up some funny job application scenarios, and run your program to
      determine whether they are successful.

2.

   a. Figure 4.4 describes a model[3] for a `Contact` system. `ContactList` can derive
      from or reuse any Qt container that you like, as long as it supports the
      operations listed.

      • `getPhoneList(int category)` accepts a value to be compared with
        a `Contact`'s category member for selection purposes. It returns a
        `QStringList` containing, for each selected `Contact`, the name and
        phone number, separated by the tab symbol: `"\t"`.

      • `getMailingList()` has a similar selection mechanism and returns a
        `QStringList` containing address label data.

---

[3] We discuss models and views in Chapter 13, "Models and Views." For now we refer to a data structure that manages information for an application (but not the acquisition, display, or transmission of that information) as a **model**.

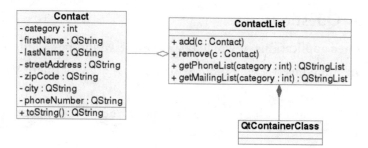

FIGURE 4.4   Contacts

b. Write a `ContactFactory` class that generates random `Contact` objects. Example 4.4 contains a substantial hint.

EXAMPLE 4.4   src/containers/contact/testdriver.cpp

```
[ . . . . ]

void createRandomContacts(ContactList& cl, int n=10) {
    static ContactFactory cf;
    for (int i=0; i<n; ++i) {
        cf >> cl;                                             1
    }
}
```

1   Adds a Contact into the Contact List.

There are many ways to generate random names/addresses. One way is to have the `ContactFactory` create lists of typical first names, last names, street names, city names, and so forth.[4] When it is time to generate a `Contact`, it can pick a random element from each list, add randomly generated address numbers, zip codes, etc. We demonstrate the use of the `random()` function in Section 1.13.3.

c. Write client code to test your classes. In particular, the client code should generate some random contacts. After that, it should test the two query methods (`getPhoneList()` and `getMailingList()`) to ensure that they return the proper sublists. Print the original list and the query results to standard output. Summarize the results by listing the number of elements in the original `ContactList` compared to the query results.

---

[4] Spam is a great source of names—just browse through your spam folder and grab names from the mail headers or from the message bodies. We have provided a starter list of spam names in the Dist directory.

4.5   Review Questions

1. Name three applications in which `QStringList` would be useful.

2. How can you convert a `QStringList` to a `QString`? Why might you want to do that?

3. How can you convert a `QString` to a `QStringList`? Why might you want to do that?

4. What is the iterator pattern? Give three examples.

5. Draw a UML diagram with three or more classes, and make sure that all these different kinds of relationships are represented.

   • Aggregation and composition

   • One-to-One and One-to-Many

   • Unidirectional and bidirectional

   The classes should represent real-world concepts, and the relationships should attempt to represent reality. Write a couple of paragraphs explaining why there is a relationship of each kind in your diagram.

6. What is the difference between composition and aggregation?

7. Read the API docs for `QList`, and find three distinct ways to add elements to the list.

8. List three methods that exist in `QStringList` but are not in `QList`.

9. Why does `QList` have an `iterator` and an `Iterator`? What is the difference between them?

10. Discuss the advantages and disadvantages of Qt or STL container classes as compared to arrays.

11. Discuss the syntax of the `QList` declaration. What should be in <angle brackets>? Why is it necessary?

12. Why does Qt support so many different kinds of iterators?

13. What is the difference between `QFile` and `QFileInfo`?

Chapter 5

Functions

This chapter discusses the essentials of function overloading, function call resolution, default/optional arguments, temporary variables and when they're created, reference parameters and return values, and `inline` functions.

Functions in C++ are similar to functions and subroutines in other languages. C++ functions, however, support many features not found in some languages, so it is worthwhile discussing them here.

5.1 Overloading Functions

As stated in Section 1.5 the **signature** of a function consists of its name and its parameter list. In C++, the return type is *not* part of the signature.

You have seen that C++ permits **overloading** of function names. Recall that a function name is overloaded if it has more than one meaning within a given scope. Overloading occurs when two or more functions within a given scope have the same name but different signatures. Also recall (Section 1.5) that it is an error to have two functions in the same scope with the same signature but different return types.

Function Call Resolution

When a function call is made to an overloaded function within a given scope, the C++ compiler determines from the arguments which version of the function to invoke. To do this, a match must be found between the number and type of the arguments and the signature of exactly one of the overloaded functions. For the purpose of signature matching, *Type* and *Type&* parameters match.

This is the sequence of steps that the compiler takes to determine which overloaded function to call.

1. If there is an exact match with one function, call it.

2. Else, match through standard type promotions (Section 19.6).

3. Else, match through conversion constructors or conversion operators (Section 2.12).

4. Else, match through *ellipsis* (. . .) (Section 5.11) (if found).

5. Else, report an error.

Example 5.1 shows a class with six member functions, each with a distinct signature. Keep in mind that each member function has an additional, implicit, parameter: this. The keyword const, following the parameter list, protects the host object (pointed to by this) from the action of the function and is part of its signature.

EXAMPLE 5.1   src/functions/function-call.cpp

```
[ . . . . ]

class SignatureDemo {
public:
    SignatureDemo(int val) : m_Val(val) {}
    void demo(int n)
        {cout << ++m_Val << "\tdemo(int)" << endl;}
    void demo(int n) const                                          1
        {cout << m_Val << "\tdemo(int) const" << endl;}
/*  void demo(const int& n)
       {cout << ++m_Val << "\tdemo(int&)" << endl;}  */            2
    void demo(short s)
        {cout << ++m_Val << "\tdemo(short)" << endl;}
    void demo(float f)
        {cout << ++m_Val << "\tdemo(float)" << endl;}
    void demo(float f) const
```

```
        {cout << m_Val << "\tdemo(float) const" << endl;}
    void demo(double d)
        {cout << ++m_Val << "\tdemo(double)" << endl;}
private:
    int m_Val;
};
```

1 Overloaded on `const`-ness.

2 Clashes with previous function.

Example 5.2 contains some client code that tests the overloaded functions from `SignatureDemo`.

EXAMPLE 5.2   src/functions/function-call.cpp

```
[ . . . . ]

int main() {
    SignatureDemo sd(5);
    const SignatureDemo csd(17);
    sd.demo(2);
    csd.demo(2);                                              1
    int i = 3;
    sd.demo(i);
    short s = 5;
    sd.demo(s);
    csd.demo(s);                                              2
    sd.demo(2.3);                                             3
    float f(4.5);
    sd.demo(f);
    csd.demo(f);
    //csd.demo(4.5);
    return 0;
}
```

1 `const` version is called.

2 Non-const short cannot be called, so a promotion to `int` is required to call the `const int` version.

3 This is `double`, not `float`.

The output should look something like this:

```
6       demo(int)
17      demo(int) const
7       demo(int)
8       demo(short)
17      demo(int) const
9       demo(double)
10      demo(float)
17      demo(float) const
```

5.1.1   Exercises: Overloading Functions

1. Experiment with Example 5.1. Start by uncommenting the third member function and compiling.

2. Try uncommenting the following line just before the end of `main()`:

```
//   csd.demo(4.5);
```

   What happened? Explain the error message.

3. Notice the compiler warnings about unused parameters when you build this application. Try deleting all the unused parameter names from the function heads that the compiler mentions. (Do not delete the parameter types!) Then rebuild the application and observe the compiler output. This is a good way to notify the compiler that you do not intend to use certain parameters. You can see this technique used in a more convincing way in Section 15.2.

4. Add other function calls and other variations on the `demo()` function.

   Explain each result.

5.2   Optional Arguments

Default (Optional) Arguments

Function parameters can have default values, making them optional. The default value for an optional argument can be a constant expression or an expression that does not involve local variables.

Parameters with default arguments must be the right-most (trailing) parameters in the parameter list. Trailing arguments with default values can be left out of the function call. The corresponding parameters will then be initialized with the default values.

From the viewpoint of the function, if it is called with one missing argument, that argument must correspond to the last parameter in the list. If two arguments are missing, they must correspond to the last two parameters in the list (and so forth).

Because an optional argument specifier applies to a function's interface, it belongs with the declaration, not the definition of the function if the declaration is kept in a separate header file. A function with default arguments can be called in more than one way. If all arguments for a function are optional, the function can be called with no arguments. Declaring a function with n optional arguments can be thought of as an abbreviated way of declaring n+1 functions—one for each possible way of calling the function.

In Example 5.3, the constructor for the Date class has three parameters; each parameter is optional and defaults to 0.

EXAMPLE 5.3   src/functions/date.h

```
[ . . . . ]
class Date {
public:
    Date(int d = 0, int m = 0, int y = 0);
    void display(bool eoln = true) const;
private:
    int m_Day, m_Month, m_Year;
};
[ . . . . ]
```

The constructor definition shown in Example 5.4 looks the same as usual; no default arguments need to be specified there. If 0 turns out to be the value of any of the supplied arguments, it will be replaced with a sensible value derived from the current date.

EXAMPLE 5.4   src/functions/date.cpp

```
#include <QDate>
#include "date.h"
#include <iostream>
```

```cpp
Date::Date(int d , int m , int y )
: m_Day(d), m_Month(m), m_Year(y) {

    static QDate currentDate = QDate::currentDate();          1

    if (m_Day == 0) m_Day = currentDate.day();
    if (m_Month == 0) m_Month = currentDate.month();
    if (m_Year == 0) m_Year = currentDate.year();
}


void Date::display(bool eoln) const {
    using namespace std;
    cout << m_Year << "/" << m_Month << '/' << m_Day;
    if (eoln)
        cout << endl;
}
```

1 We use Qt's QDate class only to get the current date.

EXAMPLE 5.5   src/functions/date-test.cpp

```cpp
#include "date.h"
#include <iostream>

int main() {
    using namespace std;
    Date d1;
    Date d2(15);
    Date d3(23, 8);
    Date d4(19, 11, 2003);

    d1.display(false);
    cout << '\t';
    d2.display();
    d3.display(false);
    cout << '\t';
    d4.display();
    return 0;
}
```

Example 5.5 demonstrates that, by defining default values you are, in effect, over-loading the function. The different versions of the function execute the same code, but with different values passed in for the later parameters.

So if you ran this program on May 14, 2011, it should show you the following output:

```
src/functions> qmake
src/functions> make
[ compiler linker messages ]
src/functions> ./functions
2011/5/14        2011/5/15
2011/8/23        2003/11/19
src/functions>
```

5.3   Operator Overloading

The keyword `operator` is used in C++ to define a new meaning for an operator symbol, such as +, -, =, *, and &. Adding a new meaning to an operator symbol is a specialized form of overloading. Overloaded operators provide a more compact syntax for calling functions, leading to more readable code (assuming the operators are used in ways that are commonly understood).

It is possible to overload nearly all the existing operator symbols in C++. For example, suppose that you want to define a class `Complex` to represent complex numbers.[1] To specify how to do the basic arithmetic operations with these objects, you could overload the four arithmetic operator symbols. In addition, you could overload the insertion symbol, <<, so that it uses a more stream-lined (if you'll pardon the pun) interface.

---

[1] The set of complex numbers comprises all numbers of the form: $a + bi$, where a and b are real numbers and i is the square root of -1. Because that set includes such numbers for which $b = 0$, this shows that the real numbers are a subset of the complex numbers.

Complex numbers were introduced initially to describe the solutions to equations like

$$x^2 - 6x + 25 = 0$$

Using the quadratic formula, you can easily determine that the roots of this equation are $3 + 4i$ and $3 - 4i$.

Example 5.6 shows a class definition with both member and nonmember operators.

EXAMPLE 5.6   src/complex/complex.h

```
#include <iostream>
using namespace std;

class Complex {
    // binary nonmember friend function declarations
    friend ostream& operator<<(ostream& out, const Complex& c);
    friend Complex operator-(const Complex& c1, const Complex & c2);
    friend Complex operator*(const Complex& c1, const Complex & c2);
    friend Complex operator/(const Complex& c1, const Complex & c2);

    public:
    Complex(double re = 0.0, double im = 0.0);                          1

    // binary member function operators
    Complex& operator+= (const Complex& c);
    Complex& operator-= (const Complex& c);


    Complex operator+(const Complex & c2);                             2

private:
    double m_Re, m_Im;
};
```

1 Default and conversion constructor.

2 This should be a nonmember friend like the other nonmutating operators.

All the operators declared in Example 5.6 are binary (accepting two operands). For the member functions, there is only one formal parameter because the first (left) operand is implicit: *this. The definitions of the member operators are shown in Example 5.7.

EXAMPLE 5.7   src/complex/complex.cpp

```
[ . . . . ]

Complex& Complex::operator+=(const Complex& c) {
    m_Re += c.m_Re;
    m_Im += c.m_Im;
```

```
        return *this;
}

Complex Complex::operator+(const Complex& c2) {
    return Complex(m_Re + c2.m_Re, m_Im + c2.m_Im);
}

Complex& Complex::operator-=(const Complex& c) {
    m_Re -= c.m_Re;
    m_Im -= c.m_Im;
    return *this;
}
```

Example 5.8 shows the definitions of the nonmember friend functions. They are defined like ordinary global functions.

EXAMPLE 5.8   src/complex/complex.cpp

```
[ . . . . ]



ostream& operator<<(ostream& out, const Complex& c) {
    out << '(' << c.m_Re << ',' << c.m_Im << ')' ;
    return out;
}

Complex operator-(const Complex& c1, const Complex& c2) {
    return Complex(c1.m_Re - c2.m_Re, c1.m_Im - c2.m_Im);
}
```

We have now expressed the mathematical rules that define each of the four algebraic operations in C++ code. These details are encapsulated and hidden so that client code does not need to deal with them. Example 5.9 shows some client code that demonstrates and tests the Complex class.

EXAMPLE 5.9   src/complex/complex-test.cpp

```
#include "complex.h"
#include <iostream>

int main() {
    using namespace std;
    Complex c1(3.4, 5.6);
    Complex c2(7.8, 1.2);
```

```
cout << c1 << " + " << c2 << " = " << c1 + c2 << endl;
cout << c1 << " - " << c2 << " = " << c1 - c2 << endl;
Complex c3 = c1 * c2;
cout << c1 << " * " << c2 << " = " << c3 << endl;
cout << c3 << " / " << c2 << " = " << c3 / c2 << endl;
cout << c3 << " / " << c1 << " = " << c3 / c1 << endl;

return 0;
}
```

Following is the output of the program in Example 5.9.

```
(3.4,5.6) + (7.8,1.2) = (11.2,6.8)
(3.4,5.6) - (7.8,1.2) = (-4.4,4.4)
(3.4,5.6) * (7.8,1.2) = (19.8,47.76)
(19.8,47.76) / (7.8,1.2) = (3.4,5.6)
(19.8,47.76) / (3.4,5.6) = (7.8,1.2)
```

Member Versus Global Operators

As you have seen, it is possible to overload operators as member functions, or as global functions. The primary difference that you notice first is how they can be called. In particular, a member function operator *requires* an object as the left operand. A global function, in contrast, *permits* the same kinds of type conversions for either operand.

Example 5.10 shows why Complex::operator+() would be better suited as a nonmember function.

EXAMPLE 5.10   src/complex/complex-conversions.cpp

```
#include "complex.h"

int main() {
    Complex c1 (4.5, 1.2);
    Complex c2 (3.6, 1.5);

    Complex c3 = c1 + c2;
    Complex c4 = c3 + 1.4;          1
    Complex c5 = 8.0 - c4;          2
    Complex c6 = 1.2 + c4;          3
}
```

1 Right operand is promoted.
2 Left operand is promoted.
3 Error: left operand is not promoted for member operators.

There are some limitations on operator overloading. Only built-in operators can be overloaded. It is not possible to introduce definitions for symbols such as $ " ' that do not already possess operator definitions. Furthermore, although new meanings can be defined for built-in operators, their associativity and precedence cannot be changed.

It is possible to overload all the built-in binary and unary operators except for these:

- The ternary conditional operator `testExpr ? valueIfTrue : valueIfFalse`
- The scope resolution operator `::`
- Member select operators `.` and `.*`

 TIP

Here is a way to remember which operators can be overloaded. If the symbol has a dot (.) in it anywhere, overloading is probably not allowed.

 NOTE

Overloading the comma operator is permitted but not recommended until you are a C++ expert.

You can find a complete table of operator symbols and their characteristics in Section 19.1.

NOTE

It is possible to define a new meaning for a built-in operator symbol so that it can be used with operands of different types. But it is *not* possible to change the associativity or the precedence of a built-in operator symbol.

5.3.1   Exercises: Operator Overloading

1. Continue the development of the `Fraction` class by adding overloaded operators for addition, subtraction, multiplication, division, and various kinds of comparison. In each case the parameter should be a `const Fraction&`. Write client code to test your new operators.

2. To be useful, a `Fraction` object should be able to interact with other kinds of numbers. Expand the definition of `Fraction` so that the operators in your solution to Problem 1 also work for `int` and `double`. It should be clear, for example, how to get `frac + num` to be correctly evaluated. How would you handle the expression `num + frac`, where `frac` is a fraction and `num` is an `int`? Write client code to test your new functions.

3. Add arithmetic and comparison operators to the class `Complex`. Write client code to test your expanded class.

5.4   Parameter Passing by Value

By default, C++ parameters are passed by value. When a function is called, a temporary (local) copy of each argument object is made and placed on the program stack. Only the local copy is manipulated inside the function, and the argument objects from the calling block are not affected by these manipulations. All the temporary stack variables are destroyed when the function returns. A useful way to think of value parameters is this: Value parameters are merely local variables initialized by copies of the corresponding argument objects specified when the function is called. Example 5.11 gives a short demonstration.

EXAMPLE 5.11   src/functions/summit.cpp

```cpp
#include <iostream>

int sumit(int num) {
    int sum = 0;
    for (; num ; --num)                          1
        sum += num;
    return sum;
}


int main() {
    using namespace std;
    int n = 10;
    cout << n  << endl;
    cout << sumit(n) << endl;
    cout << n << endl;                           2
    return 0;
}
```

Output:

```
10
55
10
```

1 The parameter gets reduced to 0.

2 See what sumit() did to n.

If a pointer is passed to a function, a temporary copy of that pointer is placed on the stack. Changes to that pointer will have no effect on the pointer in the calling block. For example, the temporary pointer could be assigned a different value (see Example 5.12).

EXAMPLE 5.12   src/functions/pointerparam.cpp

```cpp
#include <iostream>
using namespace std;

void messAround(int* ptr) {
    *ptr = 34;                                   1
    ptr = 0;                                     2
```

```
}

int main() {
    int n(12);
    int* pn(&n);
    cout << "n = " << n << "\tpn = " << pn << endl;
    messAround(pn);
    cout << "n = " << n << "\tpn = " << pn << endl;
    return 0;
}
```

3

4

5

Output:

```
n = 12  pn = 0xbffff524
n = 34  pn = 0xbffff524
```

1 Change the value that is pointed to.

2 Change the address stored by `ptr`. Better not dereference this!

3 Initialize an `int`.

4 Initialize a pointer that points to n.

5 See what is changed by `messAround()`.

The output displays the hexadecimal value of the pointer `pn` and the value of n so that there can be no doubt about what was changed by the action of the function.

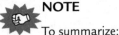 **NOTE**

To summarize:

· When an object is passed by value to a function, a **copy** is made of that object.

· The copy is treated as a local variable by the function.

· The copy is **destroyed** when the function returns.

5.5 Parameter Passing by Reference

Large objects, or objects with expensive copy constructors, should not be passed by value because the creation of copies needlessly consumes machine cycles and time. In C, you can avoid copying objects by passing pointers to them; however, using pointers requires a different syntax from using objects. Further, accidental misuse of pointers can cause data corruption, leading to runtime errors that can be difficult to find and fix. In C++ (and C99), you can pass by reference, a mechanism that offers the same performance as a pass by pointer. With objects, this permits use of the (.) operator for accessing members indirectly.

A **reference parameter** is simply a parameter that is an alias for something else. To declare a parameter to be a reference, put the ampersand character (&) between the type name and the parameter name.

A reference parameter of a function is initialized by the actual argument that is passed when the function is called. That argument must be, as with any reference, a non-const lvalue. Changes to a non-const reference parameter in the function cause changes to the argument object used to initialize the parameter. This feature can be used to define functions, which can normally return at most one value, that cause changes in several argument objects, effectively enabling the function to return several values. Example 5.13 shows how reference parameters can be used with integers.

EXAMPLE 5.13   src/reference/swap.cpp

```cpp
#include <iostream>
using namespace std;

void swap(int& a, int& b) {
    int temp = a;
    cout << "Inside the swap() function:\n"
        << "address of a: " << &a
        << "\taddress of b: " << &b
        << "\naddress of temp: " << &temp << endl;
    a = b;
    b = temp;
}


int main() {
    int n1 = 25;
    int n2 = 38;
    int n3 = 71;
    int n4 = 82;
    cout << "Initial values:\n"
        << "address of n1: " << &n1
        << "\taddress of n2: " << &n2
        << "\nvalue of n1: " << n1
```

```
        << "\t\t\tvalue of n2: " << n2
        << "\naddress of n3: " << &n3
        << "\taddress of n4: " << &n4
        << "\nvalue of n3: " << n3
        << "\t\t\tvalue of n4: " << n4
        << "\nMaking the first call to swap()" << endl;
    swap(n1,n2);
    cout << "After the first call to swap():\n"
        << "address of n1: " << &n1
        << "\taddress of n2: " << &n2
        << "\nvalue of n1: " << n1
        << "\t\t\tvalue of n2: " << n2
        << "\nMaking the second call to swap()" << endl;
    swap(n3,n4);
    cout << "After the second call to swap():\n"
        << "address of n3: " << &n3
        << "\taddress of n4: " << &n4
        << "\nvalue of n3: " << n3
        << "\tvalue of n4: " << n4 << endl;
    return 0;
}
```

There are extra output statements in this program to help keep track of the addresses of the important variables.

```
Initial values:
address of n1: 0xbffff3b4        address of n2: 0xbffff3b0
value of n1: 25                 value of n2: 38
address of n3: 0xbffff3ac       address of n4: 0xbffff3a8
value of n3: 71                 value of n4: 82
```

Initially the program stack might look something like Figure 5.1.

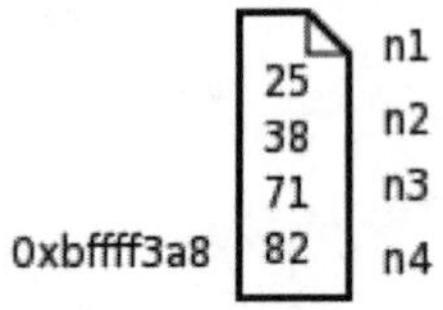

FIGURE 5.1   Before First swap()

As the program proceeds, you see output like this:

```
Making the first call to swap()
Inside the swap() function:
address of a: 0xbffff3b4        address of b: 0xbffff3b0
address of temp: 0xbffff394
```

When references get passed to functions, the values that get pushed onto the stack are *addresses*, not rvalues. Under the covers, pass-by-reference is very much like pass-by-pointer. The stack now might look like Figure 5.2.

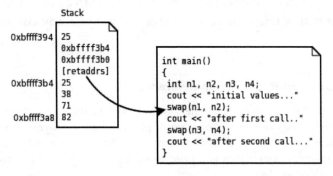

FIGURE 5.2   Inside first swap ()

```
After the first call to swap():
address of n1: 0xbffff3b4        address of n2: 0xbffff3b0
value of n1: 38                  value of n2: 25
Making the second call to swap()
Inside the swap() function:
```

Figure 5.3 shows the state of the stack after the preceding lines have been printed.

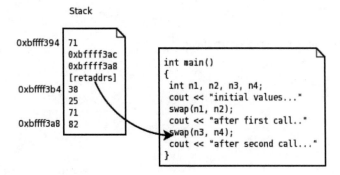

FIGURE 5.3   Inside Second swap ()

```
address of a: 0xbffff3ac         address of b: 0xbffff3a8
address of temp: 0xbffff394
After the second call to swap():
address of n3: 0xbffff3ac         address of n4: 0xbffff3a8
value of n3: 82 value of n4: 71
```

The `swap()` function is actually working with n1 and n2 during the first call, and with n3 and n4 during the second call.

Pass-by-reference syntax provides an alternative to pass-by-pointer. Under the covers, it is implemented with pointers and the value is not copied. The main difference between pass-by-pointer and pass-by-reference is that with a pointer you must dereference it, whereas with a reference you can access it in same way you would access the referred entity.

Pass-by-Pointer or Pass-by-Reference?

When you have a choice, it is generally preferable to use references instead of pointers because this can reduce the number of places where a programmer can accidentally corrupt memory. It is only when you need to manage objects (creation, destruction, adding to a managed container) that you need to operate on pointers, and those routines can usually be encapsulated as member functions.

5.6   References to `const`

Declaring a reference parameter to be `const` tells the compiler to make sure that the function does not attempt to change that object. For objects larger than a pointer, a reference to `const` is an efficient alternative to a value parameter because no data is copied. Example 5.14 contains three functions, each accepting a parameter in a different way.

EXAMPLE 5.14   src/const/reference/constref.cpp

```
#include <QString>

class Person {

public:
```

```
    void setNameV( QString newName) {
        newName += " Smith";                                1
        m_Name = newName;
    }

    void setNameCR( const QString& newName) {
//      newName += " Python";                               2
        m_Name = newName;
    }
    void setNameR( QString& newName) {
        newName += " Dobbs";                                3
        m_Name = newName;
    }
private:
    QString m_Name;
};

#include <QDebug>

int main() {
    Person p;
    QString name("Bob");
    p.setNameCR(name);                                      4
//  p.setNameR("Monty");                                    5
    p.setNameCR("Monty");                                   6
    p.setNameV("Connie");                                   7
    p.setNameR(name);                                       8
    qDebug() << name;
}
```

1 Changes a temporary that's about to be destroyed.

2 Error: Can't change const&.

3 Changes the original QString.

4 No temporaries are created.

5 Error: Cannot convert to a QString&.

6 char* converts to temporary and gets passed by const reference.

7 Temporary QString #1 is created to convert char* to QString. Temporary #2 is created when it is passed by value.

8 No temporaries are created.

5.7   Function Return Values

Some functions return a value when they finish performing the task for which they were designed. Space for a temporary return object is usually a register (if it can fit), but sometimes it is an object allocated on the stack. The temporary return object is initialized when the `return` statement is executed and exists just long enough to be used in whatever expression contains the function call. It is generally a copy of an object that is local to the function or an object constructed from an expression in the `return` statement.

5.8   Returning References from Functions

Sometimes it can be useful to design a function so that it returns a reference. For example, this makes it possible to chain operations like this:

```
cout << thing1 << thing2 << thing3 ... ;
```

A reference return (especially of `*this`) is used to provide lvalue behavior for member functions.

As with reference parameters, it is possible to protect a reference return by specifying that the object it aliases is `const`.

Example 5.15 captures the essence of reference returns.

EXAMPLE 5.15   src/reference/maxi.cpp

```cpp
#include <iostream>
using namespace std;
int& maxi(int& x, int& y) {

    return (x > y) ? x : y;
}


int main() {
    int a = 10, b = 20;
    maxi(a,b) = 5;                           1
    maxi(a,b) += 6;                          2
    ++maxi(a, b) ;                           3
    cout << a << '\t' << b << endl;
    return 0;
}
```

Output:

```
17      5
```

1 Assigns the value 5 to b.

2 Increases a by 6. a is now 16.

3 Increments a by 1.

As you see in the `main()` function, the reference return value of the function `maxi()` makes the expression `maxi(a,b)` into a **modifiable lvalue**.

CAUTION

Be careful that your function does not return a reference to a temporary (local) object. A moment's thought should make the reason for that restriction clear: When the function returns, its local variables are destroyed.

```
int& max(int i,int j) {
    int retval = i > j ? i : j;

    return retval;
}
```

If you are lucky, code like the preceding code may generate a compiler warning, but (alas) the compiler does not consider it an error. Here is the warning that a recent version of C++ gives.

```
badmax.cpp:4: warning: reference to local variable 'retval' returned
```

A more practical example showing the benefits of reference returns is shown in Example 5.16, which defines some common operators for vectors.

5.9   Overloading on `const`

`const` changes the signature of a member function. This means that functions can be overloaded on `const`-ness. Example 5.16 is an example of a homemade vector class with member functions overloaded in this way.

EXAMPLE 5.16   src/const/overload/constoverload.h

```
#ifndef CONSTOVERLOAD_H
#define CONSTOVERLOAD_H

#include <iostream>

class Point3 {                                                         1
 public:
    friend std::ostream& operator<<(std::ostream& out, const Point3& v);
    Point3(double x = 0, double y = 0, double z = 0);
    double& operator[](int index);
    const double& operator[](int index) const;                        2
    Point3 operator+(const Point3& v) const;
    Point3 operator-(const Point3& v) const;
    Point3 operator*(double s) const;                                 3
 private:
    static const int cm_Dim = 3;
    double m_Coord[cm_Dim];
};

#endif
```

1 3-dimension point (of double).

2 Overloaded on const-ness.

3 Scalar multiplication.

The operator function definitions are shown in Example 5.17.

EXAMPLE 5.17   src/const/overload/constoverload.cpp

```
[ . . . . ]
const double& Point3::operator[](int index) const {
    if ((index >= 0) && (index < cm_Dim))
        return m_Coord[index];
    else
        return zero(index);
}

double& Point3::operator[](int index) {
    if ((index >= 0) && (index < cm_Dim))
        return m_Coord[index];
    else
```

```
        return zero(index);
}
```

[. . . .]

The fact that the two function bodies are identical is worth pondering. If index is in range, each function returns m_Coord[index]. So what is the difference between them? It is important to understand that the non-const version of this operator behaves very much like the function maxi() in Example 5.15.

5.9.1   Exercises: Overloading on const

1. In Example 5.18, the compiler can tell the difference between calls to the const and to the non-const versions of operator[] based on the const-ness of the object.

EXAMPLE 5.18   src/const/overload/constoverload-client.cpp

```
#include "constoverload.h"
#include <iostream>

int main( ) {
    using namespace std;
    Point3 pt1(1.2, 3.4, 5.6);
    const Point3 pt2(7.8, 9.1, 6.4);
    double d ;
    d = pt2[2];                                          1
    cout << d << endl;
    d = pt1[0];                                          2
    cout << d << endl;
    d = pt1[3];                                          3
    cout << d << endl;
    pt1[2] = 8.7;                                        4
    cout << pt1 << endl;
    //  pt2[2] = 'd';
    cout << pt2 << endl;
    return 0;
}
```

1 _____

2 _____

3 _____

4 _____

Which operator is called for each of the notes?

2. Why is the last assignment commented out?

5.10   `inline` Functions

To avoid the overhead associated with a function call (i.e., creation of a stack frame containing copies of arguments or addresses of reference parameters and the return address), C++ permits you to declare functions to be `inline`. Such a declaration is a *request* to the compiler that it replace each call to the function with the fully expanded code of the function. For example:

```
inline int max(int a, int b){
  return a > b ? a : b ;
}


int main(){
   int temp = max(3,5);
    etc....
}
```

The compiler could substitute the expanded code for `max` as shown here.

```
int main() {
  int temp;
  {
    int a = 3;
    int b = 5;
    temp = a > b ? a : b;
  }
  etc.......
}
```

The inlining of a function can give a significant boost in performance if it is called repeatedly (e.g., inside a large loop). The penalty for inlining a function is that it might make the compiled code larger, which will cause the code to occupy more memory while it is running. For small functions that get called many times, that memory effect will be small whereas the potential performance gain might be large.

There are no simple answers to the question of whether inlining will improve the performance of your program. A lot depends on the optimization settings of the compiler. A lot depends on the nature of the program. Does it make heavy use of the processor? Does it make heavy use of system memory? Does it spend a lot of its time interacting with slow devices (e.g., input and output)? The answers to these questions affect the answer to the question of whether to inline, and we leave that to a more advanced treatment of the subject. For an overview of the complexity of this issue, visit Marshall Cline's FAQ Lite site.[2]

An inline function is similar to a #define macro with one important difference: The substitution process for a #define macro is handled by the preprocessor, which is essentially a text editor. The substitution process for an inline function is handled by the compiler, which will perform the operation much more intelligently with proper type checking. We discuss this in more detail in the next section.

Some Rules About inline Functions

- An inline function must be defined before it is called. (A declaration is not enough.)
- An inline definition can only occur once in any source code module.
- If a class member function's definition appears inside the class definition, the function is implicitly inline.

If a function is too complex, or the compiler options are switched, the compiler may ignore the inline directive. Most compilers refuse to inline functions that contain one or more of the following:

- while, for, do ... while statements
- switch statements
- More than a certain number of lines of code

If the compiler does refuse to inline a function, it treats it as a normal function and generates regular function calls.

---

[2] http://www.parashift.com/c++-faq-lite/inline-functions.html

5.10.1   Inlining Versus Macro Expansion

Macro expansion is a mechanism for placing code inline by means of a preprocessor directive:

```
#define MACRO_ID expr
```

This is different from an `inline` function.

Macro expansion provides no type-checking for arguments. It is essentially an editing operation: Each occurrence of `MACRO_ID` is replaced by *expr*. Careful use of parentheses in macros is necessary to avoid precedence errors, but parentheses won't solve all the problems associated with macros, as you see in Example 5.19. Errors caused by macros can lead to strange (and unclear) compiler errors or, more dangerously, to invalid results. Example 5.19 demonstrates the latter situation.

EXAMPLE 5.19   src/functions/inlinetst.cpp

```cpp
// Inline functions vs macros

#include <iostream>
#define   BADABS(X)    (((X) < 0)? -(X)  : X)
#define   BADSQR(X) (X * X)
#define   BADCUBE(X) (X) * (X) * (X)

using namespace std;

inline double square(double x) {
    return x * x ;
}

inline double cube(double x) {
    return x * x * x;
}

inline int absval(int n) {
    return (n >= 0) ? n : -n;
}

int main() {
    cout << "Comparing inline and #define\n" ;
    double  t = 30.0;
    int i = 8, j = 8, k = 8, n = 8;
    cout << "\nBADSQR(t + 8) = " << BADSQR(t + 8)
```

```
        << "\nsquare(t + 8) = " << square(t + 8)
        << "\nBADCUBE(++i) = " << BADCUBE(++i)
        << "\ni = " << i
        << "\ncube(++j) = " << cube(++j)
        << "\nj = " << j
        << "\nBADABS(++k) = " << BADABS(++k)
        << "\nk = " << k
        << "\nabsval(++n) = " << absval(++n)
        << "\nn = " << n << endl;
}
```

Here is its output.

```
Comparing inline and #define

BADSQR(t + 8) = 278
square(t + 8) = 1444
BADCUBE(++i) = 1100
 i = 11
cube(++j) = 729
j = 9
BADABS(++k) = 10
k = 10
absval(++n) = 9
n = 9
```

BADSQR(t+8) gives the wrong results because

```
    BADSQR(t + 8)
=   (t + 8 * t + 8)          (preprocessor)
=   (30.0 + 8 * 30.0 + 8)    (compiler)
=   (30 + 240 + 8)           (runtime)
=   278
```

More troubling, however, are the errors produced by BADCUBE and BADABS, which both have sufficient parentheses to prevent the kind of error that occurred with BADSQR. Here is what happened with BADCUBE(++i).

```
    BADCUBE(++i)
=   ((++i) * (++i)) * (++i)    // left associativity
=   ((10) * (10)) * (11)
=   1100
```

In general, code substitution macros should be avoided. They are regarded as evil by most serious C++ programmers. Preprocessor macros are used mostly for the following:

1. `#ifndef/#define/#endif` wrapping around header files to avoid multiple inclusion

2. `#ifdef/#else/#endif` to conditionally compile some parts of code but not others

3. `__FILE__` and `__LINE__` macros for debugging and profiling

As a rule, `inline` functions should be used instead of macros for code substitutions. The exception to this rule is the use of Qt macros that insert code into programs that use certain Qt classes. It is easy to see why some C++ experts look suspiciously at Qt's use of macros.

5.11   Functions with Variable-Length Argument Lists

In C and in C++, it is possible to define functions that have parameter lists ending with the **ellipsis** (...). The ellipsis enables the caller to specify the number of parameters and their types. The usual example of such a function is from `<stdio.h>`:

```
int printf(char* formatStr, ...)
```

This flexible mechanism permits calls such as

```
printf("Eschew Obfuscation!\n");
printf("%d days hath %s\n", 30, "September");
```

To define a function that uses the ellipsis, you need to include the `cstdarg` library, which adds a set of macros for accessing the items in the argument list to the `std` namespace. There must be at least one parameter other than the ellipsis in the parameter list. A variable, usually named `ap` (argument pointer), of type `va_list`, is used to traverse the list of unnamed arguments. The macro

```
va_start(ap, p)
```

where p is the last-named parameter in the list, initializes `ap` so that it points to the first of the unnamed arguments. The macro

```
va_arg(ap, typename)
```

returns the argument that `ap` is pointing to and uses the `typename` to determine (i.e., with `sizeof`) how large a step to take to find the next argument. The macro

```
va_end(ap)
```

must be called after all the unnamed arguments have been processed. It cleans up the stack of unnamed arguments and ensures that the program will behave properly after the function has terminated.

Example 5.20 shows how to use these features.

EXAMPLE 5.20   src/ellipsis/ellipsis.cpp

```
#include <cstdarg>
#include <iostream>
using namespace std;

double mean(int n ...) {                                    1
    va_list ap;                                             2
    double sum(0);
    int count(n);
    va_start(ap, n);                                        3
    for (int i = 0; i < count; ++i) {
        sum += va_arg(ap, double);
    }
    va_end(ap);                                             4
    return sum / count;
}

int main() {
    cout << mean(4, 11.3, 22.5, 33.7, 44.9) << endl;
    cout << mean (5, 13.4, 22.5, 123.45, 421.33, 2525.353) << endl;
}
```

1 First parameter is number of args.
2 Sequentially points to each unnamed arg.
3 Now, `ap` points to first unnamed arg.
4 Clean up before returning.

5.12 Exercise: Encryption

1. In Example 5.16 we declared but did not implement three operators for the `Point3` class. Add implementations for these three operators and add tests to the client code.

2. In this exercise, you reuse the `random()` function from the `<cstdlib>` (Appendix B, "Standard Headers").

   `random()` generates a pseudo-random integer in the range from `0` to `RAND_MAX` (commonly set to 2147483647).

   Write a function

   ```
   int myRand(int min, int max);
   ```

   that returns a pseudo-random `int` in the range from `min` to `max - 1`.

3. Write the function

   ```
   QVector<int> randomPerm(int n, unsigned key);
   ```

   that uses the `myRand()` function (seeded with key) to produce a permutation of the numbers `0, ... n`.

4. Encryption and privacy are becoming increasingly important. One way to think of encryption is that you start with a string of text that you pass to one or more transforming functions. The result of these transformations is a string of encrypted text that you can then transmit or store more safely. The recipient of the encrypted string then applies the inverses of the transforming functions to the string of encrypted text (i.e., decrypts it) and obtains a copy of the original string. The sender of the encrypted string must share some information with the recipient that permits the string to be decrypted (i.e., a key). The following exercises explore a few simple designs for the transforming functions. These exercises exploit the fact that the sequence of values returned by `random()` is completely determined by the initial value (seed) and is, therefore, *repeatable*.

   a. Write the function

   ```
   QString shift(const QString& text, unsigned key) ;
   ```

`shift()` uses the parameter `key` to set the random function's seed by calling `srandom()`. For each character `ch` in the given string, `text`, produce a shifted character by adding the next pseudo-random `int` to the code for `ch`. The shifted character is then put in the corresponding place in the new string. When all the characters of `text` have been processed, `shift()` returns the new string.

When you add a random `int` to the code for a character, you must do the addition "mod n," where `n` is the number of characters in the underlying character set that is being used. For this exercise, you can assume that you are working with the ASCII character set, which has 128 characters.

b. The next function to write is

```
QString unshift(const QString& cryptext, unsigned key);
```

This function reverses the process described in the previous exercise.

c. Write code to test your `shift()` and `unshift()` functions.

d. Another approach to encryption (which can be combined with the approach described earlier) is to permute (change the order of) the characters of the given string. Write the function

```
QString permute(const QString& text, unsigned key);
```

that uses the `randomPerm()` function to generate a permutation of the characters of the original string, `text`.

e. Write the function

```
QString unpermute(const QString& scrtext, unsigned key);
```

that reverses the action of the `permute()` function described earlier.

f. Write code to test your `permute()` and `unpermute()` functions.

g. Write code to test `shift()` and `permute()` being applied to the same string, followed by `unpermute()` and `unshift()`.

5. Implement a `Crypto` class that encapsulates the functions from the preceding exercises. You can use the UML diagram shown in Figure 5.4 to get you started.

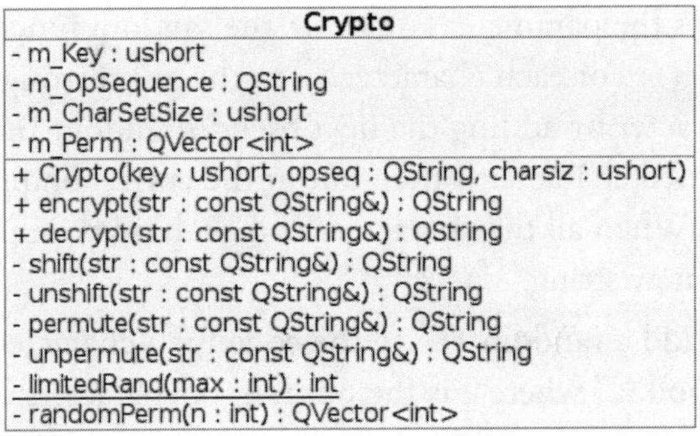

Crypto
- m_Key : ushort
- m_OpSequence : QString
- m_CharSetSize : ushort
- m_Perm : QVector<int>
+ Crypto(key : ushort, opseq : QString, charsiz : ushort)
+ encrypt(str : const QString&) : QString
+ decrypt(str : const QString&) : QString
- shift(str : const QString&) : QString
- unshift(str : const QString&) : QString
- permute(str : const QString&) : QString
- unpermute(str : const QString&) : QString
- limitedRand(max : int) : int
- randomPerm(n : int) : QVector<int>

FIGURE 5.4   Crypto UML diagram

m_OpSequence is a QString consisting of the characters 'p' and 's' that represent permute() and shift(). The encrypt() function applies those functions to the given string in the order that they appear in the m_OpSequence string. Example 5.21 contains some code to test your class.

EXAMPLE 5.21   src/functions/crypto-client.cpp

```
#include <QTextStream>
#include "crypto.h"

int main() {
   QTextStream cout(stdout);
   QString str1 ("asdfghjkl;QWERTYUIOP{}}|123456&*()_+zxcvnm,,, ./?"),
           str2;
   cout << "Original string: " << str1 << endl;
   cout << "length: " << str1.length() << endl;
   QString seqstr("pspsp");
   ushort key(12579);
   Crypto crypt(key, seqstr);
   str2 = crypt.encrypt(str1);
   cout << "Encrypted string: " << str2 << endl;
   cout << "Recovered string: " << crypt.decrypt(str2) << endl;
}
```

The topic of encryption is visited again in Section 17.1.4, which introduces a Qt class that does cryptographic hashing.

5.13 Review Questions

1. What is the difference between a function declaration and a function definition?

2. Why are default argument specifiers in the declaration but not the definition?

3. Explain why it is an error to have two functions in the same scope with the same signature but with different return types.

4. For overloading arithmetic symbols (+ - * /) on `Fraction` objects, which is preferred: member functions or nonmember global operators? Explain your answer.

5. For overloading left-modifying operators such as = and +=, which is preferred: member function operators or (nonmember) global operators?

6. Explain the difference between pass-by-value and pass-by-reference. Why would you use one instead of the other?

7. Explain the difference between preprocessor macros and inline functions.

Chapter 6

Inheritance and Polymorphism

This chapter introduces the concepts and shows some examples of how to define inheritance relationships between C++ classes. Overriding methods, the `virtual` keyword, and simple examples show how polymorphism works.

6.1 Simple Derivation

Inheritance is a particular way to organize classes that is supported by all object-oriented languages. It enables classes to **share** code in many different ways and to exploit natural relationships between classes. It can also make well-designed classes more reusable.

To employ inheritance, you place the common features of a set of related classes together in a **base class** and then **derive** other, more specialized classes from it. Each **derived class** inherits all the members of the base class and can override or extend each base class function as needed. Inheritance from a common base class significantly simplifes the derived classes and, with the use of certain design patterns, enables you to eliminate redundant code. In fact, inheritance sometimes suggests itself during the process of eliminating repeated blocks of code from a set of related classes.

We demonstrate inheritance with a simple example. The base class Student is supposed to contain the attributes common to all students. We kept the list of attributes short for this example, but you can easily imagine other attributes that might be appropriate.

We derived two classes from Student that describe particular kinds of students. The first derived class, Undergrad, contains only those properties specific to undergraduate students. The second derived class, GradStudent, contains only those properties specific to graduate students. The UML diagram shown in Figure 6.1 describes these relationships.

The pound sign (#) that precedes Student::m_Year indicates that m_Year is a protected member of that class. Recall that protected members of a class are accessible to the member functions of derived classes. The other data members of Student are private and, hence, *inaccessible to the member functions of the derived classes*. The open triangle arrowhead (pointing to the base class) indicates class inheritance. That arrow is also called **generalization** because it points from the more specific (derived) class to the more general (base) class. The derived classes are also called **subclasses** of the base class.

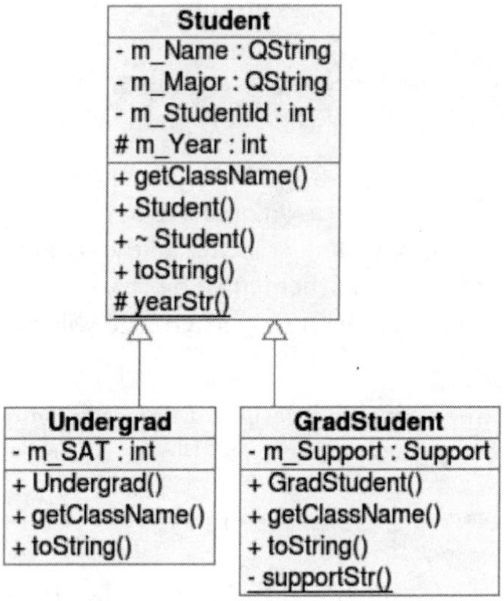

FIGURE 6.1   UML Diagram of Inheritance

Example 6.1 shows the definitions of the three classes.

EXAMPLE 6.1   src/derivation/qmono/student.h

```
#ifndef STUDENT_H
#define STUDENT_H

#include <QString>

class Student  {
 public:
    Student(QString nm, long id, QString major, int year = 1);
    ~Student() {}
    QString getClassName() const;
    QString toString() const;
 private:
    QString m_Name;
    QString m_Major;
    long m_StudentId;
 protected:
    int m_Year;
    QString yearStr() const;
};

class Undergrad: public Student {
 public:
```

```
    Undergrad(QString name, long id, QString major, int year, int sat);
    QString getClassName() const;
    QString toString() const;
 private:
    int m_SAT;   Scholastic Aptitude Test score total.|

};

class GradStudent : public Student {
 public:
    enum Support { ta, ra, fellowship, other };
    GradStudent(QString nm, long id, QString major,
                int yr, Support support);

    QString getClassName() const ;
    QString toString() const;
 protected:
    static QString supportStr(Support sup) ;
 private:
    Support  m_Support;
};

#endif        //  #ifndef STUDENT_H
```

The **classHead** of each derived class specifies the base class from which it is derived and the kind of derivation used. In this case we are using `public` derivation.[1]

Each of the three classes has a function named `getClassName()` and a function named `toString()`. The versions of those two functions in the derived classes **override** the corresponding base class functions. Each such derived class function must have the same signature and return type as the base class function it overrides.

Example 6.2 defines the member functions of `Student`.

---

[1] Section 22.4 discusses the three kinds of derivation: `public`, `protected`, and `private`.

EXAMPLE 6.2   src/derivation/qmono/student.cpp

```
[ . . . . ]

#include <QTextStream>
#include "student.h"

Student::Student(QString nm, long id, QString major, int year)
        : m_Name(nm), m_Major(major), m_StudentId(id), m_Year(year) {}



QString Student::getClassName() const {
    return "Student";
}


QString Student::toString() const {
    QString retval;
    QTextStream os(&retval);                                            1
    os << "[" << getClassName() << "]"
        << " name: " << m_Name
        << "; Id: " << m_StudentId
        << "; Year: " << yearStr()
        << "; Major: " << m_Major   ;
    return retval;
}
```

1 Write to the stream and return its string.

The `Undergrad` member functions are defined in Example 6.3. It is clear that `Undergrad::toString()` must produce a string that contains the `Student` data in addition to its own data member `m_SAT` (the combined Scholastic Aptitude Test score).[2] Keeping in mind that the data members of `Student` are `private`, the solution to this problem is for `Undergrad::toString()` to call the `public` function, `Student::toString()`. Thus, encapsulation is preserved and responsibility is properly distributed: `Student` takes care of `Student` data and `Undergrad` takes care of `Undergrad` data.

---

[2] A standardized set of exams taken by high school students and used by most college admissions offices in the United States.

EXAMPLE 6.3   src/derivation/qmono/student.cpp

```
[ . . . . ]

Undergrad::Undergrad(QString name, long id, QString major,
                                           int year, int sat)
            : Student(name, id, major, year), m_SAT(sat)        1
            { }

QString Undergrad::getClassName() const {
    return "Undergrad";
}

QString Undergrad::toString() const {
    QString result;
    QTextStream os(&result);
    os <<   Student::toString()                                 2
        << "\n   [SAT: "                                         3
        << m_SAT
        << " ]\n";
    return result;

}
```

1 The base class object is treated as a subobject of the derived object. Both class members and base classes must be initialized in an order determined by the order that they appear in the class definition.

2 Call the base class version.

3 Then add items that are specific to Undergrad.

Member Initialization for Base Classes

Because each Undergrad is a Student, whenever you create an Undergrad object, you must also create and initialize a Student. Furthermore, you must call a Student constructor to initialize the Student part of any derived object.

In the member initializers of a constructor, you can treat the base class name as an implicit member of the derived class.

- It gets initialized first, *before* the initialization of the derived class members.
- If you do not specify how the base class is initialized, its default constructor is called.
- If there is no base class default constructor, the compiler reports an error.

Look at the signature of the Undergrad constructor. The parameter list contains values for Student data members that are private, so it is not possible for an Undergrad member function to assign those values. The only way to make those assignments is to pass those values to the Student constructor, which is not private.

GradStudent has some added features that you need to handle properly, as shown in Example 6.4.

EXAMPLE 6.4   src/derivation/qmono/student.cpp

```
[ . . . . . ]

GradStudent::
GradStudent(QString nm, long id, QString major, int yr,
                   Support support) :Student(nm, id, major, yr),
           m_Support(support) { }

QString GradStudent::toString() const {                           1
    return QString("%1%2%3 ]\n")
        .arg(Student::toString())                                 2
        .arg("\n   [Support: ")                                   3
        .arg(supportStr(m_Support));
}
```

1 Another QString style.

2 Call the base class version.

3 Then add items that are specific to GradStudent.

Extending

Inside both derived class versions of toString(), before the derived class attributes are handled, we explicitly call Student::toString(), which handles the (private) base class attributes. Each derived class version of toString() *extends* the functionality of Student::toString().

It is worth repeating that, because most of the data members of Student are private, you need a nonprivate base class function (e.g. toString()) to give the derived class access to the private base class data members. A derived class object cannot directly access the private members of Student even though it contains those members. This arrangement definitely takes some getting used to!

6.1.1   Inheritance Client Code Example

GradStudent is a Student, in the sense that a GradStudent object can be used wherever a Student object can be used. The client code shown in Example 6.5 creates some instances and performs operations on a GradStudent and an Undergrad instance directly and also indirectly, through pointers.

EXAMPLE 6.5   src/derivation/qmono/student-test.cpp

```
#include <QTextStream>
#include "student.h"

static QTextStream cout(stdout);

void finish(Student* student) {
    cout << "\nThe following "
        << student->getClassName()
        << " has applied for graduation.\n "
        << student->toString() << "\n";
}

int main() {
    Undergrad us("Frodo Baggins", 5562, "Ring Theory", 4, 1220);
    GradStudent gs("Bilbo Baggins", 3029, "History", 6, GradStudent::fellowship);
    cout << "Here is the data for the two students:\n";
    cout << gs.toString() << endl;
    cout << us.toString() << endl;
    cout << "\nHere is what happens when they finish their studies:\n";
    finish(&us);
    finish(&gs);
    return 0;
}
```

To build this application, use qmake and make as follows:

```
src/derivation/qmono> qmake -project
src/derivation/qmono> qmake
src/derivation/qmono> make
```

Then run it like this:

```
src/derivation/qmono> ./qmono
Here is the data for the two students:
[Student]³ name: Bilbo Baggins; Id: 3029; Year: gradual student; Major: History
  [Support: fellowship ]

[Student] name: Frodo Baggins; Id: 5562; Year: senior; Major: Ring Theory
  [SAT: 1220 ]

Here is what happens when they finish their studies:

The following Student has applied for graduation.
  [Student] name: Frodo Baggins; Id: 5562; Year: senior; Major: Ring Theory

The following Student has applied for graduation.
  [Student] name: Bilbo Baggins; Id: 3029; Year: gradual student; Major: History
src/derivation/qmono>
```

In the `finish()` function, the parameter, `student`, is a base class pointer. Calling `student->toString()` invokes `Student::toString()` regardless of what kind of object `student` points to. But, for example, if `student` points to a `GradStudent`, there should be a mention of the fellowship in the output message. In addition, you should see `[GradStudent]` in the `toString()` messages, and you do not.

It would be more appropriate to use runtime binding for indirect function calls to determine which `toString()` is appropriate for each object.

Because of its C roots, C++ has a compiler that attempts to bind function invocations at compile time, for performance reasons. With inheritance and base class pointers, the compiler can have no way of knowing what type of object it is operating on. In the absence of runtime checking, an inappropriate function can be called. C++ requires the use of a special key word to enable runtime binding on function calls via pointers and references. The keyword is **virtual**, and it enables **polymorphism**, which is explained in the next section.

---

³ It would be nice if the output showed [GradStudent] here.

6.1.2   Exercises: Simple Derivation

1. Build and run the `Student` application described in Section 6.1 and Section 6.1.1. Then remove the base class initializer from the Undergrad constructor. Describe and explain what happens when you try to build the application.

2. Modify the client code so that it uses message boxes for output instead of standard out.

3. Modify the application so that the `finish()` function checks the year of any `Undergrad` student and gives a more appropriate message. For example, it does not make sense for a Freshman, Sophomore, or Junior to apply for graduation. How should `GradStudents` be handled?

6.2   Derivation with Polymorphism

We now introduce another powerful feature of object-oriented programming: **polymorphism**. Example 6.6 differs from the previous example in only one important way: the use of the keyword **virtual** in the base class definition.

EXAMPLE 6.6   src/derivation/qpoly/student.h

```
[ . . . . ]

class Student  {
 public:
    Student(QString nm, long id, QString major, int year = 1);
    virtual ~Student() {}                                        1
    virtual QString getClassName() const;                        2
    QString toString() const;                                    3
 private:
    QString m_Name;
    QString m_Major;
    long m_StudentId;
 protected:
    int m_Year;
    QString yearStr() const;
};
```

1 We added the keyword virtual here.

2 We added virtual here also.

3 This should also be virtual.

Adding the keyword `virtual` to at least one member function creates a **polymorphic type**. `virtual` functions are called **methods**. This terminology is consistent with the use of that term in Java, where member functions are "methods" by default. Example 6.7 shows the same client code again.

EXAMPLE 6.7   src/derivation/qpoly/student-test.cpp

```
#include <QTextStream>
#include "student.h"

static QTextStream cout(stdout);

void finish(Student* student) {
    cout << "\nThe following "
        << student->getClassName()
        << " has applied for graduation.\n "
        << student->toString() << "\n";
}

int main() {
    Undergrad us("Frodo Baggins", 5562, "Ring Theory", 4, 1220);
    GradStudent gs("Bilbo Baggins", 3029, "History", 6, GradStudent::fellowship);
    cout << "Here is the data for the two students:\n";
    cout << gs.toString() << endl;
    cout << us.toString() << endl;
    cout << "\nHere is what happens when they finish their studies:\n";
    finish(&us);
    finish(&gs);
    return 0;
}
```

When you run this slightly changed program, you get the following output:

```
Here is the data for the two students:
[GradStudent] name: Bilbo Baggins; Id: 3029; Year: gradual student; Major: History
  [Support: fellowship ]

[Undergrad] name: Frodo Baggins; Id: 5562; Year: senior; Major: Ring Theory
  [SAT: 1220 ]



Here is what happens when they finish their studies:
```

```
The following Undergrad has applied for graduation.
 [Undergrad] name: Frodo Baggins; Id: 5562; Year: senior; Major: Ring Theory⁴
```

```
The following GradStudent has applied for graduation.
 [GradStudent] name: Bilbo Baggins; Id: 3029; Year: gradual student; Major:
History⁵
```

[GradStudent] and [UnderGrad] now appear in the output, because getClassName() is virtual. There is still a problem with the output of finish() for the GradStudent, however. The Support piece is missing.

With polymorphism, **indirect** calls (via pointers and references) to methods are resolved at **runtime**. This is called **dynamic**, or **runtime binding**. **Direct** calls (*not through pointers or references*) of methods are resolved by the compiler. That is called **static binding** or **compile time binding**.

In this example, when finish() receives the address of a GradStudent object, student->toString() calls the Student version of the function. However, when the Student::toString() calls getClassName() (indirectly through this, a base class pointer), it is a virtual method call, bound at runtime.

In C++, dynamic binding is an option that you must switch on with the keyword virtual.

NOTE

Because "this" is in the process of being initialized while its constructor is executing (or destroyed while its destructor is executing), it is not reasonable to expect runtime binding to work properly under those conditions. In particular, because the virtual table (essential for runtime binding) may be incompletely set up by the constructor (or may be partially or completely destroyed by the destructor), compile-time binding will determine which method is called—as if the virtual keyword was not even there—when invoking any method of this from inside a constructor or destructor. As Scott Meyers [Meyers] likes to say: "From a constructor or destructor, virtual methods aren't."

---

⁴ Missing: SAT score.

⁵ Missing: Fellowship.

NOTE

In general, if a class has one or more `virtual` functions, it should also have a virtual destructor. This is because when operating on a collection of polymorphic objects, it is common to `delete` objects through base class pointers, which results in an indirect call to the destructor. If the destructor is not virtual, compile-time binding determines which destructor is called and may result in incomplete destruction of the derived object.

6.2.1   Exercises: Derivation with Polymorphism

1. Add the keyword `virtual` to the declaration of `toString()` in the `Student` class definition. Then build and run that program and explain the results.

2. Be the computer and predict the output of the programs shown in Example 6.8 through Example 6.12. Then compile and run the programs to check your answers.

   a. **EXAMPLE 6.8**   src/polymorphic1.cc

   ```cpp
   #include <iostream>
   using namespace std;

   class A {
   public:
       virtual ~A() { }
       virtual void foo() {
           cout << "A's foo()" << endl;
           bar();
       }
       virtual void bar() {
           cout << "A's bar()" << endl;
       }
   };

   class B: public A {
   public:
       void foo() {
           cout << "B's foo()" << endl;
           A::foo();
       }
       void bar() {
   ```

```
        cout << "B's bar()" << endl;
    }
};

int main() {
    B bobj;
    A *aptr = &bobj;
    aptr->foo();
    cout << "-------------" << endl;
    A aobj = *aptr;
    aobj.foo();
    cout << "-------------" << endl;
    aobj = bobj;
    aobj.foo();
    cout << "-------------"<< endl;
    bobj.foo();
}
```

b. **EXAMPLE 6.9**   src/polymorphic2.cc

```
#include <iostream>
using namespace std;

class A {
public:
    virtual void foo() {
        cout << "A's foo()" << endl;
    }
};

class B: public A {
public:
    void foo() {
        cout << "B's foo()" << endl;
    }
};

class C: public B {
public:
    void foo() {
        cout << "C's foo()" << endl;
    }
};
```

```
int main() {
    C cobj;
    Bx *bptr = &cobj;
    bptr->foo();
    A* aptr = &cobj;
    aptr->foo();
}
```

c. **EXAMPLE 6.10   src/derivation/exercise/Base.h**

```
[ . . . . ]
class Base {
public:
    Base();
    void a();
    virtual void b() ;
    virtual void c(bool condition=true);
    virtual ~Base() {}
};


class Derived : public Base {
public:
    Derived();
    virtual void a();
    void b();
    void c();
};
[ . . . . ]
```

EXAMPLE 6.11   src/derivation/exercise/Base.cpp

```
[ . . . . ]
Base::Base() {
    cout << "Base::Base() " << endl;
    a();
    c();
}
void Base::c(bool condition) {
    cout << "Base::c()" << endl;
}
void Base::a() {
    cout << "Base::a()" << endl;
```

```
    b();
}
void Base::b() {
    cout << "Base::b()" << endl;
}


Derived::Derived() {
    cout << "Derived::Derived() " << endl;
}


void Derived::a() {
    cout << "Derived::a()" << endl;
    c();
}
void Derived::b() {
    cout << "Derived::b()" << endl;
}


void Derived::c() {
    cout << "Derived::c()" << endl;
}
[ . . . . ]
```

EXAMPLE 6.12   src/derivation/exercise/main.cpp

```
[ . . . . ]
int main (int argc, char** argv) {

    Base b;
    Derived d;

    cout << "Objects Created" << endl;
    b.b();
    cout << "Calling derived methods" << endl;
    d.a();
    d.b();
    d.c();
    cout << ".. via base class pointers..." << endl;
    Base* bp = &d;
    bp->a();
    bp->b();
    bp->c();
    //d.c(false);
}
[ . . . . ]
```

6.3   Derivation from an Abstract Base Class

Consider Figure 6.2, which shows an inheritance diagram of a tiny portion of the animal kingdom. We use it to explain the difference between an abstract and a concrete class. An **abstract** base class is used to encapsulate common features of **concrete** derived classes. An abstract class cannot be instantiated. Nevertheless, this scheme is quite useful and efficient for organizing the accumulated knowledge of the vastly complex biological world. For example, a primate is a mammal that has certain additional characteristics, a hominid is a particular kind of primate, a gorilla is a hominid with certain additional characteristics, and so forth.

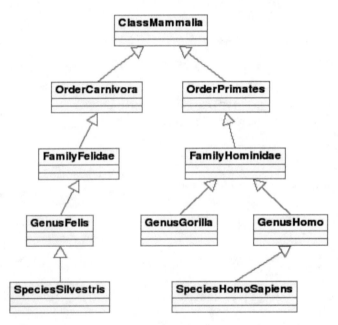

FIGURE 6.2   Animal Taxonomy

A concrete class represents a particular kind of entity—something that really exists (i.e., can be instantiated). For example, when walking through the woods, you never encounter a real, live animal that is completely described by the designation, Carnivora, or Felidae. You may, depending on where you walk, find a lion, a siamese cat, or a common housecat (*Felis silvestris*). But there is no instance of a Hominidae (i.e., of a base class) in the concrete world that is not also an instance of some particular species. If a biologist ever finds a concrete instance that does not fit into an existing species definition, then that biologist may define and name a new species and become famous.

To summarize, the more general categories (class, order, family, subfamily) are abstract base classes that cannot be instantiated in the concrete world. They were invented by people to help with the classification and organization of the concrete classes (species).

Back to Programming

At first, it might seem counterintuitive to define a class for an abstract idea that has no concrete representative. But classes are *groupings* of functions and data and are useful tools to enable certain kinds of organization and reuse. Categorizing things makes the world simpler and more manageable for humans and computers.

As you study design patterns and develop frameworks and class libraries, you will often design inheritance trees where only the leaf nodes can be instantiated, and all the inner nodes are abstract.

An **abstract base class** is a class that is impossible or inappropriate to instantiate. Features of a class that tell the compiler to enforce this rule are

- Having at least one pure `virtual` function.
- Having no public constructors.

Figure 6.3 shows an example of an abstract `Shape` class that has pure `virtual` functions.

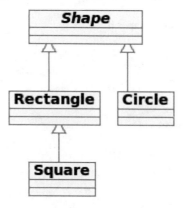

FIGURE 6.3   Shapes UML Diagram

The names of abstract classes are *italicized* in UML diagrams.

A pure `virtual` **function** has the following declaration syntax:

```
virtual returnType functionName(parameterList)=0;
```

Example 6.13 shows the base class definition.

EXAMPLE 6.13   src/derivation/shape1/shapes.h

```
[ . . . . ]

class Shape {                                              1
 public:
    virtual double area() = 0;                             2
    virtual QString getName() = 0;
    virtual QString getDimensions() = 0;
    virtual ~Shape() {}
};
```

1 An abstract base class.

2 Pure virtual function.

getName(), area(), and getDimensions() are pure virtual functions. Because they are defined to be pure virtual, no function definition is required in the Shape class. Any concrete derived class *must* override and define *all* pure virtual base class functions for instantiation to be permitted. In other words, any derived class that does not override and define *all* pure virtual base class functions is, itself, an abstract class. Example 6.14 shows the derived class definitions.

EXAMPLE 6.14   src/derivation/shape1/shapes.h

```
[ . . . . ]

class Rectangle : public Shape {
 public:
    Rectangle(double h, double w) :
        m_Height(h), m_Width(w) {}
    double area();
    QString getName();
    QString getDimensions();

 protected:                                                1
    double m_Height, m_Width;
};

class Square : public Rectangle {
 public:
    Square(double h)
```

```
           : Rectangle(h,h)                                      2
    { }
    double area();
    QString getName();
    QString getDimensions();
};

class Circle : public Shape {
 public:
    Circle(double r) : m_Radius(r) {}
    double area();
    QString getName();
    QString getDimensions();
 private:
    double m_Radius;
};
```

1 We want to access m_Height in the Square class.

2 Base class name in member initialization list—pass arguments to base class ctor.

Rectangle and Circle are derived from Shape. Square is derived from Rectangle. Their implementations are shown in Example 6.15.

EXAMPLE 6.15   src/derivation/shape1/shapes.cpp

```
#include "shapes.h"
#include <math.h>
    double Circle::area() {
        return(M_PI * m_Radius * m_Radius);            1
    }

    double Rectangle::area() {
        return (m_Height * m_Width);
    }

    double Square::area() {
        return (Rectangle::area());                    2
    }
[ . . . . . ]
```

1 M_PI comes from <math.h>, the cstdlib #include file.

2 Calling base class version on this.

Example 6.16 provides some client code to exercise these classes.

EXAMPLE 6.16   src/derivation/shape1/shape1.cpp

```
#include "shapes.h"
#include <QString>
#include <QDebug>

void showNameAndArea(Shape* pshp) {
    qDebug() << pshp->getName()
             << " " << pshp->getDimensions()
             << " area= " << pshp->area();
}

int main() {                                                    1
    Shape shp;

    Rectangle   rectangle(4.1, 5.2);
    Square      square(5.1);
    Circle      circle(6.1);

    qDebug() << "This program uses hierarchies for Shapes";
    showNameAndArea(&rectangle);
    showNameAndArea(&circle);
    showNameAndArea(&square);
    return 0;
}
```

1 ERROR—instantiation is not allowed on classes with pure virtual functions.

In the global function `showNameAndArea()`, the base class pointer, `pshp`, is successively given the addresses of objects of the three subclasses. For each address assignment, `pshp` polymorphically invokes the correct `getName()` and `area()` functions. Example 6.17 shows the output of the program.

EXAMPLE 6.17   src/derivation/shape1/shape.txt

```
This program uses hierarchies for Shapes

RECTANGLE  Height = 4.1 Width = 5.2    area = 21.32
CIRCLE  Radius = 6.1    area = 116.899
SQUARE  Height = 5.1      area = 26.01
```

6.4   Inheritance Design

Sometimes defining an inheritance relationship helps at first (e.g., by reducing redundant code) but causes problems later when other classes must be added to the hierarchy. Some up-front analysis can help make things easier and avoid problems later.

Example 6.14, in which we derive from the abstract `Shape` class, demonstrates an inheritance relationship with two levels of depth. The `Rectangle` class was used as a classification of objects and as a concrete base class.

Is a square a kind of rectangle? Geometrically it certainly is. Here are some definitions borrowed from elementary geometry.

- A shape is a closed two-dimensional object in the plane, with a graphical way of representing itself, together with a point that is considered its center.

- A rectangle is a shape consisting of four straight line segments with only 90-degree angles.

- A square is a rectangle with equal sides.

As you attempt to represent an inheritance tree of classes for an application that you are designing, it helps to list the kinds of capabilities that you need to provide for each class. For geometric shapes, they might be

- Drawable
- Scalable
- Loadable
- Savable

After you describe the interface in further detail, you may find that the classic geometric definitions for shape classification are not the ideal taxonomy for shape classes within the context of your application.

As you perform an analysis, some questions arise:

- What are the common operations you want to perform on all `Shapes`?
- What other kinds of `Shapes` might you use in your application?
- Why do you need a `Rectangle` class as the base class of a `Square`?
- Can a `Square` substitute for a `Rectangle`?
- A `Rhombus` is four-sided, like a `Rectangle`, so should `Rectangle` derive from `Rhombus`?

- Should you have a base class for all four-sided objects?
- Should you have a different base class for all five-sided objects?
- Should you have a general base class for polygons with the number of sides as an attribute?
- Is your program going to perform geometric proof searches to identify objects?

Using a UML modeling tool makes it easier to try out different ideas before writing concrete code. UML diagrams are especially useful for focusing on and describing small parts of a larger system. Figure 6.4 has concrete classes that serve as templates for creating the more "specific" shapes.

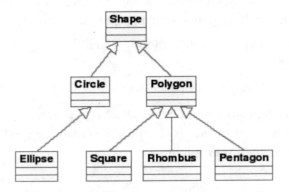

FIGURE 6.4   Another Way to Represent Shapes

In this tree diagram, the classes in leaf nodes are constrained versions of their base classes. The interface for the vector representations, drawing, and loading/saving of the objects is established in the abstract base classes.

Questions

1. In the geometric sense, given a `Circle`, you can prove it is also an `Ellipse`, because an equation exists that specifies an `Ellipse`, with its two foci being equal. In contrast, Figure 6.4 shows `Ellipse` to be a kind of `Circle`, with an extra point, or an extra degree of freedom. Would it make more sense to reverse the inheritance relationship? Or to have a completely different tree?

2. Can you describe a better *is-a* relationship between two of these classes?

3. Consider Figure 6.5: the Shape classes from the Qt GraphicsView library.[6]

---

[6] For more information about these classes, refer to the Qt Graphics View Framework Overview in the Qt Assistant.

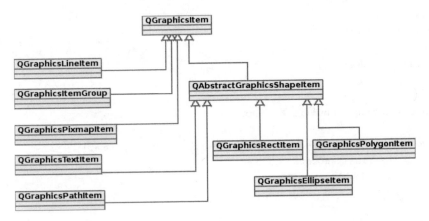

FIGURE 6.5 QGraphicsItem Inheritance

Notice, there are no concrete Circle or Square items. Why do you think that is?

Why do you think there is a Rectangle *and* a Polygon item?

6.5 Overloading, Hiding, and Overriding

First, recall the definitions of two terms that often get confused:

- When two or more versions of a function `foo` exist in the same scope (with different signatures), we say that `foo` has been **overloaded**.

- When a `virtual` function from the base class also exists in the derived class, with the *same signature and return type*, we say that the derived version **overrides** the base class version.

Example 6.18 demonstrates overloading and overriding and introduces another relationship between functions that have the same name.

EXAMPLE 6.18 src/derivation/overload/account.h

```
[ . . . . ]
class Account {
public:
    Account(unsigned acctno, double bal, QString owner);
    virtual ~Account() { }
    virtual void deposit(double amt);
    virtual QString toString() const;
    virtual QString toString(char delimiter);
```

1

```
protected:
    unsigned   m_AcctNo;
    double     m_Balance;
    QString    m_Owner;
};

class InsecureAccount: public Account {
public:
    InsecureAccount(unsigned acctno, double bal, QString owner);
    QString toString() const;                                        2
    void deposit(double amt, QDate postDate);                        3
};
[ . . . . . ]
```

1 Overloaded function.

2 Overrides base method and hides toString(char).

3 Does not override a method, but hides all Account::deposit() methods.

Function Hiding

A member function of a derived class with the same name as a function in the base class *hides* all functions in the base class with that name. In such a case

- Only the derived class function can be called directly.

- The class scope resolution operator :: must be used to call hidden base functions explicitly.

Example 6.19 shows the difference between a hidden and an inaccessible member.

EXAMPLE 6.19   src/derivation/overload/account-client.cpp

```
#include   "account.h"
#include   <QTextStream>

int main() {
    InsecureAccount acct(12345, 321.98, "Luke Skywalker");
    acct.deposit(6.23);                                              1
    acct.m_Balance += 6.23;                                          2
    acct.Account::deposit(6.23);                                     3
    // ... more client code
    return 0;
}
```

1   Error! No matching function—hidden by `deposit(double, int)`.

2   Error! Member is protected, inaccessible.

3   Hidden does not mean inaccessible. You can still access hidden public members via scope resolution.

6.6   Constructors, Destructors, and Copy Assignment Operators

Three special kinds of member functions are *never* inherited:

1. Copy constructors

2. Copy assignment operators

3. Destructors

These three functions are generated automatically by the compiler for classes that do not specify them.

Why Are These Functions Special?

The base class functions are not sufficient to initialize, copy, or destroy a derived instance.

Constructors

For a class that inherits from another, the base class constructor must be called *as part of* its initialization process. The derived constructor may specify which base class constructor is called in its initialization list.

A class with no constructors is automatically given a compiler-generated, `public`, default constructor that calls the default constructor for each of its base classes. If a class has some constructors but no default constructor, then it has no default initialization. In this case, any derived class constructor *must* make an explicit base class constructor call in its initialization list.

Order of Initialization

Initialization proceeds in the following order:

1. Base classes first, in the order in which they are listed in the *classHead* of the derived class
2. Data members, in declaration order

Copy Assignment Operators

A `public` copy assignment operator is automatically generated by the compiler for each class that does not have one explicitly defined for it. Because base class data members are generally private, the derived class copy assignment operator must call the base class assignment operator (for each base class) for memberwise copying of those data members to happen. After that, it can perform memberwise assignments of derived class data members.

Other member function operators are inherited the same way as normal member functions.

Copy Constructors

Like the copy assignment operator, a `public` copy constructor is automatically generated for classes that do not have one defined. The compiler-generated copy constructor carries out member-by-member initialization by copying the data members of its argument object.

Example 6.20 defines a class with a single constructor that requires three arguments, so `Account` has no default constructor (i.e., the compiler will *not* generate one). We declare the base class destructor `virtual` to ensure that the appropriate derived class destructor gets called when it is time to destroy a derived object accessed through a base class pointer.

EXAMPLE 6.20   src/derivation/assigcopy/account.h

```
[ . . . . ]

class Account {
 public:
    Account(unsigned acctNum, double balance, QString owner);
    virtual ~Account(){
       qDebug() << "Closing Acct - sending e-mail to primary acctholder:"
```

```
                << m_Owner; }
    virtual QString getName() const {return m_Owner;}
    // other virtual functions
private:
    unsigned  m_AcctNum;
    double    m_Balance;
    QString    m_Owner;
};
```

We did *not* define a copy constructor, which means the compiler *will* generate one for us. Therefore, this class can be instantiated in exactly two ways: (1) by calling the three-parameter constructor or (2) by invoking the compiler generated copy constructor and supplying an `Account` object argument.

Example 6.21 defines a derived class with two constructors. Both of them require base class initialization.

EXAMPLE 6.21   src/derivation/assigcopy/account.h

```
[ . . . . ]

class JointAccount : public Account {
 public:
  JointAccount (unsigned acctNum, double balance,
                QString owner, QString jowner);
  JointAccount(const Account & acct, QString jowner);
  ~JointAccount() {
     qDebug() << "Closing Joint Acct - sending e-mail to joint acctholder:"
              << m_JointOwner; }
  QString getName() const {
    return QString("%1 and %2").arg(Account::getName()).arg(m_JointOwner);
  }
  // other overrides
 private:
  QString m_JointOwner;
};
```

In Example 6.22, the compiler enables `JointAccount::JointAccount` to use `Account(const Account&)` for initialization, even though we have not defined it. The compiler-generated copy constructor does memberwise copy/initialization in the order that the data members are listed in the class definition.

EXAMPLE 6.22   src/derivation/assigcopy/account.cpp

```
[ . . . . ]

Account::Account(unsigned acctNum, double balance, QString owner) :
    m_AcctNum(acctNum), m_Balance(balance), m_Owner(owner)
    { }

JointAccount::JointAccount (unsigned acctNum, double balance,
                            QString owner, QString jowner)
    :Account(acctNum, balance, owner),
     m_JointOwner(jowner)                                          1
    { }

JointAccount::JointAccount (const Account& acc, QString jowner)
    :Account(acc),                                                 2
     m_JointOwner(jowner)
    { }
```

   1 Base class initialization required.
   2 Compiler-generated copy constructor call.

Example 6.23 defines a little `Bank` class that maintains a list of `Account` pointers.

EXAMPLE 6.23   src/derivation/assigcopy/bank.h

```
[ . . . . ]
class Account;

class Bank {
 public:
    Bank& operator<< (Account* acct);                             1
    ~Bank();
    QString getAcctListing() const;
 private:
    QList<Account*> m_Accounts;
};
[ . . . . ]
```

   1 This is how to add object pointers to `m_Accounts`.

In Example 6.24, the construction of the object a4 uses the `JointAccount` compiler-supplied copy constructor, which calls the `Account` compiler-supplied copy constructor.

EXAMPLE 6.24   src/derivation/assigcopy/bank.cpp

```
[ . . . . ]
#include <QDebug>
#include "bank.h"
#include "account.h"

Bank::~Bank() {
    qDeleteAll(m_Accounts);
    m_Accounts.clear();
}



Bank& Bank::operator<< (Account* acct) {
   m_Accounts << acct;
   return *this;
}

QString Bank::getAcctListing() const {
   QString listing("\n");
   foreach(Account* acct, m_Accounts)
      listing += QString("%1\n").arg(acct->getName());      1
   return listing;
}
int main() {
  QString listing;
   {                                                          2
     Bank bnk;
     Account* a1 = new Account(1, 423, "Gene Kelly");
     JointAccount* a2 = new JointAccount(2, 1541, "Fred Astaire",
        "Ginger Rodgers");
     JointAccount* a3 = new JointAccount(*a1, "Leslie Caron");
     bnk << a1;
     bnk << a2;
     bnk << a3;
     JointAccount* a4 = new JointAccount(*a3);               3
     bnk << a4;
     listing = bnk.getAcctListing();
   }                                                          4
```

```
    qDebug() << listing;
    qDebug() << "Now exit program" ;
}
[ . . . . ]
```

1 `getName()` is virtual.

2 Begin internal block.

3 What's this?

4 At this point, all four `Account`s are destroyed as part of the destruction of the bank.

Destructors

Destructors are not inherited. Just as with the copy constructor and copy assignment operator, the compiler generates a destructor if you do not define one explicitly. Base class destructors are automatically called when a derived object is destroyed. Destruction of data members and base class parts occurs in precisely the reverse order of initialization.

6.7   Processing Command-Line Arguments

Applications that run from the command line are often controlled through command-line arguments, which can be switches or parameters. `ls`, `g++`, and `qmake` are familiar examples of such applications.

You can handle the different kinds of command-line arguments in a variety of ways. Suppose that you write a program that supports these options:

```
Usage:
    a.out [-v] [-t] inputfile.ext [additional files]
      If -v is present then verbose  = true;
      If -t is present then testmode = true;
```

Typically, the program does not care about the order in which these optional switches appear. In usage descriptions, optional arguments are always enclosed in [square brackets], whereas required arguments are not. This program accepts an arbitrarily long list, consisting of at least one filename, and performs the same operation on each file.

In general, command-line arguments can be any of the following:

- **switches**, such as -verbose or -t
- **parameters** (typically filespecs), which are simple strings not associated with switches
- **switched parameters** such as the gnu compiler's optional -o switch, which *requires* an accompanying parameter, the name of the executable file to generate

The following line contains examples of all three kinds of arguments:

```
g++ -ansi -pedantic -Wall -o myapp someclass.cpp someclass-demo.cpp
```

Example 6.25 shows how a C program might deal with command-line arguments.

EXAMPLE 6.25   src/derivation/argumentlist/argproc.cpp

```
[ . . . . ]
#include <cstring>

bool test = false;
bool verbose = false;

void processFile(char* filename) {
[ . . . . ]
}

/*
  @param argc - the number of arguments
  @param argv - an array of argument strings
*/
int main (int argc, char* argv[]) {
  // recall that argv[0] holds the name of the executable.
  for (int i=1; i < argc; ++i) {                              1

    if (strcmp(argv[i], "-v")==0) {
      verbose = true;
    }
    if (strcmp(argv[i], "-t") ==0) {
      test = true;
    }
  }
  for (int i=1; i < argc; ++i) {                              2
    if (argv[i][0] != '-')
```

```
        processFile(argv[i]);
    }
}
[ . . . . ]
```

1 First process the switches.

2 Make a second pass to operate on the non-switched arguments.

Qt enables you to avoid the use of arrays, pointers, and `<cstring>` by using more object-oriented constructs.

In Example 6.26, you can see how code like this could be greatly simplified through the use of higher-level classes: `QString` and `QStringList`.

6.7.1   Derivation and `ArgumentList`

`ArgumentList` provides an example of a reusable class with a specific purpose derived from a more general-purpose Qt class. It reuses `QString` and `QStringList` to simplify the processing of command-line arguments.

Operationally, `ArgumentList` is a class that is initialized with the `main()` function's `int` and `char**` parameters, which capture the command-line arguments. Conceptually, `ArgumentList` is a list of `QStrings`. Structurally, it is derived from `QStringList`, with some added functionality. A Java programmer would say that `ArgumentList` is *extended* from `QStringList`. Example 6.26 contains the class definition for `ArgumentList`.

EXAMPLE 6.26   src/derivation/argumentlist/argumentlist.h

```
#ifndef ARGUMENTLIST_H
#define ARGUMENTLIST_H

#include <QStringList>

class ArgumentList : public QStringList {
  public:
    ArgumentList();

    ArgumentList(int argc, char* argv[]) {
        argsToStringlist(argc, argv);
    }
```

```
    ArgumentList(const QStringList& argumentList):
        QStringList(argumentList) {}
    bool getSwitch(QString option);
    QString getSwitchArg(QString option,
                            QString defaultRetVal=QString());
  private:
    void argsToStringlist(int argc,  char* argv[]);
};
#endif
```

Because it is publicly derived from QStringList, ArgumentList supports the full interface of QStringList and can be used wherever a QStringList is expected. In addition to its constructors, ArgumentList defines a few additional functions:

- argsToStringList() extracts the command-line arguments from the given array of char arrays and loads them into a QStringList. This function is private because it is part of the implementation of this class, not part of the public interface. It is needed by the constructors but not by client code.

- getSwitch() finds and removes a switch from the string list, if that switch exists. It returns true if the switch is found and false otherwise.

- getSwitchArg() finds and removes a switch and its accompanying argument from the string list and returns the argument if the switch is found. It does nothing and returns a defaultValue if the switch is not found.

Example 6.27 shows the implementation code for these functions.

EXAMPLE 6.27   src/derivation/argumentlist/argumentlist.cpp

```
#include <QCoreApplication>
#include <QDebug>
#include "argumentlist.h"
ArgumentList::ArgumentList() {
    if (qApp != NULL)                                             1
        *this = qApp->arguments();
}


void ArgumentList::argsToStringlist(int argc, char * argv []) {
    for (int i=0; i < argc; ++i) {
        *this += argv[i];
    }
}
```

```cpp
bool ArgumentList::getSwitch (QString option) {
   QMutableStringListIterator itr(*this);
   while (itr.hasNext()) {
     if (option == itr.next()) {
        itr.remove();
        return true;
     }
   }
    return false;
}


QString ArgumentList::getSwitchArg(QString option, QString defaultValue) {
   if (isEmpty())
      return defaultValue;
   QMutableStringListIterator itr(*this);
   while (itr.hasNext()) {
      if (option == itr.next()) {
         itr.remove();
         if (itr.hasNext()) {
            QString retval = itr.next();
            itr.remove();
            return retval;
         }
         else {
            qDebug() << "Missing Argument for " << option;
            return QString();
         }
      }
   }
   return defaultValue;
}
```

1 A global pointer to the current QApplication.

In the client code shown in Example 6.28, all argument processing code has been removed from main(). No loops, char*, or strcmp are to be found.

EXAMPLE 6.28   src/derivation/argumentlist/main.cpp

```cpp
#include <QString>
#include <QDebug>
#include "argumentlist.h"
```

```
void processFile(QString filename, bool verbose) {
    if (verbose)
        qDebug() << QString("Do something chatty with %1.")
                        .arg(filename);
    else
        qDebug() << filename;
}

void runTestOnly(QStringList & listOfFiles, bool verbose) {
    foreach (const QString &current, listOfFiles) {
        processFile(current, verbose);
    }
}

int main( int argc, char * argv[] ) {
    ArgumentList al(argc, argv);                          1
    QString appname = al.takeFirst();                     2
    qDebug() << "Running " << appname;
    bool verbose = al.getSwitch("-v");
    bool testing = al.getSwitch("-t");                    3
    if (testing) {
        runTestOnly(al, verbose);                         4
        return 0;
    } else {
        qDebug() << "This Is Not A Test";
    }
}
```

1 Instantiate the `ArgumentList` with command-line args.

2 Inherited from `QStringList`—first item in the list is the name of the executable.

3 Now all switches have been removed from the list. Only filenames remain.

4 `ArgumentList` can be used in place of `QStringList`.

Following are some sample outputs from running the program in Example 6.28:

```
src/derivation/argumentlist> ./argumentlist
Running  "./argumentlist"
This Is Not A Test
src/derivation/argumentlist> ./argumentlist item1 "item2 item3" item4 item5
Running  "./argumentlist"
This Is Not A Test
src/derivation/argumentlist> ./argumentlist -v -t "foo bar" 123 space1 "1 1"
```

```
Running  "./argumentlist"
"Do something chatty with foo bar."
"Do something chatty with 123."
"Do something chatty with space1."
"Do something chatty with 1 1."
src/derivation/argumentlist>
```

6.7.2   Exercises: Processing Command-Line Arguments

Write a birthday reminder application called `birthdays`.

- Store name/birthday pairs in any format you like, in a file called `birthdays.dat`.

- `birthdays` with no command-line arguments opens the file and lists all birthdays coming up in the next 30 days, in chronological order.

- `birthdays -a "john smith" "yyyy-mm-dd"` should add an entry to the file.

- `birthdays -n 40` shows birthdays coming up in the next 40 days.

- `birthdays nameSpec` searches for a birthday paired with *nameSpec*.

6.8   Containers

Qt's container classes collect **value types** (things that can be copied), including pointers to object types[7] (but not object types themselves). **Qt containers** are defined as template classes that leave the collected type unspecified. Each data structure is optimized for different kinds of operations. In Qt there are several template container classes to choose from.

- `QList<`*T*`>` is implemented using an array, with space preallocated at both ends. It is optimized for index-based random access and, for lists with less than a thousand items, it also gives good performance with operations like `prepend()` and `append()`.

- `QStringList` is a convenience class derived from `QList<QString>`.

---

[7] Chapter 8, "QObject, QApplication, Signals, and Slots," discusses `QObject` and object types.

- QLinkedList<T> is optimized for sequential access with iterators and quick, constant-time inserts anywhere in the list. Sorting and searching are slow. It has several convenience functions for frequently used operations.

- QVector<T> stores its data in contiguous memory locations and is optimized for random access by index. Generally, QVector objects are constructed with an initial size. There is no automatic preallocation of memory at either end, so insertions, appends, and prepends are expensive.

- QStack<T> is publicly derived from QVector<T>, so the public interface of QVector is available to QStack objects. However, the last-in-first-out semantics are offered by the push(), pop(), and top() functions.

- QMap<Key, T> is an ordered **associative container** that stores (key, value) pairs and is designed for fast lookup of the value associated with a key. It is also designed to support reasonably fast insertions and removals. It keeps its keys in sorted order, for fast searching and subranging, by means of a skip-list diction-ary[8] that is probabilistically balanced and uses memory efficiently. The Key type must have an operator<() and operator==().

- QHash<Key, T> is also an associative container that uses a hash table to facilitate key lookups. It provides fast lookups (exact key match) and insertions, but slow searching, and no sorting. The Key type must have an operator==().

- QMultiMap<Key, T> is a subclass of QMap, and QMultiHash<Key, T> is a subclass of QHash. These two classes enable multiple values to be associated with a single key.

- QCache<Key, T> is an associative container that provides fastest access to recently used items and automatic removal of infrequently used items based on cost functions.

- QSet<T> stores values of type T using a QHash with keys in T and a dummy value associated with each key. This arrangement optimizes lookups and insertions. QSet has functions for the usual set operations (e.g., union, intersec-tion, set difference, etc.). The default constructor creates an empty set.

A type parameter T for a template container class or key type for an associative con-tainer must be an **assignable data type** (i.e., a value type) (Section 8.1). This means

---

[8] ftp://ftp.cs.umd.edu/pub/skipLists/skiplists.pdf

that T must have a `public` default constructor, copy constructor, and assignment operator.

Basic types (e.g, `int`, `double`, `char`, etc.) and pointers are assignable. Some Qt types are assignable (e.g., `QString`, `QDate`, `QTime`). `QObject` and types derived from `QObject`, however, are not assignable. If you need to collect objects of some nonassignable type, you can define a container of pointers, e.g., `QList<QFile*>`.

6.9   Managed Containers, Composites, and Aggregates

Qt's value containers are containers of uniform (same-typed) values—e.g., `QString`, `byte`, `int`, `float`, etc. Pointer containers are containers of pointers to (polymorphic commonly typed) objects. They can be **managed** or **unmanaged**.

Both kinds of containers can grow at runtime by allocating additional heap memory as needed. This is always done in an exception-safe way, so you don't need to worry about possible memory leaks.

In the case of pointer containers to heap objects, however, one must decide which class is responsible for managing the heap objects. UML diagrams can distinguish between managed and unmanaged containers by using **composite** (filled diamond) and **aggregate** (empty diamond) connectors, as shown in Figure 6.6.

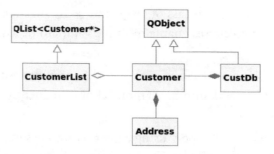

FIGURE 6.6   Aggregates and Compositions

In general, a **managed container** is a **composite**, because the container manages its pointed-to objects. In other words, when a composite is destroyed, it destroys (cleans up) its entire self because the smaller objects are part of its composition.

When one object embeds another as a subobject, it is also considered a composition.

In Figure 6.6, there are two kinds of `Customer` containers: `CustomerList` and `CustDb`. `CustDb` and `CustomerList` reuse template containers. `CustomerList` objects are aggregates—temporary structures to hold the results of a query, or a user selection. `CustDb`, on the other hand, is a singleton composite that manages all the `Customer` objects that exist.

In the case of the `Customer` and `Address` relationship, this diagram indicates that one or more `Address` objects should be associated with a particular `Customer`. When the `Customer` object is destroyed, it is reasonable to destroy all its `Address` objects at the same time. Thus, the `Customer` object manages its `Addresses`, which gives you another example of a composite relationship.

NOTE

This suggested design does impose some limitations on possible use of `Address`—in particular, there is no easy way to find all `Customers` at a particular `Address`. If `Address` and `Customer` were independently managed, then you could form bidirectional relationships between the classes.

Typically, a managed container deletes any heap objects it "owns" when the container itself is destroyed. With a Qt container of pointers, you can use `qDeleteAll(container)`, an algorithm that calls `delete` on each element in the container.

Copying a managed container can be defined in a number of ways:

- For some containers, the feature might be disabled.

- For others, it might be defined as a deep copy, where all contained objects are cloned and placed in the new container.

- Another approach, taken with the design of Qt containers, is implicit sharing, explained in Section 11.5.

An **aggregate container** is a container that provides only an indexing or reference navigation mechanism to its contents.

In this case, the container does not manage its objects—it only provides a convenient way to access them. When an aggregate container is copied, only references to the collected objects are copied. When an aggregate container is deleted, only the references are removed. There is no impact on the underlying objects in the container.

> **NOTE**
> A managed container is a composition, and an unmanaged container of objects is usually (but not always) represented in a UML diagram as aggregation.

6.9.1   Exercises: Managed Containers, Composites, and Aggregates

Playing cards have been in existence in various forms for more than 600 years. They are used for a large number of games of chance and are a favorite subject for exercises in math, statistics, and computer science.

In Europe and the West, there is a standard card set, called a **deck**, which is familiar to most people. It consists of 52 cards, divided into 4 subsets, called suits. Each suit consists of 13 cards designated by the names **A** (Ace), **2, 3, 4, 5, 6, 7, 8, 9, T** (Ten), **J** (Jack), **Q** (Queen), **K** (King). Many card games begin by supplying each player with a small set of cards (randomly extracted from the deck) called a **hand**.

In this exercise you design data types to represent a deck and a hand of cards. Later you will revisit these clases to elaborate the rules and add graphics. Figure 6.7 suggests one way of representing these classes.

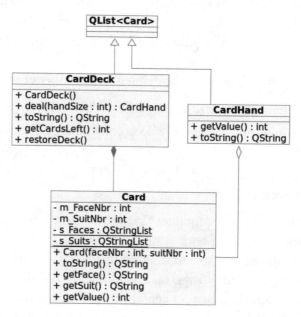

FIGURE 6.7   Card Game UML

Following are some hints:

- The `CardDeck` constructor generates a complete deck of cards in a convenient order.

- `CardDeck::deal(int k)` should use the `random()` function from `<cstdlib>` to pick k `Card` objects from the deck (removing each one from the deck after it is picked) to fill a `CardHand` object.

- Initialize the `random()` function from the system clock so that the results will be different each time you run the application. The syntax is

```
srandom(time(0));
```

- Evaluate the hand, using the rules of the game of bridge: Ace = 4, King = 3, Queen = 2, Jack = 1; all other cards have zero value. You can use this formula to calculate the return values for the `getValue()` functions.

- Example 6.29 is a piece of client code that you can start with, for testing your classes.

EXAMPLE 6.29 src/cardgame/datastructure/cardgame-client.cpp

```cpp
[ . . . . ]
#include "carddeck.h"
#include <QTextStream>
#include <QtGui>
int main(int argc, char* argv[]) {
    QApplication app(argc, argv);
    QTextStream cout(stdout);
    CardDeck deck;
    CardHand hand;
    int handSize, playerScore, progScore;
    cout << "How many cards in a hand? " << flush;
    handSize = QInputDialog::getInt(0, QString("getInt()"),
        QString("How many cards in hand?"), 1, 5);
    QMessageBox::StandardButton sb;
    do {
        hand = deck.deal(handSize);
        cout << "Here is your hand:" << endl;
        cout << hand.toString() << endl;
        playerScore = hand.getValue();
        cout << QString("Your score is: %1 points.")
                    .arg(playerScore) << endl;
```

```
    // Now a hand for the dealer:
    hand = deck.deal(handSize);
    progScore = hand.getValue();
    cout << "Here is my hand:" << endl;
    cout << hand.toString() << endl;
    cout << QString("My score is: %1 points.")
                    .arg(progScore) << endl;
    cout << QString("%1 win!!")
            .arg((playerScore > progScore)?"You":"I") << endl;
    sb = QMessageBox::question(0, QString("QMessageBox::question()"),
        QString("Another hand?"), QMessageBox::Yes | QMessageBox::No);

    } while (sb == QMessageBox::Yes);
}
```

6.10 Containers of Pointers

In Section 1.15.1, you saw that all pointers are the same (small) size. That is just one of the reasons that you should prefer to work with containers of pointers rather than containers of objects. In the remaining parts of this book, many of the classes that you will use are members of inheritance trees—especially the classes used for GUI programming. As you saw in several examples in this chapter, a base class pointer can hold the address of a derived object. So, a container of base class pointers can hold addresses of any derived objects. Polymorphism then enables the appropriate functions to be called through these pointers at runtime. To use polymorphism there *must* be a prototype in the base class for *each* function that you may want to call—even if it cannot be defined in the base class. That is why pure virtual functions are sometimes needed. The base class provides the interface that can work with the concrete, derived objects.

Containers of pointers require careful destruction procedures to avoid memory leaks. Also, access to and maintenance of the pointers must be carefully controlled so that no attempt to dereference a null or undefined pointer is ever made. This is not as difficult as it might sound.

- When you add a pointer to the container, make sure that it is initialized immediately. If that is not possible, it should be assigned a value of 0.
- When an individual pointer is no longer needed, remove it and delete it. If immediate removal is not convenient for some reason, the deleted pointer should be reassigned or set to 0.

- When it is time to destroy a Qt container of pointers, call `qDeleteAll()`.

  - `qDeleteAll()` is a generic algorithm that works with all Qt container classes.
  - Each specific Qt container class has its own `clear()` member function.

Copies, Copies, Copies

Using pointers gives rise to another important issue, which is magnified when working with containers of pointers. Always keep in mind that bad things can happen if you allow an object that contains pointers to be copied. One almost guaranteed recipe for disaster is letting the compiler supply the copy constructor and the copy assignment operator, both of which simply duplicate the host object's pointers. With that approach, if a container of pointers (or an object with a pointer member) were passed as an argument for a value parameter in a function call, the function would make a local copy of that object that would be destroyed when it returned. Assuming that the destructor properly deleted the pointers, the original object would then contain one or more pointers to deleted memory, leading to the kind of memory corruption that is notoriously difficult to trace.

One way to avoid that problem is to make sure that the copy constructor and the copy assignment operator each make a deep copy of the host object; i.e., pointers in the new copy address new memory that contains exact copies of the data addressed by the host object's pointers. Unfortunately, this approach can be prohibitively expensive in terms of system resources and is generally avoided. Section 11.5 discusses a more efficient approach that uses *resource sharing*.

The `QObject` class mentioned earlier, which can possess a container of pointers, deals with this issue by having a private copy constructor and a private copy assignment operator so that any attempt to make a copy would result in a compile error.[9]

In Chapter 8 and subsequent chapters, there are several opportunities to work with containers of various types of pointers. There you will work with containers of `QObject` pointers that can hold the addresses of an enormous variety of objects, including all the "widgets" that you will use for graphical user interfaces (GUIs). In Chapter 9, "Widgets and Designer," when you write GUI programs using many different kinds of widgets and layouts, all of which are QObjects, containers of base class pointers play a crucial role.

---

[9] Section 8.1

Extended Example: A Simple Library

For the purposes of this example, we regard a library as a collection of various kinds of reference materials. First, we define classes to implement a simplified library as suggested by the abbreviated UML diagram Figure 6.8.

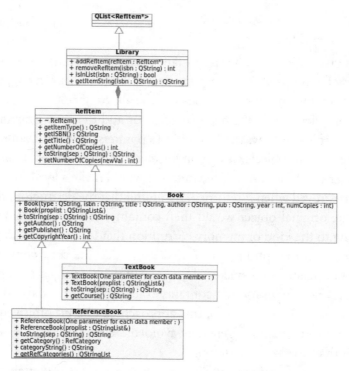

FIGURE 6.8   Reference Library UML Diagram

The base class definition is shown in Example 6.30. Because all its constructors are `protected`, no `RefItem` object can be constructed by client code. Thus, `RefItem` is an abstract base class.

EXAMPLE 6.30   src/pointer-container/library.h

```
[ . . . . . ]

class RefItem {
public:
    virtual ~RefItem();
    QString getItemType() const;
    QString getISBN() const;
```

```
    QString getTitle() const;
    int getNumberOfCopies() const;
    virtual QString toString(QString sep="[::]") const;
    void setNumberOfCopies(int newVal);
protected:
    RefItem(QString type, QString isbn, QString title, int numCopies=1);
    RefItem(QStringList& proplist);
private:
    QString m_ItemType, m_ISBN, m_Title;
    int m_NumberOfCopies;
};
```

Example 6.31 shows a few derived class definitions. The base class and each of the derived classes has a constructor that takes a single QStringList reference parameter. This greatly simplifies and facilitates the creation of objects when reading data from a file or taking information from the user. RefCategory, an enum type defined publicly within ReferenceBook, is intended to enumerate categories such as Literature, Music, Math, Science, Art, Architecture, etc. There are no input/output (I/O) operations in any of these classes. For this example, all I/O is handled by client code, leaving improvements as exercises for you.

EXAMPLE 6.31   src/pointer-container/library.h

```
[ . . . . ]

class Book : public RefItem {
public:
    Book(QString type, QString isbn, QString title, QString author,
        QString pub, int year, int numCopies=1);
    Book(QStringList& proplist);
    virtual QString toString(QString sep="[::]") const;
    QString getAuthor() const;
    QString getPublisher() const;
    int getCopyrightYear() const;
private:
    QString m_Author, m_Publisher;
    int m_CopyrightYear;
};

class ReferenceBook : public Book {
public:
    enum RefCategory {NONE = -1, Art, Architecture, ComputerScience, Literature,
                    Math, Music, Science};
```

```
    ReferenceBook(QString type, QString isbn, QString title, QString author,
        QString pub, int year, RefCategory refcat, int numCopies=1);
    ReferenceBook(QStringList& proplist);
    QString toString(QString sep="[::]") const;
    RefCategory getCategory() const;
    QString categoryString() const; //returns string version of m_Category
    static QStringList getRefCategories();  //returns a list of categories
private:
    RefCategory m_Category;
};
```

Much of the implementation code is quite routine and need not be displayed here. We focus instead on the techniques we use to facilitate transmitting and receiving data. Because that can happen in a variety of ways (e.g., to/from files, across networks), we provide two kinds of conversions: Object to QString and QStringList to Object. Specific details regarding I/O are kept outside of these classes. Example 6.32 shows the first of these conversions.

EXAMPLE 6.32   src/pointer-container/library.cpp

```
[ . . . . ]

QString RefItem::toString(QString sep) const {
    return
    QString("%1%2%3%4%5%6%7").arg(m_ItemType).arg(sep).arg(m_ISBN).arg(sep)
                        .arg(m_Title).arg(sep).arg(m_NumberOfCopies);
}
[ . . . . ]

QString Book::toString(QString sep) const {
    return QString("%1%2%3%4%5%6%7").arg(RefItem::toString(sep)).arg(sep)
                .arg(m_Author).arg(sep).arg(m_Publisher).arg(sep)
                .arg(m_CopyrightYear);
}
[ . . . . ]

QString ReferenceBook::toString(QString sep) const {
    return QString("%1%2%3").arg(Book::toString(sep)).arg(sep)
                        .arg(categoryString());
}
[ . . . . ]

QString ReferenceBook::categoryString() const {
    switch(m_Category) {
      case Art: return "Art";
```

```
        case Architecture: return "Architecture";
        case ComputerScience: return "ComputerScience";
        case Literature: return "Literature";
        case Math: return "Math";
        case Music: return "Music";
        case Science: return "Science";
      default: return "None";
      }
}
```

QString provides a convenient way to transmit data. If a QString consists of several pieces of data and has been carefully put together, it can easily be repackaged as a QString-List using the function QString::split(QString separator). In this example, the order of data items and the separator are determined by the toString(QString sep) functions. Make a careful study of Example 6.33 and think carefully about the use of a **non-const** reference parameter in each constructor. Everything happens in the member initialization lists.

EXAMPLE 6.33   src/pointer-container/library.cpp

```
[ . . . . ]

RefItem::RefItem(QStringList& plst) : m_ItemType(plst.takeFirst()),
        m_ISBN(plst.takeFirst()), m_Title(plst.takeFirst()),
        m_NumberOfCopies(plst.takeFirst().toInt())
{ }
[ . . . . ]

Book::Book(QStringList& plst) : RefItem(plst), m_Author(plst.takeFirst()),
        m_Publisher(plst.takeFirst()), m_CopyrightYear(plst.takeFirst().toInt())
{ }
[ . . . . ]

ReferenceBook::ReferenceBook(QStringList& plst) : Book(plst),
            m_Category(static_cast<RefCategory>(plst.takeFirst().toInt()))
{ }
```

Example 6.34 shows the class definition for Library. Because Library is publicly derived from QList<RefItem*> it **is a** container of pointers. The copy constructor and copy assignment operator are private. That prevents the compiler from supplying public versions (the recipe for disaster that was mentioned earlier) and, hence, guarantees that no copies can be made of a Library object. It also prevents the compiler from supplying a default constructor, so we must provide one.

EXAMPLE 6.34   src/pointer-container/library.h

```
[ . . . . . ]

class Library : public QList<RefItem*> {
public:
   Library() {}
   ~Library();                                                              1
   void addRefItem(RefItem*& refitem);
   int removeRefItem(QString isbn);
   QString toString(QString sep="\n") const;
   bool isInList(QString isbn);
   QString getItemString(QString isbn);
private:
   Library(const Library&);
   Library& operator=(const Library&);
   RefItem* findRefItem(QString isbn);
};
```

   1 A container of pointers must have a destructor!

The implementations of the Library class member functions are listed next. The first chunk, in Example 6.35, shows the implementations of the copy constructor and the copy assignment operator and how to add and remove items from the Library. The copy constructor and copy assignment operator will never be used, but we supplied just enough implementation to prevent the compiler from issuing warnings about not initializing the base class in the constructor or not returning anything in the assignment operator.

Before adding an item to the list, check to see if it is already there. If the item is already in the list, simply increment its m_NumberOfCopies. To remove an item, decrement its m_NumberOfCopies. If the result of decrementing is zero, remove it from the list and delete the pointer.[10]

EXAMPLE 6.35   src/pointer-container/library.cpp

```
[ . . . . . ]

Library::~Library() {
   qDeleteAll(*this);
   clear();
}
```

---

[10] Why not delete first and then remove?

```
Library::Library(const Library&) : QList<RefItem*>() {}

Library& Library::operator=(const Library&) {
    return *this;
}

void Library::addRefItem(RefItem*& refitem) {                      1
    QString isbn(refitem->getISBN());
    RefItem* oldItem(findRefItem(isbn));
    if(oldItem==0)
        append(refitem);
    else {
        qDebug() << isbn << " Already in list:\n"
                 << oldItem->toString()
                 << "\nIncreasing number of copies "
                 << "and deleting new pointer." ;
        int newNum(oldItem->getNumberOfCopies() + refitem->getNumberOfCopies());
        oldItem->setNumberOfCopies(newNum);
        delete refitem;                                            2
        refitem = 0;                                               3
    }
}

int Library::removeRefItem(QString isbn) {
    RefItem* ref(findRefItem(isbn));
    int numCopies(-1);
    if(ref) {
        numCopies = ref->getNumberOfCopies() - 1;
        if(numCopies== 0) {
            removeAll(ref);
            delete ref;
        }
        else
            ref->setNumberOfCopies(numCopies);
    }
    return numCopies;
}
```

1 Parameter is a pointer reference so that null assignment after delete is possible.

2 Not in a managed container.

3 Reference parameter!

For a more realistic application, Library and the RefItem classes would need more data and function members. Example 6.36 provides a few more Library member functions for inspiration. `Library::findRefItem()` is `private` because it returns a pointer and, as mentioned earlier, it is generally not a good idea to let client code work with pointers.

EXAMPLE 6.36   *src/pointer-container/library.cpp*

```
[ . . . . ]



RefItem* Library::findRefItem(QString isbn) {
   for(int i = 0; i < size(); ++i) {
      if(at(i)->getISBN().trimmed() == isbn.trimmed())
         return at(i);
   }
   return 0;
}



bool Library::isInList(QString isbn) {
   return findRefItem(isbn);
}

QString Library::toString(QString sep) const {
   QStringList reflst;
   for(int i = 0; i < size(); ++i)
      reflst << at(i)->toString();
   return reflst.join(sep);
}

QString Library::getItemString(QString isbn) {
   RefItem* ref(findRefItem(isbn));
   if(ref)
      return ref->toString();
   else
      return QString();
}
```

NOTE
   We did not have the option to use the `foreach()` macro in the implementations of `Library::findRefItem()` and `Library::toString()` because the `foreach()` macro needs to make a copy of the container that it traverses. Because the copy constructor is private, that is not possible. Keep this in mind when you work with QObjects in later chapters.

We wrote some client code to test these classes. Because we are using standard I/O, we introduced some enums to make it easier to set up a menu system, as you see in Example 6.37.

EXAMPLE 6.37 src/pointer-container/libraryClient.cpp

```
[ . . . . ]

QTextStream cout(stdout);
QTextStream cin(stdin);
enum Choices {READ=1, ADD, FIND, REMOVE, SAVE, LIST, QUIT};
enum Types {BOOK, REFERENCEBOOK, TEXTBOOK, DVD, FILM, DATADVD};
const QStringList TYPES = (QStringList() << "BOOK" << "REFERENCEBOOK"
    << "TEXTBOOK" << "DVD" << "FILM" << "DATADVD");
bool saved(false);
```

Example 6.38 shows how the enums can be used.

EXAMPLE 6.38 src/pointer-container/libraryClient.cpp

```
[ . . . . ]

Choices nextTask() {
   int choice;
   QString response;
   do {
      cout << READ << ". Read data from a file.\n"
           << ADD << ". Add items to the Library.\n"
           << FIND << ". Find and display an item.\n"
           << REMOVE << ". Remove an item from the Library.\n"
           << SAVE << ". Save the Library list to a file.\n"
           << LIST << ". Brief listing of Library items.\n"
           << QUIT << ". Exit from this program.\n"
           << "Your choice: " << flush;
   response = cin.readLine();
   choice = response.toInt();
   } while(choice < READ or choice > QUIT);
   return static_cast<Choices>(choice);
}

void add(Library& lib, QStringList objdata) {
   cout << objdata.join("[::]") << endl;
   QString type = objdata.first();
   RefItem* ref;
   switch(static_cast<Types>(TYPES.indexOf(type))) {
```

```
    case BOOK:
        ref = new Book(objdata);
        lib.addRefItem(ref);
        break;
    case REFERENCEBOOK:
        ref = new ReferenceBook(objdata);
        lib.addRefItem(ref);
            break;
[ . . . . ]

    default: qDebug() << "Bad type in add() function";
    }
}
```

You see in Example 6.39 how simple it is to save data to a file.

EXAMPLE 6.39   src/pointer-container/libraryClient.cpp

```
[ . . . . ]

void save(Library& lib) {
    QFile outf("libfile");
    outf.open(QIODevice::WriteOnly);
    QTextStream outstr(&outf);
    outstr << lib.toString();
    outf.close();
}
```

In Example 6.40 we read data from a file, one line at a time. This approach works only if Library::toString() uses the newline character to separate one object's data from the next.

EXAMPLE 6.40   src/pointer-container/libraryClient.cpp

```
[ . . . . ]

void read(Library& lib) {
    const QString sep("[::]");
    const int BADLIMIT(5); //max number of bad lines
    QString line, type;
    QStringList objdata;
    QFile inf("libfile");
    inf.open(QIODevice::ReadOnly);
    QTextStream instr(&inf);
    int badlines(0);
```

```
    while(not instr.atEnd()) {
        if(badlines >= BADLIMIT) {
            qDebug() << "Too many bad lines! Aborting.";
            return;
        }
        line = instr.readLine();
        objdata = line.split(sep);
        if(objdata.isEmpty()) {
            qDebug() << "Empty Line in file!";
            ++badlines;
        }
        else if(not TYPES.contains(objdata.first())) {
            qDebug() << "Bad type in line: " << objdata.join(";;;");
            ++badlines;
        }
        else
            add(lib, objdata);
    }
}
```

Getting data from the keyboard is necessarily more complicated because each data item must be requested and, where possible, validated. In the client code, shown in Example 6.41, we have a prompt function for each RefItem class that returns a QString-List we can then pass along to the appropriate constructor for that class.

EXAMPLE 6.41   src/pointer-container/libraryClient.cpp

```
[ . . . . ]

QStringList promptRefItem() {
    const int MAXCOPIES(10);
    const int ISBNLEN(13);
    int copies;
    QString str;
    QStringList retval;
    while(1) {
        cout << "ISBN ("<< ISBNLEN << " digits): " << flush;
        str = cin.readLine();
        if(str.length() == ISBNLEN) {
            retval << str;
            break;
        }
    }
```

```
      cout << "Title: " << flush;
      retval << cin.readLine();
      while(1) {
         cout << "Number of copies: " << flush;
         copies = cin.readLine().toInt();
         if(copies > 0 and copies <= MAXCOPIES) {
            str.setNum(copies);
            break;
         }
      }
      retval << str;
      return retval;
}

QStringList promptBook() {
   static const int MINYEAR(1900), MAXYEAR(QDate::currentDate().year());
   int year;
   QStringList retval(promptRefItem());
   QString str;
   cout << "Author: " << flush;
   retval << cin.readLine();
   cout << "Publisher: " << flush;
   retval << cin.readLine();
   while(1) {
      cout << "Copyright year: " << flush;
      year = cin.readLine().toInt();
      if(year >= MINYEAR and year <= MAXYEAR) {
         str.setNum(year);
         break;
      }
   }
   retval << str;
   return retval;
}

QStringList promptReferenceBook() {
   int idx(0);
   bool ok;
   QString str;
   QStringList retval(promptBook());
   QStringList cats(ReferenceBook::getRefCategories());
   while(1) {
      cout << "Enter the index of the correct Reference Category: ";
```

```
        for(int i = 0; i < cats.size(); ++i)
            cout << "\n\t(" << i << ") " << cats.at(i);
        cout << "\n\t(-1)None of these\t:::" << flush;
        idx = cin.readLine().toInt(&ok);
        if(ok) {
            retval << str.setNum(idx);
            break;
        }
    }
    return retval;
}
[ . . . . ]

void enterData(Library& lib) {
    QString typestr;
    while(1) {
        cout << "Library item type: " << flush;
        typestr = cin.readLine();
        if(not TYPES.contains(typestr)) {
            cout << "Please enter one of the following types:\n"
                << TYPES.join(" ,") << endl;
            continue;
        }
        break;
    }
    QStringList objdata;
    switch (TYPES.indexOf(typestr)) {
    case BOOK: objdata = promptBook();
            break;
    case REFERENCEBOOK: objdata = promptReferenceBook();
            break;
[ . . . . ]

    default:
            qDebug() << "Bad type in enterData()";
    }
    objdata.prepend(typestr);
    add(lib, objdata);
}
```

The `main()` function is shown in Example 6.42.

EXAMPLE 6.42   src/pointer-container/libraryClient.cpp

```
[ . . . . ]

int main() {
   Library lib;
   while(1) {
      switch(nextTask()) {
      case READ: read(lib);
         saved = false;
         break;
      case ADD: enterData(lib);
         saved = false;
         break;
      case FIND: find(lib);
         break;
      case REMOVE: remove(lib);
         saved = false;
         break;
      case SAVE: save(lib);
         saved = true;
         break;
      case LIST: list(lib);
         break;
      case QUIT: prepareToQuit(lib);
         break;
      default:
         break;
      }
   }
}
```

You can refine and improve this application in Section 6.10.2.

6.10.1   Exercises: Containers of Pointers

1. Suppose you need to write an inventory control system for automobile parts.

- Write a UML class diagram with a base class named AutoPart and some subclasses like EnginePart, BodyPart, Accessory, etc. and concrete part classes like Alternator, Fender, Radiator, SeatBelt, etc.

- Write (but do not implement) class definitions for your classes. What kinds of base class functions will be needed?

- How will you guarantee that only the concrete part classes can be instantiated?

2. The classes in Figure 6.9 are intended to help organize the film collection in the college library.

   a. Implement the `Film` classes. Make sure that the constructors have sufficient parameters to initialize all data members. We suggest enum types `FilmTypes` (Action, Comedy, SciFi, ...) and `MPAARatings` (G, PG, PG-13, ...) for use in the `Entertainment` class.

   b. Implement the `FilmList` class as a container of `Film` pointers. Make sure that the `addFilm()` function does not permit the same film to be added more than once.

   Is it possible to use base class functions such as `contains()` or `indexOf()` here?

   c. Write client code to test these classes. Put a mixture of `Entertainment` and `Educational` films into the `FilmList` and exercise all the member functions.

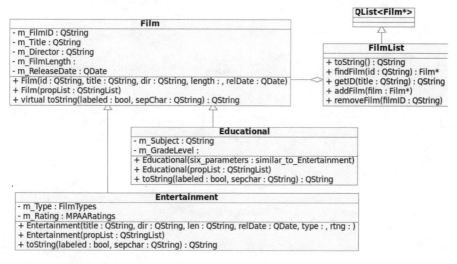

FIGURE 6.9   Film Classes

Having a container of pointers raises the question of how to destroy it. If you simply "do the right thing" and define a `FilmList` destructor that visits each of its pointers and deletes it, you must then worry about client code that contains a function with a `FilmList` value parameter. Recall that each value parameter causes a copy of the corresponding argument to be made. That copy is destroyed when the function returns. How should you deal with copying and destroying `FilmList` objects?

The `FilmList` class enables you to exploit polymorphism but exposes the `Film` pointers to client code. So far, this design violates our earlier warning regarding the use of pointers. In general, pointers must be hidden from client code. We discuss an approach to this problem in Section 16.3.

3. Refine our solution to Extended Example: A Simple Library by adding a `LibraryUI` class that handles the interactions with the user as suggested by Figure 6.10.

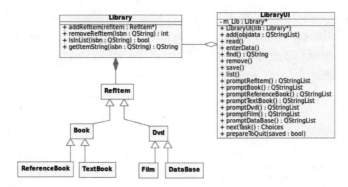

FIGURE 6.10   Library—Version 2

When you add that class, you should use the client code in Example 6.43 to test your system.

EXAMPLE 6.43   src/pointer-container/libraryClient-v2.cpp

```
#include "libraryui.h"
#include "library.h"

bool saved(false);

int main() {
   Library lib;
   LibraryUI libui(&lib);
   while(1) {
      switch(libui.nextTask()) {
      case LibraryUI::READ: libui.read();
         saved = false;
         break;
      case LibraryUI::ADD: libui.enterData();
         saved = false;
         break;
      case LibraryUI::FIND: libui.find();
         break;
      case LibraryUI::REMOVE: libui.remove();
         saved = false;
         break;
      case LibraryUI::SAVE: libui.save();
         saved = true;
         break;
      case LibraryUI::LIST: libui.list();
         break;
      case LibraryUI::QUIT: libui.prepareToQuit(saved);
         break;
      default:
         break;
      }
   }
}
```

4. Refine your solution to Problem 3 so that each class has its own corresponding UI class, as suggested by Figure 6.11.

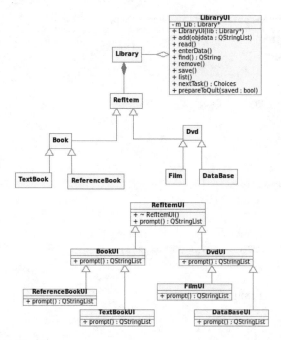

FIGURE 6.11   Library—Version 3

5. Change the implementation of the `Library` class so that it is derived from `QMap<QString, RefItem*>` where the `QString` key is the ISBN code.

6.11   Review Questions

1. What is the difference between a function and a method?

2. What does it mean for a base class function to be *hidden*? What can cause this to happen?

3. Which member functions *cannot* be inherited from the base class? Explain why.

4. Given the definitions in Example 6.44, answer the questions in Example 6.45.

EXAMPLE 6.44   src/quizzes/virtual-quiz.cpp

```cpp
class Shape {
public:
    virtual void draw(Position p);
    virtual void draw(PaintEngine* pe, Position p);
};

class Square : public Shape {
public:
    void draw(Position p);
private:
    void draw(int x, int y);
};

int main() {
    Position p(4,3);
    Position q(5,6);
    PaintEngine *pe = .....;
    Square sq;

    sq.draw(p);                                      1
    sq.draw(pe, p);                                  2
    sq.draw(3,3);                                    3

    Shape* sp = &sq;
    sp->draw(q);                                     4
    sp->draw(pe, q);                                 5
    sp->draw(3,2);                                   6


}
```

1 _____

2 _____

3 _____

4 _____

5 _____

6 _____

EXAMPLE 6.45 src/quizzes/virtual-questions.txt

1. Which method is called?
   a. Shape::draw()
   b. Square::draw()
   c. error - method is hidden
   d. error - method is inaccessible
   e. error - no such method

2. Which method is called?
   a. Shape::draw()
   b. Square::draw()
   c. error - method is hidden
   d. error - method is inaccessible
   e. error - no such method

3. Which method is called?
   a. Shape::draw()
   b. Square::draw()
   c. error - method is hidden
   d. error - method is inaccessible
   e. error - no such method

4. Which method is called?
   a. Shape::draw()
   b. Square::draw()
   c. error - method is hidden
   d. error - method is inaccessible
   e. error - no such method

5. Which method is called?
   a. Shape::draw()
   b. Square::draw()
   c. error - method is hidden
   d. error - method is inaccessible
   e. error - no such method

6. Which method is called?
   a. Shape::draw()
   b. Square::draw()
   c. error - method is hidden
   d. error - method is inaccessible
   e. error - no such method

5. Consider another shape class and answer the questions that follow. There can be more than one correct answer.

EXAMPLE 6.46   src/quizzes/abstract-quiz.cpp

```cpp
/* Consider the following header file, assume the
function definitions are in a .cpp file somewhere. */
class Shape {
public:
    explicit Shape(Point origin);
    virtual void draw(PaintDevice* pd) = 0;
    virtual void fill(PaintDevice* pd) = 0;
    virtual String name() const;
    Point origin() const;
private:
    Point m_origin;
};

class Rectangle : public Shape {
public:
    Rectangle(Point origin, int width, int height);
    void draw(PaintDevice* pd);
private:
    int m_width, m_height;
};

class Square: public Rectangle {
public:
    Square(Point origin, int width);
};

/* 1. Which methods are pure virtual in all classes?
    a. origin
    b. draw
    c. fill
    d. draw and fill
    e. draw, fill, and name. */
/* 2. Which classes are abstract?
    a. Shape
    b. Rectangle
    c. Square
    d. Shape and Rectangle
    e. All of them. */
```

```
/* 3. Which of the following constructor implementations are valid?

      Rectangle::Rectangle(Point origin, int width, int height)

   a. { m_width = width; m_height = height; }
   b. : m_origin(origin), m_width(width), m_height(height) {}
   c. : Shape(origin) {m_width = width; m_height = height; }
   d. { m_origin = origin; m_width = width; m_height = height; }
   e. : Shape(origin), m_width(width), m_height(height) {}
*/
```

6. Read the code in Example 6.47 and answer the questions in Example 6.48.

EXAMPLE 6.47   src/quizzes/virtual-destructors-quiz.cpp

```cpp
#include <QDebug>

class Base {
public:
    Base() { ++sm_bases; }
    ~Base() { --sm_bases; }
    void a();
    virtual void b();
protected:
    static int sm_bases;
};

class Derived : public Base {
public:
    Derived() { ++sm_deriveds; }
    ~Derived() { --sm_deriveds; }
    void a();
    void b();
    static void showCounts() {
        qDebug() << sm_bases << sm_deriveds;
    }
protected:
    static int sm_deriveds;
};

int Base::sm_bases(0);
int Derived::sm_deriveds(0);
void Base::a() { qDebug() << "Base::a()" ;}
void Base::b() { qDebug() << "Base::b()" ;}
```

```
void Derived::a() { qDebug() << "Derived::a()" ;}
void Derived::b() { qDebug() << "Derived::b()" ;}

void foo() {
    Derived d1;
    Base b1;
    Base* bp = new Derived();
    bp->a();
    bp->b();
    delete bp;
    Derived::showCounts();                                          1
}
int main() {
    Base b;
    Derived d;
    foo();
    Derived::showCounts();                                          2
}
```

1 _____

2 _____

EXAMPLE 6.48 src/quizzes/virtual-destructors-quiz.txt

1. What is the output from the first call to showCounts()?
   a. 4 3
   b. 3 2
   c. 2 2
   d. 1 1
   e. 3 4

2. What is the output of the second call to showCounts()?
   a. 1 2
   b. 1 1
   c. 0 0
   d. 2 2
   e. 2 1

7. In Extended Example: A Simple Library, it is likely that items will be added to the `RefCategory` enum in the class `ReferenceBook` as the collection evolves. What pitfalls should be avoided and what rules should be imposed that would enable such growth to occur without encountering those pitfalls?

Chapter 7

Libraries and Design Patterns

Libraries are groups of code modules, organized in a reusable way. This chapter discusses how they are built, reused, and designed. Design patterns are also introduced and discussed.

The term **platform** refers to a particular combination of hardware architecture, especially central processing unit (CPU),[1] and software framework, especially operating system (OS).[2] Each computer system can only execute code written in its own low-level, platform-specific language. This low-level machine language does not resemble any natural human language, and few programmers are comfortable working directly with it.

For optimal use of programming resources (especially programmer time), you write programs in a high-level language (e.g., C++) so that you can express and share your ideas and precise instructions in a form reasonably close to your own natural language (e.g., English). The task of translating each item in the high-level code into machine

---

[1] e.g., Intel Core 2 Duo or SPARC64 "Venus"

[2] e.g., Linux, Windows7, Mac_OS_X

language, so that it can be executed on a particular computer platform, is handled by a **compiler**.[3]

Widespread acknowledgment of the value of **code reuse** has steadily increased the demand for (and production of) **code libraries** that store useful, reusable, already compiled code so that programmers can exploit its functionality without having to handle any of its source code. A library module is reused when you `#include` its header file, which specifies its Application Programming Interface (API), in the appropriate source code module. You have already reused several of these from the Standard Library (e.g., `iostream` and `string`) and from Qt (e.g., `QString`, `QTextStream`, and `QList`). When you reuse an item from a library, it is the job of a **linker**, during the build process, to establish appropriate connections between the item references in your compiled code and the item definitions in the compiled library code. The resulting executable must find and dynamically link to the compiled libraries (called **runtime libraries**) at runtime. The compiled library code does not need to be incorporated into the executable file because it can be dynamically linked at runtime. This results in smaller executable files and more efficient use of memory.

A **lib** is a file that contains one or more compiled files (called **object files**) indexed to make it easy for the linker to locate symbols (e.g., names of classes, class members, functions, variables, etc.) and their definitions. Collecting several object files in a single `lib` expedites the linking process significantly.

C++ libraries can be packaged in a few different ways:

- Open source package
- `dev` package
- Runtime library

An **open source package** is usually distributed as a compressed archive containing all source code and header files plus build scripts and documentation. A **dev package**, sometimes referred to as a `-devel` package by Linux package managers, is usually distributed as an archive containing a `lib` plus its associated header files. This format enables you to distribute a library without its source code. Others can still compile their applications with it. A **runtime library**, consists of a `lib` file *without* its associated

---

[3] The Java compiler produces platform-independent code by compiling Java code to an intermediate state called byte code, which gets translated to machine language by a platform-specific Java Virtual Machine. This arrangement buys the considerable advantage of platform independence at a significant cost in performance.

headers, so it can only be used to execute an application that has already been built with the library.

To summarize, the variety of ways that C++ code can be organized and packaged facilitates code sharing and reuse.

Table 7.1 defines some terms that describe containers of code.

TABLE 7.1   Reusable Components

Term	Visible Attributes	Description
class	class `Classname` { body } ;	A collection of functions and data members, and descriptions of its lifecycle management (constructors and destructors)
namespace	namespace name { body } ;	A collection of declarations and definitions, of classes, functions, and static members, perhaps spanning multiple files
header file	`.h`	Class definitions, template definitions, function declarations (with default argument definitions), inline definitions, static object declarations
source code module	`.cpp`	Function definitions, static object definitions
compiled "object" module	`.o` or `.obj`	Each `.cpp` module is compiled into a binary module as an intermediate step in building a library or executable.
library	`.lib` or `.la` (+ `.so` or `.dll` if dynamic)	An indexed collection of object files linked together. No `main()` function must exist in any code module in a library.
devel package	`.lib` + header files	A library along with accompanying header files
application	`.exe` on Windows; no particular extension on *nix	A collection of object files, linked with libraries, to form an application. Contains exactly one function definition called `main()`.

7.1   Building and Reusing Libraries

Many of our examples link with various libraries that we have supplied. You can download the tarball `src.tar.gz` containing the code and libraries we use from our [dist] directory.[4] Unpack the tarball and create a shell/environment variable CPPLIBS that contains the absolute path to the `src/libs` directory.

---

[4] The URL can be found in the "Bibliography."

NOTE

When we set up projects that reuse these libraries, we always assume that the shell/ environment variable CPPLIBS (or %CPPLIBS% in Windows) has been properly set to contain the libs root.

This variable is used for two purposes: It is the parent directory of all the C++ source code for libraries supplied by us (or by you), and it is the destination directory of the compiled shared object code for those libraries.

qmake can access an environment variable such as CPPLIBS from inside a project file using the syntax $$(CPPLIBS). qmake can also include other project files (fragments). For example, the project file in Example 7.1 includes the file common.pri, for the common application build settings you saw earlier in Example 1.6.

EXAMPLE 7.1   src/xml/domwalker/domwalker.pro

```
# include common qmake settings
include (../../common.pri)

# this project depends on libdataobjects:
LIBS += -ldataobjects

# this directory contains the libraries:
LIBS += -L$$(CPPLIBS)

# Search here for headers:
INCLUDEPATH += . $$(CPPLIBS)/dataobjects

QT += xml gui

CONFIG += console
TEMPLATE = app

SOURCES += main.cpp slacker.cpp domwalker.cpp xmltreemodel.cpp
HEADERS += slacker.h domwalker.h xmltreemodel.h
```

In addition, the project adds some values to the LIBS and INCLUDEPATH qmake variables so the project can find dependent libraries and headers.

The command

```
qmake -project
```

produces a project file that contains information based only on the contents of the current working directory. In particular, qmake cannot know about external libraries that you may need to build your project. If your project depends on an external library, you must edit the project file and add assignments to the variables INCLUDEPATH and LIBS. After that, rerunning qmake -project clobbers those changes, so don't.

For example, suppose you develop an application that uses our dataobjects library. The header files are in $CPPLIBS/dataobjects, and the lib shared object files are in $CPPLIBS. Then you must add the following lines to the project file:

```
INCLUDEPATH += $$(CPPLIBS)/dataobjects  # the source header files
LIBS += -L$$(CPPLIBS)                    # add this to the lib search path
LIBS += -ldataobjects                    # link with libdataobjects.so
```

Assignments to the LIBS variable generally contain two kinds of linker switches that are passed directly to the compiler and the linker. For more information about what the linker switches mean, see Section C.3.

7.1.1   Organizing Libraries: Dependency Management

A **dependency** between two program elements exists if one reuses the other; that is, if building, using, or testing one (the reuser) requires the presence and correctness of the other one (the reused). In the case of classes, a dependency exists if the implementation of the reuser class must change whenever the interface of the reused class changes.

Another way of describing this relationship is to say that ProgElement1 depends on ProgElement2 if ProgElement2 is needed to build ProgElement1.

This dependency is a **compile time dependency** if ProgElement1.h must be #included in ProgElement2.cpp to compile.

It is a **link time dependency** if the object file ProgElement2.o contains symbols defined in ProgElement1.o.

Figure 7.1 shows the dependency between a reuser ClassA and a reuser ClassB with a UML diagram.

FIGURE 7.1   Dependency

A dependency between `ClassA` and `ClassB` can arise in a variety of ways. In each of the following situations, a change in the interface of `ClassB` might necessitate changes in the implementation of `ClassA`.

- `ClassA` has a data member that is a `ClassB` object or pointer.
- `ClassA` is derived from `ClassB`.
- `ClassA` has a function that takes a parameter of type `ClassB`.
- `ClassA` has a function that uses a static member of `ClassB`.
- `ClassA` sends a message (e.g., a signal) to `ClassB`.[5]

In each case, it is necessary to `#include ClassB` in the implementation file for `ClassA`.

In the package diagram shown in Figure 7.2, we display parts of our own `libs` collection of libraries. There are direct and indirect dependencies shown. This section focuses on the dependencies between libraries (indicated by dashed arrows).

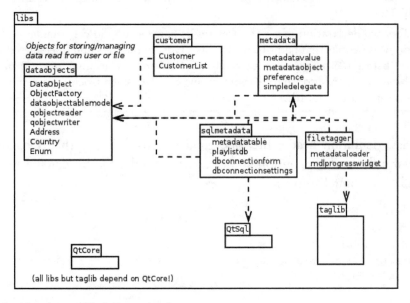

FIGURE 7.2   Libraries and Their Dependencies

---

[5] We discuss signals and slots in Section 8.5.

If you want to reuse one of the libraries shown in Figure 7.2, you need to ensure that all of its dependent libraries are also part of your project. For example, if you use the `filetagger` library, there is a chain of dependencies that requires you to also make available the `dataobjects` library (e.g., `MetaData` classes are derived from `DataObject`) and the `taglib` library (e.g., `filetagger` uses taglib to load metadata). If you want to use `sqlmetadata`, then you need QtSql, the SQL module of Qt.

Code reuse, a valuable and important goal, *always* produces dependencies. When designing classes and libraries, you need to make sure that you produce as few unnecessary or unintentional dependencies as possible because they tend to slow down compile times and reduce the reusability of your classes and libraries. Each `#include` directive produces a dependency and should be carefully examined to make sure that it is really necessary. This is especially true in header files: Each time a header file is `#included`, it brings all of its own `#includes` along with it so that the number of dependencies grows accordingly.

NOTE

A **forward declaration** of a class declares its name as a valid class name but leaves out its definition. This permits that name to be used as a type for pointers and references that are not dereferenced before the definition is encountered. Forward declarations make it possible for classes to have circular relationships without having circular dependencies between header files (which the compiler does not permit).

In a class definition header file, one good rule to follow is this: Do not use an `#include` if a forward declaration suffices. For example, the header file `"classa.h"` might look something like this:

```
#include "classb.h"
#include "classd.h"
// other #include directives as needed
class ClassC;     // forward declaration
class ClassA : public ClassB {
  public:
    ClassC* f1(ClassD);
  // other stuff that does not involve ClassC
};
```

There are (at least) two intentional reuse dependencies in this definition: ClassB and ClassD, so both #include directives are necessary. A forward declaration of ClassC is sufficient, however, because the class definition only uses a pointer to that class.

Dependency management is an important issue that is the subject of several articles and for which a variety of tools have been developed. Two open source tools are

- *cinclude2dot,*[6] a Perl script that analyzes C/C++ code and produces a dependency graph.
- *Makedep,*[7] a C/C++ dependency generator for large software projects that parses all source files in a directory tree and constructs a large dependency file for inclusion in a Makefile.

7.1.2 Installing Libraries

After a library has been written and tested, it is installed at the end of the build process in the directory specified by the qmake variable DESTDIR. For example, the project file for our dataobjects library contains the following relevant lines:

```
TEMPLATE = lib      # Build this as a library, not as an application
DESTDIR=$$(CPPLIBS) # Place the compiled shared object code here
```

For library templates, qmake can generate a Makefile with the *install* target so that the command

```
make install
```

will, after a successful build, copy the library to some particular location. For example, on a *nix platform, you can add the following lines to the project file for dataobjects:

```
target.path=/usr/lib
INSTALLS += target
```

Then, provided that you have write access there, the command

```
make install
```

---

[6] http://www.flourish.org/cinclude2dot/

[7] http://sourceforge.net/projects/makedep

will copy the `libdataobjects.so` files and their associated symlinks to the directory `/usr/lib`, making that library usable by anyone logged into that computer.

If you need to relocate a library, the procedure varies from platform to platform. In Windows, you can copy its `.dll` file into an appropriate directory listed in your PATH variable. In *nix, you can copy the shared object file and associated symbolic links into a directory listed in `/etc/ld.so.conf` or one listed in your LD_LIBRARY_PATH variable.

During development, it is usually sufficient to make and install libraries in your CPPLIBS directory, and adjust LD_LIBRARY_PATH appropriately. On a *nix system, if you have followed our advice and made consistent use of the CPPLIBS environment variable, you only need to add the line

```
export LD_LIBRARY_PATH=$CPPLIBS
```

to your `.bashrc` file, below the line in which you define CPPLIBS. At deployment time, on a *nix platform, it may be desirable to install the library in `/usr/local`, a systemwide location accessible to all other users. This would require superuser permissions.

NOTE

The environment variable QTDIR is not required by Qt, but we sometimes use it in different parts of the book to refer to the base directory of an unzipped Qt tarball. It provides a convenient way to refer to the location of the examples, tutorials, binaries, and libraries of Qt. However, on systems like Ubuntu or Debian, where Qt is split into multiple folders and installed to different locations, QTDIR should not be, and is not defined. In that case, you can interpret our usage of QTDIR to mean "the parent directory of the Qt binaries" or "the parent directory of the Qt examples" (which could be two different directories in that case).

TIP

Building Dynamic Link Libraries, or DLLs, is more complicated on Microsoft platforms, because you need to define a unique "exporter" macro for each library.

This macro expands to the appropriate `__declspec()` export or import, depending on whether the header file is included from its own library or an external program.

You can use a handy preprocessor macro, Q_DECL_EXPORT, defined in <qglobal.h> that can conditionally switch on or off the declspec and import or export the identifier at the right time.

So, for example, in `libdataobjects`, we define an export macro, shown in Example 7.2, called DOBJS_EXPORT.

EXAMPLE 7.2   src/libs/dataobjects/dobjs_export.h

```
#include <QtGlobal>
#ifndef DOBJS_EXPORT
/* This macro is only for building DLLs on Windows. */
#ifndef Q_OS_WIN
#define DOBJS_EXPORT
#elif defined(DATAOBJECTS_DLL)
#define DOBJS_EXPORT Q_DECL_EXPORT
#else
#define DOBJS_EXPORT Q_DECL_IMPORT
#endif
#endif
```

This macro only exports symbols when DATAOBJECTS_DLL is defined from dataobjects.pro:

```
win32 {
    CONFIG(dll) {
        DEFINES += DATAOBJECTS_DLL
    }
}
```

Now, for any class that you want to export to the DLL, simply place the macro between the class keyword and the classname in the class definition:

```
class DOBJS_EXPORT DataObject : public QObject {
  [ . . . ]
}
```

There is a thread on the subject[8] at qtcentre.org that might save you a lot of time when you build your first DLL.

NOTE

The QLibrary class has methods to help you load and unload dynamic libraries at run-time in a platform-independent way.

---

[8] http://www.qtcentre.org/forum/showthread.php?t=1080

7.2   Exercise: Installing Libraries

A number of examples in this book use classes found in libraries that were written for this book. The source code for these classes is available for download.[9] API documentation is included, generated with Doxygen. In this exercise, you can see how to build and install some libraries.

Instructions for installing libraries on a *nix platform for use with the book examples follow. For help installing Qt and MySQL on Windows with MinGW, check the QtCentre Wiki.[10]

As we suggested in Section 7.1 and Section 7.1.2:

- Create a directory especially for your C++/Qt work; e.g., `~/oop/projects/`.
- Download `src.tar.gz` from the [dist] directory.[11]
- Unpack this tarball in the new directory. That should result in a `libs` directory with a number of subdirectories including `libs/dataobjects` and `libs/customer`.
- Examine the `subdirs` project file, named `libs.pro`, in the `libs` directory.
- It is designed to build the libraries and the tests.
- Feel free to comment out the libraries and tests you do not plan to use, but do not change the order of the libraries.
- Create a shell/environment variable named `CPPLIBS` that contains the absolute path of your new `libs` directory. For convenience, you can place the definition for this environment variable inside a shell script, as demonstrated in Example 7.3.

NOTE

If you decide to comment out a particular library directory in `libs.pro`, you should also comment out the corresponding test dir in `libs/tests/tests.pro` (or else the tests part of libs won't build).

Reminder: You can comment out any line in a project file by inserting the poundsign char # at the beginning of that line.

---

[9] From our [dist] directory.

[10] http://wiki.qtcentre.org/index.php?title=Building_the_QMYSQL_plugin_on_Windows_using_MinGW

[11] The URL can be found in the "Bibliography."

libs.pro

```
TEMPLATE = subdirs
CPPLIBS=$$(CPPLIBS)
isEmpty(CPPLIBS) {
   error("Define CPPLIBS environment variable to point to this location.")
   }
SUBDIRS += dataobjects \
           actioneditor \
           customer \
#          metadata \
#          sqlmetadata
```

Build the libraries from the `libs` directory in two steps:

1. `qmake -recursive` // creates `Makefiles` in `$CPPLIBS` and in each subdir.
2. `make` // builds the libraries and tests (per Hc).[12]

Verify that the libraries are built and that the shared object files (e.g., `libdataobjects.so`[13]) are located in the `CPPLIBS` directory. Following is an abbreviated directory listing from a typical Linux box:

```
libs> ls -l
drwxr-xr-x  5 dataobjects
lrwxrwxrwx  1 libactioneditor.so -> libactioneditor.so.1.0.0
lrwxrwxrwx  1 libactioneditor.so.1 -> libactioneditor.so.1.0.0
lrwxrwxrwx  1 libactioneditor.so.1.0 -> libactioneditor.so.1.0.0
-rwxrwxr-x  1 libactioneditor.so.1.0.0
[...]
lrwxrwxrwx  1 libdataobjects.so -> libdataobjects.so.1.0.0
lrwxrwxrwx  1 libdataobjects.so.1 -> libdataobjects.so.1.0.0
lrwxrwxrwx  1 libdataobjects.so.1.0 -> libdataobjects.so.1.0.0
-rwxr-xr-x  1 libdataobjects.so.1.0.0
-rw-r--r--  1 libs.pro
-rw-r--r--  1 Makefile
libs>
```

---

[12] You may need to install some specialized Qt packages before building some of our libraries. For example, the `libphonon-dev` package is required for our phononmetadata library. The linker will inform you of these dependencies.

[13] Or on Windows, `libdataobjects.lib` and `dataobjects.dll`, the latter which must be in a directory listed in your PATH, so be sure to include `%CPPLIBS%` in your PATH.

Lines that begin with `drwxr-xr-x` are directories. Lines that begin with `lrwxrwxrwx` are symbolic links. Use Google to find out why each shared object file has three symbolic links.

Fixing the Linker Path

- Update the shell/environment variable `LD_LIBRARY_PATH` (*nix) or `PATH` (win32) to include `CPPLIBS` using the appropriate syntax.
- Create a `projects/tests` directory. This is where you can keep code for testing various library components.
- Run the test apps that came with the libs tarball. They are in subdirs of `libs/tests` that correspond to the libraries that you built.

 NOTE

On a *nix platform, a shell script is generally used to define environment variables. Example 7.3 shows a bash shell script that handles the job.

EXAMPLE 7.3   src/bash/env-script.sh

```
export CPPLIBS=$HOME/oop/projects/libs
export LD_LIBRARY_PATH=$CPPLIBS
```

Note the bash syntax details in this script:

- The environment variable `HOME` contains the absolute path to your personal "home" directory. You can also use the tilde symbol ~ for this.
- An environment variable on the left side of an assignment has no dollar sign $ prefix.
- An environment variable on the right of an assignment must have a $ prefix.
- The command `export` is needed if the environment variable is to become a part of the environment—and not simply be local to the script file.

You can run this script by typing one of the following commands:

```
source env-script.sh
   or
. env-script.sh
```

Notice the dot (.) at the beginning of the second version. In the bash shell, the dot is equivalent to the command source.

If you want to make sure that these environment variables are automatically set at the start of each shell, you can source the script from ~/.bashrc, which runs automatically whenever bash starts (for example, whenever you bring up a terminal or console).

Hamish Whittal has put together a nice online guide to Shell Scripting.[14]

7.3   Frameworks and Components

Organization of classes goes beyond simple inheritance. Carefully designed frameworks enable you to find and reuse components much more easily. All large software projects are built on top of frameworks, and we discuss some of the more popular ones in use today.

Code reuse has high priority in modern programming. In the past, computer time was expensive and programmer time was relatively cheap, but now things are exactly reversed. Today all software is built out of building blocks, which are themselves pieces of software. You never start from scratch to develop an app. It is a waste of a programmer's time to reinvent and reimplement things that have already been designed, implemented, refined, and tested by recognized experts.

A **framework** is a (typically large) collection of general-purpose (or domain-specific) classes and conventions designed to improve the consistency of design. Frameworks are often used to create graphical applications, database applications, or other complex pieces of software.

A framework has a well-documented public API. An API is a description of the public functions, classes, and interfaces in a library. To implement frameworks, **design patterns** are used. Development with design patterns involves looking for pertinent objects and possible hierarchies. The classes and patterns used are given good descriptive names so that you can define them once and reuse them elsewhere. We discuss design patterns shortly in Section 7.3.

---

[14] http://www.cc.puv.fi/~jd/course/Linux/Shell_Scripting/index.html

Qt is one of many open source object-oriented frameworks that provide a set of reusable components for building cross-platform applications. Some others worth knowing about are

- **boost**[15]—An open source cross-platform library of C++ utility classes.
- **mono**[16]—An open source implementation of Microsoft's .NET, the API for C#, which is built on top of libgtk.
- **libgtk**, **libgtk++**—Libraries that define the widgets used by the Gnome desktop, Mozilla, Dia, GAIM, GIMP, Evolution, OpenOffice, and many other open source programs.
- **wxWidgets**[17]—Another C++ cross-platform widget toolkit.
- **Wt**[18]—A Qt-like framework for building Web applications using boost and AJAX.[19]

With a multiplatform framework like Qt, you can gain enormous benefits from the creative efforts of others. Software built *on top of* (strictly using) Qt will be based on components that have already been tested on Windows, Linux, and Mac OS/X by thousands of programmers.

Toolkits like Qt (and also Gtk++, the cross-platform Gnu ToolKit) are implemented differently on each platform. This is why Qt-based applications look like KDE applications in Linux and like Windows applications in Windows.

7.4   Design Patterns

Design patterns are efficient and elegant solutions to common problems in object-oriented software design. They are high-level abstract templates that can be applied to particular kinds of design problems.

In their influential book *Design Patterns* [Gamma95], Erich Gamma, Richard Helm, Ralph Johnson, and John Vlissides, often (affectionately) referred to as the "Gang of Four," analyzed 23 specific patterns. Each pattern has a section devoted to it, describing the following things:

---

[15] http://www.boost.org

[16] http://www.mono-project.com/

[17] http://www.wxwidgets.org

[18] http://www.webtoolkit.eu/wt

[19] AJAX is an acronym for Asynchronous JavaScript And XML, a client-side system of JavaScript and XML-rpc that gives list/tree/table views with GUI behavior inside a Web page.

- A pattern name.
- A description of the kinds of problems to which one might apply the pattern.
- An abstract description of a design problem and how its solution can be obtained.
- A discussion of the results and trade-offs that can occur when the pattern is applied.

Design patterns are used for many different purposes. Most describe how to separate code by responsibility. They are subdivided into three categories: Creational, Structural, and Behavioral. Structural patterns describe how to organize objects and connect them. Behavioral patterns describe how to organize code. Creational patterns describe how to organize code that manages object creation.

The Gang of Four assert that design patterns are "descriptions of communicating objects and classes that are customized to solve a general design problem in a particular context." As you continue to develop applications with Qt, you will see descriptions and examples of several design patterns.

Some of the commonly encountered design patterns arose from working around limitations in the more popular languages and APIs that were in use at the time they were cataloged. On the other hand, a modern, dynamic language like Python has built-in support for several design patterns already, so implementing them in your own software is a natural benefit of learning that language. The same is true for Qt. You will work with several Qt classes that implement particular design patterns.

7.4.1 Serializer Pattern: QTextStream and QDataStream

> **Serializer Pattern**
>
> A **serializer** is an object that is responsible only for reading or writing objects. Qt has the QTextStream for reading and writing human-readable files, and the QDataStream for reading and writing structured, binary data. These classes are implementations of the **Serializer pattern**, as it is used in C++ and Qt. [Martin98]

With QDataStream, it is already possible to serialize and deserialize all QVariant-supported types, including QList, QMap, QVector, and others.[20] With QTextStream, if you want the extraction (>>) operator to work with the output of the insertion (<<) operator on your custom type, you must define proper field and record delimiters for the string types, and write and test the operators properly with sample data.

Because these streams can be created from any QIODevice, and there are many other Qt classes that use QIODevice to communicate, your operators can send objects over a network, or through pipes, or to a database.

Example 7.4 shows the friend declarations of input/output operator functions of MetaDataValue, a class used for storing song metadata. The operators are not member functions because the left operand is a QDataStream or QTextStream, classes that cannot modified. Furthermore, the operators *should not be* member functions of MetaDataValue because the idea of the serializer pattern is to separate the I/O code from the class itself. The METADATAEXPORT macro facilitates the reuse of this code on a Windows platform.[21]

EXAMPLE 7.4   src/libs/metadata/metadatavalue.h

```
[ . . . . ]
class METADATAEXPORT MetaDataValue {
public:

    friend METADATAEXPORT QTextStream& operator<< (QTextStream& os,
                                    const MetaDataValue& mdv);
    friend METADATAEXPORT QTextStream& operator>> (QTextStream& is,
                                    MetaDataValue& mdv);
    friend METADATAEXPORT QDataStream& operator<< (QDataStream& os,
                                    const MetaDataValue& mdv);
    friend METADATAEXPORT QDataStream& operator>> (QDataStream& is,
                                    MetaDataValue& mdv);
    friend METADATAEXPORT bool operator==(const MetaDataValue&,
                                    const MetaDataValue&);
[ . . . . ]
    virtual QString fileName() const ;
    virtual Preference preference() const ;
    virtual QString genre() const;
    virtual QString artist() const;
    virtual QString albumTitle() const;
```

---

[20] http://doc .qt.nokia.com/latest/datastreamformat.html

[21] We discuss such macros in the TIP in Section 7.1.2.

```
    virtual QString trackTitle() const;
    virtual QString trackNumber() const;
    virtual const QImage &image() const;
    virtual QTime trackTime() const;
    virtual QString trackTimeString() const;
    virtual QString comment() const;
[ . . . . ]
protected:
    bool m_isNull;
    QUrl m_Url;
    QString m_TrackNumber;
    QString m_TrackTitle;
    QString m_Comment;
    Preference m_Preference;
    QString m_Genre;
    QString m_Artist;
    QTime m_TrackTime;
    QString m_AlbumTitle;
    QImage m_Image;
};
Q_DECLARE_METATYPE(MetaDataValue);                                    1
[ . . . . ]
```

1 Add to `QVariant` type system.

Each operator deals with one `MetaDataValue` object. `operator<<()` inserts its data into the output stream. `operator>>()` extracts its data from the input stream. Each operator returns a reference to the left operand to enable chaining.

The `QTextStream` operators in Example 7.5 need to be concerned with whitespace and delimiters because everything is streamed out in string representations.

EXAMPLE 7.5   src/libs/metadata/metadatavalue.cpp

```
[ . . . . ]


QTextStream& operator<< (QTextStream& os, const MetaDataValue& mdv) {
    QStringList sl;
    sl << mdv.url().toString() << mdv.trackTitle() << mdv.artist() << mdv.
albumTitle()
            << mdv.trackNumber() << mdv.trackTime().toString("m:ss")
            << mdv.genre() << mdv.preference().toString() << mdv.comment();
```

```
    os << sl.join("\t") << "\n";                                        1
    return os;
}


QTextStream& operator>> (QTextStream& is, MetaDataValue& mdv) {
    QString line = is.readLine();
    QStringList fields = line.split("\t");                              2
    while (fields.size() < 9) {
        fields << "";
    }
    mdv.m_isNull = false;
    mdv.setUrl(QUrl::fromUserInput(fields[0]));
    mdv.setTrackTitle(fields[1]);
    mdv.setArtist(fields[2]);
    mdv.setAlbumTitle(fields[3]);
    mdv.setTrackNumber(fields[4]);
    QTime t = QTime::fromString(fields[5], "m:ss");
    mdv.setTrackTime(t);
    mdv.setGenre(fields[6]);
    Preference p(fields[7]);
    mdv.setPreference(p);
    mdv.setComment(fields[8]);
    return is;
}
```

1 Output to TSV (tab-separated-values)

2 Read as TSV

The QDataStream operators, shown in Example 7.6, are much simpler to use because they relieve the programmer of the responsibility of separating data items from one another.

EXAMPLE 7.6   src/libs/metadata/metadatavalue.cpp

```
[ . . . . ]


QDataStream& operator<< (QDataStream& os, const MetaDataValue& mdv) {
    os << mdv.m_Url << mdv.trackTitle() << mdv.artist() << mdv.albumTitle()
            << mdv.trackNumber() << mdv.trackTime() << mdv.genre()
            << mdv.preference() << mdv.comment() << mdv.image();
    return os;
}
```

```
QDataStream& operator>> (QDataStream& is, MetaDataValue& mdv) {
    is >> mdv.m_Url >> mdv.m_TrackTitle >> mdv.m_Artist >> mdv.m_AlbumTitle
          >> mdv.m_TrackNumber >> mdv.m_TrackTime >> mdv.m_Genre
          >> mdv.m_Preference >> mdv.m_Comment >> mdv.m_Image;
    mdv.m_isNull= false;
    return is;
}
```

Example 7.7 shows how to use these operators with the different streams. The only disadvantage to using QDataStream is that the resulting file is binary (i.e., not human readable).

EXAMPLE 7.7   src/serializer/testoperators/tst_testoperators.cpp

```
[ . . . . ]
void TestOperators::testCase1()
{
    QFile textFile("playlist1.tsv");
    QFile binaryFile("playlist1.bin");
    QTextStream textStream;
    QDataStream dataStream;

    if (textFile.open(QIODevice::ReadOnly)) {
        textStream.setDevice(&textFile);
    }
    if (binaryFile.open(QIODevice::WriteOnly)) {
        dataStream.setDevice(&binaryFile);
    }
    QList<MetaDataValue> values;
    while (!textStream.atEnd()) {
        MetaDataValue mdv;
        textStream >> mdv;                                          1
        values << mdv;                                              2
        dataStream << mdv;                                          3
    }
    textFile.close();
    binaryFile.close();
    textFile.setFileName("playlist2.tsv");
    if (binaryFile.open(QIODevice::ReadOnly)) {
        dataStream.setDevice(&binaryFile);
        for (int i=0; i<values.size(); ++i) {
            MetaDataValue mdv;
            dataStream >> mdv;                                      4
```

```
        QCOMPARE(mdv, values[i]);                               5
    }
  }
}
[ . . . . . ]
```

1 Read as TSV.

2 Add to list.

3 Write to `binaryFile`.

4 Read binary data.

5 Is it same as what we read before?

7.4.2 AntiPatterns

AntiPattern is a term first coined by [Koenig95] to describe a commonly used programming practice that has proved to be ineffective, inefficient, or otherwise counterproductive. Several antiPatterns arose as solutions to recurring problems and have been picked up and passed on by students and other inexperienced programmers. There is an informative and evolving article on this subject in Wikipedia[22] that organizes and briefly describes a substantial number of antiPatterns. Discussing examples of antiPatterns may help programmers avoid such pitfalls. Following is a small selection of named antiPatterns from the Wikipedia article.

- **Software design antiPatterns**
  - **Input kludge**—Failing to specify and implement the handling of possibly invalid input.
  - **Interface bloat**—Making an interface so powerful and complicated that it is hard to reuse or implement.
  - **Race hazard**—Failing to see the consequence of different orders of events.
- **Object-oriented design antiPatterns**
  - **Circular dependency**—Introducing unnecessary direct or indirect mutual dependencies between objects or software modules.

---

[22] http://en.wikipedia.org/wiki/AntiPattern#Programming_antiPatterns

- **God Object**—An object that has too much information or too much responsibility. This can be the result of having too many functions in a single class. It can arise from many situations, but it often happens when code for a model and view are combined in the same class.

- **Programming antiPatterns**
  - **Hard coding**—Embedding assumptions about the environment of a system in its implementation.
  - **Magic numbers**—Including unexplained numbers in algorithms.
  - **Magic strings**—Including literal strings in code, for comparisons, as event types, etc.

- **Methodological antiPatterns**
  - **Copy and paste programming**—Copying and modifying existing code without creating more generic solutions.
  - **Reinventing the (square) wheel**—Failing to adopt an existing, adequate solution and, instead, adopting a custom solution (which performs much worse than the existing one).

In Figure 7.3, `Customer` includes member functions for importing and exporting its individual data members in XML format.

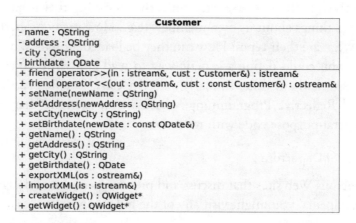

Customer
- name : QString
- address : QString
- city : QString
- birthdate : QDate
+ friend operator>>(in : istream&, cust : Customer&) : istream&
+ friend operator<<(out : ostream&, cust : const Customer&) : ostream&
+ setName(newName : QString)
+ setAddress(newAddress : QString)
+ setCity(newCity : QString)
+ setBirthdate(newDate : const QDate&)
+ getName() : QString
+ getAddress() : QString
+ getCity() : QString
+ getBirthdate() : QDate
+ exportXML(os : ostream&)
+ importXML(is : istream&)
+ createWidget() : QWidget*
+ getWidget() : QWidget*

FIGURE 7.3 AntiPattern Example

`getWidget()` provides a special GUI widget that the user can use to enter data from a graphical application. In addition, there are friend functions for input/output via `iostream`.[23]

This class is a *model* because it holds onto data and represents some abstract entity. However, this class also contains *view* code because of the `createWidget()` and `getWidget()` member functions. In addition, it contains *serialization* code specific to particular I/O streams.[24] That is too much responsibility for a data model. This is an example of the **Interface Bloat** antiPattern (and perhaps a few others also).

The problems that interface bloat can lead to become immediately apparent when you implement other data model classes such as `Address`, `ShoppingCart`, `Catalog`, `CatalogItem`, etc. Each of them would also need these methods:

- `createWidget()`
- `importXML()`
- `exportXML()`
- `operator<<()`
- `operator>>()`

This could lead to the use of **Copy-and-Paste** programming, another antiPattern.

If you ever change the data structure, corresponding changes would need to be made to all presentation and I/O methods. Bugs are likely to be introduced when maintaining this code. If `Customer` were **reflective**, meaning that it had the ability to determine useful things about its own members (e.g., How many properties? What are their names? What are their types? How can they be loaded/stored? What are the child objects?), then you could define a generic way to read and write objects that would work for `Customer` and any other similarly reflective class. Chapter 12, "Meta Objects, Properties, and Reflective Programming," discusses an example that shows how to write more general-purpose code with reflection.

7.4.2.1   Points of Departure

There are numerous Web sites that discuss and present examples of design patterns. In addition to Wikipedia, you might visit any of the following sites:

---

[23] Friends are discussed in Section 2.6.

[24] Serialization is the process of converting an object's data to a form that permits the data to be stored in a file or transmitted across a network so that it can later be used to reconstruct the object. Section 7.3.1 discusses the Serializer Pattern.

- Vince Huston's page.[25]
- Douglas Schmidt's Design Pattern Tutorials.[26]
- The Wikibooks C++ Programming/Code/Design Patterns[27] site.

The term AntiPattern has been adopted by the Pattern Community[28] which maintains a catalog of AntiPatterns.[29]

7.5 Review Questions

1. What is a platform? What platform do you use? What platform can be found in the labs at your school or work place?

2. What is code reuse? How is it done? What is good about it?

3. What is the role of a compiler?

4. What is the role of a linker?

5. Name three kinds of C++ libraries.

6. What is CPPLIBS? Why do you need it?

7. For each of these items, decide whether it would normally be found in a header (.h) file or an implementation (.cpp) file and explain why.

   a. Function definitions

   b. Function declarations

   c. static object declarations

   d. static object definitions

   e. Class definitions

   f. Class declarations

---

[25] http://www.vincehuston.org/dp/

[26] http://www.cs.wustl.edu/~schmidt/tutorials-patterns.html

[27] http://en.wikibooks.org/wiki/C++_Programming/Code/Design_Patterns

[28] http://c2.com/cgi/wiki?PatternCommunity

[29] http://c2.com/cgi/wiki?AntiPatternsCatalog

    g. `inline` function definitions

    h. `inline` function declarations

    i. Default argument specifiers

8. What is the difference between a compile time dependency and a link time dependency?

9. What is a framework? Are you using one?

10. What is a design pattern? What do most design patterns have in common?

11. What is an AntiPattern?

Chapter 8

QObject, QApplication, Signals, and Slots

QObject is the base class for many of the important classes in the Qt library, such as QEvent, QApplication, QLayout, and QWidget. We refer to any object of a class publicly derived from QObject as a QObject. A QObject can have a parent and children, providing another implementation of the *Composite pattern*. It can use signals and slots, an implementation of the *Observer pattern*, to communicate with other QObjects. QObjects make it possible to do event-based programming, which employs QApplication and Qt's event loop.

Following is an abbreviated look at its definition.

```
class QObject {
  public:
    explicit QObject(QObject* parent=0);
    QObject * parent () const;
    QString objectName() const;
    void setParent ( QObject * parent );
    const ObjectList & children () const;
    // ... more ...
};
```

QObject does *not* have a `public` copy constructor or copy assignment operator. Down toward the end of its class definition there is a macro (`Q_DISABLE_COPY(QObject)`) that explicitly makes sure that no `QObject` can be copied. `QObject`s are not meant to be copied. In general, `QObject`s are intended to represent unique objects with identity; that is, they correspond to real-world things that have some sort of persistent identity. One immediate consequence of this no-copy policy is that a `QObject` can never be passed by value to a function. Copying a `QObject`'s data members into another `QObject` is still possible, but the resulting two QObjects are considered distinct.

---

explicit **Constructors**

Single-argument constructors of `QObject` (and derived classes) should be designated `explicit` to avoid accidental conversions from taking place.[1] `QObject` is not intended to be a holder of a temporary value, and it should not be possible to create one implicitly from a pointer or a simple value.

Each `QObject` can have (at most) one **parent** `QObject`, and an arbitrarily large number of `QObject` **children**. In other words, the type of each child must be `QObject` or must be derived from `QObject`. Each `QObject` stores pointers to its children in a `QObjectList`.[2] The list itself is created in a lazy-fashion to minimize the overhead for objects that have no children. Because each child is a `QObject` and can have an arbitrarily large collection of children, it is easy to see why copying `QObject`s is not permitted.

The notion of children can help to clarify the notion of identity and the no-copy policy for `QObject`s. If you represent individual humans as `QObject`s, the idea of a unique identity for each `QObject` is clear. Also clear is the idea of children. The rule that allows each `QObject` to have at most one parent can be seen as a way to simplify the implementation of this class. Finally, the no-copy policy stands out as a clear necessity. Even if it were possible to "clone" a person (i.e., copy its data members to another `QObject`), the question of what to do with the children of that person makes it clear that the clone would be a separate and distinct object with a different identity.

Each `QObject` parent *manages* its children. This means that the `QObject`'s children are destroyed during its destructor call.

---

[1] We first discussed the keyword *explicit* in Section 2.12.

[2] `QObjectList` is a `typedef` (i.e., an *alias*) for `QList<QObject*>`.

The child list establishes a bidirectional association between QObjects:

- Each parent object knows the address of each of its child objects.
- Each child object knows the address of its parent object.

Setting the parent of a `QObject` implicitly adds its address to the child list of the parent; i.e.,

```
objA->setParent(objB);
```

adds the `objA` pointer to the child list of `objB`. If you subsequently have

```
objA->setParent(objC);
```

then the `objA` pointer is removed from the child list of `objB` and added to the child list of `objC`. We call such an action **reparenting**.

Parents Versus Base Classes

Parent objects should not be confused with **base classes**. The parent-child relationship is meant to describe containment, or management, of *objects* at **runtime**. The base-derived relationship is a static relationship between *classes* determined at **compile time**.

It is possible for a parent object to also be an instance of a base class of some of its child objects. These two kinds of relationships are distinct and must not be confused, especially considering that many of your objects will be derived directly or indirectly from `QObject`. Figure 8.1 should clarify this idea.

As you saw earlier, all the widgets of a graphical user interface (GUI) are derived from `QWidget`, which is derived from `QObject`. As with QObjects, we refer to any object of a class publicly derived from `QWidget` as a `QWidget` (or sometimes, simply, widget). In a GUI, the parent-child relationships are usually visible: Child widgets appear *inside* parent widgets. In Figure 8.1, the dialog widget has several children, including: A label widget, a line edit widget, and two pushbutton widgets. It also has a title bar widget, which may be a parent or sibling of the dialog. It is usually provided by the window manager and contains several child widgets, including the button widgets that enable a user to minimize, maximize, or close the dialog.

The need for the child management requirement is also visible in Figure 8.1. When you close the dialog (e.g., by clicking on the small x button in the upper-right corner), you want the entire dialog window to vanish from the screen (i.e., to be destroyed). You don't want pieces of it (e.g., the odd button or label widget) to linger on the screen, and you don't want to put the burden of all that cleanup on the programmer. That is why each QObject is responsible for destroying all its children when its destructor is called. This is a naturally recursive process. When a QObject is to be destroyed, it must first call the destructor for each of its children; each child object must then call the destructor for each of its children; and so forth.

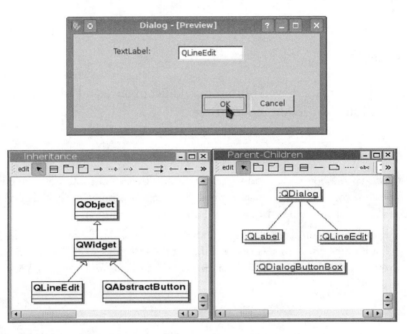

FIGURE 8.1   Parent-Child Object Versus Base-Derived Class

Now consider some of the problems that would arise if it were possible to copy a QObject. For example, should the copy have the same parent as the original? Should the copy have (in some sense) the children of the original? A shallow copy of the child list would not work because then each of the children would have two parents. In that case, if the copy needs to be destroyed (e.g., if the copy was a value parameter in a function call), each child needs to be destroyed too (because the QObject must manage its children). Even with resource sharing methods, this approach would introduce some serious difficulties. A deep copy of the child list could be a costly operation if the number of children were large and the objects pointed to were large. Because each child could also have arbitrarily many children, this questionable approach would generate serious difficulties.

NOTE

Generally speaking, QObjects without a parent should be defined on the program stack, and those with a parent should be dynamically created on the heap. This helps to guarantee that correct destruction can take place: An object on the stack, which has no parent, will be destroyed when its scope is eliminated (e.g., when the function in which it was defined returns, or when the flow of control leaves the block in which it was defined). Then, prior to its destruction, the (stack) object destroys its (heap) children.

8.1   Values and Objects

C++ types can divided into two categories: value types and object types.

Instances of **value types** are usually relatively simple, occupy contiguous memory space, and can be copied or compared quickly. Examples of value types: `Anything*`, `int`, `char`, `QString`, `QDate`, and `QVariant`.

QVariant

`QVariant` is a special union type that can hold all copyable built-in types and programmer-defined types. An interesting thing about `QVariant` and the types it already supports, such as `QList`, `QImage`, `QString`, `QMap`, `QHash`, is that they all support implicit sharing, copy on write, and reference counting. This means it is relatively cheap to copy, pass, and return them by value. See `QMetaType::Type` for a list of the supported types, and Section 11.5 for more details about how implicit sharing is achieved.

Any class that has a `public` default constructor, copy constructor, and copy assignment operator is a value type.

Instances of **object types**, on the other hand, are typically more complex and maintain some sort of identity. Object types are rarely copied (cloned). If cloning is permitted, the operation is usually expensive and results in a new object (graph) that has a separate identity from the original.

The designers of `QObject` asserted an unequivocal "no-copy" policy by designating its assignment operator and copy constructor `private`. This effectively prevents the compiler from generating assignment operators and copy constructors for QObject-derived classes. One consequence of this scheme is that any attempt to pass or return QObject-derived classes by value to or from functions results in a compile time error.

✖ TIP

There is never a good reason to create a QList, QString, QHash, QImage, or any other QVariant-related type on the heap. Don't do it. Let Qt do the reference counting and memory management for you.

8.2   Composite Pattern: Parents and Children

According to [Gamma95], the **Composite pattern** is intended to facilitate building complex (composite) objects from simpler (component) parts by representing the part-whole hierarchies as tree-like structures. This must be done in such a way that clients do not need to distinguish between simple parts and more complex parts that are made up of (i.e., contain) simpler parts.

Figure 8.2 describes the Composite pattern. In this diagram, there are two distinct classes for describing two roles:

- A **composite object** is something that can contain children.
- A **component object** is something that can have a parent.

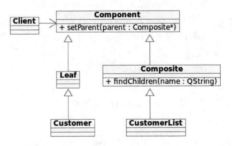

FIGURE 8.2   Components and Composites

Many Qt classes use the Composite pattern: `QObject`, `QWidget`, `QTreeWidgetItem`, `QDomNode`, `QHelpContentItem`, `QResource`. The Composite pattern can be found in just about any tree-based structure.

In Figure 8.3, you can see that `QObject` is both composite *and* component. You can express the whole-part relationship as a parent-child relationship between `QObjects`. The highest level (i.e., most "composite") `QObject` in such a tree (i.e., the **root** of the tree) will have children but no parent. The simplest `QObjects` (i.e., the **leaf** nodes of this tree) each have a parent but no children. Client code can recursively deal with each node of the tree.

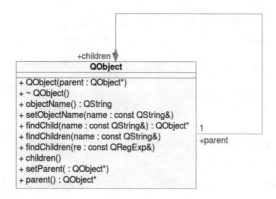

FIGURE 8.3   QObject: Composite and Component

For an example of how the Composite pattern might be used, let's look at Suffolk University. In 1906 the founder, Gleason Archer, decided to start teaching the principles of law to a small group of tradesmen who wanted to become lawyers. He was assisted by one secretary and, after a while, a few instructors. The organizational chart for this new school was quite simple: a single office consisting of several employees with various tasks. As the enterprise grew, the chart gradually became more complex with the addition of new offices and departments. Today, more than a hundred years later, the Law School has been joined with a College of Arts and Sciences, a

Business School, a School of Art and Design, campuses abroad, and many specialized offices so that the organizational chart has become quite complex and promises to become more so. Figure 8.4 shows an abbreviated and simplified subchart of today's Suffolk University.

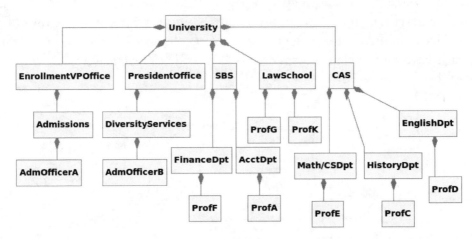

FIGURE 8.4   Suffolk University Organizational Chart

Each box in this chart is a component. It may be a composite and have subcomponents which, in turn, may be composite or simple components. For example, the PresidentOffice has individual employees (e.g., the president and his assistants) and suboffices (e.g., DiversityServices). The leaves of this tree are the individual employees of the organization.

You can use the Composite pattern to model this structure. Each node of the tree can be represented by an object of type OrgUnit.

```
class OrgUnit : public QObject {
  public:
    QString getName();
    double getSalary();
  private:
    QString m_Name;
    double m_Salary;
};
```

The QObject public interface enables you to build up a tree-like representation of the organization with code that instantiates an OrgUnit and then calls setParent() to add it to the appropriate child list.

For each OrgUnit pointer ouptr in the tree, initialize its m_Salary data member as follows:

- If ouptr points to an individual employee, use that employee's actual salary.

- Otherwise initialize it to 0.

You can implement the getSalary() method like this:

```
double OrgUnit::getSalary() {
  QList<OrgUnit*> childlst = findChildren<OrgUnit*>();
  double salaryTotal(m_Salary);
  if(!childlst.isEmpty())
    foreach(OrgUnit* ouptr, childlst)
      salaryTotal += ouptr->getSalary();
  return salaryTotal;
}
```

A call to getSalary() from any particular node returns the total salary for the part of the university represented by the subtree whose root is that node. For example, if ouptr points to University, ouptr->getSalary() returns the total salary for the entire university. If ouptr points to EnglishDpt, then ouptr->getSalary() returns the total salary for the English Department. If ouptr points to ProfE, ouptr->getSalary() simply returns ProfE's individual salary.

8.2.1 Finding Children

Each QObject can have an unlimited number of QObject children. The addresses of these children are stored in a special container of QObject pointers.[3] QObject has a member function that returns a list of pointers to all the child objects of the host object. The prototype for this function is

```
const QObjectList& QObject::children() const
```

---

[3] Recall: any object derived from QObject is called a QObject. Also, a QObject pointer can store the address of a derived object.

The order in which the child objects appear in the list is (initially) the order in which they were added to the list. There are certain runtime operations that can change that order.[4]

QObject also provides two overloaded (recursive) functions named findChildren(). Each returns a list of children that satisfy certain conditions. The prototype of one of the overloaded forms looks like this:

```
QList<T> parentObj.findChildren<T> ( const QString& name = QString() ) const
```

The function returns a list of child objects of type T that have an object name equal to *name*. If *name* is the empty string, findChildren() works as a class filter—returning a QList of pointers to all children that can can be cast[5] to type T.

Example 8.1 shows how to call this function. You must supply a template parameter after the function name.

EXAMPLE 8.1   src/findchildren/findchildren.cpp

```
[ . . . . ]
/* Filter on Customer* */
    QList<Customer*> custlist = parent.findChildren<Customer*>();
    foreach (const Customer* current, custlist) {
        qDebug() << current->toString();
    }
[ . . . . ]
```

This is a simple example so, to make it more realistic, imagine the parent object is a SalesManager whose child list may contain pointers to Supplier, SupportStaff, and SalesPerson objects which, in turn, have child lists that may contain pointers to Customer, TravelAgent, and other associated objects.

---

[4] e.g., raising (or lowering) a QWidget child, which visually places the widget in front of (or behind) all overlapping sibling widgets

[5] Section 19.7 discusses type conversion and casting.

8.2.2   QObject's Child Managment

Example 8.2 shows a `QObject` derived class.[6]

EXAMPLE 8.2   *src/qobject/person.h*

```
[ . . . . ]

class Person : public QObject {
 public:
    explicit Person(QString name, QObject* parent = 0);
    virtual ~Person();
};
[ . . . . ]
```

The complete implementation is shown in Example 8.3. Notice that `~Person()` does no explicit object deletion. It only displays the name of the object being destroyed (for teaching purposes).

EXAMPLE 8.3   *src/qobject/person.cpp*

```
#include "person.h"
#include <QTextStream>

static QTextStream cout(stdout);

Person::Person(QString name, QObject* parent)
        : QObject(parent) {
    setObjectName(name);
    cout << QString("Constructing Person: %1").arg(name)
        << endl;
}

Person::~Person() {
    cout << QString("Destroying Person: %1").arg(objectName())
        << endl;
}
```

`growBunch()`, shown in Example 8.4, creates some objects, adds them to other objects, and then exits. All its local objects get destroyed when `growBunch()` returns.

---

[6] This example is based on an American TV sitcom that originally aired from 1969 to 1974 and was in syndication for decades after that. If you were born too late to view it, you can get a bit of the flavor of it from this Wikipedia article (http://en.wikipedia.org/wiki/The_Brady_Bunch).

EXAMPLE 8.4   src/qobject/bunch.cpp

```
[ . . . . . ]
void growBunch() {
    qDebug() << "First we create a bunch of objects." << endl;
    QObject bunch;
    bunch.setObjectName("A Stack Object");                       1
    /* other objects are created on the heap */
    Person* mike = new Person("Mike", &bunch);
    Person* carol = new Person("Carol", &bunch);
    new Person("Greg", mike);                                    2
    new Person("Peter", mike);
    new Person("Bobby", mike);
    new Person("Marcia", carol);
    new Person("Jan", carol);
    new Person("Cindy", carol);
    new Person("Alice");                                         3
    qDebug() << "\nDisplay the list using QObject::dumpObjectTree()"
             << endl;
    bunch.dumpObjectTree();                                      4
    cout << "\nReady to return from growBunch() -"
         << " Destroy all local stack objects." << endl;
int main(int , char**) {
    growBunch();
    cout << "We have now returned from growBunch()."
         << "\nWhat happened to Alice?" << endl;
    return 0;
}
[ . . . . . ]
```

1 A local stack object—not a pointer

2 We do not need to keep pointers to children, because we can reach them via object navigation.

3 Alice has no parent—memory leak?

4 `dumpObjectTree()` output will appear on the screen only if the Qt library has been compiled with the debugging option turned on.

Following is the output of this program.

```
src/qobject> ./qobject
First we create a bunch of objects.
Constructing Person: Mike
Constructing Person: Carol
Constructing Person: Greg
```

```
Constructing Person: Peter
Constructing Person: Bobby
Constructing Person: Marcia
Constructing Person: Jan
Constructing Person: Cindy
Constructing Person: Alice

Display the list using QObject::dumpObjectTree()
QObject::A Stack Object
    QObject::Mike
        QObject::Greg
        QObject::Peter
        QObject::Bobby
    QObject::Carol
        QObject::Marcia
        QObject::Jan
        QObject::Cindy

Ready to return from growBunch() - Destroy all local stack objects.
Destroying Person: Mike
Destroying Person: Greg
Destroying Person: Peter
Destroying Person: Bobby
Destroying Person: Carol
Destroying Person: Marcia
Destroying Person: Jan
Destroying Person: Cindy
We have now returned from growBunch().
There is no way to access Alice.
src/qobject>
```

8.2.2.1   Exercises: QObject's Child Managment

1. In Example 8.4, what local stack objects were destroyed when `growBunch()` returned?

2. Notice that Alice does not appear in the `dumpObjectTree()` output. When does Alice get destroyed?

3. Write your own function

   ```
   void showTree(QObject* theparent)
   ```

   to `main.cpp`. The output of this function, after all objects have been created, should look like this:

```
Member: Mike - Parent: A Stack Object
Member: Greg - Parent: Mike
Member: Peter - Parent: Mike
Member: Bobby - Parent: Mike
Member: Carol - Parent: A Stack Object
Member: Marcia - Parent: Carol
Member: Jan - Parent: Carol
Member: Cindy - Parent: Carol
```

4. Modify your `showTree()` function so that it produces the same output as `dumpObjectTree()`.

8.3   `QApplication` and the Event Loop

Interactive Qt applications with GUI have a different control flow from console applications and filter applications.[7] This is because they are event-based. In such applications, objects frequently send messages to one another through an intermediate object. This can make a linear hand-trace through the code rather difficult.

Observer Pattern

When writing event-driven programs, GUI views need to respond to changes in the state of data model objects so that they can display the most current information.

When any data model object changes state, it needs an *indirect* way to alert (and perhaps send additional information to) observers. Observers are objects that are listening for (and responding to) state-change events. The design pattern that enables such a message-passing mechanism is called the **Observer pattern** (sometimes also known as the **publish-subscribe pattern**).

There are many different implementations of this pattern. Some common characteristics that tie them together are

1. They all enable concrete subject classes to be decoupled from concrete observer classes.

2. They all support broadcast-style (one to many) communication.

3. The mechanism used to send information from subjects to observers is completely specified in the subject's base class.

---

[7] A filter application is not interactive. It simply reads from standard input and writes to standard output.

The Qt class `QEvent` encapsulates the notion of a low-level event. It is the base class for several specific event classes such as `QActionEvent`, `QFileOpenEvent`, `QHoverEvent`, `QInputEvent`, `QMouseEvent`, and so forth. `QEvent` objects can be created by the window system in response to an action of the user (e.g., a `QMouseEvent`), at specified time intervals (`QTimerEvent`), or explicitly by an application program. The `type()` member function returns an `enum` that has nearly a hundred specific values to identify the particular kind of event (e.g., Close, DragEnter, DragMove, Drop, Enter, GrabMouse, HoverEnter, KeyPress, MouseButtonDblClick, MouseMove, Resize, and so on).

An **event loop** is a program structure that permits events to be prioritized, enqueued, and dispatched to objects. Writing an event-based application means implementing a **passive interface** of functions that get called in response to things such as mouse clicks, touch pad gestures, key clicks, signals being emitted, window manager events, or messages from other programs. The event loop generally continues running until a terminating event. (For example, the user invokes a `Quit` action, the last window is closed, and so on.)

A typical Qt program creates objects, connects them, and then tells the application to `exec()`. At that point, the application enters the **event loop**. The objects can then send information to each other in a variety of ways. A typical `main()` function looks like this:

```
int main(int argc, char ** argv) {
  QApplication app(argc, argv);
  FancyWidget fwidg;
  fwidg.show();        // returns immediately
  return app.exec();   // enters event loop
}
```

The call to the `QApplication::exec()` function occurs in the `return` statement at the end of `main()`. The entire active part of the application begins with that function call and ends when it returns. The details are in the definition and implementation of the `FancyWidget` class. That is quite typical of Qt event loop applications.

Events Versus Signals and Slots

Events can be thought of as low-level messages, targeted with one specific object. Signals can be thought of as higher-level messages, possibly connected to many slots. Signals can only be delivered to slots when in an event loop, typically entered via `QApplication::exec()`. This is because signals and slots use the event loop under the covers when passing messages.

8.4   `Q_OBJECT` and moc: A checklist

`QObject` supports features not normally available in C++ objects:

- Signals and Slots (Section 8.5)
- MetaObjects, MetaProperties, MetaMethods (Chapter 12, "Meta Objects, Properties, and Reflective Programming")
- `qobject_cast` (Section 12.2)

Some of these features are only possible through the use of generated code. The Meta Object Compiler, moc, generates additional functions for each `QObject`-derived class that uses the `Q_OBJECT` macro. Generated code can be found in files with names `moc_filename.cpp`.

This means that some errors from the compiler/linker may be confuscated[8] when moc cannot find or process a class in the project. To help ensure that moc processes each `QObject`-derived class in the project, following are some guidelines for writing C++ code and qmake project files:

- Each `class` definition should go in its own `.h` file.
- Its implementation should go in a corresponding `.cpp` file.
- The header file should be "wrapped" (e.g., with `#ifndef`) to avoid multiple inclusion.
- Each `.cpp` file should be listed in the SOURCES variable of the project file; otherwise it will not be compiled.
- Each header file should be listed in the HEADERS variable of the `.pro` file. Without this, moc will not preprocess the file.
- The `Q_OBJECT` macro must appear inside the `class` definition of each `QObject` derived header file so that moc knows to generate code for it.

NOTE

Because each `Q_OBJECT` macro generates code, it needs to be preprocessed by moc. moc works under the assumption that you are only deriving from `QObject` once and, further, that `QObject` is the first base class in the list of base classes. If you accidentally inherit from `QObject` more than once, or if it is not the first base class in the inheritance list, you may produce strange errors in the moc-generated code.

---

[8] confusing + obfuscated

> **NOTE**
>
> If you define a QObject-derived class, build an application, realize that you need to add the Q_OBJECT macro to the class definition, and add it after the project was built with an old Makefile, you must then rerun qmake to update the Makefile.

make is not smart enough to add the moc step on such files to your Makefile otherwise. A "clean rebuild" does not fix this problem usually. This is an issue that often causes headaches for inexperienced Qt developers. For more information about this error message, see Section C.3.1.

8.5 Signals and Slots

A **signal** is a message presented in a class definition like a void function declaration. It has a parameter list but no function body. A signal is part of the interface of a class. It looks like a function, but it is not invoked the same way—it is *emitted* by an object of that class.

A **slot** is usually a void member function. It can be called as a normal member function, or it can be invoked indirectly by the QMetaObject system.

A signal of one object can be connected to the slots of one or more objects, provided the objects exist and the parameter lists are assignment compatible from the signal to the slot.[9] The syntax of the connect statement is

```
bool QObject::connect(senderQObjectPtr,
                SIGNAL(signalName(argumentList)),
                receiverQObjectPointer,
                SLOT[10](slotName(argumentList))
                optionalConnectionType);
```

Any QObject that has a signal can emit that signal. This produces indirect calls to all connected slots.

Arguments passed in the emit statement are accessible as parameters in the slot function, similar to a direct function call. The argument list is a way to transmit information from one object to another. The optionalConnectionType enables you to

---

[9] When the lists are assignment compatible, this means that corresponding parameters must be compatible. In Qt, the slot must have at least as many paramaters as the signal. The slot can ignore extra arguments.

[10] or SIGNAL–It is possible to connect one signal to another signal.

specify if you want synchronous (blocking) or asynchronous (queued) calls to the destination slots from the `emit` point.[11]

In Section 1.11, we discussed an example that employed a `QInputDialog` widget (Figure 8.5). When running that application, the user interacts with the first dialog by entering a value and then left-clicking on either the Cancel or the OK button.

FIGURE 8.5   QInputDialog

The left mouse button release event, which is the final step in a mouse-click, causes the chosen button widget to emit the `clicked()` signal. That signal is the culmination of a sequence of lower-level mouse events that pinpoint the location of the mouse pointer (inside the button's rectangle) and verify the correct order of mouse button operations. (For example, the left mouse button was pressed and then released while still inside the rectangle.) In other words, mouse events have been combined to form a `clicked()` signal. The API of a well-designed widget should contain an adequate set of signals so that it is not necessary to work with low-level events unless you develop a custom widget.

✄ TIP

If you have multiple signals connected to the same slot and need to know which `QObject` emitted the signal, you can call `sender()` from inside the slot, and it returns a pointer to that object.

8.5.1   Points of Departure

There are other open source implementations of signals and slots, similar to the Qt `QObject` model. One is called XLObject[12] which, in contrast to Qt, does not require

---

[11] Connection is not restricted to the current thread (Section 17.2).

[12] http://sourceforge.net/projects/xlobject

any moc-style preprocessing but instead relies heavily on templates, so it is supported only by modern (post-2002) C++ compilers. The Boost library[13] also contains an implementation of signals and slots.

8.6   QObject **Lifecycle**

In this section, we have a few best practices for managing QObject lifecycle.

CAUTION

It is important to ensure that every QObject you construct is created after the QApplication and destroyed before the QApplication is destroyed. Objects created in static storage are destroyed after main() has returned, which is too late. This means you should *never* define static storage-class QObjects.

Stack or Heap?

In general, a QObject without a parent should be created on the stack or defined as an subobject of another class. A QObject with a parent should *not* be on the stack because then it might get deleted twice accidentally. All QObjects created on the heap should either have a parent or be managed somehow by another object.

TIP

It is not recommended to delete QObjects directly. In a program with an event loop, it is better to use QObject::deleteLater(). This schedules the object to be destroyed when the application is processing events, after your current slot returns.

This is actually required from slots where you may wish to delete the sender() of a signal (Example 17.20).

8.7   QTestLib

The most common way to write testing code is to organize it in a **unit-based framework**. Qt 4 introduced the QTestLib framework of helper-macros and test runners to facilitate the writing of unit tests for applications and libraries that use Qt. All public

---

[13] http://www.boost.org

methods in this framework are in the `QTest` namespace. The next examples use this framework.

A **Test Class** is a class derived from `QObject`, with some private slots for one or more test functions. A test case is a sequence of test functions to be executed. Each test case must be in its own project with a source module that contains a `QTEST_MAIN()` macro. `QTEST_MAIN()` specifies which class is the entry point of this test. It expands to a `main()` function that creates an instance and executes its private slots in order of declaration. Additional methods for initialization and cleanup can be supplied, `initTestCase()` and `cleanupTestCase()` respectively, which get called at the begining and end of the test case.

To demonstrate the use of QTestLib, we write a test for `QCOMPARE` and `QVERIFY`, two macros that are used to make assertions inside Qt test cases. These macros can be used only in test classes, whereas `Q_ASSERT` can be used anywhere. On failures of assertions, they provide more information than `Q_ASSERT`.

Any project that uses the QTestLib module must enable it in the `.pro` file with this line:

```
CONFIG += qtestlib
```

The first step, as shown in Example 8.5, is to define a `QObject` derived class that contains the test functions. It is necessary to include the `QtTest` header and to declare the test functions as `private slots`.

EXAMPLE 8.5   src/libs/tests/assert/testassertequals.h

```
[ . . . . . ]

#include <QtTest>

class TestAssertEquals:public QObject {
    Q_OBJECT
private slots:
    void test ();
};

[ . . . . . ]
```

This test tries out all the various verify expression types. Example 8.6 is the part of the implementation that deals with `bool` expressions.

EXAMPLE 8.6   src/libs/tests/assert/testassertequals.cpp

```
[ . . . . ]

void TestAssertEquals::test () {
    qDebug() << "Testing bools";
    bool boolvalue = true;
    QVERIFY (1);
    QVERIFY (true);
    QVERIFY (boolvalue);
    qDebug () << QString ("We are in file: %1  Line: %2").
            arg (__FILE__).arg (__LINE__);
    QCOMPARE (boolvalue, true);          1
```

1 Test EQUALS with boolean values.

Example 8.7 is the part of the implementation that deals with QString expressions.

EXAMPLE 8.7   src/libs/tests/assert/testassertequals.cpp

```
[ . . . . ]

    qDebug() << "Testing QStrings";
    QString string1 = "apples";                                1
    QString string2 = "oranges";
    QString string3 = "apples";
    QCOMPARE ("apples", "apples");                             2
    QCOMPARE (string1, QString("apples"));
    QCOMPARE (QString("oranges"), string2);
    QCOMPARE (string1, string3);
    QVERIFY (string2 != string3);
```

1 Test EQUALS with string values.
2 Test for char* comparisons with QStrings.

Example 8.8 deals with QDate and QVariant expressions. Normally, the test() function stops at the first failure, which occurs when QVERIFY(condition) encounters a false condition or QCOMPARE(actual, expected) encounters a mismatch between *actual* and *expected*. So, we have deliberately included a QCOMPARE() failure in Example 8.8. To enable the test to continue, we have preceded the deliberate failure with a QEXPECT_FAIL() macro.

EXAMPLE 8.8   src/libs/tests/assert/testassertequals.cpp

```
[ . . . . . ]

    qDebug() << "Testing QDates";
    QString datestr ("2010-11-21");
    QDate dateobj = QDate::fromString (datestr, Qt::ISODate);
    QVERIFY (dateobj.isValid ());
    QVariant variant (dateobj);
    QString message(QString ("comparing datestr: %1 dateobj: %2 variant: %3")
            .arg (datestr).arg (dateobj.toString ()).arg (variant.toString ()));
    qDebug() << message;
    QCOMPARE (variant, QVariant(dateobj));                                    1
    QCOMPARE (QVariant(dateobj), variant);
    QCOMPARE (variant.toString(), datestr);                                   2
    QCOMPARE (datestr, variant.toString());
    QEXPECT_FAIL("","Keep going!", Continue);
    QCOMPARE (datestr, dateobj.toString());                                   3
```

1 Comparing QDates to QVariants

2 QVariants with Strings

3 QDates and QStrings

Example 8.9 deals with expressions containing int, long, and double items. We have inserted two QVERIFY() failures in Example 8.9. We precede the first with a QEXPECT_FAIL() macro. We allow the second failure to stop the test. Note the QTEST_MAIN macro below the function definition, which generates code for an appropriate main() function.

EXAMPLE 8.9   src/libs/tests/assert/testassertequals.cpp

```
[ . . . . . ]

    qDebug() << "Testing ints and doubles";
    int i = 4;                                                               1
    QCOMPARE (4, i);
    uint u (LONG_MAX + 1), v (u / 2);
    QCOMPARE (u, v * 2);
    double d (2. / 3.), e (d / 2);
    QVERIFY (d != e);
    QVERIFY (d == e*2);
    double f(1./3.);
    QEXPECT_FAIL("","Keep going!", Continue);
```

```
    QVERIFY (f * 3 == 2);
    qDebug() << "Testing pointers";
    void *nullpointer = 0;
    void *nonnullpointer = &d;
    QVERIFY (nullpointer != 0);
    qDebug() << "There is one more item left in the test.";
    QVERIFY (nonnullpointer != 0);
}


// Generate a main program
QTEST_MAIN(TestAssertEquals)
```

1 Integer Tests

Example 8.10 shows the output of this test. Note that you do not see the output of the last qDebug() message.

EXAMPLE 8.10   src/libs/tests/assert/testassert.txt

```
********* Start testing of TestAssertEquals *********
Config: Using QTest library 4.6.2, Qt 4.6.2
PASS    : TestAssertEquals::initTestCase()
QDEBUG  : TestAssertEquals::test() Testing bools
QDEBUG  : TestAssertEquals::test() "We are in file:
testassertequals.cpp  Line: 15"
QDEBUG  : TestAssertEquals::test() Testing QStrings
QDEBUG  : TestAssertEquals::test() Testing QDates
QDEBUG  : TestAssertEquals::test() "comparing datestr: 2010-11-21
dateobj: Sun Nov 21 2010 variant: 2010-11-21"
XFAIL   : TestAssertEquals::test() Keep going!
   Loc: [testassertequals.cpp(46)]
QDEBUG  : TestAssertEquals::test() Testing ints and doubles
XFAIL   : TestAssertEquals::test() Keep going!
   Loc: [testassertequals.cpp(59)]
QDEBUG  : TestAssertEquals::test() Testing pointers
FAIL!   : TestAssertEquals::test() 'nullpointer != 0' returned FALSE.
()
   Loc: [testassertequals.cpp(63)]
PASS    : TestAssertEquals::cleanupTestCase()
Totals: 2 passed, 1 failed, 0 skipped
********* Finished testing of TestAssertEquals *********
```

8.8   Exercises: QObject, QApplication, **Signals, and Slots**

1. Rewrite the Contact and ContactList from Section 4.4 so that they both derive from QObject.

   When a Contact is to be added to a ContactList, make the Contact the child of the ContactList.

2. Port the client code you wrote for the exercise to use the new versions of Contact and ContactList.

8.9   Review Questions

1. What does it mean when QObject A is the parent of QObject B?
2. Which QObjects do not need a parent?
3. What happens to a QObject when it is reparented?
4. Why is the copy constructor of QObject not public?
5. What is the composite pattern?
6. How can QObject be both composite and component?
7. How can you access the children of a QObject?
8. What is an event loop? How is it initiated?
9. What is a signal? How do you call one?
10. What is a slot? How do you call one?
11. How are signals and slots connected?
12. In the case where multiple signals are connected to the same slot, how can you determine the QObject that emitted the signal?
13. How can information be transmitted from one object to another?
14. Deriving a class from QObject more than once can cause problems. How might that happen accidentally?
15. What is the difference between value types and object types? Give examples.

Chapter 9

Widgets and Designer

This chapter provides an overview of the graphical user interface (GUI) building blocks in the Qt library, called **widgets**, and includes some simple examples of how to use them. We use QtCreator and Designer to explore the widgets and their features and to integrate forms with user code.

A **widget** is an object of a class derived from QWidget that has a visual representation on the screen. The structural origins of QWidget are shown in Figure 9.1.

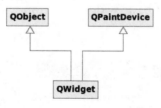

FIGURE 9.1   QWidget's Heritage

QWidget is a class that uses multiple inheritance (Section 22.3). A QWidget *is a* QObject, and thus can have a parent, signals, slots, and managed children. A QWidget *is a* QPaintDevice, the base class of all objects that can be "painted" on the screen.

`QWidgets` interact with their children in interesting ways. A widget that has no parent is called a **window**. If one widget is a parent of another widget, the boundaries of the child widget lie completely within the boundaries of the parent.[1] The contained child widget is displayed according to layout rules (Section 9.6 later in this chapter).

A `QWidget` can handle events by responding to messages from various entities in the window system (e.g., mouse, keyboard, timers, other processes, etc.). It can paint its own rectangular image on the screen. It can remove itself from the screen in a way that respects whatever else is on the screen at the moment.

A typical desktop GUI application can contain many (hundreds is not unusual) different `QWidget`-derived objects, deployed according to parent-child relationships and arranged according to the specifications of the applicable layouts.

`QWidget` is considered to be the simplest of all GUI classes because it is rendered as an empty box. The class itself, however, is quite complex, containing hundreds of functions. When you reuse `QWidget` and its subclasses, you stand on the shoulders of giants because every `QWidget` is built on top of layers of Qt code, which in turn are built on top of *different* layers of native widget libraries, depending on your platform (X11 in Linux, Cocoa on MacOS, and Win32 in Windows).

9.1   Widget Categories

Qt widgets can be categorized in a number of ways to make it easier to find classes you are likely to use. The more complex widgets may cross over into more than one category. This section provides a brief overview of some of the classes you are likely to use as you start GUI programming.

There are four categories of basic widgets. Button widgets, in "Windows style," are shown in Figure 9.2.

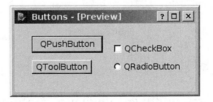

FIGURE 9.2   Buttons

---

[1] There are some exceptions to this rule. For example, a floating `QDockWidget` or `QDialog` can lie outside the boundaries of the parent widget but still be "in front" of it. Section 10.2 discusses QDocWidgets.

Input widgets, in "Plastique style," are shown in Figure 9.3.

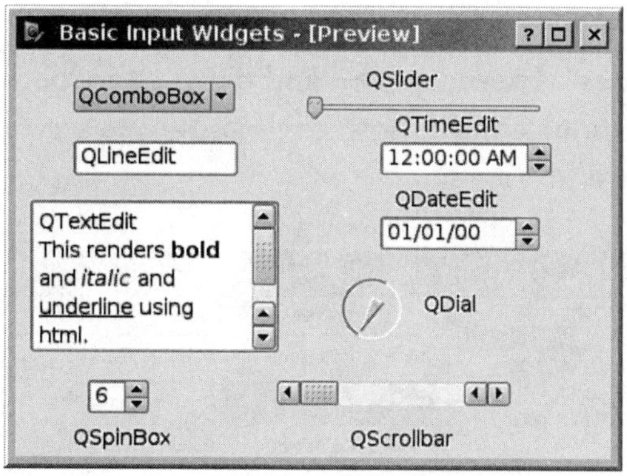

FIGURE 9.3   Input Widgets

Display widgets are noninteractive, such as QLabel, QProgressBar, and QPixmap.

Container widgets, such as the QMainWindow, QFrame, QToolBar, QTabWidget, and QStackedWidget, contain other widgets.

The widgets just described are used as building blocks to create other more complex widgets, such as

- Dialogs for asking the user questions or popping up information, such as the QFileDialog, QInputDialog, and QErrorMessage
- Views that provide displays of collections of data such as QListView, QTreeView, QColumnView, and QTableView, all four of which are shown in Figure 9.4

In addition, there are some Qt classes that do not have graphical representation (so they are not widgets) but are used in GUI development. They include

- **Qt Data types**—QPoint, QSize, QColor, QImage, and QPixMap are used when working with graphical objects.
- **Layouts**—These are objects that dynamically manage the layout of widgets. There are specific layout varieties: QHBoxLayout, QVBoxLayout, QGridLayout, QFormLayout, and so on.
- **Models**—The QAbstractItemModel and various derived classes such as QAbstractListModel and QAbstractTableModel, plus ready-made concrete derived classes such as QSqlQueryModel and QFileSystemModel, are part of Qt's

model/view framework that has built-in mechanisms for linking a model with various views so that changes to one component are automatically transmitted to the others.

- **Controller classes**—QApplication and QAction are both objects that manage the GUI application's control flow. QItemDelegate serves as a controller between Models and Views.

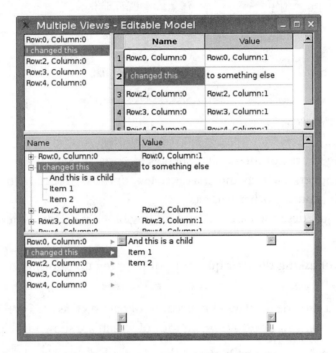

FIGURE 9.4   Four Views of One Model

To see more widgets rendered in different styles, check out The Qt Widget Gallery,[2] which contains a variety of screenshots and source code for rendering the widgets in different styles.

9.2   Designer Introduction

Designer is a graphical program for composing and editing the GUI for an application. It has a drag-and-drop interface and a complete set of features that can save lots of

---

[2] http://doc.trolltech.com/4.6/gallery.html

programming time and effort. The output of a Designer session is an XML file named `classname.ui`, where `classname` is normally specified at the beginning of the Designer session.

In QtCreator, Designer has been included as an embedded "design mode" that is invoked whenever a `.ui` file opens. Designer can also run as an embedded application inside other Integrated Development Environments (IDEs) for which an appropriate Qt integration package exists (e.g., Eclipse, Microsoft Developer Studio, Xcode).

A `classname.ui` file can describe a Designer widget with children, layout, and internal connections. The XML file is translated into a C++ header file, as explained in Section 9.7, but this section is about the use of Designer to compose a GUI.

You can drag widgets from the Widget Box into the central widget, the Widget Editor. After you have some widgets, you can select any of them in the Object Inspector and see its properties in the Property Editor, as shown in Figure 9.5.

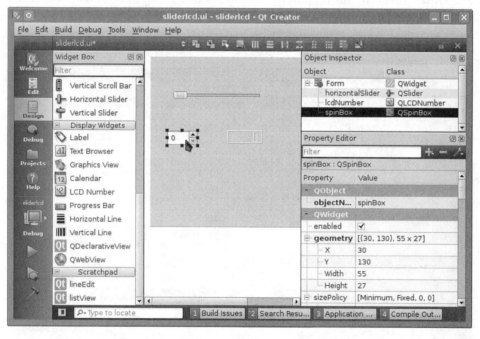

FIGURE 9.5   QtCreator in Design Mode

In the Property Editor, you can change any of the properties, and that change will cause a corresponding change in the `classname.ui` file. If the property edit changes the appearance of the widget, you can see the change immediately in the Widget Editor.

When you drag widgets from the Widget Box to the Widget Editor, Designer gives them rather uninspired and uninformative names that you can change easily.

> **NOTE**
>
> Most objects can be renamed from the Widget Editor or the Object Inspector, by either selecting the widget with a single left-click and then pressing F2, or by double-clicking on the widget. If you prefer, you can set the `objectName` from the Property Editor. Later, it will be important that the input widgets have sensible names because those will also be the data member names of the class generated by the User Interface Compiler (uic).

You can drag and drop connections between widgets by switching into Edit Signals/Slots (F4), as shown in Figure 9.6. When you enter Edit Signals/Slots mode, the Widget Box is disabled and you can drag a connection from the widget with a signal to the widget with a slot (in the Widget Editor).

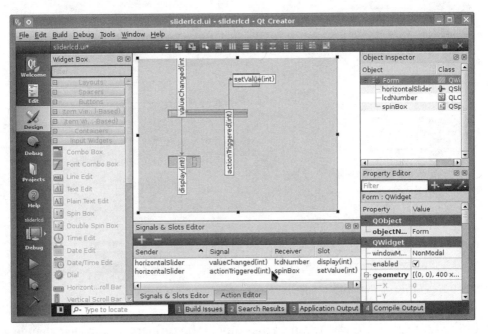

FIGURE 9.6   Designer Edit Signals/Slots Mode

When you release the mouse button, a Configure Connection dialog pops up, as shown in Figure 9.7. It first shows a list of signals in the left panel and, when one is selected, the compatible slots display in the right panel. When you select a slot and click the OK button, the connection details immediately appear in the Signal/Slot Editor.

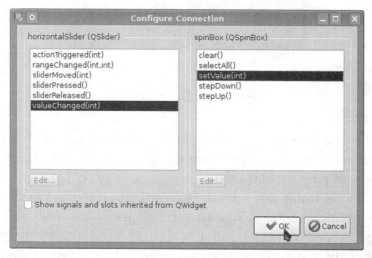

FIGURE 9.7   Configure Connection

When you finish forming new connections, you can get back into Edit Widgets by pressing F3. You can always view or edit existing connections with the Signal/Slot Editor dockable (shown near the bottom of Figure 9.6) regardless of whether the widget editor is in widget editing mode, connection mode, or buddy editing mode. You can preview the dynamic behavior of the connections you just formed with Preview Widget (Ctrl+Alt+R), as shown in Figure 9.8.

Even though no code has been written at this point, you can preview the dynamic behavior of your newly created ui file immediately with Designer. Section 9.7 describes how to integrate your ui file with your own (data handling) class.

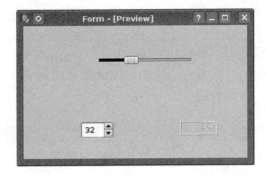

FIGURE 9.8   Widget Preview

9.3   Dialogs

QDialog is the base class for Qt dialogs. Dialog windows are mostly used for brief interactions with the user. A dialog window can be modal or nonmodal. Modal dialogs pop up when your program calls a static QMessageBox:: or QFileDialog:: convenience function. While the dialog box is on the screen, input is blocked to all other visible windows in the same application. Normal interactions with the application can resume when the user dismisses the modal dialog box. QDialog::exec() is another way to put a modal dialog on the screen. When the user completes the required response, the dialog can return data (e.g., a string or number) and/or a dialog code (QDialog::Accepted or QDialog::Rejected).

You can show() a QDialog like any QWidget. In this case, it is nonmodal, and the user can still interact with other windows of the application. Example 9.1 shows the difference between a modal dialog and and a nonmodal one that is popped up with show().

EXAMPLE 9.1   src/widgets/dialogs/modal/main.cpp

```
[ . . . . ]
#include <QtGui>
int main (int argc, char* argv[]) {
    QApplication app(argc, argv);
    QProgressDialog nonModal;
    nonModal.setWindowTitle("Non Modal Parent Dialog");
    nonModal.show();                                              1
    nonModal.connect(&nonModal, SIGNAL(finished()),
        &app, SLOT(quit()));                                      2
[ . . . . ]
```

```
QFileDialog fileDialog(&nonModal, "Modal File Child Dialog");
// 2 modal dialogs. exec() takes over all user interactions until closed.
fileDialog.exec();                                                    3
QMessageBox::question(0, QObject::tr("Modal parentless Dialog"),
        QObject::tr("can you interact with the other dialogs now?"),
        QMessageBox::Yes | QMessageBox::No);
return app.exec();                                                    4
}
[ . . . . ]
```

1 Returns immediately

2 Termination condition

3 Similar to entering an event loop; returns when window closes.

4 Quits when nonModal closes

Parents and Children

A QDialog with a parent widget always appears in front of its parent. Clicking the parent also raises the dialog. For nonmodal dialogs, this helps you avoid accidentally hiding them behind the main window. Modal dialogs always appear on top of other widgets created from that application regardless of parentage.

Input Dialogs

There are a number of predefined input dialogs you can reuse. $QTDIR/examples/ dialogs/standarddialogs, shown in Figure 9.9, uses most of them.

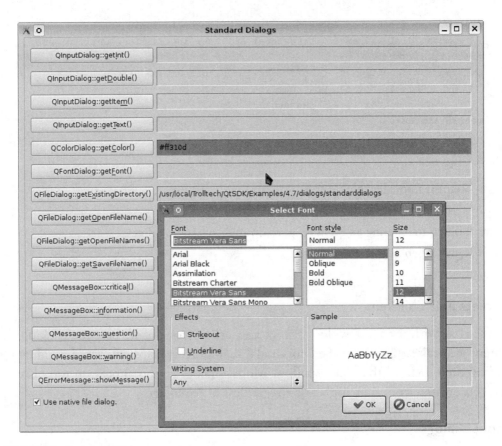

FIGURE 9.9   Standard Dialogs

9.4   Form Layout

Sometimes, you need to create your own dialogs with custom input fields. The dialog in Figure 9.10 shows a QFormLayout inside a QVBoxLayout. It gets a QString, QDate, and QColor from the user. You can use objects of type QLayout to organize widgets into grids, nested rows or columns, or forms.

The QFormLayout class is meant to simplify the creation of forms, manually or from Designer. It creates two columns: one for fixed-size labels and the other for variable-size input widgets. Following is the class definition for InputForm.

FIGURE 9.10 QFormLayout Example

EXAMPLE 9.2 src/layouts/form/inputform.h

```
#ifndef INPUTFORM_H
#define INPUTFORM_H

#include <QDialog>
class QLineEdit;
class QDateEdit;
class QPushButton;
class QDialogButtonBox;

class InputForm : public QDialog {
    Q_OBJECT
public:
    explicit InputForm(QWidget* parent = 0);
    void updateUi();
protected slots:
    void accept();
    void chooseColor();
private:
    QColor m_color;
    QLineEdit* m_name;
    QDateEdit* m_birthday;
    QPushButton* m_colorButton;
    QDialogButtonBox* m_buttons;
};

#endif // INPUTFORM_H
```

Example 9.3 displays some lines from the InputForm constructor. Each call to
addRow() adds an input widget and its corresponding QLabel to the layout in one line
of code. It is not necessary to explicitly construct the QLabels.

EXAMPLE 9.3   src/layouts/form/inputform.cpp

```
[ . . . . ]

    m_name = new QLineEdit;
    m_birthday = new QDateEdit;
    m_birthday->setDisplayFormat("dd/MM/yyyy");
    m_colorButton = new QPushButton(tr("Choose"));
    m_colorButton->setAutoFillBackground(true);

    m_buttons = new QDialogButtonBox(QDialogButtonBox::Ok |
                    QDialogButtonBox::Cancel);

    QVBoxLayout* vbox = new QVBoxLayout;
    QFormLayout* layout = new QFormLayout;

    layout->addRow(tr("Name"), m_name);                          1
    layout->addRow(tr("Birthdate"), m_birthday);
    layout->addRow(tr("Favorite Color"), m_colorButton);

    vbox->addLayout(layout);                                     2
    vbox->addWidget(m_buttons);

    Q_ASSERT(vbox->parent() == 0);
    Q_ASSERT(m_birthday->parent() == 0);
    setLayout(vbox);                                             3
    Q_ASSERT(vbox->parent() == this);
    Q_ASSERT(m_birthday->parent() == this);
```

1 Create/add a QLabel and the input widget in one line.

2 This is how we nest one layout in another.

3 Reparents previously laid-out widgets.

You can use a **QDialogButtonBox** for presenting the standard buttons to a user. This guarantees that they show up in the same order every time. It also makes it possible for the dialogs to show up in different places on different platforms, depending on the style and dimensions of the screen.

It was not necessary to set the parents of the various widgets in the form. They were all added to various layouts that form a component tree with vbox as the root. The call setLayout(vbox) sets the parent of vbox to the host InputForm object. It also reparents all QWidgets that were added to the various sublayouts of vbox to the parent of vbox (once again, the host InputForm). The Q_ASSERTs above and below that statement verify this.

9.5   Icons, Images, and Resources

You can use graphic images to add visual impact to an application. In this section, we show how to build an application or a library that includes graphic images in the project.

Qt enables projects to use binary resources, such as images, sounds, icons, text in some exotic font, and so forth. Resources such as these are generally stored on disk in separate binary files. The advantage of incorporating binary dependencies in the actual project is that they can then be addressed using paths that do not depend on the local file system and are deployed automatically with the executable.

Qt provides at least two ways to get standard icons. One is from the desktop style `QStyle::standardIcon()`, and another is from pluginable icon themes: `QIcon::fromTheme()`. But you might want to use additional icons from other sources.

The next examples show how to create and reuse a library that includes images—one for each card in a deck of playing cards.

The first step is to list the binary files you want to use in a **resource collection file**, an XML file that has the extension `.qrc`. A piece of the resource file in `libcards2` is shown here:

```
<!DOCTYPE RCC>
<RCC version="1.0"><qresource>
<file alias="images/qh.png">images/qh.png</file>
<file alias="images/qd.png">images/qd.png</file>
<file alias="images/jc.png">images/jc.png</file>
<file alias="images/js.png">images/js.png</file>
[...]
</qresource>
</RCC>
```

✒ Tip

Among other things, **QtCreator**, the Nokia open source Qt-based IDE, is an editor of qrc files, as shown in Figure 9.11. You can create new (or edit existing) resource files and add or modify resources using GUI forms and file choosers to ensure that they contain what you want.

Provided the `.qrc` file is added to your `.pro` file, and you are in QtCreator, you can access the resources from the `[...]` button in the property editor for any property that can be set to a resource.

---

qrc is an XML file format, used by QtCreator and rcc (Qt's resource compiler), that generally consists of a list of `<file>` elements enclosed by `<qresource>` tags. Each `<file>` element contains a relative path and an optional file alias.

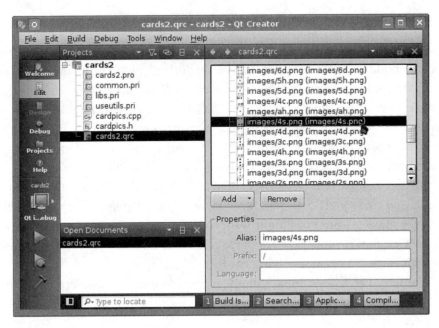

FIGURE 9.11 QtCreator Resource Editor

Add a RESOURCES line in the project file that contains the name of each qresource file, as shown in Example 9.4.

EXAMPLE 9.4 src/libs/cards2/cards2.pro

```
include (../libs.pri)

TEMPLATE = lib
QT += gui

# For locating the files.
RESOURCES = cards2.qrc
SOURCES += cardpics.cpp \
    card.cpp
HEADERS += cardpics.h \
    card.h \
    cards_export.h

win32 {
        DEFINES += CARDS_DLL
}
```

When this project is built, rcc generates an extra file named `cards2_qrc.cpp` that contains byte arrays defined in C++. This file is compiled and linked into the project binary (executable or library) instead of the original card image files. The DESTDIR line specifies that the shared object files for `libcards2` will be located in `$CPPLIBS` with the other libraries that you have built.

Attaching required binary data files to projects as resources makes the project more robust. The source code does not need to use nonportable pathnames for the resource files. To refer to a file that is stored as a resource, you can use the alias established in the `.rcc` file and precede it with the prefix `:/`. Each resource then appears (to Qt) to be located in a private virtual file system, rooted at `:/`. These benefits do come with a cost, however. The executable is larger, and the program requires more memory.

In `libcards2`, you have a class named `CardPics`, which provides `QImage`s of cards in a convenient way. Example 9.5 shows some images created with pathnames of this format.

EXAMPLE 9.5   src/libs/cards2/cardpics.cpp

```
[ . . . . ]
const QString CardPics::values="23456789tjqka";
const QString CardPics::suits="cdhs";

CardPics::CardPics(QObject* parent) : QObject(parent) {
    foreach (QChar suit, suits) {
        foreach (QChar value, values) {
            QString card = QString("%1%2").arg(value).arg(suit);
            QImage image(fileName(card));
            m_images[card]= image;
        }
    }
}

QString CardPics::fileName(QString card) {
    return QString(":/images/%1.png").arg(card);                    1
}
QImage CardPics::get(QString card) const {
    return m_images.value(card.toLower(), QImage());
}
[ . . . . ]
```

1 From resource

There are three Qt classes that facilitate the handling of images.

- `QImage`—Designed for off-screen manipulation, input and output operations, and direct pixel access
- `QPixmap`—Designed and optimized for drawing on the screen. Used only in the main thread
- `QIcon`—Designed for being cached in video memory and being used frequently, only in the main thread
- `QPicture`—Stores drawing operations rather than the actual bitmap image

In `libcards2`, each `QImage` is constructed in advance from a resource and added to `CardPics` for quick access with the `get()` function.

9.6   Layout of Widgets

A widget can be popped up on the screen, like a dialog, or it can be made a part of a larger window. Whenever you must want to arrange smaller widgets inside larger ones, you must use *layouts*. A **layout** is an object that belongs to (i.e., is a child of) exactly one widget. Its sole responsibility is to organize the space occupied by its owner's child widgets.

Although each widget has a `setGeometry()` function that enables you to set its size and position, absolute sizing and positioning are rarely used in a windowing application because they impose an undesirable rigidity on the design. Proportional resizing, splitters, scrollbars when needed, and flexible arrangement of visual space are achieved quite naturally through the use of layouts.

The process of specifying the way that your widgets display on the screen consists of dividing the screen into regions, each controlled by a `QLayout`. Layouts can arrange their widgets

- Vertically (`QVBoxLayout`)
- Horizontally (`QHBoxLayout`)
- In a grid (`QGridLayout`)
- In a form (`QFormLayout`)
- In a stack where only one widget is visible at any time (`QStackedLayout`)

Widgets are added to QLayouts using the addWidget() function. When a widget is added to a layout, it becomes the child of the widget that owns the layout. A widget can never be the child of a layout.

Layouts are not widgets and have no visual representation. Qt supplies an abstract base class named QLayout plus several QLayout subclasses: QBoxLayout (particularized to QHBoxLayout and QVBoxLayout), QGridLayout, and QStackedLayout. Each of the layout types has an appropriate set of functions to control the spacing, sizing, alignment, and access to its widgets.

For its geometry management to work, each QLayout object must have a parent that is either a QWidget or another QLayout. The parent of a QLayout can be specified when the layout is constructed by passing the constructor a pointer to the parent widget or layout. It is also possible to construct a QLayout without specifying its parent, in which case you can call QWidget::addLayout() at some later time.

Layouts can have child layouts. Layouts can be added as sublayouts to another by calling addLayout(). The exact signature depends on the kind of layout used. *If the parent of a layout is a widget, that widget cannot be the parent of any other layout.*

The CardTable class defined in Example 9.6 reuses libcards2, for easy access to QImages of playing cards (see Section 9.5). Constructing a CardTable object puts Figure 9.12 on the screen.

EXAMPLE 9.6   src/layouts/boxes/cardtable.h

```
#ifndef CARDTABLE_H
#define CARDTABLE_H
#include <cardpics.h>
#include <QWidget>

class CardTable : public QWidget {
  public:
    explicit CardTable(QWidget* parent=0);
  private:
    CardPics m_deck;
};

#endif        // #ifndef CARDTABLE_H
```

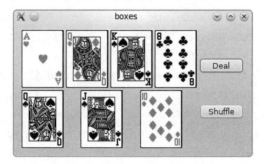

FIGURE 9.12   Rows and Columns

CardTable is implemented in Example 9.7 by constructing a QLabel for each image. This implementation demonstrates some simple but useful layout techniques.

EXAMPLE 9.7   src/layouts/boxes/cardtable.cpp
```
[ . . . . ]

CardTable::CardTable(QWidget* parent)
: QWidget(parent) {

    QHBoxLayout* row = new QHBoxLayout();                    1
    row->addWidget(new Card("ah"));                         2
    row->addWidget(new Card("qd"));
    row->addWidget(new Card("ks"));
    row->addWidget(new Card("8c"));

    QVBoxLayout* rows = new QVBoxLayout();                   3
    rows->addLayout(row);                                   4

    row = new QHBoxLayout();                                5
    row->addWidget(new Card("qs"));
    row->addWidget(new Card("js"));
    row->addWidget(new Card("td"));
    rows->addLayout(row);                                   6

    QVBoxLayout* buttons = new QVBoxLayout();               7
    buttons->addWidget(new QPushButton("Deal"));
    buttons->addWidget(new QPushButton("Shuffle"));
```

```
QHBoxLayout* cols = new QHBoxLayout();        8
setLayout(cols);                              9
cols->addLayout(rows);                       10
cols->addLayout(buttons);                    11
}
[ . . . . ]
```

1 First row.

2 Parents are set by layout, so we don't have to.

3 Lay out rows vertically.

4 Nest a row in the vertical layout.

5 Second row.

6 Nesting again.

7 A column for the buttons.

8 Bring them all together.

9 The "root layout" for this widget.

10 Add both card rows as a column.

11 Add column of buttons as another column.

The client code shown in Example 9.8 suffices to put the window on the screen.

EXAMPLE 9.8   src/layouts/boxes/boxes.cpp

```
#include <QApplication>
#include "cardtable.h"

int main(int argc, char* argv[]) {
        QApplication app (argc, argv);
        CardTable ct;
        ct.show();
        return app.exec();
}
```

If you build and run this example and use your mouse to resize the window, you notice that the width of the buttons stretches first to gobble up extra space. But there is also stretchable spacing between the cards and between the buttons. If you remove the buttons and resize, you can see that the horizontal spacing between the cards grows evenly and uniformly.

9.6.1   Spacing, Stretching, and Struts

Without using Designer, you can use the API of `QLayout` directly to specify spacers, stretches, and struts between widgets. Box layouts, for example, offer the following functions:

- `addSpacing(int size)` adds a fixed number of pixels to the end of the layout.
- `addStretch(int stretch = 0)` adds a stretchable number of pixels. It starts at a minimum amount and stretches to use all available space. In the event of multiple stretches in the same layout, this can be used as a growth factor.
- `addStrut(int size)` imposes a minimum size to the perpendicular dimension (i.e., the width of a `QVBoxLayout` or the height of an `QHBoxLayout`).

Revisiting Example 9.7, you can see how to make the layout behave a little better during resizing. Figure 9.13 shows the results of adding some stretch and some spacing to this application.

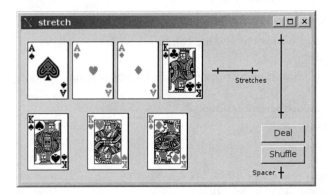

FIGURE 9.13   Improved Layout with Stretch and Spacing

Normally, layouts try to treat all widgets equally. When you want one widget to be off to a side or pushed away from another, you can use stretches and spacing to deviate from that norm. Example 9.9 demonstrates how to use stretches and spacing.

EXAMPLE 9.9   src/layouts/stretch/cardtable.cpp

```
[ . . . . . ]
    row = new QHBoxLayout();
    row->addWidget(new Card("td"));
    row->addWidget(new Card("js"));
```

```
    row->addWidget(new Card("kc"));
    rows->addLayout(row);
    rows->addStretch(1);                                      1
    QVBoxLayout* buttons = new QVBoxLayout();
    buttons->addStretch(1);                                   2
    buttons->addWidget(new QPushButton("Deal"));
    buttons->addWidget(new QPushButton("Shuffle"));
    buttons->addSpacing(20);                                  3
    QHBoxLayout* cols = new QHBoxLayout();
    setLayout(cols);
    cols->addLayout(rows);
    cols->addLayout(buttons);
    cols->addStretch(0);                                      4
}
[ . . . . ]
```

1 Stretchable space for rows.

2 Stretchable space before buttons in column.

3 Fixed spacing after buttons.

4 How does this affect the size of the buttons?

If you build and run this application using Example 9.9 instead of Example 9.7, you can resize the main window and observe that the buttons no longer grow and are pushed off to the corner. The horizontal spacing between the cards does not grow, but the vertical spacing does.

9.6.2   Size Policy and Size Hint

Each `QWidget` has several attributes that relate to its size on the screen. Some widgets can use extra space at runtime in one or both directions. You can control the default resizing behavior of your custom widget by setting its **sizePolicy** and **sizeHint**.

The `sizeHint` holds the recommended `QSize` for your widget; i.e., the size that it has when it first appears on the screen. A `QSize` defines the size of a widget by holding its width and height. There are several member functions that give you complete control of your widget's size at runtime, including `setMinimumSize()`, `setMaximumSize()`, `setMinimumHeight()`, `setMaximumWidth()`, `setSizeHint()`, etc.

Each `QWidget` and `QLayout` can have a horizontal and a vertical `QSizePolicy`. The size policies `Minimum`, `Maximum`, `Fixed`, `Preferred`, `Expanding`, `MinimumExpanding`, and `Ignore` express the willingness of the widget or layout to be resized. The default policy is `Preferred/Preferred`, which indicates that the `sizeHint` has the preferred size for the widget. `Ignore` indicates that `minimumHeight` and `minimumWidth` do not constrain resizing operations.

Widgets that display something fixed in size would not benefit from extra space given to a resized widget. Therefore, they should have Fixed or Preferred horizontal and vertical size policies. In contrast, scrollable widgets, container widgets, and text editing widgets should have an expanding size policy, so they can display more information to the user, because this is why the user probably made the widget bigger in the first place. Extra space is given or taken from the widgets that have a flexible size policy.

Widgets in the same layout, with expanding policies, are given extra space at a different rate from others, based on stretch factor.

In Figure 9.14, you can see that pushbuttons normally do not eat up extra space in either dimension. On the first two rows, some buttons have a horizontal expanding size policy. The second row demonstrates how stretch factors can affect the expanding buttons. On the third row, you can see that one button eats up all the extra vertical space and forces the first two rows as high up as possible.

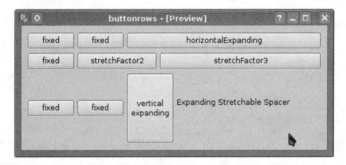

FIGURE 9.14   Stretchy Buttons

9.6.3   Exercises: Layout of Widgets

1. In Designer, try to reproduce a layout of buttons resembling that in Figure 9.14.

2. The 15 puzzle (or n^2-1 puzzle) involves a 4×4 (*nxn*) grid that contains 15 tiles numbered 1 to 15 (1 to n^2-1) and one empty space. The only tiles that can move are those next to the empty space.

- Create a 15 puzzle with QPushButtons in a `QGridLayout`, as shown in Figure 9.15.

- At the start of the game, the tiles are presented to the player in "random" order. The object of the game is to rearrange them so that they are in ascending order, with the lowest numbered tile in the upper-left corner.

- If the player solves the puzzle, pop up a `QMessageBox` saying "YOU WIN!" (or something more clever).

- Add some buttons:
    - **Shuffle**—Randomize the tiles by performing a large number (at least 50) of legal tile-slides.
    - **Quit**—Terminate the game.

FIGURE 9.15   Sample 15 Puzzle

⚔ TIP

To avoid connecting a signal to a slot for each button, you can group the buttons in a `QButtonGroup`, which has a 1-argument signal for `QAbstractButton`.

⚔ TIP

Start with classes shown in Figure 9.16, and try to partition your code properly into them. The "view" classes should deal with GUI, while the "model" classes should have no `QWidget` code or dependency at all and deal only with the logic of the game.

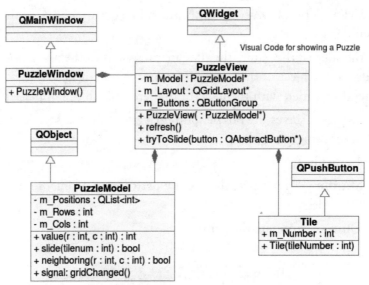

FIGURE 9.16   Model-View-Controller Design for Puzzle

9.7   Designer Integration with Code

Consider the ProductForm, a form for Product instances, shown in Figure 9.17.

FIGURE 9.17   Product Form

QFormLayout is a convenience widget that facilitates organizing QLabel and input widgets in a two-column format.

The `ProductForm` widget can accept data from the user for a new `Product` object. It can be used to display (read-only) or edit the values of a stored `Product` instance. The buttons can have text and roles that depend upon the usage mode. For example, in response to the user adding a new Product, the OK should result in the values in the form being used to create a new `Product` instance. If instead the user clicks Cancel, the values would be discarded. In edit mode, when the user clicks OK, the values in the form would replace the values in the already stored instance. In info mode, when the user clicks OK, the form should dismiss, and the Cancel button should be hidden.

While it is used, the `ProductForm` has a reference to the `Product` it is editing, as shown in Figure 9.18.

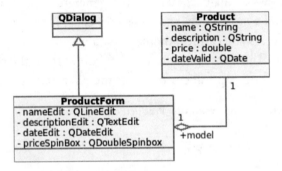

FIGURE 9.18   Product and Its Form

Using Designer to Design the Form

The first step is to pick a base classname (e.g., `ProductForm`) and write a header (`ProductForm.h`) and implementation file (`ProductForm.cpp`) for it, as usual. Next, create a form in Designer with the same base name (`ProductForm.ui`). Setting the `objectName` for the root object of this form (`ProductForm`) then enables `uic` to generate a header file for a corresponding Ui class (`Ui_ProductForm`).

Figure 9.19 shows how `uic` takes as input the special XML file with a `.ui` extension produced by Designer and generates a header file that you can include in your code.

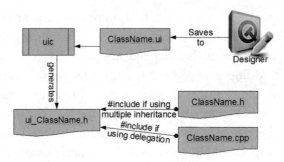

FIGURE 9.19   Designer to Code

Example 9.10 shows a small segment of the generated code. It defines both a `Ui_ProductForm` class and a `Ui::ProductForm` derived class. It is your choice which one to use in your C++ code. As you can see, there is a data member that points to each widget in the Designer form. The **name** of each member comes from the object name as set in the Designer form, giving you full control over member names in generated code.

EXAMPLE 9.10   src/designer/productform/ui_ProductForm.h

```
[ . . . . ]
class Ui_ProductForm
{
public:
    QVBoxLayout *verticalLayout;
    QFormLayout *formLayout;
    QLabel *label;
    QDoubleSpinBox *priceSpinbox;
    QLabel *label_2;
    QLabel *label_3;
    QLineEdit *nameLineEdit;
    QLabel *label_4;
    QTextEdit *descriptionEdit;
    QDateEdit *dateEdit;
    QSpacerItem *verticalSpacer;
    QDialogButtonBox *buttonBox;

    void setupUi(QDialog *ProductForm)
[ . . . . ]
};
namespace Ui {
    class ProductForm: public Ui_ProductForm {};
} // namespace Ui
[ . . . . ]
```

What Is a Ui Class?

A Ui class is a class that contains only auto-generated code produced by the `uic` tool. It can be used as a base class or as a data member of the custom form. Its members are initialized from the `setupUi()` method.

NOTE

Designer initially connects a couple of signals from the `QDialogButtonBox` to the `QDialog` `accept()` and `reject()` slots. You can see this from the Signals and Slots Editor dockable. What this means is that as long as the underlying `Product` object is not changed until OK is pressed, the `reject()` base class behavior closes the dialog, as you probably want. You still might want to override `accept()`, but you do not need to connect a button's signal to it. The base class version also closes the dialog.

Approaches to Integration

Following are three approaches to integration of a Ui class with a custom `QWidget`-based form class.

1. Aggregation as a pointer member
2. Multiple (private) Inheritance
3. Aggregation as an embedded object

Aggregation by pointer is the recommended (and default) approach because it makes it possible to change the Ui file without causing binary breakage with the `ProductForm` header file. Example 9.11 shows aggregation by pointer member. `ProductForm.h` uses a forward class declaration instead of including the `Ui_ProductForm.h` directly.

EXAMPLE 9.11   src/designer/delegation/productform.h

```
[ . . . . ]
#include <QDialog>
class Product;
class Ui_ProductForm;
class QWidget;
class QAbstractButton;
class ProductForm : public QDialog {
        Q_OBJECT
public:
```

```
    explicit ProductForm(Product* product = 0, QWidget* parent=0); 1
    void setModel(Product* model);

public slots:
    void accept();
    void commit();
    void update();

private:
    Ui_ProductForm *m_ui;
    Product* m_model;
};
[ . . . . . ]
```

1 Mark explicit to avoid implicit conversions between pointers!

Only the implementation file, shown in Example 9.12, depends on the uic-generated header file. This makes it easier to place this class into a library, for example.

EXAMPLE 9.12 src/designer/delegation/productform.cpp

```
#include <QtGui>
#include "productform.h"
#include "ui_ProductForm.h"
#include "product.h"

ProductForm::ProductForm(Product* product, QWidget* parent)
: QDialog(parent), m_ui(new Ui::ProductForm),  m_model(product) {
    m_ui->setupUi(this);                                              1
    update();
}

void ProductForm::setModel(Product* p) {
    m_model =p;
}

void ProductForm::accept() {
    commit();
    QDialog::accept();                                               2
}
```

```
void ProductForm::commit() {
    if (m_model == 0) return;
    qDebug() << "commit()";
    m_model->setName(m_ui->nameLineEdit->text());
    QTextDocument* doc = m_ui->descriptionEdit->document();
    m_model->setDescription(doc->toPlainText());
    m_model->setDateAdded(m_ui->dateEdit->date());
    m_model->setPrice(m_ui->priceSpinbox->value());
}

void ProductForm::update() {
    if (m_model ==0) return;
    qDebug() << "update()";
    m_ui->nameLineEdit->setText(m_model->name());
    m_ui->priceSpinbox->setValue(m_model->price());
    m_ui->dateEdit->setDate(m_model->dateAdded());
    m_ui->descriptionEdit->setText(m_model->description());
}
```

1 Populate the Ui object with valid instances with properties set from values in the .ui file.

2 Closes the dialog.

9.7.1   QtCreator Integration with Designer

QtCreator integrates Designer with an IDE in a convenient way, generating the integration code and function bodies of slots for you, for classes where it understands the correspondence between the Ui file and its class files. You can create new `.ui` files, header files, and corresponding `.cpp` files all at once, from QtCreator's **File -> New -> Qt -> Designer Form Class**. Figure 9.20 shows you the three styles of code generation that it supports.

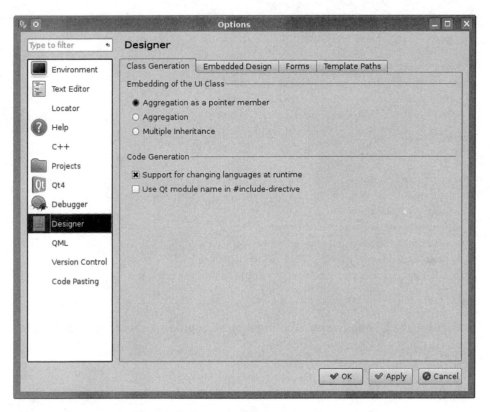

FIGURE 9.20   QtCreator Designer Code Generation Options

For child objects that need to connect to one another (e.g., GUI components of a `QMainWindow`), QtCreator has a nice convenience feature, shown in Figure 9.21. You can right-click on any signal-emitting component in the Widget editor (e.g., the Save pushbutton) or any action in the Action Editor (e.g., actionSave), and select Go to slot. Next, select a signal from the list that pops up (e.g., `triggered()`). QtCreator generates a private slot for you—a prototype in the header file and a stub in the implementation file—if you do not already have one with the name that is generated (e.g., `on_actionOpen_triggered()`). You can complete the definition of the new slot by adding the necessary operational details. The signal you select is automatically connected to that newly defined slot at runtime. You will not find the `connect` statement in the implementation (`.cpp`) file. Instead, the connections are made by the `QMetaObject::connectSlotsByName()` function.

FIGURE 9.21   QtCreator: Go to Slot

Section 10.5 discusses an application written entirely in QtCreator using these tools.

9.8   Exercise: Input Forms

1. Implement the missing methods from the `OrderForm` class to construct an input dialog form for Order objects. A starting point is provided in `src/handouts/forms/manual`. The dialog should look something like Figure 9.22.

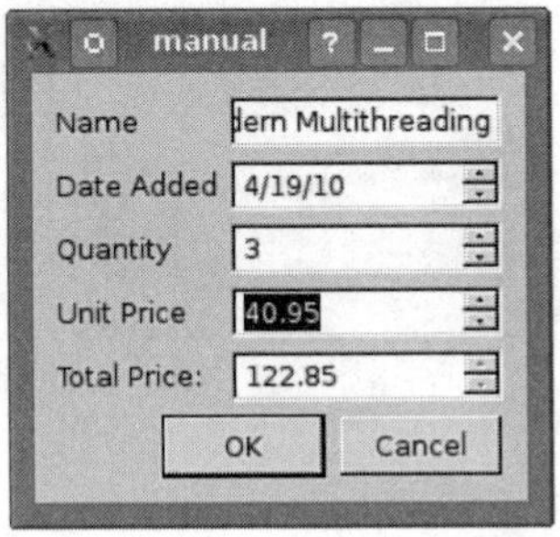

FIGURE 9.22   Order Form Dialog

The code goes in `orderform.cpp`.

The user should click OK to send data into the Order, or Cancel to dismiss the dialog and do nothing to the Order.

The `totalPrice` field should be read-only and calculated based on the quantity and unitPrice.

2. Next, use Designer to create the same input dialog, and integrate it with your code using either delegation or multiple inheritance, as described in Section 9.7.

9.9   The Event Loop: Revisited

In Section 8.3, we introduced `QApplication` and the event loop. Now that you have had some experience with GUI programming, you are ready to look at events in more detail.

`QWidgets` send `QEvents` to other `QObjects` in response to user actions such as mouse events and keyboard events. A widget can also respond to events from the window manager such as repaints, resizes, or close events. Events are **posted** (i.e., added to the **event queue**) and can be filtered and prioritized. Furthermore, it is possible to post a custom event directly to any `QObject` or selectively respond to events that were posted to other objects. You can delegate the handling of an event to a specially defined *handler* object.

Each `QWidget` can be specialized to respond to keyboard and mouse events in its own way. Figure 9.23 is a screenshot of a `QWidget` named `KeySequenceLabel` that captures a `QKeySequence` and displays it for the user.

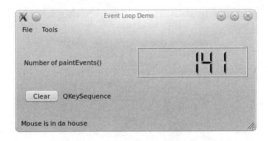

FIGURE 9.23   KeySequenceLabel Widget

In Example 9.13, you can see from the names of the private slots that QtCreator was used to compose the GUI. Also, we chose the Multiple Inheritance option for embedding the Ui class, so the `KeySequenceLabel` class is derived from `QMainWindow` and from the designer-generated Ui class.

EXAMPLE 9.13   src/eventloop/keysequencelabel.h

```
[ . . . . . ]
#include "ui_keysequencelabel.h"
#include <QList>
#include <QPair>
class QObjectBrowserAction;

class KeySequenceLabel : public QMainWindow, private Ui::KeySequenceLabel {
    Q_OBJECT
 public:
    explicit KeySequenceLabel(QWidget* parent = 0);
 protected:                                                      1
    void changeEvent(QEvent* e);
    void keyPressEvent(QKeyEvent*);
    void leaveEvent(QEvent*);
    void enterEvent(QEvent*);
    void paintEvent(QPaintEvent*);
    void timerEvent(QTimerEvent*);                              2
    void updateUi();
 private slots:
    void on_actionShow_ObjectBrowser_triggered(bool checked);
    void on_m_clearButton_clicked();
    void on_actionQuit_triggered();
 private:
    QObjectBrowserAction* m_browserAction;
    QList<QPair<int, int> > m_keys;
    int m_paints;
};
[ . . . . . ]
```

1 `QWidget` event handler overrides

2 `QObject` event handler override

The implementation of this class contains some interesting items.

There is a `QLabel` in the dialog used for display of a `QKeySequence`. The `QKeySequence` class encapsulates a sequence of up to four keystrokes, typically used as shortcuts to invoke QActions. The base class keyPressEvent() handler is overridden in the KeySequenceLabel widget. In Example 9.14, you can see that it catches the keystrokes and saves them to a list before the child widgets see them. In updateUi(), those events convert to a QKeySequence and then to a QString, which is sent to the QLabel for display via setText().

EXAMPLE 9.14   src/eventloop/keysequencelabel.cpp

```
[ . . . . ]

void KeySequenceLabel::keyPressEvent(QKeyEvent* evt) {
    bool doNothing = false;

    if (evt->key() == 0) doNothing = true;
    if (m_keys.size() > 3) doNothing = true;
    if (doNothing) {
        QMainWindow::keyPressEvent(evt);                              1
        return;
    }
    QPair<int, int> pair = QPair<int, int>(evt->modifiers(), evt->key());
    m_keys << pair;
    evt->accept();
    updateUi();
}

void KeySequenceLabel::updateUi() {
    if (!m_keys.isEmpty()) {
        int keys[4] = {0,0,0,0};
        for (int i=0; i<m_keys.size(); ++i) {
            QPair<int, int> pair = m_keys[i];
            keys[i] = pair.first | pair.second;
        }
        QKeySequence seq = QKeySequence(keys[0], keys[1], keys[2], keys[3]);
        m_label->setText(seq.toString());
    }
    else m_label->clear();
}
```

1 QWidget's base class handler responds to ESC for pop-up windows.

We defined mouse event handlers, shown in Example 9.15, that tell you when the mouse pointer enters or leaves the widget.

EXAMPLE 9.15   src/eventloop/keysequencelabel.cpp

```
[ . . . . ]

void KeySequenceLabel::enterEvent(QEvent* evt) {

    statusBar()->showMessage(tr("Mouse is in da house"));
    evt->accept();

}

void KeySequenceLabel::leaveEvent(QEvent* evt) {
    statusBar()->showMessage(tr("Mouse has left the building"));
    evt->accept();
}
```

In Example 9.16, the constructor uses the `QObject` built-in timer and calls `QObject::startTimer()`, which generates a timer event every 2 seconds. You can handle the `timerEvent()` by updating a `QLCDNumber`, once every 2 seconds, with the number of paint events that have been performed so far. For example, whenever the value of the LCDNumber changes, this indirectly causes the widget to repaint. You can run this app and try moving and resizing the widget to see how it effects the number of paint events.

EXAMPLE 9.16   src/eventloop/keysequencelabel.cpp

```
[ . . . . ]

KeySequenceLabel::KeySequenceLabel(QWidget* parent) :
    QMainWindow(parent), m_browserAction(new QObjectBrowserAction(this)) {

    setupUi(this);
    startTimer(2000);                                              1
    m_paints = 0;
}

void KeySequenceLabel::timerEvent(QTimerEvent*) {
    m_lcdNumber->display(m_paints);
}

void KeySequenceLabel::paintEvent(QPaintEvent* evt) {
    ++m_paints;
    QMainWindow::paintEvent(evt);
}
```

1 A timer event occurs every 2 seconds.

All of the GUI activity discussed so far was accomplished with events and event handlers. There is one more interesting feature of this example that we now discuss.

From the Tools menu you can select Show ObjectBrowser and see the widget in Figure 9.24.

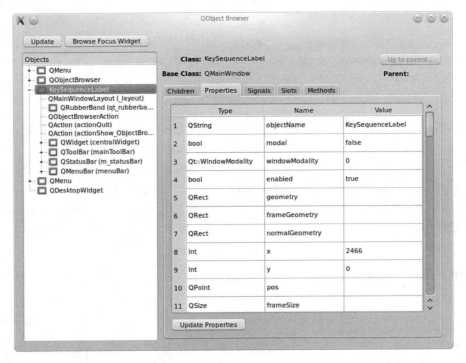

FIGURE 9.24   QObjectBrowser Widget

QObjectBrowser is an open source debugging tool that gives a graphic display of properties, signals, and slots of a QObject tree during the execution of a program.[3] One easy way to use it is by adding the QObjectBrowserAction directly to the QMainWindow's menu.

We have included a slightly modified version of this tool in src/libs.

---

[3] Contributed by Jeremy Magland, you can follow the development of this utility from its initial posting and see some community suggestions and the author's responses at http://tinyurl.com/2a6qkpy.

Custom Events Versus Signals and Slots

In general, you can think of signals as higher-level messages from objects, with semantics, whereas events are lower-level messages from the user or the system. Both mechanisms implement the Publish/Subscribe Pattern.

It's possible to define custom events or custom signals and slots. With custom events, you can publish to any `QObject` with `QObject::postEvent()` and subscribe to events intended for any `QObject` with `installEventFilter()`. Perhaps you are wondering which mechanism to use if you need to transmit a custom message.

In most situations, if you have a choice, a signal-slot connection is preferable to a custom `QEvent` because signals and slots are safer, higher-level, and more flexible mechanisms for message passing. Signals and slots are more flexible because the `emit` statement does not need a destination object, and the signal can be destined for multiple slots.

Signals and Slots also depend on an event loop, something you notice immediately if you try to connect signals from an object in one thread to slots of objects created in another thread. Signals can be transmitted (in a blocking or a nonblocking way) to slots within the same thread or in another thread (with its own event loop).

9.9.1   QTimer

Section 9.9 shows an example that uses the `QObject` built-in timer. Qt also has the class `QTimer`, which provides a high-level interface for timers. A `QTimer` object is a countdown timer started with a time interval in milliseconds. When it reaches zero, it emits a `timeout()` signal.

A `QTimer` can be used to emit a `timeout()` signal at regular intervals or, if the `singleShot` property has been set to `true`, to emit a signal only once after a specified `interval`. `QTimer` has a static `singleShot()` function that calls a slot once after a given time interval. If the countdown interval is set to zero, the `QTimer` emits its `timeout()` signal as soon as all the events in the event queue have been processed.

The following example uses `QTimer` to write an application for training the user to read faster. The designers of this approach also claimed that it increases the user's reading comprehension. The idea is to briefly display a sequence of character strings, one at a time, and let the user try to type each string as soon as it is no longer visible. The user specifies the string length and the exposure time. The program compares the displayed string with the typed string and keeps score in some appropriate way. The user gradually increases the string length and decreases the exposure times to build a kind of strength in this realm which, presumably, translates into an enhanced ability to read text.

This application is relatively simple, as can be seen from the UML diagram in Figure 9.25.

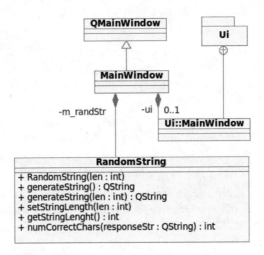

FIGURE 9.25   Speed-reader UML

The class definition of MainWindow is shown in Example 9.17. You can see that several of its slots use naming conventions that enable `QMetaObject::connectSlotsByName` `(MainWindow)` to work properly. Those names were generated by QtCreator based on this convention—which is why you see no `connect` statements for them in the code.

EXAMPLE 9.17   src/timer/speed-reader/mainwindow.h

```
[ . . . . ]
class MainWindow : public QMainWindow {
    Q_OBJECT
public:
    explicit MainWindow(QWidget* parent = 0);
    ~MainWindow();
protected:
    void changeEvent(QEvent* e);
    void processTrial();
private:
    Ui::MainWindow* ui;
private slots:
    void on_nextButton_clicked();
    void on_responseString_returnPressed();
```

```
        void on_startButton_clicked();
        void on_lengthSlider_valueChanged(int value);
        void on_exposureSlider_valueChanged(int value);
        void timerDisplayRandStr();
private:
        int m_expInterval;
        RandomString m_randStr;
        int m_trials;
        int m_correctChars;
        int m_totTrials;
        int m_totCorrectChars;
};
[ . . . . ]
```

This application uses the static QTimer function singleShot() to control the expo-sure time for each random string. singleShot() sends a timeout() signal to the slot timerDisplayRandStr() after the slider-selected time interval elapses. processTrial(), shown in Example 9.18 shows how the connection is made without an explicit connect statement.

EXAMPLE 9.18   src/timer/speed-reader/mainwindow.cpp

```
[ . . . . ]
void MainWindow::processTrial() {
    //clear response text editor
    ui->responseString->setText("");
    //display the random string
    ui->targetString->setText(m_randStr.generateString());
    ui->responseString->setEnabled(false);
    ui->nextButton->setEnabled(false);
    //count the number of trials
    m_trials++;
    m_totTrials++;
    ui->nextButton->setText(QString("String %1").arg(m_trials));
    //begin exposure
    QTimer::singleShot(m_expInterval, this, SLOT(timerDisplayRandStr()));
}


void MainWindow::timerDisplayRandStr() {
    ui->targetString->setText(QString(""));
    //enable the response line editor and next button
    ui->responseString->setEnabled(true);
```

```
    ui->responseString->setFocus();
    ui->nextButton->setEnabled(true);
}


[ . . . . ]
```

Figure 9.26 is a screenshot of the running program after the exposure time and string length have been selected.

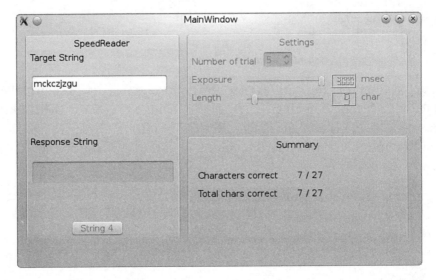

FIGURE 9.26   Speed Reader Screenshot

9.9.1.1   Exercises: QTimer

1. Modify the speed-reader application (beginning with Example 9.17) so that the amount of time for typing in the response string is limited to an amount specified by the user. You need to add another input widget to the user interface.

2. Give the user the option of working with words in some language instead of random strings of characters. For this problem, feel free to use the file src/handouts/canadian-english-small, which contains words from a peculiar dialect of English. You can download the src tarball from our [dist] directory. How can you control the string length for these words?

9.10   Paint Events, Drawing Images

A widget should perform the appropriate painting inside its `paintEvent()` method. This is the *only* place where a `QWidget` can create a `QPainter(this)`.

As you may have observed, a `QPaintEvent` can be sent to a `QWidget` for a number of reasons:

1. Widget is hidden and then exposed.
2. Widget is resized or re-laid out.
3. `update()` or `repaint()` is called.

Example 9.19, defines a custom `QWidget` that overrides `paintEvent()`.

EXAMPLE 9.19   src/widgets/life/lifewidget.h

```
[ . . . . ]
class LifeWidget : public QWidget
{
    Q_OBJECT
public:
    explicit LifeWidget(QWidget* parent = 0);
    ~LifeWidget();
    QSize sizeHint() const;
    void paintEvent(QPaintEvent* evt);                              1
public slots:
    void setImage(const QImage& image);
private:
    QImage m_image;
    QSize m_size;
};
[ . . . . ]
```

1 Custom paint event

Steps to get a `QPainter` for a `QWidget`:

1. Create a `QPainter(this)`.
2. Use the `QPainter` API to draw on `QWidget`.

Example 9.20 shows a `paintEvent()` that takes an off-screen `QImage` and paints it directly onto the `QWidget`.

EXAMPLE 9.20   src/widgets/life/lifewidget.cpp

```
[ . . . . ]

void LifeWidget::paintEvent(QPaintEvent* evt) {
    QPainter painter(this);                                        1
    if (!m_image.isNull())
        painter.drawImage(QPoint(0,0), m_image);
}
```

1 First line of most `paintEvents`.

This program paints successive generations of population maps based on the rules described in Conway's Game of Life.[4] Figure 9.27 shows a snapshot of one generation. We revisit this game when we parallelize it in Section 17.2.3.

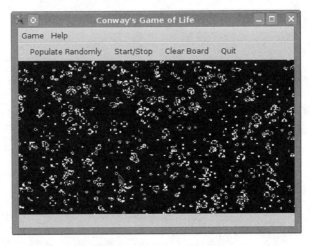

FIGURE 9.27   Conway's Game of Life

Normally, `paintEvent()` is not called directly, but you can schedule it to be called, synchronously or asynchronously. `repaint()` does not return until `paintEvent()` has been called. `update()` returns immediately after a `QPaintEvent` is placed on the event queue. Example 9.21 scales the image to the correct size and saves it, before calling `update()`, ensuring that `LifeWidget` shows the new image sometime soon.

---

[4] http://en.wikipedia.org/wiki/Conway%27s_Game_of_Life

EXAMPLE 9.21 src/widgets/life/lifewidget.cpp

```
[ . . . . ]

void LifeWidget::setImage(const QImage& image) {
    m_size = image.size();
    m_image = image.scaled(size());
    update();                                          1
}
```

1 Asynchronous—return immediately.

9.11 Review Questions

1. List six things that `QWidgets` have in common.

2. What is a dialog? Where is an appropriate place to use it?

3. What is a `QLayout`? What is its purpose? What is an example of a concrete `QLayout` class?

4. Can a widget be a child of a layout?

5. Can a layout be a child of a widget?

6. Can a layout be a child of another layout?

7. What are the advantages of listing your images in a resources file?

8. What is the difference between a spacer and a stretch?

Chapter 10

Main Windows and Actions

Most QApplications manage a single QMainWindow. As Figure 10.1 shows, the QMainWindow has some features that are common to most desktop applications:

- Central widget
- Menu bar
- Toolbars
- Status bar
- Dock regions

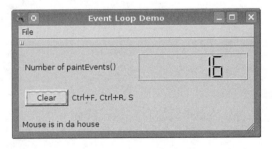

FIGURE 10.1   A Main Window

In most applications, the `QMainWindow` is the (grand)parent object of all `QAction`, `QWidget`, and `QObject` heap objects. It is common practice to extend that class for applications, as shown in Example 10.1.

EXAMPLE 10.1   src/widgets/mainwindow/mymainwindow.h

```
[ . . . . ]
class MyMainWindow : public QMainWindow {
    Q_OBJECT
 public:
    explicit MyMainWindow(QWidget* parent=0);
    void closeEvent(QCloseEvent* event);                    1

 protected slots:
    virtual void newFile();
    virtual void open();
    virtual bool save();
[ . . . . ]
```

1 Overridden from base class to capture when the user wants to close the window

10.1   QActions, QMenus, and QMenuBars

`QAction`, derived from `QObject`, is a base class for user-selected actions. It provides a rich interface that can be used for a variety of actions, as you soon see. The `QWidget` interface enables each widget to maintain a `QList<QAction*>`.

All `QWidgets` can have `QActions`. Some widgets provide the list of `QActions` via a context menu, others via menu bar. See `setContextMenuPolicy()` API docs for details on how to provide context menus from widgets.

A `QMenu` is a `QWidget` that provides a particular kind of view for a collection of `QActions`. A `QMenuBar` is a collection of menus, usually found in a `QMainWindow`.

When the parent of a `QMenu` is a `QMenuBar`, the `QMenu` appears as a pull-down menu with a familiar interface. When its parent is not a `QMenuBar` it can pop up, like a dialog, in which case it is considered a **context menu**.[1] A `QMenu` can have another `QMenu` as its parent, in which case it becomes a **submenu**.

---

[1] A context menu is usually activated by clicking the right mouse button or by pressing the menu button. It is called a context menu because the menu always depends on the context (which `QWidget` or item is currently selected or focused).

To help the user make the right choice, each `QAction` can have the following:

- Text and/or icon that appears on a menu and/or button
- An accelerator, or a shortcut key
- A "What's this?" and a tooltip
- A way to toggle the state of the action between visible/invisible, enabled/disabled, and checked/not checked
- `changed()`, `hovered()`, `toggled()`, and `triggered()` signals

The `QMainWindow` in Figure 10.2 has a single menu bar that contains a single menu that offers two choices.

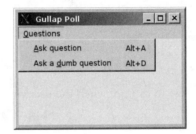

FIGURE 10.2 QMenu

Example 10.2 shows the code that sets up that menu bar. The function `QMainWindow::menuBar()` returns a pointer to the `QMenuBar`, which is a child of the `QMainWindow`. The `menuBar()` function creates and returns a pointer to an empty `QMenuBar` child if the menu bar does not already exist.

EXAMPLE 10.2 src/widgets/dialogs/messagebox/dialogs.cpp

```
[ . . . . ]

    /* Insert a menu into the menubar. */
    QMenu* menu = new QMenu(tr("&Questions"), this);

    QMainWindow::menuBar()->addMenu(menu);

    /* Add some choices to the menu. */
    menu->addAction(tr("&Ask question"),
                    this, SLOT(askQuestion()), tr("Alt+A"));
    menu->addAction(tr("Ask a &dumb question"),
                    this, SLOT(askDumbQuestion()), tr("Alt+D"));
}
```

Each call to `QMenu::addAction(text, target, slot, shortcut)` creates an unnamed `QAction` and adds it to the `QMenu`. It then calls its hidden base class function, `QWidget::addAction(QAction*)`, which adds the newly created `QAction` to the list of `QActions` of the `QMenu` for use in a context menu. The latter call adds the new action to the menu's `QList<QAction*>`.

10.1.1   QActions, QToolbars, and QActionGroups

Because an application might provide a variety of different ways for the user to issue the same command (e.g., menus, toolbar buttons, keyboard shortcuts), encapsulating each command as an *action* helps to ensure consistent, synchronized behavior across the application. `QAction` emits signals and connects to slots as needed.

In Qt GUI applications, actions are typically "triggered" in one of the following ways:

- A user clicks on a menu choice.
- A user presses a shortcut key.
- A user clicks on a toolbar button.

There are several overloaded forms of `QMenu::addAction()`. We use the version inherited from `QWidget`, `addAction(QAction*)`, in Example 10.3.

Here you can see how to add actions to menus, action groups, and toolbars. We started by deriving a class from `QMainWindow` and equipping it with several `QAction` members plus a `QActionGroup` and a `QToolBar`.

EXAMPLE 10.3   src/widgets/menus/study.h

```
[ . . . . . ]
class Study : public QMainWindow {
    Q_OBJECT
 public:
    explicit Study(QWidget* parent=0);
 public slots:
    void actionEvent(QAction* act);
 private:
    QActionGroup* actionGroup;                              1
    QToolBar* toolbar;                                      2

    QAction* useTheForce;
    QAction* useTheDarkSide;
    QAction* studyWithObiWan;
```

```
    QAction* studyWithYoda;
    QAction* studyWithEmperor;
    QAction* fightYoda;
    QAction* fightDarthVader;
    QAction* fightObiWan;
    QAction* fightEmperor;
protected:
    QAction* addChoice(QString name, QString text);


};
[ . . . . ]
```

1 For catching the signals

2 For displaying the actions as buttons

The constructor for this class sets up the menus and installs them in the QMenuBar that is already part of the base class, as you can see in Example 10.4.

EXAMPLE 10.4   src/widgets/menus/study.cpp

```
[ . . . . ]

Study::Study(QWidget* parent) : QMainWindow(parent) {
    actionGroup = new QActionGroup(this);
    actionGroup->setExclusive(false);
    statusBar();

    QWidget::setWindowTitle( "to become a jedi, you wish?  " );
                                                              1

    QMenu* useMenu = new QMenu("&Use", this);
    QMenu* studyMenu = new QMenu("&Study", this);
    QMenu* fightMenu = new QMenu("&Fight", this);

    useTheForce = addChoice("useTheForce", "Use The &Force");
    useTheForce->setStatusTip("This is the start of a journey...");
    useTheForce->setEnabled(true);
    useMenu->addAction(useTheForce);                          2
[ . . . . ]

    studyWithObiWan = addChoice("studyWithObiWan", "&Study With Obi Wan");
    studyMenu->addAction(studyWithObiWan);
    studyWithObiWan->setStatusTip("He will certainly open doors for you...");
```

```
fightObiWan = addChoice("fightObiWan", "Fight &Obi Wan");
fightMenu->addAction(fightObiWan);
fightObiWan->setStatusTip("You'll learn some tricks from him"
                          " that way for sure!");
[ . . . . ]

QMainWindow::menuBar()->addMenu(useMenu);
QMainWindow::menuBar()->addMenu(studyMenu);
QMainWindow::menuBar()->addMenu(fightMenu);

toolbar = new QToolBar("Choice ToolBar", this);          3
toolbar->addActions(actionGroup->actions());

QMainWindow::addToolBar(Qt::LeftToolBarArea, toolbar);


QObject::connect(actionGroup, SIGNAL(triggered(QAction*)),
        this, SLOT(actionEvent(QAction*)));              4

QWidget::move(300, 300);
QWidget::resize(300, 300);
}
```

1 Some of the `ClassName::` prefixes used here are not necessary, because the functions can be called on `this`. The class names can be used to explicitly call a baser-version, or show the reader which version is called.

2 It's already in a `QActionGroup`, but we also add it to a `QMenu`.

3 This gives us visible buttons in a dockable widget for each of the `QActions`.

4 Instead of connecting each action's signal, perform one connect to an `ActionGroup` that contains them all.

It is possible to connect individual `QAction triggered()` signals to individual slots. In Example 10.5, we group related `QActions` in a `QActionGroup`. If any member of this group is triggered, `QActionGroup` emits a single signal, `triggered(QAction*)`, which makes it possible to handle all those actions in a uniform way. The signal carries a pointer to the particular action that was triggered so that the appropriate response can be chosen.

EXAMPLE 10.5   src/widgets/menus/study.cpp

```
[ . . . . ]


// Factory function for creating QActions initialized in a uniform way
QAction* Study::addChoice(QString name, QString text) {
    QAction* retval = new QAction(text, this);
    retval->setObjectName(name);
    retval->setEnabled(false);
    retval->setCheckable(true);
    actionGroup->addAction(retval);                                1
    return retval;
}
```

1 Add every action to a QActionGroup so we need only one signal connected to one slot.

After being created, each QAction is added to three other objects (via addAction()):

1. A QActionGroup, for signal handling
2. A QMenu, one of three possible pull-down menus in a QMenuBar
3. A QToolBar, where it is rendered as a button

To make this example a bit more interesting, we established some logical dependencies between the menu choices to make them consistent with the plots of the various movies. This logic is expressed in the actionEvent() function shown in Example 10.6.

EXAMPLE 10.6   src/widgets/menus/study.cpp

```
[ . . . . ]

void Study::actionEvent(QAction* act) {
    QString name = act->objectName();
    QString msg = QString();

    if (act == useTheForce ) {
        studyWithObiWan->setEnabled(true);
        fightObiWan->setEnabled(true);
        useTheDarkSide->setEnabled(true);
    }
    if (act == useTheDarkSide) {
```

```
        studyWithYoda->setEnabled(false);
        fightYoda->setEnabled(true);
        studyWithEmperor->setEnabled(true);
        fightEmperor->setEnabled(true);
        fightDarthVader->setEnabled(true);
    }


    if (act == studyWithObiWan) {
        fightObiWan->setEnabled(true);
        fightDarthVader->setEnabled(true);
        studyWithYoda->setEnabled(true);
    }
[ . . . . ]

    if (act == fightObiWan ) {
        if (studyWithEmperor->isChecked()) {
            msg = "You are victorious!";
        }
        else {
            msg = "You lose.";
            act->setChecked(false);
            studyWithYoda->setEnabled(false);
        }
    }
[ . . . . ]

    if (msg != QString()) {
        QMessageBox::information(this, "Result", msg, "ok");
    }
}
```

Because all actions are in a `QActionGroup`, a single `triggered(QAction*)` results in a call to `actionEvent()`.

All menu choices except one are initially disabled. As the user selects from the available choices, other options become enabled or disabled, as shown in Figure 10.3. Notice that there is consistency between the buttons and the choices in the menus. Clicking an enabled button causes the corresponding menu item to be checked. `QAction` stores the state (enabled/checked), and the `QMenu` and `QToolBar` provide views of the `QAction`.

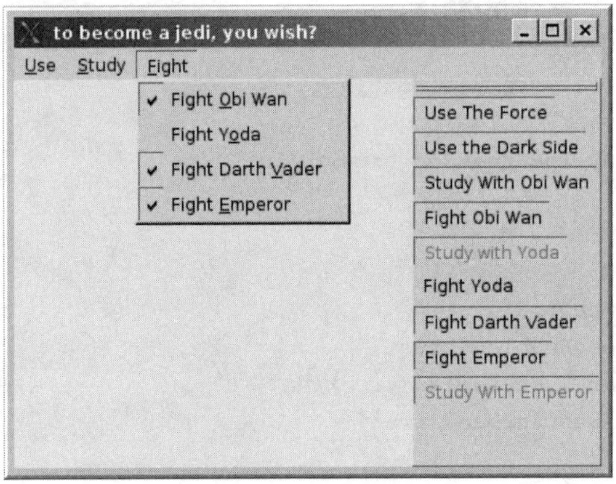

FIGURE 10.3   Checkable Actions in Menus and Toolbars

10.1.2   Exercise: CardGame GUI

Write a blackjack game, with the following actions:

- New game
- Deal new hand
- Shuffle deck
- Hit me—ask for another card
- Stay—evaluate my hand
- Quit—stop playing

These actions should be available via the menu bar as well as the toolbar, in a main window application like Figure 10.4. The rules of the game are explained next.

When the game starts, the user and the dealer are each dealt a "hand" of cards. Each hand initially consists of two cards. The user plays her hand first by deciding to add cards to her hand with the Hit Me action zero or more times. Each Hit adds one card to her hand. The user signals that she wants no more cards with the Stay action.

The object of the game is to achieve the highest point total that is not greater than 21.

For the purposes of evaluation of a hand, a "face card" (Jack, Queen, and King) counts as 10 points, and an Ace can count as 1 or 11 points, whichever is better. Each other card has a number and a point value equal to that number. If the hand consists of an Ace plus a Jack, then it is better to count the Ace as 11 so that the total score is

21. But if the hand consists of an 8 plus a 7, and an Ace is added to the hand, it is better to count the Ace as 1.

FIGURE 10.4 Blackjack Screenshot

If a player gets a point total greater than 21, that player is "busted" (loses) and the hand ends.

If a player gets five cards in her hand with a total that is not greater than 21, then that player wins the hand.

After the user either wins, loses, or Stays, the dealer can take as many hits as necessary to obtain a point total greater than 18. When that state is reached, the dealer must Stay and the hand ends. The player whose score is closer to, but not greater than, 21 wins. If the two scores are equal, the dealer wins.

When the hand is over, the user can select only Deal Hand, New Game, or Quit. (Hit Me and Stay are disabled.)

After the user selects `Deal Hand`, that choice should be disabled until the hand is finished.

Keep track of the number of games won by the dealer and by the user, starting with zero for each player, by adding one point to the total for the winner of each hand. Display these totals above the cards.

Deal more cards without resetting the deck until the deck becomes empty or the user chooses Shuffle Deck.

Try to reuse or extend the `CardDeck` and related classes that you developed earlier in Section 6.9.1. Add a graphical representation to your game by showing an image for each card, perhaps as shown in Section 9.5 and Section 9.6.

Provide a pull-down menu and a toolbar for each of the `QActions`. Make sure that Hit and Stay are enabled only after the game has started.

Show how many cards are left in the deck in a read-only `QSpinBox` at the top of the window.

A new game should zero the games won totals and reset the deck.

Design Suggestions

Try to keep the model classes separate from the view classes, rather than adding GUI code to the model classes. Keeping a strong separation between model and view is good programming style and makes your project easier to manage from start to finish.

Figure 10.5 shows one possible design for the solution.

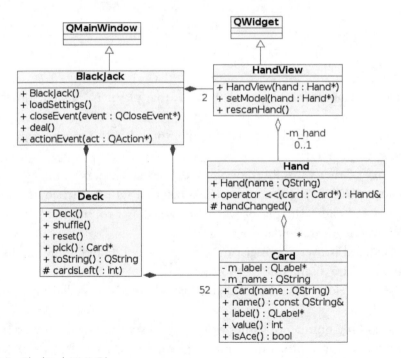

FIGURE 10.5   BlackJack UML Diagram

10.2 Regions and QDockWidgets

Any class that derives from QMainWindow has dock window regions, one on each of the four sides of the **central widget**, as shown in Figure 10.6. These regions are used for attaching secondary windows, also called **dock windows**, to the central widget.

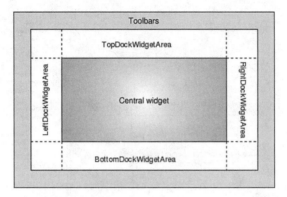

FIGURE 10.6 QMainWindow Regions

A QDockWidget can be thought of as an envelope for another widget. It has a title bar and a content area to contain the other widget. Depending on how its attributes are set, a QDockWidget can be undocked (so that it "floats"), resized, closed, dragged to a different location, or docked to the same or to a different dock widget region by the end user. It's okay to have several dockwidgets occupying the same dock region.

The QMainWindow correctly creates slidable QSplitters between the central widget and the QDockWidgets. The two principal QMainWindow functions for managing the dock widget regions are

1. setCentralWidget(QWidget*), which establishes the central widget
2. addDockWidget(Qt::DockWidgetAreas, QDockWidget*), which adds the given QDockWidget to the specified dock window region

Dock windows are important in integrated development environments because different tools or views are needed in different situations. Each dock window is a widget that can be "plugged" into the main window quite easily with the docking mechanism, as shown in Figure 10.7.

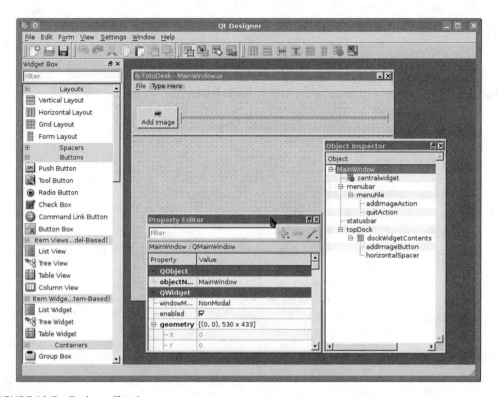

FIGURE 10.7   Designer Floating QDockWindows

Like most Qt applications, Designer, the tool for designing and building GUIs, makes heavy use of dock windows. Designer has a widget editor (central widget) and dockable views for tools such as

- Widget Box
- Object Inspector
- Property Editor
- Signal/Slot Editor
- Action Editor
- Resource Editor

These dockables do not all need to be visible at the same time, so there is a View menu that enables you to select or deselect them as needed. QMainWindow::createPop upMenu() returns this menu, permitting you to use it from context menus or add it to toolbars or to pull-down menus.

10.3   `QSettings`: **Saving and Restoring Application State**

Most desktop applications have a way for users to configure the settings. The settings/preferences/options need to be persistent. The mechanism for that is included with `QSettings`.

A `QSettings` must be initialized with an application name, organization name, and organization domain before it is used for the first time. This prevents settings from one application from accidentally overwriting those from another. If, however, the `QApplication` itself is set with this information, as shown in Example 10.7, the `QSettings` default constructor uses it.

EXAMPLE 10.7   src/widgets/mainwindow/mainwindow-main.cpp

```
#include "mymainwindow.h"
#include <QApplication>

int main( int argc, char ** argv ) {
    QApplication app( argc, argv );
    app.setOrganizationName("objectlearning");
    app.setOrganizationDomain("objectlearning.net");
    app.setApplicationName("mainwindow-test");
    MyMainWindow mw;
    mw.show();
    return app.exec();
}
```

Now that the `QApplication` is initialized, you can create `QSettings` instances using the default constructor.

As you develop a new `QMainWindow` application, the first persistent settings you may want to save are probably the window size and position. You may also want to save the names of the most recent documents that were opened by the application.

`QSettings` manages persistent maps of key/value pairs. It is a `QObject` and uses something similar to `QObject`'s property interface, `setValue()` and `value()`, to set and get its values. It can be used to store any data that needs to be remembered across multiple executions.

The `QSettings` needs an organization name and an application name, but when you use the default constructor, `QSettings` gets those values from the `QApplication`. Each combination of names defines a unique persistent map that does not clash with settings from other-named Qt applications.

Monostate Pattern

A class that enables multiple instances to share the same state is an implementation of the **Monostate pattern**. Two instances of QSettings with the same organization/application name can be used to access the same persistent map data. This makes it easy for applications to access common settings from different source files.

QSettings is an implementation of the Monostate pattern.

The actual mechanism for the persistent storage of QSettings data is implementation-dependent and quite flexible. Some possibilities for its storage include the Win32 registry (in Windows) and your $HOME/.settings directory (in Linux). For more detailed information, see the Qt QSettings API documentation.

QMainWindow::saveState() returns a QByteArray that contains information about the main window's toolbars and dockwidgets. Doing this uses the objectName property for each of those subwidgets, thus making it important that each name be unique. saveState() has an optional int versionNumber parameter. The QSettings object stores that QByteArray with the key string "state".

QMainWindow::restoreState() takes a QByteArray, presumably created by saveState(), and uses the information that it holds to put the toolbars and dockwidgets into a prior arrangement. It, too, has an optional versionNumber parameter. Read the settings after constructing the object, as shown in Example 10.8.

EXAMPLE 10.8   src/widgets/mainwindow/mymainwindow.cpp

```
[ . . . . ]

void MyMainWindow::readSettings() {
    QSettings settings;
    QPoint pos = settings.value("pos", QPoint(200, 200)).toPoint();
    QSize size = settings.value("size", QSize(400, 400)).toSize();
    QByteArray state = settings.value("state", QByteArray()).toByteArray();
    restoreState(state);
    resize(size);
    move(pos);
}
```

You should write settings after the user wants to quit but before the window is closed. The appropriate place for that is in an event handler, so that you can handle the event before the widget itself does. Example 10.9 shows an event handler for `closeEvent()` that saves this information to `QSettings`.

EXAMPLE 10.9   src/widgets/mainwindow/mymainwindow.cpp

```
[ . . . . . ]

void MyMainWindow::closeEvent(QCloseEvent* event) {
    if (maybeSave()) {
        writeSettings();
        event->accept();
    } else {
        event->ignore();
    }
}


void MyMainWindow::writeSettings() {
    /* Save postion/size of main window */
    QSettings settings;
    settings.setValue("pos", pos());
    settings.setValue("size", size());
    settings.setValue("state", saveState());
}
```

10.4   Clipboard and Data Transfer Operations

Sometimes it is necessary to take data from one place and "send" it to another. One way is clipboard "cut and paste," and another is "drag and drop." The data transfer classes used are the same for both.

Every Qt application has access to the system **clipboard** from `qApp->clipboard()`. The clipboard holds onto typed data (text, graphics, URLs, or custom data). To place data into the clipboard, you create a `QMimeData`, encode the data somehow, and call `QClipBoard->setMimeData()`.

- `setText()` to store text
- `setHtml()` to store rich text

- `setImageData()` for an image
- `setUrls()` for a list of URLs or filenames

In Example 10.10, we connect the system clipboard's `changed` signal to the `MainWindow` `clipboardChanged()` slot. That signal is emitted whenever any application copies something into the clipboard. You can run this example and see what data types are available when you copy data from the `QTextEdit` or from other applications.

EXAMPLE 10.10   src/clipboard/mainwindow.cpp

```
[ . . . . ]
MainWindow::MainWindow(QWidget* parent) :
    QMainWindow(parent),
    ui(new Ui::MainWindow)
{
    ui->setupUi(this);
    connect (qApp->clipboard(), SIGNAL(changed(QClipboard::Mode)),
            this, SLOT(clipboardChanged(QClipboard::Mode)));
}

void MainWindow::clipboardChanged(QClipboard::Mode) {
    QStringList sl;
    QClipboard *cb = qApp->clipboard();
    const QMimeData *md = cb->mimeData();
    sl << "Formats: " + md->formats().join(",");
    foreach (QString format, md->formats()) {
        QByteArray ba = md->data(format);
        sl << "    " + format + ": " + QString(ba);
    }
    ui->clipboardContentsEdit->setText(sl.join("\n"));
}
[ . . . . ]
```

Figure 10.8 shows what happens when text is copied from the `QTextEdit`. In this case, clipboard data is encoded in three ways: plain text, HTML, and an OASIS open-document format. You can choose which format to use depending on what kind of data you need in the paste or drop object.

FIGURE 10.8   System Clipboard Demo

10.5   The Command Pattern

Providing reversal actions (undo) in your software reduces anxiety and encourages experimentation in your users. This can be a better choice than a confirmation dialog. Qt provides classes that make it easier to write your application with undo capability.

Command Pattern

The **Command pattern**, as described in [Gamma95], encapsulates operations as objects with a common execution interface. This can make it possible to place operations in a queue, log operations, and undo the results of an already executed operation. A successful implementation of this pattern may also provide a common location for handling errors or unexpected conditions.

Qt classes that may be considered to implement this pattern to some degree are QUndoCommand, QRunnable, and QAction.

Implementing the Command pattern is particularly easy with Qt:

- You can create several commands and queue them in an appropriate container (e.g., QQueue).

- A QUndoCommand can be executed by pushing it onto a QUndoStack.

- If commands need to be executed concurrently, you can derive them from QRunnable and schedule them in a thread pool with QtConcurrent::Run().[2]

- You might serialize commands to a file and load them again later (perhaps on another machine) for batch or distributed execution.[3]

10.5.1   QUndoCommand and Image Manipulation

The following example demonstrates the use of QUndoCommand. This program uses image manipulation operations.[4] This example uses the QImage class, a hardware-independent representation of an image that enables you to manipulate individual pixels. QImage supports several of the most popular formats for images, including JPEG,[5] a lossy compression system for photographic images that we use in this example.

First, as you see in Example 10.11, we derive a couple of typical image manipulation operations from QUndoCommand. The first operation adjusts the color of each pixel by applying double multipliers to its red, green, and blue components. The second operation replaces half of the image by the mirror image of its other half, either horizontally or vertically, depending on the user-supplied argument. The constructor for each operation takes a reference to the source QImage and instantiates an empty QImage with the same size and format.

EXAMPLE 10.11   src/undo-demo/image-manip.h

```
[ . . . . . ]
class AdjustColors : public QUndoCommand {
public:
    AdjustColors(QImage& img, double radj, double gadj, double badj)
      : m_Image(img), m_Saved(img.size(), img.format()), m_RedAdj(radj),
      m_GreenAdj(gadj), m_BlueAdj(badj)    {setText("adjust colors"); }
    virtual void undo();
    virtual void redo();
```

---

[2] Section 17.2 discusses threads.

[3] Section 7.4.1 discusses the Serializer Pattern.

[4] This example was inspired by the work of Guzdial and Ericson [Guzdial07] and their MediaComp project.

[5] http://www.jpeg.org

```
private:
    QImage& m_Image;
    QImage m_Saved;
    double m_RedAdj, m_GreenAdj, m_BlueAdj;
    void adjust(double radj, double gadj, double badj);

};

class MirrorPixels : public QUndoCommand {
public:
    virtual void undo();
    virtual void redo();
[ . . . . . ]
```

Each of the two operations makes a copy of the original image before changing any of its pixels. Example 10.12 shows the implementation of one of the operation classes, `AdjustColors`. Its constructor iterates through the pixels of the `QImage` and calls the `pixel()` function on each one. `pixel()` returns the color as an ARGB quad, an unsigned, 8-byte `int` in the format AARRGGBB, where each pair of bytes represents a component of the color. We operate on this quad (which has been given the `typedef QRgb`) using the functions `qRed()`, `qGreen()`, and `qBlue()` to tease out the individual values, each between 0 and 255, for the three basic colors.[6] It then replaces the pixel with adjusted values for red, green, and blue. Keep in mind that the color adjustment operation multiplies `int` values by `double` values and then assigns the products to `int` variables, which results in truncation. In other words, the adjustment cannot be reversed by performing the inverse multiplication.

The `undo()` method reverts to the saved copy of the image. The `redo()` method calls the pixel-changing function.

EXAMPLE 10.12   src/undo-demo/image-manip.cpp

```
[ . . . . . ]

void AdjustColors::adjust(double radj, double gadj, double badj) {
    int h(m_Image.height()), w(m_Image.width());
    int r, g, b;
    QRgb oldpix, newpix;
    m_Saved = m_Image.copy(QRect()); // save a copy of entire image
    for(int y = 0; y < h; ++y) {
        for(int x = 0; x < w; ++x) {
```

---

[6] The fourth pair holds the value for the *alpha* component, which expresses the transparency of the pixel. It has a default value of ff (255), i.e., opaque.

```
        oldpix = m_Image.pixel(x,y);
        r = qRed(oldpix) * radj;
        g = qGreen(oldpix) * gadj;
        b = qBlue(oldpix) * badj;
        newpix = qRgb(r,g,b);
        m_Image.setPixel(x,y,newpix);
    }
  }
}

void AdjustColors::redo() {
   qDebug() << "AdjustColors::redo()";
   adjust(m_RedAdj, m_GreenAdj, m_BlueAdj);
}

void AdjustColors::undo() {
    qDebug() << "AdjustColors::undo()";
    m_Image = m_Saved.copy(QRect());
}
```

We designed the GUI using QtCreator. The QImage displays on the screen in a QLabel after being converted to a QPixmap. Figure 10.9 shows a photo before this program worked on it.

FIGURE 10.9   The Undisturbed Original Photo

Figure 10.10 shows the unfortunate scene after the `AdjustColors` and both kinds of `MirrorPixels` operations have been applied to it.

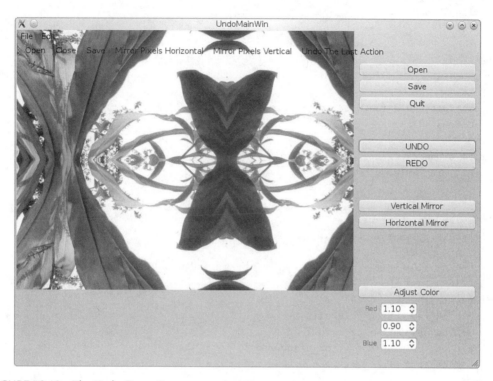

FIGURE 10.10   The Undo-Demo Screen

The `UndoMainWin` class is derived from `QMainWindow` and uses `QUndoStack`. By default, QtCreator embeds the Ui class as a pointer member of `UndoMainWin`. In Example 10.13, the private slots started out as stubs that QtCreator generated when we employed the `Go to slot` feature on widgets and actions from Designer.

EXAMPLE 10.13   src/undo-demo/undomainwin.h

```
#ifndef UNDOMAINWIN_H
#define UNDOMAINWIN_H

#include <QMainWindow>
#include <QUndoStack>

class QWidget;
class QLabel;
```

```cpp
class QImage;
class QEvent;
namespace Ui {
    class UndoMainWin;
}

class UndoMainWin : public QMainWindow {
    Q_OBJECT
 public:
    explicit UndoMainWin(QWidget* parent = 0);
    ~UndoMainWin();

 public slots:
    void displayImage(const QImage& img);

 private:
    Ui::UndoMainWin* ui;
    QLabel* m_ImageDisplay;
    QImage m_Image;
    QUndoStack m_Stack;

 private slots:
    void on_redoButton_clicked();
    void on_openButton_clicked();
    void on_actionAdjust_Color_triggered();
    void on_actionUndo_The_Last_Action_triggered();
    void on_actionHorizontal_Mirror_triggered();
    void on_actionVertical_Mirror_triggered();
    void on_actionQuit_triggered();
    void on_actionSave_triggered();
    void on_actionClose_triggered();
    void on_saveButton_clicked();
    void on_quitButton_clicked();
    void on_adjustColorButton_clicked();
    void on_undoButton_clicked();
    void on_verticalMirrorButton_clicked();
    void on_horizontalMirrorButton_clicked();
    void on_actionOpen_triggered();
};

#endif // UNDOMAINWIN_H
```

In Example 10.14, you can see the implementation style that QtCreator uses to tie the parts together. Notice also the compact completions of the `private slots` that were listed in Example 10.13.

`QImage` is optimized for pixel manipulation. `QPixmap` uses video memory and is the class used by various widgets for images that need to be on-screen. As mentioned earlier, you can convert a `QImage` to a `QPixmap` and display it in a `QLabel`.

EXAMPLE 10.14   src/undo-demo/undomainwin.cpp

```
[ . . . . ]
#include "image-manip.h"
#include "ui_undomainwin.h"
#include "undomainwin.h"

UndoMainWin::UndoMainWin(QWidget *parent)
: QMainWindow(parent), ui(new Ui::UndoMainWin),
  m_ImageDisplay(new QLabel(this)), m_Image(QImage()) {
  ui->setupUi(this);
  m_ImageDisplay->setMinimumSize(640,480);
}

UndoMainWin::~UndoMainWin() {
  delete ui;                                                    1
}

void UndoMainWin::displayImage(const QImage &img) {
    m_ImageDisplay->setPixmap(QPixmap::fromImage(img));
}

void UndoMainWin::on_actionOpen_triggered() {
    m_Image.load(QFileDialog::getOpenFileName());
    displayImage(m_Image);
}

void UndoMainWin::on_horizontalMirrorButton_clicked() {
    MirrorPixels* mp = new MirrorPixels(m_Image, true);
    m_Stack.push(mp);
    displayImage(m_Image);
}
```

```
void UndoMainWin::on_adjustColorButton_clicked() {
    double radj(ui->redSpin->value()), gadj(ui->greenSpin->value()),
    badj(ui->blueSpin->value());
    AdjustColors* ac = new AdjustColors(m_Image, radj, gadj, badj);
    m_Stack.push(ac);
    displayImage(m_Image);
}
[ . . . . . ]
```

1 Neither a `QObject` nor a child, it must be deleted explicitly.

10.5.1.1   Exercises: QUndoCommand and Image Manipulation

Add some other undoable image manipulation operations to Example 10.11. Here are some ideas to try:

1. **Monochrome**—Convert a three-color image to a monochrome image with a grayscale. Gray is produced by setting all three color components to the same value. Unfortunately, if you simply replace each color value by the average of the three for all pixels in the image, the overall effect is to make the image seem too dark. The standard approach to producing an acceptable grayscale image is to correct for the fact that blue is considered to be a "darker" color than red. You can adjust each pixel by applying commonly used weight factors to each of the three colors[7]

   ```
   redVal *= 0.30; greenVal *= 0.59; blueVal *=0.11;
   ```

   Then you can compute the luminance of that pixel. Luminance (or intensity) is an `int` equal to the weighted average of the three color values. In this case, because you have already weighted them,

   ```
   luminance = redVal + greenVal + blueVal
   ```

   Finally, replace each of the three color values of the pixel with the luminance.

2. **Negative**—Convert a three-color image to its negative. To do this, simply replace each color value v by 255 - v.

3. **Scramble colors**—For each pixel, permute the color values so that the red value gets the original blue value, the green value gets the original red value, and the blue value gets the original green value.

---

[7] For example, http://tinyurl.com/ydpjvgk discusses luminance.

4. **TriColor**—For each pixel, compute its color intensity (average value of its three colors) c_i. If c_i is below 85, reduce its red and blue values to 0. If c_i is 85 or higher but below 170, reduce its blue and green values to 0. If c_i is 170 or higher, reduce its red and green values to 0.

5. **Expose edges**—For each pixel, compare its color insensity with that of the pixel below it. If the absolute value of the difference exceeds the threshold value (supplied as an argument), set its color to black (all three color values to 0); otherwise set its color to white (all three color values to 255).

10.6 `tr()` and Internationalization

If you write a program that might be translated into another language (**internationalization**), Qt Linguist and Qt translation tools have already solved the problem of how to organize and where to put the translated strings. To prepare your code for translation, you can use `QObject::tr()` to surround any translatable string in your application. When used as a non-static function, it takes the object's class name, as provided by `QMetaObject`, as a "context" for grouping translated strings.

`tr()` serves two purposes:

1. It makes it possible for Qt's `lupdate` tool to extract all the translatable string literals.

2. If a translation is available, and the language has been selected, the function returns the translated string.

If no translation is available, `tr()` returns the original string.

NOTE

It is important that each translatable string is indeed fully inside the `tr()` function and extractable at compile time. For strings that have parameters, use the `QString::arg()` function to place parameters inside translated strings. For example:

```
statusBar()->message(tr("%1 of %2 complete. progress: %3%")
                    .arg(processed).arg(total).arg(percent));
```

This way, translations can place the parameters in a different order in the situations where language changes the order of words/ideas.

The following tools are used for translation:

1. `lupdate`—Scans designer `.ui` files and C++ files for translatable strings. Generates a `.ts` file.

2. `linguist`—Edits `.ts` files and enables user to enter translations.

3. `lrelease`—Reads `.ts` files and generates `.qm` files, which are used by the application to load translations.

See the linguist manual[8] for further details on how to use these tools.

10.7 Exercises: Main Windows and Actions

1. Write a text editor application, with a `QTextEdit` as its central widget.
   - Show the filename and whether there are changes to be saved in the window title.
   - File Menu: Add actions for Open, Save as, and Quit.
   - Help Menu: Add actions for About and About Qt
   - If there are changes to be saved, ask the user to confirm the quit.

2. Write an application that lets the user select and Open a text (or rich text) file from the disk and view the contents by scrolling through it. The scrolling view should expose at least ten lines at a time.

   It should also permit the user to search for a string in that file. If the string is found, the line that contains it should appear in the scrolling view so that the user can see its context within the file. If it is not found, an appropriate message should appear in the status bar.

   The user should click a button to search for the Next occurrence or the Previous occurrence of the search string.

   There should also be a Close button that removes the file from the display and invites the user to select another file or Quit.

   Figure 10.11 is a screenshot of one possible solution. The two menus contain actions that duplicate all of the pushbuttons except for Clear Search (which just clears the search text).

---

[8] http://doc.qt.nokia.com/latest/internationalization.html

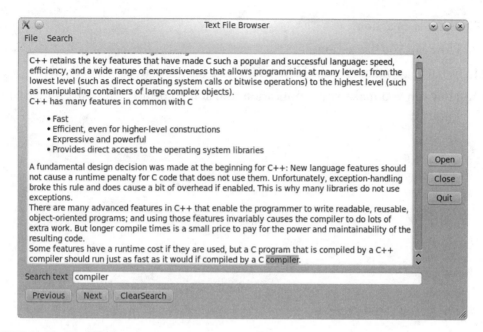

FIGURE 10.11   Text File Browser

3. QTextEdit provides methods for undo and redo. Investigate these features and discuss the operations that can be undone or redone.

10.8   Review Questions

1. What are the main features of a QMainWindow?

2. How can you install a QMenuBar in a QMainWindow?

3. How can you save and later restore the size, position, and arrangements of widgets for a GUI app?

4. What is a central widget?

5. How does a widget become the central widget?

6. What are dock widgets for?

7. How many dock widgets can you have in one application?

8. How can you use dock widgets?

9. What is an action?

10. How can you use actions?

11. What is an action group? Why would you have one in your application?

12. How can you make your application available to people who can't understand English?

## Chapter 11

Generics and Containers

This chapter covers more deeply the subject of generics. Generics are classes and functions that can operate just as easily on objects as on primitive types. Qt container classes are generic, template-based classes, and we show the use of lists, sets, and maps. This chapter also discusses overloaded operators, managed containers, and implicit sharing.

11.1 Generics and Templates

C++ supports four distinct categories of types:

- Primitives: `int, char, float, double,` etc.
- Pointers
- Instances of `class/struct`
- Arrays

Because there is no common base type for these four distinct type categories, writing generic functions and classes that can operate on multiple type categories would be difficult without the use of **templates**. Templates provide a means for the C++ compiler to generate different versions of classes and functions with parameterized types and common behavior. They are distinguished by the use of the keyword `template` and a template parameter enclosed in angle brackets `<>`.

A **template parameter** differs from a function parameter in that it can be used to pass not only variables and values, but also type expressions.

```
template <class T > class String { ... };
template <class T, int max > Buffer { ...
    T v[max];
};
String <char> s1;
Buffer <int, 10> intBuf10;
```

11.1.1   Function Templates

Function templates create type-checked functions that work on the same pattern. Example 11.1 defines a template function that raises a value of type *T* to the power *exp* by repeatedly applying the `operator*=`.

EXAMPLE 11.1   src/templates/template-demo.cpp

```
[ . . . . ]

template <class T> T power (T a, int exp) {
  T ans = a;
  while (--exp > 0) {
    ans *= a;
  }
  return (ans);
}
```

Once again, the compiler must do extra work to provide this convenient feature of C++. The compiler scans your code and generates as many different function bodies as necessary, based on the argument types supplied in the function calls, so that all calls can be resolved at compile-time, as shown in Example 11.2. Even though the word `class` is in the template parameter, `T` can be a class *or* a primitive type. In this example, the only limitation on the type `T` is that it must be a type for which the `operator*=` is defined.

EXAMPLE 11.2 src/templates/template-demo.cpp

```
[ . . . . ]


int main() {
  Complex z(3,4), z1;
  Fraction f(5,6), f1;
  int n(19);
  z1 = power(z,3);                                      1
  f1 = power(f,4);                                      2
  z1 = power<Complex>(n, 4);                            3
  z1 = power(n,5);                                      4


}
```

1 First instantiation: T is Complex.

2 Second instantiation: T is Fraction.

3 Supply an explicit template parameter if the actual argument is not "specific" enough. This results in a call to a function that was already instantiated.

4 Which version gets called?

Each time the compiler sees a template function used for the first time with a specific combination of parameter types, we say the template is **instantiated**. Subsequent uses of power(Complex, int) or power(Fraction, int) translate into ordinary function calls.

> **NOTE**
> One important difference between overloaded functions and multiple specializations of the same template function is that overloaded functions must return the same type. Example 11.2 shows different versions of the template power() function with different return types. Overloaded functions must have the same return type.

11.1.1.1 Exercises: Function Templates

1. Complete Example 11.2. In particular, write a generic Complex and Fraction class, and fix main() so that it works and uses those classes.

2. Write a template version of `swap()`, based on Example 5.13. Write client code to test it thoroughly.

3. Are there any types for which `swap()` does not work?

4. Specify the restrictions on the class parameter in your template swap function.

11.1.2   Class Templates

Like functions, classes can use parameterized types. A class template specifies how to produce generic data structures of a particular type. All Qt container classes and, of course, all containers in the Standard Template Library (STL), are parameterized. The parameter is the answer to the question, "Container of what?" Figure 11.1 shows a UML diagram of two template classes.

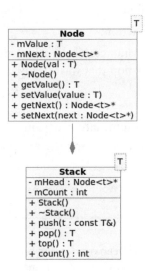

FIGURE 11.1   Template-Based Stack

UML locates the template parameter in a small offset box in the upper-right corner of the class box. Example 11.3 contains definitions for these classes.

EXAMPLE 11.3   src/containers/stack/stack.h

```
[ . . . . ]

#include <QDebug>
template<class T> class Node {
 public:
    Node(T invalue): m_Value(invalue), m_Next(0) {}
    ~Node() ;
    T getValue() const {return m_Value;}
    void setValue(T value) {m_Value = value;}
    Node<T>* getNext() const {return m_Next;}
    void setNext(Node<T>* next) {m_Next = next;}
 private:
    T m_Value;
    Node<T>* m_Next;
};


template<class T> Node<T>::~Node() {
    qDebug() << m_Value << " deleted " << endl;
    if(m_Next) {
        delete m_Next;
    }
}


template<class T> class Stack {
 public:
    Stack(): m_Head(0), m_Count(0) {}
    ~Stack<T>() {delete m_Head;} ;
    void push(const T& t);
    T pop();
    T top() const;
    int count() const;
 private:
    Node<T>* m_Head;
    int m_Count;
};
```

All template definitions (classes *and* functions) must appear in the header file. This is necessary for the compiler to generate code from a template declaration.

Notice in both Example 11.3 and Example 11.4 the required template declaration code: `template<class T>` precedes each class or function definition that has a template parameter in its name.

EXAMPLE 11.4   src/containers/stack/stack.h

```
[ . . . . ]


template <class T> void Stack<T>::push(const T& value) {
    Node<T>* newNode = new Node<T>(value);
    newNode->setNext(m_Head);
    m_Head = newNode;
    ++m_Count;
}

template <class T>  T Stack<T>::pop() {
    Node<T>* popped = m_Head;
    if (m_Head != 0) {
        m_Head = m_Head->getNext();
        T retval = popped->getValue();
        popped->setNext(0);
        delete popped;
        --m_Count;
        return retval;
    }
    return 0;
}
```

The creation of objects is handled generically in the template function, push(). The destructor for the Node<T> class recursively deletes Node pointers until it reaches one with a zero m_Next pointer.[1] Controlling creation and destruction of Node<T> objects this way enables Stack<T> to completely manage its dynamic memory. Example 11.5 contains some client code to demonstrate these classes.

EXAMPLE 11.5   src/containers/stack/main.cpp

```
#include <QDebug>
#include <QString>
#include "stack.h"

int main() {
    Stack<int> intstack1, intstack2;
```

---

[1] This is a consequence of the fact that calling delete on a pointer automatically invokes the destructor associated with that pointer.

```
    int val;
    for (val = 0; val < 4; ++val) {
        intstack1.push(val);
        intstack2.push(2 * val);
    }
    while (intstack1.count()) {
        val = intstack1.pop();
        qDebug() << val;
    }
    Stack<QString> stringstack;
    stringstack.push("First on");
    stringstack.push("second on");
    stringstack.push("first off");
    QString val2;
    while (stringstack.count()) {
        val2 = stringstack.pop();
        qDebug() << val2;
    }
    qDebug() << "Now intstack2 will self destruct.";
    return 0;
}
```

When you run the program, you should see the following output:

```
3 deleted
3
2 deleted
2
1 deleted
1
0 deleted
0
first off deleted
"first off"
second on deleted
"second on"
First on deleted
"First on"
Now intstack2 will self destruct.
6 deleted
4 deleted
2 deleted
0 deleted
```

NOTE

Because additional code needs to be generated by moc for each Q_OBJECT, and moc is not smart enough to know how to generate specializations of a template class, it is not permitted to make a class template that is also marked Q_OBJECT.

11.1.3   Exercises: Generics and Templates

1. Place the function definitions for stack in a separate file (stack.cpp), modify the project file appropriately, and then build the application. Explain the results.

2. How general is this application (i.e., what conditions must the class T satisfy to be used here)?

3. What limits the size of a Stack<T>?

4. Write a template Queue<T> class and client code to test it.

11.2   Generics, Algorithms, and Operators

Overloading operator symbols makes it possible to define a common interface for our classes that is consistent with that of the basic types. Many generic algorithms take advantage of this by using the common operators to perform basic functions such as comparison.

qSort

The qSort() function is a generic algorithm implemented using the heapsort algorithm.[2] Example 11.6 shows how it can be used on two similar but different containers.

qSort() can be applied to any Qt container of objects that have publicly defined functions operator<() and operator==(). Containers of primitive numeric types can also be sorted with this function.

---

[2] There is a nice article about heapsort in Wikipedia (http://en.wikipedia.org/wiki/Heapsort).

EXAMPLE 11.6   src/containers/sortlist/sortlist4.cpp

```cpp
#include <QList>
#include <QtAlgorithms>    // for qSort()
#include <QStringList>
#include <QDebug>

class CaseIgnoreString : public QString {
public:
    CaseIgnoreString(const QString& other = QString())
    : QString(other) {}
    bool operator<(const QString & other) const {
        return toLower() < other.toLower();
    }
    bool operator==(const QString& other) const {
        return toLower() == other.toLower();
    }
};

int main() {
    CaseIgnoreString s1("Apple"), s2("bear"),
                     s3 ("CaT"), s4("dog"), s5 ("Dog");

    Q_ASSERT(s4 == s5);
    Q_ASSERT(s2 < s3);
    Q_ASSERT(s3 < s4);

    QList<CaseIgnoreString> namelist;

    namelist << s5 << s1 << s3 << s4 << s2;                      1

    qSort(namelist.begin(), namelist.end());
    int i=0;
    foreach (const QString &stritr, namelist) {
        qDebug() << QString("namelist[%1] = %2")
                        .arg(i++).arg(stritr) ;
    }

    QStringList strlist;
    strlist << s5 << s1 << s3 << s4 << s2;                       2

    qSort(strlist.begin(), strlist.end());
    qDebug() << "StringList sorted: " + strlist.join(", ");
    return 0;
}
```

1 Insert all items in an order that is definitely not sorted.

2 The value collection holds QString but, if you add CaseIgnoreString, a conversion is required.

operator<<(), which is the **left shift** operator from C, has been overloaded in the QList class to append items to the list.

Example 11.7 shows the output of this program.

EXAMPLE 11.7 src/containers/sortlist/sortlist-output.txt

```
namelist[0] = Apple
namelist[1] = bear
namelist[2] = CaT
namelist[3] = dog
namelist[4] = Dog
StringList sorted: Apple, CaT, Dog, bear, dog
```

Notice that CaseIgnoreString objects get case-sensitive sorting when they are added to a QStringList. This is because each CaseIgnoreString must be converted into a QString as it is added to strlist. Therefore, when strlist's elements are compared, they are compared as QStrings and sorted with case sensitivity.

11.2.1 Exercises: Generics, Algorithms, and Operators

1. A QStringList is a value container of objects that have lazy copy-on-write. In a way, it is like a pointer-container, but smarter. In Example 11.6, a CaseIgnoreString was added to a QStringList, which required a conversion. Does this require a copy of the actual string data? Why or why not?

2. Add some more functions to ContactList (Figure 11.2).

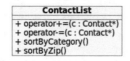

FIGURE 11.2 ContactList UML

operators += and -= should add() and remove() respectively.

Write some client-code that tests these functions.

11.3   Sorted Map Example

As mentoned earlier, QMap is an associative array that maintains key sorting-order as items are added and removed. Key-based insertions and deletions are fast (*log(n)*), and iteration is done in key order.

QMap is a value container, but pointers are simple values, so you can use a QMap to store pointers to heap allocated QObjects. By default, however, value containers do not manage heap objects so, to avoid memory leaks, you must ensure they are deleted at the proper time. Figure 11.3 describes a class that extends a QMap to contain information about textbooks. By deriving from QMap, the entire public interface of QMap becomes part of the public interface of TextbookMap. We added only a destructor plus two convenience functions to facilitate adding and displaying Textbooks in the container. This convenience also creates some problems, as you can see next.

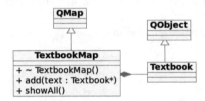

FIGURE 11.3   TextbookMap

TextbookMap consists of <key,value> pairs with ISBN numbers as keys and Textbook pointers as values. Example 11.8 shows the class definitions.

EXAMPLE 11.8   src/containers/qmap/textbook.h

```
#ifndef _TEXTBOOK_H_
#define _TEXTBOOK_H_

#include <QObject>
#include <QString>
#include <QMap>

class Textbook : public QObject {
    Q_OBJECT
  public:
    Textbook(QString title, QString author, QString isbn, uint year);
[ . . . . ]
private:
```

```
    uint m_YearPub;
    QString m_Title, m_Author, m_Isbn;
};


/* Managed collection of pointers */
class TextbookMap : public QMap<QString, Textbook*> {
  public:
    ~TextbookMap();
    void add(Textbook* text);
    QString toString() const;


};
#endif
```

In Example 11.9, the destructor uses `qDeleteAll()` on the `values()` of the `QMap`, deleting each pointer. This is necessary for a value container to manage its objects.

EXAMPLE 11.9   src/containers/qmap/qmap-example.cpp

```
[ . . . . ]


TextbookMap::~TextbookMap() {
    qDebug() << "Destroying TextbookMap ..." << endl;
    qDeleteAll(values());
    clear();
}


void TextbookMap::add(Textbook* text) {
    insert(text->getIsbn(), text);
}


QString TextbookMap::toString() const {
    QString retval;
    QTextStream os(&retval);
    ConstIterator itr = constBegin();
    for ( ; itr != constEnd(); ++itr)
        os << '[' << itr.key() << ']' << ": "
        << itr.value()->toString() << endl;
    return retval;
}
```

More Than One Way to Traverse a Map

Iterating through each element in a map, and getting the value, can be done in a number of ways. Example 11.9 uses the C-style `for` loop and an STL-style `iterator`. It happens to be quite efficient on single-core machines. The same method written here uses a Qt `foreach` loop and looks nice on paper, but at runtime, it creates a temporary list and requires $n(log2(n))$ tree lookups, so it's not as efficient with space or time.

```cpp
void TextbookMap::showAll() const {
    foreach (QString key, keys()) {
        Textbook* tb = value(key);
        cout << '[' << key << ']' << ":"
            << tb->toString() << endl;
    }
}
```

It is important to understand, as you can see in the client code shown in Example 11.10, that when you `remove()` a pointer from the `TextbookMap`, you also remove its responsibility for managing that pointer. Once you remove it, *you* have the responsibility for deleting that pointer! In other words, client code can easily produce memory leaks. The same problem arises with other `QMap` member functions (e.g., `QMap::erase()` and `QMap::take()`). You can diminish these particular problems by *hiding* the dangerous `QMap` functions with `TextbookMap` versions that remove *and* delete or reparent no longer needed `Textbook` pointers. Another (perhaps safer) option would be to use `private` derivation instead of `public` derivation. Then the `TextbookMap` public interface would contain only *safe* `public` member functions that you (carefully) defined.

EXAMPLE 11.10 src/containers/qmap/qmap-example.cpp

```cpp
[ . . . . ]

int main() {
    Textbook* t1 = new Textbook("The C++ Programming Language",
        "Stroustrup", "0201700735", 1997);
    Textbook* t2 = new Textbook("XML in a Nutshell",
        "Harold","0596002920", 2002);
    Textbook* t3 = new Textbook("UML Distilled",
        "Fowler", "0321193687", 2004);
    Textbook* t4 = new Textbook("Design Patterns", "Gamma",
        "0201633612",1995);
```

```
{                                                                      1
    TextbookMap m;
    m.add(t1);
    m.add(t2);
    m.add(t3);
    m.add(t4);
    qDebug() << m.toString();
    m.remove (t3->getIsbn());                                          2
}                                                                      3
qDebug() << "After m has been destroyed we still have:\n"
    << t3->toString();
return 0;
}
```

1 Inner block for demonstration purposes

2 Removed but not deleted

3 End of block—local variables destroyed

When `TextbookMap::ShowAll()` iterates through the container, you can see from the output in Example 11.11 that the `Textbooks` have been placed in order by ISBN (the key).

EXAMPLE 11.11   src/containers/qmap/qmap-example-output.txt

```
src/containers/qmap> ./qmap
[0201633612]:Title: Design Patterns; Author: Gamma; ISBN: 0201633612;
Year: 1995
[0201700735]:Title: The C++ Programming Language; Author: Stroustrup;
ISBN: 0201700735; Year: 1997
[0321193687]:Title: UML Distilled; Author: Fowler; ISBN: 0321193687;
Year: 2004
[0596002920]:Title: XML in a Nutshell; Author: Harold; ISBN:
0596002920; Year: 2002
Destroying TextbookMap ...
After m has been destroyed we still have:
Title: UML Distilled; Author: Fowler; ISBN: 0321193687; Year: 2004
src/containers/qmap>
```

11.4   Function Pointers and Functors

Functors are generalized callable structures that can be invoked. Regular C and C++ functions, which readily convert to function pointers, fall into this category. Generic algorithms are typically overloaded to accept various categories of callables as parameters. Example 11.12 demonstrates how to invoke functions indirectly via function pointers.

EXAMPLE 11.12 src/functors/pointers/main.cpp

```
#include <QtGui>

QString name() {
    return QString("Alan");
}

typedef QString (*funcPtr)();                                    1
Q_DECLARE_METATYPE(funcPtr);                                     2

int main() {
    qRegisterMetaType<funcPtr>("funcPtr");                      3
    funcPtr ptr = name;                                         4

    QString v = (*ptr)();                                       5
    qDebug() << v << endl;                                      6
}
```

1 A function that returns QString and takes no args.
2 Declare, so we can use in QVariant.
3 Register, so we can use in queued signal parameters.
4 Function names evaluate to pointers to functions.
5 Invoke a method by dereferencing function ptr.
6 Prints "Alan"

Pointers to functions are frequently used in C for callbacks, or functions that need to be called in response to certain events. In C++, it is possible to use object-oriented, template-based mechanisms as well. This way, you can specify the types of the arguments and return type at compile-time, making their use type-safe.

A *functor* in C++ is a callable object that behaves like a function pointer, in the sense that it can be dereferenced and *called* like a function. The C++ standard libs that comply with TR1[3] or later provide base class types for these in the <functional> header

---

[3] C++ Technical Report 1 (TR1) is a draft document containing proposed additions to the C++ Standard Library that are likely to be included in the next official standard. See this Wikipedia article [http://en.wikipedia.org/wiki/C%2B%2B_Technical_Report_1] for more information.

file. The C++ function call operator provides part of the syntactic sugar that makes objects act like functions. The types `std::unary_function` and `std::binary_function` provide additional type information on C++ functors. They are parameterized base class types you can extend, for use in QtAlgorithms, C++ STL, and the Qt Concurrent library. Example 11.13, shows how to define functors that can be used in places where function pointers are found.

EXAMPLE 11.13   src/functors/operators/functors.h

```
[ . . . . . ]
class Load : public std::unary_function<QString, QImage> {          1
public:
    QImage operator() (const QString& imageFileName) const {
        return QImage(imageFileName);
    }
};
class Scale {
    public:
    typedef QImage result_type;                                     2
    QImage operator() (QImage image) const {
        for (int i=0; i<10; ++i) {
            QImage copy = image.copy();
            copy.scaled(100, 100, Qt::KeepAspectRatio);
        }
        if (image.width() < image.height()) {
            return image.scaledToHeight(imageSize,
                                    Qt::SmoothTransformation);
        }
        else {
            return image.scaledToWidth(imageSize,
                                    Qt::SmoothTransformation);
        }
    }
};
class LoadAndScale : public std::unary_function<QString, QImage> { 3
public:
    Scale scale;
    QImage operator() (const QString& imageFileName) const {
        QImage image(imageFileName);
        return scale(image);
    }
};
[ . . . . . ]
```

1 Defines `result_type`.

2 A trait required for functor objects.

3 Also defines `result_type`.

In Example 11.14 a temporary instance of LoadAndScale is created and passed to a `QtConcurrent` algorithm, which is overloaded to accept function pointers and `std::unary_function` objects for its mapping function. `QtConcurrent` is discussed in more detail in Section 17.2.

EXAMPLE 11.14   src/functors/operators/imagefunctor.cpp

```
[ . . . . . ]


    connect(m_futureWatcher, SIGNAL(progressValueChanged(int)),
        this, SIGNAL(progressCurrent(int)));
    emit statusMessage("Loading and Transforming in parallel");
    m_futureWatcher->setFuture(QtConcurrent::mapped(files,
                                        LoadAndScale()));
```

11.5   Flyweight Pattern: Implicitly Shared Classes

Unlike Java, C++ has no garbage collection. Garbage collection is a thread that recovers heap memory that is no longer referenced. It runs when the CPU is relatively idle or when it is running out of memory. When an object is no longer referenced, it is deleted, and the memory that it occupied is made available for use by other objects. It has the benefit of being less work for the developer, who does not need to worry about memory leaks,[4] but it is certainly more work for the CPU.

The next examples show a way of building garbage collection into the design of a class by means of **reference counting**. Reference counting is an example of **resource sharing**. It is considered much more efficient, in terms of both developer and CPU time, than depending on a garbage collector to manage the heap.

Each object keeps track of its active references. When an object is created, its reference counter is set to 1. Each time the object is newly referenced, the reference counter is incremented. Each time it loses a reference, the reference counter is decremented. When the reference count becomes 0, the shared object can be deallocated.

---

[4] Actually, Java developers do worry and often try many tricks to create fewer heap objects. They also have ways to force the garbage collector to run more frequently (and, of course, consume more CPU cycles).

NOTE

If the object is about to be changed (e.g., a non-const member function is called), and its reference count is greater than 1, it must be detached first so that it is no longer shared.

Implicitly shared classes work by reference-counting, to prevent the accidental deletion of shared managed objects. Clients using this class need not be concerned with reference counts or memory pointers.

QString, QVariant, and QStringList are all implemented this way, meaning that it is fast to pass and return these by value. If you need to change objects from inside a function, you should pass by reference, rather than by pointer.

It is still slightly faster to pass by const reference, which enables C++ to optimize out the copy operation entirely. With const reference, the function cannot make changes to the reference, and automatic conversions do not happen.

Flyweight Pattern

To avoid the need to store multiple copies of the same object, there are many situations in which a lightweight wrapper can be used in place of the actual object. The wrapper class holds a pointer to shared data instead of maintaining a copy of the data. Classes that work this way implement the **Flyweight Pattern**, sometimes called the **Bridge pattern** or the **Private Implementation pattern**.

As you examine the source code of Qt, you undoubtedly notice file_p.cpp and file_p.h files that contain the implementation details of most Qt classes. This pattern helps ensure both source and binary compatibility when changing implementations of a class. In addition, it is used to achieve implicit sharing, where the data is shared across multiple implementations.

The flexibility that the Bridge pattern gives you comes at a cost: the code is more complex (twice as many classes to manage) and you must implement a wrapper with the same interface as the original class.

To make your own implicitly shared flyweight, you can write your own reference counting code, or reuse two Qt classes: QSharedData and QSharedDataPointer.

QSharedData provides a public QAtomicInt ref member, for a reference count. QAtomicInt provides a deref() operation, which is used by QSharedDataPointer to decrement and test, to determine if it can safely delete the shared data. QSharedDataPointer updates the reference count of its shared data depending on whether it is being copied or detached.

The next example, pictured in Figure 11.4, starts with a relatively mundane, non-sharing MyString class that implements strings with dynamic arrays of char, shown in Example 11.15.

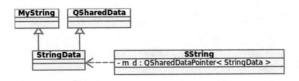

FIGURE 11.4   Example QSharedData Private Implementation

EXAMPLE 11.15   src/mystring/shareddata/mystring.h

```
#ifndef MYSTRING_H
#define MYSTRING_H
#include <iostream>
class MyString {
public:
    MyString(const MyString& str);
    MyString& operator=(const MyString& a);
    MyString();
    MyString(const char* chptr);
    explicit MyString(int size);
    virtual ~MyString();
    friend std::ostream& operator<<(std::ostream& os, const MyString& s);
    int length() const;
    MyString& operator+= (const MyString& other);
    friend MyString operator+(const MyString&, const MyString&);
protected:
    int   m_Len;
    char* m_Buffer;                                                   1
    void  copy(const char* chptr);
};
#endif          //  #ifndef MYSTRING_H
```

1 Pointer to the start of dynamic array

Example 11.16 extends the MyString class by adding reference counting capability. This is the private implementation class.

EXAMPLE 11.16　src/mystring/shareddata/stringdata.h

```
[ . . . . . ]
class StringData : public QSharedData, public MyString {
public:
    friend class SString;
    StringData() {}
    StringData(const char* d) : MyString(d) {}
    explicit StringData(int len) : MyString(len) {}
    StringData(const StringData& other)
              : QSharedData(other), MyString(other) {}
};
[ . . . . . ]
```

The implicitly shared sstring, shown in Example 11.17, is an example of a class that uses the QSharedDataPointer to achieve copy on write.

EXAMPLE 11.17　src/mystring/shareddata/sstring.h

```
[ . . . . . ]
class SString {
public:
    SString();
    explicit SString(int len);
    SString(const char* ptr);
    SString& operator+= (const SString& other);
    int length() const;
    int refcount() const {return m_d->ref;}
    friend SString operator+(SString, SString);
    friend std::ostream& operator<< (std::ostream&, const SString&);
[ . . . . . ]
private:
    // Private Implementation Pattern
    QSharedDataPointer<StringData> m_d;

};
[ . . . . . ]
```

The public methods of sstring delegate to StringData. The actual shared data is copied automatically whenever m_d is dereferenced in a non-const way. Example 11.18 demonstrates that the refcount() decreases when one of the shared flyweights is modified.

EXAMPLE 11.18   src/mystring/shareddata/sharedmain.cpp

```
#include <iostream>
#include "sstring.h"
using namespace std;

void passByValue(SString v) {
    cout << v << v.refcount() << endl;                     1
    v = "somethingelse";
    cout << v << v.refcount() << endl;                     2
}

int main (int argc, char* argv[]) {
    SString s = "Hello";
    passByValue(s);
    cout << s << s.refcount() << endl;                     3
}
```

1 refcount=2

2 refcount=1

3 refcount=1

`QExplicitlySharedDataPointer` is the same as `QSharedDataPointer`, but you must explicitly call `detach()` on the `QSharedData` each time that a copy is needed.

Most Qt classes implement the Flyweight pattern, for either implicit sharing or for other reasons. Only when the copy is actually modified are the collected objects cloned and detached from the original container. That is when there will be a time/memory penalty.

11.6   Exercise: Generics

This exercise requires you to come up with data structures that keep track of relationships between symbols. Our relationship is a boolean operator `frop` on a set s of symbols that has two properties:

1. **Reflexivity**—For any symbol s in s,

   s frop s   is always true.

2. **Symmetry**—For any symbols s and t in s,

   if s frop t is true, then t frop s is also true.

`frop` is similar to the boolean operator `is-friends-with` between people on a social networking site. `is-friends-with` is not transitive; you do not automatically become friends with all your friends' friends.[5]

In this problem, you build a data structure for storing the relationships between symbols. Each symbol is an arbitrary string of alphanumerics. This data structure should use one or more `QSet`, `QMap`, or `QMultiMap`.

1. Write a program that repeatedly asks the user to enter relationships or commands and keeps track of relationships between all pairs of symbols that it sees. The interface should be pretty simple: The user enters a string that is parsed and processed by the dispatching function, `processLine()`. In other words, `processLine()` should expect strings of the following forms:

    a. To add a *frop* between two strings: `string1=string2`

    b. To list the friends of `string1`: `string1` (no = symbol in the line)

2. Add another function, `takeback(int n)`, where n refers to the nth assertion. If the nth assertion added a `frop`, the function should "undo" that assertion, ensuring that relational integrity is kept. After this, show the updated friend lists of both symbols (`string1` and `string2`) involved.

    Have the `processLine()` function scan for messages of the form "takeback n" and call the `takeback()` function in response.

11.7   Review Questions

1. Explain an important difference between a template parameter and a function parameter.

2. What does it mean to instantiate a template function? Describe one way to do this.

3. Normally, you need to place template definitions in header files. Why is this?

4. Some compilers support `export`. What is it for?

---

[5] **Transitivity** is a third property of boolean operators that we are *not* assuming—for any symbols s, t, and u in *S*, if s *op* t and t *op* u are both true, then s *op* u is also true.

If a boolean operator op is Reflexive, Symmetric, and Transitive, then it is an *Equivalence Relation*.

5. Qt's container classes are used to collect value types. What kinds of things are not appropriate to store by value in a value collection?

6. Which containers provide a mapping from key to value? List and describe at least two, and tell how they are different from one another.

7. What does it mean for a container to "manage" its heap objects? How can a container of pointers to heap objects become a "managed container"?

8. Give at least three examples of Qt classes that implement the Flyweight pattern.

9. When defining a class template, how should the code be distributed between the header (.h) file and the implementation (.cpp) file? Explain your answer.

Chapter 12

Meta Objects, Properties, and Reflective Programming

This chapter introduces the idea of reflection, the self-examination of an object's members. Using reflective programming, you can write general-purpose operations that work on classes of varied structures. Using `QVariant`, a generic value-holder, you can operate on built-in types and other common types in a uniform way.

12.1 QMetaObject—The MetaObject Pattern

A **meta object** is an object that describes the structure of another object.[1]

The MetaObject Pattern

`QMetaObject` is Qt's implementation of the **MetaObject pattern**. It provides information about the properties and methods of a `QObject`. The MetaObject pattern is sometimes known as the **Reflection pattern**.

---

[1] *Meta*, the Latin root meaning *about*, is used for its literal definition here.

A class that has a MetaObject supports reflection. This is a feature found in many object-oriented languages. It does not exist in C++, but Qt's MetaObject compiler, moc, generates the code to support this for specially equipped QObjects.

As long as certain conditions apply,[2] each class derived from QObject has a QMetaObject generated for it by moc, similar to those we have for Customer and Address, shown in Figure 12.1. QObject has a member function that returns a pointer to the object's QMetaObject. The prototype of that function is

```
QMetaObject* QObject::metaObject() const [virtual]
```

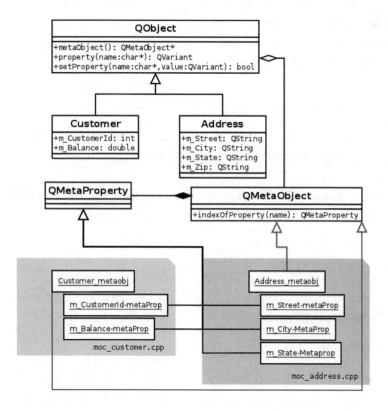

FIGURE 12.1   MetaObjects

---

[2] Each class must be defined in a header file, listed in the project file's HEADERS, and must include the Q_OBJECT macro in its class definition.

You can use these methods of `QMetaObject` to get information about a `QObject`:

- `className()`, which returns the class name as a `const char*`
- `superClass()`, which returns a pointer to the `QMetaObject` of the base class if there is one (or `0` if there is not)
- `methodCount()`, which returns the number of member functions of the class
- Several other useful functions that we discuss in this chapter

The signal and slot mechanism also relies on the `QMetaObject`. Figure 12.1 shows the inheritance relationships between the Qt base classes, the derived `QObjects`, and the `moc`-generated meta classes for them.

By using the `QMetaObject` and `QMetaProperty`, you can write code that is generic enough to handle all self-describing classes.

12.2   Type Identification and `qobject_cast`

RTTI, or Run Time Type Identification, as its name suggests, is a system for determining at runtime the actual type of an object, to which you may have only a base class pointer.

In addition to C++'s RTTI operators, `dynamic_cast` and `typeid` (Section 19.10), Qt provides two mechanisms for runtime type identification.

1. `qobject_cast`
2. `QObject::inherits()`

`qobject_cast` is an ANSI-style typecast operator (Section 19.8). ANSI typecasts look a lot like template functions:

```
DestType* qobject_cast<DestType*> ( QObject* qoptr )
```

A **typecast** operator converts an expression from one type to another, following certain rules and restrictions imposed by the types and the language. Like other cast operators, `qobject_cast` takes the destination type as a template parameter. It returns a `DestType` pointer to the same object. If at runtime, the actual pointer type cannot be converted to `DestType*`, the conversion fails and the value returned is `NULL`.

As the signature suggests, qobject_cast is type-restricted to arguments of type ObjectType*, where ObjectType is derived from QObject and the class was fully processed by moc (which requires it to have the Q_OBJECT macro in its class definition).

qobject_cast is actually a **downcast** operator, similar to dynamic_cast. It permits you to cast pointers and references from a more general to a more specific type. You may find that qobject_cast works 5 to 10 times faster than dynamic_cast, depending on what compiler you use.

In situations where you have base class pointers to derived class objects, downcasting makes it possible to call derived class methods that do not exist in the base class interface.

A common place to find qobject_cast is in concrete implementations of QAbstractItemDelegate, such as Example 12.1. Most of the virtual functions take QWidget* as an argument, so you can do dynamic type checking to determine which kind of widget it is.

EXAMPLE 12.1   src/modelview/playlists/stardelegate.cpp

```
[ . . . . . ]


void StarDelegate::
    setEditorData(QWidget* editor,
                    const QModelIndex& index) const {
    QVariant val = index.data(Qt::EditRole);
    StarEditor* starEditor = qobject_cast<StarEditor*>(editor);        1
    if (starEditor != 0) {
        StarRating sr = qVariantValue<StarRating>(val);                2
        starEditor->setStarRating(sr);
        return;
    }
    TimeDisplay* timeDisplay = qobject_cast<TimeDisplay*>(editor);     3
    if (timeDisplay != 0) {
        QTime t = val.toTime();
        timeDisplay->setTime(t);
        return;
    }
    SUPER::setEditorData(editor, index);                              4
    return;
}
```

1   Dynamic type checking.

2   Extract user type value from QVariant.

3   Dynamic type checking.

4   Let base class handle other types.

NOTE

The implementation of qobject_cast makes no use of C++ RTTI. The code for this operator is generated by the MetaObject Compiler (moc).

NOTE

For qobject_cast to work for the non-QObject base classes, you need to place each base class in a Q_INTERFACES(BaseClass1 BaseClass2) line, in the class definition after the Q_OBJECT macro.

QObject also offers a deprecated, Java-style typechecking function, inherits(). Unlike qobject_cast, inherits() accepts a char* type name instead of a type expression. This operation is slower than qobject_cast because it requires an extra hashtable lookup, but it can be useful if you need input-driven type checking. Example 12.2 shows some client-code that uses inherits().

EXAMPLE 12.2   src/qtrtti/qtrtti.cpp

```
[ . . . . ]

//  QWidget* w = &s;                                              1

    if (w->inherits("QAbstractSlider"))  cout << "Yes, it is ";
    else cout << "No, it is not";
    cout << "a QAbstractSlider" << endl;

    if (w->inherits("QListView")) cout << "Yes, it is ";
    else  cout << "No, it is not ";
    cout << "a QListView" << endl;

    return 0;
}
```

1   A pointer to some widget

12.3   Q_PROPERTY Macro—Describing QObject Properties

The property facility gives you a choice of ways to access data members:

- Directly, through the classic getters/setters (faster, more efficient)
- Indirectly, through the QObject/QMetaObject interface (enables more reusable code)

You can specify read-only access to some properties, by leaving out a WRITE function. In addition, you can provide a NOTIFY signal to emit when the property is changed.

In Example 12.3, we have a customer class with a Qt property defined for each data member. The possible types for a property are those listed in QVariant::Type, plus user types added with Q_DECLARE_METATYPE (see Section 12.6). We have adopted the common practice of basing the name of each property that corresponds to a data member on the corresponding member name. For the member m_DataItem, we named the corresponding property dataItem.

EXAMPLE 12.3   src/properties/customer-props.h

```
[ . . . . ]
class Customer : public QObject {
    Q_OBJECT                                                            1

    /* Each property declaration has the following syntax:

    Q_PROPERTY( type name READ getFunction [WRITE setFunction]
    [RESET resetFunction] [NOTIFY notifySignal] [DESIGNABLE bool]
    [SCRIPTABLE bool] [STORED bool] )
    */

    Q_PROPERTY( QString id READ getId WRITE setId NOTIFY valueChanged);
    Q_PROPERTY( QString name READ getName WRITE setName
            NOTIFY valueChanged);
    Q_PROPERTY( QString address READ getAddress WRITE setAddress
            NOTIFY addressChanged);
    Q_PROPERTY( QString phone READ getPhone WRITE setPhone
            NOTIFY phoneChanged);
    Q_PROPERTY( QDate dateEstablished READ getDateEstablished );        2
    Q_PROPERTY( CustomerType type READ getType WRITE setType
            NOTIFY valueChanged);
```

```
public:
    enum CustomerType
    { Corporate, Individual, Educational, Government };        3
    Q_ENUMS( CustomerType ) ;                                  4

    explicit Customer(const QString name = QString(),          5
        QObject* parent = 0);

    QString getId() const {
        return m_id;
    }
[ . . . . ]
    // Overloaded, so we can set the type two different ways:
    void setType(CustomerType newType);
    void setType(QString newType);
signals:
    void addressChanged(QString newAddress);
    void phoneChanged(QString newPhone);
    void typeChanged(CustomerType type);
    void valueChanged(QString propertyName,
        QVariant newValue, QVariant oldValue = QVariant());
private:
    QString m_id, m_name, m_address, m_phone;
    QDate m_date;
    CustomerType m_type;
};
[ . . . . ]
```

1 Macro required for moc to preprocess class.

2 Read-only property

3 The enum type definition must be in the same class definition as the Q_ENUMS macro.

4 Special macro to generate string-to-enum conversion functions; must be in same class.

5 Declared explicit because we do not want accidental conversions from QString to Customer.

Notice the enum CustomerType defined in the public section of the class Customer. Just above that definition, the Q_ENUMS macro tells moc to generate some functions for this property in the QMetaProperty to aid in string conversions for enum values.

The setters and getters, defined in Example 12.4, are implemented in the usual way.

EXAMPLE 12.4   src/properties/customer-props.cpp

```
[ . . . . ]
Customer::Customer(const QString name, QObject* parent)
:QObject(parent) {
    setObjectName(name);
}


void Customer::setId(const QString &newId) {
    if (newId != m_id) {
        QString oldId = m_id;
        m_id = newId;
        emit valueChanged("id", newId, oldId);
    }
}
[ . . . . ]
void Customer::setType(CustomerType theType) {
    if (m_type != theType) {
        CustomerType oldType = m_type;
        m_type = theType;
        emit valueChanged("type", theType, oldType);
    }
}


/* Method for setting enum values from Strings. */
void Customer::setType(QString newType) {                        1

    static const QMetaObject* meta = metaObject();              2
    static int propindex = meta->indexOfProperty("type");
    static const QMetaProperty mp = meta->property(propindex);

    QMetaEnum menum = mp.enumerator();                          3
    const char* ntyp = newType.toAscii().data();
    CustomerType theType =
                static_cast<CustomerType>(menum.keyToValue(ntyp));

    if (theType != m_type) {                                    4
        CustomerType oldType = m_type;
        m_type = theType;
        emit valueChanged("type", theType, oldType);
    }
}
```

```
QString Customer::getTypeString() const {
    return property("type").toString();
}
[ . . . . ]
```

1 Overloaded version that accepts a string as an argument. Sets value to -1 if unknown.

2 Because they are static locals, the initializations happen only once.

3 This code gets executed each time.

4 Always check if valueChanged signal is needed.

The implementation of the overloaded function setType(QString) takes advantage of QMetaProperty's Q_ENUMS macro to convert the QString to the proper enumerated value. To obtain the correct QMetaProperty object for an enum, you first get the QMetaObject and call indexOfProperty() and property() to find it. QMetaProperty has a function called enumerator() that returns an object you can use to convert strings to enums. If the given QString argument does not match one of the enumerators, the keyToValue() function returns -1.

---

static Local Variables

Observe that we have declared the three local (block scope) variables—meta, propindex, and mp—to be static. static local variables are initialized only once, which is our intention; repeated calls to this function will use the same QMetaProperty object to do the conversion. Using static local variables this way in a function can greatly improve the runtime performance for that function.[3]

12.4   QVariant **Class: Accessing Properties**

To retrieve the value of any property, you call this method:

```
QVariant QObject::property(QString propertyName);
```

---

[3] Of course, this depends on how expensive creating the objects is and how often the function is called.

QVariant is a union[4] wrapper for all the basic types and all permitted Q_PROPERTY types. You can create a QVariant as a wrapper around another typed value. A QVariant remembers its type and has member functions for getting and setting its value.

QVariant has a rich interface for data conversion and validity checking. In particular, there is a toString() function that returns a QString representation for many of its supported types.[5] This class greatly simplifies the property interface.

Example 12.5 shows how you can get and set the same property values via the direct getters and setters, or via the indirect property() and setProperty() methods.

EXAMPLE 12.5   src/properties/testcustomerprops.cpp

```
[ . . . . ]

#include "customer-props.h"
void TestCustomerProps::test() {
    Customer cust;
    cust.setObjectName("Customer");                                    1
    cust.setName("Falafal Pita");                                      2
    cust.setAddress("41 Temple Street; Boston, MA; 02114");
    cust.setPhone("617-555-1212");
    cust.setType("Government");                                        3
    QCOMPARE(cust.getType(), Customer::Government);                    4
    QString originalid = "834";                                       5
    cust.setId(originalid);
    QVariant v = cust.property("id");                                 6
    QString str = v.toString();
    QCOMPARE(originalid, str);
    QDate date(2003, 7, 15);
    cust.setProperty("dateEstablished", QVariant(date));             7
    QDate anotherDate = cust.getDateEstablished();                   8
    QEXPECT_FAIL("", "These are different dates", Continue);
    QCOMPARE(date, anotherDate);
    cust.setId(QString("anotherId"));
    qDebug() << objToString(&cust);
    cust.setType(Customer::Educational);
    qDebug() << " Educational=" << cust.getType();
    cust.setType("BogusType");
```

---

[4] In C and C++, a **union** is a struct that can declare two or more alternative data members to be allocated at the same address. This means that the union will occupy only enough memory to accommodate the largest of the declared data members. When instantiated, a union can store a value only for one of the declared members.

[5] See QVariant::canConvert() for more details.

```
    qDebug() << " Bogus= " << cust.getType();
    return;
}
```

```
QTEST_MAIN(TestCustomerProps)
```

1 QObject function call.

2 Setting some simple properties.

3 Setting enum property as a string.

4 Comparing to enum value.

5 Setting a string property.

6 Getting it back as a QVariant through the QObject base class method.

7 Setting date properties, wrapped in QVariants.

8 The date comes back through the type-specific getter.

Example 12.6 shows a reflective objToString() method that works on any class with Qt properties defined. It works by iterating through the indexed property() values in a way that is comparable to the java.lang.reflect interface. Only the variant types that canConvert(QVariant::String) will be printed.

EXAMPLE 12.6   src/properties/testcustomerprops.cpp

```
[ . . . . ]

QString objToString(const QObject* obj) {
    QStringList result;
    const QMetaObject* meta = obj->metaObject();                         1
    result += QString("class %1 : public %2 {")
        .arg(meta->className())
        .arg(meta->superClass()->className());
    for (int i=0; i < meta->propertyCount(); ++i) {                      2
        const QMetaProperty qmp = meta->property(i);
        QVariant value = obj->property(qmp.name());
        if (value.canConvert(QVariant::String))
            result += QString("   %1 %2 = %3;")
            .arg(qmp.typeName())
            .arg(qmp.name())
            .arg(value.toString());
    }
    result += "};";
    return result.join("\n");
}
```

1 Introspect into the object via the `QMetaObject`.

2 Each property has a `QMetaProperty`.

To build this program, it is necessary for the project file to contain the line

```
CONFIG += qtestlib
```

The program outputs an object's state in a C++-style format:

EXAMPLE 12.7   src/properties/output.txt

```
********* Start testing of TestCustomerProps *********
Config: Using QTest library 4.6.2, Qt 4.6.2
PASS    : TestCustomerProps::initTestCase()
QDEBUG : TestCustomerProps::test() "class CustProps : public QObject {
  QString objectName = Customer;
  QString id = anotherId;
  QString name = Falafal Pita;
  QString address = 41 Temple Street; Boston, MA; 02114;
  QString phone = 617-555-1212;
  QDate dateEstablished = 2003-07-15;
  CustomerType type = 3;
};"
QDEBUG : TestCustomerProps::test()  Educational= 2
QDEBUG : TestCustomerProps::test()  Bogus=  -1
PASS    : TestCustomerProps::test()
PASS    : TestCustomerProps::cleanupTestCase()
Totals: 3 passed, 0 failed, 0 skipped
********* Finished testing of TestCustomerProps *********
```

12.5 Dynamic Properties

It is possible to load and store properties in a `QObject` without having to define them on the class with `Q_PROPERTY`.

Up to this point, we have been dealing exclusively with properties that are defined with the `Q_PROPERTY` macro. These properties are known to the `QMetaObject` of that class and have a `QMetaProperty` defined. All objects of the same class share the same `metaObject` and thus have the same set of meta properties.

Dynamic properties, on the other hand, are acquired at runtime and are specific to the object that acquired them. In other words, two objects of the same class have the same meta property list, but they can have different lists of dynamic properties. In Example 12.8, we define a class with a single Q_PROPERTY, which we name someString.

EXAMPLE 12.8   src/properties/dynamic/dynoprops.h

```
[ . . . . ]
class DynoProps : public QObject {
    Q_OBJECT
    Q_PROPERTY(QString someString READ someString WRITE setSomeString);
 public:
    friend QDataStream& operator<<(QDataStream& os, const DynoProps& dp);
    friend QDataStream& operator>>(QDataStream& is, DynoProps& dp);
    QString someString() { return m_someString; }
    void setSomeString(QString ss) { m_someString = ss; }
    QString propsInventory();
 private:
    QString m_someString;
};
[ . . . . ]
```

In Example 12.9, the implementation of propsInventory() shows a way to display fixed and dynamic properties. The list of the fixed properties comes from the QMetaObject. You can access property values using QMetaProperty::read() or QObject::property(). The propertyCount() function sets a limit for iteration through the QMetaProperty list.

The dynamic properties are *not* known by the QMetaObject. Instead, you must use QObject methods. You can iterate through the QList returned by QObject::dynamicPropertyNames() for the list of names and use QObject::property() to obtain values.

EXAMPLE 12.9   src/properties/dynamic/dynoprops.cpp

```
[ . . . . ]

QString DynoProps::propsInventory() {
    static const QMetaObject* meta = metaObject();
    QStringList res;
    res << "Fixed Properties:";
    QString propData;
    for(int i = 0; i < meta->propertyCount(); ++i) {
        res << QString("%1\t%2").arg(QString(meta->property(i).name()))
```

```
            .arg(meta->property(i).read(this).toString());        1
  }
  res << "Dynamic Properties:";
  foreach(QByteArray dpname, dynamicPropertyNames()) {
     res << QString("%1\t%2").arg(QString(dpname))
             .arg(property(dpname).toString());
  }
  return res.join("\n");
}
```

1 We could also use `property(propName)` here.

Aside from the slight awkwardness of accessing them, dynamic properties can be used in much the same way as fixed properties; for example, they can be serialized. The implementations of the two serialization operators are shown in Example 12.10. We employ a similar technique for serialization that we used for the `propsInventory()` function.

EXAMPLE 12.10   src/properties/dynamic/dynoprops.cpp

```
[ . . . . ]
QDataStream& operator<< (QDataStream& os, const DynoProps& dp) {
   static const QMetaObject* meta = dp.metaObject();
   for(int i = 0; i < meta->propertyCount(); ++i) {
       const char* name = meta->property(i).name();
       os << QString::fromLocal8Bit(name)                          1
          << dp.property(name);
   }
   qint32 N(dp.dynamicPropertyNames().count());                    2
   os << N;
   foreach(QByteArray propname, dp.dynamicPropertyNames()) {
      os << QString::fromLocal8Bit(propname) << dp.property(propname);
   }
   return os;
}

QDataStream& operator>> (QDataStream& is, DynoProps& dp) {
   static const QMetaObject* meta = dp.metaObject();
   QString propname;
   QVariant propqv;
   int propcount(meta->propertyCount());
   for(int i = 0; i < propcount; ++i) {
      is >> propname;
```

```
      is >> propqv;
      dp.setProperty(propname.toLocal8Bit(), propqv);              3
   }
   qint32 dpcount;
   is >> dpcount;
   for(int i = 0; i < dpcount; ++i) {
      is >> propname;
      is >> propqv;
      dp.setProperty(propname.toLocal8Bit(), propqv);
   }
   return is;
}
```

   1 To serialize a `char*` as a `QString`

   2 To serialize an `int`

   3 De-serialize `char*` using reverse `QString` conversion

Client code to demonstrate the use of dynamic properties is shown in Example 12.11.

EXAMPLE 12.11   src/properties/dynamic/dynoprops-client.cpp

```cpp
#include <QtCore>
#include "dynoprops.h"

int main() {
   QTextStream cout(stdout);
   DynoProps d1, d2;
   d1.setObjectName("d1");
   d2.setObjectName("d2");
   d1.setSomeString("Washington");
   d1.setProperty("AcquiredProp", "StringValue");
   d2.setProperty("intProp", 42);
   d2.setProperty("realProp", 3.14159);
   d2.setProperty("dateProp", QDate(2012, 01, 04));
   cout << d1.propsInventory() << endl;
   cout << d2.propsInventory() << endl;
   cout << "\nNow we save both objects to a file, close the file,\n"
           "reopen the file, read the data from the file, and use it\n"
           "to create new DynoProps objects.\n" << endl;
   QFile file("file.dat");
   file.open(QIODevice::WriteOnly);
   QDataStream out(&file);
```

```
    out << d1 << d2;
    file.close();
    DynoProps nd1, nd2;
    file.open(QIODevice::ReadOnly);
    QDataStream in(&file);
    in >> nd1 >> nd2;
    file.close();
    cout << "Here are the property inventories for the new objects.\n";
    cout << nd1.propsInventory() << endl;
    cout << nd2.propsInventory() << endl;
}
```

Example 12.12 shows the output of the program.

EXAMPLE 12.12   src/properties/dynamic/output.txt

```
Fixed Properties:
objectName      d1
someString      Washington
Dynamic Properties:
AcquiredProp    StringValue
Fixed Properties:
objectName      d2
someString
Dynamic Properties:
intProp 42
realProp        3.14159
dateProp        2012-01-04


Now we save both objects to a file, close the file,
reopen the file, read the data from the file, and use it
to create new DynoProps objects.


Here are the property inventories for the new objects.
Fixed Properties:
objectName      d1
someString      Washington
Dynamic Properties:
AcquiredProp    StringValue
Fixed Properties:
objectName      d2
someString
```

```
Dynamic Properties:
intProp 42
realProp      3.14159
dateProp      2012-01-04
```

12.6   MetaTypes, Declaring, and Registering

QMetaType is a helper class for working with value types. For more than 60 built-in types, QMetaType associates a type name to a type ID, enabling construction and destruction to occur dynamically at runtime. There is a public enum named QMetaType::Type that has values for all the QVariant compatible types. The enumerator values in QMetaType::Type agree with those in QVariant::Type.

We have added custom enumerated types to the QVariant system, through the use of the Q_ENUMS macro. It is also possible to add value types of our own to the QMetaType list using the macro Q_DECLARE_METATYPE(MyType). If MyType has public default and copy constructors and a public destructor, the Q_DECLARE_METATYPE macro enables it to be used as a custom type in QVariant.

In Example 12.13, we introduce a new value type, Fraction, to the known metatypes of the program that contains its definition. We did not need to explicitly define default and copy constructors or a destructor because the compiler-generated ones, which do memberwise copy or assignment, are exactly what we need for this class. Placing the macro in the header file below the class definition is standard practice.

EXAMPLE 12.13   src/metatype/fraction.h

```
[ . . . . ]
class Fraction : public QPair<qint32, qint32> {
public:
    Fraction(qint32 n = 0, qint32 d = 1) : QPair<qint32,qint32>(n,d)
    { }
};

Q_DECLARE_METATYPE(Fraction);
[ . . . . ]
```

12.6.1   qRegisterMetaType()

A *registered metatype* must be already declared with Q_DECLARE_METATYPE. The template function qRegisterMetaType<T>() registers the type T and returns the internal ID used by QMetaType. There is an overloaded version of this function, qRegisterMetaType<T>(const char* *name*), that enables you to register *name* as the name of type T. The call to this function must occur early in the main program, before any attempt is made to use the registered type in a dynamic way.

When a metatype is declared, it is possible to store a value in a QVariant. Example 12.14 shows how to store and get declared metatype values back from a QVariant.

EXAMPLE 12.14   src/metatype/metatype.cpp

```
[ . . . . ]

int main (int argc, char* argv[]) {
    QApplication app(argc, argv);
    qRegisterMetaType<Fraction>("Fraction");
    Fraction twoThirds (2,3);
    QVariant var;
    var.setValue(twoThirds);
    Q_ASSERT (var.value<Fraction>() == twoThirds);

    Fraction oneHalf (1,2);
    Fraction threeQuarters (3,4);

    qDebug() << "QList<Fraction> to QVariant and back."

    QList<Fraction> fractions;
    fractions << oneHalf << twoThirds << threeQuarters;
    QFile binaryTestFile("testMetaType.bin");
    binaryTestFile.open(QIODevice::WriteOnly);
    QDataStream dout(&binaryTestFile);
    dout << fractions;
    binaryTestFile.close();
    binaryTestFile.open(QIODevice::ReadOnly);
    QDataStream din(&binaryTestFile);
    QList<Fraction> frac2;
    din >> frac2;
    binaryTestFile.close();
    Q_ASSERT(fractions == frac2);
    createTest();
    qDebug() << "If this output appears, all tests passed.";
}
```

Values of a registered type can be constructed dynamically via QMetaType::construct(), as shown in Example 12.15.

EXAMPLE 12.15   src/metatype/metatype.cpp

```
[ . . . . ]

void createTest() {
    static int fracType = QMetaType::type("Fraction");
    void* vp = QMetaType::construct(fracType);
    Fraction* fp = reinterpret_cast<Fraction*>(vp);                    1
    fp->first = 1;
    fp->second = 2;
    Q_ASSERT(*fp == Fraction(1,2));
}
```

1 Note: This is our first use of reinterpret_cast in this book!

QMetaType::construct() returns a void pointer, so we use reinterpret_cast to convert it to a Fraction pointer.

12.7   invokeMethod()

Qt's capability to connect signals to slots requires a mechanism to indirectly call the slots in a type-safe way, by name. When a slot is called, it is actually done by invokeMethod(). Example 12.16 shows how it accepts a string for the method name. In addition to slots, regular methods marked Q_INVOKABLE can be invoked indirectly this way.

EXAMPLE 12.16   src/reflection/invokemethod/autosaver.cpp

```
void AutoSaver::saveIfNecessary() {
    if (!QMetaObject::invokeMethod(parent(), "save")) {
        qWarning() << "AutoSaver: error invoking save() on parent";
    }
}
```

Similar to QObject::connect(), invokeMethod() takes an optional argument, the Qt::ConnectionType, which enables you to decide if you want synchronous or asynchronous invocation. The default, Qt::AutoConnection, executes the slot synchronously when the sender and receiver are in the same thread.

To pass typed arguments to a function via `invokeMethod()`, you can create values with the `Q_ARG` macro in Example 12.17, which returns a `QGenericArgument`, encapsulating type, and value information for a single argument.

EXAMPLE 12.17   src/reflection/invokemethod/arguments.cpp

```
QByteArray buffer= ... ;
const bool b = QMetaObject::invokeMethod(m_thread, "calculateSpectrum",
                Qt::AutoConnection,
                Q_ARG(QByteArray, buffer),
                Q_ARG(int, format.frequency()),
                Q_ARG(int, bytesPerSample));
```

12.8   Exercises: Reflection

1. Write a program that creates instances of the following classes—`QSpinBox`, `QProcess`, `QTimer`—and shows the user a list of properties (and values, for those that can convert to a `QString`), plus a list of all the method names.

2. Rewrite a previous GUI application to use `invokeMethod()` to `show()` the initial widget from `main()` instead of using a direct call.

12.9   Review Questions

1. What kinds of information can you obtain from a `QMetaObject`?

2. What Qt classes are used to do data reflection? Explain why.

3. How is the `QMetaObject` code for each of your `QObject`-derived classes generated?

4. What is a downcast? In what situations would you use them?

5. What is RTTI? How does Qt provide RTTI?

6. Discuss the differences between the `dynamic_cast` and `qobject_cast` operators.

7. What is a `QVariant`? How might you use one?

8. What are the advantages of using `property()` and `setProperty()` over direct getters and setters?

9. What does the `property()` function return? How do you obtain the actual stored value?

10. Explain how it is possible to add new properties, acquired at runtime, to a `QObject`.

11. Explain how dynamic properties can be serialized.

## Chapter 13

Models and Views

A model-view design framework provides tools and techniques for separating the set of underlying data classes (the model) from the set of classes that present the user with a GUI (the view). Models typically organize the data, which can be tabular or hiearchical. In this chapter, we will show how to use the model classes in Qt to represent many different kinds of data.

In several earlier examples, you saw code that attempted to keep a clean separation between **model** classes that represent data and **view** code that presented a user interface. There are several important reasons for enforcing this separation.

First, separating model from view reduces the complexity of each. Model and view code have completely different maintenance imperatives—changes are driven by completely different factors—so it is much easier to maintain both when they are kept separate. Furthermore, the separation of model from view makes it possible to maintain several different, but consistent, views of the same data. The number of sophisticated view classes that can be reused with well-designed models is constantly growing.

Most GUI toolkits offer list, table, and tree view classes but require the developer to store data inside them. Qt has widget classes derived from corresponding view classes, as shown in Figure 13.1. For developers who have not used model-view frameworks, these widget classes may be easier to learn than their view counterparts. Storing data inside these widgets, however, leads to a strong dependency between the user interface and the underlying structure of the data. This dependency makes it difficult to reuse the widgets for other types of data or to reuse them in other applications. It also makes it difficult to maintain multiple consistent views of the same data. So, the price for the ease of use and convenience (especially in Qt Designer) is a decrease in flexibility and reusability.

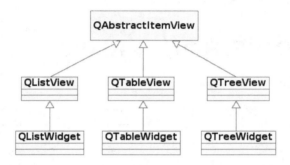

FIGURE 13.1 Widgets and Views

13.1 Model-View-Controller (MVC)

MVC: A Classic Design Pattern

The Gang of Four [Gamma95] provides a brief but precise description of MVC:

MVC consists of three kinds of objects. The model is the application object, the view is its screen presentation, and the controller defines the way the user interface reacts to user input. Before MVC, user interface designs tended to lump these objects together. MVC decouples them to increase flexibility and reuse.

Controller code manages the interactions among events, models, and views. Factory methods, delegates, and creation and destruction code in general fall into the realm of the controller. In the Qt framework, much of the controller mechanism can be found in **delegates**. Delegates control the rendering and editing of individual items in views. Views supply default delegates that are sufficient for most purposes, although you can, if necessary, refine the ways that the default delegates render items by deriving a custom model from `QAbstractItemModel`.

Data and Roles

When you get and set data, there is an optional *role* parameter that lets you specify values for particular *roles* from `Qt::ItemDataRole`, used by the view when it requires data from the model. Some roles specify general-purpose data values, such as `Qt::DisplayRole` (the default), `Qt::EditRole` (the data in a `QVariant` suitable for editing), or `Qt::ToolTipRole` (the data is a `QString` displayed in a tooltip). Other roles can describe appearance, such as `Qt::FontRole`, which enables the default delegate to specify a particular `QFont`, or `Qt::TextAlignmentRole`, which enables the default delegate to specify a particular `Qt::AlignmentFlag`. `Qt::DecorationRole` is used for icons that can decorate values in a view. Typically, you would use a `QColor`, `QIcon`, or `QPixmap` for this role type. Values of `Qt::UserRole` and above can be defined for your own purposes. Think of these as extra columns of data in the table model.

A model-view-controller framework, illustrated in Figure 13.2, uses a number of design patterns to make it possible to write applications that provide more than one view of the same data. It specifies that the model code (responsible for maintaining the data), the view code (responsible for displaying all or part of the data in various ways), and the controller code (responsible for handling events that impact both the data and the model, such as delegates) be kept in separate classes. This separation enables views and controllers to be added or removed without requiring changes in the model. It enables multiple views to be kept up to date and consistent with the model, even if the data is being interactively edited from more than one view. It maximizes code reuse by enabling subtitution of one model for another, or one view for another.

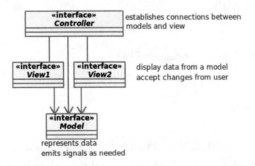

FIGURE 13.2   Model-View-Controller Classes

The primary purpose of a **controller class** is to encapsulate controller code. A complex application might have multiple controllers for different subcomponents, or layers, of the application.

In Qt, the base class for a variety of controller classes is `QAbstractItemDelegate`. Code that `connects` signals to slots can also be considered controller code. As you will see, keeping controller code out of model and view classes can yield additional design benefits.

13.2   Qt Models and Views

Qt includes a model/view framework that maintains separation between the way data is organized and managed and the way that it is presented to the user. Classes for the three most common types of views (lists, trees, and tables) are provided. In addition, there are abstract and concrete data models that can be extended and customized to hold different kinds of data. It is not unusual for an application to have a model that can be viewed in several different ways simultaneously.

Views are objects for acquiring, changing, and displaying the data. Figure 13.3 shows four kinds of view types in the Qt model-view framework.

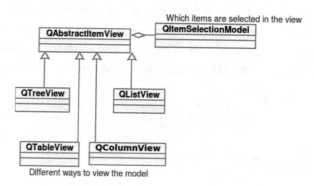

FIGURE 13.3   Qt View Classes

`QAbstractItemModel` defines the standard interface that enables views (and delegates) to access data. Item models store the actual data that is to be viewed and manipulated (e.g., sorted, edited, stored, retrieved, transmitted, and so on). Using signals and slots, they notify all associated views of changes to the data. Each view object holds a pointer to a model object. View objects make frequent calls to item model methods to get or set data or to do various other operations. Figure 13.4 shows the model classes that are designed to work closely with the various view classes.

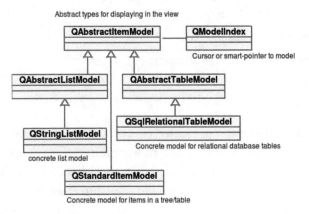

FIGURE 13.4   Qt Model Classes

Selection models are objects that describe which items in the model are selected in the view. Each view has a pointer to a selection model. QModelIndex acts like a cursor, or a smart pointer, providing a uniform way to iterate through list, tree, or table items inside the model.

After setModel() is called, the view should automatically update itself whenever the model changes (assuming the model is written properly).

There are two approaches to implementing the data model. Each has advantages.

1. Implement the passive interface of a QAbstractItemModel, including the data representation.

2. Reuse a general-purpose concrete data model, such as QStandardItemModel, and fill in the data.

The passive interface offers more flexibility in implementation. It is possible to use data structures that are optimized for specific access patterns or data distributions.

The second approach, reusing the QStandardItem (Model) classes, makes it possible to write tree/item code in a style similar to that used by QListWidget, QTableWidget, and QTreeWidget.

Views

QAbstractItemView provides an interface for the common features of the three different model types:

- Lists in various arrangements
- Tables, perhaps with interactive elements
- Trees representing objects in a parent-child hierarchy

Model Index

Each piece of data in a model is represented by a model index. Model indexes give views and delegates indirect access to data items in the model without relying on knowledge of the underlying structure of the data. Only the model needs to know how to directly access its data. The QModelIndex class provides an interface for indexing and accessing data in models derived from QAbstractItemModel. It works equally well for lists, tables, and trees. Each index has a pointer to the model that created it and may have a parent index, in case of hierarchically structured data (e.g., in a tree). QModelIndex treats model data as if it were arranged in a rectangular array with row and column indices, regardless of what underlying data structure actually holds the data.

QModelIndex objects, created by the model, can be used by model, view, or delegate code to locate particular items in the data model. QModelIndex objects have short life spans and can become invalid shortly after being created, so they should be used immediately and then discarded.

QModelIndex::isValid() should be called before using a QModelIndex object that has existed for more than a few operations. QPersistentModelIndex objects have longer life spans but still should be checked with isValid() before being used.

13.2.1   QFileSystemModel

The QFileSystemModel can be viewed as a list, table, or tree. Figure 13.5 shows one in a QTreeView.

QFileSystemModel is already populated with data, so we can simply create one, create a view, and view->setModel(model). Example 13.1 shows what may be the simplest Qt model-view example.

FIGURE 13.5   QFileSystemModel in a `QTreeView`

EXAMPLE 13.1   src/modelview/filesystem/main.cpp

```
#include <QtGui>
int main(int argc, char *argv[]) {
    QApplication app(argc, argv);
    QFileSystemModel model;
    model.setRootPath("/");
    QTreeView tree;
    tree.setModel(&model);
    tree.setSortingEnabled(true);                                    1
    tree.header()->setResizeMode(QHeaderView::ResizeToContents);
    tree.resize(640, 480);
    tree.show();
    return app.exec();
}
```

1 Enable HeaderView sort buttons.

By setting the `resizeMode` in the `headerView`, the columns of the table or tree will be resized whenever the window is. These classes are the basic building blocks for writing a file browser widget.

13.2.2   Multiple Views

Example 13.2 is a function that creates a QStandardItemModel that can be viewed as a tree, a table, or a simple list. This function also demonstrates the use of QStandardItem.

EXAMPLE 13.2   src/modelview/multiview/createModel.cpp

```
#include <QtGui>

QStandardItemModel* createModel(QObject* parent, int rows,
                              int cols, int childNodes) {
    QStandardItemModel*
        model = new QStandardItemModel(rows, cols, parent);
    for( int r=0; r<rows; r++ )
        for( int c=0; c<cols; c++)   {
            QStandardItem* item = new QStandardItem(
                QString("Row:%0, Column:%1").arg(r).arg(c) );
            if( c == 0 )                                          1
                for( int i=0; i<childNodes; i++ ) {
                    QStandardItem* child = new QStandardItem(
                                          QString("Item %0").arg(i) );
                    item->appendRow( child );
                }
            model->setItem(r, c, item);
        }
    model->setHorizontalHeaderItem( 0, new QStandardItem( "Name" ));
    model->setHorizontalHeaderItem( 1, new QStandardItem( "Value" ) );
    return model;
}
```

1 Add child nodes to elements in the first column

The main program, shown in Example 13.3, creates four different views: QListView, QTableView, QTreeView, and QColumnView. Notice that the QTableView and QListView do not display child nodes. In addition, the QColumnView and QListView do not display the table model's columns beyond column 0. The QColumnView displays tree *children* of selected nodes in the column to the right, similar to the way that the MacOS X *Finder* displays files in a selected folder.

All views share the same model, so edits in a cell are immediately visible in the other views. In addition, all views share a selection model so that selections happen simultaneously in all four views.

EXAMPLE 13.3   src/modelview/multiview/multiview.cpp

```
[ . . . . ]

#include "createModel.h"

int main( int argc, char** argv ) {
  QApplication app( argc, argv );
  QStandardItemModel* model = createModel(&app);
  QSplitter vsplitter(Qt::Vertical);
  QSplitter hsplitter;                                          1

  QListView list;
  QTableView table;
  QTreeView tree;
  QColumnView columnView;
  [ . . . . ]

  list.setModel( model );
  table.setModel( model );
  tree.setModel( model );                                       2
  columnView.setModel (model);
  [ . . . . ]

  list.setSelectionModel( tree.selectionModel() );
  table.setSelectionModel( tree.selectionModel() );            3
  columnView.setSelectionModel (tree.selectionModel());
  table.setSelectionBehavior( QAbstractItemView::SelectRows );
  table.setSelectionMode( QAbstractItemView::SingleSelection );
```

1 By default, children lay out horizontally.

2 Share the same model.

3 Common selection model.

When you run this code, you should see a window similar to Figure 13.6. Notice that selecting an item from one of the views causes selection to occur in the others. Because we use the concrete `QStandardItemModel`, items are editable from any of the views. Furthermore, changes from any view are automatically propagated to the other views, thus ensuring that each view is consistent with the model.

You can *trigger* an edit via the F2 key, a double-click, or by simply entering the cell, depending on how `QAbstractItemView::EditTriggers` has been set. You might notice that other keyboard shortcuts (cut, copy, paste, Ctrl+cursor keys, and so on) familiar from your native window environment will also work inside these views and text areas.

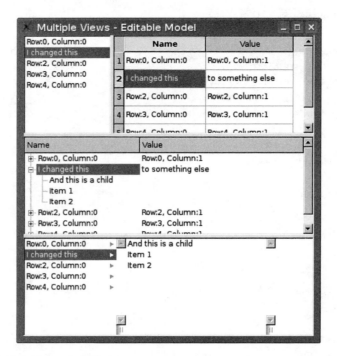

FIGURE 13.6 Multiple Views, One Model

For this application, we used `QSplitter` widgets. A `QSplitter` has some of the features of a layout, but the widgets that it manages are its children. Splitters permit the user to resize the subspaces that contain child widgets at runtime by dragging the boundary between them. Example 13.4 includes the code that sets up the splitter widgets.

EXAMPLE 13.4   src/modelview/multiview/multiview.cpp

```
[ . . . . ]

hsplitter.addWidget( &list );
hsplitter.addWidget( &table );
vsplitter.addWidget( &hsplitter );
vsplitter.addWidget ( &tree );
vsplitter.addWidget ( &columnView );

vsplitter.setGeometry(300, 300, 500, 500);
vsplitter.setWindowTitle("Multiple Views - Editable Model");
```

13.2.3 Delegate Classes

The delegate, shown in Figure 13.7, provides another level of indirection between the model and view, which increases the possibilities for customization.

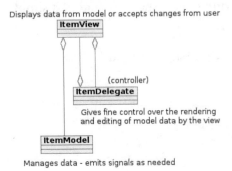

FIGURE 13.7   Model, View, and Delegate

A delegate class, usually derived from `QAbstractItemDelegate`, adds several kinds of controller features to the Qt model-view framework. A delegate class can provide a factory method that enables view classes to create editors and virtual getters and setters for moving editor data to and from the model. It can also provide a virtual `paint()` method for custom display of items in the view. Delegates can be set up for an entire `QAbstractItemView` or for just one of its columns.

Figure 13.8 shows a modified version of the StarDelegate example from `$QTDIR/examples/modelview/stardelegate`.

FIGURE 13.8   Star Delegates

In Example 13.5, we extended from QStyledItemDelegate. This is a concrete class that is used by default in Q(List|Table|Tree)Views. It provides a QLineEdit for editing QString properties, and other appropriate editors for the native style, when the type is a boolean, QDate, QTime, int, or double. The custom delegate shows the virtual methods one must override to get "stars" instead of a simple integer in the table for a custom StarRating value.

EXAMPLE 13.5   src/modelview/playlists/stardelegate.h

```
#ifndef STARDELEGATE_H
#define STARDELEGATE_H

#include <QStyledItemDelegate>
#include <QStyleOptionViewItem>
class StarDelegate : public QStyledItemDelegate {
    Q_OBJECT
public:
    typedef QStyledItemDelegate SUPER;
    StarDelegate(QObject* parent=0) : SUPER(parent) {};
    QWidget* createEditor(QWidget* parent,
                          const QStyleOptionViewItem& option,
                          const QModelIndex& index) const;
    void paint(QPainter* painter,
               const QStyleOptionViewItem& option,
               const QModelIndex& index) const;

    void setEditorData(QWidget* editor,
                       const QModelIndex& index) const;
    void setModelData(QWidget* editor,
                      QAbstractItemModel* model,
                      const QModelIndex& index) const;
};

#endif // STARDELEGATE_H
```

Delegates give full control over how the item in a view appears when displayed, via the paint() method, overridden in Example 13.6.

EXAMPLE 13.6   src/modelview/playlists/stardelegate.cpp

```
[ . . . . ]

void StarDelegate::
    paint(QPainter* painter,
            const QStyleOptionViewItem& option,
            const QModelIndex& index) const {
    QString field = index.model()->headerData(index.column(),
                                        Qt::Horizontal).toString();
    if (field == "length") {
        QVariant var = index.data(Qt::DisplayRole);
        Q_ASSERT(var.canConvert(QVariant::Time));
        QTime time = var.toTime();
        QString str = time.toString("m:ss");
        painter->drawText(option.rect, str, QTextOption());
        // can't use drawDisplay with QStyledItemDelegate:
        // drawDisplay(painter, option, option.rect, str);
        return;
    }
    if (field != "rating") {
        SUPER::paint(painter, option, index);
        return;
    }
    QVariant variantData = index.data(Qt::DisplayRole);
    StarRating starRating = variantData.value<StarRating>();
    if (option.state & QStyle::State_Selected)
        painter->fillRect(option.rect, option.palette.highlight());
    starRating.paint(painter, option.rect, option.palette,
                    StarRating::ReadOnly);
}
```

In addition, delegates can determine what kind of widget shows up when the user triggers editing of an item. For this, you need to either override createEditor(), as shown in Example 13.7, or supply a custom QItemEditorFactory.

EXAMPLE 13.7   src/modelview/playlists/stardelegate.cpp

```
[ . . . . ]

QWidget* StarDelegate::
    createEditor(QWidget* parent,
                const QStyleOptionViewItem& option,
```

```
                          const QModelIndex& index) const {
      QString field = index.model()->headerData(index.column(),
                                     Qt::Horizontal).toString();
      if (field == "rating")  {
             return new StarEditor(parent);
      }
      if (field == "length") {
          return new TimeDisplay(parent);
      }
      return SUPER::createEditor(parent, option, index);
}v
```

What Is an Edit Trigger?

There are various ways to "trigger" the view into going into edit mode. On most desktop platforms, the F2 key is a "platform edit" key. On handhelds, it may be a gesture such as double-tap, or a special button. See the API documentation for `QAbstractItemView::setEditTriggers(EditTriggers triggers)` http:// doc.qt.nokia.com/latest/qabstractitemview.html#editTriggers-prop.

When you trigger an edit request, you want to see an editor that initially has the value from the model for you to see or change. This is done by `setEditorData()`, as shown in Example 13.8.

EXAMPLE 13.8   src/modelview/playlists/stardelegate.cpp

```
[ . . . . ]


void StarDelegate::
    setEditorData(QWidget* editor,
                const QModelIndex& index) const {
    QVariant val = index.data(Qt::EditRole);
    StarEditor* starEditor = qobject_cast<StarEditor*>(editor);              1
    if (starEditor != 0) {
        StarRating sr = qVariantValue<StarRating>(val);                      2
        starEditor->setStarRating(sr);
        return;
    }
```

```
    TimeDisplay* timeDisplay = qobject_cast<TimeDisplay*>(editor);     3
    if (timeDisplay != 0) {
        QTime t = val.toTime();
        timeDisplay->setTime(t);
        return;
    }
    SUPER::setEditorData(editor, index);                               4
    return;
}
```

1 Dynamic type checking.

2 Extract user type value from QVariant.

3 Dynamic type checking.

4 Let base class handle other types.

When the user finishes editing, setModelData(), shown in Example 13.9, is called to put the data back into the QAbstractItemModel.

EXAMPLE 13.9   src/modelview/playlists/stardelegate.cpp

```
[ . . . . ]

void StarDelegate::
    setModelData(QWidget* editor, QAbstractItemModel* model,
                 const QModelIndex& index) const {
    StarEditor* starEditor = qobject_cast<StarEditor*>(editor);
    if (starEditor != 0) {
        StarRating r = starEditor->starRating();
        QVariant v;
        v.setValue<StarRating>(r);
        model->setData(index, v, Qt::EditRole);
        return;
    }
    TimeDisplay* td = qobject_cast<TimeDisplay*>(editor);
    if (td != 0) {
        QTime t = td->time();
        model->setData(index, QVariant(t));
        return;
    }
    SUPER::setModelData(editor, model, index);
    return;
}
```

13.3   Table Models

The next example, pictured in Figure 13.9, is a table model with a view for displaying and editing actions and their corresponding shortcuts. To demonstrate the use and display of the different data roles supported in the Qt Model-View classes, we take a list of QActions and display it in a table. Each action can have an icon, tooltips, status tip, and other user data. These directly correspond to four of the available data roles.

FIGURE 13.9   Shortcut Editor

13.3.1   Standard or Abstract?

When programmers first get acquainted with QStandardItem, they sometimes use it in situations where it might not be the best choice. Although QStandardItemModel can make it a bit easier to build a model without the need for inheritance from an abstract base class, if you are concerned about QStandardItem data's failing to stay in sync with other data in memory, or that it takes too long to create the standard items initially, these could be indicators that you should derive directly or indirectly from a QAbstractItemModel instead.

Example 13.10 is an example of a QStandardItem-based class for a shortcut table model.

EXAMPLE 13.10   src/modelview/shortcutmodel-standarditem/actiontableeditor.h

```
[ . . . . ]
class ActionTableEditor : public QDialog {
    Q_OBJECT
public:
    ActionTableEditor(QWidget* parent = 0);
    ~ActionTableEditor();
protected slots:
    void on_m_tableView_activated(const QModelIndex& idx=QModelIndex());
    QList<QStandardItem*> createActionRow(QAction* a);
protected:
    void populateTable();
    void changeEvent(QEvent* e);
private:
    QList<QAction*> m_actions;
    QStandardItemModel* m_model;
    Ui_ActionTableEditor* m_ui;
};
[ . . . . ]
```

Because this is a Designer form, the widgets were created and instantiated in generated code that looks like Example 13.11.

EXAMPLE 13.11   src/modelview/shortcutmodel-standarditem/actiontableeditor_ui.h

```
[ . . . . ]
class Ui_ActionTableEditor
{
public:
  QVBoxLayout *verticalLayout;
  QTableView *m_tableView;
  QSpacerItem *verticalSpacer;
  QDialogButtonBox *m_buttonBox;

  void setupUi(QDialog *ActionTableEditor)
  {
    if (ActionTableEditor->objectName().isEmpty())
      ActionTableEditor->setObjectName(QString::
                                  fromUtf8("ActionTableEditor"));
    ActionTableEditor->resize(348, 302);
    verticalLayout = new QVBoxLayout(ActionTableEditor);
    verticalLayout->setObjectName(QString::fromUtf8("verticalLayout"));
    m_tableView = new QTableView(ActionTableEditor);
```

```
    m_tableView->setObjectName(QString::fromUtf8("m_tableView"));
    verticalLayout->addWidget(m_tableView);
[ . . . . ]
```

Example 13.12 shows how to create rows of data, one per `QAction`, in a `QStandardItemModel`.

EXAMPLE 13.12   src/modelview/shortcutmodel-standarditem/actiontableeditor.cpp

```
[ . . . . ]

QList<QStandardItem*> ActionTableEditor::
createActionRow(QAction* a) {
    QList<QStandardItem*> row;
    QStandardItem* actionItem = new QStandardItem(a->text());
    QStandardItem* shortcutItem =
        new QStandardItem(a->shortcut().toString());                1
    actionItem->setIcon(a->icon());                                 2

    actionItem->setToolTip(a->toolTip());                           3
    actionItem->setFlags(Qt::ItemIsSelectable | Qt::ItemIsEnabled); 4
    shortcutItem->setFlags(Qt::ItemIsSelectable| Qt::ItemIsEnabled);
    shortcutItem->setIcon(a->icon());                               5
    row << actionItem << shortcutItem;
    return row;
}


void ActionTableEditor::populateTable() {
    foreach (QWidget* w, qApp->topLevelWidgets())                   6
        foreach (QAction* a, w->findChildren<QAction*>()) {         7
            if (a->children().size() > 0) continue;                 8
            if (a->text().size() > 0) m_actions << a;
        }

    int rows = m_actions.size();
    m_model = new QStandardItemModel(this);
    m_model->setColumnCount(2);
    m_model->setHeaderData(0, Qt::Horizontal, QString("Action"),
                           Qt::DisplayRole);
    m_model->setHeaderData(1, Qt::Horizontal, QString("Shortcut"),
                           Qt::DisplayRole);
    QHeaderView* hv = m_ui->m_tableView->horizontalHeader();
```

```
m_ui->m_tableView->
    setSelectionBehavior(QAbstractItemView::SelectRows);
m_ui->m_tableView->
    setSelectionMode(QAbstractItemView::NoSelection);
hv->setResizeMode(QHeaderView::ResizeToContents);
hv->setStretchLastSection(true);
m_ui->m_tableView->verticalHeader()->hide();
for (int row=0; row < rows; ++row ) {
    m_model->appendRow(createActionRow(m_actions[row]));
}
m_ui->m_tableView->setModel(m_model);                              9
}
```

1 Duplicating data from `QAction` to `QStandardItem`.
2 More duplicate data.
3 More duplicate data.
4 Read-only model without `Qt::ItemIsEditable`.
5 More duplicate data.
6 All top-level widgets.
7 All QActions that can be found.
8 Skip groups of actions.
9 Connect the view to its model.

`QStandardItem` has its own properties, so we copy values from each `QAction` into two corresponding Items. This kind of duplication of data can have huge performance and memory impact when working with large data models. The main point of this is that there is a significant overhead just creating the model, and we throw it away when we are done with it.

This example does not use the editing features of the view to change data in the model. That requires writing a delegate to provide a custom editor widget and is left as an exercise for you (Exercise 4 in Section 13.6). Instead, a dialog is popped up when the user activates a row, as shown in Example 13.13. When the dialog is `Accepted`, the `QAction`'s shortcut is set directly, bypassing the model entirely. The next time you display this shortcut table, the model must be regenerated from the action list again, or else we need to handle changes properly.

EXAMPLE 13.13 src/modelview/shortcutmodel-standarditem/actiontableeditor.cpp

```
[ . . . . ]

void ActionTableEditor::
on_m_tableView_activated(const QModelIndex& idx) {
    int row = idx.row();
    QAction* action = m_actions.at(row);
    ActionEditorDialog aed(action);
    int result = aed.exec();                                        1
    if (result ==  QDialog::Accepted) {                             2
        action->setShortcut(aed.keySequence());                    3
        m_ui->m_tableView->reset();
    }
}
```

1 Pop-up modal dialog for editing an action's shortcut.

2 This would be a good place to check for duplicate/ambiguous bindings.

3 Skip the model and set the QAction property directly.

A Better Approach...

Example 13.14 is an example of a table model that extends QAbstractTableModel by implementing data() and flags(), the pure virtual methods that provide access to model data. The model is a proxy for a list of QActions that are already in memory. This means there is no duplication of data in the model.

EXAMPLE 13.14 src/libs/actioneditor/actiontablemodel.h

```
[ . . . . ]
class ACTIONEDITOR_EXPORT ActionTableModel : public QAbstractTableModel {
    Q_OBJECT
 public:
    explicit ActionTableModel(QList<QAction*> actions, QObject* parent=0);
    int rowCount(const QModelIndex&  = QModelIndex()) const {
        return m_actions.size();
    }
    int columnCount(const QModelIndex& = QModelIndex()) const {
        return m_columns;
    }
    QAction* action(int row) const;
```

```
QVariant headerData(int section, Qt::Orientation orientation,      1
    int role) const;
QVariant data(const QModelIndex& index, int role) const;           2
Qt::ItemFlags flags(const QModelIndex& index) const;               3
bool setData(const QModelIndex& index, const QVariant& value,
    int role = Qt::EditRole);                                      4

protected:
  QList<QAction*> m_actions;
  int m_columns;
};
[ . . . . ]
```

1 Optional override.

2 Required override.

3 Required override.

4 Required for an editable model.

Example 13.15 shows the implementation of data(). Notice that for many of the different properties of a QAction, there is an equivalent *data role*. You can think of a role (especially a user role) as an additional column of data.

EXAMPLE 13.15   src/libs/actioneditor/actiontablemodel.cpp

```
[ . . . . ]

QVariant ActionTableModel::
data(const QModelIndex& index, int role) const {
    int row = index.row();
    if (row >= m_actions.size()) return QVariant();
    int col = index.column();
    if (col >= columnCount()) return QVariant();
    if (role == Qt::DecorationRole)
        if (col == 0)
            return m_actions[row]->icon();

    if (role == Qt::ToolTipRole) {
        return m_actions[row]->toolTip();
    }
    if (role == Qt::StatusTipRole) {
        return m_actions[row]->statusTip();
    }
```

```
    if (role == Qt::DisplayRole) {
        if (col == 1) return m_actions[row]->shortcut();
        if (col == 2) return m_actions[row]->parent()->objectName();
        else return m_actions[row]->text();
    }
    return QVariant();
}
```

The `ActionTableModel` is lightweight, in the sense that it creates/copies no data. It presents the data to the view only when the view asks for it. This means it is possible to implement sparse data structures behind a data model. This also means models can fetch data in a lazy fashion from another source, as is the case with `QSqlTableModel` and `QFileSystemModel`.

13.3.2   Editable Models

For editable models, you must override `flags()` and `setData()`. If you want in-place editing (in the actual view), you would return `Qt::ItemIsEditable` from `flags()`. Because we still pop up an `ActionEditorDialog` when an item is clicked, we do not need in-place editing so, Example 13.16 simply returns `Qt::ItemIsEnabled`.

EXAMPLE 13.16   src/libs/actioneditor/actiontablemodel.cpp

```
[ . . . . ]

Qt::ItemFlags ActionTableModel::
flags(const QModelIndex& index) const {
    if (index.isValid()) return Qt::ItemIsEnabled;
    else return 0;
}
```

Example 13.17 shows how, in `setData()`, you can check for ambiguous shortcuts before actually setting new values. After the data is changed, it is important to emit a `dataChanged()` signal so that views that may be showing old data know it is time to fetch newer data from the model.

EXAMPLE 13.17   src/libs/actioneditor/actiontablemodel.cpp

```
[ . . . . ]

bool ActionTableModel::
setData(const QModelIndex& index, const QVariant& value, int role) {
```

```
    if (role != Qt::EditRole) return false;
    int row = index.row();
    if ((row < 0) | (row >= m_actions.size())) return false;
    QString str = value.toString();
    QKeySequence ks(str);
    QAction* previousAction = 0;

    if (ks != QKeySequence() ) foreach (QAction* act, m_actions) {
        if (act->shortcut() == ks) {
            previousAction = act;
            break;
        }
    }
    if (previousAction != 0) {
        QString error = tr("%1 is already bound to %2.").
                arg(ks.toString()).arg(previousAction->text());
        bool answer = QMessageBox::question(0, error,
                    tr("%1\n Remove previous binding?").arg(error),
                    QMessageBox::Yes, QMessageBox::No);
        if (!answer) return false;
        previousAction->setShortcut(QKeySequence());
    }
    m_actions[row]->setShortcut(ks);
    QModelIndex changedIdx = createIndex(row, 1);                  1
    emit dataChanged(changedIdx, changedIdx);                     2
    return true;
}
```

1 Column 1 displays the shortcut.

2 Required for views to know when/what to update.

To support inserting/removing rows, there are analogous signals, rowsInserted() and rowsRemoved(), that you must emit from our implementations of insertRows()/removeRows().

After one or more shortcuts have been changed, you save them to QSettings. Example 13.18 shows how to keep track of the modified QActions that need to be saved.

EXAMPLE 13.18   src/libs/actioneditor/actiontableeditor.cpp

```
[ . . . . . ]

void ActionTableEditor::
on_m_tableView_activated(const QModelIndex& idx) {
```

```
    int row = idx.row();
    QAction* action = m_model->action(row);
    ActionEditorDialog aed(action);

    int result = aed.exec();
    if (result ==  QDialog::Accepted) {
        QKeySequence ks = aed.keySequence();
        m_model->setData(idx, ks.toString());
        m_changedActions << action;
    }
}
```

Example 13.19 shows how those shortcuts are saved to QSettings, but only if the user accepts the dialog.

EXAMPLE 13.19   src/libs/actioneditor/actiontableeditor.cpp

```
[ . . . . ]

void ActionTableEditor::accept() {
    QSettings s;
    s.beginGroup("shortcut");
    foreach (QAction* act, m_changedActions) {
        s.setValue(act->text(), act->shortcut() );
    }
    s.endGroup();
    QDialog::accept();
}
```

13.3.3   Sorting and Filtering

Don't bother looking for the code creating the QLineEdit, the Clear button, or the connect between the two in Figure 13.10. Those were all defined in Designer and generated by uic.

Thanks to QSortFilterProxyModel, you can add sorting/filtering capability to an existing model with fewer than five lines of code. Figure 13.11 shows how the proxy sits between the view and the model.

FIGURE 13.10   Filtered Table View

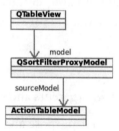

FIGURE 13.11   Sort Filter Proxy

Example 13.20 shows what is needed to set up the sort filter proxy in the preceding action table example.

EXAMPLE 13.20   src/libs/actioneditor/actiontableeditor.cpp

```
[ . . . . . ]

void ActionTableEditor::setupSortFilter() {
    m_sortFilterProxy = new QSortFilterProxyModel(this);
    m_sortFilterProxy->setSourceModel(m_model);                    1
```

```
    m_ui->m_tableView->setModel(m_sortFilterProxy);                2
    m_sortFilterProxy->setFilterKeyColumn(-1);                     3

}
void ActionTableEditor::on_m_filterField_textChanged             4
    (const QString& newText) {
    m_sortFilterProxy->setFilterFixedString(newText);            5
}
```

1 `SortFilterProxy` source model set to `ActionTableModel`.
2 Table view model set to proxy model instead of `ActionTableModel`.
3 Filter on all fields.
4 Auto-connected slot.
5 Change the filter string.

The `filterField_textChanged` is an auto-connected slot that gets called whenever the `textChanged` signal is emitted by the `filterField QLineEdit`.

13.4   Tree Models

To display trees of data in a `QTreeView` (parents and children), you have a few options:

1. `QAbstractItemModel` is a general-purpose abstract model used with `QTreeView`, `QListView`, or `QTableView`.

2. `QStandardItemModel`, used in Example 13.2, is a concrete class that can store `QStandardItems`, making it convenient to populate a concrete model with tree nodes.

3. `QTreeWidgetItem` is not a model class, but it can build trees in a `QTreeWidget`, derived from `QTreeView`.

WidgetItem Classes

`QTreeWidget` and `QTreeWidgetItem` classes are used primarily in Designer when populating views with items. The APIs are similar to how things were done in the Qt3 days. They're recommended only for simple kinds of data and for single views. This is because with the widget/item classes, it is not possible to separate the model from the view or have multiple views automatically update themselves in response to changes in data.

The `QStandardItemModel` and `QTreeWidgetItem` classes are tree nodes that can be instantiated or extended. The individual objects connect in a tree-like fashion, similar to `QObject` children (Section 8.2) or `QDomNodes` (Section 15.3). In fact, these classes are implementations of the Composite pattern.

Figure 13.12 is a screenshot of the next example, which shows the objects currently in memory that compose the user interface of the application.

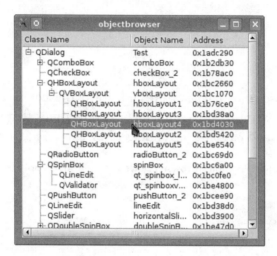

FIGURE 13.12   ObjectBrowser Tree

The class definition for this application is shown in Example 13.21. `ObjectBrowserModel` is a concrete tree model extended from `QAbstractItemModel`. It implements all the necessary methods to provide a read-only object browser tree.

EXAMPLE 13.21   src/modelview/objectbrowser/ObjectBrowserModel.h

```
[ . . . . ]
#include <QAbstractItemModel>
class ObjectBrowserModel :public QAbstractItemModel {
 public:
    explicit ObjectBrowserModel (QObject* rootObject);
    int columnCount ( const QModelIndex& parent = QModelIndex() ) const;
    int rowCount ( const QModelIndex& parent = QModelIndex() ) const;
    QVariant data ( const QModelIndex& index,
                    int role = Qt::DisplayRole ) const;
    QVariant headerData(int section, Qt::Orientation,
                    int role = Qt::DisplayRole) const;
```

```
    QModelIndex index ( int row, int column,
                        const QModelIndex& parent = QModelIndex()) const;
    QModelIndex parent ( const QModelIndex& index ) const;

 protected:
    QList<QObject*> children( QObject* parent ) const;
    QString label( const QObject* widget, int column ) const;
    QObject* qObject ( const QModelIndex& ) const;
 private:
    QObject *rootItem;
};
[ . . . . ]
```

To enable tree views to navigate up and down the parent-child hierarchy of a QAbstractItemModel, you need to implement two methods that were not needed for table views: index() and parent(). Example 13.22 shows their implementation.

EXAMPLE 13.22   src/modelview/objectbrowser/ObjectBrowserModel.cpp

```
[ . . . . ]

QModelIndex ObjectBrowserModel::
index(int row, int col, const QModelIndex& parent) const {
    if ((row < 0) || (col < 0) || row >= rowCount() ||
    col >= columnCount()) return QModelIndex();
    return createIndex( row, col, qObject(parent) );             1
}

QModelIndex ObjectBrowserModel::parent( const QModelIndex& index ) const {
    if (!index.isValid()) return QModelIndex();
    QObject* obj = qObject(index)->parent();                     2
    if ( obj == 0 )
        return QModelIndex();

    QObject* parent = obj->parent();
    int row = children( parent ).indexOf( obj );
    return createIndex( row, 0, parent );
}

QObject* ObjectBrowserModel::
```

```
qObject(const QModelIndex& index) const {                                3
    if ( index.isValid() ) {
        QObject* parent = reinterpret_cast<QObject*>( index.internalPointer() );
        return children(parent)[index.row()];                            4
    }
    return 0;                                                            5
}
```

1 Store an `internalPointer` in the index.

2 `qObject()` returns the row child of this index, but you want this index's parent `QObject` pointer, which is stored in `index.internalPointer()`.

3 My index's `internalPointer` is my parent `QObject` pointer. I am the `row()` child of my parent.

4 This is me!

5 This is the root.

`index()` can also be thought of as "childIndex," as it is used to find `QModelIndex` of children in the tree, while `parent()` calculates one step in the other direction. It is not important to implement these methods in table models that are only used with table views, but `index()` and `parent()` are necessary if you ever want to view the model with a tree view.

13.4.1 Trolltech Model Testing Tool

The methods you implement in a model are called by views you may not have tested or use cases that you have not tried. Because the data values are often driven by the user, it can be helpful to test your model with the "modeltest" tool. It finds common implementation errors quickly and gives you an indication of how to fix them.

Figure 13.13 shows what happens when you run the `ObjectBrowser` example from Example 13.21 in the debugger from QtCreator, with the `ModelTest` tool. The failed assertions and aborts might be deeper in the stack trace, so you need a debugger to see the full stack trace. Typically, there will be code comments right before the aborted line that indicate what test it was performing at that point. The included `readme.txt` file, shown in Example 13.23, contains brief instructions for using `ModelTest`.

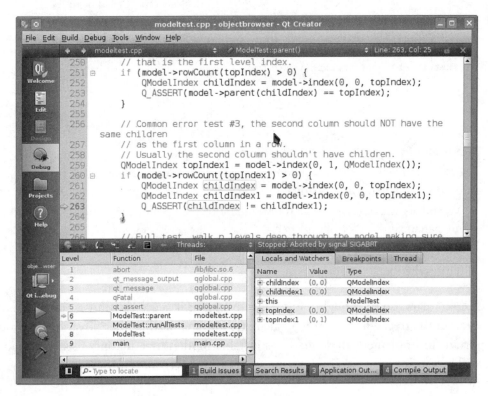

FIGURE 13.13   ModelTest in the Debugger

EXAMPLE 13.23   src/libs/modeltest/readme.txt

```
To use the model test do the following:

1) Include the pri file at the end of your project pro file using the
include() command like so:

include(../path/to/dir/modeltest.pri)

2) Then in your source include "modeltest.h" and instantiate ModelTest
with your model so the test can live for the lifetime of your model.
For example:
```

```
#include <modeltest.h>

QDirModel *model = new QDirModel(this);
new ModelTest(model, this);
```

3) That is it. When the test finds a problem it will assert.
modeltest.cpp contains some hints on how to fix problems that the test
finds.

13.5 Smarter Pointers

Although C++ does not support garbage collection, automatic memory management
of C++ objects can be achieved in a number of ways, primarily through the use of
smart pointers and reference counting. Qt offers many different smart pointer types,
suited for different purposes.

A class is called a **smart pointer** if it overrides `operator*()` and `operator->()`, the
pointer dereference operators. This enables instances to act as if they were built-in
pointers. Such classes are almost always template classes, so in definitions, we must supply the referenced type in template arguments. The most common places to find these
operators overloaded are in iterators and smart pointers. What makes them smart is
usually due to customized behavior during construction, destruction, or assignment.

`QScopedPointer` is a smart pointer that automatically deletes the referenced object
when the pointer goes out of scope. It is similar to `std::auto_ptr`. It makes no sense to
copy `QScopedPointer`s because then the referenced object would be deleted twice. The
scope of the pointer clearly shows the lifetime and ownership of the referenced object.

`QSharedPointer`, like `QScopedPointer`, is a smart pointer that deletes its referenced
object, but copies are permitted, and the `QSharedPointer` keeps a reference count. The
shared heap object is deleted only when the last shared pointer to it is destroyed.

One place we have used `QSharedPointer` is in `DataObjectTableModel`, shown in
Example 13.24.

EXAMPLE 13.24   src/libs/dataobjects/dataobjecttablemodel.h

```
[ . . . . ]

class DOBJS_EXPORT DataObjectTableModel : public QAbstractTableModel {
    Q_OBJECT
  public:
```

```
    explicit DataObjectTableModel(DataObject* headerModel = 0,
                                   QObject* parent=0);
    virtual bool insertRecord(QSharedPointer<DataObject> newRecord,
                              int position = -1,
                              const QModelIndex& = QModelIndex());
    QStringList toStringList() const;

    QString toString() const;

    virtual int fieldIndex(const QString& fieldName) const;
    virtual ~DataObjectTableModel();
[ . . . . ]

  public slots:
    void clear();
    void rowChanged(const QString& fileName);

  protected:
    QList<QSharedPointer<DataObject> > m_Data;
    QList<bool> m_isEditable;
    QStringList m_Headers;
    DataObject* m_Original;
    void extractHeaders(DataObject* hmodel);
  public:
    DataObjectTableModel& operator<<(QSharedPointer<DataObject> newObj) {
        insertRecord(newObj);
        return *this;
    }
};
```

You can invoke `property()` and `setProperty()` on the `DataObject` indirectly with the smart pointer, just like a regular pointer, using `operator->`, as shown in Example 13.25.

EXAMPLE 13.25   src/libs/dataobjects/dataobjecttablemodel.cpp

```
[ . . . . ]

QVariant DataObjectTableModel::
data(const QModelIndex& index, int role) const {
    if (!index.isValid())
        return QVariant();
    int row(index.row()), col(index.column());
```

```
    if (row >= rowCount()) return QVariant();
    QSharedPointer<DataObject> lineItem(m_Data.at(row));
    if (lineItem.isNull()) {
        qDebug() << "lineitem=0:" << index;
        return QVariant();
    }
    if (role == Qt::UserRole || role == Qt::ToolTipRole)
        return lineItem->objectName();
    else if (role == DisplayRole || role == EditRole) {
        return lineItem->property(m_Headers.at(col));
    } else
        return QVariant();
}


bool DataObjectTableModel::
setData(const QModelIndex& index, const QVariant& value, int role) {
    if (index.isValid() && role == EditRole) {
        int row(index.row()), col(index.column());
        QSharedPointer<DataObject> lineItem(m_Data.at(row));
        lineItem->setProperty(m_Headers.at(col), value);
        emit dataChanged(index, index);
        return true;
    }
    return false;
}
```

If each row is represented by a `DataObject`, which could exist in more than one `DataObjectTableModel`, by using reference-counted pointers, the table can clean up the `DataObject`s when it has the last shared pointer to the object.

13.6   Exercises: Models and Views

1. Write a file system browser, with an address bar, **Up** button, and optionally other commonly found buttons and features of your favorite file browser. Use the `QFileSystemModel` and at least two view classes separated by a `QSplitter`. One of the views should be a `QTableView`. You can choose a Windows Explorer-style tree on the side of the table, or a Mac OSX-style browser with a `QColumnView` and a table, as shown in Figure 13.14. Make it possible to select a directory in the tree/columnview, addressbar, or with the **Up** button, so that

any of them will update the contents of the table to reflect the newly selected directory.

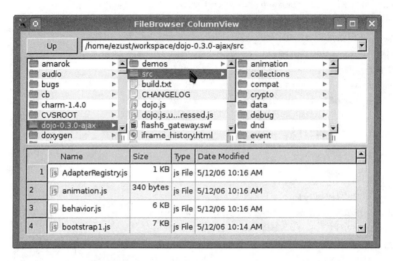

FIGURE 13.14   ColumnView File Browser

2. Extend `QAbstractTableModel` and define a `PlayListModel`. It should represent a list of `MetaDataValue` (or `MetaDataObject`) objects. These can be based on audio tracks or videos, your choice.

   Generate and display test data either based on real media files and `MetaDataLoader` or using your own test data/factory method. Implement actions for load/save playlist to disk.

3. Revisiting the program in Section 11.6, implement a GUI for showing friends lists or a bidirectional relationship between symbols. The GUI should show two `QListViews` or `QListWidgets`, like Figure 13.15.

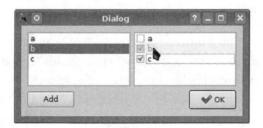

FIGURE 13.15   Friends Lists

- Both lists should show the set of symbols available.
- Click add to add a new symbol to both lists.
- When a symbol is selected on the left, the right list shows the friends checked and the strangers unchecked.
- Checking/unchecking a box on the right adds/removes a relationship between the two people.
- Do not allow the user to uncheck a contact if it is the same as the selected one on the left. Always show it as checked.

4. Rewrite the ShortcutEditor example to use in-place editing. You need to write a delegate class for the table view, which provides a custom editor when the user wants to change a shortcut.

13.7   Review Questions

1. What are model classes? What are view classes? What relationship should be maintained between them?

2. What tools are provided by Qt to work with models and views?

3. What is MVC?

4. What is controller code? Which Qt classes are controller classes?

5. What are delegates? Where are they found?

6. In relation to delegates, what are roles?

7. How do you determine what item(s) is/are selected in a `QListView`?

8. If you want to iterate through items in an `QAbstractItemModel`, what would be a good class to use?

9. There are two hierarchies of classes for storing and displaying tree-like data: *Widget/Item and *ItemModel/View. What reasons might you have for using one rather than the other?

10. Why would you use the `QStandardItemModel` rather than the `QAbstractItemModel`? Or vice versa?

Chapter 14

Validation and Regular Expressions

Input data generally needs to be screened, or *validated*, to make sure that it is appropriate. Numeric data generally needs to be within certain ranges. String data often must have a certain format. Validation of input data is an important issue that can be handled in an object-oriented way by a combination of Qt classes. This chapter discusses some efficient ways of validating input, including the use of regular expressions.

Validators and input masks give the developer fine-grained control over behavior of a `QLineEdit`, for the purpose of restricting certain kinds of inputs. Before working with them, keep in mind that Qt also offers predefined input widgets and input dialogs for many common value types already (`QDateEdit`, `QTimeEdit`, `QCalendarWidget`, `QColorDialog`, `QSpinBox`, `QDoubleSpinBox`) that permit the user to easily select values, while permitting the developer to restrict the input and narrow the range of valid values. In the case of `QDateEdit`, the developer can also choose from a variety of locale-aware date formats to use. See Figure 9.9, or run Qt's Standard Dialogs Example to demonstrate some of them.

14.1   Input Masks

An **input mask** is an active pattern that controls what can be typed into an input widget by the user. It can help to prevent certain types of incorrect data from being entered. Each `QLineEdit` has a `QString` property for storing a string of mask characters that can be applied to the data that is being typed into it. An input mask can specify what kinds of characters are allowed in certain positions of a string that is being typed into a `QLineEdit`. The string consists of special, predefined mask characters and (optional) ordinary characters that occupy corresponding positions in the entered string.

The set of predefined mask characters consists of the following:

TABLE 14.1   Mask Characters

Character	Required Character in That Position
A	ASCII alphabetic character—uppercase or lowercase
N	ASCII alphanumeric character—uppercase or lowercase
X	ASCII any character
D	ASCII nonzero digit
9	ASCII digit
H	Hexadecimal digit
B	Binary digit

Lowercase versions of the mask letters listed in Table 14.1 specify that the corresponding input characters are permitted in that position but not required. Using zero (0) instead of nine (9) indicates that an ASCII digit is permitted in that position but not required. # indicates that an ASCII digit or a plus (+) or a minus (–) is permitted in that position but not required. In addition, there are a few meta characters, shown in Table 14.2.

TABLE 14.2   Mask Meta Characters

Character	Effect
>	The following alphabetic characters are uppercased
<	The following alphabetic characters are lowercased
!	No further case conversion
\	Escape char

To demonstrate the use of the input mask, we present a short application that permits the user to specify the characters of the input mask and then see how the input is restricted. Example 14.1 shows the class definition.

EXAMPLE 14.1 src/validate/inputmask/masktestform.h

```
[ . . . . ]
class MaskTestForm : public QWidget {
    Q_OBJECT
public:
    MaskTestForm();
public slots:
    void showResult();
    void installMask();
    void again();
private:
    QLineEdit* m_InputMask;
    QLineEdit* m_StringEntry;
    QLabel* m_Result;
    void setupForm();
};
[ . . . . ]
```

In Example 14.2 we implement the class.

EXAMPLE 14.2 src/validate/inputmask/masktestform.cpp

```
[ . . . . ]
MaskTestForm::MaskTestForm(): m_InputMask(new QLineEdit),
    m_StringEntry(new QLineEdit), m_Result(new QLabel) {
    setupForm();
    move(500, 500); /*Start in mid screen (approx). */
}

void MaskTestForm::setupForm() {
    setWindowTitle("Mask Test Demo");
    QPushButton* againButton = new QPushButton("Another Input Mask", this);
    QPushButton* quitButton = new QPushButton("Quit", this);
    QFormLayout *form = new QFormLayout(this);
    form->addRow("Mask String:", m_InputMask);
    form->addRow("Test Input: ", m_StringEntry);
```

```
    form->addRow("Result:", m_Result);
    connect(m_InputMask, SIGNAL(returnPressed()),
            this, SLOT(installMask()));
    connect(m_StringEntry, SIGNAL(returnPressed()),
            this, SLOT(showResult()));
[ . . . . ]
}
void MaskTestForm::installMask() {
    m_StringEntry->setInputMask(m_InputMask->text());
}
[ . . . . ]
```

Figure 14.1 shows a screenshot of the running application.

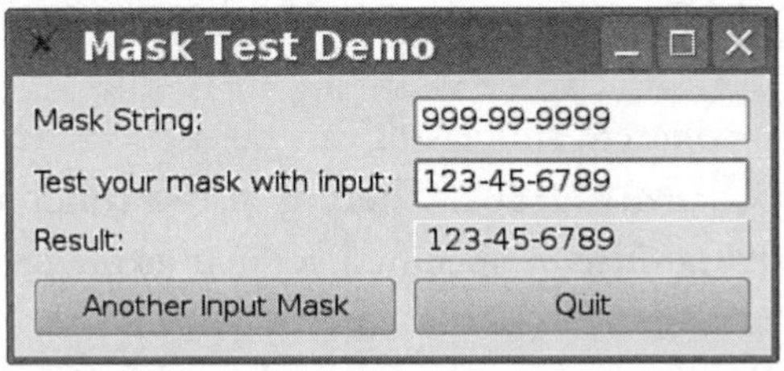

FIGURE 14.1   Input Masks

14.1.1 Exercises: Input Masks

1. Build and run the `MaskTestForm` application and use it to explore the following `inputMask` values:

   a. `AV99e77`

   b. `\AV99e77`

2. Provide an input mask that accepts the following (and use the form to test your answers):

   a. Only valid Social Security numbers in the format 123-45-6789

   b. Only Canadian postal codes in the format 2K3 Y4W (alternating numbers and letters)

   c. Only U.S. Zip+4 codes in the format 02114-5678

   d. Only U.S. phone numbers in the format (234)345-4567

   e. Only U.S. phone numbers in the format 1-123-234-5678

3. Can you make the 1- at the beginning of the last U.S. phone number format optional (i.e., so that it also accepts phone numbers like 123-456-5678)?

14.2   Validators

Validators are objects that can be attached to input widgets (such as `QLineEdit`, `QSpinBox`, and `QComboBox`) to provide a general framework for checking user input. Qt has an abstract class named `QValidator` that establishes the interface for all built-in and custom validators.

Two of `QValidator`'s concrete subclasses can be used for numeric range checking: `QIntValidator` and `QDoubleValidator`. There is also a concrete subclass that can be used for validating a string with a specified regular expression. We discuss regular expressions in the next section.

`QValidator::validate()` is a pure virtual method that returns one of the following enumerated values:

- `Invalid`—The expression does not satisfy the required conditions, and further input will not help.

- `Intermediate`—The expression does not satisfy the required conditions, but further input might produce an acceptable result.

- `Acceptable`—The expression satisfies the required conditions.

Other member functions enable the setting of the values that `validate()` uses (e.g., range limits).

Generally, a working validator will not permit the user to enter data that causes it to return the value `Invalid`.

Example 14.3 is a short *Work-Study Salary Calculator* application that uses the two numerical validators. It takes an `int` and a `double` from the user and displays their product. Total Pay is computed and displayed when the user presses **Enter**.

EXAMPLE 14.3   src/validate/numvalidate/inputform.h

```
[ . . . . ]
class InputForm : public QWidget {
    Q_OBJECT
```

```
public:
    InputForm(int ibot, int itop, double dbot, double dtop);
public slots:
    void computeResult();
private:
    void setupForm();
    int m_BotI, m_TopI;
    double m_BotD, m_TopD;
    QLineEdit* m_IntEntry;
    QLineEdit* m_DoubleEntry;
    QLabel* m_Result;
};
[ . . . . ]
```

In Example 14.4, validators are initialized with range values in the constructor and are assigned to their respective input widgets in the setupForm() function.

EXAMPLE 14.4   src/validate/numvalidate/inputform.cpp

```
[ . . . . ]
InputForm::InputForm(int ibot, int itop, double dbot, double dtop):
    m_BotI(ibot), m_TopI(itop), m_BotD(dbot), m_TopD(dtop),
    m_IntEntry(new QLineEdit("0")),
    m_DoubleEntry(new QLineEdit("0")),
    m_Result(new QLabel("0")) {
    setupForm();
    move(500, 500); /*Start in mid screen (approx). */
}

void InputForm::setupForm() {
    [ . . . . ]
    QIntValidator* iValid(new QIntValidator(m_BotI, m_TopI, this));
    QDoubleValidator*
            dValid(new QDoubleValidator(m_BotD, m_TopD, 2, this));
    m_IntEntry->setValidator(iValid);
    m_DoubleEntry->setValidator(dValid);
    connect(m_IntEntry, SIGNAL(returnPressed()),
            this, SLOT(computeResult()));
    connect(m_DoubleEntry, SIGNAL(returnPressed()),
            this, SLOT(computeResult()));
}
[ . . . . ]
```

The running program looks like Figure 14.2.

14.2.1 Exercises: Validators

1. Build and run the *Work-Study Salary Calculator* application. Try to enter a non-`int` in the first LineEdit, or a non-`float` in the second.
2. For each of the LineEdits, find out what happens when you try to enter a value that is out of range. For example, what total pay is calculated for 2 hours of work at $3 per hour?

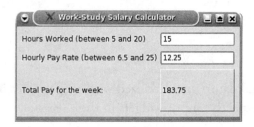

FIGURE 14.2 Work Study Calculator

14.3 Regular Expressions

Regular expressions are powerful tools for validating input, for extracting data from input, and for searching and replacing. A regular expression, **regexp** (or **regex** for short), describes constraints on the way a string is composed, using a formal language for pattern matching.

Regular expressions were first available in tools such as `vi`, `emacs`, `awk`, `sed`, and the POSIX Standard Library. Perl was the first mainstream programming language to integrate regular expressions so tightly into the language that it caused many people to learn regular expressions for the first time. Many enhancements have been made to the version of regular expressions that Perl recognizes. The enhancements are part of what is called Perl-style *extended* regular expressions. These extended regular expressions are also available in Java and Python. C++0x and boost also offer C++ regular expression tools.

Qt provides `QRegExp`, which implements most of the Perl-style *extended* regular expression language.

14.3.1 Regular Expression Syntax

Much like a string, a regular expression is a series of characters; however, not all characters are taken literally. For example, while an `'a'` in a regular expression will match an `'a'` in the target string, the character `'.'` will match any character. Here `'.'` is called a **meta-character**. Another common meta-character is '*', which is used to indicate that zero or more of the preceding character may exist in the target string. For example, 'a*' would match any number of 'a's (including zero) in a row. There are many different kinds of meta-characters, as illustrated next.

Following are some of the most commonly used meta-characters.

1. Special characters
   - . (the dot matches any character)
   - \n (matches the newline character)
   - \f (matches the form feed character)
   - \t (matches the tab character)
   - \x*hhhh* (matches the Unicode character whose code is the hexadecimal number *hhhh* in the range 0x0000 to 0xFFFF)

2. **Quantifiers**—Modifiers that specify the number of occurrences of the preceding character (or group) that may appear in the matching expression.
   - + (1 or more occurrences)
   - ? (0 or 1 occurrences)
   - * (0 or more occurrences)
   - {*i,j*} (at least *i* but not more than *j* occurrences)

3. **Character Sets**—Sets of allowable values for the character in the specified position of the matching expression. Several character sets are predefined:
   - \s (matches any whitespace character)
   - \S (matches any non-whitespace character)
   - \d (matches any digit character: 0 to 9)
   - \D (matches any non-digit character)
   - \w (matches any "word" character; i.e., any letter or digit or the underscore _)
   - \W (matches any non-word character)

   Character sets can also be specified in square brackets:
   - [AEIOU] (matches any of the characters A, E, I, O, or U)
   - [a-g] (the dash makes this a range from a to g)
   - [^xyz] (matches any character *except* for x, y, and z)

4. **Grouping and Capturing Characters**—(round parentheses) can be used to form a group. Groups can be back-referenced, meaning that if there is a match, the grouped values can be captured and accessed in various ways.

   For convenience, up to nine groups can be referenced within the regular expression by using the identifiers `\1` thru `\9`.

   There is also a `QRegExp` member function `cap(int nth)`, which returns the nth group (as a `QString`).

5. **Anchoring Characters**—Assertions that specify the boundaries of a matching effort.

   - The caret (`^`), if it is the first character in the regex, indicates that the match starts at the beginning of the string.

   - The dollar sign (`$`), when it is the last character in the regex, means that the effort to match must continue to the end of the string.

   - In addition, there are word boundary (`\b`) or non-word boundary (`\B`) assertions that help to focus the attention of the regex.

TABLE 14.3   Examples of Regular Expressions

Pattern	Meaning
hello	Matches the literal string `hello`
c*at	Quantifier: zero or more occurrences of `c`, followed by at: at, cat, ccat, etc.
c?at	Matches or one occurrences of `c`, followed by at: at or cat only.
c.t	Matches `c` followed by any character, followed by `t`: cat, cot, c3t, c%t, etc.
c.*t	Matches `c` followed by zero or more characters, followed by `t`: ct, caaatttt, carsdf$#S8ft, etc.
ca+t	+ means one or more of the preceding "thing," so this matches cat, caat, caaaat, etc., but not ct.
c\.*t	Backslashes precede special characters to "escape them," so this matches only the string `"c.*t"`
c\\\.t	Matches only the string `"c\.t"`
c[0-9a-c]+z	Between the `c` and the `z` one or more of the characters in the set [0-9a-c] matches strings like `"c312abbaz"` and `"caa211bac2z"`
the (cat|dog) ate the (fish|mouse)	(Alternation) the cat ate the fish or the dog ate the mouse or the dog ate the fish, or the cat ate the mouse
\w+	A sequence of one or more alphanumerics (word characters); same as [a-zA-Z0-9]+
\W	A character that is not part of a word (punctuation, whitespace, etc.)
\s{5}	Exactly five whitespace characters (tabs, spaces, or newlines)

Pattern	Meaning
^\s+	Matches one or more whitespace characters at the beginning of the string
\s+$	Matches one or more whitespace characters at the end of the string
^Help	Matches Help if it occurs at the beginning of the string
[^Help]	Matches any single character except one of the letters in the word Help, anywhere in the string (a different meaning for the metacharacter ^)
\S{1,5}	At least one, at most five non-whitespace (printable characters)
\d	A digit `[0-9]` (and `\D` is a non-digit, i.e., `[^0-9]`)
\d{3}-\d{4}	7-digit phone numbers: `555-1234`
\bm[A-Z]\w+	`\b` means word boundary: matches `mBuffer` but not `StreamBuffer`

> **NOTE**
> Backslashes are used for escaping special characters in C++ strings as well, so regular expression strings inside C++ strings must be "double-backslashed"—i.e. every \ becomes \\, and to match the backslash character itself you need four: \\\\.

> **NOTE**
> If your compiler supports C++0x, you may want to use raw quoted strings for regular expressions to avoid the need to double-escape backslashes.

```
R"(The String Data \ Stuff " )"
R"delimiter(The String Data \ Stuff " )delimiter"
```

There is much more to regular expressions, and it is well worth investing the time to learn about them. The documentation for QRegExp is a good place to start; we also recommend [Friedl98] for a more in-depth examination of the subject.

In the meantime, you can explore the capabilities of QRegExp and test your own regular expressions with a Qt example from Nokia. You can find the code in src/regex-tester. Figure 14.3 shows a screenshot of the running program.

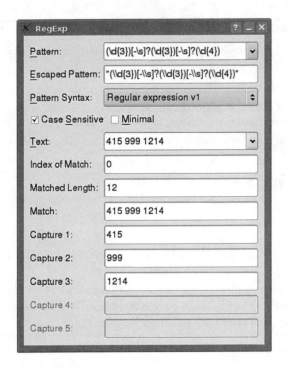

FIGURE 14.3   Regular Expression Tester

14.3.2   Regular Expressions: Phone Number Recognition

14.3.2.1   The Problem

In almost any application, there is a need for an easy but general-purpose way to specify conditions that must be satisfied by input data at runtime. For example:

- In a U.S. Address, every ZIP code can have five digits, followed by an optional dash (-) and four more digits.

- A U.S. phone number consists of ten digits, usually grouped 3+3+4, with optional parentheses and dashes and an optional initial 1.

- A U.S. state abbreviation must be one from the set of 50 approved abbreviations.

How can you impose conditions such as these on incoming data in an object-oriented way?

Suppose that you want to write a program that recognizes phone number formats and could accept a variety of phone numbers from various countries. You would need to take the following things into consideration:

- For any U.S./Canada format numbers, we extract *AAA EEE NNNN*, where *A* = area code, *E* = exchange, and *N* = number.
- These have been standardized so that each of the three pieces has a fixed length.
- For phone numbers in other countries,[1] assume that there must be *CC MM* (or *CCC MM*) followed by either *NN NN NNN* or *NNN NNNN*, where *C* = country code, *M* = municipal code, and *N* = localNumberDigits.
- There might be dashes, spaces, or parentheses delimiting number clusters.
- There might be + or 00 in front of the country code.

Imagine how you would write this program using the standard tools available to you in C++. It would be necessary to write lengthy parsing routines for each possible format. Example 14.5 shows the desired output of such a program.

EXAMPLE 14.5   src/regexp/testphone.txt

```
src/regexp> ./testphone
Enter a phone number (or q to quit): 16175738000
 validated: (US/Canada) +1 617-573-8000
Enter a phone number (or q to quit): 680111111111
 validated: (Palau) + 680 (0)11-11-11-111
Enter a phone number (or q to quit): 777888888888
 validated: (Unknown - but possibly valid) + 777 (0)88-88-88-888
Enter a phone number (or q to quit): 86333333333
 validated: (China) + 86 (0)33-33-33-333
Enter a phone number (or q to quit): 962444444444
 validated: (Jordan) + 962 (0)44-44-44-444
Enter a phone number (or q to quit): 56777777777
 validated: (Chile) + 56 (0)77-77-77-777
Enter a phone number (or q to quit): 351666666666
 validated: (Portugal) + 351 (0)66-66-66-666
Enter a phone number (or q to quit): 31888888888
 validated: (Netherlands) + 31 (0)88-88-88-888
```

---

[1] The phone number situation in Europe is quite complex, and specialists have been working for years to develop a system that would work and be acceptable to all EU members. You can get an idea of what is involved by visiting this Wikipedia page. [http://en.wikipedia.org/wiki/Telephone_numbers_in_Europe]

```
Enter a phone number (or q to quit): 20398478
Unknown format
Enter a phone number (or q to quit): 2828282828282
Unknown format
Enter a phone number (or q to quit): q
src/regexp>
```

Example 14.6 is a procedural C-style solution that shows how to use QRegExp to handle this problem.

EXAMPLE 14.6   src/regexp/testphoneread.cpp

```
[ . . . . ]
QRegExp filtercharacters ("[\\s-\\+\\(\\)\\-]");                              1

QRegExp usformat                                                             2
("(\\+?1[- ]?)?\\(?(\\d{3})\\)?[\\s-]?(\\d{3})[\\s-]?(\\d{4})");

QRegExp genformat                                                            3
("(00)?([[3-9]\\d{1,2})(\\d{2})(\\d{7})$");

QRegExp genformat2                                                           4
("(\\d\\d)(\\d\\d)(\\d{3})");


QString countryName(QString ccode) {
   if(ccode == "31") return "Netherlands";
   else if(ccode == "351") return "Portugal";
[ . . . . ]
   //Add more codes as needed ..."
   else return "Unknown - but possibly valid";
}

QString stdinReadPhone() {                                                   5
   QString str;
   bool knownFormat=false;
   do {                                                                      6
      cout << "Enter a phone number (or q to quit): ";
      cout.flush();
      str = cin.readLine();
      if (str=="q")
         return str;
      str.remove(filtercharacters);                                         7
```

```
        if (genformat.exactMatch(str)) {
            QString country = genformat.cap(2);
            QString citycode = genformat.cap(3);
            QString rest = genformat.cap(4);
            if (genformat2.exactMatch(rest)) {
                knownFormat = true;
                QString number = QString("%1-%2-%3")
                                    .arg(genformat2.cap(1))
                                    .arg(genformat2.cap(2))
                                    .arg(genformat2.cap(3));
                str = QString("(%1) + %2 (0)%3-%4").arg(countryName(country))
                        .arg(country).arg(citycode).arg(number);
            }
        }
[ . . . . ]
        if (not knownFormat) {
            cout << "Unknown format" << endl;
        }
    } while (not knownFormat) ;
    return str;
}

int main() {
    QString str;
    do {
        str =  stdinReadPhone();
        if (str != "q")
            cout << " validated: " << str << endl;
    } while (str != "q");
    return 0;
}
[ . . . . ]
```

1 Remove these characters from the string that the user supplies.

2 All U.S. format numbers have country-code 1 and have 3 + 3 + 4 = 10 digits. Whitespaces, dashes, and parantheses between these digit groups are ignored, but they help to make the digit groups recognizable.

3 Landline country codes in Europe begin with 3 or 4, Latin America with 5, Southeast Asia and Oceania with 6, East Asia with 8, and Central, South, and Western Asia with 9. Country codes may be 2 or 3 digits long. Local phone numbers typically have 2 (or 3) + 2 + 7 = 11 (or 12) digits. This program does not attempt to interpret city codes.

4 The last seven digits will be be arranged as 2 + 2 + 3.

5 Ensures the user-entered phone string complies with a regular expression and extracts the proper components from it. Returns a properly formatted phone string.

6 Keep asking until you get a valid number.

7 Remove all dashes, spaces, parentheses, and so on.

In a stream-based program like this, the complete response of the user is examined by the QRegExp after s/he has typed it and pressed the Enter key. There is no way to prevent the user from entering inappropriate characters into the input stream.

14.3.3   Exercises: Regular Expressions

1. Many operating systems come with a reasonably good list of words that are used by various programs to check spelling. On *nix systems, the word list is generally named (at least indirectly) `words`. You can locate the file on your *nix system by typing the command

```
locate words | grep dict
```

Piping the output of this command through grep reduces the output to those lines that contain the string `"dict"`.

After you locate your system word list file, write a program that will read lines from the file and, using a suitable regex (or, if that is not possible, another device), display all the words that

a. Begin with a pair of repeated letters

b. End in "gory"

c. Have more than one pair of repeated letters

d. Are palindromes

e. Consist of letters arranged in strictly increasing alphabetic order (e.g., knot)

If you cannot find such a suitable word list on your system, you can use the file `src/downloads/canadian-english-small` in the source package.[2] If you have not done so already, you will need to uncompress it with the command `gunzip canadian-english-small.gz`.

---

[2] Downloaded from our [dist] directory.

2. Write a program that extracts the hyperlinks from HTML files using regular expressions. A hyperlink looks like this:

```
<a href="http://www.web.www/location/page.html">The Label</a>
```

For each hyperlink encountered in the input file, print just the URL and label, separated by a tab.

Keep in mind that optional whitespace can be found in different parts of the preceding example pattern. Test your program on a variety of different Web pages that contain hyperlinks, and verify that your program does indeed catch all the links.

3. You have just changed companies, and you want to reuse some open source code that you wrote for the previous company. Now you need to rename all the data members in your source code. The previous company wanted data members named like this: mVarName. However, your new company wants them named like this: m_varName. Use QDirIterator and perform a substitution in the text of each visited file so that all data members conform to the new company's coding standards.

14.4 Regular Expression Validation

The class QRegExpValidator uses a QRegExp to validate an input string. Example 14.7 shows a main window class that contains a QRegExpValidator and some input widgets.

EXAMPLE 14.7 src/validate/regexval/rinputform.h

```
[ . . . . ]

class RinputForm : public QWidget {
    Q_OBJECT
public:
    explicit RinputForm(QWidget* parent=0);
    void setupForm();
public slots:
    void computeResult();
private:
    QLineEdit* m_PhoneEntry;
    QLabel* m_PhoneResult;
```

```
    QString m_Phone;
    static QRegExp s_PhoneFormat;
};
[ . . . . ]
```

We borrowed a regex from Example 14.6 and used it to initialize the static QRegExp in Example 14.8. The program takes a phone number from the user and displays it only if it is valid. Note that, in reference to the question we raised in problem 3 [438] of Section 14.1.1, the initial 1- is optional for U.S. phone numbers.

EXAMPLE 14.8   src/validate/regexval/rinputform.cpp

```
[ . . . . ]
QRegExp RinputForm::s_PhoneFormat (
  "(\\+?1[- ]?)?\\(?(\\d{3,3})\\)?[\\s-]?(\\d{3,3})[\\s-]?(\\d{4,4})");

RinputForm::RinputForm(QWidget* parent)
:   QWidget(parent),
    m_PhoneEntry(new QLineEdit),
    m_PhoneResult(new QLabel) {
    setupForm();
    move(500, 500); /*Start in mid screen (approx). */
}

void RinputForm::setupForm() {
    [ . . . . ]
    QRegExpValidator*
        phoneValid(new QRegExpValidator(s_PhoneFormat, this));
    m_PhoneEntry->setValidator(phoneValid);
    connect(m_PhoneEntry, SIGNAL(returnPressed()),
            this, SLOT(computeResult()));
}

void RinputForm::computeResult() {
    m_Phone = m_PhoneEntry->text();
    if (s_PhoneFormat.exactMatch(m_Phone)) {
        QString areacode = s_PhoneFormat.cap(2);
        QString exchange = s_PhoneFormat.cap(3);
        QString number = s_PhoneFormat.cap(4);
        m_PhoneResult->setText(QString("(US/Canada) +1 %1-%2-%3")
                .arg(areacode).arg(exchange).arg(number));
    }
}
[ . . . . ]
```

The `QRegExpValidator` will not permit entry of characters that would produce an `Invalid` result. Figure 14.4 shows a screenshot of the running program.

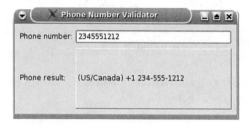

FIGURE 14.4   Phone Number Validator

The `QValidator` classes provide a powerful mechanism for validating input data. Qt provides two numerical range validators and a regular expression validator. If validation is not possible via numeric ranges or regular expressions, it is not difficult to extend and customize `QValidator` for custom conditions.

14.5   Subclassing QValidator

When the requirements for validating user input go beyond simple numeric range-checking or validation with a regular expression, you can define your own validator class by deriving from `QValidator`. For the next example, we define a palindrome as a string that reads the same backward or forward, ignoring case, whitespace, and punctuation. Unfortunately, it is not possible for a single regular expression to determine whether strings of arbitrary size are palindromes. Example 14.9 shows `Palindate`, a `QValidator` that can used to verify if a given string is a palindrome.

EXAMPLE 14.9   src/validate/palindrome/palindate.h

```
#include <QValidator>
#include <QString>

class Palindate : public QValidator {
   Q_OBJECT
public:
   explicit Palindate(QObject* parent = 0);
   QValidator::State validate(QString& input, int&) const;
};
```

The QValidator class has one required override, validate(), defined in Example 14.10. It makes a lowercase copy, inpStr, of the given string, and it removes all whitespace and punctuation from it. It then compares inpStr with the string revStr, which contains the same characters but in reverse order.

EXAMPLE 14.10   src/validate/palindrome/palindate.cpp

```
[ . . . . ]
QValidator::State Palindate::validate(QString& str, int& ) const {
   QString inpStr(str.toLower());
   QString skipchars("-_!,;. \t");
   foreach(QChar ch, skipchars)
      inpStr = inpStr.remove(ch);                              1
   QString revStr;                                             2
   for(int i=inpStr.length(); i > 0; --i)
      revStr.append(inpStr[i-1]);
   if(inpStr == revStr)
      return Acceptable;
   else
      return Intermediate;
}
```

1 You could do this faster with a regex.

2 It's surprising there is no reverse() function.

Example 14.11 defines a widget that contains a QLineEdit to test the validator.

EXAMPLE 14.11   src/validate/palindrome/palindromeform.h

```
[ . . . . ]
class PalindromeForm : public QWidget {
   Q_OBJECT
public:
   PalindromeForm(QWidget* parent=0);
   QString getPalindrome();
public slots:
   void showResult();
   void again();
private:
   Palindate* m_Palindate;
   QLineEdit* m_LineEdit;
   QLabel* m_Result;
```

```
    QString m_InputString;
    void setupForm();
};
[ . . . . ]
```

In Example 14.12, the widgets are set up, and a Palindate validator is set on the QLineEdit.

EXAMPLE 14.12   src/validate/palindrome/palindromeform.cpp

```
[ . . . . ]
PalindromeForm::PalindromeForm(QWidget* parent) : QWidget(parent),
  m_Palindate(new Palindate),
  m_LineEdit(new QLineEdit),
  m_Result(new QLabel) {
    setupForm();
}

void PalindromeForm::setupForm() {
    setWindowTitle("Palindrome Checker");
    m_LineEdit->setValidator(m_Palindate);
    connect(m_LineEdit, SIGNAL(returnPressed()),
            this, SLOT(showResult()));
[ . . . . ]
}
void PalindromeForm::showResult() {
    QString str = m_LineEdit->text();
    int pos(0);
    if(m_Palindate->validate(str,pos) == QValidator::Acceptable) {
        m_InputString = str;
        m_Result->setText("Valid Palindrome!");
    }
    else {
        m_InputString = "";
        m_Result->setText("Not a Palindrome!");
    }
}
[ . . . . ]
```

Figure 14.5 shows a screenshot of the running application.

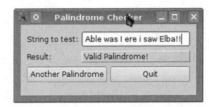

FIGURE 14.5   Palindrome Checker

14.6   Exercises: Validation and Regular Expressions

1. Design an Address Form like that shown in Figure 14.6.

FIGURE 14.6   Address Form

When the user selects a country from the combo box, the program must set an appropriate validator on the `stateEdit`, `zipEdit`, and `phoneEdit` QLineEdit widgets. Also, the dialog labels should change in the following ways:

a. USA:

- Set the `zipLabel` to Zip.
- Set the `stateLabel` to State.

b. Canada:

- Set the `zipLabel` to Postal Code.
- Set the `stateLabel` to Province.

c. Add another country of your choice with appropriate validators.

Make sure that invalid inputs are never accepted (disable the OK button, too). When the user clicks Ok, close the dialog and print out the value of each field. You can start with `handout/validation/addressform.ui` if you like.

2. International Standard Book Number (ISBN) is a coding system for books and other publications. ISBNs come in different sizes (10-digit and 13-digit), and they break down into substrings that identify language group, publisher, and title. In addition, the rightmost digit is a check digit that is computed from the other digits for error detection.[3]

Assume that the ISBN-10 code (including the check digit) looks like this:

`d1d2d3...d9d10`

Then the following equation must balance:

`(10*d1 + 9*d2 + 8*d3 + ... + 2*d9 + d10) % 11 = 0`

If the required value for the check digit is 10, use the letter X in that position.

Define a `QValidator` that accepts an ISBN-10 code if and only if it has a correct check digit. You can test it with 0-306-40615-2 (valid) and 0-306-40615-5 (invalid).

3. Find out (e.g., from the Wikipedia article[4]) how to validate the check digit for an ISBN-13 code and define a `QValidator` that accepts one if and only if its check digit is correct.

4. Can you make a single `QValidator` that can handle both ISBN-10 and ISBN-13 codes (validating only the check digit)?

---

[3] There is an interesting article in Wikipedia [http://en.wikipedia.org/wiki/ISBN] that explains the system.

[4] http://en.wikipedia.org/wiki/ISBN

14.7   Review Questions

1. What is an input mask? What can an input mask do for you?

2. What is a regular expression? What can you use it for?

3. What is a validator? What is it used for?

4. Describe three different kinds of validators.

5. What is a regular expression meta-character? There are four kinds of meta-characters: quantifier, character set, group, and anchor. Give examples of each type and explain what they mean.

6. Why would you want to extend `QValidator`?

## Chapter 15

Parsing XML

This chapter demonstrates three different ways to parse XML data: two available from Qt's XML module, and a new, improved one from Qt's core module. These examples show parse-event-driven parsing with SAX (the Simple API for XML), tree-style parsing with DOM (the Document Object Model), and stream-style parsing with `QXmlStreamReader`.

XML is an acronym for Extensible Markup Language. It is a markup language similar to HTML (Hypertext Markup Language), but with stricter syntax and no semantics (i.e., no meanings associated with the tags).

XML's stricter syntax is in strong contrast to HTML. For example:

- Each XML `<tag>` must have a closing `</tag>`, or be self-closing, like this: `<br/>`.

- XML tags are case-sensitive: `<tag>` is not the same as `<Tag>`

- In an XML document, the characters > and < that are not actually part of a tag must be replaced by their passive equivalents `&gt;` and `&lt;` to avoid confusing the parser.

- In addition, the ampersand character (`&`) must be replaced by its passive equivalent, `&amp;` for the same reason.

Example 15.1 is an HTML document that does not conform to XML rules.

EXAMPLE 15.1   src/xml/html/testhtml.html

```
<html>
<head> <title> This is a title </title>

 <!--Unterminated <link> and <input> tags are commonplace
         in HTML code:      -->
 <link rel="Saved Searches" title="oopdocbook"
   href="buglist.cgi?cmdtype=runnamed&amp;namedcmd=oopdocbook">
 <link rel="Saved Searches" title="queryj"
   href="buglist.cgi?cmdtype=runnamed&amp;namedcmd=queryj">
</head>
<body>
<p> This is a paragraph. What do you think of that?

HTML makes use of unterminated line breaks: <br>
And those do not make XML parsers happy. <br>

<ul>
<li> HTML is not very strict.
<li> An unclosed tag doesn't bother HTML parsers one bit.
</ul>

</body>
</html>
```

If we combined XML syntax with HTML element semantics, we would get a language called XHTML. Example 15.2 shows Example 15.1 rewritten as XHTML.

EXAMPLE 15.2   src/xml/html/testxhtml.html

```
<!DOCTYPE xhtml >
<html>
<head>
<title> This is a title </title>
<!-- These links are now self-terminated: -->
<link rel="Saved Searches" title="oopdocbook"
  href="buglist.cgi?cmdtype=runnamed" />
<link rel="Saved Searches" title="queryj"
  href="buglist.cgi?namedcmd=queryj" />
</head>
<body>

<p> This is a paragraph. What do you think of that? </p>
```

```
<p>
Html self-terminating line breaks are ok: <br/>
They don't confuse the XML parser. <br/>
</p>

<ul>
<li> This is proper list item </li>
<li> This is another list item </li>
</ul>


</body>
</html>
```

XML is a whole class of file formats that is understandable and editable by humans and by programs. XML has become a popular format for storing and exchanging data from Web applications. It is also a natural language for representing hierarchical (tree-like) information, which includes most documentation.

Many applications (e.g., Qt Designer, Umbrello, Dia) use an XML file format for storing data. Qt Designer's `.ui` files use XML to describe the layout of Qt widgets in a graphical user interface (GUI). This book is written in a flavor of XML called Slacker's DocBook.[1] It's like DocBook,[2] an XML language for writing books, but it adds some shorthand tags from XHTML and custom tags for describing courseware.

An XML document consists of **nodes**. Elements are nodes and look like this: `<tag>` `text` or `elements` `</tag>`. An opening tag can contain **attributes**. An attribute has the form `name="value"`. Elements nested inside one another form a parent-child tree structure.

EXAMPLE 15.3   src/xml/sax1/samplefile.xml

```
<section id="xmlintro">
    <title> Intro to XML </title>
    <para> This is a paragraph </para>
    <ul>
        <li> This is an unordered list item. </li>
        <li c="textbook"> This only shows up in the textbook </li>
    </ul>
    <p> Look at this example code below: </p>
    <include src="xmlsamplecode.cpp" mode="cpp"/>
</section>
```

---

[1] http://slackerdoc.tigris.org

[2] http://www.docbook.org

In Example 15.3, the `<ul>` has two `<li>` children, and its parent is a `<section>`. Elements with no children can be self-terminated with a `/>`, e.g., `<include/>`. Some elements, such as `<section>` and `<include>`, have attributes. Most parsers ignore extra whitespace, but indenting nested elements makes the code more readable by humans.

QUESTION

How many direct children are there of the `<section>`?

XML Editors

There are several open source XML editors available. We encourage you to try them before you invest in a commercial solution.

1. jEdit[3] has an XML plugin that works quite well. (Be sure to enable Sidekick.)

2. For KDE users, there is quanta.[4] Like Kdevelop, this is based on **kate**, the KDE advanced text editor. If you are accustomed to using emacs keys, be sure to get this Kate plugin: ktexteditor-emacsextensions.[5]

TIP

The free tool `xmllint` is handy for checking an XML file for errors. It reports descriptive error messages (mismatched start/end tags, missing characters, and so on) and points out where the errors are. It can be used to indent, or "pretty print," a well-formed XML document. It can also be used to join multipart documents that use XInclude or external entity references—two features that are not supported by the Qt XML parsers.

15.1   The Qt XML Parsers

XML is widely used as a medium of exchange between programs and as a convenient way to store and transmit hierarchical data. This implies that, for each program that produces XML output, there must be a corresponding program that reads it and produces something meaningful from it. For example: converting the `.xmi` file produced by Umbrello to a graphic diagram, converting the `.ui` file produced by Designer to a

---

[3] http://www.jedit.org

[4] http://quanta.kdewebdev.org/

[5] http://www.kde-apps.org/content/show.php?content=21706

Widget on the screen, converting the `.xml` files produced by docbook to a `.pdf` file for printing or to a set of `.html` files for reading on the Web, and so on. To accomplish such a conversion requires the XML file to be parsed. Each of the applications mentioned has a way of parsing XML that uses SAX, DOM, or another XML parsing application programming interface (API). Some APIs, such as DOM and `QXmlStreamWriter`, have a higher level way of generating XML documents also.

QXmlStreamReader and QXmlStreamWriter

As of Qt 4.3, there is another XML API: `QXmlStreamReader` and `QXmlStreamWriter`. These stream-based classes are available from QtCore and are recommended when writing new applications, because they provide more flexibility and better performance than the Qt XML module. An example using it to build element trees is coming up in Section 15.4.

Qt's XML module includes Qt implementations of two standard (cross-language) XML APIs:

SAX[6] specifies a parse event-driven API for a set of classes that enable low-level, sequential-access parsing for an XML document. It was originally developed in and intended for parsers written in Java. To utilize the SAX API, it is necessary to define callback functions that are passively called in response to various SAX events such as

- Start tag, end tag
- Character data (content)
- XML processing instructions (enclosed with <? and ?>)[7]
- XML comments (enclosed with <!-- and -->)

SAX can process an XML file of almost any size. SAX parsing can proceed only in the forward direction, and SAX applications are expected to do their processing sequentially while the document is being parsed.

The DOM[8] is a standard API that can represent XML elements as objects (i.e., nodes) in a navigable tree structure. Because DOM loads the entire XML file into memory, the maximum file size document that an application can handle is limited by

---

[6] http://www.saxproject.org

[7] A processing instruction is an XML note type that can occur anywhere in a document. It is intended to contain instructions to the application.

[8] http://www.w3.org/DOM/

the amount of available RAM. DOM is especially suitable for applications that require random access (as opposed to sequential access) to the various parts of an XML document. It does not provide a way of handling parse errors or modifying elements, but it does provide an API for creating documents.

To use Qt's XML module, add the following line to your project file:

```
QT += xml
```

15.2   SAX Parsing

When using SAX-style XML parsers, the flow of execution depends entirely on the data being read sequentially from a file or stream. This **inversion of control** means that tracing the thread of execution requires a stack to keep track of passive calls to callback functions. Furthermore, your code (overrides of virtual functions) will be called by parsing code inside the Qt library.

Invoking the parser involves creating a reader and a handler, hooking them up, and calling parse(), as shown in Example 15.4.

EXAMPLE 15.4   src/xml/sax1/tagreader.cpp

```cpp
#include "myhandler.h"
#include <QFile>
#include <QXmlInputSource>
#include <QXmlSimpleReader>
#include <QDebug>

int main( int argc, char **argv ) {
    if ( argc < 2 ) {
        qDebug() << QString("Usage: %1 <xmlfile>").arg(argv[0]);
        return 1;
    }
    MyHandler handler;
    QXmlSimpleReader reader;                             1
    reader.setContentHandler( &handler );               2
    for ( int i=1; i < argc; ++i ) {
        QFile xmlFile( argv[i] );
        QXmlInputSource source( &xmlFile );
        reader.parse( source );                         3
    }
```

```
    return 0;
}
```

1 The generic parser.

2 Hook the objects together.

3 Start parsing.

The interface for parsing XML is described in the abstract base class QXmlContentHandler. We call this a **passive interface** because it is not our own code that calls MyHandler methods. A QXmlSimpleReader object reads an XML file and generates parse events, to which it then responds by calling MyHandler methods. Figure 15.1 shows the main classes involved.

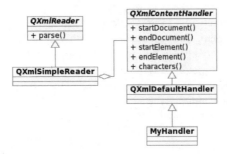

FIGURE 15.1   Abstract and Concrete SAX Classes

For the XML reader to provide useful information, it needs an object to receive parse events. This object, a **parse event handler**, must implement the interface specified by its abstract base class, so it can "plug into" the parser, as shown in Figure 15.2.

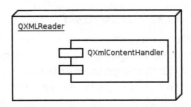

FIGURE 15.2   Plugin Component Architecture

The handler derives (directly or indirectly) from QXmlContentHandler. The virtual methods get called by the parser when it encounters various elements of the XML file during parsing. This is **event-driven** parsing: *You do not call these functions directly.* Example 15.5 shows a class that extends the default handler so that it can respond to parse events in the particular way required by your application.

EXAMPLE 15.5   src/xml/sax1/myhandler.h

```
[ . . . . ]
#include <QXmlDefaultHandler>
class QString;
class MyHandler : public QXmlDefaultHandler {
  public:
    bool startDocument();
    bool startElement( const QString & namespaceURI,
                       const QString & localName,
                       const QString & qName,
                       const QXmlAttributes & atts);
    bool characters(const QString& text);
    bool endElement( const QString & namespaceURI,
                     const QString & localName,
                     const QString & qName );
  private:
    QString indent;
};
[ . . . . ]
```

Functions that are called passively are often referred to as **callbacks**. They respond to events generated by the parser. The client code for MyHandler is the QXmlSimpleReader class, inside the Qt XML module.

ContentHandler or DefaultHandler?

QXmlContentHandler is an abstract class with many pure virtual functions, all of which must be overridden by a concrete derived class. Qt has provided a concrete class named QXmlDefaultHandler that implements the base class pure virtual functions as empty, do-nothing bodies. You can use this as a base class. Handlers derived from this class are not required to override all the methods but must override some to accomplish anything.

If you do not properly override each handler method that will be used by your application, the corresponding `QXmlDefaultHandler` method, which does nothing, is called instead. In the body of a handler function, you can

- Store the parse results in a data structure.
- Create objects according to certain rules.
- Print or transform the data in a different format.
- Do other useful things.

Example 15.6 contains the definition of a concrete event handler.

EXAMPLE 15.6   src/xml/sax1/myhandler.cpp

```cpp
[ . . . . ]
QTextStream cout(stdout);

bool MyHandler::startDocument() {
    indent = "";
    return TRUE;
}

bool MyHandler::characters(const QString& text) {
    QString t = text;
    cout << t.remove('\n');
    return TRUE;
}

bool MyHandler::startElement( const QString&,                        1
                              const QString&, const QString& qName,
                              const QXmlAttributes& atts) {
    QString str = QString("\n%1\\%2").arg(indent).arg(qName);
    cout << str;
    if (atts.length()>0) {
        QString fieldName = atts.qName(0);
        QString fieldValue = atts.value(0);
        cout << QString("(%2=%3)").arg(fieldName).arg(fieldValue);
    }
    cout << "{";
    indent += "      ";
    return TRUE;
}
```

```
bool MyHandler::endElement( const QString&,
    const QString& , const QString& ) {
    indent.remove( 0, 4 );
    cout << "}";
    return TRUE;
}
[ . . . . ]
```

1 We have omitted the names of the parameters that we don't use. This prevents the
   compiler from issuing "unused parameter" warnings.

The QXmlAttributes object passed into the startElement() function is a map used
to hold the *name = value* attribute pairs that were contained in the XML elements.

As it processes the file, the parse() function calls characters(), startElement(),
and endElement() as these events are encountered in the file. Whenever a string of
ordinary characters is found between the beginning and end of a tag, it's passed to the
characters() function.

We ran this program on Example 15.3, and it transformed that document into
Example 15.7, something that looks a little like LaTex, another document format.

EXAMPLE 15.7   src/xml/sax1/tagreader-output.txt

```
\section(id=xmlintro){
    \title{ Intro to XML }
    \para{ This is a paragraph }
    \ul{
        \li{ This is an unordered list item. }
        \li(c=textbook){ This only shows up in the textbook }      }
    \p{ Look at this example code below: }
    \include(src=xmlsamplecode.cpp){}}
```

15.3   XML, Tree Structures, and DOM

The DOM is a higher-level interface for operating on XML documents. Working with
and navigating through DOM documents is straightforward (especially if you are
familiar with QObject children).

The main classes in DOM are shown in Figure 15.3. The function setContent()
parses the file, after which the QDomDocument contains a structured tree consisting of

QDomNode objects. Each QDomNode could be an instance of QDomElement, QDomAttr, or QDomText. Every QDomNode has a parent except the root, which is a QDomDocument. Every node is reachable from the parent. DOM is another application of the Composite pattern.

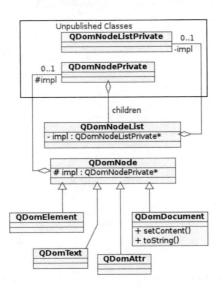

FIGURE 15.3   QDom UML Model

NOTE

The QDom classes are wrappers around private implementation classes. They contain no data except a pointer. This makes it possible to pass around QDomNodes by value to other functions that can change the addressed objects (by adding attributes or children or by changing attributes). This gives QDom a more Java-like interface.

15.3.1   DOM Tree Walking

Qt provides full read/write access to trees of XML data. Nodes can be navigated through an interface that is similar to, *but slightly different from*, the QObject interface. Under the surface, SAX performs the parsing, and DOM defines a content handler that creates the tree of objects in memory. All client code needs to do is call setContent(), which causes the input to be parsed and the tree to be generated.

Example 15.8 transforms an XML document in-place. After the tree is manipulated, it is serialized to a QTextStream, where it becomes savable and parsable again. Figure 15.4 shows the main classes used in this example.

EXAMPLE 15.8   src/xml/domwalker/main.cpp

```
[ . . . . ]
int main(int argc, char **argv) {
    QApplication app(argc, argv);
    QString filename;
    if (argc < 2) {
        cout << "Usage: " << argv[0] << " filename.xml" << endl;
        filename = "samplefile.xml";
    }
    else {
        filename = argv[1];
    }
    QFile f(filename);
    QString errorMsg;
    int errorLine, errorColumn;
    QDomDocument doc("SlackerDoc");
    bool result = doc.setContent(&f, &errorMsg,
        &errorLine, &errorColumn);                           1
    QDomNode before = doc.cloneNode(true);                   2
    Slacker slack(doc);                                      3
    QDomNode after = slack.transform();                      4
    cout << QString("Before: ") << before << endl;
    cout << QString("After: ") << after << endl;
    QWidget * view = twinview(before, after);               5
    view->show();
    app.exec();
    delete view;
}
[ . . . . ]
```

1 Parse the file into a DOM tree, and store the tree in an empty doc.

2 Deep copy.

3 Send the tree to slack.

4 Start the visitation.

5 Create a pair of QTreeView objects separated by slider, using the QDomDocuments as models.

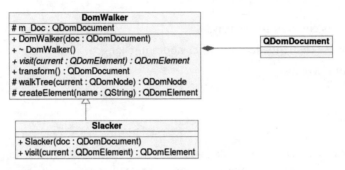

FIGURE 15.4   Domwalker and Slacker

Slacker is derived from DomWalker, an application specialized for walking through DOM trees.

The walkTree() method, defined in Example 15.9, contains no pointers or type-casts. The QDom(Node|Element|Document|Attribute) types are smart-pointers. We "downcast" from QDomNode to QDomElement, or QDom*XXX*, using QDomNode::toElement() or to*XXX*() conversion functions.

EXAMPLE 15.9   src/xml/domwalker/domwalker.cpp

```
[ . . . . . ]
QDomDocument DomWalker::transform() {
    walkTree(m_Doc);
    return m_Doc;
}


QDomNode DomWalker::walkTree(QDomNode current) {
    QDomNodeList dnl = current.childNodes();                        1
    for (int i=dnl.count()-1; i >=0; --i)
        walkTree(dnl.item(i));
    if (current.nodeType() == QDomNode::ElementNode) {             2
        QDomElement ce = current.toElement();                      3
        return visit(ce);
```

```
    }
    return current;
}
[ . . . . ]
```

1 First process children recursively.

2 Only process elements, leaving other nodes unchanged.

3 Instead of a typecast.

⚓ TIP

When traversing a tree, it is possible to use only the QDomNode interface, but "casting down" to QDomElement adds some convenient functions for dealing with the element as a whole, with its attributes (which are QDomNode child objects themselves).

Even though in this example QDomNode/QDomElement objects are being passed and returned by value, it is still possible to change the underlying DOM objects through the temporary copies. Through interface trickery, QDom objects look and feel like Java-style references and hold pointers inside, rather than actual data.

Slacker defines how to transform documents from one XML format to another. It is an extension of DomWalker and overrides just one method, visit(). Defined in Example 15.10, this method has a special rule for each kind of element.

EXAMPLE 15.10 src/xml/domwalker/slacker.cpp

```
[ . . . . ]
QDomElement Slacker::visit(QDomElement element) {
    QString name = element.tagName();


    QString cvalue = element.attribute("c", QString()) ;
    if (cvalue != QString()) {                                            1
        element.setAttribute("condition", cvalue);
        element.setAttribute("c", QString());
    }
    [ . . . . ]
    if (name == "b") {
        element.setAttribute("role", "strong");
        element.setTagName("emphasis");
        return element;
```

```
}
if (name == "li") {                                          2
    QDomNode parent = element.parentNode();
    QDomElement listitem = createElement("listitem");
    parent.replaceChild(listitem, element);                  3
    element.setTagName("para");                              4
    listitem.appendChild(element);
    return listitem;
}
[ . . . . ]
```

1 Modifying attributes—any c= becomes condition=.

2 This transformation is more interesting because we replace <li> text </li> with <listitem><para> text </para></listitem>.

3 Remove the li tag; put a listitem in its place.

4 Modify tag name in-place.

When run, this example pops up a window like Figure 15.5, with two tree views shown side-by-side, letting us inspect the XML documents before and after the transformation.

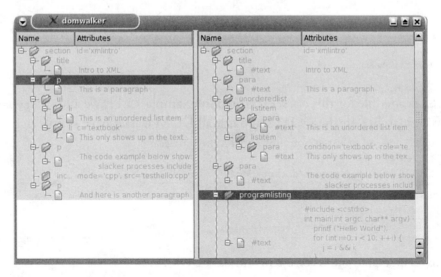

FIGURE 15.5   XML Tree Views

15.3.2   Generation of XML with DOM

DOM documents are normally created by parsers to represent XML from an input stream, but DOM can also generate XML structures as output. It is preferable to generate XML through an API rather than by printing formatted strings because DOM generation guarantees that the resulting document will be parsable again.

In Figure 15.6, DocbookDoc is a factory for QDomElements. It is derived from QDomDocument and specialized for creating Docbook/XML documents.

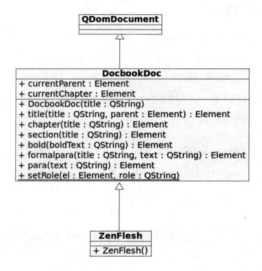

FIGURE 15.6   DocbookDoc

In the header file for this class, excerpted in Example 15.11, we added a typedef to improve readability. In the DOM standard, all DOM classes have simple names such as example Node, Element, Document, and Attribute.

EXAMPLE 15.11   src/libs/docbook/docbookdoc.h

```
[ . . . . ]
```

```
typedef QDomElement Element;   1
```

1 Saves on typing and is consistent with Java DOM.

As shown in Example 15.12, you can build documents by creating chapters, sections, and paragraphs.

EXAMPLE 15.12   src/xml/dombuilder/zenflesh.cpp

```cpp
#include <QTextStream>
#include <docbookdoc.h>

class ZenFlesh : public DocbookDoc {
    public: ZenFlesh();
};

ZenFlesh::ZenFlesh() :
    DocbookDoc("Zen Flesh, Zen Bones") {

    chapter("101 Zen Stories");
    section("A cup of tea");
    para("Nan-in served a cup of tea.");
    section("Great Waves");
    QDomElement p = para("o-nami the wrestler sat in meditation and "
            "tried to imagine himself as a bunch of great waves.");
    setRole(p, "remark");
    chapter("The Gateless Gate");
    formalpara("The Gateless Gate",
      "In order to enter the gateless gate, you must have a ");
    bold(" mindless mind.");

    section("Joshu's dog");
    para("Has a dog buddha nature or not?");

    section("Haykujo's Fox");
    QDomElement fp = formalpara("This is a special topic",
      "Which should have a role= remark attribute");
    setRole(fp, "remark");
}

int main() {
    QTextStream cout(stdout);
    ZenFlesh book;
    cout << book << endl;
}
```

The constructor generates a little book in XML which, after pretty-printing, could look like Example 15.13.

EXAMPLE 15.13   src/xml/zen.xml

```
<book>
    <title>Zen Flesh, Zen Bones</title>
    <chapter>
        <title>101 Zen Stories</title>
        <section>
            <title>A cup of tea</title>
            <para>Nan-in served a cup of tea.</para>
        </section>
        <section>
            <title>Great Waves</title>
            <para>
            o-nami the wrestler sat in meditation and tried
            to imagine himself as a bunch of great waves.
            </para>
        </section>
    </chapter>
    <chapter>
        <title>The Gateless Gate</title>
        <formalpara>
            <title>The Gateless Gate</title>
            In order to enter the gateless gate,
            you must have a <emphasis role="strong">
            mindless mind</emphasis>
        </formalpara>
        <section>
            <title>Joshu's dog</title>
            <para>Has a dog buddha nature or not?</para>
        </section>
        <section>
            <title>Haykujo's Fox</title>
            <formalpara role="remark">
                <title>This is a special topic</title>
                Which should have a role="remark" attribute
            </formalpara>
        </section>
    </chapter>
</book>
```

The advantage of this format is that it can be easily converted into HTML[9] (or PDF, or LaTEX) using `xsltproc` and the Docbook/XSL stylesheets [docbookxsl]. Example 15.14 shows the invocation for generating an HTML version.

---

[9] ../docs/src/xml/zen.html

EXAMPLE 15.14 src/xml/zen2html

```sh
#!/bin/sh
# Translates zen.xml into index.html.
# Requires gnu xsltproc and docbook-xsl.
# DOCBOOK=/usr/share/docbook-xsl
xsltproc $DOCBOOK/html/onechunk.xsl zen.xml
```

Now look at Example 15.15, where the elements are created. Each major Docbook language element has a corresponding Factory method in `DocbookDoc`.

EXAMPLE 15.15 src/libs/docbook/docbookdoc.cpp

```cpp
[ . . . . ]

Element DocbookDoc::bridgehead(QString titleStr) {
    Element retval = createElement("bridgehead");
    Element titleEl = title(titleStr);
    currentParent.appendChild(retval);
    return retval;
}
Element DocbookDoc::title(QString name, Element parent) {
    Element retval = createElement("title");
    QDomText tn = createTextNode(name);
    retval.appendChild(tn);
    if (parent != Element())
        parent.appendChild(retval);
    return retval;
}

Element DocbookDoc::chapter(QString titleString) {
    Element chapter = createElement("chapter");
    title(titleString, chapter);
    documentElement().appendChild(chapter);
    currentParent = chapter;
    currentChapter = chapter;
    return chapter;
}

Element DocbookDoc::para(QString textstr) {
    QDomText tn = createTextNode(textstr);
    Element para = createElement("para");
```

```
    para.appendChild(tn);
    currentParent.appendChild(para);
    currentPara = para;
    return para;
}
```

In addition, there are some character-level elements that only modify text, as shown in Example 15.16.

EXAMPLE 15.16   src/libs/docbook/docbookdoc.cpp

```
[ . . . . ]

Element DocbookDoc::bold(QString text) {
    QDomText tn = createTextNode(text);
    Element emphasis = createElement("emphasis");
    setRole(emphasis, "strong");
    emphasis.appendChild(tn);
    currentPara.appendChild(emphasis);
    return emphasis;
}

void  DocbookDoc::setRole(Element el, QString role) {
    el.setAttribute("role", role);
}
```

Because each `QDomNode` must be created by `QDomDocument`, it makes sense to extend `QDomDocument` to write your own DOM factory.

Depending on what kind of element is being created, `DocbookDoc` adds newly created elements as children to previously created elements.

15.4   XML Streams

`QXmlStreamReader` and `QXmlStreamWriter` provide a faster and more powerful API for reading and writing XML. They are not part of Qt's XML module either—they have been in QtCore since Qt 4.3.

Why Not Use the "Standard" APIs?

DOM, although convenient and standard, has high memory and processing requirements and could be much simpler. SAX, although fast and relatively memory efficient,
could be faster but for the need to create certain standard structures during parsing, and it is not
very simple because it requires an understanding of inheritance and pure virtual functions to use
properly.

The interfaces in Qt's XML module are based on interfaces that are part of the Java standard and
are also available in other languages, so they are easy to pick up if you've used them before. But
if you already know them, it should be easy to pick up another XML parsing API such as this one.

There is no tree structure generated by the `QXmlStreamReader` API. Example 15.17
shows a class that uses it to build one. It is itself a `QStandardItemModel` and creates
instances of `QStandardItem` for each tree node.

EXAMPLE 15.17   src/xml/streambuilder/xmltreemodel.h

```
[ . . . . . ]
class XmlTreeModel : public QStandardItemModel {
    Q_OBJECT
public:
    enum Roles {LineStartRole = Qt::UserRole + 1,
                LineEndRole};                                    1
    explicit XmlTreeModel(QObject *parent = 0);
public slots:
    void open(QString fileName);
private:
    QXmlStreamReader m_streamReader;
    QStandardItem* m_currentItem;
};
[ . . . . . ]
```

1 Custom roles for `data()`

The code that does the actual parsing is shown in Example 15.18.

EXAMPLE 15.18   src/xml/streambuilder/xmltreemodel.cpp

```
[ . . . . . ]
void XmlTreeModel::open(QString fileName) {
    QFile file (fileName);                                       1
    if (!file.open(QIODevice::ReadOnly)) {
```

```
            qDebug() << "Can't open file: " << fileName;
            abort();
        }
    m_streamReader.setDevice(&file);                                          2
    while (!m_streamReader.atEnd()) {
        QXmlStreamReader::TokenType tt = m_streamReader.readNext();
        switch (tt) {
            case QXmlStreamReader::StartElement: {
                QString name = m_streamReader.name().toString();
                QStandardItem* item = new QStandardItem(name);
                item->setData(m_streamReader.lineNumber(),
                              LineStartRole);                                 3
                QXmlStreamAttributes attrs = m_streamReader.attributes();
                QStringList sl;
                sl << tr("Line# %1").arg(m_streamReader.lineNumber());
                foreach (QXmlStreamAttribute attr, attrs) {
                    QString line = QString("%1='%2'").arg(attr.name().toString())
                                    .arg(attr.value().toString());
                    sl.append(line);
                }
                item->setToolTip(sl.join("\n"));
                if (m_currentItem == 0)
                    setItem(0, 0, item);                                      4
                else
                    m_currentItem->appendRow(item);                          5
                m_currentItem = item;
                break; }
            case QXmlStreamReader::Characters: {
                QString tt = m_currentItem->toolTip();
                tt.append("\n");
                tt.append(m_streamReader.text().toString());
                m_currentItem->setToolTip(tt);
                break; }
            case QXmlStreamReader::EndElement:
                m_currentItem->setData(m_streamReader.lineNumber(), LineEndRole);
                m_currentItem = m_currentItem->parent();                     6
                break;
            case QXmlStreamReader::EndDocument:
            default:
                break;
        }
    }
}
```

1 Closes automatically when out of scope.

2 Start parsing—can use any `QIODevice`.

3 Custom `data()`

4 Set root item in model.

5 Add as a child to the current item.

6 Go up the tree.

If you run the example, you can see the `QTreeView` on the left populated with elements that show the structure of the XML file in a text editor on the right, similar to Figure 15.7. Hovering over an element in the tree shows you the text inside it, and clicking on it moves the text editor's cursor to the corresponding position in the document.

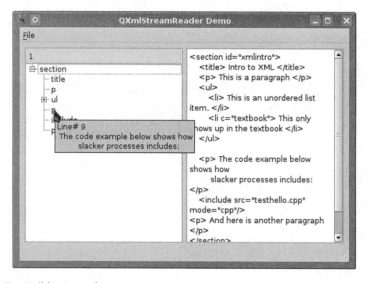

FIGURE 15.7   TreeBuilder Example

15.5   Review Questions

1. If there is a syntax error in your XML file, how do you determine the cause and location?

2. SAX is an event-driven parser. What kinds of events does it respond to?

3. Compare and contrast SAX and DOM. Why would you use one rather than the other?

4. If you have a QDomNode and it is actually "pointing" to a QDomElement, how do you get a reference to the QDomElement?

5. What are the advantages of using QXmlStreamReader over SAX?

6. What are the advantages of using QXmlStreamReader over DOM?

16

More Design Patterns

This chapter presents design patterns from two categories: creational and structural.

16.1 Creational Patterns

By using patterns to manage object creation, we gain flexibility that makes it possible to choose or change the kinds of objects created or used at runtime and to manage object deletion, especially in large software systems. Proper management of the creation of objects is an essential part of managing the separation between layers of code and ensuring the proper disposal of objects at destruction time.

In C++, a **factory** is a program component, generally a class, that is responsible for creating objects. The idea of a factory is to separate object creation from object usage.

A factory class generally has a function that obtains dynamic memory for the new object and returns a (base class) pointer to that object. This approach enables new derived types to be introduced without necessitating changes to the code that uses the factory.

This section will discuss several design patterns that use factories and show examples of these design patterns.

When the responsibility for heap object creation is delegated to a `virtual` function, we call this a **Factory method**.

By making the factory method pure `virtual` and writing concrete derived factory classes, the base factory class becomes an **abstract factory**.

> The **Abstract Factory pattern** provides an interface for defining factories that share abstract features but differ in concrete details. Client code can instantiate a particular subfactory and then use the abstract interface to create objects.

By imposing **creation rules** that prevent direct instantiation of a class, we can force clients to use Factory methods to create all instances. For example, there may be times when it is necessary to restrict the number of objects of a particular class that can exist at one time. In fact, making use of classes that can be instantiated exactly once is quite common.

> The **Singleton** pattern restricts a class so that only one instance can be created. This can be accomplished by making its constructor `private` or `protected` and providing an `instance()` member that returns a pointer to a new instance if one does not already exist but returns a pointer to that instance if it does.

We have already seen and worked with a singleton discussed in Section 8.3. A Qt application that uses an event loop instantiates a `QApplication` first, creates some other objects, and then calls `QApplication::exec()` to start the event loop. To refer to the object elsewhere in the program, you can use the `qApp` macro, which returns a pointer to the singleton `QApplication`.[1] Section 16.1.4 discusses singletons further.

Object Creation

Consider three ways to create an instance of the `QObject`-derived class `Customer`:

- `Customer* c1 = new Customer(name);`
- `QMetaObject meta = Customer::staticMetaObject; Customer* cust = qobject_cast<Customer*>(meta.newInstance());`
- `Customer* cust = CustomerFactory::instance()->newCustomer(name);`

---

[1] `QApplication` is derived from `QCoreApplication`. When you include `<QApplication>`, you are including the macro `#define qApp (static_cast<QApplication*>(QCoreApplication::instance()))`.
`QCoreApplication::instance()` returns a pointer to the already defined instance or `null`, if no instance has been created.

In the first case, the class name is hard-coded in the constructor call. The object will be created in memory using the default heap storage. Hard-coded class names in client code can limit the reusability/flexibility of the code.

In the second case, `QMetaObject::newInstance()` is called. This is an abstract factory, overridden in each `QMetaObject` derived class, generated by `moc`. `newInstance()` returns a `QObject` pointer to a new instance of `Customer`.

In the third case, a `Customer` object is constructed indirectly using a specialized Factory method called `CustomerFactory::newCustomer()`. This interface might be more convenient to use than the Qt library, but it is simply a wrapper around another factory.

Before `QMetaObject::newInstance()`,[2] it was necessary to write a `switch` statement to handle each supported class in a factory.

16.1.1   Abstract Factory

`AbstractFactory`, defined in Example 16.1, is a simple class.

EXAMPLE 16.1   src/libs/dataobjects/abstractfactory.h

```
[ . . . . ]
class DOBJS_EXPORT AbstractFactory
{
  public:
    virtual QObject* newObject (QString className,
                                QObject* parent=0) = 0;
    virtual ~AbstractFactory();

};
[ . . . . ]
```

The `newObject()` method is pure `virtual`, so it must be overridden in derived classes. Example 16.2 shows a concrete class derived from `AbstractFactory`.

EXAMPLE 16.2   src/libs/dataobjects/objectfactory.h

```
[ . . . . ]
class DOBJS_EXPORT  ObjectFactory : public AbstractFactory {
  public:
    ObjectFactory();
```

---

[2] Introduced in Qt 4.5

```
    virtual QObject* newObject (QString className, QObject* parent=0);
protected:
    QHash<QString, QMetaObject> m_knownClasses;
};
[ . . . . . ]
```

QMetaObject::newInstance()

By marking a constructor Q_INVOKABLE, you can create instances of the QObject-derived class with QMetaObject::newInstance(). The QMetaObject::newInstance() method is *itself* another example of the Abstract Factory pattern.

We have defined ObjectFactory so that it knows how to create two concrete types. Because it is possible for any QString to be supplied to newObject(), ObjectFactory handles the case when an unknown class is passed. In this case, it returns a pointer to a generic QObject and sets the dynamic property, className, to let other functions (such as the XML export routine) know that this object is "spoofing" an object of another class.

EXAMPLE 16.3   src/libs/dataobjects/objectfactory.cpp

```
[ . . . . . ]

ObjectFactory::ObjectFactory() {
    m_knownClasses["UsAddress"] = UsAddress::staticMetaObject;
    m_knownClasses["CanadaAddress"] = CanadaAddress::staticMetaObject;
}

QObject* ObjectFactory::newObject(QString className, QObject* parent) {
    QObject* retval = 0;
    if (m_knownClasses.contains(className)) {
        const QMetaObject& mo = m_knownClasses[className];
        retval = mo.newInstance();                                      1
        if (retval == 0) {
            qDebug() << "Error creating " << className;
            abort();
        }
    } else {
        qDebug() << QString("Generic QObject created for new %1")
                    .arg(className);
```

```
      retval = new QObject();
      retval->setProperty("className", className);
   }
   if (parent != 0) retval->setParent(parent);
   return retval;
}
```

1 Requires Qt 4.5 or later.

Example 16.4 shows an example use of the Q_INVOKABLE macro with the constructor for the UsAddress class.

EXAMPLE 16.4   src/libs/dataobjects/address.h

```
[ . . . . ]

class DOBJS_EXPORT UsAddress : public Address {
    Q_OBJECT
  public:
    Q_PROPERTY( QString State READ getState WRITE setState );
    Q_PROPERTY( QString Zip READ getZip WRITE setZip );
    explicit Q_INVOKABLE UsAddress(QString name=QString(), QObject* parent=0)
                              : Address(name, parent) {}
  protected:
    static QString getPhoneFormat();
  public:
[ . . . . ]

  private:
    QString m_State, m_Zip;
};
```

16.1.2   Abstract Factories and Libraries

Now consider two libraries, libdataobjects and libcustomer, each with its own (concrete) object factory, as shown in the UML diagram in Figure 16.1.

CustomerFactory, defined in Example 16.5, *extends* the functionality of ObjectFactory.

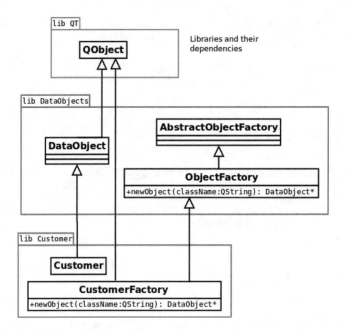

FIGURE 16.1   Libraries and Factories

EXAMPLE 16.5   src/libs/customer/customerfactory.h

```
[ . . . . . ]
class CUSTOMER_EXPORT CustomerFactory :
                          public QObject, public ObjectFactory {
  public:
    static CustomerFactory* instance();                              1
    Customer* newCustomer(QString name, QObject* parent=0);          2
    Address* newAddress(QString countryType = "USA", QObject* parent=0);
  private:
    CustomerFactory(QObject* parent=0);
};
[ . . . . . ]
```

1 Singleton factory method.

2 Regular factory method; does not require a typecast.

CustomerFactory inherits the ability to create Address objects from ObjectFactory. In addition, it knows how to create Customer objects. CustomerFactory needs only to add some `QMetaObjects` to `ObjectFactory::m_knownClasses` from the constructor (which is possible because that container is `protected`). The base-class `newObject()` method is smart enough to handle the classes added by `Customer` provided they are properly registered in that container.

EXAMPLE 16.6   src/libs/customer/customerfactory.cpp

```
[ . . . . ]



CustomerFactory::CustomerFactory(QObject* parent) : QObject(parent) {
    m_knownClasses["Customer"] = Customer::staticMetaObject;
    m_knownClasses["CustomerList"] = Customer::staticMetaObject;
}
```

16.1.3   `qApp` and Singleton Pattern

As discussed earlier, the Singleton pattern is a specialized factory used in situations where you wish to limit the number or type of instances created.

The `CustomerFactory::instance()` method, defined in Example 16.7, is an example of a singleton factory. It creates an object if needed, but only the first time that the method is called. On subsequent calls it always returns a pointer to the same object.

EXAMPLE 16.7   src/libs/customer/customerfactory.cpp

```
[ . . . . ]

CustomerFactory* CustomerFactory::instance() {
    static CustomerFactory* retval = 0;
    if (retval == 0) retval = new CustomerFactory(qApp);        1
    return retval;
}
```

1 Ensures this object and all its children are cleaned up when the `QApplication` exits.

It is important when dealing with heap objects that you do not leave memory leaks behind. You can use `QObject`'s parent-child relationship to help in this regard.

As mentioned earlier, `qApp` is a pointer to a singleton instance of `QApplication`, which was presumably created in `main()`. The `QApplication` instance exists precisely as long as the application is running.

Why Not Use a `static` Parent?

If you make the parent of your heap objects a `static` `QObject`, children of this object will be destroyed *after* the `QApplication` is destroyed. Unless there is a compelling reason to the contrary, *a program should not do anything with QObjects after the QApplication has been destroyed*—including object cleanup. Static objects from different files of a multifile application are destroyed in a linker-dependent order. That order of destruction may cause unintended side effects (e.g., segmentation faults at termination). See Section 8.6 for more details.

16.1.4   Benefits of Using Factories

One of the benefits of factory patterns is that we can manage the created objects in a pool (reusing the ones that can be reused).

Indirect object creation also makes it possible to decide at runtime which class objects to create. This enables the "plugging in" of replacement classes without requiring changes in the client code. Section 16.2 shows an example of a method that uses factory objects to create trees of connected, client-defined objects based on the contents of an XML file. In `src/libs/metadata/abstractmetadataloader.h`, there is another example of a factory method that manages singleton instances of `MetaDataLoader` in such a way that it becomes easy to write programs that can switch between derived metadata loaders without code breakage.

Libraries and Plugins

When building a large system, it's good to design libraries to contain classes that share some common features or need to be used together. Substantial applications generally use components from several libraries, some supplied by the development team and some supplied by third-party developers (e.g., Qt from Nokia). Only the public interface of a library class appears in the client code of reusers. Library designers should be able to change the implementation of a library class without breaking client code.

A **plugin** is an integrated set of software components that adds specific capabilities to a larger application. An example of a plugin is the *Adobe Flash Player*, which enables various web browsers to show certain types of videos. Good plugin support enables the user to customize the functionality of an application. Many libraries enable the "plugging in" of outside classes by publishing interfaces and documenting how to implement them. Libraries can facilitate the creation of such plugin classes by providing a factory base class from which specialized factory classes can be derived as needed.

Another benefit of the Factory method (or indirect object creation in general) is that it can enforce post-constructor initialization of objects, including the invocation of virtual functions.

Polymorphism from Constructors

An object is not considered "fully constructed" until the constructor has finished executing. An object's *vpointer* does not point to the correct vtable until the end of the constructor's execution. Therefore, calls to methods of this from the constructor cannot use polymorphism!

Factory methods are required when any polymorphic behavior is needed during object initialization. Example 16.8 demonstrates this problem.

EXAMPLE 16.8   src/ctorpoly/ctorpoly.cpp

```cpp
#include <iostream>
using namespace std;

class A {
public:
    A() {
        cout << "in A ctor" << endl;
        foo();
    }
    virtual void foo() {
        cout << "A's foo()" << endl;
    }
};

class B: public A {
public:
    B() {
        cout << "in B ctor" << endl;
    }
    void foo() {
        cout << "B's foo()" << endl;
    }
};

class C: public B {
public:
    C() {
```

```
        cout << "in C ctor" << endl;
    }

    void foo() {
        cout << "C's foo()" << endl;
    }
};

int main() {
    C* cptr = new C;
    cout << "After construction is complete:" << endl;
    cptr->foo();
    return 0;
}
```

Its output is given in Example 16.9.

EXAMPLE 16.9　src/ctorpoly/ctorpoly-output.txt

```
src/ctorpoly> ./a.out
in A ctor
A's foo()
in B ctor
in C ctor
After construction is complete:
C's foo()
src/ctorpoly>
```

Notice that the wrong version of `foo()` was called when the new C object was constructed. Section 22.1 discusses vtables in more detail.

16.1.5　Exercises: Creational Patterns

1. Complete the implementation of the `Address`, `Customer`, and `CustomerList`
classes.

Apply the ideas that we discussed in Section 7.4.1 to write a `CustomerWriter`
class. Make sure that you use the `Q_PROPERTY` features of `Customer` and `Address`
so that your `CustomerWriter` class will not need to be rewritten if you change
the implementation of `Customer`.

Keep in mind that `Address` objects are stored as children of `Customer` objects. Here is one output format that you might consider using:

```
Customer {
    Id=83438
    DateEstablished=2004-02-01
    Type=Corporate
    objectName=Bilbo Baggins
    UsAddress {
        Line1=52 Shire Road
        Line2=Suite 6
        City=Brighton
        Phone=1234567890
        State=MA
        Zip=02201
        addressName=home
    }
}
```

Another possibility arises if you use the `Dataobject::toString()` function.

2. Write a `CustomerReader` class that creates all its new objects by reusing the `CustomerFactory` class that we supplied.

   Write a `CustomerListWriter` and a `CustomerListReader` class that serialize and deserialize lists of `Customer` objects. How much of the `CustomerWriter/Reader` code can you reuse here?

   Write client code to test your classes.

16.2 Memento Pattern

This section combines `QMetaObjects` with the SAX2 parser to show how to write a general-purpose XML encoding/decoding tool that works on `QObjects` with well-defined `Q_PROPERTY`s and children. This gives us an example that combines the Meta-Object pattern with the Memento pattern. And because both XML and QObjects can represent hierarchical structures, these ideas are combined with the Composite and Abstract Factory patterns, to save and load entire trees of polymorphic objects.

The goal of this section is to come up with serializers and deserializers for many different kinds of classes, where the encoding and decoding is handled by QMetaObject-aware methods, separate from the logic of the model.

To encode and decode trees of QObjects as XML, we must define a mapping scheme. Such a mapping must capture not only the QObject's properties, types, and values, but the existing relationships between the object and its children, between each child and all of its children, and so on.

The parent-child relationships of XML elements naturally map to QObject parents and children. These relationships define a tree structure.

You may recall that both XML and QObject already use the Composite pattern, to support a tree-like hierarchy of objects. Figure 16.2 shows Customer and CustomerList, both derived from QObject. We use the Composite pattern here to map children of QObjects to corresponding child elements in XML.

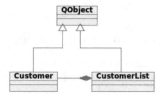

FIGURE 16.2   CustomerList UML

An example of the desired XML format for storing the data of a CustomerList is shown in Example 16.10.

EXAMPLE 16.10   src/xml/propchildren/customerlist.xml

```
<object class="CustomerList" name="Customers" >

   <object class="Customer" name="Simon" >
     <property name="Name" type="QString" value="Simon" />
     <property name="Date" type="QDate" value="1963-11-22" />
     <property name="LuckyNumber" type="int" value="834" />
     <property name="State" type="QString" value="WA" />
     <property name="Zip" type="QString" value="12345" />
     <property name="FavoriteFood" type="QString" value="Donuts" />
     <property name="FavoriteDrink" type="QString" value="YooHoo"/>
   </object>
```

```
<object class="Customer" name="Raja" >
  <property name="Name" type="QString" value="Raja" />
  <property name="Date" type="QDate" value="1969-06-15" />
  <property name="LuckyNumber" type="int" value="62" />
  <property name="State" type="QString" value="AZ" />
  <property name="Zip" type="QString" value="54321" />
  <property name="FavoriteFood" type="QString" value="Mushrooms" />
  <property name="FavoriteDrink" type="QString" value="Jolt" />
</object>

</object>
```

With this kind of information in an input file, it is possible to fully reconstruct not only the properties and their types, but the tree structure of parent-child relationships between QObjects in a `CustomerList`.

16.2.1   Exporting to XML

Memento Pattern

When an object's internal state is captured and externalized so that it can be restored later, that is an implementation of the Memento pattern.

Example 16.11 shows a reflective recursive `toString()`, which constructs strings for each of the object's properties and then iterates over the object's children, recursively calling `toString()` on each child.

EXAMPLE 16.11   src/libs/dataobjects/qobjectwriter.cpp

```
[ . . . . ]
QString QObjectWriter::
toString(const QObject* obj, int indentLevel) const {
    QStringList result;
    QString indentspace;
    indentspace.fill(' ', indentLevel * 3 );
    QString className = obj->metaObject()->className();
    QString objectName = obj->objectName();
    QStringList propnames = propertyNames(obj);
```

```
    foreach (const QString &propName, propnames) {
        if (propName == "objectName") continue;
        QVariant qv = obj->property(propName.toAscii());

        if (propName == "className") {
                className = qv.toString();
                continue;
        }
        const QMetaObject* meta = obj->metaObject();
        int idx = meta->indexOfProperty(propName.toAscii());
        QMetaProperty mprop = meta->property(idx);

        result <<
        QString("%1   <property name=\"%2\" type=\"%3\" value=\"%4\" />")
            .arg(indentspace).arg(propName).
            arg(qv.typeName()).arg(toString(qv, mprop));
    }
    /* Query over QObjects */
    if (m_children) {
        QList<QObject*> childlist =
                qFindChildren<QObject*>(obj, QString());

        foreach (const QObject* child, childlist) {
            if (child->parent() != obj) {
//                  qDebug() << "This is not my child!!";
                continue;
            }
            if (child != 0) {
                result << toString(child, indentLevel+1);
            }
        }
    }

    result.insert(0, QString("\n%1<object class=\"%2\" name=\"%3\" >")
        .arg(indentspace).arg(className).arg(objectName));
    result << QString("%1</object>\n").arg(indentspace);
    return result.join("\n");
}
[ . . . . ]
```

Example 16.11 shows a toString() that uses Qt's properties and QMetaObject facilities to reflect on the class. As it iterates, it appends each line to a QStringList.

When iteration is complete, the `<object>` is closed. The returned `QString` is then produced quickly by calling `QStringList::join("\n")`.

16.2.2   Importing Objects with an Abstract Factory

Prerequisites

- Section 15.2

The importing routine is more sophisticated than the exporting routine, and it has some interesting features.

- It parses XML using the SAX parser.
- Depending on the input, it creates objects.
- The number and types of objects with their parent-child relationships must be reconstructed from the information in the file.

Example 16.12 shows the class definition for `QObjectReader`.

EXAMPLE 16.12   src/libs/dataobjects/qobjectreader.h

```
[ . . . . ]
#include "dobjs_export.h"
#include <QString>
#include <QStack>
#include <QQueue>
#include <QXmlDefaultHandler>

class AbstractFactory;
class DOBJS_EXPORT  QObjectReader : public QXmlDefaultHandler {
  public:
    explicit QObjectReader (AbstractFactory* factory=0) :
                     m_Factory(factory), m_Current(0) { }
    explicit QObjectReader (QString filename, AbstractFactory* factory=0);
    void parse(QString text);
    void parseFile(QString filename);
    QObject* getRoot();
    ~QObjectReader();
```

```
    // callback methods from QXmlDefaultHandler
    bool startElement( const QString& namespaceURI,
                       const QString& name,
                       const QString& qualifiedName,
                       const QXmlAttributes& attributes );
    bool endElement(  const QString& namespaceURI,
                      const QString& localName,
                      const QString& qualifiedName);
    bool endDocument();
  private:
    void addCurrentToQueue();
    AbstractFactory* m_Factory;
    QObject* m_Current;
    QQueue<QObject*> m_ObjectList;
    QStack<QObject*> m_ParentStack;
};
[ . . . . ]
```

Figure 16.3 shows the relationships between the various classes in the example.

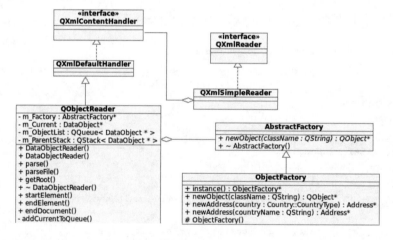

FIGURE 16.3   QObjectReader and Its Related Classes

QObjectReader is derived from QXmlDefaultHandler, which is a plugin for the QXmlSimpleReader. AbstractFactory is a plugin for QObjectReader. When you create a QObjectReader, you must supply it with a concrete instance of ObjectFactory or DataObjectFactory.

`QObjectReader` is now completely separate from the specific types of objects that it can create. To use it with your own types, just derive a factory from `AbstractFactory` for them.

Keep in mind the XML output file in Example 16.10 as you read the code that constructs objects from it, starting with Example 16.13.

EXAMPLE 16.13   src/libs/dataobjects/qobjectreader.cpp

```
[ . . . . ]

bool QObjectReader::startElement ( const QString&,
    const QString& elementName, const QString&,
    const QXmlAttributes& atts) {                                    1
  if (elementName == "object") {
      if (m_Current != 0)                                           2
          m_ParentStack.push(m_Current);                           3
      QString classname = atts.value("class");
      QString instancename = atts.value("name");
      m_Current = m_Factory->newObject(classname);
      m_Current->setObjectName(instancename);
      if (!m_ParentStack.empty()) {                                 4
          m_Current->setParent(m_ParentStack.top());
      }
      return true;
  }
  if (elementName == "property") {
      QString fieldType = atts.value("type");
      QString fieldName = atts.value("name");
      QString fieldValue = atts.value("value");
      QVariant qv = QVariant(fieldValue);
      m_Current->setProperty(fieldName.toAscii(), qv);

  }
  return true;
}
```

1 No need to name unused parameters.

2 If already inside an <object>.

3 Push previous current onto stack.

4 Top of `ParentStack`, or previous current, should be my parent.

startElement() is called when the SAX parser encounters the initial tag of an XML element. The parameters to this function contain all the information needed to create an object. All other objects encountered between startElement() and the matching endElement() are children of m_Current. The object is "finished" when we reach endElement(), as shown in Example 16.14.

EXAMPLE 16.14   src/libs/dataobjects/qobjectreader.cpp

```
[ . . . . ]


bool QObjectReader::endElement( const QString& ,
                         const QString& elementName,
                         const QString& ) {
    if (elementName == "object") {
        if (!m_ParentStack.empty())
            m_Current = m_ParentStack.pop();
        else {
            addCurrentToQueue();
        }
    }
    return true;
}
```

QObjectReader uses an Abstract Factory to do the actual object creation.

The callback function, newObject(QString className), creates an object that can hold all the properties described in className. ObjectFactory creates properly classed objects for the types for which it has a QMetaObject. For other classes, it creates a regular QObject but tries to "mimic" the type by setting its className dynamic property. To support your own types, you can write a concrete derived factory that maps the correct strings to QMetaObject.

16.3   Façade Pattern

A class that uses the Façade pattern provides "a unified interface to a set of interfaces in a subsystem. Façade defines a higher-level interface that makes the subsystem easier [and safer] to use." [Gamma95] When a class interface is too complicated to use effectively (leads to hard-to-debug errors from improper use) or does not use a programming style that fits into your larger framework, a façade should be used. Another use of the Façade is to keep the code that uses a particular library separate from the rest of the application, for the purposes of reducing inter-library dependencies. A Façade is a class (or set of classes) with a clear simple interface that encapsulates and hides a complicated set of classes and/or functions. Two closely related design patterns are **wrapper** and **adaptor**, and it is possible that some examples of one can be demonstrated to be examples of another.

Many of the core Qt classes are Façades around native classes that would be different to use on each platform, or much more complex under the covers. For example, QString is a wrapper around a growable, implicitly shared array of characters. A QWidget is a wrapper around a native widget, and QThread, QFile, QProcess, and QSqlDatabase are all wrappers around lower-level libraries that could have quite different implementations across platforms. By using them only through the Qt API, your code can run on all platforms.

Experience gained from the struggle to reuse classes with difficult interfaces can provide valuable motivation for designing elegant, friendly, and useful interfaces for your own classes. In this example, we discuss a Qt wrapper for a multimedia metadata system.

A **multimedia** file contains audio and/or video content: sound effects, music, graphic images, animation, movies, and so on. **Metadata** is information that describes the audio or video content of a multimedia file. Metadata is often referred to as tag data or, simply, tags.

Multimedia files typically store metadata in the same file that contains the media. Tag information can be used by a media player to display pertinent information (e.g., title, artist, genre, and so on) about a selection that is currently being played or that is being queued for play. It can also be used to organize collections of files or to create playlists.

There are many libraries that can be used to read metadata from files. Earlier versions of this book used id3lib, which is no longer supported. Now there is Phonon, which was added to Qt 4.4. Phonon supports more file formats but did not work well with MP3s on Windows, and only reads, but does not write back tag data. There is also **Taglib 1.6**, a library that is similar to id3lib but supports modern file formats and builds on Windows, Linux, and Mac OS/X. TagLib is used by many open source tools such as Amarok and kid3.

We have organized our code in such a way that we can easily switch between Phonon and TagLib in our applications. Figure 16.4 shows the way that MetaDataLoader and MetaDataValue fit together, providing a façade between our applications and the underlying metadata library used. If we wanted a way of dynamically choosing one of these in our program (depending perhaps, on the platform or file format that is used), we might further package `phononmetadata` and `filetagger` into plugins.

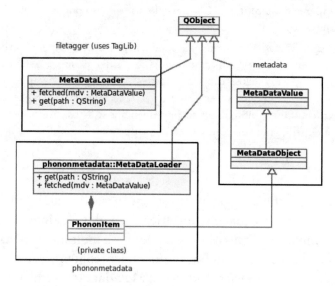

FIGURE 16.4   `MetaDataLoader` and `MetaDataValue`

`MetaDataValue`, shown in Example 16.15, is the base class interface for working with metadata values.

EXAMPLE 16.15   src/libs/metadata/metadatavalue.h

```
[ . . . . ]
class METADATAEXPORT MetaDataValue {
public:

    friend METADATAEXPORT QTextStream& operator<< (QTextStream& os,
                                    const MetaDataValue& mdv);
    friend METADATAEXPORT QTextStream& operator>> (QTextStream& is,
                                    MetaDataValue& mdv);
    friend METADATAEXPORT QDataStream& operator<< (QDataStream& os,
                                    const MetaDataValue& mdv);
    friend METADATAEXPORT QDataStream& operator>> (QDataStream& is,
                                    MetaDataValue& mdv);
    friend METADATAEXPORT bool operator==(const MetaDataValue&,
                                    const MetaDataValue&);
```

```
[ . . . . ]
    virtual QString fileName() const ;
    virtual Preference preference() const ;
    virtual QString genre() const;
    virtual QString artist() const;
    virtual QString albumTitle() const;
    virtual QString trackTitle() const;
    virtual QString trackNumber() const;
    virtual const QImage &image() const;
    virtual QTime trackTime() const;
    virtual QString trackTimeString() const;
    virtual QString comment() const;
[ . . . . ]
protected:
    bool m_isNull;
    QUrl m_Url;
    QString m_TrackNumber;
    QString m_TrackTitle;
    QString m_Comment;
    Preference m_Preference;
    QString m_Genre;
    QString m_Artist;
    QTime m_TrackTime;
    QString m_AlbumTitle;
    QImage m_Image;
};
Q_DECLARE_METATYPE(MetaDataValue);                                    1
[ . . . . ]
```

1 Add to `QVariant` type system.

`MetaDataValue` objects can come from tags on disk, a database, or the user. Different libraries supply a custom `MetaDataLoader` class that emits a value of this type in a signal parameter.

EXAMPLE 16.16   src/libs/metadata/abstractmetadataloader.h

```
[ . . . . ]
namespace Abstract {
class METADATAEXPORT MetaDataLoader : public QObject {
    Q_OBJECT
public:
```

```
    explicit MetaDataLoader(QObject *parent = 0)
        : QObject(parent) {}
    static MetaDataLoader* instance();
    virtual MetaDataLoader* clone(QObject* parent=0) = 0;
    virtual ~MetaDataLoader();
    virtual const QStringList &supportedExtensions() = 0;
    virtual void get(QString path) = 0;
    virtual void get(QStringList path) = 0;
    virtual bool isRunning() const = 0;
public slots:
    virtual void cancel() = 0;

signals:
    void fetched(const MetaDataValue & mdv);
    void progressValueChanged(int);
    void progressRangeChanged(int, int);
    void finished();

};
}


#endif // AMETADATALOADER_H
```

AbstractMetaDataLoader, shown in Example 16.16, has a simple, nonblocking get() method that will return immediately. It emits a fetched(MetaDataValue) signal, which can be connected to a slot of another object, such as a PlayListModel. Example 16.17 shows a concrete MetaDataLoader for TagLib.

EXAMPLE 16.17   src/libs/filetagger/tmetadataloader.h

```
[ . . . . ]
class FILETAGGER_EXPORT MetaDataLoader
                        : public Abstract::MetaDataLoader {
    Q_OBJECT
public:
    typedef Abstract::MetaDataLoader SUPER;
    explicit MetaDataLoader(QObject *parent = 0);
    static MetaDataLoader* instance();
    virtual ~MetaDataLoader() {}
    const QStringList &supportedExtensions() ;
    MetaDataLoader* clone(QObject *parent) ;
    void get(QString path);
    void get(QStringList path);
```

```
    bool isRunning() const {return m_running;}
public slots:
    void cancel();
private slots:
    void checkForWork();

private:
    bool m_running;
    bool m_canceled;
    int m_processingMax;
    QStringList m_queue;
    QTimer m_timer;
};
}


[ . . . . ]
```

Example 16.18 shows the checkForWork() method that performs its operation in a loop. It calls qApp->processEvents() to enable the GUI to remain responsive in long-running loops such as this one.

EXAMPLE 16.18   src/libs/filetagger/tmetadataloader.cpp

```
[ . . . . ]

TagLib::MetaDataLoader::MetaDataLoader(QObject *parent) :
    SUPER(parent) {
    m_processingMax = 0;
    m_running = false;
    qDebug() << "TagLib::MetaDataLoader created.";
    connect (this, SIGNAL(finished()), this, SLOT(checkForWork()),
            Qt::QueuedConnection);
}


void TagLib::MetaDataLoader::get(QString path) {
    m_queue << path;
    m_timer.singleShot(2000, this, SLOT(checkForWork()));
}


void TagLib::MetaDataLoader::checkForWork() {
    MetaDataFunctor functor;
    if (m_queue.isEmpty() && !m_running) {
        m_processingMax = 0;
        return;
```

```
    }
    if (m_running ) return;
    m_running = true;
    m_canceled = false;
    QStringList sl = m_queue;
    m_queue = QStringList();
    m_processingMax = sl.length();
    emit progressRangeChanged(0, m_processingMax);
    for (int i=0; i<m_processingMax;++i) {
        if (m_canceled) break;
        emit fetched(functor(sl[i]));
        emit progressValueChanged(i);
        qApp->processEvents();                                        1
    }
    m_running = false;
    emit finished();
}
```

1 Allow the GUI to process events (and our signals to be delivered).

In Example 16.19, the actual TagLib code can be found. We have it in a functor because this was originally going to be used in a `QtConcurrent` algorithm. After some testing, we found that the functor was not thread-safe, so now we call it in sequence from a loop. All conversions between TagLib types and Qt's types are done here. Clients do not need to be concerned about how the data is fetched or the string library that was used and may continue using the `MetaDataValue` interface from `libmetadata`.

EXAMPLE 16.19   src/libs/filetagger/tmetadataloader.cpp

```
[ . . . . ]

MetaDataValue MetaDataFunctor::operator ()(QString path) {
    using namespace TagLib;
    MetaDataValue retval;
    FileRef f(path.toLocal8Bit().constData());
    const Tag* t = f.tag();
    Q_ASSERT( t != NULL ) ;
    retval.setFileName(path);
    retval.setTrackTitle(toQString(t->title()));
    retval.setArtist(toQString(t->artist()));
    retval.setAlbumTitle(toQString(t->album()));
```

```
[ . . . . ]

    QTime time(0,0,0,0);
    const AudioProperties* ap = f.audioProperties();
    time = time.addSecs(ap->length());
    retval.setTrackTime(time);
    return retval;
}
```

NOTE

You must call `qRegisterMetaType<MetaDataValue>("MetaDataValue")` before emitting signals over queued connections with `MetaDataValue` parameters. This is because under the covers, another instance is being created dynamically by `QMetaType::construct()`.

16.4 Review Questions

1. How can a creational pattern help manage object destruction?
2. How can properties help you write a more general-purpose `Writer`?
3. How can an Abstract Factory help you write a more general-purpose `Reader`?
4. What Qt classes are implementations of the Façade pattern? Explain why they are façades or wrappers.

16.4.1 Points of Departure

- Try to come up with another `UserType` you might want to add to `QVariant` for a new type of `InputField`.
- Further discussion of moc and marshalling objects using metaobjects can be found in *Qt Quarterly*.[3]

---

[3] http://doc.trolltech.com/qq/qq14-metatypes.html

## Chapter 17

Concurrency

`QProcess` and `QThread` provide two approaches to concurrency. This chapter discusses how to create and communicate with processes and threads and offers techniques for monitoring and debugging them.

17.1   `QProcess` and Process Control

`QProcess` is a convenient (and cross-platform) class for starting and controlling other processes. It is derived from `QObject` and takes full advantage of signals and slots to make it easier to "hook up" with other Qt classes.

Now consider a simple example that starts a process and views its continually running output.[1] Example 17.1 shows the definition of a simple class derived from `QProcess`.

---

[1] `tail -f` runs forever showing whatever is appended to a file and is useful for showing the contents of a log file of a running process.

EXAMPLE 17.1   src/logtail/logtail.h

```
[ . . . . ]
#include <QObject>
#include <QProcess>
class LogTail : public QProcess {
    Q_OBJECT
  public:
    LogTail(QString fn = QString());
    ~LogTail();
  signals:
    void logString(const QString &str);

  public slots:
    void logOutput();
};
[ . . . . ]
```

A `QProcess` can launch[2] another process using the `start()` function. The new process is a child process that terminates when the parent process does.[3] Example 17.2 shows the implementation of the constructor and destructor of the `LogTail` class.

EXAMPLE 17.2   src/logtail/logtail.cpp

```
[ . . . . ]

LogTail::LogTail(QString fn) {
    connect (this, SIGNAL(readyReadStandardOutput()),
        this, SLOT(logOutput()));                          1
    QStringList argv;

    argv << "-f" << fn;                                    2
    start("tail", argv);                                   3
}
LogTail::~LogTail() {
    terminate();                                           4
}
```

---

[2] Underscoring the value of the cross-platform `QProcess` API is the fact that the mechanism for one process to launch another differs considerably in the two leading operating system families. For more information about how it is handled in *nix systems, see the Wikipedia article Fork [http://en.wikipedia.org/wiki/Fork_%28operating_system%29]. The Microsoft Windows approach is described in Spawn[http://en.wikipedia.org/wiki/Spawn_%28computing%29].

[3] It is also possible to use `startDetached()` to start a process that can live after the parent process dies.

1 When there is input ready, call this slot.

2 tail -f filename.

3 Returns immediately, and now there is a child process running, "attached" to this process. When this process exits, the child tail process will also terminate.

4 Attempts to terminate this process.

The child process can be treated as a sequential I/O device with two predefined output channels that represent two separate streams of data: stdout and stderr. The parent process can select an output channel with setReadChannel() (default is stdout). The signal readyReadStandardOutput() is emitted when data is available on the selected channel of the child process. The parent process can then read its output by calling read(), readLine(), or getChar(). If the child process has standard input enabled, the parent can use write() to send data to it.

Example 17.3 shows the implementation of the slot logOutput(), which is connected to the signal readyReadStandardOutput() and uses readAllStandardOutut() so that it pays attention only to stdout.

EXAMPLE 17.3   src/logtail/logtail.cpp

```
[ . . . . ]

// tail sends its output to stdout.
void LogTail::logOutput() {                                            1
    QByteArray bytes = readAllStandardOutput();
    QStringList lines = QString(bytes).split("\n");
    foreach (QString line, lines) {
        emit logString(line);
    }
}
```

1 Slot called whenever there is input to read.

The use of signals eliminates the need for a read loop. When there is no more input to be read, the slot will no longer be called. Signals and slots make concurrent code much simpler to read, because they hide the event-handling and dispatching of code. Some client code is given in Example 17.4.

EXAMPLE 17.4 src/logtail/logtail.cpp

```
[ . . . . ]

int main (int argc, char* argv[]) {
    QApplication app(argc, argv);
    QStringList al = app.arguments();
    QTextEdit textEdit;
    textEdit.setWindowTitle("Debug");
    textEdit.setWindowTitle("logtail demo");
    QString filename;
    if (al.size() > 1) filename = al[1];
    LogTail tail(filename);                                             1
    tail.connect (&tail, SIGNAL(logString(const QString&)),
        &textEdit, SLOT(append(const QString&)));
    textEdit.show();
    return app.exec();
}
```

1 Create object and starts process.

This application appends lines to the QTextEdit whenever they appear in the specified log file. To demonstrate the LogTail application, you need a text file that constantly grows as lines are added to it, such as some kind of active log file. If you can't find one, you can create one using a tool such as top, a utility available on a typical *nix host. Normally top, with no command-line arguments, produces a plain-text, formatted screen that lists, in descending order of resource usage, the 25 running processes that use the most system resources at the moment. The display starts with a summary of system usage specs, and the entire display is updated every few seconds. top continues until it is terminated by the user. In this example, we launch top with command-line arguments:

- -b, which puts it into batch mode so that we can redirect its output
- -d 1.0, which specifies the number of seconds between updates
- > toplog, which redirects output to the file toplog
- &, which runs top as a background process

After that, run the logtail example on the result file:

```
top -b -d 1.0 > toplog &
./logtail toplog
```

Figure 17.1 is a screenshot of the running program.

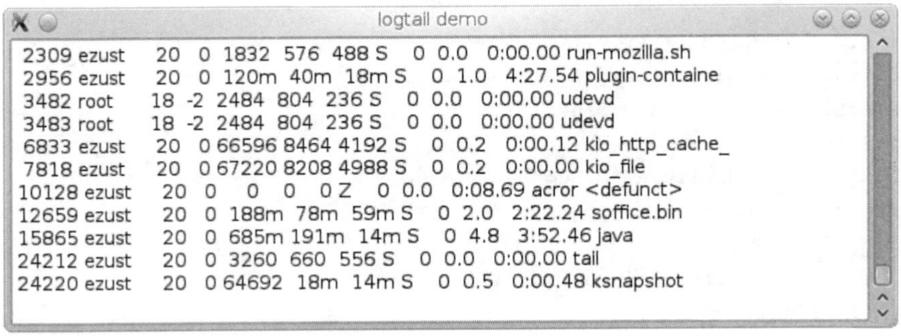

```
 2309 ezust   20  0 1832 576  488 S   0 0.0  0:00.00 run-mozilla.sh
 2956 ezust   20  0 120m 40m 18m S    0 1.0  4:27.54 plugin-containe
 3482 root    18 -2 2484 804  236 S   0 0.0  0:00.00 udevd
 3483 root    18 -2 2484 804  236 S   0 0.0  0:00.00 udevd
 6833 ezust   20  0 66596 8464 4192 S 0 0.2  0:00.12 kio_http_cache_
 7818 ezust   20  0 67220 8208 4988 S 0 0.2  0:00.00 kio_file
10128 ezust   20  0   0   0   0 Z     0 0.0  0:08.69 acror <defunct>
12659 ezust   20  0 188m 78m 59m S    0 2.0  2:22.24 soffice.bin
15865 ezust   20  0 685m 191m 14m S   0 4.8  3:52.46 java
24212 ezust   20  0 3260 660  556 S   0 0.0  0:00.00 tail
24220 ezust   20  0 64692 18m 14m S   0 0.5  0:00.48 ksnapshot
```

FIGURE 17.1   LogTail in Use

The demo runs until terminated, after which you must also kill the top job, whose [job number] and process ID were displayed just after it was launched. Using bash, you need only the job number (%1) to kill the job.

```
src/logtail> top -b -d 1.0 > toplog &
[1] 24209
src/logtail> ./logtail toplog
      [[ logtail was terminated here. ]]
QProcess: Destroyed while process is still running.
src/logtail> kill 24209
src/logtail>
```

17.1.1   Processes and Environment

Environment variables are <name, value> string pairs that can be stored quite easily in a map or a hash table. The variable name must be a legal identifier and, by convention, it usually does not contain lowercase letters. Every running process has an **environment**, consisting of a collection of environment variables. Most programming languages support a way of getting and setting these variables.

Some environment variables that we use are

1. PATH, a list of directories to search for executables (also dynamic link libraries (DLLs) on Windows).

2. HOME, the location of your home directory.

3. CPPLIBS, where the C++ Libraries from this book's source examples[4] are installed.

4. HOSTNAME (*nix) or COMPUTERNAME (win32), which usually gives you the name of your machine.

5. USER (*nix) or USERNAME (Win32), which usually gives you the currently logged in user ID.

Environment variables and their values are generally set by the parent process. Programs that depend on specific variables or values are generally not portable but depend somehow on their parent process. Variables provide a convenient cross-language mechanism for communicating information between processes.

Operating system shells enable the user to set environment variables for a process and its future children. Here are some examples.

- **Microsoft Windows desktop**—Start -> Settings -> System -> Advanced -> Environment Variables gives you something like Figure 17.2.

- **Microsoft Command Prompt**—set VARIABLE=value and echo %VARIABLE%. Also see the setx command in newer versions of Windows.

- **bash command-line**—export VARIABLE=value and echo $VARIABLE

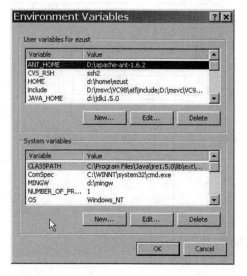

FIGURE 17.2 Windows Environment Variables

---

[4] http://www.distancecompsci.com/dist/

Most programming languages support getting and setting environment variables, too, as shown here.

- C++ / Qt: `QProcess::environment()` and `setEnvironment()`.

- Python: `os.getenv()` and `os.putenv()`

- Java: `ProcessBuilder.environment()`

- C: `getenv()` and `putenv()` from <cstdlib> (see Appendix B, "Standard Headers")

Changing the environment does not affect other processes that are already running. Environments are inherited from the parent process at process creation time.

Any program that you run is quite possibly a few levels deep in the process tree. This is because the typical desktop operating system environment consists of many processes running concurrently. In Figure 17.3, indentation levels indicate the parent-child relationships. Processes that are at the same indentation level are siblings (i.e., children of the same parent). Figure 17.3 shows the lifetimes and the parent-child relationships between processes running on a typical KDE/Linux system while the `environment` example runs from `konsole`.

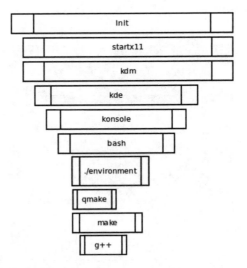

FIGURE 17.3   KDE/Linux Process Hierarchy

Whenever program A runs program B, A is the parent process of B. B inherits (a copy of) A's environment when B is created. Changes to B's environment from inside B affects only B and B's future children and are always invisible to A.

Example 17.5 demonstrates that the value given to setenv() is propagated to its child process.

EXAMPLE 17.5 src/environment/setenv.cpp

```cpp
#include <QCoreApplication>
#include <QTextStream>
#include <QProcess>
#include <QCoreApplication>
#include <QTextStream>
#include <QStringList>
#include <cstdlib>

class Fork : public QProcess {
    public:
    Fork(QStringList argv = QStringList() ) {
        execute("environment", argv);                              1
    }
    ~Fork() {
        waitForFinished();
    }
};

QTextStream cout(stdout);
int main(int argc, char* argv[]) {

    QCoreApplication qca(argc, argv);
    QStringList al = qca.arguments();
    al.removeAt(0);
    bool fork=al.contains("-f");
    if(fork) {
        int i = al.indexOf("-f");
        al.removeAt(i);
    }

    QStringList extraVars;
    if (al.count()  > 0) {
        setenv("PENGUIN", al.first().toAscii(), true);
    }
    cout << " HOME=" << getenv("HOME") << endl;
```

```
    cout << " PWD=" << getenv("PWD") << endl;
    cout << " PENGUIN=" << getenv("PENGUIN") << endl;

    if (fork) {
        Fork f;
    }
}
```

1 Runs this same app as a child.

When this program is run, the output looks like this:

```
src/environment> export PENGUIN=tux
src/environment> ./environment -f
HOME=/home/lazarus
PWD=src/environment
PENGUIN=tux
HOME=/home/lazarus
PWD=src/environment
PENGUIN=tux
src/environment> ./environment -f opus
HOME=/home/lazarus
PWD=src/environment
PENGUIN=opus
HOME=/home/lazarus
PWD=src/environment
PENGUIN=opus
src/environment> echo $PENGUIN
tux
src/environment>
```

17.1.2   Qonsole: Writing an Xterm in Qt

A command-line shell reads commands from the user and prints the output. In this example, we have a `QTextEdit` providing a view of the output of another running process, in this case, `bash`, the default command-line shell interpreter for most *nix systems (`cmd` on Windows). The `QProcess` is a model, representing a running process. Figure 17.4 shows a screenshot of `Qonsole`, our first attempt at a graphical user interface (GUI) for a command shell.[5]

---

[5] There is a small disagreement between the authors about the pronunciation of `Qonsole`. The two choices seem to be "Chonsole" (using the standard Chinese transliteration convention, as in Qing) and "Khonsole" (using the standard Arabic transliteration, as in Qatar).

FIGURE 17.4   `Qonsole1`

Because it connects signals to slots and handles user interactions, `Qonsole` is considered a **controller**. Because it derives from `QMainWindow`, it also contains some view code. The UML diagram in Figure 17.5 shows the relationships between the classes in this application.

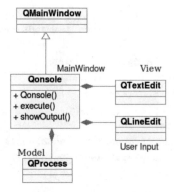

FIGURE 17.5   `Qonsole` UML: Model and View

Example 17.6 shows the class definition for `Qonsole`.

EXAMPLE 17.6   src/qonsole/qonsole1/qonsole.h

```
[ . . . . ]
class Qonsole : public QMainWindow {
    Q_OBJECT
 public:
    Qonsole();
```

```
public slots:
    void execute();
    void showOutput();
private:
    QTextEdit* m_Logw;
    QLineEdit* m_InputArea;
    QProcess* m_Shell;
};
[ . . . . . ]
```

Example 17.7 shows how the constructor establishes the structure of Qonsole and the important connections between its components.

EXAMPLE 17.7   src/qonsole/qonsole1/qonsole.cpp

```
[ . . . . . ]

Qonsole::Qonsole() {
    m_Logw = new QTextEdit();
    m_Logw->setReadOnly(true);
    setCentralWidget(m_Logw);
    m_InputArea = new  QLineEdit();
    QDockWidget* qdw = new QDockWidget("Type commands here");
    qdw->setWidget(m_InputArea);
    addDockWidget(Qt::BottomDockWidgetArea, qdw);
    connect (m_InputArea, SIGNAL(returnPressed()),
                        this, SLOT(execute()));

    m_Shell = new QProcess(this);
    m_Shell->setReadChannelMode(QProcess::MergedChannels);          1
    connect (m_Shell, SIGNAL(readyReadStandardOutput()),
                        this, SLOT(showOutput()));
#ifdef Q_OS_WIN
    m_Shell->start("cmd", QStringList(), QIODevice::ReadWrite);
#else
    m_Shell->start("bash", QStringList("-i"), QIODevice::ReadWrite);  2
#endif

}
```

1 Merge stdout and stderr.
2 Run bash in interactive mode.

Whenever the `Shell` outputs anything, `Qonsole` sends it to the `QTextEdit`. Whenever the user presses the Enter key, `Qonsole` grabs any text that is in the `QLineEdit` and sends it to the `Shell`, which interprets it as a command, as shown in Example 17.8.

EXAMPLE 17.8   src/qonsole/qonsole1/qonsole.cpp

```
[ . . . . ]

void Qonsole::showOutput() {                                              1
    QByteArray bytes = m_Shell->readAllStandardOutput();
    QStringList lines = QString(bytes).split("\n");
    foreach (QString line, lines) {
        m_Logw->append(line);
    }
}

void Qonsole::execute() {
    QString cmdStr = m_InputArea->text() + "\n";
    m_InputArea->setText("");
    m_Logw->append(cmdStr);
    QByteArray bytes = cmdStr.toUtf8();                                    2
    m_Shell->write(bytes);                                                3
}
```

1 A slot that gets called whenever input is ready

2 8-bit Unicode Transformation Format

3 Send the data into the stdin stream of the Shell child process

Example 17.9 shows the client code that launches this application.

EXAMPLE 17.9   src/qonsole/qonsole1/qonsole.cpp

```
[ . . . . ]

#include <QApplication>

int main(int argc, char* argv[]) {
    QApplication app(argc, argv);
    Qonsole qon;
    qon.show();
    return app.exec();
}
```

17.1.3 `Qonsole` with Keyboard Events

In the preceding example, `Qonsole` had a separate widget for user input. For a more authentic console experience, the user should be able to type commands directly in the command output window. To accomplish this, `Qonsole` needs to capture keyboard events. The first step is to override the `QObject` base class `eventFilter()` method, as shown in Example 17.10, the revised class definition.

EXAMPLE 17.10   src/qonsole/keyevents/qonsole.h

```
[ . . . . ]
class Qonsole : public QMainWindow {
    Q_OBJECT
 public:
    Qonsole();
 public slots:
    void execute();
    void showOutput();
    bool eventFilter(QObject *o, QEvent *e)   ;
 protected:
    void updateCursor();
 private:
    QString m_UserInput;
    QTextEdit* m_Logw;
    QProcess* m_Shell;
};
[ . . . . ]
```

As discussed in Section 8.3, an event is an object derived from `QEvent`. Within the context of an application, such a `QEvent` is associated with a `QObject` that is its intended receiver. The receiving object has a handler to process the event. An **event-Filter** examines a `QEvent` and determines whether to permit it to be processed by the intended receiver. We have provided our revised `Qonsole` application with an `eventFilter()` function that can be used to filter keyboard events from `m_Logw`, an extended `QTextEdit`. `Qonsole`, an extended `QMainWindow`, is the intended recipient of those events. The implementation of this function is shown in Example 17.11.

EXAMPLE 17.11   src/qonsole/keyevents/qonsole.cpp

```
[ . . . . ]

bool Qonsole::eventFilter(QObject* o, QEvent* e) {
    if (e->type() == QEvent::KeyPress) {
        QKeyEvent* k = static_cast<QKeyEvent*> (e);
        int key = k->key();
        QString str = k->text();
        m_UserInput.append(str);
        updateCursor();
        if ((key == Qt::Key_Return) || (key == Qt::Key_Enter) ) {
#ifdef Q_WS_WIN                                                          1
            m_UserInput.append(QChar(0x000A));
#endif
            execute();
            return true;                                                2
        }
        else {
            m_Logw->insertPlainText(str);
            return true;
        }
    }
    return false;                                                       3
}
```

1 Windows processes need a Carriage Return + Line Feed, not just a CR.

2 We processed the event. This prevents other widgets from seeing it.

3 Don't touch the event.

When the Enter key is pressed, the member function `execute()` is called so that the command string can be sent to the shell and then reset. Example 17.12 shows the implementation of these two functions.

EXAMPLE 17.12   src/qonsole/keyevents/qonsole.cpp

```
[ . . . . ]

void Qonsole::updateCursor() {
    QTextCursor cur = m_Logw->textCursor();
    cur.movePosition(QTextCursor::End, QTextCursor::KeepAnchor);
    m_Logw->setTextCursor(cur);
}
```

```
void Qonsole::execute() {
    QByteArray bytes = m_UserInput.toUtf8();
    m_Shell->write(bytes);
    m_UserInput = "";
}
```

All that remains to be done is to call the base class function `installEventFilter()` on `m_Logw`, the widget whose events you want to capture. This is done in the constructor, as shown in Example 17.13.

EXAMPLE 17.13 src/qonsole/keyevents/qonsole.cpp

```
[ . . . . . ]

Qonsole::Qonsole() {
    m_Logw = new QTextEdit;
    setCentralWidget(m_Logw);
    m_Logw->installEventFilter(this);                                      1
    m_Logw->setLineWrapMode(QTextEdit::WidgetWidth);
    m_Shell = new QProcess();
    m_Shell->setReadChannelMode(QProcess::MergedChannels);
    connect(m_Shell, SIGNAL(readyReadStandardOutput()),
               this, SLOT(showOutput()));
#ifdef Q_WS_WIN
    m_Shell->start("cmd", QStringList(), QIODevice::ReadWrite);
#else
    m_Shell->start("bash", QStringList("-i"), QIODevice::ReadWrite);
#endif
}
```

1 Intercept events going to the `QTextEdit`.

17.1.4 Exercises: QProcess and Process Control

1. Backspace is not handled properly in this version of `Qonsole`. Add an event handler that does the proper thing in response to Backspace.

2. Modify the `Qonsole` to support multiple simultaneous terminals in separate tabs.

3. According to NIST,[6] the U.S. National Institute of Standards and Technology:

> A hash function takes binary data, called the message, and produces a condensed representation, called the message digest. A cryptographic hash function is a hash function that is designed to achieve certain security properties. The Federal Information Processing Standard 180-2, Secure Hash Standard, specifies algorithms for computing five cryptographic hash functions: SHA-1, SHA-224, SHA-256, SHA-384, and SHA-512.

For any given chunk of data, a good cryptographic hash function must reliably produce a digest that is essentially unique; that is, no other chunk of data would yield the same digest using that function. Hashing is a one-way operation; that is, it is generally not possible to reverse the process and produce the data chunk from the digest.

Secure passwords can be handled by storing only the digest for each password. When a user logs in and enters a password, that string is immediately hashed, and the resulting digest is compared with the stored digest. If they match, the user has been validated. Otherwise, the login is not successful. **The user's password is never stored and exists in memory only long enough to compute its digest.**

Qt has a class named `QCryptographicHash` that provides a hash function for computing the cryptographic hash of a given `QByteArray`. As of QT 4.7, the algorithms SHA-1, MD4, and MD5 are supported.[7]

a. Write a simple application that takes two command-line arguments: a string to be hashed and an argument that specifies the algorithm to be used. The application should send the resulting digest to standard output. For example:

```
crhash "my big secret" md5
```

would result in the output of a digest consisting of "binary" data.

b. Using the `crhash` application from part (a) as a separate process, write an application that manages club member data, including user ID, password,

---

[6] http://csrc.nist.gov/groups/ST/hash/index.html

[7] MD4 and MD5 are Message-Digest algorithms designed by Ron Rivest prior to the development of SHA-1, which has since been superceded by the SHA-2 family of hash functions. See http://en.wikipedia.org/wiki/MD5 for more details.

email address, street address, city, state, ZIP, and phone number. Passwords should be stored only as digests. Make sure that you serialize the club member data properly.

17.2   QThread **and** QtConcurrent

Before Qt, cross-platform threads were not generally available for C++ open source developers because threads were relatively new concepts and were handled differently in each operating system. Threads are now found in most operating systems and many modern programming languages. Multicore processors have also become quite common, so threads from the same process can be scheduled to run on different cores by modern operating systems.

Qt's thread model permits the prioritizing and control of threads. QThread provides a low-level class that can be used for explicit creation of long-running threads.

QtConcurrent is a namespace that provides higher-level classes and algorithms for writing concurrent software. One important class in this namespace is QThreadPool, a class that manages a pool of threads. Every Qt application has a QThreadPool::globalInstance() with a suggested maximum thread count that defaults, on most systems, to the number of cores.

Using QtConcurrent's functional map/filter/reduce algorithms, which apply functions in parallel to each item in a container, you can write a program that automatically takes advantage of the system's multiple cores by distributing the processing across the threads managed by the thread pool. Alternatively, you can use QRunnable as a base class for the Command pattern and schedule work with QtConcurrent::run(). In these cases, you do not need to create threads explicitly or manage them directly—you can simply describe the pieces of work as objects with the right interface.

Why Use Threads?

Sometimes, complexity added to software from using threads can outweigh the performance benefits. If a program is bound by the I/O, chances are that distributing the CPU's work across multiple threads will not show noticeable improvement in the program's overall performance. If, however, there is a significant amount of advance calculation that can be done, and you have idle cores, threads can improve performance.

Guidelines for Threads

In general, it is possible to avoid the use of threads and use instead the Qt Event Loop combined with `QTimer`s, nonblocking I/O operations, signals, and short-duration slots. In addition, you can call `QApplication::processEvents()` from a long-running loop in the main thread to enable the GUI to remain responsive[8] while that work is being done.

For driving animations, `QTimer`, `QTimeLine`, or the Animation Framework[9] is recommended. These APIs do not require additional threads to be created. They permit you to access GUI objects from your animation code and do not interfere with the responsiveness of your GUI.

If you have CPU-bound work to do and want to distribute it across multiple cores, you can break up your work into QRunnables and make those thread-safe by following these recommendations:

- Distribute the CPU-heavy calculations across multiple threads using `QtConcurrent` algorithms whenever possible, instead of writing your own `QThread` code.

- Do not access the GUI (this includes any `QWidget`-derived class, `QPixmap`, and other graphics-card specific classes) from any thread other than the main thread. This includes read access like querying the text entered into a `QLineEdit`.

- For processing images in other threads, use `QImage` instead of `QPixmap`.

- Do not call `QDialog::exec()` or create `QWidget` or `QIODevice` subclasses from any thread other than the main thread.

- Prevent simultaneous access to critical variables from more than one thread with a `QMutex`, `QReadWriteLock`, or `QSemaphore`.

- Use a `QMutexLocker` (or `QReadLocker`, `QWriteLocker`) in a function that has multiple `return` statements to ensure the function releases the lock from any possible execution path.

- The thread that creates a `QObject`, also known as its *thread affinity*, is responsible for executing slots of that `QObject`.

- You cannot link `QObject`s in parent-child relationships if they have different thread affinities.

- A thread enters an event loop by calling `QThread::exec()` directly or indirectly from `run()`.

- Posting events with `QApplication::postEvent()`, or using queued signal/slot connections, are both safe mechanisms for communicating across threads but require the receiving thread to be in an event loop.

- Be sure to `qRegisterMetaType()` each type used in signal/slot arguments of cross-thread connections.

---

[8] http://doc.trolltech.com/qq/qq27-responsive-guis.html#manualeventprocessing

[9] Introduced in Qt 4.6

17.2.1   Thread Safety and `QObjects`

A **reentrant** method is one that can be called simultaneously by multiple threads, provided no two invocations of the method attempt to reference the same data. A **thread-safe** method can be called simultaneously by multiple threads at any time, because any shared data is protected somehow (e.g., by `QMutex`) from simultaneous access. A class is reentrant or thread-safe if all of its non-static functions are reentrant or thread-safe.

A `QObject` that was created in a particular thread "belongs to," or has an affinity to, that thread. Its children must also belong to the same thread. Having parent-child relationships that cross over threads is forbidden by Qt.

- `QObject::thread()` returns its owner thread, or its affinity.
- `QObject::moveToThread()` moves it to another thread.

---

moveToThread(this)

Because a `QThread` is a `QObject`, and you create `QThread` when an additional thread for processing is needed, it is understandable that you might *think* of one as representing the other. However, the additional thread is not actually *created* until `QThread::exec()` is called, which confuses the issue.

Recall that each `QThread`, by virtue of being a `QObject`, has an affinity to its creating thread, rather than the one that it started.

It is for this reason that some people say a `QThread` is not the thread itself, but rather, a *manager* of that thread. It might help you to think of it that way also. In effect, the `QThread` is a wrapper for an underlying thread API and serves to manage a single thread via an API that is based on `java.lang.thread`.

This implies that when signals are connected to slots of this `QThread`, *the processing of the slot is done in the creating thread, not in the managed thread.*

Some programs have changed the definition of `QThread` so that it represents the thread that it manages and executes its slots in its managed thread. Such programs use a workaround: `moveToThread(this)` from the `QThread`'s constructor. The main problem with this workaround is that it leaves undefined what should happen to events that are posted to this object after the thread has exited.

This article[10] discusses the issue in more detail and says that even though the documentation and some older examples from Qt itself use this, it is no longer recommended. For one thing, it is undefined what happens to events and signals when the managed thread terminates. For another, it mixes the purpose of `QThread` with `QRunnable` and puts too much responsibility on a single class.

---

[10] http://labs.qt.nokia.com/2010/06/17/youre-doing-it-wrong/

A **thread-safe** object is one that can be accessed concurrently by multiple threads and is guaranteed to be in a "valid" state. QObjects are not thread safe by default. To make an object thread safe, there are a number of approaches to take. Some are listed here, but we recommend the Qt Thread Support documentation[11] for further details.

1. QMutex, for mutual exclusion, along with QMutexLocker, enables an individual thread T to protect (lock) an object or a section of code so that no other thread can access it until T releases (unlocks) it.

2. QWaitCondition, combined with QMutex, can be used to put a thread into a non-busy block state where it can wait for another thread to wake it up.

3. A QSemaphore is a more generalized QMutex for situations where a thread may need to lock more than one resource before doing its work. Semaphores make it possible to ensure that a thread locks resources only when enough are available for it to do its job.

There are more examples demonstrating how to use QtConcurrent in the Qt examples: $QTDIR/examples/qtconcurrent.

---

volatile Correctness

volatile, like const, can be used by the compiler to enforce a certain degree of thread safety in your program. When an object is volatile, only methods marked volatile can be called on it. volatile is used in Qt to implement some atomic operations, which in turn are used to implement higher-level locking structures such as QMutex, QSharedPointer, and QReadWriteLock. More info about volatile can be found in the following two articles.

- "Using Volatile with User Defined Types"[12]
- "Volatile Almost Useless for Multithreaded Programming"[13]

---

[11] http://doc.qt.nokia.com/latest/threads.html

[12] http://www.drdobbs.com/184403766

[13] http://software.intel.com/en-us/blogs/2007/11/30/volatile-almost-useless-for-multi-threaded-programming/

17.2.2   Parallel Prime Number Calculators

This section presents two different approaches to calculating prime numbers, while sharing work across multiple threads.

The first approach is a producer-consumer model, with a mediator object that is responsible for collecting the results.

Example 17.14 shows a producer class, `PrimeServer`.

EXAMPLE 17.14   src/threads/PrimeThreads/primeserver.h

```
[ . . . . ]
class PrimeServer : public QObject
{
    Q_OBJECT
public:
    explicit PrimeServer(QObject* parent =0);
    void doCalc(int numThreads, int highestPrime, bool concurrent = false);
    int nextNumberToCheck();
    void foundPrime(int );
    bool isRunning() const;
public slots:
    void cancel();
private slots:
    void handleThreadFinished();
signals:
    void results(QString);
private:
    int m_numThreads;
    bool m_isRunning;
    QList<int> m_primes;
    int m_nextNumber;
    int m_highestPrime;
    QTime m_timer;
    QMutex m_nextMutex;
    QMutex m_listMutex;
    QSet<QObject*> m_threads;
private slots:
    void handleWatcherFinished();
    void doConcurrent();
private:
    bool m_concurrent;
    int m_generateTime;                                          1
    QFutureWatcher<void> m_watcher;
};
[ . . . . ]
```

1 Time spent generating input data.

The `PrimeServer` creates `PrimeThreads` (consumers) to do the actual work. Child `PrimeThreads` are created and started in Example 17.15.

EXAMPLE 17.15   src/threads/PrimeThreads/primeserver.cpp

```
[ . . . . ]

void PrimeServer::
doCalc(int numThreads, int highestPrime, bool concurrent) {
    m_isRunning = true;
    m_numThreads = numThreads;
    m_concurrent = concurrent;
    m_highestPrime = highestPrime;
    m_primes.clear();
    m_primes << 2 << 3;
    m_threads.clear();
    m_nextNumber = 3;
    m_timer.start();
    if (!concurrent) {
        for (int i=0; i<m_numThreads; ++i) {
            PrimeThread *pt = new PrimeThread(this);            1
            connect (pt, SIGNAL(finished()), this,
                    SLOT(handleThreadFinished()));
            m_threads << pt;
            pt->start();                                        2
        }
    }
    else doConcurrent();
}
```

1 Child thread is not started yet.

2 Child thread executes `run()`.

`PrimeThread`, shown in Example 17.16, is a custom `QThread` that overrides `run()`.

EXAMPLE 17.16   src/threads/PrimeThreads/primethread.h

```
#ifndef PRIMETHREAD_H
#define PRIMETHREAD_H

#include <QThread>
#include "primeserver.h"
```

```
class PrimeThread : public QThread
{
    Q_OBJECT
public:
    explicit PrimeThread(PrimeServer *parent);
    void run();                                                      1
private:
    PrimeServer *m_server;

};


#endif // PRIMETHREAD_H
```

1 Required override.

The `run()` method, shown in Example 17.17, is doing a single prime number test between two method calls to the `QMutexLocker` methods of `PrimeServer`, in a tight loop.

EXAMPLE 17.17   src/threads/PrimeThreads/primethread.cpp

```
[ . . . . ]
PrimeThread::PrimeThread(PrimeServer *parent)
: QThread(parent), m_server(parent) { }

void PrimeThread::run() {
    int numToCheck = m_server->nextNumberToCheck();
    while (numToCheck != -1) {
        if (isPrime(numToCheck))
            m_server->foundPrime(numToCheck);
        numToCheck = m_server->nextNumberToCheck();
    }
}
[ . . . . ]
```

PrimeServer locks a `QMutex` via a `QMutexLocker`, which safely locks and unlocks its `QMutex` as the program enters and leaves the enclosing block scope, as shown in Example 17.18. Originally, this program used a single mutex to protect both methods, but because the data accessed is independent, you can increase parallelism possibilities by using independent mutexes for each method.

EXAMPLE 17.18   src/threads/PrimeThreads/primeserver.cpp

```
[ . . . . ]

int PrimeServer::nextNumberToCheck() {
    QMutexLocker locker(&m_nextMutex);                          1
    if (m_nextNumber >= m_highestPrime) {
        return -1;
    }
    else {
        m_nextNumber+= 2;
        return m_nextNumber;
    }
}

void PrimeServer::foundPrime(int pn) {
    QMutexLocker locker(&m_listMutex);                          2
    m_primes << pn;
}
```

1 Scope-based mutex works from multiple return points.

2 This method also must be made thread safe.

These methods are thread safe because simultaneous calls from multiple threads block one another. This is one way of serializing access to critical shared data.

EXAMPLE 17.19   src/threads/PrimeThreads/primeserver.cpp

```
[ . . . . ]

void PrimeServer::cancel() {
    QMutexLocker locker(&m_nextMutex);
    m_nextNumber = m_highestPrime+1;
```

The `cancel` method, shown in Example 17.19 is meant to be called in a nonblocking way, so that a GUI can continue responding to events while the `PrimeThread` safely exits its loop and returns from `run()`.

In Example 17.20, the server cleans up each `finished` thread and reports the results when all of them have finished. It uses `QObject::sender()` to obtain the signal sender and deletes it safely with `deleteLater()`. This is a recommended and safe way to terminate and clean up threads.

EXAMPLE 17.20   src/threads/PrimeThreads/primeserver.cpp

```
[ . . . . . ]

void PrimeServer::handleThreadFinished() {
    QObject* pt = sender();                                        1
    m_threads.remove(pt);
    pt->deleteLater();
    if (!m_threads.isEmpty()) return;                              2
    int numPrimes = m_primes.length();
    QString result = QString("%1 mutex'd threads %2 primes in %3"
                             "miliseconds. ").arg(m_numThreads)
                           .arg(numPrimes).arg( m_timer.elapsed());
    QString r2 = QString(" %1 kp/s")
                   .arg(numPrimes / m_timer.elapsed());
    qDebug() << result << r2;
    emit results(result + r2);
    m_isRunning = false;
}
```

1 The `QThread` is our sender.

2 Others are still running.

Some results from testing 100,000,000 numbers are summarized in Figure 17.6. The line marked `Mutex'd` shows the speedup factor observed from running the producer-consumer algorithm above with *n* worker threads. As you can see, the best speedup factor we have is at 3, and the performance goes down after that. This could be because there is also a producer thread that could be quite busy and not counted in the graph.

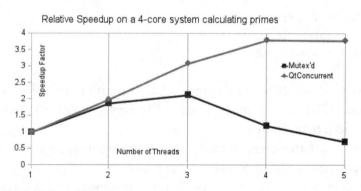

FIGURE 17.6   Speedup Factor of `PrimeThreads`

The other line marked QtConcurrent shows almost optimal speedup factors (1:1) as we reach 4 threads on a 4-core system, and no noticable degradation as we increase the number of threads beyond that. This is from using the same isPrime() function concurrently, in Example 17.22.

This graph is focused on *relative* speedup factors compared to the same algorithm running with a single thread, but what it does show is the absolute speeds. If you try running the example, you will find that the QtConcurrent approach runs at least 10 times faster overall, in all tests.

The efficiency of a parallel algorithm depends on keeping all cores busy doing calculations, rather than waiting for each other to synchronize. The more relative time is spent in synchronization points, the worse an algorithm performs as you add more threads.

QtConcurrent **Approach**

Instead of creating and managing your own threads, you can use the QtConcurrent filter() algorithm to filter non-primes from a list of numbers. QtConcurrent algorithms automatically distribute the work across an arbitrary number of threads, as specified by the global QThreadPool. The algorithms accept a container and function pointer, or a *functor*, which gets performed on each item in the container.

Example 17.21 shows the data members used by the concurrent algorithm in PrimeServer. You can use a QFutureWatcher to perform non-busy waiting for the end of the calculation.

EXAMPLE 17.21   src/threads/PrimeThreads/primeserver.h

```
[ . . . . ]

private slots:
    void handleWatcherFinished();
    void doConcurrent();
private:
    bool m_concurrent;
    int m_generateTime;                                  1
    QFutureWatcher<void> m_watcher;
};
```

1 Time spent generating input data.

Example 17.22 shows a functional programming-style approach to the solution. The nonblocking `filter()` function returns immediately with a value of type `QFuture`. You can send that to a `QFutureWatcher` to monitor progress of the calculation.

EXAMPLE 17.22   src/threads/PrimeThreads/primeserver.cpp

```
[ . . . . ]

void PrimeServer::doConcurrent() {
    QThreadPool::globalInstance()->setMaxThreadCount(m_numThreads);
    m_primes.clear();
    m_primes << 2;
    for (m_nextNumber=3; m_nextNumber<=m_highestPrime;
        m_nextNumber += 2) {
      m_primes << m_nextNumber;
    }
    m_generateTime = m_timer.elapsed();
    qDebug() << m_generateTime << "Generated "
            << m_primes.length() << " numbers";
    connect (&m_watcher, SIGNAL(finished()), this,
            SLOT(handleWatcherFinished()));
    m_watcher.setFuture(                                          1
        QtConcurrent::filter(m_primes, isPrime));                2
}


void PrimeServer::handleWatcherFinished() {
    int numPrimes = m_primes.length();
    int msecs = m_timer.elapsed();
    QString result =
      QString("%1 thread pool %2 primes in %4/%3 milliseconds"
            "(%5% in QtConcurrent).") .arg(m_numThreads)
            .arg(numPrimes) .arg(msecs) .arg(msecs-m_generateTime)
            .arg((100.0 * (msecs-m_generateTime)) / msecs);
    QString r2 = QString(" %1 kp/s").arg(numPrimes / msecs);
    qDebug() << result << r2;
    m_watcher.disconnect(this);
    emit results(result + r2);
    m_isRunning = false;
}
```

1 `QFutureWatcher` for monitoring progress.

2 Non-blocking, in-place `filter()` returns a `QFuture`.

17.2.3   Concurrent Map/Reduce Example

Revisiting Conway's Game of Life from Section 9.10, we will parallelize the computation using a `QtConcurrent mapReduce()` algorithm. For this to work, we must first break up the puzzle into smaller pieces. We define each piece as a `LifeSlice`, shown in Example 17.23.

EXAMPLE 17.23   src/threads/life/lifeslice.h

```
[ . . . . ]
struct LifeSlice {
    LifeSlice() {};
    LifeSlice(QRect r, QImage i) : rect(r), image(i) {}
    QRect rect;
    QImage image;
};
[ . . . . ]
```

A `LifeSlice` consists of a `QImage` with a `QRect` indicating which piece it came from. This is the argument and return type of the mapping function (Example 17.24). Do not use `QPixmap` in LifeSlice.[14]

EXAMPLE 17.24   src/threads/life/lifemainwindow.cpp

```
[ . . . . ]
struct LifeFunctor : public std::unary_function<LifeSlice, LifeSlice> {
    LifeSlice operator() (LifeSlice slice);
};

LifeSlice LifeFunctor::operator()(LifeSlice slice) {              1
    QRect rect = slice.rect;
    QImage image = slice.image;
    QImage next = QImage(rect.size(), QImage::Format_Mono);
    next.fill(DEAD);
    int h = rect.height();  int w = rect.width();

    for (int c=0; c<w; ++c) {
        for (int r=0; r<h; ++r) {
            int x = c+rect.x();
```

---

[14] This restriction is discussed in Section 17.2. In general, it is not safe to use `QPixmap` outside the GUI (main) thread.

```
            int y = r+rect.y();
            bool isAlive = (image.pixelIndex(x, y) == ALIVE);
            int nc = neighborCount(image, x, y);
            if (!isAlive && nc == 3)
                next.setPixel(c, r, ALIVE);
            if (!isAlive) continue;
            if (nc == 2 || nc == 3)
                next.setPixel(c,r, ALIVE);
        }
    }
    slice.image = next;
    return slice;
}
```

1 Mapping function

Deriving a *unary function object*, LifeFunctor from the Standard Library template unary_function gives our functor additional type "traits," used by generic algorithms to get the argument and return type of the functor. This functor defines an operator() that takes a LifeSlice argument and returns a LifeSlice value.

The return type of the mapping function must be the (second) argument type of the reduce function shown in Example 17.25.

EXAMPLE 17.25   src/threads/life/lifemainwindow.cpp

```
[ . . . . ]
void stitchReduce(QImage& next, const LifeSlice &slice) {
    if (next.isNull())
        next = QImage(boardSize, QImage::Format_Mono);
    QPainter painter(&next);
    painter.drawImage(slice.rect.topLeft(), slice.image);          1
}
```

1 Draw one piece of an image onto another.

The reduce function must somehow take together the partial results produced by each of the worker threads and reassemble them into a coherent QImage. As in the collage exercise, the mapping function uses the high-level QPainter API to draw one image onto another, avoiding the need for nested loops of individual pixel assignments.

The main loop in Example 17.26 must break up the problem into smaller pieces, send them to a `QtConcurrent` `blockingMappedReduced()`, and send the results to the `LifeWidget`.

EXAMPLE 17.26   src/threads/life/lifemainwindow.cpp

```
[ . . . . . ]

void LifeMainWindow::calculate() {
    int w = boardSize.width();
    // This might not be optimal, but it seems to work well...
    int segments = QThreadPool::globalInstance()->maxThreadCount() * 2;
    int ws = w/segments;                                                    1
    LifeFunctor functor;                                                    2
    while (m_running) {
        qApp->processEvents();                                              3
        m_numGenerations++;
        QList<LifeSlice> slices;                                            4
        for (int c=0; c<segments; ++c) {
            int tlx = c*ws;
            QRect rect(tlx, 0, ws, boardSize.height());
            LifeSlice slice(rect, m_current);
            slices << slice;                                                5
        }
        m_current = QtConcurrent::blockingMappedReduced(slices, functor,
                    stitchReduce, QtConcurrent::UnorderedReduce );          6
        m_lifeWidget->setImage(m_current);
    }
}
```

1 Width of a segment.
2 Map functor.
3 Ensure GUI is still responsive.
4 Break up into smaller pieces.
5 Add the pieces to a collection to be processed in parallel.
6 Do the work in parallel. `stitchReduce` can be called on each piece as it is ready.

The `qApp->processEvents()` is required in this loop for the main event loop to receive and process other GUI events. If you comment that line out and try running the application, you notice that as soon as the calculations start, there is no way to stop or quit.

This program gets 10 frames per second (fps) with four threads, compared to 4fps with one thread, on a 1024 × 768 board. Not quite a factor of 4, but with a larger life board, you might observe better improvements. Keep in mind, there is a synchronization point that cannot be avoided after each generation is computed.

17.3 Exercises: `QThread` and `QtConcurrent`

1. Without using `QtConcurrent`, write a multithreaded Game of Life example, where `LifeServer` creates and manages `LifeWorker` threads (up to `QThreadPool::maxThreadCount()`) and distributes the calculations across those threads to get faster speed. Let the user set the number of threads from a `QSpinBox`.

   Use `QMutex` or `QReadWriteLock` to synchronize access to shared data. Use the `PrimeThreads` producer-consumer example from Example 17.14 as a guide, and reuse any code you want from the Life example in Section 17.2.4. Figure 17.7 shows a possible high-level design in UML.

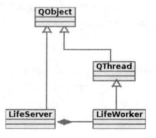

FIGURE 17.7   Multithreaded Life UML

2. Start with the application shown in Section 17.2.2 and add a progress bar to the GUI that works using either algorithm.

3. In this exercise you revisit some of the image manipulation techniques that were introduced in Section 10.5.1 and apply them in parallel, across several threads, to produce random collages.

   Write an application that lets the user select as many images as desired from the disk and then uses a `QtConcurrent` algorithm to distribute the labor of randomly applying image manipulation functions (with random arguments if appropriate) to random numbers of copies of the images.

After the image manipulations have been completed, use a `QtConcurrent` algorithm to randomly scale down each of the manipulated images and paint them into random locations inside an initially blank image—the collage.

After the collage has been produced and saved to disk, display it on the screen.

Figure 17.8 was produced using 28 photos, each of which was copied from one to five times, manipulated, scaled, and inserted into a (default) 640×480 image. The size of the final collage can (optionally) be set with command-line arguments.

FIGURE 17.8   Collage Example

17.4   Review Questions

1. List and explain at least two mechanisms by which a parent process communicates information to its child process.

2. List and explain at least two mechanisms by which threads synchronize with each other.

3. In what situations can a `QTimer` be used instead of a `QThread`? Why would you want to do that?

4. What does it mean for a function to be thread safe?

5. Which class can be used in non-GUI threads? `QImage` or `QPixmap`?

6. What does it mean for a function to be reentrant?

7. How do you tell a non-GUI thread to enter into an event loop?

8. Without using extra threads, how can you keep the GUI responsive while still performing a long-running loop?

## Chapter 18

Database Programming

This chapter gives a general introduction to the capabilities of Qt's SQL classes, using Sqlite as an example back-end.

Learning Structured Query Language (SQL)?

Do not bother learning SQL with any book that claims to be on "standard" SQL. The best manual to read is the reference guide for your chosen database server software because each server supports slightly different syntax and data types. Fortunately, with the exception of creating tables and other DDL queries, mapping between SQL values and `QVariant` is made quite easy for you by the QSql application programming interface (API). When you have used more than one database, you should either look for an abstraction layer (which might end up being an obstruction layer, depending on how well it is written) or write SQL for the least common denominator (SQLite).

Qt provides a platform-neutral database interface similar to JDBC.[1] It requires a **driver** for each specific database that it can connect to. To build the driver against a specific database, the development header files of the database and its libraries must be

---

[1] Java Database Connectivity API

available. You can use Qt to connect to a variety of different SQL databases, including Oracle, PostgreSQL, and Sybase SQL. In the examples that follow, we have tested our code with MySQL and SQLite on Linux.

If you develop something new with QtSQL, we recommend using SQLite syntax because it

1. Is open source
2. Comes with Qt
3. Does not require building Qt from source, building a plugin, or setting up a standalone server
4. Maps each database to a single file on disk
5. Supports a subset of SQL that is available on most other systems

SQLite is an in-process, zero-configuration database library. It does not run as a separate server. For concurrency, reliability, higher performance, faster startup/shutdown, and smaller memory requirements for your application, it is recommended that you connect instead to an external database process such as MySQL. But SQLite is probably sufficient for simple labs and for learning SQL.

What About Other Drivers?

For more information, see the Qt SQL drivers[2] documentation page.

What Drivers Are Already Supported?

To find out which drivers are available to the current version of Qt:

1. Run `$QTDIR/demos/sqlbrowser`, and you can see a driver list in a combobox on the initial Connection Settings dialog, as shown in Figure 18.1.
2. Call `QSqlDatabase::drivers()` from code.

---

[2] http://doc.qt.nokia.com/latest/sql-driver.html

FIGURE 18.1   Sql Browser Connection Settings Dialog

TIP

If you want to completely isolate yourself from SQL and map objects directly to persistent storage, you might be interested in Code Synthesis ODB,[3] an open source object-relational mapping layer with support for Qt types.

18.1   QSqlDatabase: **Connecting to SQL from Qt**

QSqlDatabase is a somewhat misleading name for this class. It does not represent a database on disk, but rather a *connection* to a database. A better name for this class would be QSqlConnection.

Connecting initially to a database server requires these pieces of information: driver type, host name, username, password, and database name, as shown in Example 18.1. In the case of SQLite, you need only a filename, which is passed to QSqlDatabase:: setDatabaseName().

A connection (i.e., an instance of QSqlDatabase) is created initially with the static QSqlDatabase::addDatabase(). The instance can be given an optional connection name and can later be retrieved again using that name. The default connection can be reused with the QSqlDatabase::database() method.

---

[3] http://www.codesynthesis.com/products/odb/

EXAMPLE 18.1   src/sql/testprepare/testprepare.cpp

```
[ . . . . . ]

void testprepare::testPrepare() {
    QSqlDatabase db = QSqlDatabase::addDatabase("QMYSQL");
    db.setHostName("localhost");
    db.setUserName("amarok");
    db.setPassword("amarok");
    db.setDatabaseName("amarok");
    QVERIFY(db.open());
```

Data Definition Language (DDL) Statements: Defining a Table

Each database has a collection of **tables**. A query statement that changes the definition of a table is called a DDL statement. A table is very much like an array of `struct`, where each data member corresponds to a column, and each object roughly corresponds to a **record**, or a row in the table. To define a table, we must describe what a record looks like. That means describing each of the columns, which can also be thought of as fields, properties, or data members. Example 18.2 defines a table in SQL called `MetaData`.

EXAMPLE 18.2   src/libs/sqlmetadata/metadatatable.cpp

```
[ . . . . . ]

bool MetaDataTable::createMetadataTable() {
    QSqlDatabase db = DbConnectionSettings::lastSaved();
    if (m_driver == "QMYSQL")
        m_createTableQStr = QString("CREATE TABLE if not exists %1 ("
          "TrackTitle  text, Artist text, "
          "AlbumTitle  text, TrackTime integer, TrackNumber integer, "
          "Genre varchar(30),  Preference integer, Comment  text, "
          "FileName  varchar(255) PRIMARY KEY, INDEX(Genre) ) "
          "DEFAULT CHARSET utf8").arg(m_tableName);
    else m_createTableQStr = QString("CREATE TABLE IF NOT EXISTS %1 ("   1
          "TrackTitle  text, Artist text, AlbumTitle  text, "
          "TrackTime integer, TrackNumber integer, Genre varchar(30), "
          "Preference integer, Comment  text, FileName  varchar(255) "
          "PRIMARY KEY").arg(m_tableName);
    QSqlQuery q(m_createTableQStr);
    if (!q.isActive()) {
        qDebug() << "Create Table Fail: " << q.lastError().text()
                << q.lastQuery();
```

```
        return false;
    }
    db.commit();
    return true;
}
```

<hr/>

1 Tested with SQLite3.

We have different SQL create strings depending on which QSqlDriver is in use. Each additional database we want to support must be tested separately, because SQL syntax can vary from one server to another. For example, we started out using `time` as the type for the `TrackTime` column in MySQL, but we changed it to `integer`[4] so that we can use the same schema with both databases.

After the database connection is opened, we use a powerful class called `QSqlQuery`, which has a member function `exec()`.

18.1.2   Prepared Statements: Inserting Rows

Using the `QSqlQuery`, there are two ways to execute SQL statements:

1. QSqlQuery.exec(QString)
2. QSqlQuery.prepare(QString)

`exec(QString)` is slower because it requires the server to parse each SQL statement. **Prepared statements** are safer because you do not need to escape strings. They are also faster, especially when the same SQL statement is executed repeatedly with different parameter values. The SQL driver needs to *parse* the query string only once.

Example 18.3 shows use of prepared statements to insert or update rows. We use named parameters here, but positional parameters are also possible with the use of `addBindValue` and parameters of the form of `:1`, `:2`, etc. The SQL syntax for a single operation that can insert or update a row in MySQL is slightly different from that of SQLite, so again, we have two different `insert` strings.

<hr/>

[4] Note the divergence from C++ type names.

EXAMPLE 18.3   src/libs/sqlmetadata/metadatatable.cpp

```
[ . . . . ]

MetaDataTable::MetaDataTable(QObject* parent)
    : QObject(parent), m_tableName("MetaData") {
    setObjectName(m_tableName);
    m_mdl = Abstract::MetaDataLoader::instance();
    m_driver = DbConnectionSettings::lastSaved().driverName();
    Q_ASSERT(createMetadataTable());
    QString preparedQuery = "INSERT into MetaData"                   1
        "(Artist, TrackTitle, AlbumTitle, TrackNumber, TrackTime, Genre,"
        "Preference, FileName, Comment) VALUES (:artist, :title, :album,"
        ":track, :time, :genre, :preference, :filename, :comment) "
        "ON DUPLICATE KEY UPDATE Preference=VALUES(Preference),"
        "Genre=VALUES(Genre), AlbumTitle=VALUES(AlbumTitle),"
        "TrackTitle=VALUES(TrackTitle), TrackNumber=VALUES(TrackNumber),"
        "Artist=VALUES(Artist), COMMENT=VALUES(Comment)";
    if (m_driver == "QSQLITE") {
        preparedQuery = "INSERT or REPLACE into MetaData"
            "(Artist, TrackTitle, AlbumTitle, TrackNumber, TrackTime, "
            "Genre, Preference, FileName, Comment)"
            "VALUES (:artist, :title, :album, :track, :time, :genre, "
            ":preference, :filename, :comment)";
    }
    bool prepSuccess = m_insertQuery.prepare(preparedQuery);
    if (!prepSuccess) {
        qDebug() << "Prepare fail: " << m_insertQuery.lastError().text()
                << m_insertQuery.lastQuery();
        abort();
    }
}
```

1 Tested with MySQL5.

In some cases, the Qt SQL driver may not support server-side prepared queries, but with Qt SQL you can still use prepared queries for client-side character escaping, which is the safest way to insert data or process user-supplied data. Prepared statements protect you from SQL injection attacks and other possible parsing errors and should be faster than regular queries that need to be parsed every time they are executed.

Example 18.4 shows the prepared statement in use. First, we call bindValue() on the query for each column, and then we call **exec()**.

EXAMPLE 18.4   src/libs/sqlmetadata/metadatatable.cpp

```
[ . . . . ]

bool MetaDataTable::insert(const MetaDataValue &ft) {
    using namespace DbUtils;

    QSqlDatabase db = DbConnectionSettings::lastSaved();
    QSqlRecord record = db.record(m_tableName);
    if (record.isEmpty() && !createMetadataTable()) {
        qDebug() << "unable to create metadata: "
                 << db.lastError().text();
        return false;
    }

    m_insertQuery.bindValue(":artist", ft.artist());
    m_insertQuery.bindValue(":title", ft.trackTitle());
    m_insertQuery.bindValue(":album", ft.albumTitle());
    m_insertQuery.bindValue(":track", ft.trackNumber());
    QTime t = ft.trackTime();
    int secs = QTime().secsTo(t);
    m_insertQuery.bindValue(":time", secs);
    m_insertQuery.bindValue(":genre", ft.genre());
    m_insertQuery.bindValue(":filename", ft.fileName());
    int pref = ft.preference().intValue();
    m_insertQuery.bindValue(":preference", pref);
    m_insertQuery.bindValue(":comment", ft.comment());

    bool retval = m_insertQuery.exec();

    if (!retval) {
        qDebug() << m_insertQuery.lastError().text()
                 << m_insertQuery.lastQuery();
        abort();
    }
    emit inserted(ft);
    return retval;
}
```

As you can see, the Qt SQL does not provide a way for you to "write once, run anywhere" against different database engines. And although it is possible to map columns to properties, you still write the object-relational mapping code and must test on different servers.

18.2   Queries and Result Sets

In Example 18.4, we inserted rows into a `MetaData` table. In this application, we try to encapsulate all the SQL operations we may need on MetaData SQL table in a class called `MetaDataTable`. Example 18.5 shows a simple query that is returned as a `QStringList`.

EXAMPLE 18.5   src/libs/sqlmetadata/metadatatable.cpp

```
[ . . . . ]

QStringList MetaDataTable::genres() const {
    QStringList sl;
    QSqlDatabase db = DbConnectionSettings::lastSaved();
    QSqlQuery q("SELECT DISTINCT Genre from MetaData");
    if (!q.isActive()) {
        qDebug() << "Query Failed: " << q.lastQuery()
                 << q.lastError().text();
    } else while (q.next()) {
        sl << q.value(0).toString();
    }
    return sl;
}
```

When we want to return a row of data, what is the best way to present it in our API? I prefer returning an object with getters and setters, but whether it should be a heap `MetaDataObject` or a stack `MetaDataValue` is open to debate. If you return pointers to heap objects from here, you have to worry about who owns and is responsible for deleting them afterward. Example 18.6 shows another approach, where we convert the `QObject` to its base class value type and return that.

EXAMPLE 18.6   src/libs/sqlmetadata/metadatatable.cpp

```
[ . . . . ]

MetaDataValue MetaDataTable::findRecord(QString fileName) {
    using namespace DbUtils;
    QFileInfo fi(fileName);
    MetaDataObject f;
    if (!fi.exists()) return f;
    QString abs = fi.absoluteFilePath();
```

1

```cpp
QSqlDatabase db = DbConnectionSettings::lastSaved();
QString qs = QString("select * from %1 where FileName = \"%2\"")
              .arg(m_tableName).arg(escape(abs));
QSqlQuery findQuery(qs);
if (!findQuery.isActive()) {
    qDebug() << "Query Failed: " << findQuery.lastQuery()
             << findQuery.lastError().text();
    return f;
}
if (!findQuery.first()) return f;
QSqlRecord rec = findQuery.record();
for (int i=rec.count() -1; i >= 0; --i) {                    2
    QSqlField field = rec.field(i);
    QString key = field.name();
    QVariant value = field.value();
    if (key == "Preference") {
        int v = value.toInt();
        Preference p(v);
        f.setPreference(p);
    }
    else if (key == "TrackTime") {                          3
        QTime trackTime;
        trackTime = trackTime.addSecs(value.toInt());
        f.setTrackTime(trackTime);
    }
    else {
        f.setProperty(key, value);                          4
    }

}
return f;                                                   5
}
```

1   Return a `QObject` by value? Don't forget, `MetaDataValue` is the base class of this particular `QObject`.

2   Properties in `QObject` map to column names / field values in the table!

3   SQLite has no time type, so we must store as `int`.

4   Using `QObject` `setProperty` for other columns.

5   Create a value type from this local stack `QObject` about to be destroyed.

In this example, we create a stack `MetaDataObject` for the purposes of setting properties. Then we return it *by value*, so a temporary `MetaDataValue` is returned. This illustrates how derived objects can be implicitly converted to base class types.[5]

18.3   Database Models

Figure 18.2 shows the concrete model classes for connecting to a `QTableView`.

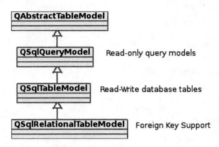

FIGURE 18.2   SQL Table Models

If you want to show a table that was created after calling Example 18.4, it takes five lines of code with the `QSqlTableModel`.

EXAMPLE 18.7   src/libs/tests/testsqlmetadata/testsqlmetadata.cpp

```
[ . . . . . ]

void TestSqlMetaData::showTable() {
    QSqlTableModel model;
    model.setTable("MetaData");
    model.select();
    QTableView *view = new QTableView;
    view->setModel(&model);
    view->setItemDelegate(new SimpleDelegate(view));
```

---

[5] Provided the copy constructor is not `private`.

The testcase, excerpted in Example 18.7, scans a directory of your choice, as set by an environment variable, TESTTRACKS, and adds metadata for each mp3 file found to the table model. It is included in the source tarball from our [dist] directory.

18.4   Review Questions

1. Which database is included with Qt on all platforms?

2. How can you determine what databases are supported by your version of Qt?

3. What is QSqlDatabase an abstraction for: a file, connection, user, or table?

4. What is the difference between a DDL query and a regular query?

5. Why are prepared queries preferred over regular queries?

6. What would be a better name for the class QSqlDatabase?

7. If the database driver's hasFeature(QSqlDriver::PreparedQueries) reports false, can you use prepared queries?

8. Can a non-DDL query modify table rows?

PART II

C++ Language Reference

## Chapter 19

Types and Expressions

This chapter seeks to provide a deeper understanding of C++'s strong typing system and shows how expressions are evaluated and converted.

Here we formally define some terms that we have been using. **Operators** are special kinds of functions that perform calculations on operands and return results. **Operands** are the arguments supplied to an operator.

Operators can be thought of as ordinary functions, except that you can call some of them using infix operator symbols (e.g., +, -, *, /, etc.). Thus, in addition to the longer function-call syntax (e.g., `str3 = operator+(str1, str2);`) you can use the more readable infix systax (e.g., `str3 = str1 + str2;`).

An **expression** can consist of a single operand, multiple operands with operators interspersed, or functions with arguments. Each expression has a type and a value. The value is obtained by applying the definitions of the operators (and/or functions) to the operands (and/or arguments).

19.1 Operators

Operators fall into broad classifications according to their primary use:

Assignment operators	=, +=, *=, ...
Arithmetic operators	+, -, *, /, %
Relational operators	<, <=, >, >=, ==, !=
Logical operators	&&, ||, !
Bitwise operators	&, |, ^, ~, <<, >>
Memory management operators	new, delete, sizeof
Pointer and access operators	*, &, ., ->, [], ()
Scope resolution operators	::
Miscellaneous operators	conditional (? :), comma (,)

As shown in Table 19.1, the C++ standard defines certain keywords that act as aliases for some of the operator symbols.

TABLE 19.1 Operator Aliases

Operator	Alias
&&	and
&	bitand
&=	and_eq
||	or
|	bitor
|=	or_eq
^	xor
^=	xor_eq
!	not
!=	not_eq
~	compl

Operators have predefined meanings for built-in types, but not all operators are defined for all built-in types.

Operator Characteristics

Operators have the following special characteristics:

- Precedence
- Associativity
- Number of required operands

Table 19.2 lists all the C++ operators and their characteristics, grouped by precedence and purpose, with groups of highest precedence listed first:

- The **Operands** column contains the number of operands that the operator requires.
- The **Description** column contains the conventional meaning of the operator for built-in types.
- The **A** column indicates the associativity that governs how an expression is evaluated if the same operator occurs more than once.
  - **L** indicates left-to-right associativity. Example:
    ```
    d = a + b + c;  // a+b is evaluated first, then (a+b)+c
    ```
    Assignment is evaluated last because of lower precedence.
  - **R** indicates right-to-left associativity:
    ```
    c = b = a;     // a is assigned to b, then to c.
    ```
- The **Ovl** column indicates whether the operator may be overloaded (redefined) for custom types.

  The possible values for that column are

  - Y: This operator can be overloaded as a global or member function.
  - M: This operator can be overloaded only as a class member function.
  - N: This operator cannot be overloaded.

19.1.1 Table of Operators

TABLE 19.2 C++ Operators

Operator	Operands	Description	Example	A	Ovl
::	one	Global Scope Resolution	`:: name`	R	N
::	two	class/namespace scope resolution	`className::memberName`	L	N
->	two	Member selector via ptr	`ptr->memberName`	L	N
.	two	Member selector via obj	`obj.memberName`	L	N
->	one	Smart ptr	`obj->member`	R	M
[ ]	two	Subscript operator	`ptr[expr]`	L	M
( )	any[a]	Function call	`function(argList)`	L	N
( )	any	Value construction	`className(argList)`	L	M
++	one	Post increment	`varName++`	R	Y
--	one	Post decrement	`varName--`	R	Y
typeid	one	Type identification	`typeid(type)` or `typeid(expr)`	R	N
dynamic_cast	two	runtime checked conv	`dynamic_cast<type>(expr)`	L	N
static_cast	two	compile time checked conv	`static_cast<type>(expr)`	L	N
reinterpret_cast	two	unchecked conv	`reinterpret_cast<type>(expr)`	L	N
const_cast	two	const conv	`const_cast<type>(expr)`	L	N
sizeof	one	Size in bytes	`sizeof expr` or `sizeof(type)`	R	N
++	one	Pre Increment	`++varName`	R	Y
--	one	Pre Decrement	`--varName`	R	Y
~	one	Bitwise negation	`~ expr`	R	Y
!	one	Logical negation	`! expr`	R	Y
+, -	one	Unary plus, unary minus	`+expr` or `-expr`	R	Y
*	one	Pointer dereference	`* ptr`	R	Y
&	one	Address-of	`& lvalue`	R	Y
new	one	Allocate	`new type` or `new type(expr-list)`	R	Y
new [ ]	two	Allocate array	`new type [ size ]`	L	Y
delete	one	Deallocate	`delete ptr`	R	Y
delete [ ]	one	Deallocate array	`delete [ ] ptr`	R	M

Operator	Operands	Description	Example	A	Ovl
( )	two	C-style type cast	`( type ) expr`	R	N [b]
->*	two	Member ptr selector via ptr	`ptr->*ptrToMember`	L	M
.*	two	Member ptr selector via obj	`obj.*ptrToMember`	L	N
*	two	Multiply	`expr1 * expr2`	L	Y
/	two	Divide	`expr1 / expr2`	L	Y
%	two	Remainder	`expr1 % expr2`	L	Y
+	two	Add	`expr1 + expr2`	L	Y
-	two	Subtract	`expr1 - expr2`	L	Y
<<	two	Bitwise left shift	`expr << shiftAmt`	L	Y
>>	two	Bitwise right shift	`expr >> shiftAmt`	L	Y
<	two	Less than	`expr1 < expr2`	L	Y
<=	two	Less or equal	`expr1 <= expr2`	L	Y
>	two	Greater	`expr1 > expr2`	L	Y
>=	two	Greater or equal	`expr1 >= expr2`	L	Y
==	two	Equals [c]	`expr1 == expr2`	L	Y
!=	two	Not equal	`expr1 != expr2`	L	Y
&	two	Bitwise AND	`expr1 & expr2`	L	Y
^	two	Bitwise XOR (exclusive OR)	`expr1 ^ e2`	L	Y
|	two	Bitwise OR (inclusive OR)	`expr1 | expr2`	L	Y
&&	two	Logical AND	`expr1 && expr2`	L	Y
||	two	Logical OR	`expr1 || expr2`	L	Y
=	two	Assign	`expr1 = expr2`	R	Y
*=	two	Multiply and assign	`expr1 *= expr2`	R	Y
/=	two	Divide and assign	`expr1 /= expr2`	R	Y
%=	two	Modulo and assign	`expr1 %= expr2`	R	Y
+=	two	Add and assign	`expr1 += expr2`	R	Y
-=	two	Subtract and assign	`expr1 -= expr2`	R	Y
<<=	two	Left shift and assign	`expr1 <<= expr2`	R	Y
>>=	two	Right shift and assign	`expr1 >>= expr2`	R	Y
&=	two	And and assign	`expr1 &= expr2`	R	Y
|=	two	Inclusive or and assign	`expr1 |= expr2`	R	Y

Operator	Operands	Description	Example	A	Ovl
`^=`	two	Exclusive or and assign	`expr1 ^= expr2`	R	Y
`? :`	three	Conditional expression	`bool ? expr : expr`	L	N
`throw`	one	Throw exception	`throw expr`	R	N
`,`	two	Sequential Evaluation (comma)	`expr , expr`	L	Y

[a] The function call operator may be declared to take any number of operands.

[b] The type-cast operator may use constructors or conversion operators to convert custom types.

[c] This operator should not be used for `float` or `double` operands. It requires an "exact" match, which is architecture-dependent and can give unexpected results.

19.2   Statements and Control Structures

Statements are pieces of executable code. Control structures are statements that control the way other statements are executed. This chapter formally defines the language elements and shows what kind of control structures are available.

19.2.1   Statements

A C++ program contains **statements** that alter the state of the storage managed by the program and determine the flow of program execution. There are several types of C++ statements, most of which are inherited from the C language. First, there is the simple statement, terminated with a semicolon:

```
x = y + z;
```

Next, there is the **compound statement**, or **block**, consisting of a sequence of statements enclosed in curly braces:

```
{
    int temp = x;
    x = y;
    y = temp;
}
```

The preceding example is a single compound statement that *contains* three simple statements that are executed in sequence, top to bottom. The variable `temp` is local to the block and is destroyed when the end of the block is reached. A compound statement may contain other compound statements.

In general, a compound statement can be placed wherever a simple statement can go. The reverse is not always true, however. In particular, the function definition

```
double area(double length, double width) {
    return length * width;
}
```

cannot be replaced by

```
double area(double length, double width)
    return length * width;
```

The body of a function definition must always be a block.

19.2.2   Selection Statements

Every programming language has at least one control structure that enables the flow of the program to branch depending on the outcome of a boolean condition. C and C++ have if and switch. The if statement typically has the following form:

```
if(boolExpression)
  statement
```

It can have an optional else attached.

```
if(boolExpression)
  statement1
else
  statement2
```

Conditional statements can be nested, which means they can get quite complicated. An important rule to keep in mind is that an else or else if clause is activated when the boolExpression of the *immediately preceding* open if evaluates to false. This can be confusing when your program logic allows you to omit some else clauses. Consider the following badly indented example, where x is an int:

```
if (x>0)
    if (x > 100)
        cout << "x is over a hundred";
else
    if (x == 0)  // no! this cannot be true -the indentation is misleading
        cout << "x is 0";
```

```
    else
        cout << "x is negative"; // no! x is between 1 and 100 inclusive!
```

You can clarify and repair this logic with braces:

```
if (x>0) {
    if (x > 100)
        cout << "x is over a hundred";
}
else
    if (x == 0)  // now this is possible.
        cout << "x is 0";
    else
        cout << "x is negative";
```

An `if` without an `else` can be closed by enclosing the `if` statement in braces {}, making it a compound statement.

switch

`switch` is another branching construct, which permits the execution of different code depending on the value of a parameter.

```
switch(integralExpression) {
    case value1:
        statement1;
        break;
    case value2:
        statement2;
        break;
        ...
    case valuen:
        statementn;
        break;
    default:
        defaultStatement;
}
nextStatement;
```

The `switch` statement is a computed `goto` statement. Each `case` is followed by a unique label value, which is compared to the `integralExpression`.

When the `switch` causes a jump to a `case` label whose value matches the *integralExpression*, statements are executed from that point on until the end of the `switch` block or a branching statement (e.g. `break`) is reached.

The optional `default` label is the jump destination when the *integralExpression* does not match a `case` label value. If `default` is omitted and no matching `case` label exists, then the jump destination is *nextStatement*.

The *integralExpression* must be an expression that evaluates to an integer. Each `case` label, except `default`, must be an integer constant.[1]

Any `switch` statement such as the previous one can be rewritten as a long `if` ... `else` statement. However, the runtime performance of a `switch` is considerably better because it requires only a single comparison and performs only one branch:

```
if(integralExpression == value1)
    statement1;
else if(integralExpression == value2)
    statement2;
...
else if(integralExpression == valuen)
    statementn;
else
    defaultStatement;
```

> **NOTE**
>
> Long compound conditional statements and `switch` statements should be avoided in object-oriented programming (unless they are isolated in factory code) because they tend to make functions complex and hard to maintain.
>
> If each case can be rewritten as a method of a different class, you can use the Strategy pattern (and the virtual table) instead of writing your own `switch` statement.

19.2.2.1   Exercises: Selection Statements

Be the computer and predict the output of Example 19.1. Then run it and compare your predicted output with the output produced by the computer.

---

[1] case labels are not the same as goto labels, which are used as destinations for the infamous goto statement. goto labels must be identifiers. In particular, they cannot be integers.

EXAMPLE 19.1   src/early-examples/nestedif.cpp

```cpp
#include <iostream>
using namespace std;

void nestedif1 () {
    int m = 5, n = 8, p = 11;
    if (m > n)
        if (p > n)
            cout << "red" << endl;
        else
            cout << "blue"  << endl;
}


void nestedif2() {
    int m = 5, n = 8,  p = 11;
    if (m > n) {
        if (p > n)
            cout << "red"  << endl;
    } else
        cout << "blue" << endl;
}


int main() {
    nestedif1();
    nestedif2();
    return 0;
}
```

Iteration

C++ provides three iteration structures:

1. `while` loop:

```cpp
while ( loopCondition ) {
    loopBody
}
```

a. Evaluate `loopCondition` first.

b. Execute `loopBody` repeatedly until `loopCondition` is `false`.

2. `do..while` loop:

```
do {
    loopBody
} while ( loopCondition ) ;
```

a. Execute `loopBody` first.

b. Evaluate `loopCondition`.

c. Execute `loopBody` repeatedly until `loopCondition` is `false`.

3. `for` loop:

```
for ( initStatement; loopCondition; incrStmt ) {
    loopBody
}
```

a. Execute `initStatement` first.

b. Execute `loopBody` repeatedly until `loopCondition` is `false`.

c. After each execution of `loopBody`, execute `incrStmt`.

With each of these iteration structures, the `loopBody` code gets repeated as long as `loopCondition` evaluates to `true`. The `do` loop differs from the other two in that its `loopCondition` gets checked at the bottom of the loop, so its `loopBody` is always executed at least once.

A common programming error is to place a semicolon after the `while`:

```
while (notFinished()) ;
    doSomething();
```

The first semicolon terminates the `while` statement entirely and produces a loop with an empty `loopBody`. Even though `doSomething()` is indented, it does not get executed inside the loop. The `loopBody` is responsible for changing the `loopCondition`. If `notFinished()` is initially `true`, then the empty `loopBody` causes an infinite loop. If `notFinished()` is initially `false`, then the loop terminates immediately and `doSomething()` gets executed exactly once.

C++ provides `break` and `continue` for finer control over code executed inside loops:

```
while ( moreWorkToDo ) {
    statement1;
    if ( specialCase ) continue;
    statement2;
```

```
    if ( noMoreInput ) break;
    statement3;
// continue jumps here
}
// break jumps here
```

break jumps out of the current control structure, whether it is a switch, for, while, or do..while.

continue operates only inside loops. It skips the remaining statements in the current iteration and checks the *moreWorkToDo* condition. Example 19.2 shows how you might use continue and break.

EXAMPLE 19.2   src/continue/continue-demo.cpp

```
#include <QTextStream>
#include <cmath>

int main() {
    QTextStream cout(stdout);
    QTextStream cin(stdin);
    int num(0), root(0), count;
    cout << "How many perfect squares? "<< flush;
    cin >> count;
    for(num = 0;; ++num) {                                    1
        root = sqrt(num);
        if(root * root != num)
            continue;
        cout << num << endl;
        --count;
        if(count == 0)
            break;
    }
}
```

1 Convert sqrt to int.

19.2.3.1   Exercises: Iteration

1. Write the function isPrime(int n) that returns true if n is prime and false otherwise. Supply an interactive main() to test your function.

2. Write the function `primesBetween(int min, int max)` that displays on the screen all the prime numbers that are between `min` and `max`. Supply an interactive `main()` to test your function.

3. Write the function `power2(int n)` that computes and returns the value of 2 raised to the power `n`. Supply an interactive `main()` to test your function.

4. Write a binary logarithm function `binLog(int n)` that computes and returns an `int` equal to the integral part of $\log_2(n)$, where `n` is positive. This is equivalent to finding the exponent of the largest power of 2 that is less than or equal to n. For example, `binLog(25)` is 4. There are at least two simple, iterative ways to do this computation. Supply an interactive `main()` to test your function.

19.2.4   Review Questions

1. What is the difference between a compound statement and a simple statement?

2. How can you guarantee that at least one case will be executed for any given `switch` value?

3. What are the advantages and disadvantages of the three iteration structures? For each, discuss the kinds of situations that would lead you to prefer using it rather than the other two.

19.3   Evaluation of Logical Expressions

In C and C++, evaluation of a logical expression stops as soon as the logical value of the entire expression is determined. This shortcut mechanism may leave some operands unevaluated. The value of an expression of the form

$expr_1$ && $expr_2$ && ... && $expr_n$

is `true` if and only if all the operands are `true`. If one or more of the operands are `false`, the value of the expression is `false`. Evaluation of the expression proceeds sequentially, from left to right, and is *guaranteed to stop* (and return the value `false`) if it encounters an operand that has the value `false`.

Similarly, an expression of the form

$expr_1$ || $expr_2$ || ... || $expr_n$

is `false` if and only if all the operands are `false`. Evaluation of the expression proceeds sequentially, from left to right, and is *guaranteed to stop* (and return the value `true`) if it encounters an operand, that has the value `true`.

Programmers often exploit this system with statements like

```
if( x != 0 &&  y/x < z) {
// do something ...
}
else {
// do something else ...
}
```

If x were equal to 0, evaluating the second expression would produce a runtime error. Fortunately, that cannot happen.

Logical expressions often use both && and ||. It is important to remember that && has higher precedence than ||. In other words,

$expr_1$ || $expr_2$ && $expr_3$

means

$expr_1$ || ($expr_2$ && $expr_3$)

not

($expr_1$ || $expr_2$) && $expr_3$.

19.4 Enumerations

In Chapter 2, "Top of the class," we discussed at some length how you can add new types to the C++ language by defining classes. Another way to add new types to C++ deserves some more discussion.

The keyword enum is used for assigning integral values to C++ identifiers. For example, when designing data structures that perform bitwise operations, it is convenient to give names to the various bitmasks. Qt frequently uses enums for this. A good example can be seen in QFileDialog::Option. The main purpose for an enum is to make the code more readable and, hence, easier to maintain. For example:

```
enum {UNKNOWN, JAN, FEB, MAR };
```

defines three constant identifiers, numbered in ascending order, starting at 0. It is equivalent to

```
enum {UNKNOWN=0, JAN=1, FEB=2, MAR=3};
```

The identifiers JAN, FEB, and MAR are called **enumerators**. They can be defined and initialized to arbitrary integer values. Because enumerators are const items, their names are frequently spelled with uppercase letters. (Qt does not follow this convention, however.)

```
enum Ages {MANNY = 10, MOE, JACK = 23,
        SCOOTER = JACK + 10};
```

If the first enumerator, MANNY, had not been initialized, it would automatically get the value 0. Because MANNY has been initialized to 10 and MOE was not assigned a value, the value of MOE is 11. The values of enumerators need not be distinct.

Assigning a name to an enum defines a new type. For example:

```
enum Winter {JAN=1, FEB, MAR, MARCH = MAR };
```

The name Winter is called a **tag name**. Now it is possible to declare variables of type Winter.

```
Winter m = JAN;
int i = JAN;    // OK - enum can be implicitly converted to int.
m = i;          // error - explicit cast is required.
m = static_cast<Winter>(i);  // OK
i = m;          // OK
m = 4;          // error
```

The tag name and the enumerators must be distinct identifiers within their scope.

Enumerator values can be implicitly converted to ordinary integer types, but the reverse is not possible without an explicit cast. Example 19.3 demonstrates the use of enum and shows how enumerators look when they are printed out.

EXAMPLE 19.3   src/enums/enumtst.cpp

```
#include <iostream>
using namespace std;

int main(int, char** ) {
    enum Signal { off, on } sig;                    1
    sig = on;
    enum Answer { no, yes, maybe = -1 };            2
    Answer ans = no;                                3
//    enum Neg {no,false} c;                        4
    enum { lazy, hazy, crazy } why;                 5
```

```
    int  i, j = on;                                    6
    sig = off;
    i = ans;
//  ans = s                                            7
    ans = static_cast<Answer>(sig);                    8
    ans = (sig ? no : yes);
    sig = static_cast<Signal>(9);                      9
    Signal sig2(sig);                                 10
    why = hazy;
    cout << "sig2, ans, i, j, why "
         << sig2 << ans << i << j << why << endl;
    return 0;
}
```

Output:

```
src/enums> ./enums
sig2, ans, i, j, why 91011
src/enums>
```

1 A new type, two new enum identifiers, and a variable definition all in one line.
2 Just the type/enum definitions.
3 An instance of an enum.
4 Illegal redefinitions of identifiers.
5 An unnamed enum variable.
6 An enum can always convert to int.
7 Conversions between enum types cannot be done implicitly.
8 Conversion is okay with a cast.
9 Bad news!
10 Have we added an unnamed enumerator?

19.5   Signed and Unsigned Integral Types

This section explains the differences between signed and unsigned integral types.

The underlying binary representation of an object x of any integral type looks like this (assuming n-bit storage):

$$d_{n-1}d_{n-2}\ldots d_2d_1d_0$$

where each d_i is either 0 or 1. The computation of the decimal equivalent value of x depends on whether x is an unsigned or signed type. If x is unsigned, the decimal equivalent value is

$$d_{n-1}*2^{n-1} + d_{n-2}*2^{n-2} +\ldots+ d_2*2^2 + d_1*2^1 + d_0*2^0$$

The largest (positive) value that can be expressed by an unsigned integer is, therefore,

$$2^n - 1 = 1*2^{n-1} + 1*2^{n-2} +\ldots+ 1*2^2 + 1*2^1 + 1*2^0$$

If x is signed, the decimal equivalent value is

$$d_{n-1}*-(2^{n-1}) + d_{n-2}*2^{n-2} +\ldots+ d_2*2^2 + d_1*2^1 + d_0*2^0$$

The largest (positive) value that can be expressed by a signed integer is

$$2^{n-1} - 1 = 0*-(2^{n-1}) + 1*2^{n-2} +\ldots+ 1*2^2 + 1*2^1 + 1*2^0$$

This is called **two's complement** representation. To determine the representation of the negative of a signed integer,

1. Compute the **one's complement** of the number (i.e., replace each bit with its complement).

2. Add 1 to the one's complement produced in the first step.

8-Bit Integer Example

Suppose that you have a tiny system that uses only 8 bits to represent a number. On this system, the largest unsigned integer would be

```
11111111 = 128 + 64 + 32 + 16 + 8 + 4 + 2 + 1 = 255
```

But that same number, interpreted as a signed integer, would be

```
11111111 = -128 + 64 + 32 + 16 + 8 + 4 + 2 + 1 = -1
```

19.5.1   Exercises: Signed and Unsigned Integral Types

You be the computer.

For Example 19.4, Example 19.5, and Example 19.6, simulate the action of the computer as it executes the given code and specify what you think the output will be. Then compile and run the code yourself to see if your output is correct. If you disagree with the computer, try to explain why.

1. EXAMPLE 19.4   src/types/tctest1.cpp

```cpp
#include <iostream>
using namespace std;
int main() {
  unsigned n1 = 10;
  unsigned n2 = 9;
  char *cp;
  cp = new char[n2 - n1];
  if(cp == 0)
    cout << "That's all!" << endl;
  cout << "bye bye!" << endl;
}
```

2. EXAMPLE 19.5   src/types/tctest2.cpp

```cpp
#include <iostream>
using namespace std;

int main() {
  int x(7), y = 11;
  char ch = 'B';
  double z(1.34);
  ch += x;
  cout << ch << endl;
  cout << y + z << endl;
  cout << x + y * z << endl;
  cout << x / y * z << endl;
}
```

3. EXAMPLE 19.6   src/types/tctest3.cpp

```cpp
#include <iostream>
using namespace std;

bool test(int x, int y)
{ return x / y; }

int main()
{ int m = 17, n = 18;
  cout << test(m,n) << endl;
  cout << test(n,m) << endl;
  m += n;
  n /= 5;
  cout << test(m,n) << endl;
}
```

4. It is generally a bad idea to mix signed and unsigned numbers in any computation or comparison. Predict the output of running Example 19.7.

EXAMPLE 19.7   src/types/unsigned.cpp

```cpp
#include <iostream>
using namespace std;
int main() {
  unsigned u(500);
  int i(-2);
  if(u > i)
    cout << "u > i" << endl;
  else
    cout << "u <= i" << endl;
  cout << "i - u = " << i - u << endl;
  cout << "i * u = " << i * u << endl;
  cout << "u / i = " << u / i << endl;
  cout << "i + u = " << i + u << endl;
}
```

19.6   Standard Expression Conversions

This section discusses expression conversions, including implicit type conversions through promotion or demotion, and explicit casting through a variety of casting mechanisms.

Suppose *x* and *y* are numeric variables. An expression of the form *x op y* has both a value and a type. When this expression is evaluated, temporary copies of *x* and *y* are used. If *x* and *y* have different types, the one with the shorter type may need to be converted (widened) before the operation can be performed.

An implicit conversion of a number that preserves its value is called a **promotion**.

Automatic Expression Conversion Rules for *x op y*

1. Any `bool`, `char`, `signed char`, `unsigned char`, `enum`, `short int`, or `unsigned short int` is promoted to `int`. This is called an **integral promotion**.

2. If, after the first step, the expression is of mixed type, then the operand of the smaller type is promoted to that of the larger type, and the value of the expression has that type.

3. The hierarchy of types is indicated by the arrows in Figure 19.1.

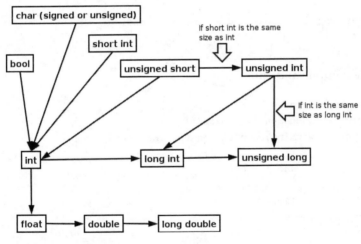

FIGURE 19.1   Hierarchy of Basic Types

The relationship between `unsigned` and `long` depends on the implementation. For example, on a system that implements `int` with the same number of bytes as `long`, it would not be possible to promote `unsigned` to `long`, so the promotion process would bypass `long` and promote `unsigned` to `unsigned long`. Now assume that you have the following declarations:

```
double d;
int i;
```

In general, a promotion such as `d = i;` will be well behaved. An assignment that causes a demotion such as `i = d;` can result in a loss of information. Assuming the compiler permits the assignment, the fractional part of `d` would be discarded. Example 19.8 demonstrates some of the conversions we have discussed.

EXAMPLE 19.8   src/types/mixed/mixed-types.cpp

```
#include <iostream>
using namespace std;

int main() {
    int i, j = 88;
    double d = 12314.8723497;
    cout << "initially d = " << d
        << "  and j = " << j << endl;
    cout << "The sum is: " << j + d << endl;
    i = d;
    cout << "after demoting d,  i = " << i << endl;
    d = j;
    cout << "after promoting j,  d = " << d << endl;
}
```

Here is the compile and run.

```
src> g++ mixed-types.cpp
mixed-types.cpp: In function `int main()':
mixed-types.cpp:10: warning: converting to `int' from `double'
src> ./a.out
initially d = 12314.9  and j = 88
The sum is: 12402.9
after demoting d,  i = 12314
after promoting j,  d = 88
src>
```

There is another kind of implicit conversion that is made whenever necessary. An expression that evaluates to a pointer or to an integral or floating-point value can be converted to `bool`. If that value is `0`, the result is `false`; otherwise the result is `true`. Example 19.9 demonstrates this conversion.

EXAMPLE 19.9 src/types/convert2bool.cpp

```cpp
#include <iostream>
using namespace std;

int main() {
   int j(5);
   int* ip(&j);
   int* kp(0);
   double y(3.4);
   if(y)
      cout << "y looks like true to me!" << endl;
   else
      cout << "y looks like false to me!" << endl;
   cout << "ip looks like " << (ip ? "true" : "false") << endl;
   cout << "kp looks like " << (kp ? "true" : "false") << endl;
   while(--j) {
      cout << j << '\t';
   }
   cout << endl;
}
```

The output is

```
src> ./a.out
y looks like true to me!
ip looks like true
kp looks like false
4       3       2       1
src>
```

19.6.1 Exercises: Standard Expression Conversions

Assume that you have the following declarations:

```cpp
double d = 123.456;
int i = 789, j = -1;
uint k = 10;
```

- What is the type and what is the value of d + i?
- What is the type and what is the value of j + k?

- What happens with a promotion such as d = i;?
- What happens with a demotion such as i = d;?

19.7   Explicit Conversions

Explicit conversions are called **casts**. Casting is sometimes necessary, but it tends to be overused and can be a major source of errors. Bjarne Stroupstrup, the creator of C++, is on record recommending that they be used as little as possible.

Because of its roots in the C language, C++ supports the old-style (unsafe) C-style casting

```
(type)expr
```

For example:

```
double d=3.14;
int i = (int)d;
```

C++ also supports an alternative constructor-style syntax for casts:

```
Type t = Type(arglist)
```

A cast causes a temporary value of the specified type to be created and pushed onto the program stack. If `Type` is a class, a temporary object is created and initialized by the appropriate conversion constructor. If `Type` is a native type, `Type(arg)` is equivalent to `(Type)arg`. The temporary is kept on the stack just long enough to evaluate the expression it is in. After that, it is destroyed.

For example:

```
double d = 3.14;
Complex c = Complex(d);
```

19.8   Safer Typecasting Using ANSI C++ Typecasts

ANSI C++ adds four cast operators, with template-style syntax, that more clearly express the intentions of the programmer and make casts easier to spot in the code.

TABLE 19.3   ANSI Typecasts

`static_cast<type>(expr)`	For converting between related types
`const_cast<type> expr`	For casting away `const` or `volatile`
`dynamic_cast<type>(expr)`	For safe navigation through an inheritance hierarchy
`reinterpret_cast<type>(expr)`	For type conversions of pointers between unrelated types

19.8.1   `static_cast` and `const_cast`

`static_cast<DestType>(expr)` converts the value `expr` to type `DestType`, provided that the compiler knows of an implicit conversion from `expr` to `DestType`. All type-checking is done at compile time.

```
static_cast<char>('A' + 1.0);
static_cast<double>(static_cast<int>(y) + 1);
```

The `static_cast` operator converts between related types such as one pointer type to another, an enumeration type to an integral type, or a floating-point type to an integral type. These conversions are well defined, portable, and invertible. The compiler can apply some minimal type checking for each `static_cast`.

`static_cast` cannot cast away const ness. For that you must use `const_cast<Dest Type>(expr)`, which creates a non-const version of `expr`.

In that case, the `DestType` can differ from the type of `expr` only in the presence or absence of `const/volatile`.

For an `int i`, `static_cast<double>(i)` creates a temporary of type `double` that has the value of `i`. The variable `i` itself is not changed by this cast. Example 19.10 contains both kinds of casts.

EXAMPLE 19.10   src/ansicast/m2k.cpp

```
// Miles are converted to kilometers.
#include <QTextStream>

QTextStream cin(stdin);
QTextStream cout(stdout);
QTextStream cerr(stderr);

const double  m2k = 1.609;     // conversion constant
```

```
inline double mi2km(int miles) {
    return (miles * m2k);
}

int main() {
    int  miles;
    double kilometers;
    cout << "Enter distance in miles: " << flush;
    cin >> miles ;
    kilometers = mi2km(miles);
    cout << "This is approximately "
         <<  static_cast<int>(kilometers)
         << "km."<< endl;
    cout << "Without the cast, kilometers = "
         << kilometers << endl;
    double* dp = const_cast<double*>(&m2k);
    cout << "m2k: " << m2k << endl;
    cout << "&m2k: " << &m2k << "  dp: " << dp << endl;
    cout << "*dp: " << *dp << endl;
    *dp = 1.892;                                              1
    cout << "Can we reach this statement? " << endl;
    return 0;
}
```

Output:

```
Enter distance in miles: 23
This is approximately 37km.
Without the cast, kilometers = 37.007
m2k: 1.609
&m2k: 0x8049048  dp: 0x8049048
*dp: 1.609
Segmentation fault
```

1 What are we attempting to do here?

Here are some observations regarding the previous example:

- The mixed expression `miles * m2k` is implicitly widened to `double`.
- The safe cast `static_cast<int>(kilometres)` truncates the `double` value to `int`.

- The cast did not change the variable `kilometres`.
- The results of our attempt to assign to `*dp` are undefined.

Casting away `const`

In general, `const_cast` is used only on `const`-references and pointers to non-`const` objects. Using `const_cast` to change `const` objects has undefined behavior because `const` objects may be stored in read-only memory (which the operating system protects). In the case of `const int`, trying to change it by casting away `const` depends on compiler optimization techniques, which frequently optimize them out of existence (by doing precompilation value replacement). Example 19.11 gives some indication of the strange behavior that can occur.

EXAMPLE 19.11   src/casts/constcast1.cpp

```
#include <iostream>
using namespace std;

int main() {
    const int N = 22;
    int* pN = const_cast<int*>(&N);
    *pN = 33;
    cout << N << '\t' << &N << endl;
    cout << *pN << '\t' << pN << endl;
}
```

Output:

```
22      0xbf91cfa0
33      0xbf91cfa0
```

The preceding output, obtained with gcc version 4.4.5, might be different on your system because the behavior is undefined.

In this example, we used `const_cast` to obtain a regular pointer to a `const int`. Because the `const int` is in stack storage class, attempting to change its memory does not cause a segmentation fault. The compiler is unable to "optimize out" the `int`, and the `const_cast` tells it not to even try.

19.8.1.1 Exercises: `static_cast` and `const_cast`

1. In Example 19.11, try moving the

```
const int N = 22;
```

above or below

```
int main() {
```

Observe and explain the difference in output.

2. a. Predict the output of Example 19.12.

EXAMPLE 19.12 src/casts/constcast2.cpp

```
#include <iostream>

void f2(int& n) {
    ++n;
}

void f1(const int& n, int m) {
    if (n < m)
        f2(const_cast<int&>(n));
}

int main() {
    using namespace std;
    int num1(10), num2(20);
    f1(num1, num2);
    cout << num1 << endl;
}
```

b. Remove the `const_cast` from the call to `f2()` inside `f1()`, and predict the output again.

19.8.2 `reinterpret_cast`

`reinterpret_cast` is used for casts that are representation- or system-dependent. Examples are conversions between unrelated types such as `int` to pointer, or between unrelated pointer types such as `int*` to `double*`. It cannot cast away `const`.

`reinterpret_casts` are dangerous, generally not portable, and should be avoided.

Consider the following situation:

```
Spam spam;
Egg* eggP;
eggP = reinterpret_cast<Egg*>(&spam);
eggP->scramble();
```

reinterpret_cast takes some spam and gives us an Egg-shaped pointer, without concern for type-compatibility. eggP is *reinterpreting* the bits of spam as if they were bits of egg. In some countries, this would be sacrilege!

What Is It Really Used For?

Sometimes, a C function returns a void* pointing to a type that is known to the developer. In such a case, a typecast from void* to the actual type is needed. If you are sure it is pointing to an Egg, reinterpret_cast<Egg*> is the appropriate cast to use. There is no compiler or runtime checking on such a cast.

For example, we use reinterpret_cast on a void* in the QMetaType example, Example 12.15.

19.8.3   Why Not Use C-Style Casts?

C-style casts are deprecated and should not be used anymore. Consider the following situation, quite similar to the previous example:

```
Apple apple;
Orange* orangeP;
// other processing steps ...
orangeP = (Orange*) &apple;
orangeP->peel();
```

The problem is that you cannot tell from looking at this code whether the developer is aware that an apple is compatible with an orange. From looking at it, it is unclear whether this is a proper type conversion or a nonportable pointer conversion. Sure, they might both have peel() functions, but can you peel an apple like an orange?

Errors caused by such a cast can be difficult to understand and correct. If a system-dependent cast is necessary, it is preferable to use reinterpret_cast over a C-style cast so that, when troubles arise, it will be easier to spot the likely source of those troubles in the source.

19.8.4   More About `explicit` Conversion Constructors

Section 2.12 has `explicit` conversion constructors. Following is another example that uses one.

Suppose that, for some reason, you needed to write your own `String` class.[2] You might produce a class definition with several constructors such as these:

```
class String {
    String();                  // Creates an empty string of length 0
    String(const char* str);   // Converts a char array to a String
    explicit String(int n);    // Creates length n string, filled
                               // with spaces
    ... other member functions - but not constructors ...
};
```

Describe the `string` objects `str1` and `str2` produced by the following client code lines.

```
...
String str1, str2;          // construct two empty strings
str1 = "A";
str2 = 'A';
...
```

It would not be illogical for you to expect `str1` and `str2` to be quite similar after those assignments: both short `string` objects, each containing a single character 'A.' However, depending on how you implemented the conversion constructor (i.e., how the terminating `null char` is handled), `str1` will indeed contain a single `'A'` and perhaps a `null`. But the `str2` assignment is a completely different story. If the keyword `explicit` were removed, `str2` would become a length 65 `string` filled with spaces. That is because char `'A'` would be promoted to the `int` 65 (the ASCII code for `'A'`) so that the third constructor could be (implicitly) called.

Specifying that the third constructor is `explicit` is a good way to avoid such a misunderstanding. Doing so causes the `str2` assignment to generate a compile error; i.e., the third constructor cannot be called *implicitly*—it can only be called *explicitly*. Hence, the `string` class would have no way to handle that line of code, and the compiler would report an error.

---

[2] Voice of screaming Sgt. Major: "So, `QString` not good enough for you, eh?"

19.9   Overloading Special Operators

This section discusses how to use operator overloading as a form of "syntactic sugar," to make complex objects appear as if they are simple types, arrays [square brackets], or functions (round brackets).

19.9.1   Conversion Operators

You saw earlier in Section 2.12 that you can introduce type conversions into the compiler's type system through the use of conversion constructors. This makes it possible to convert from an already existing type to a new type. To define a conversion in the opposite direction, a **conversion operator** is needed. In Section 5.3, you saw how to define the behavior of operators on nonsimple types. A conversion operator uses the same mechanism to overload a typecast.

A conversion operator looks quite different from other member functions. It has no return type (not even `void`) and no parameters. When a conversion operator is applied, it returns an object of its named type: a conversion of the host object as specified in the function body. Conversion operators are generally intended for implicit use so that automatic conversions can be made as needed (e.g., when function calls are being resolved, as you saw in Section 5.1).

When the program in Example 19.13 is run, you can see the use of user-defined conversions from `Fraction` to `double` and to `QString`.

EXAMPLE 19.13   src/operators/fraction/fraction-operators.cpp

```
#include <QString>
#include <QTextStream>

QTextStream cout(stdout);

class Fraction {
public:
    Fraction(int n, int d = 1)                              1
        : m_Numerator(n), m_Denominator(d) {}

    operator double() const {                              2
        return (double) m_Numerator / m_Denominator;
    }
```

```
    operator QString () const {
        return  QString("%1/%2").arg(m_Numerator).arg(m_Denominator);
    }
private:
    int m_Numerator, m_Denominator;
};


QTextStream& operator<< (QTextStream& os, const Fraction& f) {
    os << static_cast<QString> (f);                              3
    return os;
}


int main() {

    Fraction frac(1,3);
    Fraction frac2(4);                                           4
    double d = frac;                                             5
    QString fs = frac;                                           6
    cout << "fs= " << fs << "  d=" << d << endl;
    cout << frac << endl;                                        7
    cout << frac2 << endl;
    return 0;
}
```

1 Conversion constructor.

2 Conversion operator.

3 Explicit cast calls conversion operator.

4 Conversion constructor call.

5 Calls conversion operator.

6 Another conversion operator call.

7 Operator <<() called directly.

Here is the output of this program:

```
src/operators/fraction> ./fraction
fs= 1/3   d=0.333333
1/3
4/1
src/operators/fraction>
```

19.9.2   The Subscript `operator[]`

Many lists and array-like classes offer an interface consistent with arrays but with additional functionality. The **subscript operator** `operator[]` is limited to a single parameter. It is usually used to provide index access to the elements of a container as you saw in Example 5.16. Example 19.14 defines a container class that has built-in protection against out-of-range array indices and that uses the subscript operator `operator[]()`.

EXAMPLE 19.14   src/operators/vect1/vect1.h

```
[ . . . . ]
class Vect {
public:
    explicit Vect(int n = 10);
    ~Vect() {
        delete []m_P;
    }
    int& operator[](int i) {                                    1
        assert (i >= 0 && i < m_Size);
        return m_P[i];
    }
    int  ub() const {
        return (m_Size - 1);
    }                                                           2
private:
    int*  m_P;
    int   m_Size;
};

Vect::Vect(int n) : m_Size(n) {
    assert(n > 0);
    m_P = new int[m_Size];
}
[ . . . . ]
```

1 Access m_P[i].

2 Upper bound.

The client code in Example 19.15 defines an array of vect objects. This provides something similar to a matrix-like structure, where there is one fixed dimension and one that is possibly variable, or sparse, depending on the implementation details of Vect. main() also contains a simple right-justification method for numerical output.

EXAMPLE 19.15   src/operators/vect1/vect1test.cpp

```
#include "vect1.h"

int main() {
    Vect a(60), b[20];

    b[1][5] = 7;
    cout << " 1 element 5 = "<< b[1][5] << endl;
    for (int i = 0; i <= a.ub(); ++i)
        a[i] = 2 * i + 1;
    for (int i = a.ub(); i >= 0; --i)
        cout << ((a[i] < 100) ? " " : "" )
        << ((a[i] < 10) ? " " : "" )
        << a[i]
        << ((i % 10) ? " " : "\n");
    cout << endl;
    cout << "Now try to access an out-of-range index"
    << endl;
    cout << a[62] << endl;
}
```

Following is the output of the program:

```
src/operators/vect1> ./vect1
 1 element 5 = 7
119  117  115  113  111  109  107  105  103  101
 99   97   95   93   91   89   87   85   83   81
 79   77   75   73   71   69   67   65   63   61
 59   57   55   53   51   49   47   45   43   41
 39   37   35   33   31   29   27   25   23   21
 19   17   15   13   11    9    7    5    3    1

Now try to access an out-of-range index
vect1: vect1.h:16: int& Vect::operator[](int):
Assertion `i >= 0 && i < m_Size' failed.
Aborted
src/operators/vect1>
```

19.9.3 The Function Call operator

The **function call operator** operator() is overloadable as a nonstatic member function. It is frequently used to provide a callable interface, an iterator, or a multiple index subscript operator. It is more flexible than operator[] because it can be overloaded with respect to different signatures. In Example 19.16, there is a multiple-subscript operator for a Matrix class.

EXAMPLE 19.16   src/operators/matrix/matrix.h

```
[ . . . . ]
class Matrix {
public:
    Matrix(int rows, int cols);                          1
    Matrix(const Matrix& mat);                           2
    ~Matrix();
    double& operator()(int i, int j);
    double operator()(int i, int j) const;
    // Some useful Matrix operations
    Matrix& operator=(const Matrix& mat);                3
    Matrix operator+(const Matrix& mat) const;           4
    Matrix operator*(const Matrix& mat) const;           5
    bool operator==(const Matrix& mat) const;
    int getRows() const;
    int getCols() const;
    QString toString() const;
private:
    int m_Rows, m_Cols;
    double  **m_NumArray;
    //Some refactoring utility functions
    void sweepClean();                                   6
    void clone(const Matrix& mat);                       7
    double rcprod(int row, const Matrix& mat, int col) const;
                              /* Computes dot product of the
                              host's row with  mat's col. */
};
[ . . . . ]
```

1 Allocates and zeros all cells.

2 Copy constructor; clones mat.

3 Deletes host content; clones mat.

4 Matrix addition.

5 Matrix multiplication.

6 Deletes all cells in the host.

7 Makes a copy of the host using new memory.

Example 19.17 implements the two versions of the multiple-subscript operator that are needed—one for getting and one for setting values from the Matrix. Notice that this implementation uses the (unprotected) array subscripting that is the native equipment of C/C++ arrays. This cautious code for proper handling of the underlying array helps to produce a safe and reliable public interface that uses (range-checking) function-call subscripting for the Matrix class.

EXAMPLE 19.17   src/operators/matrix/matrix.cpp

```
[ . . . . ]

double Matrix::operator()(int r, int c) const {
    assert (r >= 0 && r < m_Rows && c >= 0 && c < m_Cols);
    return m_NumArray[r][c];
}

double& Matrix::operator()(int r, int c) {
    assert (r >= 0 && r < m_Rows && c >= 0 && c < m_Cols);
    return m_NumArray[r][c];
}
```

Example 19.18 shows the implementation of the constructor, which needs to know how many rows and how many columns are wanted for this Matrix.

EXAMPLE 19.18   src/operators/matrix/matrix.cpp

```
[ . . . . ]

Matrix:: Matrix(int rows, int cols):m_Rows(rows), m_Cols(cols) {
    m_NumArray = new double*[rows];
    for (int r = 0; r < rows; ++r) {
        m_NumArray[r]  = new double[cols];
        for(int c = 0; c < cols; ++c)
            m_NumArray[r][c]  = 0;
    }
}
```

The constructor allocates space for `double` values in each of the cells of the `Matrix`, so the destructor, implemented in Example 19.19, must delete each of those cells. We factored out the deletion code in case it is needed to implement other member functions.

EXAMPLE 19.19   src/operators/matrix/matrix.cpp

```
[ . . . . ]

void Matrix::sweepClean() {
    for (int r = 0; r < m_Rows; ++r)
        delete[] m_NumArray[r] ;
    delete[] m_NumArray;
}

Matrix::~Matrix() {
    sweepClean();
}
```

19.9.3.1   Exercises: The Function Call `operator`

Complete the implementations of the member functions of the `Matrix` class and write client code that thoroughly tests the class.

19.10   Runtime Type Identification

This section covers `dynamic_cast` and `typeid`, two operators that enable runtime type identification (RTTI).

The conversion of a base class pointer to a derived class pointer is called **downcasting** because casting from the base class to a derived class is considered moving *down* the class hierarchy.

When operating on hierarchies of types, sometimes it is necessary to downcast a pointer to a more specific type. Without a downcast, only the interface of the pointer type (the base class) is available. One common situation where downcasting is used is inside functions that accept base class pointers.

RTTI enables programmers to safely convert pointers and references to objects from base to derived types.

`dynamic_cast<D*>(ptr)` takes two operands: a pointer type `D*` and a pointer `ptr` of a polymorphic type `B*`. If `D` is a base class of `B` (or if `B` is the same as `D`)

dynamic_cast<*D**>(ptr) is an *upcast* (or not a cast at all) and is equivalent to static_
cast<*D**>(ptr). But if ptr has the address of an object of type *D*, where *D* is derived
from *B*, the operator returns a *downcast* pointer of type *D**, pointing to the same object.
If the cast is not possible, a null pointer is returned.

dynamic_cast performs runtime checking to determine whether the pointer/reference
conversion is valid. For example, suppose you are processing a collection of QWidget*.
Example 19.20 shows operations on a collection of QWidgets. Further suppose that you
want to operate only on buttons and spinboxes, leaving the other widgets alone.

EXAMPLE 19.20   src/rtti/dynamic_cast.cpp

```
[ . . . . . ]
int processWidget(QWidget* wid) {

    if (wid->inherits("QAbstractSpinBox")) {                          1
        QAbstractSpinBox* qasbp =
            static_cast <QAbstractSpinBox*> (wid);
        qasbp->setAlignment(Qt::AlignHCenter);
    }
    else {
        QAbstractButton* buttonPtr =
            dynamic_cast<QAbstractButton*>(wid);
        if (buttonPtr) {                                              2
            buttonPtr->click();
            qDebug() << QString("I clicked on the %1 button:")
                .arg(buttonPtr->text());
        }
        return 1;
    }
    return 0;
}
[ . . . . . ]
    QVector<QWidget*> widvect;

    widvect.append(new QPushButton("Ok"));
    widvect.append(new QCheckBox("Checked"));
    widvect.append(new QComboBox());
    widvect.append(new QMenuBar());
    widvect.append(new QCheckBox("With Fries"));
    widvect.append(new QPushButton("Nooo!!!!"));
    widvect.append(new QDateTimeEdit());
    widvect.append(new QDoubleSpinBox());
```

```
    foreach (QWidget* widpointer, widvect) {
        processWidget(widpointer);
    }
    return 0;
}
```

1 Only for QObjects processed by moc.

2 If non-null, it's a valid `QAbstractButton`.

NOTE

`qobject_cast` (Section 12.2) is faster than `dynamic_cast` but only works on QObject-derived types.

In terms of runtime cost, `dynamic_cast` is considerably more expensive—perhaps 10 to 50 times the cost of a `static_cast`. However, they are not interchangable operations and are used in different situations.

19.10.1 `typeid` **operator**

Another operator that is part of RTTI is `typeid()`, which returns type information about its argument. For example:

```
void f(Person& pRef) {
    if(typeid(pRef) == typeid(Student) {
        // pRef is actually a reference to a Student object.
        // Proceed with Student-specific processing.
    }
    else {
        // Nope! The object referred to by pRef is not a Student.
        // Proceed to do whatever alternative stuff is required.
    }
}
```

`typeid()` returns a `type_info` object that corresponds to the argument's type.

If two objects are the same type, their `type_info` objects should be equal. The `typeid()` operator can be used for polymorphic types or nonpolymorphic types. It can also be used on basic types and custom classes. Furthermore, the arguments to `typeid()` can be type names or object names.

Following is one possible implementation of the `type_info` class, based on g++ 4.4:

```
class type_info {
 private:
    type_info(const type_info& );
    // cannot be copied by users
    type_info& operator=(const type_info&);
    // implementation-dependent representation
 protected:
    explicit type_info(const char *name);
 public:
    virtual ~type_info();
    bool operator==(const type_info&) const;
    bool operator!=(const type_info&) const;
    bool before(const type_info& rhs) const;
    const char* name() const;
    // returns a pointer to the name of the type
    // [...]
}
```

19.11   Member Selection Operators

There are two forms of the member selection operator:

- *pointer->memberName*
- *object->memberName*

They look similar but differ in important ways:

- The first is binary, the second is unary.
- The first is global and not overloadable; the second is an overloadable member function.

When it is defined for a class, the unary `operator->()` should return a pointer to an object that has a member whose name is *memberName*.

An object that implements `operator->` is typically called a **smart pointer**. Smart pointers are so called because they can be programmed to be "smarter" than ordinary pointers. For example, a `QSharedPointer` is a smart pointer that maintains reference-counting pointers to `QObject`. The shared `QObject` is deleted if the last shared pointer is deleted.

Examples of smart pointers include

- STL-style iterators
- QPointer, QSharedDataPointer, QSharedPointer, QWeakPointer, QScopedPointer, QExplicitlySharedDataPointer
- auto_ptr, the STL smart pointer

These smart pointers are template classes.
Example 19.21 shows part of the definition of QSharedPointer.

EXAMPLE 19.21   src/pointers/autoptr/qsharedpointer.h

```
template <class T>
class QSharedPointer {
public:
    QSharedPointer();
    explicit QSharedPointer(T* ptr);
    T& operator*() const;
    T* operator->() const;

    bool isNull() const;
    operator bool() const;
    bool operator!() const;
    // [ ... ]
};
```

A pointer <T> is said to be a *guarded* pointer to a QObject of type T if the pointer is automatically set to 0 when its object is destroyed. QSharedPointer, QPointer, and QWeakPointer all provide this functionality as well. Here is a code fragment that shows how a smart pointer can be used in a similar way to a regular pointer:

```
[. . .]
QPointer<QIntValidator> val = new QIntValidator(someParent);
val->setRange(20, 60);
[. . .]
```

In the second line of code, val->() returns a pointer to the newly allocated object, and it is used to access the setRange() member function.

19.12   Exercises: Types and Expressions

1. Imagine you are required to use a library of classes that have been poorly written and you have no way to improve them. (It could happen!) Example 19.22 includes one such badly written example class and a small program that uses it. The program logic shows some objects being created and passed to a function that receives them as const references (an implicit vow not to change them) and then prints an arithmetic result. Unfortunately, because the class was badly written, something goes wrong along the way.

EXAMPLE 19.22   src/const/cast/const.cc

```
#include <iostream>
using namespace std;

class Snafu {
public:
    Snafu(int x) : mData(x) {}
    void showSum(Snafu & other) const {
        cout << mData + other.mData << endl;
    }

private:
    int mData;
};

void foo(const Snafu & myObject1,
         const Snafu & myObject2) {
    // [ . . . ]
    myObject1.showSum(myObject2);
}

int main() {

    Snafu myObject1(12345);
    Snafu myObject2(54321);

    foo(myObject1, myObject2);

}
```

Answer these questions:

a. What went wrong?

b. What change to the class would fix it?

Unfortunately, you can't change the class. Come up with at least two ways to fix the program without changing the class definition. What would be the best of these and why?

c. Example 19.23 is an incomplete attempt to create a class that counts, for each instantiation, the number of times an object's data is printed. Review the program and make it work properly.

EXAMPLE 19.23   src/const/cast/const2.cc

```
#include <iostream>
using namespace std;

class Quux {
public:
    Quux(int initializer) :
        mData(initializer), printcounter(0) {}
    void print() const;
    void showprintcounter() const {
      cout << printcounter << endl;
    }

private:
    int mData;
    int printcounter;
};

void Quux::print() const {
    cout << mData << endl;
}

int main() {
    Quux a(45);
    a.print();
    a.print();
    a.print();
    a.showprintcounter();
    const Quux b(246);
```

```
    b.print();
    b.print();
    b.showprintcounter();
    return 0;
}
```

19.13   Review Questions

1. What is the difference between a statement and an expression?
2. What is the difference between an overloaded operator and a function?
3. What ways can you introduce a new type into C++?
4. Which cast operator is best suited for numeric values?
5. What happens when you assign an `int` variable to a `double` value?
6. Which cast operator is best suited for downcasting through polymorphic hierarchies?
7. Why are ANSI casts preferred over C-style casts?
8. When might you might find the `reinterpret_cast` used in a reasonable way?

Chapter 20

Scope and Storage Class

Identifiers have *scope*, objects have a *storage class*, and variables have both. In this chapter, we discuss the difference between declarations and definitions and how to determine the scope of identifiers and the storage class of objects.

20.1 Declarations and Definitions

Any identifier must be declared or defined before it is used. **Declaring a name** means telling the compiler what type to associate with that name.

Defining an object, or variable, means allocating space and (optionally) assigning an initial value. For example,

```
double x, y, z;
char* p;
int i = 0;
QString message("Hello");
```

Defining a function means completely describing its behavior in a block of C++ statements. For example,

```
int max(int a, int b) {
  return a > b ? a : b;
}
```

Defining a class means specifying its structure in a sequence of declarations of function and data members, as you can see in Example 20.1. Among other things, a class definition tells the compiler how much memory is required for an object of that class.

EXAMPLE 20.1   src/early-examples/decldef/point.h

```
class Point {                                                    1
 public:
    Point(int x, int y, int z);                                  2
    int distance(Point other);                                   3
    double norm() const {                                        4
        return distance(Point(0,0,0));
    }
 private:
    int m_Xcoord, m_Ycoord, m_Zcoord;                            5
};
```

1 Class head.

2 A constructor declaration.

3 A function declaration.

4 Declaration and definition.

5 Data member declaration.

Example 20.2 contains some declarations that are not definitions.

EXAMPLE 20.2   src/early-examples/decldef/point.cpp

```
extern int step;                                                 1
class Map;                                                       2
int max(int a, int b);           3
```

1 An object (variable) declaration.

2 A (forward) class declaration.

3 A global (non-member) function declaration.

Each declaration that is not a definition conveys an implicit promise to the compiler (which will be enforced by the linker) that the declared name will be defined in an appropriate location somewhere else in the program.

Each definition is a declaration. There can be only one definition of any name in any scope, but there can be multiple declarations.

NOTE

Variable initialization might seem to be "optional" in C++. But initialization of variables always takes place—regardless of whether it is specified. A statement of the form

```
TypeT var;
```

results in **default initialization** of the variable var. Default initialization means that a value is supplied by the compiler. For simple types (e.g., int, double, char) the default value is *undefined*; i.e., that value might be zero and it might be some random garbage that happens to be in the memory assigned to var. For class objects, the value is determined by the default constructor, if one exists; otherwise, the compiler reports an error. Consequently, it is strongly recommended that a well-chosen initial value be provided for all variable definitions; otherwise, invalid results or strange runtime errors can occur that might be difficult to locate. It is worth repeating this rule: *All objects and variables should be properly initialized at (or immediately after) creation time.*

20.2   Identifier Scope

Every identifier has a scope determined by where it was declared. The **scope** of an identifier in a program is the region(s) of the program within which it can be recognized and used. Attempting to use a name outside of its scope is an error.

The same name may be declared/used in different scopes. Ambiguities are resolved as follows:

1. The name from the most local scope is used.
2. If the name is not defined in the most local scope, the same name defined in the nearest enclosing scope will be used.
3. If the name is not defined in any enclosing scope, the compiler reports an error.

We discuss six different scopes in C++:

1. Block scope (local to a block of statements)
2. Function scope (the entire extent of a function)[1]
3. Class scope (the entire extent of a class, including its member function definitions)
4. Namespace scope (an extensible block scope with features of class scope)
5. File scope (from the declaration to the bottom of one source code file)
6. Global scope (similar to file scope but can be extended to multiple source code files)

20.2.1   Default Scope of Identifiers—More Detail

We examine the six principal scopes and provide some examples:

1. **Block Scope.**

   An identifier declared inside curly braces { ... } (excluding `namespace` blocks) or in a function parameter list has **block scope**. Block scope extends from the declaration to the enclosing right brace.

2. **Function Scope.**

   A **label** is an identifier followed by a colon (:). Labels in C/C++ functions have their own scope. They are recognizable before and after their declaration, throughout the function definition. C and C++ support a very rarely used and (justifiably) shunned `goto` statement that requires a label. The thing that makes its scope unique is that the label (i.e., the self-declaration) can appear *after* the first statement (e.g., `goto`) that refers to it. Example 20.3 shows an example of the use of the strongly deprecated `goto` statement and its related label.

EXAMPLE 20.3   src/goto/goto.cpp

```
[ . . . . ]
int look() {
    int i=0;
    for (i=0; i<10; ++i) {
        if (i == rand() % 20)
```

---

[1] Only labels have function scope.

```
            goto found;                                      1
     }
     return -1;                                              2
found:
     return i;
}
[ . . . . ]
```

1 It would be better to use break or continue.

2 goto serves as a forward declaration for a label.

A related but less dangerous use of labels is in the switch statement block. The switch statement is a computed goto statement that, because its action is contained within a single block, does not create the same kinds of validation problems that goto can create. Example 20.4 shows an example of switch usage.

EXAMPLE 20.4   src/switch/switchdemo.cpp

```
#include <QTextStream>
#include "usermanager.h"

QTextStream cout(stdout);
QTextStream cin(stdin);
enum  Choices {LOAD = 1, ADD, CHANGE, CHECK, SAVE, LIST, QUIT};    1

// Function Prototypes
void addUsers(UserManager&);
void changePassword(UserManager&);
Choices menu();

//etc.

int main() {
  // some code omitted
  while (1) {
    switch (menu()) {                                                2
    case LOAD:
       cout << "Reading from file ...\n"
            << um.loadList() << " loaded to list"
            << endl;
      break;
    case ADD:
```

```
      cout << "Adding users to the list ..." << endl;
      addUsers(um);
      break;
   case SAVE:
      cout << "Saving changes ...\n"
           << um.saveList() << " users in file" << endl;
      break;
   case CHANGE:
      cout << "Changing password ..." << endl;
      changePassword(um);
      break;
   case CHECK:
      cout << "Checking a userid/pw combo ..." << endl;
      checkUser(um);
      break;
   case LIST:
      cout << "Listing users and passwords ...\n";
      um.listUsers();
      break;
   case QUIT:
      cout << "Exiting the program ..." << endl;
      return 0;
   default:
      cout << "Invalid choice! " << endl;
   }
  }
}
```

---

1 enums are discussed in Chapter 19, "Types and Expressions."

2 menu() obtains a value from the user.

As we observed in Section 19.2.2, case labels (other than default) differ from ordinary labels because they are required to be integral constants. The scope of a case label is the entire switch statement, so you might call it **switch scope**.

Labels are sometimes used to solve various compatability problems. For example, labels are used to prevent the C++ compiler from choking on the signals: and slots: declarations in certain class definitions (Section 8.3).

 NOTE

Even though goto is part of the C++ language, you should not use it.

3. Namespace Scope.

An identifier declared inside a `namespace` has **namespace scope**. It can be used anywhere, **below** the declaration, inside the `namespace` definition. `namespace` definitions are *open* and can be expanded. A subsequent definition of the same `namespace` simply adds items to it, as you can see in Example 20.5. Any attempt to redefine items *inside* the `namespace` produces a compile error.

EXAMPLE 20.5   src/namespace/openspace/opendemo.txt

```
//File:  a.h"
#ifndef _A_H_
#define _A_H_

#include <iostream>
namespace A {
  using namespace std;
  void f() { cout << "f from A\n"; }
  void g() { cout << "g from A\n"; }
}
#endif

//File:  new-a.h
#ifndef NEW_A_H_
#define NEW_A_H_
#include <iostream>

namespace A {
  //void k() { h(); }                              1
  //void g() { cout << "Redefine g()/n"; }         2
  void h() {
    cout << "h from newA\n";
    g();
  }
}
#endif

File: opendemo.cpp
#include "a.h"
#include "new-a.h"

int main() {
  using namespace A;
```

```
  f();
  h();
}

/*Run

openspace> ./a.out
f from A
h from newA
g from A
openspace>

*/
```

1 Error!

2 Error!

4. Class Scope.

An identifier declared inside a `class` definition has **class scope**. Class Scope is anywhere in the `class` definition[2] or in the bodies of member functions.[3]

5. File Scope.

An identifier whose declaration is not between curly braces can have **file scope** if it is declared `static`. Its scope extends from the declaration to the end of the file. The keyword `static` *hides* the identifier from other source files and restricts its scope to the file in which it was declared. File Scope variables *cannot* be declared `extern` and accessed from another file.

File Scope variables, because they are not exported, do not expand (pollute) the global namespace. They are often used in C programs because C does not have an implementation hiding feature like `private` for class members.

---

[2] Including `inline` function definitions above the declaration of referred members.

[3] Keeping in mind that the scope of non-`static` members *excludes* the bodies of `static` member functions.

> **NOTE**
>
> File scope is available in C++ for backward compatibility with C, but namespaces or static class members should be used instead whenever possible.

6. Global Scope.

An identifier whose declaration is not between curly braces and is not declared `static` is said to have **global scope.** The scope of such an identifier begins at the declaration and extends from there to the bottom of the source code file, but it can be extended to other source files with the use of the `extern` keyword. The `extern` declaration may be used to access a globally defined identifier in other source files.

Use of global scope for variables is unnecessary in C++. In general, only classes and namespaces should be defined in global scope. If you need a "global" variable, you can achieve something similar through the use of a `public` `static` class member or a `namespace` member. Because a compiler deals with one source file at a time, only the linker (or a template-compiler) makes a strong distinction between global and file scope, as Example 20.6 shows.

EXAMPLE 20.6   Global Versus File Scope

```
In file 1:

int g1;        // global
int g2;        // global
static int g3; // keyword static limits g3 to file scope
(etc.)


In file 2:

int g1;          // linker error!
extern int g2;   // OK, share variable space
static int g3;   // okay, 2 different variable spaces
(etc.)
```

An identifier in a `namespace` can be made available globally through the use of the **scope resolution operator**, `NamespaceName::`. It can also be made available to other scopes without using scope resolution through the `using` keyword.

Namespace variables and static class members have static storage and can be made accessible globally. They are like global variables, except they do not enlarge (pollute) the global namespace. See Section 20.4 for more details.

20.2.2   File Scope Versus Block Scope and `operator::`

You have seen and used the scope resolution operator to extend the scope of a class or access its members with `ClassName::`. A similar syntax is used to access the individual symbols in a namespace with `NamespaceName::`. C++ also has a (unary) filescope resolution operator, `::`, that provides access to global, namespace, or file scope objects from inside an enclosed scope. The following exercises deal with the use of this operator with various scopes.

20.2.2.1   Exercises: File Scope Versus Block Scope and `operator::`

1. Determine the scope of each of the variables in Example 20.7.
2. Be the computer and predict the output of the program.

EXAMPLE 20.7   src/early-examples/scopex.cpp

```
#include <iostream>
using namespace std;

long x = 17;
float y = 7.3;                                          1
static int z = 11;                                      2

class Thing {
    int m_Num;                                          3
public:
    static int s_Count;                                 4
    Thing(int n = 0) : m_Num(n) {++s_Count;}
    ~Thing() {--s_Count;}
    int getNum() { return m_Num; }
};

int Thing::s_Count = 0;
Thing t(11);
```

```
int fn(char c, int x) {                          5
    int z = 5;                                   6
    double y = 6.933;
    { char y;                                    7
    Thing z(4);                                  8
    y = c + 3;
    ::y += 0.3;                                  9
    cout << y << endl;                          10
    }
    cout << Thing::s_Count
        << endl;                                11
    y /= 3.0;                                    12
    ::z++;                                       13
    cout << y << endl;
    return x + z;
}

int main() {
    int x, y = 10;
    char ch = 'B';                              14
    x = fn(ch, y);
    cout << x << endl;
    cout << ::y << endl;                        15
    cout << ::x / 2 << endl;
    cout << ::z << endl;
}
```

1 Scope: _____

2 Scope: _____

3 Scope: _____

4 Scope: _____

5 Scope: _____

6 Scope: _____

7 Scope: _____

8 Scope: _____

9 Scope: _____

10 Scope: _____

11 Scope: _____

12 Scope: _____

13 Scope: _____

14 Scope: _____

15 Scope: _____

20.3   Storage Class

Whenever an object is created, space is allocated in one of four possible places. Each of these places is called a **storage class**.

> **NOTE**
>
> **Scope** refers to a region of code where an identifier is accessible. **Storage class** refers to a location in memory.

1. The **static** area—Global variables, `static` locals, and `static` data members are stored in the `static` storage area. The lifetime of a static object begins when its object module loads and ends when the program terminates.

   Used often for pointers, simple types, and string constants, less often for complex objects.

2. The program **stack** (automatic storage—`auto`[4])—Function parameters, local variables, return values, and other temporary objects are stored on the stack. Stack storage is allocated automatically when an object definition is executed. Objects in this storage class are local to a function or a block of statements.[5] For local (block-scope) variables, the lifetime is determined by the braces around the code that is executed.

3. The **heap** or free storage (dynamic storage)—Objects created via `new`. The lifetime of a heap object is determined entirely by the use of `new` and `delete`.

   In general, the allocation and freeing of heap objects should be kept inside carefully encapsulated classes.

---

[4] The optional keyword `auto` is almost never used.

[5] Or a member of another object that is.

4. Another storage class, left over from C, is called `register`. It is a specialized form of automatic storage that consists of a relatively small quantity of the fastest memory available—usually located on the CPU.

This category of storage can be requested by using the keyword `register` in the variable declaration. Most C++ compilers ignore this keyword and put such variables on the stack but possibly with higher priority for access to register memory. Requesting this storage class for an object means that you cannot take its address with the address-of operator (`&`).

20.3.1 Globals, `static`, and `QObject`

There are two reasons generally used to justify giving an object global scope:

1. It needs a lifetime that is the same as the application.

2. It needs to be accessible from several places in the application.

In C++, you should avoid the use of global scope as much as possible and instead use other mechanisms. However, you can still use global scope identifiers for the following:

- Class names
- Namespace names
- The global pointer `qApp`, which points to the running `QApplication` object.

By turning a global object into a `static class` member or a `namespace` member, you can avoid increasing the size of the global namespace while keeping the object accessible to several source code modules.

---

static and QObject

When creating `QObject` or other interesting classes,[6] it is important that their destructors do not get called after `qApp` (the singleton `QApplication`) has been destroyed (i.e., after `main()` is finished).

---

[6] By "interesting" we mean any class with a destructor that has some important cleaning up to do.

> static QObjects (and other complex objects) that continue to exist after qApp has been destroyed, could have cleanup-code problems. This is because when it is destroyed, qApp takes a lot of other objects with it.
>
> In general, you need to have control over the order of destruction of all complex objects. One way to ensure this is to make sure that each QObject allocated on the stack (or on the heap) is a child/grandchild/etc of a QObject that is already on the stack.
>
> The QApplication (or its derived instance) is the "rootiest" stack object of them all, so you should try to make it the "last QObject standing." This makes qApp a good choice for "ultimate ancestor" of any orphan QObject in an application.

20.3.1.1   Globals and const

The scope of const global variables is slightly different from the scope of regular globals.

A global object that has been declared const has *file scope*, by default. Unlike static objects declared outside of all blocks, it is possible to export a global const to other files by declaring it extern at the point where it is initialized. For example, in one file, you could have the code in Example 20.8.

EXAMPLE 20.8   src/const/globals/chunk1.cpp

```
const int NN = 10;      // file scope
const int MM = 44;      // file scope
extern const int QQ = 7; // can be accessed from other files

int main() {
// NN = 12;         // error
   int array[NN];   // okay
// QQ++;            // error
   double darray[QQ];
   return 0;
}
```

In another file, you might have the code in Example 20.9

EXAMPLE 20.9   src/const/globals/chunk2.cpp

```
extern const int NN = 22;     // a different constant
extern const int MM;          // error
// declare global constant - storage allocated elsewhere
extern const int QQ;     // external declaration
```

```
void newFunction() {
    int x = QQ + NN;
}
```

Example 20.9 has a `const int NN` that is separate and distinct from the `const` with the same name in Example 20.8. Example 20.9 can share the use of the `const int QQ` because of the `extern` modifier. Example 20.9 cannot access the file scope `const MM` by declaring MM with the `extern` modifier.

20.3.2 Exercises: Storage Class

In Example 20.10, identify the scope/storage class of each object's creation/definition. If there is a name clash, describe the error.

EXAMPLE 20.10 src/storage/storage.cpp

```
#include <QString>


int i;                                                      1
static int j;                                               2
extern int k;                                               3
const int l=10;                                             4
extern const int m=20;                                      5

class Point                                                 6
{
    public:
    QString name;                                           7
    QString toString() const;
    private:
    static int count;
    int x, y;                                               8
};

int Point::count = 0;                                       9

QString Point::toString() const {
    return QString("(%1,%2)").arg(x).arg(y);
                          /* Scope: _____   Storage class: _____
*/
}
```

```
int main(int argc, char** argv)                          10
{
    int j;                                               11
    register int d;
    int* ip = 0;                                         12
    ip = new int(4);                                     13
    Point p;                                             14
    Point* p2 = new Point();                             15
}
```

1 Scope: _____ Storage class: _____

2 Scope: _____ Storage class: _____

3 Scope: _____ Storage class: _____

4 Scope: _____ Storage class: _____

5 Scope: _____ Storage class: _____

6 Scope: _____ Storage class: _____

7 Scope: _____ Storage class: _____

8 Scope: _____ Storage class: _____

9 Scope: _____ Storage class: _____

10 S/SC of argc and argv: _____

11 Scope: _____ Storage class: _____

12 Scope: _____ Storage class: _____

13 Scope: _____ Storage class: _____

14 Scope: _____ Storage class: _____

15 Scope: _____ Storage class: _____

20.4   Namespaces

In C and C++ there is one global scope that contains

- The names of all global functions and variables
- Class and type names that are commonly available to all programs

Classes are one way of grouping names (members) under a common heading (the classname), but sometimes it is desirable to have a higher-level grouping of names.

The **namespace** mechanism provides a way to partition the global scope into individually named sub-scopes. This helps avoid naming conflicts that can arise when developing a program that uses modules with name conflicts. The syntax for defining a namespace is

```
namespace namespaceName { decl1, decl2, ...}
```

Any legal identifier can be used for the optional *namespaceName*. Example 20.11 and Example 20.12 define two separate namespaces in different files, each containing functions with the same name.

EXAMPLE 20.11   src/namespace/a.h

```
#include <iostream>
namespace A {
    using namespace std;
    void f() {
        cout << "f from A\n";
    }

    void g() {
        cout << "g from A\n";
    }
}
```

EXAMPLE 20.12   src/namespace/b.h

```
#include <iostream>

namespace B {
    using namespace std;
    void f() {
        cout << "f from B\n";
    }

    void g() {
        cout << "g from B\n";
    }
}
```

Example 20.13 includes both header files and uses scope resolution to call functions declared in either file.

EXAMPLE 20.13   src/namespace/namespace1.cc

```
#include "a.h"
#include "b.h"

int main() {
    A::f();
    B::g();
}
```

Output:

```
f from A
g from B
```

The `using` keyword enables individual members of a namespace to be referenced without scope resolution. The syntax can take two forms:

1. The `using` directive

```
using namespace namespaceName
```

imports the entire namespace into the current scope.

2. The `using` declaration

```
using namespaceName::identifier
```

imports a particular identifier from that namespace into the current scope.

Care must be exercised to make sure that ambiguities are not produced when identifiers are present in more than one included namespace. We show an example of such an ambiguous function call in Example 20.14.

EXAMPLE 20.14   src/namespace/namespace2.cc

```
#include "a.h"
#include "b.h"

int main() {
    using A::f;                                              1
    f();
    using namespace B;                                      2
```

```
    g();                                                          3
    f();                                                          4
}
```

Output:

```
f from A
g from B
f from A
```

1 Declaration—brings `A::f()` into scope.

2 Brings all of B into scope.

3 Okay.

4 Ambiguous!

⚔ TIP

To make sure that the names of various namespaces are unique, programmers sometimes need to produce extremely long namespace names. You can easily introduce an alias for a long namespace name with a command such as this:

```
namespace xyz = verylongcomplicatednamespacename;
```

20.4.1 Anonymous Namespaces

A `namespace` without a name is an **anonymous namespace**. This is similar to a `static` global, or file scope identifier. It is accessible from that point, down to the end of the file.[7]

Example 20.15 shows how anonymous namespaces can eliminate the need for `static` globals.

---

[7] Unless it appears inside another namespace (which the language permits), in which case the scope is further narrowed by the brackets of its enclosing namespace.

EXAMPLE 20.15 src/namespace/anonymouse.h

```
namespace {
    const int MAXSIZE = 256;
}

void f1() {
    int s[MAXSIZE];
}
```

20.4.2 Open Namespaces

Any namespace definition is **open** in the sense that you can add members to an existing namespace by declaring a second namespace with the same name but with new items. The new items will be appended to the namespace in the order in which the namespace declarations are encountered by the compiler.

Classes are similar to namespaces, but classes are not open because they must serve as a pattern for the creation of objects.

The `using` directive does not extend the scope in which it is used; it imports names from the specified namespace into the current scope.

Names locally defined take precedence over names from the `namespace` (which are still accessible using the scope resolution operator).

20.4.3 `namespace`, `static` **objects, and** `extern`

Objects declared inside namespaces are implicitly `static`, meaning they are created once for the entire application. The initialization of a `static` object must exist in only one C++ module. To declare a `static` (global or `namespace`) object without defining it, use the keyword `extern`.[8] Example 20.16 shows how to declare `namespace` variables.

EXAMPLE 20.16 src/qstd/qstd.h

```
[ . . . . ]
namespace qstd {

    // declared but not defined:
```

---

[8] Even inside namespaces!

```
    extern QTextStream cout;
    extern QTextStream cin;
    extern QTextStream cerr;

    // function declarations:
    bool yes(QString yesNoQuestion);
    bool more(QString prompt);
    int promptInt(int base = 10);
    double promptDouble();
    void promptOutputFile(QFile& outfile);
    void promptInputFile(QFile& infile);
};
[ . . . . ]
```

Functions and classes can be declared or defined in the header file of a namespace. But each top-level object (that is not local to a namespace function) in a namespace must be defined in a .cpp file, as shown in Example 20.17, if it has not been defined in the header file.

EXAMPLE 20.17   src/qstd/qstd.cpp

```
[ . . . . ]
QTextStream qstd::cout(stdout, QIODevice::WriteOnly);
QTextStream qstd::cin(stdin, QIODevice::ReadOnly);
QTextStream qstd::cerr(stderr, QIODevice::WriteOnly);

/* Namespace members are like static class members */
bool qstd::yes(QString question) {
    QString ans;
    cout << QString(" %1 [y/n]? ").arg(question);
    cout.flush();
    ans = cin.readLine();
    return (ans.startsWith("Y", Qt::CaseInsensitive));
}
```

20.5   Review Questions

1. What is a scope? What kinds of "things" have a scope?

2. What is a storage class? What kinds of "things" have a storage class?

3. When are `static` objects initialized? Be sure to consider both globals and block scope objects.

4. How does `const` act as a scope modifier?

5. What does `extern` mean?

6. The keyword `static` has many meanings depending on where it is used.

   a. Explain how `static` can be used as a scope modifier.

   b. Explain how `static` can be used as a storage-class modifier.

   c. Give another use for the keyword `static`.

7. What is the storage class of an object defined in a `namespace`?

8. What is special about a pointer to an object declared using the keyword `register`?

9. What is the difference between a `class` and a `namespace`?

10. What must you do if you want to declare an object in the header file of a `namespace` without defining it?

Chapter 21

Memory Access

Arrays and pointers are low-level building blocks of C programs that provide fast access to hardware memory. This chapter discusses the different ways to organize and access memory.

Direct manipulation of memory entails some serious risks and requires good practices and thorough testing to avoid serious errors. Improper use of pointers and dynamic memory can cause program crashes that result from heap corruption and memory leaks. Heap corruption is especially difficult to debug because it generally leads to **segmentation faults** that halt the program at a point in the code that may be far from the point at which the heap became corrupted.

Both Qt and Standard Library container classes permit the safe use of dynamic memory without adversely affecting performance.[1] Arrays implement most container classes but are hidden from client code. The safety factors come from the careful design of each container API so that actions that might produce memory problems are not permitted.

Qt offers many containers, ranging from high-level template classes such as the ones discussed in Section 6.8 to low-level containers such as `QBitArray` and `QByteArray`.

---

[1] In the sequel, whenever we use the term container, with no further qualification, we mean Qt or Standard Library container.

Generally, when writing applications that reuse those containers, it is easy to avoid the use of arrays entirely. When Qt is not available, or when you need to write an interface to C code, you may need to use arrays and pointers and work directly with allocated memory.

Modern software often has colorful graphics and sound that require rapid processing for proper execution. That generally means heavy use must be made of dynamic memory. Vast quantities of memory and secondary storage are available on the typical computing device—quantities that were unimaginable just a few years ago. But graphics, animation, and sound all require substantial amounts of memory that must be handled carefully and efficiently. That is why we focus on the proper management of memory resources and on the dire consequences of mismanagement.

21.1   Pointer Pathology

In Section 1.15, we introduced pointers and demonstrated some of the basics of working with them. We now look at two short code examples to demonstrate some of the weird and dangerous things that can happen when pointers are not handled correctly. Example 21.1 shows a few of the many ways you can declare pointers.

EXAMPLE 21.1   src/pointers/pathology/pathologydecls1.cpp

```
[ . . . . ]

int main() {
    int a, b, c;                                                1
    int* d, e, f;                                               2
    int *g, *h;                                                 3
    int* i, * j;                                                4

    return 0;
}
```

1 As expected, this line creates three `int`s.
2 This line creates one pointer to an `int` and two `int`s.
3 This line creates two pointers to `int`.
4 This line also creates two pointers to `int`.

A beginner would be forgiven for thinking the second line of `main()` creates three pointers—after all, in line one, similar syntax creates three integers. However, when multiple variables are declared on one line, the * type modifier symbol applies only to the variable that immediately follows it, not the type that precedes it. That is why we recommend having a separate declaration (on a separate line) for each pointer. Example 21.2 contains three groups of statements.

EXAMPLE 21.2   src/pointers/pathology/pathologydecls2.cpp

```
[ . . . . ]
int main() {
    int myint = 5;
    int* ptr1 = &myint;
    cout << "*ptr1 = " << *ptr1 << endl;
    int anotherint = 6;
//  *ptr1 = &anotherint;                                1

    int* ptr2;                                          2
    cout << "*ptr2 = " << *ptr2 << endl;
    *ptr2 = anotherint;                                 3

    int yetanotherint = 7;
    int* ptr3;
    ptr3 = &yetanotherint;                              4
    cout << "*ptr3 = " << *ptr3 << endl;
    *ptr1 = *ptr2;                                      5
    cout << "*ptr1 = " << *ptr1 << endl;

    return 0;
}
[ . . . . ]
```

1 Error, invalid conversion from int* to int.

2 Uninitialized pointer.

3 Unpredictable results.

4 Regular assignment.

5 Dangerous assignment!

This code illustrates some serious pointer issues, the worst of which are not detected by the compiler. The first is simply a type mismatch.

```
src/pointers/pathology> g++ pathologydecls2.cpp
pathologydecls.cpp: In function `int main()':
pathologydecls.cpp:17: error: invalid conversion from `int*' to `int'
src/pointers/pathology>
```

After commenting out the invalid conversion, we try again:

```
*ptr1 = 5
*ptr2 = -1218777888
*ptr3 = 7
*ptr1 = 6
Segmentation fault
```

Dereferencing the uninitialized pointer ptr2 gives unpredictable (i.e., undefined) results.

Dereferencing uninitialized pointers for read purposes is bad enough, but then we *wrote* to it. This is a form of **memory corruption**, which can cause problems later in the program's execution. The Segmentation fault was caused by the memory corruption that occurred when we dereferenced ptr2.

The Segmentation fault is not the worst thing that could happen. At least it warns the programmer that there is a serious problem. A worse thing would be if the program did not abort but, instead, ran and produced wrong, but feasible, results. Not many people take the time and trouble to check the computer's arithmetic! With corrupted memory, anything can happen and, because the results are undefined, you can't even rely on the program aborting.

21.2   Further Pointer Pathology with Heap Memory

The result of applying delete to a pointer that holds the address of a valid object in the heap is to change the status of that heap memory from "in use" to "available." After delete has been applied to a pointer, the state of that pointer itself is *undefined*. The pointer may or may not still store the address of the deleted memory, so a second application of delete to the same pointer may cause runtime problems, possibly heap corruption.

In general, the compiler cannot detect attempts to apply delete repeatedly to the same object, especially if that piece of memory (or a part thereof) has since been real-located. To help avoid the undesirable consequences of a repeated delete, it is good practice to assign 0 or NULL to a pointer immediately after it has been deleted.

If `delete` is applied to a null pointer, there is no error and no action.

Applying `delete` to a non-null pointer that was not returned by `new` produces undefined results. In general, the compiler cannot determine whether the pointer was returned by `new`, so undefined runtime behavior can result. Bottom line: *It is the programmer's responsibility to use `delete` correctly.*

One of the richest sources of runtime errors is the production of **memory leaks**. A memory leak is produced when a program causes memory to be allocated and then loses track of that memory so that it can neither be accessed nor deleted. An object that is not properly deleted will occupy memory until the process terminates.

Some programs (e.g., servers, operating systems) stay active for a long time. Suppose such a program contains a frequently executed routine that produces a memory leak each time it is run. The heap gradually becomes perforated with blocks of inaccessible, undeleted memory. At some point a routine that needs a substantial amount of contiguous dynamic memory may have its request denied. If the program is not prepared for an event like that, it will abort.

The operators `new` and `delete` give the C++ programmer increased power and increased responsibility.

Following is some sample code that illustrates a memory leak. After defining a couple of pointers, memory looks like Figure 21.1.

```
int* ip = new int;        // allocate space for an int
int* jp = new int(13);    // allocate and initialize
cout << ip << '\t' << jp << endl;
```

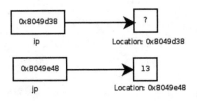

FIGURE 21.1   Initial Values of Memory

After executing the following line of code, memory looks like Figure 21.2.

```
jp = new int(3);    // reassign the pointer - MEMORY LEAK!!
```

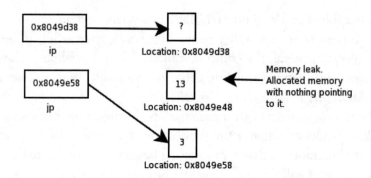

FIGURE 21.2   Memory After Leak

In Example 21.3, we delete the pointer jp twice.

EXAMPLE 21.3   src/pointers/pathology/pathologydemo1.cpp

```
#include <iostream>
using namespace std;

int main() {
    int* jp = new int(13);                          1
    cout << jp << '\t' << *jp << endl;
    delete jp;
    delete jp;                                      2
    jp = new int(3);                                3
    cout << jp << '\t' << *jp << endl;
    jp = new int(10);                               4
    cout << jp << '\t' << *jp << endl;
    int* kp = new int(17);
    cout << kp << '\t' << *kp << endl;
    return 0;
}
```

Output:

```
OOP> g++ pathologydemo1.cpp
OOP> ./a.out
0x8049e08       13
0x8049e08       3
0x8049e08       10
Segmentation fault
OOP>
```

1 Allocate and initialize.

2 Error: pointer already deleted.

3 Reassign the pointer, memory leak.

4 Reassign the pointer, memory leak.

The second deletion is a serious error, but the compiler did not catch it. That error corrupted the heap, made any further memory allocation impossible, and made the behavior of the program beyond that point **undefined**. For example, notice that when we attempted to produce a memory leak by reassigning the pointer `jp`, we did not get new memory. When we attempted to introduce another pointer variable, we got a segmentation fault. This is all undefined behavior and may be different on another platform or with another compiler.

21.3   Memory Access Summary

Following is a list of the most important points we have raised about memory access:

- The operators `new` and `delete` give the C++ programmer increased power and increased responsibility.

- Improper use of pointers and dynamic memory can cause program crashes that result from heap corruption and memory leaks.

- Qt and STL container classes permit the safe use of dynamic memory without adversely affecting performance.

- In a multiple variable declaration, the unary `*` operator applies only to the variable that immediately follows it, not the type that precedes it.

- Dereferencing an uninitialized pointer is a serious error that may not be caught by the compiler.

- After `delete` has been applied to a pointer, the state of that pointer is undefined.

- It is good practice to assign `0` or `NULL` to a pointer immediately after you delete it.

- Applying `delete` to a non-null pointer that was not returned by `new` produces undefined results.

- The compiler cannot be relied upon to detect the improper use of `delete`, so it is the programmer's responsibility to use `delete` correctly.

- A memory leak is produced when a program causes memory to be allocated
  and then loses track of that memory so that it can neither be accessed nor
  `deleted`.

21.4 Introduction to Arrays

An **array** is a sequence of contiguous memory cells, all of the same size. Each cell is
called an array **element** or entry.

When an array is declared, the size of the array must be made known. This can be
done explicitly or by initialization:

```
int a[10]; // explicitly creates uninitialized cells a[0], a[1],..., a[9]
int b[] = {1,3,5,7}; // implicitly creates and initializes b[0],..., b[3]
```

The array name is an *alias* for a `const` typed pointer to the first cell of the array. A
pointer declaration such as

```
int* ptr;
```

only creates the pointer variable. There is no automatic default initialization of
pointer variables. It is an error to attempt to dereference an uninitialized pointer.

Array indices are relative offsets from the base address:

```
a[k] is equivalent to *(a + k)
```

The following bit of code demonstrates an interesting aspect of array indices.

EXAMPLE 21.4   src/pointers/pathology/pathologydemo2.cpp

```
#include <iostream>
using namespace std;
int main(){
  int a[] = {10, 11, 12, 13, 14, 15};

  int* b = a + 1;
  cout << "a[3] = " << a[3] << '\n'
       << "b[3] = " << b[3] << endl;

  //It gets even worse.
  int c = 123;
  int* d = &c;
  cout << "d[0] = " << d[0] << '\n'
```

```
                << "d[1] = " << d[1] << '\n'
                << "d[2] = " << d[2] << endl;


}
```

Compiling and running produces the following output:

```
pointers/pathology> g++ -ansi -pedantic -Wall pathologydemo2.cpp
pointers/pathology>
a[3]  = 13
b[3]  = 14
d[0]  = 123
d[1]  = -1075775392
d[2]  = -1219610235
```

Notice that neither b nor d was declared as an array, but the compiler allows us to use the subscript [] operator anyway. c is an ordinary int variable, and d is an ordinary int pointer. d[0], d[1], and d[2] are undefined, but the compiler did not even give any warnings about their presence in the program—even with the three command-line switches that we used.

There is a special syntax for defining a dynamic array consisting of a given number of elements of some type:

```
uint n;
ArrayType* pt;
pt = new ArrayType[n];
```

This version of new allocates n contiguous blocks of memory, each of size sizeof(ArrayType), and returns a pointer to the first block. Each element of the newly allocated array is given default initialization. To properly deallocate this array, it is necessary to use the syntax:

```
delete[] pt;
```

Using delete without the empty brackets to delete a dynamic array produces undefined results.

We discuss exceptions and what happens when a request for dynamic memory cannot be fulfilled by the system in a separate article[2] in our [dist] directory.

---

[2] articles/exceptions.html

21.5   Pointer Arithmetic

The result of applying the operators +, -, ++, or -- to a pointer depends on the type of object pointed to. When an arithmetic operator is applied to a pointer p of type T*, p is assumed to point to an element of an array of objects of type T.

- p+1 points to the next element of the array.
- p-1 points to the preceding element of the array.
- In general, the address p+k is k*sizeof(T) bytes larger than the address p.

Subtraction of pointers is defined only when both pointers point to elements of the same array. In that case, the difference is an int equal to the number of array elements between the two elements.

The results of pointer arithmetic are undefined outside the context of an array. It is the responsibility of the programmer to ensure that pointer arithmetic is used appropriately. Example 21.5 demonstrates this point.

EXAMPLE 21.5   src/arrays/pointerArith.cpp

```
[ . . . . ]
int main()  {
    using namespace std;
    int y[] = {3, 6, 9};
    int x = 12;
    int* px;
    px = y;                                              1
    cout << "What's next: " << *++px << endl;
    cout << "What's next: " << *++px << endl;
    cout << "What's next: " << *++px << endl;
    cout << "What's next: " << *++px << endl;
    return 0;
}
```

1   y, or any array name, is an "alias" for a pointer to the first element in the array

Compiling and running Example 21.5 produced the following output.[3]

```
src/arrays> g++ -ansi -pedantic -Wall pointerArith.cpp
pointerArith.cpp: In function 'int main()':
```

___

[3] In general, accessing memory beyond the boundary of an array produces undefined results and, because that is what we are doing (on purpose), the results are undefined.

```
pointerArith.cpp:6: warning: unused variable 'x'
src/arrays> ./a.out
What's next: 6
What's next: 9
What's next: -1080256152
What's next: 12
```

Notice that neither the compiler nor the runtime system reported an error message. There was a warning that we did not use the variable x for anything, however. C++ happily reads from arbitrary memory addresses and reports them in the type of your choice, giving the C++ developer great power and many opportunities to make great errors.

21.6 Arrays, Functions, and Return Values

As in C, the declared return type of a function cannot be array (e.g., it cannot look like int[] or char[] or Point[]). Returning (addresses of) arrays from functions that are pointer-typed is allowed. However, this is not recommended in the public interface of a class.

You have seen that an array is a piece of unprotected memory. A class that encapsulates that memory should not have public member functions that return pointers to it. Doing so opens up the possibility for incorrect use of the memory by client code. A properly designed class completely encapsulates all interactions with any arrays used in the implementation of that class.

Arrays are never passed to functions by value; i.e., the array elements are not copied. If a function is called with an array in its argument list, for example,

```
int a[] = {10, 11, 12, 13, 14, 15};
void f(int a[]) {
    [ ... ]
}
    [ ... ]
f(a);
```

then the actual value passed is only a pointer to the first element in the array. Example 21.6 demonstrates this by showing functions that pass and return arrays.

EXAMPLE 21.6 src/arrays/returningpointers.cpp

```
#include <assert.h>

int paramSize;

void bar(int* integers) {
    integers[2]=3;                                                  1
}

int* foo(int arrayparameter[]) {
    using namespace std;
    paramSize = sizeof(arrayparameter);
    bar(arrayparameter);                                            2
    return arrayparameter;                                          3
}

int main(int argc, char** argv) {
    int intarray2[40] = {9,9,9,9,9,9,9,2,1};
    char chararray[20] = "Hello World";                             4
    int intarray1[20];                                              5
    int* retval;                                                    6

//  intarray1 = foo(intarray2);                                     7

    retval = foo(intarray2);
    assert (retval[2] == 3);
    assert (retval[2] = intarray2[2]);
    assert (retval == intarray2);
    int refSize = getSize(intarray2);
    assert(refSize == paramSize);
    return 0;
}
```

1 Change the third element in the incoming array.

2 Pass an array by pointer to a function.

3 Return an array as a pointer from a function.

4 Special syntax for initializing char array.

5 Uninitialized memory.

6 Uninitialized pointer.

7 Error: intarray1 is like a char* const. It cannot be assigned to.

21.7   Different Kinds of Arrays

Arrays of primitive types, such as `int`, `char`, and `byte`, are used to implement caches. Arrays of objects are supported in the C++ language for backward compatibility with C's arrays of `structs`, but they are used only for uniform collections of identical structures, rather than collections of similar polymorphic objects.

If you need random access to the stored items, `QList` (from Qt) or `vector` (from STL) can be used instead of an array. Both are implemented using **dynamic arrays** under the covers. It is preferable to use such containers rather than arrays whenever possible, because containers correctly and safely allocate and free memory for you.

21.8   Valid Pointer Operations

Following is a list of the operations that can properly be performed with pointers:

Creation—The initial value of a pointer has three possible sources:

- A stack address obtained by declaring a pointer variable or a `const` pointer such as an array name
- An address obtained by using the address-of operator, `&`
- A heap address obtained by a dynamic memory allocation operator (e.g., `new`)

Assignment

- A pointer can be assigned the address stored by a pointer of the same type or of a derived type.
- A variable of type `void*` can be assigned a pointer of any type without an explicit cast.
- A (non-`void*`) pointer can be assigned the address stored by a pointer of a different (and nonderived) type only with an explicit cast.
- An array name is a `const` pointer and cannot be assigned to.
- A `NULL` pointer (value 0) can be assigned to any pointer. (Note: Stroustrup recommends that 0 be used instead of `NULL`.)

Arithmetic

- A pointer can be incremented or decremented: `p++` or `p--`.
- An integer can be added to or subtracted from a pointer: `p + k` or `p - k`.

- Such expressions are defined only if the resulting pointer value is within the range of the same array. The only exception to this rule is that a pointer is allowed to point to the memory cell that is one position beyond the end of the array as long as no attempt is made to dereference that address.

- One pointer can be subtracted from another. Two pointers that point to two members of an array can be subtracted, yielding an `int` that represents the number of array elements between the two members.

Comparison

- Pointers to entries of the same array can be compared using `==`, `!=`, `<`, `>`, etc.

- Any pointer can be compared with 0.

Indirection

- If `p` is a pointer of type `T*`, then `*p` is a variable of type `T` and can be used on the left side of an assignment.

Indexing:

- A pointer `p` can be used with an array index operator `p[i]` where `i` is an `int`. The compiler interprets such an expression as `*(p+i)`.

- Indexing makes sense and is defined only in the context of an array, but the compiler will not prevent its use with nonarray pointers where the results are undefined.

Example 21.7 demonstrates this last point rather clearly.

EXAMPLE 21.7   src/arrays/pointerIndex.cpp

```cpp
#include <iostream>
using namespace std;

int main() {
    int x = 23;
    int y = 45;
    int* px = &x;
    cout << "px[0] = " << px[0] << endl;
    cout << "px[1] = " << px[1] << endl;
    cout << "px[2] = " << px[2] << endl;
    cout << "px[-1] = " << px[-1] << endl;
    return 0;
}
```

Output:

```
// g++ on Mac OSX:
px[0]  = 23
px[1]  = 1606413624
px[2]  = 32767
px[-1] = 45

// g++ on Linux (Ubuntu):
px[0]  = 23
px[1]  = -1219095387
px[2]  = -1216405456
px[-1] = 45

// g++ on Windows XP (mingw)
px[0]  = 23
px[1]  = 45
px[2]  = 2293588
px[-1] = 2009291924

// Windows XP with MS Visual Studio compiler:
px[0]  = 23
px[1]  = 45
px[2]  = 1245112
px[-1] = 1245024
```

Here we have a small, concrete example of what we mean when we talk about undefined behavior. A beginner might be forgiven for making some assumptions about how consecutively defined variables are arranged on the program stack. Using array subscripts on a nonarray pointer or using subscripts that are beyond the range of the array are just naughty ways of exploring that imagined landscape, right? Well, now try to fit the subscript -1 into that intuitive map. Then try to reconcile the different results on the different platforms. This example is too short to show the complete picture, however. Undefined behavior of pointers generally leads to corrupted memory—and corrupted memory is a programming nightmare—with runtime abort as one of the more desirable outcomes.

21.9   Arrays and Memory: Important Points

Following is a list of the most important points that we have raised in this chapter:

- An array is a sequence of contiguous memory cells, all of the same size.
- The array name is an alias for a const-typed pointer to the first cell of the array.
- There is no automatic default initialization of pointer variables.
- Array indices are relative offsets from the base address.
- Array subscripts are valid only when used to access members of an array and only within the declared limits of the array.
- The standard does not guarantee that the compiler can catch attempts to use the subscript operator with a pointer that is not an array.
- Arrays are passed to and returned from functions as pointers.
- It is possible to apply the arithmetic operators +, -, ++, and -- to an array pointer, subject to sensible limitations.
- The results of pointer arithmetic are undefined outside the context of an array.
- The standard does not guarantee that the compiler can catch attempts to misuse pointer arithmetic.
- Pointers can acquire values only in the following ways:
  - By initialization when they are created.
  - By assignment after they exist.
  - As a result of pointer arithmetic.
- A dynamic array of size elements of ArrayType is allocated using the syntax

```
uint size;
ArrayType* pt;
pt = new ArrayType[size] ;
```

- Each element of the dynamic array is given default initialization when the array is allocated.
- To deallocate such a dynamic array, it is necessary to use the syntax

```
delete[] pt;
```

The ANSI/ISO standard requires the free store operator `new` to throw a `bad_alloc` exception instead of returning `NULL` if it cannot carry out an allocation request. For more details about exceptions, see this article[4] in our [dist] directory. The qualified operator `new` `(nothrow)` can return 0 if it cannot carry out an allocation request. Dynamic arrays should be carefully encapsulated in classes that are designed with proper destructors, copy constructors, and copy assignment operators.

21.10   Exercises: Memory Access

Predict the output of Example 21.8. Then build and run it. Explain the output. If it differs from your prediction, explain the difference(s).

EXAMPLE 21.8   src/arrays/arrayVSptr.cpp

```
#include <iostream>
using namespace std;

int main()  {
    int a[] = {12, 34, 56, 78};
    cout << a << "\t" << &a[1] - a << endl;
    int x = 99;
//    a = &x;
    int* pa;
    cout << pa << endl;
    pa = &x;
    cout << pa << "\t" << pa - &a[3] << endl;
    cout << a[4] << "\t" << a[5] << endl;
    cout << *(a + 2) << "\t" << sizeof(int) <<endl;
    void* pv = a;
    cout << pv << endl;
    int* pi = static_cast<int*>(pv);
    cout << *(pi + 2) << endl;
    return 0;
}
```

---

[4] articles/exceptions.html

21.11   Review Questions

1. What is defined in the following statement?
   ```
   int* p, q;
   ```

2. What is a memory leak? How does it happen?

3. Compare the way that +, -, ++, and -- operators work on pointers with the way that they work on `int` or `double`.

4. What happens if `delete` is applied to a pointer that has just been deleted?

5. When an array is passed to a function as a parameter, what is copied onto the stack?

6. What is dynamic memory? How do you obtain it in C++?

22

Inheritance in Detail

This chapter formalizes and details some of the concepts introduced earlier in Chapter 6, "Inheritance and Polymorphism." We explain how constructors, destructors, and copy assignment operators are generated and used by derived classes. We discuss how the keywords `public`, `private`, and `protected` can be used for base classes and members. We also provide examples of multiple inheritance.

22.1 `virtual` Pointers, `virtual` Tables

Each class that contains methods (`virtual` functions) has a virtual jump table, or **vtable**, which is generated as part of the "lightweight" C++ execution environment. The vtable can be implemented in a number of ways, but the simplest implementation (which is often the fastest and most lightweight) contains a list of pointers to all methods of that class. Depending on the optimization policies, it may contain additional information to aid in debugging. The compiler substitutes function names with indirect (relative to the vtable list) references to method calls.

With this in mind, we define **polymorphic type** explicitly as a class that contains one or more methods, and thus, requires the use of a vtable. Each instance of a polymorphic type has a `typeid`, which can be quite naturally implemented as the address of the vtable for the class.

---

vtable instead of `switch`

To implement indirect method-calling through vtables, the compiler generates a jump table, which is similar to a `switch` statement, for each polymorphic class. Programmers can often exploit vtables instead of writing their own `switch` statements or large compound conditionals. This is implicit in a number of design patterns, such as the Command, Visitor, Interpreter, and Strategy patterns.

A vtable cannot be built for a class unless the method definitions for all overrides are fully defined and findable by the linker.

The `typeid` of an object is set *after* the object's constructor has executed. If there are base classes, the `typeid` for an object may be set multiple times, after each base class initialization.

We use the classes defined in Example 22.1 to demonstrate that calling a `virtual` function from a constructor or destructor can have unexpected consequences.

EXAMPLE 22.1   src/derivation/typeid/vtable.h

```
[ . . . . . ]
class Base {
 protected:
    int m_X, m_Y;
 public:
    Base();
    virtual ~Base();
    virtual void virtualFun() const;
};

class Derived : public Base {
    int m_Z;
 public:
    Derived();
    ~Derived();
    void virtualFun() const ;
};
[ . . . . . ]
```

Example 22.2 shows what happens when a `virtual` function is called from a base class constructor or destructor.

EXAMPLE 22.2   src/derivation/typeid/vtable.cpp

```cpp
#include <QDebug>
#include <QString>
#include "vtable.h"

Base::Base() {
    m_X = 4;
    m_Y = 12;
    qDebug() << " Base::Base: " ;
    virtualFun();
}

Derived::Derived() {
    m_X = 5;
    m_Y = 13;
    m_Z = 22;
}

void Base::virtualFun() const {
    QString val=QString("[%1,%2]").arg(m_X).arg(m_Y);
    qDebug() << " VF: the opposite of Acid: " << val;
}

void Derived::virtualFun() const {
    QString val=QString("[%1,%2,%3]")
        .arg(m_X).arg(m_Y).arg(m_Z);
    qDebug() << " VF: add some treble: " ;
}

Base::~Base() {
    qDebug() << " ~Base() " ;
    virtualFun();
}

Derived::~Derived() {
    qDebug() << " ~Derived() " ;
}
```

```
int main() {
    Base *b = new Derived;                                              1
    b->virtualFun();                                                    2
    delete b;                                                           3
}
```

1 Base::virtualFun() is called.
2 Calls Derived::virtualFun() using the vtable and runtime binding.
3 Base::virtualFun() is called.

In the output that follows, you can see that the derived `virtualFun()` does not get called from `Base::Base()` because the base class initializer is inside an object that is *not yet* a `Derived` instance.

```
Base::Base:
VF: the opposite of Acid:   "[4,12]"
VF: add some treble:
~Derived()
~Base()
VF: the opposite of Acid:   "[5,13]"
```

Calling `virtual` methods from destructors is not recommended either. In the previous output, you can see that the base `virtualFun` is always called from the base class constructors or destructor. Dynamic binding does not happen inside constructors or destructors. "From a constructor or destructor, virtual methods aren't. [Meyers]."

22.2   Polymorphism and `virtual` Destructors

When operating on classes in inheritance hierarchies, we often maintain containers of base class pointers that hold addresses of derived objects. Example 22.3 defines a `Bank` class that has a container of various kinds of `Accounts`.

EXAMPLE 22.3   src/derivation/assigcopy/bank.h

```
[ . . . . . ]
class Account;

class Bank {
 public:
    Bank& operator<< (Account* acct);                                  1
    ~Bank();
    QString getAcctListing() const;
```

```
private:
    QList<Account*> m_Accounts;
};
[ . . . . ]
```

1 This is how to add object pointers to `m_Accounts`.

The `Account` classes are defined in Example 22.4.

EXAMPLE 22.4   src/derivation/assigcopy/account.h

```
[ . . . . ]
class Account {
 public:
    Account(unsigned acctNum, double balance, QString owner);
    virtual ~Account(){
      qDebug() << "Closing Acct - sending e-mail "
              << "to primary acctholder:" << m_Owner; }
    virtual QString getName() const {return m_Owner;}
    // other virtual functions
 private:
    unsigned   m_AcctNum;
    double     m_Balance;
    QString    m_Owner;
};
class JointAccount : public Account {
 public:
  JointAccount (unsigned acctNum, double balance,
                 QString owner, QString jowner);
  JointAccount(const Account & acct, QString jowner);
  ~JointAccount() {
     qDebug() << "Closing Joint Acct - sending e-mail "
             << "to joint acctholder:" << m_JointOwner; }
  QString getName() const {
    return QString("%1 and %2").arg(Account::getName())
                   .arg(m_JointOwner);
  }
  // other overrides
 private:
  QString m_JointOwner;
};
[ . . . . ]
```

Bank can perform uniform operations on its collected Accounts by calling virtual methods on each one. In Example 22.5, delete acct causes an indirect call to the destructor of Account and the subsequent release of allocated memory.

EXAMPLE 22.5 src/derivation/assigcopy/bank.cpp

```
[ . . . . ]

#include <QDebug>
#include "bank.h"
#include "account.h"

Bank::~Bank() {
    qDeleteAll(m_Accounts);
    m_Accounts.clear();
}


Bank& Bank::operator<< (Account* acct) {
    m_Accounts << acct;
    return *this;
}

QString Bank::getAcctListing() const {
    QString listing("\n");
    foreach(Account* acct, m_Accounts)
        listing += QString("%1\n").arg(acct->getName());    1
    return listing;
}
```

1 getName() is virtual.

Although every address in the list is an Account, some (perhaps all) might point to derived-class objects and therefore require derived-class destructor calls.

If the destructor is virtual, the compiler enables runtime binding on any destructor call through an Account pointer, instead of simply calling Account::~Account() on each one. Without declaring ~Account() to be virtual in the base class, you would get an incorrect result from running Example 22.6.[1]

---

[1] Compilers report a missing virtual in the destructor as a warning, and the behavior is undefined, so you may not see the same thing on your system.

EXAMPLE 22.6   src/derivation/assigcopy/bank.cpp

```
[ . . . . . ]

int main() {
  QString listing;
  {                                                               1
    Bank bnk;
    Account* a1 = new Account(1, 423, "Gene Kelly");
    JointAccount* a2 = new JointAccount(2, 1541, "Fred Astaire",
        "Ginger Rodgers");
    JointAccount* a3 = new JointAccount(*a1, "Leslie Caron");
    bnk << a1;
    bnk << a2;
    bnk << a3;
    JointAccount* a4 = new JointAccount(*a3);                     2
    bnk << a4;
    listing = bnk.getAcctListing();
  }                                                               3
  qDebug() << listing;
  qDebug() << "Now exit program" ;
}
```

1 Begin internal block.

2 What's this?

3 At this point, all four Accounts are destroyed as part of the destruction of the bank.

Following is the output from this program with virtual removed from ~Account:

```
Closing Acct - sending e-mail to primary acctholder:Gene Kelly
Closing Acct - sending e-mail to primary acctholder:Fred Astaire
Closing Acct - sending e-mail to primary acctholder:Gene Kelly
Closing Acct - sending e-mail to primary acctholder:Gene Kelly
[ ... ]
```

By making the destructor virtual, both types of Account will get destroyed properly and, in this example, both account holders of a joint account will get proper e-mail notifications when the Bank is destroyed.

```
Closing Acct - sending e-mail to primary acctholder:Gene Kelly
Closing Joint Acct - sending e-mail to joint acctholder:Ginger Rodgers
```

```
Closing Acct - sending e-mail to primary acctholder:Fred Astaire
Closing Joint Acct - sending e-mail to joint acctholder:Leslie Caron
Closing Acct - sending e-mail to primary acctholder:Gene Kelly
Closing Joint Acct - sending e-mail to joint acctholder:Leslie Caron
Closing Acct - sending e-mail to primary acctholder:Gene Kelly
[ ... ]
```

> **NOTE**
>
> If you declare one or more `virtual` methods in a class, you should define a `virtual` destructor for that class, even if it has an empty body.

22.3 Multiple Inheritance

Multiple inheritance is a form of inheritance in which a class inherits the structure and behavior of more than one base class.

Common uses of multiple inheritance:

- For combining the functionalities of different classes that have little overlap, such as in Figure 22.1.

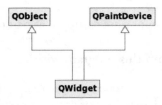

FIGURE 22.1 `QWidget`'s Inheritance

- For implementing a common "pure interface" (class with only pure `virtual` functions) in a variety of different ways.

As with single inheritance, multiple inheritance defines a static relationship among classes. It cannot be changed at runtime.

Multiple inheritance hierarchies are more complex and are harder to design, implement, and understand than single inheritance hierarchies. They can be used to solve some difficult design problems but should not be used if a simpler approach (such as aggregation) is feasible.

22.3.1 Multiple Inheritance Syntax

The example in this section demonstrates multiple inheritance syntax and usage.

The two base classes shown in Figure 22.2, Rectangle and ScreenRegion, each have particular roles to play on the screen. One class is concerned with shape and location, whereas the other is concerned with color and visibility characteristics. A Window must be a Rectangle *and* a ScreenRegion. They are defined in Example 22.7.

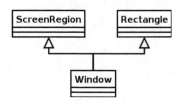

FIGURE 22.2 Window and ScreenRegion

EXAMPLE 22.7 src/multinheritance/window.h

```
[ . . . . ]

class Rectangle {
 public:
    Rectangle( Const Point& ul, int length, int width);
    Rectangle( const Rectangle& r) ;
    void move (const Point &newpoint);
 private:
    Point m_UpperLeft;
    int m_Length, m_Width;
};

class ScreenRegion {
 public:
    ScreenRegion( Color c=White);
    ScreenRegion (const ScreenRegion& sr);
    virtual color Fill( Color newColor) ;
    void show();
    void hide();
 private:
    Color m_Color;
    // other members...

};
```

```
class Window: public Rectangle, public ScreenRegion {
 public:
    Window( const Point& ul, int len, int wid, Color c)
        : Rectangle(ul, len, wid), ScreenRegion(c) {}          1

    Window( const Rectangle& rect, const ScreenRegion& sr)
        : Rectangle(rect), ScreenRegion(sr) {}                 2

    // Other useful member functions ...
};
```

1 Use base class ctors.

2 Use base class copy ctors.

There are some syntax items in the *classHead* of Window that deserve some attention:

- An access specifier (public or protected) must appear before each base class name if the derivation is not private.
  - Default derivation is private
  - It is possible to have a mixture of public, protected, and private derivations.
- The comma (,) character separates the base classes.
- The order of base class initialization is the order in which the base classes are listed in the *classHead*.

Example 22.8 has some client code for the Window class.

EXAMPLE 22.8   src/multinheritance/window.cpp

```
#include "window.h"

int main() {
    Window w(Point(15,99), 50, 100, Color(22));
    w.show();                                                 1
    w.move (Point(4,6));                                      2
    return 0;
}
```

1 Calls ScreenRegion::show();

2 Calls Rectangle::move();

Order of Member Initialization

Default initialization or assignment proceeds member-by-member in the order that data members are declared in the class definition: base classes first, followed by derived class members.

22.3.2   Multiple Inheritance with QObject

Many classes in Qt use multiple inheritance. Figure 22.3 shows the inheritance relationship between classes used in QGraphicsView. QGraphicsItem is a lightweight object, which does not support signals or slots. QGraphicsObject inherits from QObject first and QGraphicsItem second and can offer the best of both worlds: a QGraphicsObject that supports signals and slots, typically used in animation. QWidget, shown earlier in Figure 22.1, is another class that uses multiple inheritance from QObject.

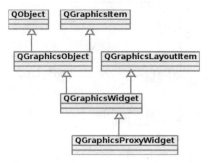

FIGURE 22.3   QGraphicsObject and Multiple Inheritance

NOTE

In Figure 22.3, QObject is one of the base classes that is multiply inherited. One restriction Qt has is that QObject must be inherited only once by any class. (virtual inheritance is not supported.) Furthermore, the QObject-derived base must be listed first in the list of base classes. Breaking this rule can lead to strange errors from the code generated by the MetaObject compiler (moc).

22.3.3   Resolving Multiple Inheritance Conflicts

Figure 22.4 shows a UML diagram where multiple inheritance is used incorrectly for both interface and implementation. To make things even more complicated, one class inherits from the same base class twice.

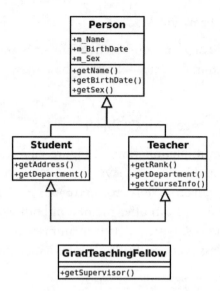

FIGURE 22.4   Person—Student—Teacher

Here, the class GradTeachingFellow is derived from two classes: Student and Teacher.

```
class GradTeachingFellow : public Student,
                           public Teacher {
    // class member functions and data members
};
```

Name conflicts and design problems can arise from the improper use of multiple inheritance. In this example, the getDepartment() function exists in both Student and Teacher. The student could be studying in one department and teaching in another, for example.

QUESTION

What happens when you call getDepartment() on a GraduateTeachingFellow?

```
GraduateTeachingFellow gtf;
Person* pptr = &gtf;
Student * sptr = &gtf;;
Teacher* tptr = &gtf;
gtf.Teacher::getDepartment();
gtf.Student::getDepartment();
sptr->getDepartment()
tptr->getDepartment()
pptr->getDepartment();   // Ambiguous: runtime error if virtual
gtf.getDepartment();  // Compiler error: ambiguous function call
```

The problem, of course, is that we have provided no getDepartment() function in the GradTeachingFellow class. When the compiler looks for a getDepartment() function, Student and Teacher have equal priority.

Inheritance conflicts like these should be avoided because they lead to great design confusion later. However, in this case they can also be resolved with the aid of scope resolution.

22.3.3.1 virtual Inheritance

In Figure 22.4, GraduateTeachingFellow inherited more than once from the same base class. There is another problem with that model: redundancy. Instances of this multiply inherited class might look like Figure 22.5.

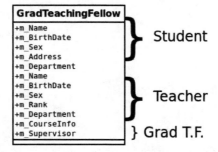

FIGURE 22.5   GradTeachingFellow—Nonvirtual

`Person` has attributes that should be inherited only once. It makes no sense for a `GradTeachingFellow` to have two birthdates and two names. **virtual inheritance** eliminates the redundancy.

The strange problems that can arise when multiple inheritance is used in controversial ways, especially with the added complexities of `virtual` versus non-`virtual` inheritance/functions, seem to have prompted the designers of Java to exclude multiple inheritance from their language. Instead, Java permits the programmer to define an `interface`, which consists only of abstract (pure `virtual`) functions. A Java class can then use the `implements` clause to implement as many interfaces as it needs.

22.3.3.2 virtual **Base Classes**

A base class may be declared `virtual`. A `virtual` base class shares its representation with all other classes that have the same `virtual` base class.

Adding the keyword `virtual` in the *classHeads* of `Student` and `Teacher`, and leaving all the other details of the class definitions the same, produces Example 22.9.

EXAMPLE 22.9   src/multinheritance/people.h

```
#include "qdatetime.h"

class Person {
public:
    Person(QString name, QDate birthdate)
    QObject(name.ascii()),
    m_Birthdate(birthdate) {}

    Person(const Person& p) : QObject(p),
    m_Birthdate(p.m_Birthdate) {}

private:
    QDate m_Birthdate;
};

class Student : virtual public Person {          1
    // other class members
};

class Teacher : virtual public Person {          2
    // other class members
}
```

```
class GraduateTeachingFellow :
    public Student, public Teacher {                           3
public:
    GraduateTeachingFellow(const Person& p,
                        const Student& s, const Teacher& t):
    Person(p), Students(s), Teacher(t) {}                      4
}
```

1 Note keyword `virtual` here.

2 `virtual` inheritance.

3 `virtual` not needed here.

4 It is necessary to initialize all `virtual` base classes explicitly in multiply-derived classes, to resolve ambiguity about how they should be initialized.

After using `virtual` inheritance, an instance of `GradTeachingFellow` might look like Figure 22.6.

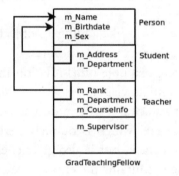

FIGURE 22.6   GradTeachingFellow—`virtual`

Each instance of a class that virtually inherits from another has a pointer (or a variable offset) to its `virtual` base class subobject. The `virtual` base class pointer is invisible to the programmer, and in general, not necessary to change.

With multiple inheritance, each `virtual` base class pointer points to the same object, effectively enabling the base class object to be shared among all of the derived-class "parts."

For any class with a `virtual` base among its base classes, a member initialization entry for that virtual base must appear in the member initialization for that class. Otherwise, the `virtual` base gets default initialization.

22.4 `public`, `protected`, and `private` Derivation

Most of the time, you are likely to see classes using `public` derivation; for example

```
class Square : public Shape {
// ...   };
```

`public` derivation describes an **interface relationship** between two classes. This means that the interface (`public` part) of the base class merges with the interface of the derived class. When it is correct to say that a derived object **is a** base class object, `public` derivation is appropriate. For example, a square **is a** shape (with certain additional attributes).

Much less commonly you might see `protected` or `private` derivation. This is considered an **implementation relationship**, rather than an **is a** relationship. The base class interface (`public` part) gets merged with the implementation (`private` or `protected`, depending on the kind of derivation) of the derived class.

In effect, `private` derivation is like adding an extra object as a `private` data member to the derived class.

Similarly, `protected` derivation is like adding an object as a `protected` data member to the derived class, but it shares the `this` pointer.

Example 22.10 is a concrete example of a situation in which `private` derivation might be appropriate. The template class `Stack` is privately derived from `QList`. The rationale for doing this is that a stack is, by definition, a datastructure that limits access to the top item. The class `QStack`, which is publicly derived from `QVector`, has the expected `public` interface for a stack, but it also gives client code unlimited access to the items in the stack because it contains the entire `public` interface of `QVector`. Our `Stack` class is privately derived from `QList`, so its public interface limits client code access to the handful of stack operations that are consistent with the definition of that data structure.

EXAMPLE 22.10   src/privatederiv/stack.h

```
#ifndef _STACK_H_
#define _STACK_H_

#include <QList>

template<class T>
class Stack : private QList<T> {
```

```
public:
    bool isEmpty() const {
        return QList<T>::isEmpty();
    }
    T pop() {
        return takeFirst();
    }
    void push(const T& value) {
        prepend(value);
    }
    const T& top() const {
        return first();
    }
    int size() const {
        return QList<T>::size();
    }
    void clear() {
        QList<T>::clear();
    }
};
#endif
```

Example 22.11 shows that an attempt by client code to use the `Stack`'s base class (`QList`) interface is not allowed.

EXAMPLE 22.11   src/privatederiv/stack-test.cpp

```
#include "stack.h"
#include <QString>
#include <qstd.h>
using namespace qstd;

int main() {
    Stack<QString> strs;
    strs.push("hic");
    strs.push("haec");
    strs.push("hoc");
//  strs.removeAt(2);                                          1
    int n = strs.size();
    cout << n << " items in stack" << endl;
    for (int i = 0; i < n; ++i)
        cout << strs.pop() << endl;
}
```

1 Error: inherited `QList` methods are private.

So, `private` derivation provides a way to hide the `public` interface of a base class, when the base class is needed only for implementation purposes. What about `protected` derivation?

Suppose you want to derive `xStack`, a particular kind of stack, from this `stack` class. With `stack` privately derived from `QList`, you will not be able to use any `QList` member functions in the implementation of `xStack`. If you need to use some of the `QList` functions when you implement `xStack`, then you must use `protected` derivation when you derive `stack` from `QList`. `protected` derivation makes the `public` interface of `QList` `protected` in `stack`. Internally, this enables classes derived from `stack` to use the inherited `QList` `protected` interface.

22.5   Review Questions

1. What is a vtable?
2. What is a polymorphic type?
3. Which kinds of member functions are not inherited? Why?
4. Under what circumstances should you have `virtual` destructors?
5. What happens when a `virtual` function is called from a base class constructor?
6. What is `virtual` inheritance? What problems can it be used to solve?
7. Why would you use nonpublic derivation?

Part III

Programming Assignments

## Chapter 23

MP3 Jukebox Assignments

In the assignments in this chapter, you will write, in stages, a main window program that serves as an MP3 playlist generator and database manager. It will generate and play selections of MP3 songs based on what it can find on your file system and it will permit filter-queries based on data stored in ID3v2 (meta) tag information.

Prerequisites: You can start on this once you have covered the material up to Chapter 13, "Models and Views."

The features you will implement are inspired by open source programs such as amaroK and aTunes, and commercial programs such as iTunes and MusicMatch Jukebox. All these programs provide similar features but very different user interfaces. There is a lot of creativity that can go into a player. Few of them are equally easy to use with a keyboard or a mouse. Try to make yours work with either.

You can find an example of a media player in $QTDIR/examples/phonon/qmusicplayer and use it as a starting point. Then you can add extra components to it as you work through the following assignments. As of this writing, qmusicplayer lets you add files to a playlist and play the list of songs on your computer.

The simplest media player, shown in Figure 23.1, has two major components:

- A Player view, which consists of
  - A dockable that shows the user what is currently playing and provides some controls for changing volume and position of the song
  - **Play/Pause** and **Stop** buttons. (**Next** and **Previous** buttons would also be nice.)
- A song list view, as the central widget, for displaying a list of songs

FIGURE 23.1 Example Screenshot

Each of these components is a view for displaying the data, and it is suggested you use separate classes to hold the actual data, maintaining a separation between model and view code.

> ### Qt MultiMedia Kit
>
> There is another library, Qt MultimediaKit,[1] which is available as an add-on to Qt. It is included in the Qt Software Development Kit (SDK) and can be downloaded from Qt Mobility.[2]
>
> Qt MultiMediaKit offers a higher-level API for media players, including the ability to make recordings and access raw sound vector data. It provides implementations of playlists and

---

[1] http://doc.qt.nokia.com/qtmobility/multimedia.html

[2] http://qt.nokia.com/products/qt-addons/mobility/

readers and writers for many popular playlist formats. If you want to reuse this library instead of Phonon, a better starting point is the demos/player example from Qt Mobility. Some parts of Qt Mobility only work on mobile devices such as phones, but Qt MultiMediaKit runs on all platforms.

Qt MultiMediaKit is still under development, but it is planned to replace Phonon in future versions of Qt.

As of Qt 4.6, there is a library, called libqtmultimedia, that is included in the Qt installation. This contains a *subset* of libqtmultimediakit, the library previously mentioned. As of Qt 4.7, this library does not include M3u playlist classes and certain other classes you might want for your media player.

23.1 Phonon/MultiMediaKit Setup

The first step is to ensure that you have a version of Qt built with Phonon (or Mobility's MultiMediaKit) and that the correct codecs are available on your system to play MP3 files. If you are currently able to play MP3 files on your computer, you are all set. Otherwise, as of Qt 4.7, the Qt SDK provides ready-built binaries of both libraries for most platforms, and they seem to work quite well.

Build and run the starting point example program that you have chosen to ensure that your Qt installation is properly set up for this project.

If you cannot play media of your desired format, see the "Installing Phonon" documentation.[3]

23.2 Playlist

1. Take your starting point example and make it possible to **load**, **save**, and **clear** the current playlist. The model for a playlist should be stored in a class derived (directly or indirectly) from QAbstractItemModel, called PlayListModel.

   The PlayListModel should provide a model for MetaDataValue (or similar) instances.

   Instead of using a QTableWidget, as the Qt Phonon example does, extend a QTableView and call it PlayListView.

---

[3] http://doc.qt.nokia.com/latest/phonon-overview.html#installing-phonon

Figure 23.2 shows the relationships between these classes.

If you wish, reuse the classes `MetaDataObject`, `DataObjectTableModel`, `SimpleDelegate`, and others you find in **libmetadata** from dist.[4]

2. Make the application remember in `QSettings` the current playlist filename, table column widths, and size/position of the main window when the user exits.

3. Restore these `QSettings` values on startup.

4. Implement the following player/playlist actions: **next**, **previous**, **playNext** (after this one is done), **addFiles**, **clear**, **save as**, **save**, and **open**. Put these actions in the main menu and the context menu of the playlist view. Ensure that the named actions actually control the player.

5. (Optional): Implement a clipboard and actions that work on multiple selections in the table view: **removeFiles**, **copy**, **cut**, and **paste here**.

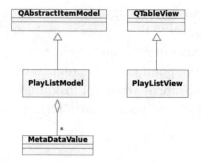

FIGURE 23.2   Single Playlist

23.3   Playlists

In this assignment, we define some data types and some means to load and save playlists in m3u format.

M3u files are quite simple; they consist of one URL per line, which may be a relative path to a local track on disk. Optional extended information and comments appear after a # on the preceding line.

---

[4] http://www.distancecompsci.com/dist/

The preceding assignment started with an example media player program that you enhanced. Now you add some load/save playlist actions to that program.

The `Phonon` library has no code for handling M3u files, so you need to write serialization code yourself. The Qt Mobility example has a `QMediaPlaylist->load()` method that can load M3u files.

Some example code for loading and saving m3u files to disk is provided in `src/handouts`. Feel free to reuse that code.

The `MetaDataLoader` classes used in our code come from our [dist] directory. There are three versions available: one that uses `Phonon`, one that uses `Taglib`, and another that uses Qt Mobility. You can choose one based on what works best on your platform. All three work on Linux. At press time, neither `Phonon` nor Mobility could read ID3 tags of MP3s on Windows, which is why we also offer a Taglib implementation.

This link[5] has information to help you determine which tag is used to store song ratings by other popular MP3 players, if you want to make your player compatible with other players.

Write some test cases using QtTestLib to verify that you can read and write playlists.

23.4   Source Selector

Selecting from a variety of different "sources" is what makes a player very powerful and useful. A source could be any of the following:

- A playlist
- A library of mp3s, stored in a database
- A list of online radio stations
- Tracks on a CD
- A folder of tracks
- A subset of the library, filtered on genre, artist, or album

One interesting thing they all have in common is that each can be viewed with a `QAbstractItemView`.

---

[5] http://help.mp3tag.de/en/main_tags.html

The `SourceSelector` widget, shown docked on the left in Figure 23.3, permits the user to select the currently viewed "source," which in this case corresponds to a list of songs.

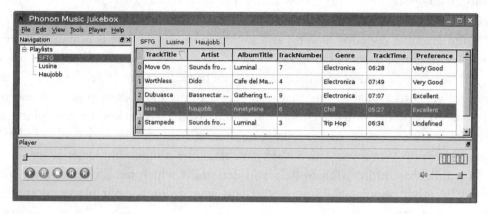

FIGURE 23.3   Source Selector View

At any given time, if the user clicks on another "source" in that widget, then the "current playlist" should switch to the chosen one, and the MP3 player should start playing songs from this new playlist next.

By clicking on a source in the selector model, the application should change the currently visible table or list view in the central widget. Figure 23.4 shows one possible way to design the classes that provide a view and a selector of a collection of sources.

At any given time, the user can perform an action, **Show Now Playing**, that changes the central widget so that it is showing what is currently playing instead of what was last selected by the user in the source selector.

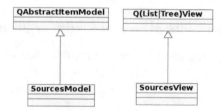

FIGURE 23.4   Source Selector and Related Classes

23.5 Database Playlists

Load and store your playlists in a database. You can reuse the code in `$CPPLIBS/`
`sqlmetadata` if you do not want to write SQL.

- Add a queue and a history playlist.
- Add QActions to enqeue and dequeue tracks.
- Show the queue position as a decoration role in the play list view.
- Test that next/previous work as expected while playing a track.

23.6 Star Delegates

1. In the Qt examples, there is a stardelegate app that provides a `QItemDelegate`
   for `StarRating` instances.
2. Instead of using a word like "bad" or "great" to rate a song, you can give the
   song from zero to N stars that are displayed in the tabular output instead of or
   in addition to the `Preference`.
3. Write a class or namespace that provides a bidirectional conversion between
   `Preference` and `StarRating`.
4. Write a `StarDelegate` that works for `Preference`.

23.7 Sorting, Filtering, and Editing Playlists

1. Add sorting and filtering capabilities on your table views. Let the user select
   some or all fields to filter on.
2. Implement cut/copy/paste, drag/drop url-lists.

Appendix A

C++ Reserved Keywords

Keywords are identifiers that are part of the basic syntax of the language. These names have fixed meanings and cannot be used in any way that attempts to change those meanings.

Here is a list of keywords in C++. Those in **bold** are also part of ANSI C89.

and	**extern**	**signed**
and_eq	FALSE	**sizeof**
asm	**float**	**static**
auto	**for**	static_cast
bitand	friend	**struct**
bitor	**goto**	**switch**
bool	**if**	template
break	inline	this
case	**int**	throw
catch	**long**	TRUE
char	mutable	try
class	namespace	**typedef**
compl	new	typeid

const	not	typename
const_cast	not_eq	**union**
continue	operator	**unsigned**
default	or	using
delete	or_eq	virtual
do	private	**void**
double	protected	**volatile**
dynamic_cast	public	wchar_t
else	**register**	**while**
enum	reinterpret_cast	xor
explicit	**return**	xor_eq
export	**short**	

Appendix B

Standard Headers

This book uses a small subset of the **Standard Template Library** (STL, also called the Standard Library). The standard header files we use are listed here. To use these classes and functions effectively, it is useful to know where to look for documentation.

Table B.1 shows a list of standard header files. For some header files, there is a man page for the whole file. In other cases, you might find a man page for the individual function also.

If you use Microsoft Developer's Studio, the documentation for the standard libraries comes with the MSDN documentation.

For other platforms, it helps to have one, but you don't need a local copy of man or the man pages because there are many copies of the documentation available on the Web.[1]

We ran the standard header files through doxygen to get this table.

---

[1] For examples, see cplusplus.com [http://www.cplusplus.com/ref/] or Dinkumware [http://www.dinkumware.com/manuals/reader.aspx?lib=cpp].

TABLE B.1   Standard Headers

Header File	Library	man Pages
	C++ STL	
string	STL strings type	std::string
sstream	stringstream, for writing to strings as if they are streams	std::stringstream
iostream	C++ standard stream library	std::ios, std::iostream
memory	C++ memory-related routines	std::bad_alloc, std::auto_ptr
	C Standard Library	
cstring, string.h	Functions for C char* strings	string, strcpy, strcmp
cstdlib, stdlib.h	C Standard Library	random, srandom, getenv, setenv
cstdio, stdio.h	Standard input/output	stdin, stdout, printf, scanf
cassert	Assert macros	assert

NOTE

By default, the C++ Standard Library documentation might not be installed on your system. Search for the string libstdc with your favorite package manager, so you can install something like libstdc++6-4.5-doc.

Development Tools

This appendix contains articles about the C++ development environment.

C.1   make **and** Makefile

You saw earlier that qmake (without arguments) reads a project file and builds a Makefile. Example C.1 is a slightly abbreviated look at the Makefile generated from a simple project called qapp.

EXAMPLE C.1   src/qapp/Makefile-abbreviated

```
# Exerpts from a makefile


####### Compiler, tools and options


CC            = gcc      # executable for C compiler
CXX           = g++      # executable  for c++ compiler
LINK          = g++      # executable for linker


# flags that get passed to the compiler
CFLAGS        = -pipe -g -Wall -W -D_REENTRANT $(DEFINES)
CXXFLAGS      = -pipe -g -Wall -W -D_REENTRANT $(DEFINES)
```

```
INCPATH       = -I/usr/local/qt/mkspecs/default -I. \
                -I$(QT4)/include/QtGui -I$(QT4)/include/QtCore \
                -I$(QT4)/include

# Linker flags
LIBS          = $(SUBLIBS) -L$(QT4)/lib -lQtCore_debug -lQtGui_debug -lpthread
LFLAGS        = -Wl,-rpath,$(QT4)/lib

# macros for performing other operations as part of build steps:
QMAKE         = /usr/local/qt/bin/qmake

####### Files

HEADERS       =    # If we had some, they'd be here.
SOURCES       = main.cpp
OBJECTS       = main.o
[snip]
QMAKE_TARGET  = qapp
DESTDIR       =
TARGET        = qapp  # default target to build

first: all          # to build "first," we must build "all"

####### Implicit rules

.SUFFIXES: .c .o .cpp .cc .cxx .C

.cpp.o:
        $(CXX) -c $(CXXFLAGS) $(INCPATH) -o $@ $<

## Possible targets to build

all: Makefile $(TARGET)   # this is how to build "all"

$(TARGET):  $(OBJECTS) $(OBJMOC)    # this is how to build qapp
        $(LINK) $(LFLAGS) -o $(TARGET) $(OBJECTS) $(OBJMOC) $(OBJCOMP) \
    $(LIBS)

        qmake:  FORCE               # "qmake" is a target, too!
        @$(QMAKE) -o Makefile qapp.pro  # what does it do?

dist:                               # Another target
        @mkdir -p .tmp/qapp \
```

```
         && $(COPY_FILE) --parents $(SOURCES) $(HEADERS) \
            $(FORMS) $(DIST) .tmp/qapp/ \
         && (cd `dirname .tmp/qapp` && $(TAR) qapp.tar qapp \
            && $(COMPRESS) qapp.tar) \
         && $(MOVE) `dirname .tmp/qapp`/qapp.tar.gz . \
         && $(DEL_FILE) -r .tmp/qapp


clean:compiler_clean                    # yet another target
         -$(DEL_FILE) $(OBJECTS)
         -$(DEL_FILE) *~ core *.core



####### Dependencies for implicit rules

main.o: main.cpp
```

The command **make** checks the dependencies and performs each build step specified in the Makefile. The name and location of the final result can be set with the project variables, TARGET and target.path. If TARGET is not specified, the name defaults to the name of the directory in which the project file is located. If target.path is not specified, the location defaults to the directory in which the project file is located.

Cleaning Up Files

qmake produces a Makefile that enables make to issue several useful commands (sometimes called *"phony" targets*.[1] The first of these, make clean, removes any object files and core dump files that may have been produced in the process of building or executing the project.[2]

```
src/early-examples/example0> make clean
rm -f fac.o
rm -f *~ core *.core
src/early-examples/example0> ls
example0   example0.pro   fac.cpp   Makefile
src/early-examples/example0>
```

---

[1] They are called "phony" to distinguish them from "genuine" targets that are generally filenames such as the name of the executable that is to be produced by the build process.

[2] Core dump files are sometimes produced when an executing program encounters a runtime error and is forced to abort. They give a snapshot of main memory at the moment of the crash, which may help to identify the cause of the crash.

The second, `make distclean`, removes all the files that `make clean` removes, plus the `Makefile` and the executable, leaving only the files needed to build the project on a different machine.

```
src/early-examples/example0> make distclean
rm -f fac.o
rm -f *~ core *.core
rm -f example0
rm -f Makefile
src/early-examples/example0> ls
example0.pro  fac.cpp
src/early-examples/example0>
```

`qmake` produces other "phony" targets in the `Makefile`, but the two we just described will be the ones that you use most frequently. You can acquaint yourself with the other targets by examining the `Makefile` and looking for labels; i.e., lines that begin with an indentifier followed by a colon (e.g., `clean:`). To learn more about `make`, we recommend the book [Rehman03].

NOTE

If you modify a project file after the last execution of `make`, you should run `qmake` to regenerate the `Makefile` before your next invocation of `make`.

TIP

The command `make dist` creates a tarball (dirname.tar.gz) that contains all the source files that the project file knows about.

C.2 The Preprocessor: For `#including` Files

In C++, code reuse is indicated by the presence of a preprocessor directive, `#include`, at the top of source code files. You `#include` header files that contain things like `class` or `namespace` definitions, `const` definitions, function prototypes, and so forth. These files are literally *included* in your own files before the compiler begins to translate your code.

The compiler reports an error if it sees any identifier defined more than once. It will tolerate repeated declarations but not repeated definitions.[3] To prevent repeated definitions, be careful to use an *#ifndef wrapper* around each header file. This tells the preprocessor to skip the contents if it has already seen them. Let's examine the following class definition in Example C.2.

EXAMPLE C.2   src/preprocessor/constraintmap.h

```
#ifndef CONSTRAINTMAP_H
#define CONSTRAINTMAP_H

#include <QHash>
#include <QString>

class Constraint;                                           1

class ConstraintMap : public QHash<QString, Constraint*> {  2

private:
    Constraint* m_Constraintptr;                            3
    Constraint m_ConstraintObj;                             4
    void addConstraint(Constraint& c);                      5
};
#endif         //  #ifndef CONSTRAINTMAP_H
```

1 Forward declaration.

2 Needs definitions of QHash and QString, but only the declaration of Constraint, because it's a pointer.

3 No problem, it's just a pointer.

4 Error: incomplete type.

5 Using forward declaration.

As you can see, inside function parameter lists, you can use pointers or references to classes that were only declared, not defined. The pointer dereferencing and member accessing operations are performed in the implementation file shown in Example C.3. There, you must #include the full definitions of each type it uses.

---

[3] Section 20.1 discusses the difference between *declaration* and *definition*.

EXAMPLE C.3   src/preprocessor/constraintmap.cpp

```
#include "constraintmap.h"

ConstraintMap map;                                                      1
#include "constraintmap.h"                                              2

Constraint* constraintP;                                               3

Constraint p;                                                          4
#include <constraint.h>
Constraint q;                                                          5

void ConstraintMap::addConstraint(Constraint& c) {
    cout << c.name();                                                  6
}
```

1 Okay, `ConstraintMap` is already included.

2 Redundant but harmless if `#ifndef` wrapped.

3 Using forward declaration from `constraintmap.h`.

4 Error: incomplete type.

5 Now it is a complete type.

6 Complete type required here.

To minimize the number of "strong dependencies" between header files, you should try to declare classes instead of `#including` header files whenever possible. Here are some guidelines to help decide whether you need a forward declaration, or the full header file `#included`.

- If `ClassA` derives from `ClassB`, the definition of `ClassB` must be known by the compiler when it processes the definition of `ClassA`. Therefore, the header file for `ClassA` must include the header file for `ClassB`.

- If the definition of `ClassA` contains a member that is an object of `ClassD`, the header file for `ClassA` must `#include` the header file for `ClassD`. If the definition of `ClassA` contains a function that has a parameter or a return object of `ClassD`, the header file for `ClassA` must `#include` the header file for `ClassD`.

- If the definition of `ClassA` only contains nondereferenced `ClassE` pointers or references, then a **forward declaration** of `ClassE` is sufficient in the `ClassA` header file:

```
class ClassE;
```

A class that is *declared* but not *defined* is considered an **incomplete type**.

Any attempt to dereference a pointer or define an object of an incomplete type results in a compiler error.[4]

The implementation file, `classa.cpp`, for `ClassA` should `#include "classa.h"` and also `#include` the header file for each class that is used by `ClassA` (unless that header file has already been included in `classa.h`). Any pointer dereferencing should be performed in the `.cpp` file. This helps reduce dependencies between classes and improves compilation speed.

- A `.cpp` file should *never* `#include` another `.cpp` file.

- A header file should `#include` as few other header files as possible so that it can be included more quickly and with fewer dependencies.

- A header file should always be `#ifndef` wrapped to prevent it from being included more than once.

Circular Dependencies versus Bidirectional Relationships

Whenever one file `#includes` another, there is a strong **dependency** created between the files. When a dependency like this exists between header files, it cannot be bidirectional: the preprocessor cannot cope with a **circular dependency** between header files, where each one `#includes` the other. One of the `#include` statements must be replaced by a forward class declaration.

Forward declarations help remove circular dependencies between classes, and in the process, enable bidirectional relationships to exist between them.

C.3   Understanding the Linker

Figure C.1 shows how the linker accepts binary files, which were generated by the compiler, and creates executable binaries as its output. The linker executable, on *nix machines, is called `ld`. It is run by g++ after all source files have been compiled successfully.

All these steps are performed when you run `make`, which prints out every command before it executes. By reading the output of `make`, you can see what arguments are

---

[4] The actual error message may not always be clear, and with `QObjects`, it might come from the MOC-generated code, rather than your own code.

passed to the compiler and linker. If an error occurs, it immediately follows the command line that produced the error.

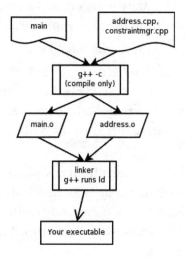

FIGURE C.1   The Linker's Inputs and Outputs

Example C.4 shows the command-line options passed to g++ and attempts to show how g++ runs the linker, known as `ld`, and passes some arguments to it.

EXAMPLE C.4   linker-invocation.txt

```
g++ -Wl,-rpath,/usr/local/qt-x11-free-3.2.3/lib            1
   -o hw7                                                   2
   .obj/address.o .obj/ca_address.o .obj/constraintgroup.o
   .obj/customer.o .obj/dataobject.o .obj/dataobjectfactory.o
   .obj/hw07-demo.o .obj/us_address.o .obj/moc_address.o    3
   .obj/moc_ca_address.o .obj/moc_customer.o .obj/moc_dataobject.o
   .obj/moc_us_address.o
   -L/usr/local/qt-x11-free-3.2.3/lib  -L/usr/X11R6/lib
   -L/usr/local/utils/lib                                   4
   -lutils -lqt -lXext -lX11 -lm                            5
```

1 Tells g++ to run the linker and pass these options to ld.

2 Specify the output to be called `hw7`.

3 Link these object files into the executable.

4 Add another location for the linker to search for libraries.

5 Link this app with four more libraries: `qt utils`, `ext`, `X11`, and `m`.

Linking entails the following:

- For each library name passed with the -1 switch, find the corresponding library file, searching the library path and all -L switched arguments (which were generated by qmake from the LIB qmake variable).

  - For static libraries, it contains the binary code to be linked into the executable.

  - For dynamic libraries, it is a catalog listing (often in readable ascii format) that describes where the actual shared objects are for each label definition. The linker checks to make sure the shared object is where it should be and reports an error if not.

- For each function call that is called from any place in the code we are linking, find the object where that code is located and do a simple, fast check to determine that there is, indeed, a completely defined function with the proper name/signature at that location. Report an error if it can't be found or isn't the correct type/name/size.

- For each reference to a variable name, find the object-address where that variable is located and do a simple, fast check to make sure the address is a valid one for an object of that type.

This is the general idea. The linker resolves references to names by finding their real addresses in files and checking the addresses to see if they're valid for the type ID. It's like a directory lookup service for C++ compilers.

C.3.1 Common Linker Error Messages

C++ programmers sometimes spend lots of time trying to understand and repair compiler and linker errors. If you can't understand the message, you're stuck. With a compiler error, the problem is easier to diagnose because it is related to the compilation of one source code module and the header files it includes. The compiler generally tells you the exact location of any error that it detects. With a linker error, the problem is related to how your source code modules link together. When the linker stage is reached, all the individual modules have compiled without errors. Linker errors can be caused by bugs in C++ code, but they can also be a result of mistakes in the project file.

`Error: Unable to find libxxx.so.x`

For Win32 Users

At compile time, your IDE needs to find the .DLL. To remedy this situation, drill into your menu structure until you find `project -> properties -> C/C++ build -> libraries`. Here, you can *add* a third party library, and you'll be asked in a dialog for the location of headers and DLL files.

At runtime, your `PATH` system environment variable must contain the directory where the required DLLs are located.

Installing a library means making it available for more than a single user on a system. It is also possible to reuse a library without installing it. All libraries that you reuse must either be installed or placed in a directory listed in your `LD_LIBRARY_PATH`.

When you reuse a library for the first time, you will probably see this error message. It means that the linker cannot find the library. When the gnu linker looks for a shared object, it checks at least two places:

1. The directories specified in `LD_LIBRARY_PATH`
2. Installed libraries referenced from a cache file called `/etc/ld.so.cache`

The Cache File: `ld.so.cache`

The cache file provides fast lookup of shared objects found in the directories specified in `/etc/ld.so.conf`. Some directories you might find there are

```
/lib
/usr/lib
/usr/X11R6/lib
/usr/i486-linuxlibc1/lib
/usr/local/lib
/usr/lib/mozilla
```

If you use a Linux package installer to install a library, it probably makes the proper changes to `ld.so.conf` and rebuilds your cache file. However, if you manually compile and install libraries, it may be necessary for you to edit this file. Afterward, you can rebuild the cache file with the command `ldconfig`.

Error: undefined reference to *identifier*

This is the most common and, probably, the most annoying linker error of all. It means that the linker cannot find the definition of some named entity in your code. Following is some output from make:

```
.obj/ca_address.o(.gnu.linkonce.t._ZN10DataObject16getConstraintGroupEv+0x4):
In function `DataObject::getConstraintGroup()':
/usr/local/qt-x11-free-3.2.3/include/qshared.h:50:
undefined reference to `DataObject::s_Cm'
collect2: ld returned 1 exit status
make: *** [hw7] Error 1
```

The compiler found the declaration, but the linker can't find the corresponding definition. In some part of your code, you have a *reference* symbol, but no *definition* can be found. The useful bits of information in the error message follow:

- The symbol it can't find is DataObject::s_Cm.
- The function that tried to use it is DataObject::getConstraintGroup.

The first step is to see if you can find the missing definition. If you can't find it, how can the linker? If you find it in a .cpp file, you must make sure that

- Both the .cpp and the .h file are mentioned in the project.
- The file is included in a library with which you are linking.

Because you use good naming conventions (Section 3.1), you can immediately tell that s_Cm is a static data member of class DataObject. The compiler found the declaration, but the linker can't find the definition.

Because it is static (Section 2.9), the definition for s_Cm belongs in dataobject. cpp. The compiler expects to find a definition statement of the form

```
ConstraintGroup DataObject::s_Cm;
```

If it's there, and the linker still can't find it, the most likely causes for this error are

- The .cpp file that contains the definition is not listed in qmake's SOURCES in the project file.
- The code is located in another library, but the linker can't find the library. This can be solved by adding a missing LIBS argument in the project file.

- `-lmyLib` adds a library to be linked.
- `-LmyLibDir` adds a directory to the linker's lib search path list.

Error: unresolved external symbol

When linking against your own library, from a Microsoft compiler, you might find a linker error like this:

```
customer.obj : error LNK2001: unresolved external symbol
"public: virtual bool __thiscall DataObject::readFrom(class QObject const &)"
(?readFrom@DataObject@@UAE_NABVQObject@@@Z)
```

This often means that the symbol was not exported when the DLL was built. Be sure that there is a `Q_DECL_EXPORT` macro for the library before the class or function declaration, and rebuild the DLL. See Section 7.1.2.

Error: undefined reference to vtable for ClassName

This is one of the most confusing errors. It generally means that a `virtual` function definition is missing. Literally, the vtable for that class (which has addresses of each of the virtual functions) cannot be fully constructed.

This error can arise from missing function definitions in your code, but it can also be caused by a missing `HEADERS` or `SOURCES` entry in your make/project file. If you recently added a `Q_OBJECT` macro to one of your existing headers, then re-run qmake, because the `Makefile` needs to be rebuilt! See Section 8.4 for more details on this.

✐ TIP

After this kind of linker error, check first that all files are listed properly in the project file. All QObjects have a proper `Q_OBJECT` macro, do a "qmake && make clean," and see if you can reproduce the error.

> **All-Inline Classes**
>
> For polymorphic classes there should be at least one non-`inline` definition (a function or a `static` member) in a source (`.cpp`) file for that header file.[5] Without this, many linkers cannot find any of their `virtual` method definitions and, instead, report a similar error.
>
> Classes that contain only inline functions are legal in C++, but they do not work in their intended way when mixed with polymorphism.

C.4   Debugging

The compiler can locate and describe syntax errors. The linker can reveal the existence of inconsistencies among program components and give some help as to how to locate them. One of the most challenging aspects to using C++ is learning how to find and fix various kinds of runtime errors.

Runtime errors are logical errors that can exist in a program that is syntactically correct and contains no undefined objects or functions. Effective use of a **debugger**, a program specifically designed for tracking down runtime errors, can greatly reduce the amount of time spent dealing with these kinds of errors.

A debugger permits the stepwise execution of your code and the inspection of object values. Because debuggers work with compiled code, the early versions could only be used by programmers who were familiar with assembly language. Modern debuggers can step concurrently through the compiled machine code *and* the original source code. The GNU family of developer tools includes gdb, the source-level GNU debugger, which you can use for C/C++ applications. gdb has been designed with a command-line interface that is quite powerful but not particularly user friendly. Fortunately, there are several open source graphical facades for gdb, one of which we discuss next. Commercial C++ IDEs (e.g., Visual Studio) generally have built-in source-level debuggers.

C.4.1   Building a Debuggable Target

For gdb to work, debugging symbols must be built into the code at compile time. Otherwise, the machine instructions will not be mapped to locations in C++ source

---

[5] A class with at least one `virtual` method is polymorphic.

files. This is easily accomplished by using the appropriate command-line switch (-g) when invoking the compiler:

```
g++ -g filename.cpp
```

This often results in a *significantly* larger executable file. Generally, the growth is proportional to the size and complexity of the source code files. The expanded executable contains symbol table information that the debugger can use to find source code that corresponds to machine instructions. To get qmake to generate makefiles with the debugging options switched on, add the following line to your qmake project file:

```
CONFIG += debug
```

When the Qt library has been built with debugging symbols, you can step through the Qt source code just as easily as your own code. You may need to build Qt with debugging symbols to debug programs that contain code called from the Qt library (most GUI programs, for example).

✗ TIP

In Win32, it's a menu choice you can click on. On *nix platforms, after unpacking the source code tarball, pass a parameter to the configure script before building, and your Qt library can be built with debug symbols.

```
./configure --enable-debug
make
make install
```

C.4.1.1 Exercises: Building a Debuggable Target

To get a better feeling for the cost of debugging

- Compare the size of an executable file created with and without the CONFIG += debug line in the project file.
- Make a mental note to try this again later with a more complex application.

C.4.2   gdb **Quickstart**

Imagine you are running a program and, for some mysterious reason, it crashes.

```
[lazarus] app> ./playlistmgr
Segmentation fault
[lazarus] app>
```

When your application aborts, or crashes, it is helpful to know (as quickly as possible) exactly where it happened. You can use gdb to locate the trouble spot quickly and easily. Following is a short example of a command-line gdb session.

```
[lazarus] app> gdb playlistmgr
GNU gdb 6.3-debian
Copyright 2004 Free Software Foundation, Inc.
This GDB was configured as "i386-linux"...Using host libthread_db library "/lib/
tls/libthread_db.so.1".

(gdb)  r⁶
Starting program: ftgui/app/playlistmgr
[Thread debugging using libthread_db enabled]
[New Thread -1227622176 (LWP 17021)]
Qt: gdb: -nograb added to command-line options.
        Use the -dograb option to enforce grabbing.
This is a debug message

Program received signal SIGSEGV, Segmentation fault.
[Switching to Thread -1227622176 (LWP 17021)]
0xb7f03320 in FormDialog::createActions (this=0x80ae2a0) at formdialog.cpp:53
53          delete m_OkAction;
(gdb)
```

gdb shows you not only the filename and line number, but also the corresponding line in the source code. However, you still might want to get some context for this error. The command list shows you the surrounding source code for the current file:

```
(gdb) list
51      void FormDialog::createActions() {
52
```

---

⁶ r is the command for "run"

```
53              delete m_OkAction;
54              delete m_CancelAction;
55              m_OkAction = new OkAction(m_Model, m_View);
56              m_CancelAction = new CancelAction(m_Model, m_View);
57              QHBoxLayout *buttons = new QHBoxLayout(0);
(gdb)
```

The command `where` shows you the stack trace, or how you got to that error spot:

```
(gdb) where
#0  0xb7f03320 in FormDialog::createActions (this=0x80ae2a0) at formdialog.cpp:53
#1  0xb7f03058 in FormDialog::setModel (this=0x80ae2a0, fmodel=0x80c80d0)
    at formdialog.cpp:34
#2  0x080664bd in SettingsDialog (this=0x80ae2a0, parent=0x0) at settingsdialog.
cpp:14
#3  0x0805f313 in MainWindow (this=0xbfffdec8) at mainwindow.cpp:42
#4  0x08066f14 in Controller (this=0xbfffdec0, argc=1, argv=0xbfffdfe4) at
controller.cpp:25
#5  0x0805a8a4 in main (argc=1, argv=0xbfffdfe4) at main.cpp:7
(gdb)
```

Most open source IDEs such as Eclipse and QtCreator, use `gdb` under the hood. They each offer a user interface that makes certain features easier to learn and use. ccdebug[7] is written in Qt and designed specifically for debugging Qt applications, including `QString` support.

✎ TIP

`QStrings` are hard to see inside some debuggers because they are indirect pointers to Unicode data. The debugger needs to know extra things about a `QString` to display it properly.

If you use an IDE with Qt integration installed, you should be able to see `QStrings` in your debugger.

If you are using QtCreator and can't see them, go to the Qt settings and check if the **debugging helpers** can be built for the version of Qt you are using.

If you are using command-line `gdb`, you can download kde-devel-gdb,[8] a collection of Qt helper macros from the KDE subversion repository, and put the following lines in your `~/.gdbinit` file:

---

[7] http://sourceforge.net/projects/ccdebug
[8] http://websvn.kde.org/*checkout*/trunk/KDE/kdesdk/scripts/kde-devel-gdb

```
source /path/to/kde/kde-devel-gdb
define pqs
    printq4string $arg0
end
```

The pqs macro should enable you to print QStrings while you are debugging.

 TIP

You can use the file .gdbinit to automate the loading of a particular executable, the setting of breakpoints, and the starting up of your debugging session. Whenever you find yourself running gdb and entering the same commands repeatedly, try adding that sequence of commands to the .gdbinit in the same directory as your project.

C.4.3 Finding Memory Errors

Memory errors are difficult to track down without the aid of a runtime analysis tool. A program that analyzes the running performance of a program is called a **profiler**. valgrind is an open source profiling tool for Linux that tracks the memory and CPU usage of your code and detects a variety of runtime errors. These include

- Memory leaks—memory that is no longer accessible but which has not been deleted
- Invalid pointer use for heap memory, such as
  - Out of bounds index
  - Mismatches between allocation and deallocation syntax (e.g., allocating with new[] but deallocating with delete)
- Use of uninitialized memory

Any of these errors can cause catastrophic results in a piece of software. Profilers can also be used for performance tuning and determining which code is responsible for slowing down a program (i.e., finding bottlenecks).

Example C.5 is a short program that contains a deliberate memory usage error.

EXAMPLE C.5   src/debugging/wrongdelete.cpp

```
void badpointer1(int* ip, int n) {
  ip = new int[n];
  delete ip;                                              1
}

int main() {
  int* iptr;
  int num(4);
  badpointer1(iptr, num);
}
```

1 Wrong delete syntax.

For the output to be human readable, compile with debugging symbols (-g).

```
debugging/wrongdelete> g++ -g -Wall wrongdelete.cpp
debugging/wrongdelete> ./a.out
debugging/wrongdelete>
```

The compiler didn't complain, and even after running the program, no error behavior appears. However, memory is corrupted by this program.

Here is a (slightly abbreviated) look at valgrind's analysis of Example C.5. We have removed the process ID of the valgrind job from the beginning of each line. The process ID is, of course, different each time you run valgrind.

```
src/debugging> valgrind a.out
--3332-- DWARF2 CFI reader: unhandled CFI instruction 0:50
--3332-- DWARF2 CFI reader: unhandled CFI instruction 0:50
 Mismatched free() / delete / delete []
    at 0x401C1CB: operator delete(void*) (vg_replace_malloc.c:246)
    by 0x80484BD: badpointer1(int*, int) (wrongdelete.cpp:3)
    by 0x80484F4: main (wrongdelete.cpp:9)
  Address 0x4277028 is 0 bytes inside a block of size 16 alloc'd
    at 0x401BBF4: operator new[](unsigned) (vg_replace_malloc.c:197)
    by 0x80484AC: badpointer1(int*, int) (wrongdelete.cpp:2)
    by 0x80484F4: main (wrongdelete.cpp:9)
```

`valgrind` found the errors and, with debugging symbols, could point you to the location of the problem code. Example C.6 is a little more interesting because it contains memory leaks and array index errors.

EXAMPLE C.6   src/debugging/valgrind-test.cpp

```
#include <iostream>

int badpointer2(int k) {
  int* ip = new int[3];
  ip[0] = k;
  return ip[3];                                            1
}                                                          2


int main() {
  using namespace std;
  int* iptr;                                               3
  int num(4), k;                                           4
  cout << iptr[num-1] << endl;                             5
  cout << badpointer2(k) << endl;                          6
}
```

1 Out of bounds index

2 Memory leak: allocated memory is no longer accessible.

3 `iptr` is uninitialized.

4 `k` is uninitialized.

5 What is the state of `iptr`?

6 Sending uninitialized `arg` to function.

Running Example C.6 through `valgrind` shows you the exact locations of some errors:

```
For more details, rerun with: -v

--2164-- DWARF2 CFI reader: unhandled CFI instruction 0:50
--2164-- DWARF2 CFI reader: unhandled CFI instruction 0:50
 Use of uninitialised value of size 4
   at 0x80486AF: main (valgrind-test.cpp:17)
68500558
```

```
Invalid read of size 4
   at 0x804867C: badpointer2(int) (valgrind-test.cpp:8)
   by 0x80486DD: main (valgrind-test.cpp:18)
 Address 0x4277034 is 0 bytes after a block of size 12 alloc'd
   at 0x401BBF4: operator new[](unsigned) (vg_replace_malloc.c:197)
   by 0x8048667: badpointer2(int) (valgrind-test.cpp:6)
   by 0x80486DD: main (valgrind-test.cpp:18)
0


ERROR SUMMARY: 2 errors from 2 contexts (suppressed: 19 from 1)
malloc/free: in use at exit: 12 bytes in 1 blocks.
malloc/free: 1 allocs, 0 frees, 12 bytes allocated.
For counts of detected errors, rerun with: -v
searching for pointers to 1 not-freed blocks.
checked 120,048 bytes.


LEAK SUMMARY:
   definitely lost: 12 bytes in 1 blocks.
     possibly lost: 0 bytes in 0 blocks.
   still reachable: 0 bytes in 0 blocks.
        suppressed: 0 bytes in 0 blocks.
Use --leak-check=full to see details of leaked memory.
```

If this is not enough information to find where the memory leak is, you can rerun valgrind with `--leak-check=full`. We repaired some of the errors in Example C.7.

EXAMPLE C.7 src/debugging/valgrind-test2.cpp

```
#include <iostream>

int notSoBadPointer(int k) {
  int* ip = new int[3];
  ip[0] = k;
  delete[] ip;                                          1
  return k;                                             2
}



int main() {
  using namespace std;
  int* iptr;                                            3
  int num(4), k(4);                                     4
  cout << iptr[num-1] << endl;                          5
  cout << notSoBadPointer(k) << endl;
}
```

1 Clean up memory leak.

2 A returnable value.

3 Uninitialized pointer!

4 At least k is no longer uninitialized.

5 Here's trouble!

Compiling and running the slightly repaired test without `valgrind` produces no warnings or errors and one nonsense output value:

```
src/debugging> g++ -g -Wall valgrind-test2.cpp
src/debugging> ./a.out
-1078391036
4
```

Running it with valgrind produces fewer complaints than before:

```
src/debugging> valgrind ./a.out
 For more details, rerun with: -v

 Use of uninitialised value of size 4
    at 0x8048794: main (valgrind-test2.cpp:18)
-1096641724
4

 ERROR SUMMARY: 1 errors from 1 contexts (suppressed: 18 from 1)
 malloc/free: in use at exit: 0 bytes in 0 blocks.
 malloc/free: 1 allocs, 1 frees, 12 bytes allocated.
 For counts of detected errors, rerun with: -v
 All heap blocks were freed -- no leaks are possible.
src/debugging>
```

Finally, in Example C.8, we eliminate the last error.

EXAMPLE C.8   src/debugging/valgrind-test3.cpp

```
#include <iostream>

int notSoBadPointer(int k) {
  int* ip = new int[3];
  ip[0] = k;
  delete[] ip;                                              1
  return k;                                                 2
}
```

```
int main() {
  using namespace std;
  int num(4), k(4);                              3
  int* iptr = new int[num] ;                     4
  for (int i = 0; i < num; ++i)
     iptr[i] = i;
  cout << iptr[num-1] << endl;                   5
  cout << notSoBadPointer(k) << endl;
  delete[] iptr;
}
```

1 Clean up memory leak.

2 A returnable value.

3 At least k is no longer uninitialized.

4 No longer uninitialized pointer.

5 No more trouble!

We compile, run, and then run with `valgrind`:

```
src/debugging> g++ -g -Wall valgrind-test3.cpp
src/debugging> ./a.out
3
4
src/debugging> valgrind ./a.out
3
4

 ERROR SUMMARY: 0 errors from 0 contexts (suppressed: 18 from 1)
 malloc/free: in use at exit: 0 bytes in 0 blocks.
 malloc/free: 2 allocs, 2 frees, 28 bytes allocated.
 For counts of detected errors, rerun with: -v
 All heap blocks were freed -- no leaks are possible.
src/debugging>
```

`valgrind` is not readily available for MacOSX,[9] but the Mac Developer Tools include a graphical tool, called MallocDebug.app, that can replace a number of `valgrind`'s functions.

---

[9] It can be installed from source code, which you can find at http://valgrind.org/downloads/repository.html.

C.5   Open Source Development Tools, Libraries, IDEs

Following are some open source libraries built on top of Qt, which provide you with additional reusable components:

- Qwt[10]—Qt Widgets for Technical Applications
- Qxt[11]—Qt eXTension Library

IDEs

It is not practical to do object-oriented development with an ordinary text editor. Object-oriented development typically involves working with many classes and many more files (headers + sources). Writing code in an edit window is just a small part of the development process. A good programmer's editor or Integrated Development Environment (IDE) should support many of the following features:

- Tree-like structured navigation to object/members in any file.
- Refactoring assistance for moving/renaming members.
- Integrated debugger.
- Context-sensitive help linked to API documentation.
- A built-in command-line shell window, so you can run programs without leaving your environment.
- A project manager, to help manage groups and subgroups of related files.
- Editing modes in other programming languages.
- Easy keyboard customization, the ability to make any keystroke perform any task (cursor movement especially, but also window movement).
- An open plugin architecture, so you can easily add other components.
- Integration with a version control facility is desirable. Look for Subversion,[12] or one of the more advanced distributed vcs systems such as bzr, mercurial, git, monotone, or darcs.

---

[10] http://qwt.sourceforge.net/

[11] http://docs.libqxt.org/index.html

[12] http://subversion.tigris.org/

- Learnable and scriptable macros.
- Language-aware navigation to different files (with shortcuts such as find declaration, find definition, and find references).

An Open Source IDE

Nokia/Qt Software has released its free, open source, QtCreator,[13] now included with the Qt SDK. It is an IDE written in C++ within Qt. It has full support for qmake/cmake projects, context-sensitive completion, code navigation, refactoring, and integrated debugging. We think that it is the ideal IDE for developing projects in C++ with Qt on all of the major platforms—for beginners and experts.

Mac OSX users may want to install XCode before doing any development in C++/Qt.

For all platforms, there is Eclipse[14], a free Java-based open source IDE. Nokia makes available an Eclipse integration package[15] that provides many features to make Eclipse a proper Qt IDE. You need to install the C/C++ Development Tools (CDT) or the plugins for C++ development first.[16] The Qt Integration enables you to import qmake .pro files directly into Eclipse as projects and dock Designer's dockables in the Eclipse main window, so that you can use all the features of Designer without leaving Eclipse. In addition, it is possible to integrate the Qt API documentation into Eclipse's context sensitive help system.

UML Modeling Tools

For creating diagrams in this book using the Unified Modeling Language, we use two open source tools: Umbrello[17] and Dia.[18] Each tool uses an XML dialect as its native file format.

Umbrello, shown in Figure C.2, is the KDE UML Modeler - it can directly import C++ code, making it very easy to drag and drop imported classes into diagrams.

---

[13] http://qt.nokia.com/products/developer-tools

[14] http://www.eclipse.org

[15] http://qt.nokia.com/developer/eclipse-integration

[16] http://www.eclipse.org/cdt/

[17] http://uml.sourceforge.net/index.php

[18] http://www.gnome.org/projects/dia/

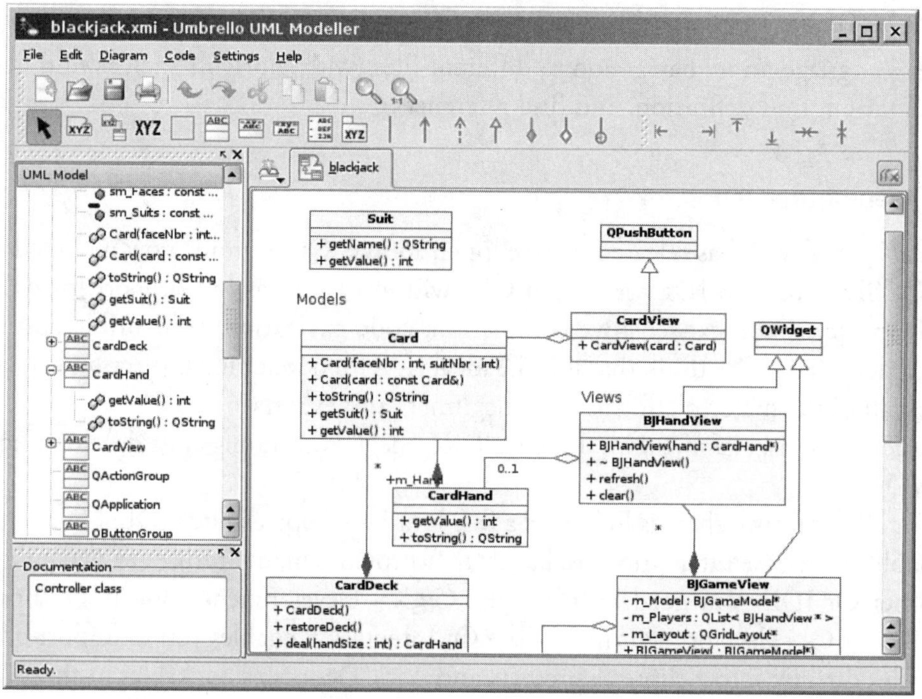

FIGURE C.2   Umbrello Screenshot

Dia, a Gnome utility, is a more general-purpose diagram tool with some UML features. There are many plugins and utilities that enable you to import code and export diagrams to/from Dia to other languages and formats.

Alan's Quick Start Guide to Debian for Programmers

This article is a summary of steps I take to set up a new Debian desktop for development. It is useful for the developer who is new to the Debian Linux desktop environment and wants to take advantage of the `apt` system.

After trying out a number of different Linux distributions, I currently use a Debian Testing KDE installer,[1] which I find ideal for my purposes: C++ / Java / Python / Qt / KDE development.

QUESTION
Why Debian?

1. There is a ridiculously huge number of packages available—many that are hard to find from other distributions. This means that you can grab already-compiled binary packages of almost every library instead of building your own from source.

2. Debian testing seems to contain reasonably up-to-date Qt and KDE packages.

---

[1] KDE is a desktop and set of utilties written entirely in Qt, in contrast to Gnome, which is based on Gtk.

3. Many KDE/Qt developers do their work in Debian or Kubuntu.

4. Debian and Ubuntu distributions offer a powerful package management system known as apt, which is quite straightforward to use and easy to fix when you break it.

QUESTION

Why KDE?

KDE is the favorite desktop environment of both authors of this book. Both of us use and prefer many of the desktop utilities that come with KDE to the comparable apps that come with other desktop environments (e.g., Gnome). In addition to being a well-designed, user-friendly environment, it has the advantage of having been written in C++ with Qt.

Recommended Debian-Based Linux Distributions

The distributions that follow have important things in common: they are *bootable*, which means you can boot your computer from the CD or USB Stick image and run Linux without installing anything on your hard drive. But you can also install a full Debian-based Linux on your hard drive from the same CD or USB Stick. All of these recommended distributions are free and can be easily downloaded from various Web sites:

1. Debian[2] has been one of the main "basic" distributions for several years. Initially, Debian's excellence was recognized, but it was thought to be too difficult for beginners to install. Several other distributions that are essentially façades for Debian, with simplified, user-friendly setup scripts, have come and gone over the years. Hardware detection and recognition has been one of the principal areas of difficulty in setting up a system. One of Debian's strengths (you can customize your installation so that it is exactly tailored to your hardware) was also its main drawback (you had to know how to find drivers for your hardware to set up your system). Recent versions of Debian have much friendlier setup scripts. You can download a "netinst" iso image, burn it to a CD or USB Stick, boot from it, and install to your hard drive with a

---

[2] http://www.debian.org

minimum of difficulty. I would recommend the latest `debian-live-kde-desktop.iso` cd image from debian.org[3] because it boots as a liveCD and installs a recent KDE Desktop.

2. Ubuntu[4] is probably the most popular Gnome-based distribution as we go to press.

3. Kubuntu[5] (KDE-based Ubuntu) is like Ubuntu, but it's KDE-based instead of Gnome-based.

QUESTION

Stable? Testing? Unstable? That sounds scary. Why would anyone use an operating system that is anything but stable?

Many people new to Debian are intimidated by the use of the word "unstable" to describe any distribution of Linux. Because the other two choices are "testing" and "stable," it's natural that people would try the stable first. Unfortunately, the versions of most applications and libraries offered in stable are fairly old (at least a year, sometimes more), and some of your favorite packages may not be available. It might be preferable to use newer software for a desktop/development system. "Testing" is a nice compromise between unstable and stable. Typically, the Debian testing installers support more recent hardware, too. As they are being developed, the Debian versions are given nicknames that have origins in the various *Toy Story* movies.[6]

stable ("squeeze") is the current stable release. It includes Qt 4.6. The versions available are tested thoroughly.

The *testing* ("wheezy" in 2011) distribution is currently using Qt 4.7 and contains versions that will not end up in stable but will be in the next major release.

The `unstable` distribution ("sid") contains more recent versions than testing, but depending on the time you decide to upgrade your system, you may find yourself with broken packages that need to be fixed. Sid is only recommended when you are quite comfortable using the `apt` system.

---

[3] http://cdimage.debian.org/debian-cd/current-live

[4] http://www.ubuntu.com/

[5] http://www.kubuntu.org/

[6] The article at http://en.wikipedia.org/wiki/Debian explains this in some detail.

D.1   The apt System

The apt system is a tool for managing packages and their dependencies. The following programs can be used to manage your apt-based package library:

- apt-get—A convenience program that makes it easy to get and update your packages.

- dpkg—A lower layer of software. Many simple apt commands are translated into more complex commands and executed by dpkg.

- apt-cache—A tool to help you search through the local apt package info database.

- aptitude—apt-get with a little more intelligence. It can be used to get and remove packages when apt fails. It is another convenience layer on top of dpkg.

Following are some handy tips and basic information about the apt system and how to use it.

⚔ etc/apt/sources.list

This file contains a list of sources that apt checks for packages. There are two things you should do with this sources list after a new install:

Fix your main mirrors so that they point to a local mirror[7] instead of a remote one. There are many ways to do this, but the most user-friendly way is to run apt-setup.

Optional: Set the sources to "unstable" (Debian) or "edgy" (Kubuntu) if you want the latest and greatest versions of everything.[8]

apt-get update downloads the package lists from your package sources so that you have a local copy of the lists, dependency relationships, and descriptions in your own dpkg database.

Sometimes you know you want a package, but you can't remember its exact name. apt-cache search search-string searches through the locally downloaded package list for occurances of a string in the name or description of each package. If the returned list contains the package you were looking for, you can easily pull it down from the network and install it.

Once you know the name of a package, you can read its full description with apt-cache show pkgname.

---

[7] http://www.debian.org/mirror/list

[8] Ubuntu only: Be sure to add a "universe" after main so that you get the full packages offered by Ubuntu.

`apt-get install` *packageName* is one of the most powerful commands you have, and it's only available if you have root access on a Debian-based system.

`apt-get remove` *packageName*, as the name suggests, removes the named package in its entirety.

To save you time, I've listed a few packages that I suggest installing on a Debian system for C++ development. Note the use of the pound sign (#) to insert comments.

```
# alias for following commands:
alias agi='apt-get install -y'
# Database Stuff
agi mysql-server mysql-client libmysqlclient15-dev
agi sqlite3 libsqlite3-dev

# For development
agi build-essential manpages-dev # manual pages for stdlib
agi global cscope exuberant-ctags # For C++ development - navigation and doc
generation
agi libqt4-dev qt4-dev-tools libphonon-dev
agi gstreamer0.10-fluendo-mp3 # for playing mp3 files in phonon
agi libtag1-dev libtag1-doc # taglib used by libfiletagger
agi gdb # gnu debugger
agi umbrello # UML Diagramming tool that reads/writes XMI and imports C++ source
```

More apt Tips

apt-get (dist-|dselect-) upgrade

As time goes on, new packages are made available in your repository. When you want to upgrade your system, it is appropriate to do a `dist-upgrade`. To give apt permission to remove what are probably obsolete packages in favor of newer ones, use the command `apt-get dselect-upgrade` (which is similar but not exactly the same as what `aptitude upgrade` does).

✒ `apt-get source` *packageName*

Unless you need a specific version that is not served by your package source, you can grab a copy of the sourcecode in a convenient tarball for any available package by simply asking for it from apt.

✒ I Just Installed Something. Where Did It Go?

For this command, we drop down a level into dpkg land. dpkg is a quite powerful tool in its own right, but most of the time, we use it indirectly via apt-get. One useful option is dpkg -L *packageName*. This command lists all the files that were extracted from this package and shows you the locations they now reside on your system.

✒ `apt-get build-dep` *packageName*

Sometimes, when compiling large packages (such as Qt), the build fails due to missing libraries (or their -dev packages). When I was still learning my way around my first Debian-based system, I was building apps and libraries by following a brute-force iterative process: configure, encounter and examine each error message, try to figure out what library is missing, install it, and repeat until no more errors. After I learned about apt-get build-dep, I realized immediately how much time I could have saved, and it was not insignificant!

You already know that the apt system is aware of which packages depend on which other packages, but with the apt-get build-dep *packageName* command, apt automatically downloads all the dependent libraries *and their -dev packages*, so that you have everything you need to build *packageName*. In other words, there's no more tracking down missing header files!

To see a list of all dependency relationships between packages, try apt-cache showpkg *packageName*.

```
apt-get build-dep libqt4-dev # grabs what you need to build qt4 from source
apt-get build-dep amarok # grabs headers and libs you need to build amarok
apt-get source amarok    # grabs the source tarball
```

✒ `aptitude`: When Your apt System Is Broken

Sometimes you try to install something, and you get an error, but apt is also left in a state that is invalid. This is quite common when running unstable, less so when using testing. You might be instructed to try apt-get -f install, but after trying that, and also trying to remove the offending package, you are still stuck.

It is important to read the error message carefully: You almost always see references to specific package names that are causing the problems. By removing *all of them*, using apt-get remove `pkg1 pkg2 pkg3`, in one line, you can sometimes bring your system back into a valid state.

Another way to fix this is by using aptitude remove pkgN for each package. aptitude can help you by finding and removing sets of related packages that are also causing problems.

D.2 update-alternatives

Because there can coexist alternative versions of the same program on a Debian system (especially programs like qmake and java), there are symbolic links from /usr/bin to the desired versions of these programs. To manage these links and change them to point to alternative versions, root can use the command update-alternatives.

For example, to choose a default version of qmake to run, root can use

```
update-alternatives --config qmake
```

To see a list of alternatives for each installed program that has alternatives, root can type

```
update-alternatives --all
```

and select defaults for all of the alternatives.

Appendix E

C++/Qt Setup

To make the best use of this book, you need to have Qt 4.6 or later and also a C++ compiler installed on your computer. The following sections describe our recommended procedures for setting up Qt for the three major desktop platforms.

E.1 C++/Qt Setup: Open Source Platforms

Open source development tools (`ssh`, `bash`, `gcc`) are available natively on most UNIX-derived platforms.[1]

When we discuss something that's specific to UNIX-derived platforms (Linux, BSD, Solaris, etc.), we will use the shorthand ***nix** for "most flavors of UNIX."

Another important acronym is **POSIX**, which stands for *Portable Operating System Interface for UNIX*. The development of this family of Application Programming Interface (API) standards was sponsored by the IEEE (*Institute of Electrical and Electronics Engineers*), an organization for engineers, scientists, and students, best known for developing standards for the computer and electronics industry.[2]

---

[1] On Mac OSX, you need to install xcode to get the C++ compiler and `make` tool.

[2] If we want to write a POSIX regular expression (Section 14.3), for *nix*, it might look like this: `(lin|mac-os|un|solar|ir|ultr|ai|hp)[iu]?[sx]`.

This section is for readers who use a computer with a *nix system installed.

The first step to prepare your computer for this book is to make sure that the full installation of Qt is available to you. This includes, in addition to the source and compiled library code, the Qt Assistant documentation system, program examples, and the Qt Creator program.

Qt SDK

The Qt SDK includes the Qt libraries, assistant, designer, and qtcreator, built for a particular compiler. It is recommended for a quick setup on your chosen development platform.

To see which (if any) version of Qt has already been installed on your system, start with the commands

```
which qmake
qmake -v
```

The output of the first command tells you where the `qmake` executable is located. If that output looks like this: `bash: qmake: command not found`, it is possible that

1. The "full" Qt (including development tools) is not installed.
2. It is installed, but your PATH does not include `/path/to/qt/bin`.
3. It is installed by your package manager as `qmake-qt4`, to avoid conflict with same-named executables from Qt3.

If you can run it, `qmake -v` provides version information. If it reports `Using Qt version 4.x.y`, use the `which` command to check whether these other Qt tools are available: `moc`, `uic`, `assistant`, `designer`, and `qtcreator`.

If all these executables are found and match versions, Qt is installed and ready to use.

If these tests indicate that you have an earlier version or no Qt installed, or that you are missing some components of Qt, then you need to build or install the latest release of Qt and select the Qt executables as defaults in your path.

Installing Qt from Packages

Using your *nix package manager (e.g., apt, zypper, aptitude, kpackage, synaptic, yum, etc.), you can easily and quickly install the packages that compose Qt. Just keep in mind that it may be broken up into many little pieces, and you probably need them all. Here is a list of Qt 4.7 packages available on Debian wheezy systems in 2011:

```
[ROOT@lazarus]# apt-cache search qt4
libqt4-assistant - transitional package for Qt 4 assistant module
libqt4-core - trans pkg for Qt 4 core non-GUI runtime libraries
libqt4-dbg - Qt 4 library debugging symbols
libqt4-dbus - Qt 4 D-Bus module
libqt4-declarative - Qt 4 Declarative module
libqt4-declarative-folderlistmodel - Qt 4 folderlistmodel QML plugin
libqt4-declarative-gestures - Qt 4 gestures QML plugin
libqt4-declarative-particles - Qt 4 particles QML plugin
libqt4-designer - Qt 4 designer module
libqt4-dev - Qt 4 development files
libqt4-gui - transitional package for Qt 4 GUI runtime libraries
libqt4-help - Qt 4 help module
libqt4-network - Qt 4 network module
libqt4-opengl - Qt 4 OpenGL module
libqt4-opengl-dev - Qt 4 OpenGL library development files
libqt4-phonon - Qt 4 Phonon module
libqt4-qt3support - Qt 3 compatibility library for Qt 4
libqt4-script - Qt 4 script module
libqt4-scripttools - Qt 4 script tools module
libqt4-sql - Qt 4 SQL module
libqt4-sql-ibase - Qt 4 InterBase/FireBird database driver
libqt4-sql-mysql - Qt 4 MySQL database driver
libqt4-sql-odbc - Qt 4 ODBC database driver
libqt4-sql-psql - Qt 4 PostgreSQL database driver
libqt4-sql-sqlite - Qt 4 SQLite 3 database driver
libqt4-sql-sqlite2 - Qt 4 SQLite 2 database driver
libqt4-sql-tds - Qt 4 FreeTDS database driver
libqt4-svg - Qt 4 SVG module
libqt4-test - Qt 4 test module
libqt4-webkit - transitional package for Qt 4 WebKit module
libqt4-webkit-dbg - trans pkg for Qt 4 WebKit debugging symbols
libqt4-xml - Qt 4 XML module
libqt4-xmlpatterns - Qt 4 XML patterns module
libqt4-xmlpatterns-dbg - Qt 4 XML patterns library debugging symbols
qt4-demos - Qt 4 examples and demos
```

```
qt4-demos-dbg - Qt 4 examples and demos debugging symbols
qt4-designer - graphical designer for Qt 4 applications
qt4-dev-tools - Qt 4 development tools
qt4-doc - Qt 4 API documentation
qt4-doc-html - Qt 4 API documentation (HTML format)
qt4-qmake - Qt 4 qmake Makefile generator tool
qt4-qmlviewer - Qt 4 QML viewer
qt4-qtconfig - Qt 4 configuration tool
[ROOT@lazarus]#
```

As you can see, in Debian, Qt 4 has been split into many separate packages to give package maintainers more flexibility when they deploy. When developing, you need most Qt 4 packages, especially -core, -dev, -doc, -dev-tools, -designer, and -dbg for debug symbols, if you want to debug programs using the distro's version of Qt.

Downloading from Source

You can download, unpack, and compile the latest open source tarball from qt.nokia. com.[3] If you have the Qt SDK, you can run the Updater and select Qt Sources, to download it into your Qt SDK directory. Be sure to also select demos and examples.

✂ TIP

In Debian, it is possible with a single command to automatically install all the tools and libraries you need to build another Debian package. You can take advantage of this, when you want to build any popular open source tool from source. For more information, see Appendix D, "Alan's Quick Start Guide to Debian for Programmers."

```
apt-get build-dep libqt4-dev
```

💥 NOTE

A **tarball** is a file produced by the **tar** command (tape archive) that can combine many files, as specified in the command line, into one file (which is generally given the extension .tar) for ease of storage or transfer. The combined file is generally compressed using a utility like gzip or bzip2, which appends the extension .gz or .bz to the tar file.

---

[3] http://qt.nokia.com/downloads

The command line for unpacking a tarball depends on how it was created. You can usually determine this from its extension.

```
tar -vxf  whatever.tar          // uses the "verbose" switch
tar -zxf  whatever.tar.gz       // compressed with gzip
tar -zxf  whatever.tgz          // also compressed with gzip
tar -jxf  whatever.tar.bz2      // compressed with bzip2
```

A tar file can preserve directory structures and has many options and switches. You can read the online documentation for these utilities by typing

info tar
info gzip
info bzip

The Qt source tarball contains the complete source code of the Qt library, plus numerous examples, tutorials, and extensions with full reference documentation. The tarball contains simple installation instructions (in the README and INSTALL files) and a configure --help message. Be sure to read the README file before you attempt to install software from any open source tarball.

Compiling from source can take two to three hours (depending on the speed of your system), but it is worth the time. Example E.1 shows the options we used to configure Qt 4.7.

EXAMPLE E.1   /bin/qtconfigure

```
#!/bin/sh
# specify -phonon if you want to build the audiojukebox exercise or
any of the Phonon examples.
# replace username with your username, and Qt473 with your version of
Qt
./configure -phonon -fast -prefix /home/username/Trolltech/Qt473
```

After Qt is configured, type make and then install it.

TIP

If you have a four-core processor, try typing

```
make -j 4
```

and the compiler will run four compile processes simultaneously, taking full advantage of your extra cores.

In the final step, `make install` copies the executables and headers into another location from the unzipped tarball source tree. If you are installing in a common location, you need to be root to do this.

Checking Qt's Installation

 TIP

After installation, type the command `qmake -v` to determine which version of qmake is found by your shell. For systems that have more than one version installed, this is especially important to do.

```
[ezust@stan] /home/ezust> which qmake
 which qmake
/usr/local/Trolltech/QtSDK/Desktop/Qt/473/gcc/bin/qmake
[ezust@cerberus] /home/ezust> qmake -version
QMake version 2.01a
Using Qt version 4.7.3
   in /usr/local/Trolltech/QtSDK/Desktop/Qt/473/gcc/lib
```

Environment Variables

After installing, check your environment variables, and make sure that your PATH contains proper references to the installed Qt.

 TIP

The bash command env displays the current values of all your environment variables. Environment variables are discussed and used in Section 7.2.

Example E.2 shows how you can set the values of environment variables with `bash`, but the actual values depend on where the files are located on your system.

EXAMPLE E.2   /bin/qt.sh

```
# Using the Qt SDK 1.1
# None of the variables below are required by Qt
# I just like having variables pointing to these locations for easy access:
export QTSDK=/opt/QtSDK
export QTCREATOR=$QTSDK/QtCreator
export QTDIR=$QTSDK/Desktop/Qt/473/gcc
export QTSRC=$QTSDK/QtSources/4.7.3

# make sure SDK's qmake and qtcreator are found first in the path:
export PATH=$QTDIR/bin:$QTCREATOR/bin:$PATH

# Location of your shared libraries:
export CPPLIBS=~/cs331/projects/libs

# Where to search for shared object libraries at runtime:
export LD_LIBRARY_PATH=$CPPLIBS
```

E.2   C++/Qt Setup: Win32

There are two versions of Qt available on Win32 platforms:

1. The mingw edition, built for g++ from MinGW[4] (the *Minimalist Gnu for Windows*), can be downloaded and used for free with open source projects.

2. The Microsoft Visual C++ version, built for a Microsoft compiler such as Microsoft Visual Studio 2008.

Installing either edition is easy: The Win32 installer guides you through the process, registers extensions, and sets environment variables for you.

✒ TIP

If you do not already have a compiler or IDE installed, then you can install the Qt SDK, which includes the libraries, mingw compiler, and QtCreator in one bundle.

---

[4] http://www.mingw.org/

After Qt is installed, you should click

```
Start -> Programs -> Qt by Nokia -> Build debug symbols
```

This may take a couple of hours.
Next, open a shell window by clicking

```
Start -> Programs -> Qt by Nokia -> Command Prompt
```

Now you can run `qmake -v` from the command prompt to see the currently installed version of Qt.

`qmake`, `assistant`, `designer`, `qtdemo`, `qtconfig`, `g++`, and `make` (or `nmake` if you use MS Developer's Studio) should be findable in your search path now.

Try the `qtdemo`, also available from the Start menu.

E.3   C++/Qt Setup: Mac OSX

1. Install **xcode** from Developer.apple.com.[5]
2. Install qtsdk from qt.nokia.com.[6]
3. Run qtcreator from previously installed qtsdk.

✒ QMAKESPEC

- `qmake` creates xcode projects by default instead of `makefiles`.

- Use `qmake -spec macx-g++` to generate a command line `Makefile`.

- Put `CONFIG -= app_bundle` in your .pro file to avoid creating an executable deep in the MacOS app directory structure.

- If you installed `make` with **fink**, read the assistant documentation on how to rebuild/set up your Qt environment properly.

---

[5] developer.apple.com

[6] qt.nokia.com

Bibliography

C++ References

[Stroustrup97] *The C++ Programming Language*. Special Edition. Bjarne Stroustrup 1997. Addison Wesley. 0-201-70073-5

[Meyers] *Effective C++*. Scott Meyers. 1999-2005. Addison Wesley Professional Software Series. 0321334876.

[Morris06] "The C++ Interpreter Pattern for Grammar Management" Stephen Morris. 2006. informit.com.

Qt References

[Blanchette08] *C++ GUI Programming with Qt 4*. Jasmin Blanchette and Mark Summerfield. Second Edition. 2008 Prentice Hall.

[Summer11] *Advanced Qt Programming*. Mark Summerfield. 2011. Prentice Hall.

[Thelin07] *Foundations of Qt Development*. Johan Thelin. 2007. Apress.com.

[Molkentin06] *The Book of Qt 4*. Daniel Molkentin 2006. No Starch Press.

[kdestyle] "KDE Style Guidelines." Coding Style.kde.org.[1]

[qtapistyle] "Designing Qt-Style C++ APIs." Matthias Ettrich. 2005. Trolltech.[2]

[qtapistyle] "Qt Coding Style" Community Project. 2010. Trolltech.[3]

[qttestlib] "Writing Unittests for Qt 4 and KDE4 with QtTestLib." Brad Hards. 2005. developer.kde.org[4]

OOP References

[Buschmann96] *Pattern-Oriented Software Architecture*. First Edition. Frank Buschmann, Regine Meunier, Hans Rohnert, Peter Sommerlad, and Michael Stal. 1996. John Wiley & Sons. 0-471-95869-7.

[Fowler04] *UML Distilled*. Third Edition. Martin Fowler. 2004. Addison Wesley. 0-321-19368-7.

[Gamma95] *Design Patterns: Elements of Reusable Object-Oriented Software*. Erich Gamma, Richard Helm, Ralph Johnson, and John Vlissides. 1995. Addison-Wesley 0-201-63361-2.

[Koenig95] *Patterns and Antipatterns*. Andrew Koenig. 1995. Journal of Object-Oriented Programming 8(1) pgs 46-48.

[Martin98] *Pattern Languages of Program Design 3*. Robert C. Martin, Dirk Riehle, and Frank Buschmann. 1998. Addison-Wesley. pgs 293-312. 0-201-31011-2.

Docbook References

[docbook] *Docbook: The Definitive Guide*. Norman Walsh. 2006. O'reilly Associates.[5]

[docbookxsl] *Docbook XSL: The Complete Guide*. Bob Stayton. 2005. SageHill Enterprises.[6]

---

[1] http://techbase.kde.org/Policies/Kdelibs_Coding_Style

[2] http://doc.trolltech.com/qq/qq13-apis.html

[3] http://qt.gitorious.org/qt/pages/QtCodingStyle

[4] http://developer.kde.org/documentation/tutorials/writingunittests/writingunittests.html

[5] http://www.docbook.org/tdg/en/html/docbook.html

[6] http://www.sagehill.net/docbookxsl/

Miscellaneous References

[xhtmlw3c] "w3c Recommendation: XHTML 1.0 The Extensible HyperText Markup Language." 2005. W3C (World Wide Web Consortium).[7]

[dist] The web accessible site from which you can download example source code and other useful resources: http://informit.com/title/9780132826457

[Friedl98] *Mastering Regular Expressions*. Second Edition. Jeffrey Friedl. 1998. O'Reilly. 1-56592-257-3.

[Rehman03] *The Linux Development Platform*. Rafeeq Ur Rehman. Christopher Paul. 2003. Prentice Hall. 0-13-009115-4.

[Guzdial07] *Introduction to Computing & Programming with Java, A Multimedia Approach*. Mark Guzdial and Barbara Ericson. 2007. Prentice Hall. 0-13-149698-0.

---

[7] http://www.w3.org/TR/xhtml1/

Index

Symbols

... (ellipsis), in variable-length argument lists, 162-163

<< operator, overloading, 9

>> operator, overloading, 9-10

A

abstract base classes, derivation from, 184-188

abstract factories, importing with, 495-498

Abstract Factory design pattern, 482, 483-487

abstract table models, standard table models versus, 414-424

accept() slot (QDialog class), 309

access specifiers, 71-74, 169, 644. *See also* scope

accessibility, visibility versus, 72

accessing memory. *See* memory access

accessing properties via QVariant class, 386-389

actions

    exercises, 334-336

    menus and, 327-336

    toolbars and, 329-333

addDockWidget() function, 337

address-of operator (&), 54-57

addSpacing() function, 302

addStretch() function, 302

addStrut() function, 302

addWidget() function, 299

aggregates, 206-210

aggregation by pointer, 309-311

aggregation relationship, 130

AJAX (Asynchronous JavaScript And XML), 248

algorithms, generics and, 362-364

aliases

    for namespaces, 613

    for operators, 553

alternative versions on Debian systems, symbolic links to, 697

ampersand (&), reference variables and, 61

anchoring characters in regular expressions, 442

anonymous namespaces, 613-614

ANSI C++ typecasts, 574-580

    const_cast operator, 575-578

    dynamic_cast operator, 587-589

    reinterpret_cast operator, 578-579

    static_cast operator, 575-577

antiPatterns, 254-257

API (Application Programming Interface), 247

Application Programming Interface (API), 247

application state, saving and restoring, 339-341

applications. *See also* QApplication class

    definition of term, 236

    interactive applications, event loop and, 272-273

    QMainWindow class, 326-327

        actions and menus, 327-336

        application state, 339-341

        clipboard and data transfer, 341-343

        dock windows, 337-338

        exercises, 334-336, 352-353

        internationalization, 351-352

        undo capability, 343-351

apt-cache program, 694, 696

apt-get program, 694-696

apt system, 694-697

aptitude program, 694, 696-697

argsToStringList() function, 201

ArgumentList class, 200-204

arguments. *See* command-line arguments; parameters

arithmetic operations, 46-50, 626-627, 629-630

arithmetic operators, 553